PRAISE FOR *THE LIFE OF CHRIST*

Since all sanctification and perfection are contained in the life of the God-Man, Jesus Christ Our Lord, the better we get to know His life, the closer we will be to the sublime goal God had in mind when He created us. Ludolph's *Life of Christ* is a priceless companion to the Gospels and leads to that goal.

—DOM PIUS MARY NOONAN, OSB, Prior of Notre Dame Priory, Tasmania, author of *Fig Leaves Are Not Enough, Whilst It Is Day, The Grace to Desire It* and *Divine Providence and Human Freedom* (Cana Press)

This spiritual classic is addressed to all. It aims to be practical, rather than speculative, Wilmart, the famous Benedictine scholar, said, "It is no exaggeration to say that it is one of the most beautiful and learned works to have come to us from the Middle Ages... almost the whole of Patristic literature is included in it." Its holy Carthusian author—never canonised, because the Carthusians don't bother to keep a score of their saints—offers an historical vision of salvation, from Christ's going out from the Father to his final glory. Its popularity and influence is shown by the fact that by the late 19th century, it had already gone through something like sixty complete editions. May this translation continue the good work!

—FR. GILES GONACHER, OSB, Pluscarden Abbey

The Carthusian Ludolph's *Life of Christ* is not so much a biography of the Lord as a compendium of contemplative Christology. Saying even this does not do it justice. Influential across centuries, it was foundational in St. Ignatius of Loyola's conversion of life, and a strong influence on Ignatian spirituality, especially its particular method of meditation. The influence it could have in our day resides in those who would take time to read this fine modern edition of a classic of Christian spirituality.

—FR. HUGH SOMERVILLE KNAPMAN, OSB, author of *Ecumenism of Blood: Heavenly Hope for Earthly Communion* (Paulist Press)

I am thrilled that Ludolph the Carthusian's masterpiece *The Life of Christ* is available in this convenient Reader's Edition. *The Life of Christ* marked a breakthrough in pious imagination, zooming in on the details of the Gospel and bringing them to life. Ludolph claims no mystical insight but simply draws from the Fathers and Doctors of the Church to inform his reading of the sacred text. And by doing so, he went on to influence later saints such as Ignatius of Loyola, Teresa of Ávila, and Francis de Sales. Thanks to these two affordable volumes, he can influence us as well.

—MICHAEL P. FOLEY, Professor of Patristics at Baylor University and author of *Lost in Translation: Meditating on the Orations of the Traditional Roman Rite* (Angelico Press, 2023)

THE LIFE OF CHRIST

THE ✤ LIFE of CHRIST

VITA IESU CHRISTI

VOLUME 1 ✤ *READER'S EDITION*

🍀 LUDOLPH 🍀
THE CARTHUSIAN

TRANSLATED BY VICTOR CAUCHI

AROUCA
PRESS

Source material for Volume 1:
Manuscript at the London, British Library,
Ms. Additional 16609, for chapters
1 to 43, excluding chapters 35 to 39.

Sections II/1 to II/5 from the manuscript at
the Edinburgh, University Library, Ms. 22,
presently numbered as chapters 35 to 39.

ISBN: 978-1-998492-12-1 (pbk)
ISBN: 978-1-998492-13-8 (hc)

Arouca Press
PO Box 55003
Bridgeport PO
Waterloo, ON N2J 0A5
Canada
www.aroucapress.com
Send inquiries to info@aroucapress.com

To Marie Therese
and Rebekah

CONTENTS

🌿 *Chapters 1 to 43, excluding chapters 35 to 39, contained in this Volume have been culled from the manuscript at the London, British Library, Ms. Additional 16609.*

CHAPTERS

🐚 *Chapters 35 to 39, as here renumbered, have been collated from sections II/1 to II/5 from the manuscript at the Edinburgh, University Library, Ms. 22.*

TRANSLATOR'S INTRODUCTION

UDOLPH the Carthusian was born in Saxony at about 1295. He entered the Order of Preachers at about 1310, and was a Dominican friar for some thirty years before entering the Carthusian monastery near Strasbourg in 1340. There, he professed and was elected prior in 1343, an office from which he resigned in 1348 over a matter of procedural requirements laid by the Constitution of the Carthusian Order. He also obtained permission to change charterhouse, going into a cell-house in Mainz before returning to his original charterhouse in Strasbourg where he died on April 13, 1378.

Besides the *Vita Jesu Christi* Ludolph might have also been a spiritual beacon to the *Imitation of Christ* by Thomas à Kempis, although its authorship is uncertain. This book was a most popular and best known devotional book in medieval Christendom borrowing on the religious thought of Ludolph's meditative writings.

Ludolph penned the *Vita Jesu Christi* taking forty desert years to complete in 1374. It was first printed in 1472, very soon after the invention of the printing press in 1440. Since those early years of going to the press in Latin it has been translated into some sixty editions and translations.

Soon after being translated in 1502 from its original Latin into Castilian, which later developed into the standard form of European Spanish, the book was read by Ignatius of Loyola while recovering from a serious leg injury in 1521. The book was also influential in the early sixteenth century on saints Teresa of Avila and Francis de Sales, other than Ignatius Loyola himself who used the text as an inspirational source of meditation, contemplation and prayer in his *Spiritual Exercises*.

The connection between Ignatius of Loyola and the Carthusians dates back to the time when Ignatius, having borne witness to the topography of the Holy Land in his pilgrimage to Jerusalem, also known as a journey within the boundaries of the "Fifth Gospel", applied to become a Carthusian monk. Given his former military character and overbearing temperament he was dissuaded from joining due to the austerity of life the Order led and his ongoing physical ailments.

To this effect in founding the Society of Jesus, Ignatius included a provision in the Order's constitution that any member may try his vocation in a charterhouse, still with an option of returning to being a Jesuit if he did not feel inclined to continue along the Carthusian way of life. So great was the influence of Ludolph's *Vita Jesu Christi* on Ignatius that he thought a plan for any of his society of priests who felt unfulfilled by active life and wanted to pursue a contemplative life.

In his essay *The Vita Christi of Ludolph of Saxony and its influence on the Spiritual Exercises of Ignatius of Loyola* (St. Louis, MO: Seminar on Jesuit Spirituality, 1998), Paul J. Shore examines the book as a teaching document studying Ludolph's imagery and theology. He also places it in its historical and cultural context identifying, above all, its influence on the composition of Ignatius' *Spiritual Exercises*.

It is said that the *Vita Jesu Christi*, also known as the *Speculum Vitae Christi* or the Mirror of the Life of Christ, is not a mere living commentary expounding the facts surrounding Jesus' life but also, besides a possible collection of homilies, an invitation to meditate and contemplate on the life of the divine Son of God.

At a time when spirituality was mainly rooted on Gospel recounts, a visual rendering of the events and teachings of Jesus was presented along with an abundant commentary culled from Bible references, the Fathers of the Church and later spiritual authors. Although most comments may seem rather outdated as to modern-day spirituality, yet they still present a broad view of medieval thought about what it took to follow Jesus in mind and body.

The theology might have been obfuscated by modern trends of more practical and utilitarian considerations about what it involves to be a practising Christian, yet the basic truths are all there as a vector between Patristic writings and pre-1600 theology, and the more volatile practices and credos emerging in post-Vatican II applications and outright belief. Times do change but the essential truth carried along by them remains solid and ever enlightening.

This translation of the *Life of Christ* has been culled from two different sources and edited into 91 consecutive chapters. The Prologue and the first 43 chapters have been translated from the Middle English as contained in the manuscript at the London, British Library, Ms. Additional 16609. These chapters also include an interlude starting at the end of chapter 34, and numbered as chapters 35 to 39, as kept in the manuscript at the Edinburgh, University Library, Ms. 22.

The second part contained in Volume II of this edition corresponds to Volume 3 of *The Life of Our Adorable Redeemer Jesus Christ*, illustrated with several notes by Juan Dadreo, Doctor of Theology at The University of Paris, and translated and supplemented from Spanish by Fr. Antonio Rosello y Sureda, an apostolic missionary priest.

The styles of both linguistic original version may be different, but the present translator has done his best to keep a coherent style and syntax as prevailing in both texts and, possibly, in the original Latin version. Certain concepts and words may be too convoluted for modern-day rendering, yet they had to be retained to avoid digressions which might have been somewhat of a loss to Ludolph's original frame of mind.

The devotional prayers at the end of each chapter have been omitted in order to keep the volume of this work as slim as possible and to provide for unimpeded reading from one chapter to the next. A collation of these prayers has been made by Sister Mary Immaculate Bodenstedt, SND, in *Praying the Life of Christ* (1973).

The Latin quotes of Gospel verses in the first part have been retained as they are followed by an English explanation which does not always fully correspond to the exact wording of the text. In the second part containing the translated Spanish text, however, Gospel quotes are italicised.

Concomitant with this translation is the recent commendable work translated and introduced by Milton T. Walsh published in four volumes by the Liturgical Press—Cistercian Publications (2022). It is a very erudite work with constant referencing similar to that found in bible editions and, being more of an exacting work, it definitely deserves

a great place of honour on scholars' bookshelves than any
fluent reading edition.

The sayings and doings of Jesus Christ on their own
suffice to portend the spirituality contained in this work,
and any greater union with God the reader might feel, or
indeed conversion, are the sole work of the Holy Spirit
operating through mortal hands.

V.C. 🐾🐾🐾

THE LIFE *of* CHRIST

VITA IESU CHRISTI

VOLUME 1 ✽ *READER'S EDITION*

PROLOGUE

Following is *THE PROLOGUE* of the worshipful Father Ludolph of Saxony, Author of this Book about the *Meditations on the Life of Jesus Christ*, also known as the *Mirror of the Life of Christ*.

HE Apostle Saint Paul says that no one may put any other foundation to a spiritual building than that already set, namely our redeemer Jesus Christ. As Saint Augustine says, God is sufficient in sovereignty, while man is greatly failing. And God is so good that no good may come to those who despise or forsake Him. And therefore, it does not suit anyone who flees or escapes from falling into his failures and sins, and to be reconciled within his soul, to depart from the said foundation, where he shall find remedy for all his needs.

The sinner desiring to discharge himself of the burden and number of his sins and to put his soul at rest, ought to first hear and understand our God, who calls sinners to pardon, saying to them, "Come to me all you who labour in sin and vice and are laden with the bundle of many sins, and I shall refresh you by healing your wounds and giving you new strength. And in so doing, you shall find rest in your souls, in this world and in the next." First, the sick man gladly hears the sweet and occupied physician, and comes to him with deep contrition, sincere confession and studious purpose that he may for ever be torn asunder from evil and to do good. Secondly, the sinner, who by true repentance is reconciled and made the loyal servant of God, ought to diligently seek how to unite himself and connect with his doctor, and to become familiar with him, thinking with all due devotion of the holy life of the said doctor. Yet let him be always aware that when he meditates on the life of Jesus, he should not move on to other reading lest he fails to think on what he is reading about Jesus. Rather, he ought to take one element each day from his holy and heart-rending meditation of Jesus Christ, and apply it to his whole day's thoughts, affections, prayers and feelings. The reading he would have chosen for that day as his meditation of the life of Our Lord Jesus Christ would induce him to delight in it and rest from the troubles and challenges of worldly and outwardly things, and to rest and sleep sweetly in such meditation. And in such manner he also ought to exercise himself as he would do in all assaults and temptations of the enemy, and in several human passions, which continually attack the servants of God, ever finding his sure and heart-rending refuge in the life of Our Lord Jesus Christ. And if he cannot have this good and holy life in mind and in his understanding, let him at least resort to the principal elements, such as the Incarnation, nativity, circumcision, presentation in the temple, passion, resurrection, ascension, the infusion of the Holy Spirit and judgment day, which would be worth recalling as fair and special elements, for spiritual enjoyment and comfort. In order to be able to profit further from the life of Our Lord Jesus Christ, he ought to read it so that according to his ability he would discern how to follow the noble methods and doctrines it contains. For it would be of little profit to read a holy life and not to follow it. Saint Bernard says about this: "Of what avail is it to read in books and to learn about the name of sweet Jesus, saviour of the world, if you do not follow his methods and his life?" And Chrysostom says: "Whoever in reading books will find God, let him hasten to live in the ways of God, for the purpose that his good conduct would serve him like a lantern before the eyes of his understanding and of his heart, opening the way of truth for him."

The life of sweet Jesus ought to be greatly desired by the sinner for many and various causes, first being for the remission of his sins. For when he has brought judgment to himself by good and true confession, by accusing and doing justice to himself, in taking wilful penance and walking in his spirit with his God while meditating on Our Lord's life, he receives a great cleansing for his sins. For God, to whom he cleaves, is the fire that consumes all sins. The second cause is to be enlightened. For God, whom the penitent desires, is light shining in the darkness. He is instructed by this light to put his life in order according to Our Lord's life and heavenly things, for himself, for his neighbour, and as to earthly matters. The third is to obtain grace, weeping many tears, as required of a sinner to do in this vale of misery. All this Our Lord, who is the fountain in gardens and the spring of living waters, is wont to give to sinners who cleave to him. The fourth cause is to put to rights frequent sins, from which Our Lord daily releases those who unite themselves to him. For as he said to Moses, "Make a brazen serpent and set it for a sign. And whoever is bitten by other serpents and looks up to it, shall live and not die of that bite." The fifth cause is for the sweet and desirable taste which is in the Lord, as written in the *Psalms*: "Taste you and behold, for Our Lord is sweet and amiable." The sixth cause is to know about the sovereign majesty of the Heavenly Father, as this knowledge could only pertain to Our Saviour, as it is said in Saint Matthew's Gospel: "No one knows the Father but the Son, and he to whom the son will show him." The seventh cause is to have safe passage out of this world which is so perilous. Certainly, a true sinner who repents, who daily receives Our Lord in the home of his whole heart while still in this world, prepares within himself a bed flourished with sweet and devout meditations. After this life God shall similarly do to him, receiving him eternally in his great heavenly palace, so that his desire may be fully accomplished.

This life is the good life, full of rivers cleansing and renewing in a new life the sinners fording them, making them citizens of God's realm. It is a life to be loved, and sweet to be followed. This life has neither bitterness nor envy. It is delicious and pleasant, giving to the soul all the vigour in which it exercises itself, also scorning all that which is unhelpful. For, according to Saint Ambrose, whoever receives Our Lord in the amiable secrets of his soul is fed with great and spiritual delicacies.

This life is also very pleasant for those who are cut off from the world and are solitary, and not without reason; whoever has this life in him is accompanied by all gladness, receiving solace and comfort against all tribulations and temptations, and becoming a strong tower and dungeon against all enemies. Also, the life of Our Lord Jesus Christ is strong, plain and swift and could be inwardly meditated upon by the Creature, and no man can excuse himself for not doing such contemplation; but every man may reasonably accuse himself of failing to contemplate God's sovereign majesty. For the creature, being imperfect of understanding, cannot lightly come to this high contemplation unless he trains himself to mainly gain in contemplating the life of Our Saviour; all would then change themselves from those who understand little to those who profit and gain from this life. And there they may find special help as well as a nest wherein to hide their amorous and chaste desires, like little chicks inasmuch as they can.

This life makes the blessed saints of paradise commendable, sweet and gentle to those who contemplate about them. For an example, the Blessed Virgin Mary, mother of mercy, mother of pity and grace, may never, oh you creature, despise you or cast her gaze away from you, although you may be a sinner, when she shall see, not only once in the day but oftentimes, her blessed child, whom she loves above all things, abiding by holy remembrance between her two arms and between her breasts, that is to say in her heart. How, I say, may she leave you, she who so bears her son, keeps him in her heart so constantly without possibly ever showing him any anger while serving him in all stillness and devotion? Certainly, she can never do it. Similarly as with other saints, who we gladly regard as those with whom God will dwell by His grace. It will so happen after death that this life will turn those who labour in it companions of the saints, for this is their life and joy.

Clearly then, this may be said to be the life of Our Lord's mother. For she sweetly nourished him when he was young. It is also the life of the apostles, who abode with Our Sovereign Lord in all perseverance until the end. It is the life of the saints of paradise, who ever think of God, and marvel in his great deeds, and assist him endlessly.

This life is the good portion, namely to sit at Our Sovereign Lord's feet and to hear his holy word. And whoever instantly possesses it by grace, that grace shall never be taken from him, for that is the reward of a wise servant. And briefly, no tongue can sufficiently and worthily praise the nobleness of such life, which is so good and holy that it is the worthiest of all other lives, and also the beginning of all higher contemplation and life of the angels, as we hope to have after life in this world.

Do you think it a small thing to be constantly with Jesus Christ, whom the angels desire to see? If you then wish to eternally reign with him, start reigning right now and do not depart from following his holy life; for serving him is nothing else but to reign with him.

Draw near to him with a pitiful heart so that you can verbally witness how he descended from the right hand of the Father into the Virgin Mary, his mother. And enjoy yourself in the pure faith of the holy conception, in thinking on the glorious Virgin, bearing in her blessed womb the sovereign son of justice. Be in his nativity and circumcision as the good attendant Joseph. And go into Bethlehem with the three kings in order to worship the child and king as they did. Help to bear the child to the temple, and there to present him with his ancestors. Take company with the sweet herdsmen and the apostles, in beholding with the eyes of your understanding the glorious miracles he did. Be at his death with his truly sweet mother and Saint John, in compassion and beholding pitifully the wounds that your blessed saviour suffered for you. Seek him in his resurrection with the blessed Magdalene until the time comes that you may find him. Marvel about his glorious ascension. And stay in the house perched on the Mount of Olives, sitting with the apostles, and leaving all worldly things, with the intent that you deserve receiving the grace of the blessed Holy Spirit. And if you so follow for some time with a sweet, humble and devout heart your maker on earth, he shall lift you up to himself in heaven, where he sits on the right hand of the Father, as he has promised those who shall serve him, when he said, "Whosoever will serve me, let him follow me. And where I am, I want my servant to be."

Then any sinner can study amiably to follow Our Lord's life, not doubting that in the end God will know him as his child. For it is written in Solomon's *Proverbs*, "I love those who love me," God says. And Saint Bernard says: "God is not pleased with a person who fails to study to please Him. For whosoever studies to please God, God will not despise him." Yet always be wisely aware of the true servant that he might never, in whatever state in which he finds himself, put sure trust in his merits. But as a poor beggar, all naked and as a person not owning anything, let him ask alms of the Lord from whom all good proceeds. And that he does not act in pretending to be meek when he shows his merits and works, but let him know for certain that no creature may be justified before the sovereign judge. For were He to contend against us in judgment we could not give an account just by our thoughts. In this manner whoever judges himself to go to God with all fear and reverence is not called presumptuous. For He calls the sinners the same as He does the poor men of this world who, the more naked they are, the more worthy they judge themselves to ask the rich for alms. And although they are somewhat pestering, yet being aware of their great poverty, they are never reputed to be presumptuous when good rich men regard them with pity.

This glorious Saint Bernard had especially recommended this life, out of which he made a load of myrrh, that is an assembly of all the bitterness which he gathered out of Our Lord's life and labours. He set them between his breasts, that is to say among his affections, saying "It is expected of you, whosoever you are, desiring to find some taste in this life, that you follow the wisdom of the spouse, holding within the kernel of your soul a load of so precious myrrh that you would not for a single instant forget about it; this burden is the bitterness of sorrows which the blessed Son of God has suffered for you; for the purpose that you must say, 'My friend's sorrows are as a load of myrrh between my breasts for those who abide in continuous remembrance.' "And Saint Bernard further says: "I tell you my brethren, that from when I started this way of life I have studied to gather this load of myrrh and to put it between my two arms and my breasts, to increase and put together a truly great assembly of merits, which I know not to be presently in me. And I have gathered the same load of the sorrows, pains and all bitterness of my Lord Jesus. That is to say, first of all, the needs which he had in his infancy, and afterwards the labours which he had in preaching, the weariness in walking, the prayer vigils, the temptations in fasting, the tears in having compassion, the backbiters and false listeners of his speech, the perils in his false brethren, the evil language in his passion, all the scratches, striking, scorning, mocking, reprimands, the pain inflicted by the nails with which his blessed body was pierced, and many other similar things which he has suffered in great abundance to save mankind, as it appears in the forest of his Gospel; in which forest and sweet wood there are so many sweet smelling trees that I have no will to pass by without gathering some branches, especially myrrh branches, of which he drank in his passion and with which he was anointed in his burial; the myrrh he drank was due to the bitterness of my sins, and the anointing myrrh was to show the incorruptibility through which my body shall pass. And because of that, while I live I shall utter the memory of the abundance of his sorrow." And yet Saint Bernard says that to think of these things is wisdom itself. "And as for me, I have put the perfectness of my justice in these things, for there are abundant riches in them and great merits. Certainly there was a time when I had a full regal drink of them full of bitterness, and made an ointment for myself out of the residue full of sweetness and comfort. In return, thinking about these things rewards and uplifts me in my adversities, keeping me low in success and between the joy and sorrow of my present life. This is a royal life to whoever has a sure hand and foot, that is to say for any person who is quite sure of himself, certainly walking in the ways of prosperity and adversity, being aware of the evils that might come to him. Thinking about these things appeases towards me the judge of the whole world, and shows me him in whom the heavenly powers believe and him who is inaccessible and feared among the earth's kings and princes, whom they also believe to be sweet, courteous, amiable and easy to please.

"And you know well, my brethren, that I have often spoke of the above and, as God knows, these things have always been held familiarly in my heart. This is my great philosophy which I have studied, namely to know well my Lord Jesus, and him crucified. And therefore I pray you, my well beloved brethren, that you gather a load of his life and place it in the depth of your heart. Embellish the inner chamber of your heart well with the aforesaid, for the purpose that all may dwell within your breasts. Have them not always behind your back, but before your eyes, for the purpose that in bearing these things you worship his life and that will make it for you the sweeter to bear. Remember when Simeon took him in his arms. Mary, his mother, carried him in her womb and nourished him in her lap, and her husband hugged him closely and intimately. I also think that when Joseph, the Virgin Mary's good husband, often held the child in his lap, the child laughed. Behold then how Mary, Simeon and the good man Joseph had him before their eyes and not behind their backs, giving you an example how to act in the same manner. For if you keep before your eyes him who you bear for certain, seeing the sorrows and anguish of your Lord, you should more easily bear your own." All these fair words were said by Saint Bernard. And since many think only a little on these things, they shall be slightly weary in spiritual life. For if they thought well on all that has been said, they should not be weary so soon of good conduct.

The virgin Saint Cecilia kept this life well in her memory, for it is written about her that among the virtues she held within her there was one which surpassed all others; it was that she always carried the Gospel of Our Lord hidden in her heart. It must be understood that she had chosen some devout meditations written in the Gospels on Our Lord's life, about which she thought day and night with pure and whole heart, with absolute and perfect intent. And when she had done with her meditation, she then started all over again. For in searching these meditations she had, in all sweetness and pleasantness and by wise counsel, set them deep in her heart. I advise you to act similarly. For certain, among all the exercises of spiritual life I believe that such meditations are most needed and profitable and that they bring man to a more perfect salvation than anything else. For you shall never find where you can be so well learned against tribulations and adversities, against temptations of the diabolical enemy, and against vices and sins, as in Our Lord Jesus Christ's life, who was all so perfect and without fault. By continual meditation the soul is inflamed in his love, finds trust and familiarity in him and sets itself against

all vain and transitory things of this wretched world, despising and defying them. This was done by the blessed virgin
Cecilia who had filled her heart with so much of Our Lord
Jesus Christ's life that no vanity might enter it, as witnessed
in the pomp of her marriage where so many vain things
were done. For she being among the angels' chorus, sang
only to Our Lord, with a firm and steadfast heart, saying
"Alas Lord, I pray you that my heart be not unclean and foul,
that I will not be confounded before you."

Also, by leading this life a person is fortified against all
tribulations and adversities, in such manner that they are
not feared at all, as can be seen by the glorious martyrs.
Saint Bernard says about this: "The spouse is called a dove
because it abides upon the whole stone. For all the devotion of the soul — the devout spouse of God and dove — is
in the wounds of his love in which it abides by continual
meditation. And in so doing, it has great trust towards the
sovereign Lord. For the sweet king desires his knight to
cast away his mask and eyes when he sees his wounds, so
that he may have even more and stronger courage to bear
the assaults and temptations of the diabolical enemy. For in
clearly seeing Our Lord's wounds, he shall also find his own.
Although a martyr's body is torn and all parts are cut off,
yet he keeps himself in constant joy beholding his worthy
blood issue out of all parts of his body." Yet Saint Bernard
says: "Where is the soul of a martyr now? It is safe enough,
for it is in Our Lord's wounds, which are always open for
those desiring to enter them. And if the soul is in perfect
syntony with the sorrows and feelings of the wounds he had,
it should not feel no sorrow and would be so enraptured.
For since it abides in the stone which is God, it is no marvel
if it is as hard as a stone and feels no bodily sorrow, seeing
that it is out of it. And what is the cause of all this? Love,
certainly, to which it submits its intelligence. And although
having great pain, it always despises it. And so it appears
that all of a martyr's strength comes from the stone which
is Jesus Christ." All this is said by Saint Bernard. And it is
also said that many confessors are and were found not only
patient in their labours, but also so joyful that by devout
meditation of Our Lord Jesus Christ' life and passion their

soul was not in their body, but completely drowned in the wounds of the blessed Son of God.

Yet this life is set against the enemy's temptations and against vices, so that a person may know what to do and what to omit from doing; and so that nobody may fall into error or fail, the perfection of all virtues are found in this life. For you shall never find such matter, example or doc- trine relating to poverty, humility, charity, piety, patience, obedience and other virtues as in the life of the lord of virtues, from whom the Church draws all its perfection. Saint Bernard says about this: "Oh you who boast of your virtues, tell me what perfectness of virtues you may have if you do not know Jesus Christ who is God's utmost virtue? Oh man, tell me where you can find true wisdom other than only in the doctrine of Jesus Christ? Where is true justice other than in God's mercy? Where is true self-denial other than in the life of Jesus Christ? And where is true strength other than in the passion of the blessed Son of God? Then it is only those who are taught by his doctrine who ought to be called wise; and only those who have obtained the remission of their sins by his mercy who ought to be called righteous; only those who study to follow his life are mild; and only those who in all their adversities are steadfast in the complete learning of his heavenly wisdom are strong. For certainly it is vain labour for anyone to obtain virtues if one thinks having them from anyone else than from the lord of virtues, whose doctrine is called the work of justice, whose life is the mirror of self-denial, and whose death is the true sign of strength." And Saint Gregory also says about this: "How is it that the spouse does not name his love myrrh, but a load of myrrh, unless it is only to show that when the holy soul wholly considers the life of our Saviour and Redeemer Jesus Christ and follows it in its own life, it collects all virtues which abhor vice, out of which a load of myrrh is made, which cleanses all of sin's filth found in it." Saint Augustine also says about this: "How is it that God by his infinite wisdom helps the soul according to the opportune time, yet he never did greater benefit to mankind than when the bountiful wisdom of God, who is His only eternal and equal Son, deigned to take our nature, when the Word, which

is the Son of God, was made man and inhabited among us."
These tyrants and worldly people have an evil appetite for
the riches and sensual pleasure of the world, but the Son
of God desired to be poor. They strive to for reverence and
lordship, and the Son of God would not be king in this
world. They think themselves to be very blessed to have a
great family, and Jesus despised such lineage and marriage.
They hold in great disgrace the wrongs and afflictions of this
world, and the Son of God has suffered all kinds of torments.
They think it impossible to suffer injuries; but what injury
may be greater than to condemn an innocent man to death,
to have him scourged and tormented until he was dead? The
people of this world repute death on the cross as the most
shameful death of all, and yet the Son of God was crucified.
All that we desire, he despises and scorns. For one can do no
sin other than to desire things which one despises, or else
to refuse suffering. Then all the life he led on earth according to the nature of man, he did pleasingly to teach us the
right path. Saint Augustine says, "And because we men are
not worthy to follow or ensue the life of so great a king and
lord, unless we view him in our mind's eye as having been
made man with the intent of teaching us how we ought to
live, behold and think therefore what Saint John says, namely
that whoever dwells with Jesus Christ ought to walk as he
walked, and in that manner he shall not fail to follow him."
And also the Venerable Bede said: "Whoever wants to dwell
with Jesus Christ, ought to go about as he went. That is to
say, not to seek the honours of the world, nor follow vain
riches, but to desire bearing all the world's ills to obtain
everlasting joy, and to be willing to have every man avail
himself of good things and to hurt no man; and if anyone
wrongs you, to suffer patiently and to call and ask for God's
pardon for those who trouble you. Then shall we follow the
life and conduct of sweet Jesus." For, as Saint Ambrose says,
by knowing him we have all wisdom and salvation, and
inversely we have all things in him and he has all things
in us. If you desire to be helped in your wounds, he is the
medicine. If you pass through fiery heat, he is the fountain.
If you are grieved with sin, he is justice. If you desire heaven,
he is the way. If you have need of help, he is the virtue and

strength. If you fear death, he is life. If you refuse darkness, he is light. If you desire meat, he is nourishment. And there-fore it is well said by a wise man, *Hoc est nescire*, that is to say that the person who knows many things but does not know the blessed Jesus Christ, is reputed to be ignorant as to really knowing the soul well. But if he knows well Our Lord, that is enough, although he cannot know anything else. Would, that it be to God, that the wise men of this world tasted and understood these things and changed what they knew to accept this! He then that follows Jesus Christ can neither err nor fail. For the heart is inflamed and loves by continual meditation to follow his life and to obtain the virtues within it, so that many simple and unlettered men have been enlightened by heavenly virtue, and have known great and profound things of God's secrets. For it is there that one shall find an ointment, which little by little purifies and lifts up the soul and instructs it about everything. For which reason in all virtue and good ways keep this before you which is a fair and clear mirror and example of full holiness, namely the life and methods of the Son of God, our Saviour and Redeemer Jesus Christ, who was sent to us from heaven in order to go before us in the way of virtues. And he gave us the law of life and discipline by his example, and deemed us as himself, so that just as we have naturally been created in his image, which we have fouled with sin, so should we be reformed by bearing a resemblance to his ways by following them as much as we can. For as much as a person studies to conform himself by imitating the virtues found in Jesus, so much the nearer shall he be to him and even more lifted up to the land of glory.

Consider then the whole lifetime of our blessed Saviour and Redeemer Jesus Christ, and study as a true disciple and follow as you can the virtues you find in them. And in all your inner and outward labours think of his sorrows and labours. And when you think you have been grieved about anything, resort at once to him who is the pitiful Father of poor people, as a pretty baby in his mother's lap turns to her, and show and commit to him all your works; and without doubt he will make the tempest cease and he will relieve you. And you ought not only abide in the life of our blessed saviour Jesus Christ when you resist, but also when you are in bed. And in your dinner, be within yourself like Saint John the Evangelist, with your head bowed upon his breast to sleep and take your rest with him in peace. And for you to gain, in whatever you say and do always behold Our Lord Jesus Christ as your example, in going, in standing, in sitting, in lying down, in drinking, in eating, in speaking, in holding your peace, in being alone or in company. And in doing this you shall love him even more, you shall have greater familiarity of him, grace and faith, and you shall be more perfect in all virtue. And act in such manner that your knowledge and study are always concentrated on something relating to Jesus Christ, by which you may be moved to follow him and to have affection to love him. And in occupying yourself in good and holy studies and in thinking on the works of Jesus Christ, you shall employ your time usefully and you shall correct yourself to be like those of his life, when you shall always gaze upon him in all your deeds as the mirror and example of all perfection. And the more often that you shall exercise these meditations, even more shall they be familiar to you and be ever lighter for you and make you more glad in your affection.

You have now seen, devote creature, what excellent and high degree of meditation of Our Lord's life brings to a man. Now I shall somewhat try to put you in the same manner of meditations, not speaking of all that is written in the Gospels, but in selecting from them some elements of devotion to imprint them even better in your mind. Even so, you ought not to believe that we may meditate on all that is written that Our Lord Jesus Christ did or said. But to inflame your affection even more, I shall recount to you some events which happened as one may believe, or else which have been truly done, or imagined to have been done as to some, or portrayals which the intellect may grasp in various ways. For certain, in many methods we may expound, understand or meditate on the Holy Scripture, since we see that it is expedient, according to what we see not to go against the truth of life and justice or of doctrine, that is to say against the faith or against good ways. For to say anything of God, our maker, that is not certain by natural reason or by true imagination or by faith or by Holy Scripture, is presumption and sin. And so, if you see that I recount anything done or said by Our Lord Jesus Christ, and I do not prove it by Scripture, then do not take it otherwise than as required by holy meditation, as if I said, "I say and think that Our Lord Jesus has done and said such a thing, and so of other similar ones." And if you desire to have fruit of these things, you ought, with all your affection, diligently and repeatedly, and casting out of your soul all other affections or worldly occupations, to be as present at all that was done and said by Our Lord Jesus Christ as if you had heard them with your own ears and seen them with your own eyes; for they are very sweet for those who meditate upon them by great desire, and proper taste to those who have grace to savour them with affection. And although many of those things are recounted as having been done and past, yet you ought to meditate upon them as being presently said and done, for without doubt you shall thereby find greater sweetness and refinement. Read, then, those things that have been done, as if they were being presently done. Set before the eyes of your mind the deeds done as in the present, and so you shall find all things having taste and joy. And then take it as a general rule that when you shall not find in those contents any source of general meditation, you ought to be happy that you set before your eyes Our Lord Jesus Christ's action. But study so as to know and be familiar with him, who is the fruit of all meditation about him.

So then, devoutly behold Our Lord Jesus Christ in all places, in all his deeds and in all his methods, as when he is with his disciples, when he is with sinners, when he speaks, when he preaches, when he goes hither, when he sits, when he sleeps, when he wakes up, when he eats, when he ministers to others, when he heals sickness or when he does other miracles. And write in your heart his methods and his deeds, how meekly he behaved himself amongst men and how sweetly amongst his disciples, how mercifully towards the poor, to whom he was willing to do mercy in everything alike. How he held no one in contempt nor abhorred anyone, were he a leper or any other person. How he did not flatter rich men. How he was delivered from all the cares of the world. How he punished himself as to bodily needs. Oh, how patient he was in troubles and how sweet in his answers! How he never avenged himself by sharp or biting words, but only gave good and sweet answers to downplay malice. How he was well vested in all his clothing. What inward business he had for the salvation of many souls, leading to his death and passion. How he set himself as an example of full goodness. Of what compassion he had on those who were sorrowful. How he deigned accept our infirmity although we are imperfect. How he never despised sinners. With what sweetness he received penitents. How he was obedient to his parents, and ready to serve and tend to all, saying "I am in your midst as he that serves." How he put away all boasting, pride and outward appearances. How he abstained from all slander. How temperate he was in his drinking and eating. How he had a modest countenance. How he was wholly given to devout prayer. How sober he was in keeping vigils, patient in labours and pains. How courteous he was to all people. And similarly, in all the deeds and sayings that you shall read or hear of Our Lord and Redeemer Jesus Christ, you must think upon his conditions and his manner of conduct in everything, befitting and in truly great perfection, as you may think and consider, for he acted very perfectly in everything, being the perfection of all things. He was of a sweet countenance, good to be spoken to and gentle in all his conversation. And especially, if you cannot behold and contemplate an image of his face, how on being hit it was harder than anything else, yet the same holy face should give joyful vigour to your soul.

Let all these things be of good memory to you for learning, recollection and course of action as to the following chapters. That is to say when you shall hear recounted any saying or deed of Our Saviour on which you could not meditate, or else you forget the general meditations which are mentioned, resort then to this part and what is being generally said ought to suffice your needs.

And so as to be able to better contemplate Our Lord Jesus Christ's face, stature or figure, and to see in it his conditions, his deeds and his manner, you would benefit from them in seeing figured in them some of the things which are written here and elsewhere. We read that Our Lord Jesus Christ, who was called prophet by the peasants, was truly a man of great stature, high-spirited, always pleasant to behold, having an adorable face, by which those who behold it might believe, fear and love him. His hair was like a very ripe walnut, shading between green and black to the hue of the sea, crisp, and hanging to his ears, and lying broad over his shoulders. His hair split down the middle of his head, in the manner of the Nazarenes, keeping his forehead plain and pleasant to behold. His face, without wrinkles, wounds or spot, was red to a certain extent; his nose easily long; his mouth quite large, definitely. His beard was not long, but fitting, and of the same colour as his hair, forked at the chin. His look was simple and ripe or like that of a mother, his eyes clear. He was dreadful in reprimanding, and sweet and amiable in admonishing, ever so helpful in all grief. There were times when he wept, but never laughed. In the manner of his body he was well made and straight. His arms and hands were so pleasant to behold. In speech he was mighty and reasonable, of few words, good tempered and well ordered in everything. And for that, it is not in vain that the Psalmist says about him that he is of fair stature above all the sons of men.

Before studying other Scripture have always with you the Holy Gospel, which, according to Saint Augustine, exceeds all other Scripture and religious authorities contained in the holy books; and keep them constantly close to your heart. For there you must be clearly taught of the life and ways of Our Saviour and Redeemer Jesus Christ and of all that you need for your salvation. And, according to Chrysostom, the Gospel contains all the perfection of the reasonable creature. And Saint Jerome says that the Gospel is the completeness of the law and that it shows it, as it plainly shows the commandments and examples of good living. And Chrysostom says: "It is not required to have the Letters and Scripture, but it is necessary to have a pure life and be clean in everything to have the grace of the Holy Spirit, as taught to us by the Scripture, as books are only written by the pen. But as we are not happy with that grace, but have cast it out of us, it suits us to take heed of the Scripture. And the Scripture was written for that purpose, not that it should simply remain in the books but that we may set it and assemble it in our hearts. For if the devil dare not come near or approach the place where the Gospels are placed or written, it is stronger to believe that he shall never touch anyone who meditates God's Gospel in his heart, nor any sin shall come to him. Then by reading the Gospel make your body and soul holy, speaking always about it and keeping it in your heart. For if it is said that stinking and deceptive speech fouls the soul and calls the devils, then it is clear that the spiritual lesson makes it holy and increases the grace of the Holy Spirit. Let us all then take heed and study the Holy Scripture; and if not all, yet at least the Holy Gospel, which we should always have in our hands and shown in our deeds. Certainly, if you keep on studying it until the end, you shall despise all worldly things and you shall have scorn of all that is in the world. And if you are rich, you shall own nothing to your riches. And if you are poor, you shall gladly endure it. For then you shall not desire to be miserly or to plunder; but in despising all riches you shall embrace poverty. This is well known by those who have passed through it.

And yet do tell me what equals the Holy Gospels in this world? In the Holy Gospel it is shown how God was considered on earth; how man went up to heaven; how men, angels and all heavenly spirits are all together. There one may see that the beauty of the old enemy has all been brought to nothing, and that God is reconciled to man. The devil is confused by the Gospel, enemies fly, death is cast away, paradise is opened, cursing is cast out, error is put down, truth comes back, the word of piety is sown in all places, the heavenly way of life is planted on earth, the heavenly virtues become familiar with us and often descend to earth for our salvation. In looking in all these things we may lay our sure trust in the life to come. And for all this we call this history the Gospel. For all other disciplines teaching the vanities of the world and through which one learns to despise its manners, have been taught by successive masters. But the words shown by the preachers, who are Our Lord's apostles, are properly called Gospels, since they are shown in a straightforward manner, for we have not received them by our labours, sorrow or pain, but only by the grace, charity and love which God had for us." All this is said by Chrysostom.

And Saint Augustine says that the name Gospel is as much to say in Latin as a good messenger or a good precursor. And therefore if one were to show any good, he may always be called a Gospel-bearer, although the name of Gospel-bearer properly pertains to the precursor who came before Our Saviour and Redeemer Jesus Christ. For those who have written of the coming and passion of Our Lord Jesus Christ are properly called Evangelists.

It should be known, before starting the Gospel story, that the Evangelists, wholesomely being directed by the Holy Spirit, have sometimes written an event before it actually happened. At other times they remembered what they had left out, while at others they repeated what they had said before; since God would not permit that they should have written otherwise. And all this is done as an example of our great meekness. Saint Augustine says about this: "It can be proven that each one of the Evangelists believed that he ought to write in the order which pleased God to show him."

In the Gospel you shall find the mystery of the Incarnation of the Son of God, the commandments and promises, by which you have the way, truth and life. Then if you desire to live well, take the example of Our Lord Jesus Christ. Keep his commandments, and learn from them how to live well. Think of his promises. To achieve these three aims it is necessary to put in the forefront the following three elements, namely lack of power, ignorance and negligence. For the ignorant shall be unknown, the negligent shall not be known, and the evil hypocrite who excuses himself of lacking ability shall be cast out from the company of righteous persons.

Devout Christian soul, lift up yourself to walk along this pleasant way of God's commandments. lift up yourself attentively, and discuss diligently what has been said above about Our Lord and Saviour Jesus. Have them in hand and think about them in great haste, in following Our Lord's legacy and way. For he descended from his heavenly seat to earth; and so do flee from earthly things and desire heavenly ones. The world is foul, so arise from it and flee it. Walk and do not be idle, that you may not lose the place in the land of paradise. ✦✦✦

CHAPTER 1
OF THE GODLY AND ETERNAL GENERATION OF JESUS CHRIST

 E, desiring and coveting to sprinkle a few drops of rain of Gospel abundance, shall start with the godly generation of the Son of God, about which the Evangelist John specifically speaks, by recalling all of his Gospel sayings, for the purpose that the Word's person as Son of God in the Trinity, is universally shown; and the more so against some heretics who say that Our Lord Jesus Christ was only human, and that consequently, because of his temporal nativity, he did not exist prior to his mother Mary. And to this end, the Evangelist begins with the eternity of the Word, showing Jesus Christ's Trinitarian nature, by which he was eternally before his mother. And he lists five things about the divine persons, which here follow in order.

First, he declares the eternal generation of the Son of God proceeding from the Father, saying *In principio erat Verbum*, "At the beginning was the Word," that is to say the Father, who is supposed to be the cause and beginning of all things, their first principle. That is to say that the Son together with the Father is everlasting. Wherefore he has not his beginning of the Virgin Mary, but of the Father, who is beginning without beginning. And the Son too is beginning without beginning. Saint John calls the Son of God the Word, more often than calling him Son or Wisdom or Virtue of God. For the Son has only regard and comparison to the Father. And the word has comparison both to him who speaks, and to what is spoken by the Word, and to the voice from where the word comes and works together, and, fourthly, to the doctrine that one administers to another person heeding the word. And since the Son of God ought not to be spoken of here only with regard to him proceeding from the Father, but also with regard to the creatures which he has made and created, and to the nature which he has taken, and to the teachings which he has given and left to us, he is readily referred to under the name Word; since that name regards all aforesaid things, one might not find even under heaven a more appropriate name for him. Since verily God is properly and perfectly called the Word of his nature, and that there proceeds from Him the one of whom it is said that the Word and the Son are one thing, it truly follows that there is eternal generation in the Trinity, and that the Word of God is God the Son, of his own nature in the Trinity, equal and infinite with and as the Father.

Secondly, the Evangelist declares the difference in persons between the Father and the Son, saying *Et Verbum erat apud Deum*; that is to say that the Word was in God the Father. This name God in this clause is a personal name, for when he says that the Word was in God, he means the Father, with whom the Son always is, and the Father always with the Son. This preposition *apud* is not a sign of the diversity of being, but of persons. For no person is properly said to be in itself, as it is not said that one man is in himself. And therefore between the Word and the beginning, who is the Word, there is a personal difference. And this Word proceeds not from the Father as does the word of him that speaks it out, but always abides within him. And after this, the Son always abides within the Father, of whom he is the Word. For the Word is in God as one thing is in another, although as a different person from Him, as it is said.

Thirdly, the Evangelist declares the Father and the Son to be of one substance, saying *Et Deus erat Verbum*, "And God was the Word." This name God in this clause is essential, as when one says that God is Word, and that his nature is of Trinitarian substance. And this is said for the purpose that one might not say that he is with God and not God, for nothing is in God that is not God. Then although the Word is in God, yet it is not a distinct thing from his heavenly nature, like as is our saying. But it is of the heavenly nature, which cannot be but one, undivided and truly single. And likewise in this clause the three persons are implied; the Father here called *Deus*, the Son here called *Verbum*, and the Holy Spirit called *apud* in this preposition.

Fourthly, he declares the co‑eternity of the Father and the Son, saying *Hoc erat in principio apud Deum*; that is to say that the Word of whom he has previously spoken, is in

God the Father from the beginning of his eternity, that is to say before the worlds, and everlastingly. As though he said, "This Son of God, whom I call here Word, was never severed from God the Father." For certainly, the Father was never without his Son, as he can never be without his virtue or without his wisdom. We call father whoever has a son, for there is no other reason in being a father but to have a son. And since God the Father, who has conceived this Word, God the Son, is eternal, we say that the Word that he has begotten is equal to him, everlastingly and not by any time. On this it is said that God at the beginning created heaven and earth, namely at the beginning of his eternity. It is also said about this, *Ex utero ante Luciferum genui te*; that is to say, God the Father said to his Son, "I have begotten you of my substance before the creation of the world." And so when he says *Hodie*, "This day I have engendered you," *Hodie* must be taken to mean the day of his eternity which comprehends all time, as this noun *principium* is taken here for eternity, and here above for the Father.

Morally, we learn from the above that God ought to be the beginning of all our intent. For the Word was at the beginning, and the Word was God. And if you desire to know your work inwardly and outwardly, if it is heavenly or that God works in you, examine whether God is the purpose of your intent. And if you find this to be so, then your work is heavenly. For the beginning and the end are all one thing, namely God.

After the Evangelist has declared the generation of the Word and Son of God, he then declared his working, show-ing the fifth element, that is the undivided working of the Father and the Son. And he says *Omnia per ipsum facta sunt*, "All things were made by him as well as by the Father." *Et sine ipso factum est nihil*, "And without him, the Father did noth-ing," whether it was a visible or intelligible thing. Here this preposition *per* signifies the efficient cause, without any help, service or instrument. But God has made all things by his wisdom, without which nothing is made. And similarly, the Holy Spirit with them. For the works of the Holy Trinity are undivided, and all things are done by them together. If then all things are made by him, and he did not make himself (for he should be even as he was), it follows then that the Word was not made of this. And, according to Saint Augustine, if the Son of God is not made, he is not a creature. And if he is not a creature, then it follows that he is of one same substance with the Father. For any substance that is not God, is a creature. And any substance that is not a creature, is God.

After that the Evangelist has shown that the Word is the cause of bringing forth all things, he now shows how the Word causes this to happen, saying *Quod factum est in ipso vita erat,* "All that is made by this Word had life and lived in him," just like the smith or mason first conceives his work in his intellect, and afterwards produces it. And that, namely in his intellect, has life together with him, and what he does changes in time. All things that are made do not have life, nor is there any life in them, that is to say in their own nature, in which they exist as creatures. So that in being in God and in God's thought, who is life in Himself, they have life. For there they have a stimulating example and purpose. All existing things and those made temporally, have ever been ordained to be done. For God knew them before they were made. And they lived in His intellect and in His presence, and had some efficacy. And before the making of the world, all things were imagined to be made. In his *Book of Consolation* Boethius says *O qui perpetue,* "Oh you who are the fairest of all who are fair, you have all things everlastingly in you, as in an example, bearing the world in your thought and forming it in your imagination."

To speak morally, we should here note that the work of virtue is the work of life, as the works of sin are the works of death. Then no man may do virtuous work but in God. And therefore, if you desire to know whether your work lives on, that is to say whether it is a work of virtue, take heed whether it is done in God and for love of Him. For it is written in the Gospel that all things that are made in Him have life and live. Then it must be known that all that is done in charity, is done in God. And all that is not done in God, has neither beginning nor end deserving merit.

After the Evangelist showed how the Word acts in proper manner with all creatures in general, he then shows how he acts with men especially, saying *Et vita erat lux hominum,*

"And life was the light of men." For the Son, who was in himself life in which and by which all creatures live, was the light of men, with which reasoning creatures ought to be enlightened for the purpose that they may be blessed. This light does not fail to send his beams and his brightness upon all men who prepare and turn themselves to him by knowledge or by love.

To speak morally, the good life is the light of men, for the holy life illuminates and edifies the next of kin more than words do. Saint Jerome says about this: "One understands better that which he sees with his eyes, than that which he hears with his ears." And also Seneca says: "That the way of commanding is very long, but that of example is very short and greatly effective." And therefore Our Saviour and Redeemer Jesus Christ first started doing and afterwards teaching.

Et lux in tenebris lucet, "And this light shines in the darkness," that is to say in sinners, for the Word of himself enlightened them by the light of grace, but they are dark, for they are so far from the effect of divine light. And therefore it here follows, *Et tenebre eam non comprehenderunt*. As if saying "Those who are dark or in darkness do not understand anything of this light," referring to those who are sinners. In not following this light they may not in any way succeed in achieving it, not for any fault within it, but owing to their own faults. Whereupon Saint Augustine says: "Similarly as when a blind man sits facing the sun, with the light of the sun shining before him, he never lacks light; so it is with all those who are wicked and have blind folly in their hearts, so that they may neither see nor perceive the divine wisdom which is ever present and never withdraws from any creature, unless it is the creature who first withdraws himself from it. Then what shall this person who is so blinded do? It suits him to purify and cleanse himself from sin, so that he may see God; and to abandon his sins and iniquities. And in this manner he may see the divine wit or eternal wisdom, which is ever present. For this good wit is God, of whom it is said: "Blessed be them who are clean of heart, for they shall see their creator." As Origen says: "Light has lit in darkness." For in our nature, which is neither firm nor stable in itself, there are many various forms of darkness, which the Son, who is the Word of God, life and light of man, never leaves him not to be enlightened. And because this light is to every creature incomprehensible, it is said *Tenebre eam non comprehenderunt,* "Its darkness could not be understood."

And as regards this it should be noted that there are three ways of understanding it. First, by shutting up or covering, as if to say, if a man covers over anything, they say it has been understood. Secondly, by clear vision or sight. And the third, by acceptance or by having faith and charity. In the first manner, God may not be understood by any creature. For He is infinite and all creatures are finite and come to an end. In the second, He is understood by the blessed saints who are in heaven. And thirdly, He is understood by those who are yet in the paths of this world. But never, in no way, nor in any of these methods, is He understood by those who are evil. And because of that, it is said that those who are dark, or in darkness, have not understood him. As it is true to say that a thing is understood when it is perfectly known. And it is only divine understanding that likewise has knowledge of this light.

Morally, the light shines in darkness for virtue shows itself and is perfect in adversity. As Saint Gregory says, no man knows how much he profits but for those who are in tribulation, as a creature may only know in his heart. And inasmuch as no adversity may either suppress or overcome the holy saints, nor separate them from the love of Jesus Christ, it is said that "The darkness has not understood it." And so adversity molests the blessed holy men in this world, in such manner that it never vanquishes or overcomes them, but they keep on enjoying and delighting themselves in it. Thus, a man may say that the light shines in darkness whenever God gives comfort or consolation to those who are in tribulation, as it is written that Our Lord is ready and ever with those who patiently suffer tribulation. And there is no darkness to be found in them. For all the pains of this world and all that any creature may suffer on earth, are of no account compared to the joys and happiness ordained and prepared at the very end for those leading a good life.

For God rewards and pays man more than he would have won or deserved by his merits, and punishes him less than he would have deserved by his grievous sins. So that no tongue can tell on what the light shines in darkness, for the Creator lights and appears in his creatures. For just as God is in paradise a mirror for all creatures to whom He gives light, by which light we shall see and perceive all things bringing us joy, so in this life and oppositely creatures mirror their Creator. For not only true faith, Scripture or testimony come from no other source than from God, for with them created things and natural reason give witness to Him, the holy men preach it, and every creature says according to his nature that He has created it and not that he has created Him. God is the way of nature, as all fair things give witness that He is very fair. And all sweet things testify that He is very sweet, that He is high that is very high, that He is pure that is very pure, that He is strong that is very strong, and so for everything else. And as the Apostle says, the invisible things of God are known by the creature through the things of the world made visible.

Be well aware when you hear of the things above, namely that the Son of God is begotten of the Father, to keep your- self from thinking about this. And that you neither ask nor be concerned to know how that might have come about, for there is neither prophet nor angel who ever knew how it happened. So just believe simply in contemplation that the Son, that is the Father's splendour or light, is of this most resplendent and very secret light. Wherefore he is eternal, and of the same single substance of the Father. For he is the sovereign virtue and wisdom by which God the Father has disposed all everlasting things, and by which he has made the world in order and rule, and has ordained all things to his eternal glory, some by nature and some by grace, and some by righteousness and others by His mercy, for the purpose that in this world there would be nothing left without order. And Saint Augustine says about this: "We understand that the Son of God is begotten of the substance of the Father similarly as the shine or brightness proceeds from the substance of the sun. And as with creatures if any- thing is found to be proceeding from one another, and ever existing once only, as is the sun and its brightness, the fire and its heat thereof (for it may not be said that the splen-dour or shine of the sun or the heat of the fire issue from the sun or fire, although they originate from them); so why do you doubt that it should not be said, nor that it should not be made, by the Creator of all creatures? Also that the sun's splendour or brightness shines over all the earth with its splendorous light, and yet it does not leave that from which it was engendered? Similarly the Son, begotten of the Father, is over the whole world, and yet he never departs from the Father, for he dwells evermore in Him. And also that substantially the lucidity is in the Son and the Son is in the lucidity, substantially in the same manner the Father is where the Son is and the Son is where the Father is. And in the same manner these are but one substance, although the brightness and the substance are not one person, for we do not say that the lucidity or sunshine is exactly the sun, nor that the sun is the lucidity; so do the Father and the Son, although they are of only one essence or being, they are still not one person. And in the same manner as the sun by its shining and brightness warms, lights, dries, whitens and burns, and it works according to how it is ordained by God; we also read that the Father has made all things by his Only Son." These things are said by Saint Augustine, that there was a disciple of the philosopher Plato who said that this Prologue of the Holy Gospel of Saint John ought to be written with golden letters, and that it ought to be put in the highest places of every Church, so that it might be there openly seen by everybody.

CHAPTER 2

HOW REMEDY WAS FOUND FOR THE SAL-VATION OF THE HUMAN RACE OR MAN-KIND FROM THE SLAVERY OF THE ENEMY'S BONDAGE, AND OF THE NATIVITY OF OUR BLESSED LADY

HEN at the beginning of the world, by the Eternal Word, Lucifer was created, he ele-vated himself against his maker with great pride and disobedience. And so, he was cast into hell with the twinkle of an eye. And for that cause, God ordained and made mankind in order to restore and fill again the site and place from where Lucifer and his company were cast out. And this is why the devil is such a great enemy of man and strongly against him. And he thought of finding means how to deceive our forefather Adam and to make him break God's commandment. And he took the likeness of a serpent crawling on his belly and having the head and face of a maid. And he deceived man with many false and deceiving words with his mouth. And he did so much that we were all cast into the prison of hell, out of which we could redeem ourselves. This was until the Father of redemption and Lord of all consolation pitifully beheld the state of our damnation and was determined to redeem us. This was when he gave us the sign or marking with the olive branch which was brought by the dove to the prisoners in Noah's Ark, this being a sign of God's great mercy to descend on those who dwelt in darkness.

At the beginning of the world Adam was created out of earth in the field of Damascus near Hebron, and set in paradise with a plenty of pleasures and delights. Eve was formed out of Adam's rib, and they were placed there to labour and keep the mentioned paradise. And they were cast out from there by God's righteousness for eating from the forbidden tree. Yet heavenly mercifulness did not suffice to kindle and move mankind to a good life, and wanted to repel and call back to penance all those who erred in faith, giving them hope of pardon and remission and promising them the coming of the Saviour. Man's action was done by chance, ignorance or ingratitude, so that God's piety would not be without effect, but sufficient for our salvation. And it never ceases but keeps on showing the coming of the Son of God through the five ages of the world, that is those of the Patriarchs, Judges, Priests, Kings and Prophets, from the first just one, Abel, to Saint John the Baptist. So that throughout many thousands of years and of periods and in different ways God enhanced our intellect of true faith, and kindled our affections by great and lovely desires.

Pope Leo says about this: "Now let the quarrel and mur-muring cease about why the Son of God tarried and was late in coming, saying that men of past times were not forbid-den from what was made in the last age of the world. The sacrament of human salvation, which is the incarnation of the Word, did not cease to show at any time that he who should have been made long before has been made. The sacrament of man's salvation was never in the remotest age at a standstill. What the apostles had preached, the proph-ets had announced; nor has what has always been believed fulfilled too late. God's wisdom and goodness in his works had made us more receptive and truthful of His call for a delay in the work which brought salvation, so that what had been foretold by many signs, utterances and mysteries for many ages might not be doubted by men by believing the Holy Gospel. And also because the Saviour's nativity has engendered in us a much firmer faith in the belief of having been made, it was preceded by long and marvellous past times. So God did not have to be moved or changed, nor did he need any new advice as to human matters. And He did not only show salvation in a more recent age, but since the beginning of the world He has instituted and set only one cause for the salvation of all mankind. For the grace of God, by which every creature is justified, though increasing in the nativity of Our Lord, did not have there its first beginning. And this sacrament of pity has of itself been so mighty in its meaning, that those who believed that he ought to come and that he had been promised, have no less merit than those who believed after it was accomplished." These things were said by Pope Leo.

And also, as Saint Augustine says, stating that Our Lord had no will to come any sooner than man, both by natural law and by written Law, was defeated. For if the Son of God had come so soon, mankind would have said that it might have been saved by natural law, and after that it would have been superfluous to have believed that Christ was to come. The same may be said of the written Law. But when the creature is aware that in this manner he may not be saved, but sees all descend into hell, than comes the Son of God. For that would be the time when he ought to have pity upon his creatures. And before, it was not necessary that he come, for spiritual medicine is of no use in any way unless those who should receive it had desired it before. Neither does he come any later, nor wait any longer, so that the hope and belief man had of his promise should not perish. And if he had tarried and deferred his coming, the desire of the holy men would have grown cold from day to day; on this Saint Augustine himself says, they had great desire to see his coming into this world, for they knew well enough that he ought to come. And not only the Patriarchs and Prophets desired his coming, but also all holy and devout uplifting persons, saying "Oh, that this nativity of the Son of God might yet find me in this world, or that I might see with my eyes what I believe!" If then these true believers and holy ancient Fathers desired to see Our Saviour Jesus, who was still to come, what ought all these do who have long before now received him unworthily? But all such persons may say they are cursed and unhappy poor souls living presently and neither having the mind nor the devotion for the great grace which God has given them, similarly as he did to the afore mentioned holy Fathers.

Saint Bernard says about this: "When many a time I think upon the hope and heartfelt desires of those who had to see the presence of Our Lord in his human nature, I feel such compunction and I am so confounded within me, such that I sustain great pain to keep myself from weeping for the very shame and negligence of the present time with regard to the desires of the most fortunate ancient Fathers about the coming of the Son of God. Oh, now that he is amongst us would we be so inflamed and filled with joy and grace and benefits as were the holy ancient Fathers about the promise which was to them only made?" This was said by Saint Bernard.

Then when during a long time, namely for some five thousand and two hundred years, man was in hell's captivity, and none could attain eternal glory because of Adam's sins, the blessed Holy Spirit having compassion seeing such loss and ruin, was the glorious solicitor of our redemption and restoration. And although great petitions and prayers were made many times before to Our Lord, ever as the time began drawing near, even more instantly and more devoutly he prayed. So that Mercy struck the Father's heart, having with him Peace, for the purpose that he should help the poor creatures. But Righteousness, having with him Justice, said the contrary. And there was a division of opinion among them, as Saint Bernard recounts in a quite lengthy sermon about the Annunciation, whose long narration may be substantially summarised as follows. Mercy said to God, "Every reasonable creature, being made very poor and unfortunate, endeavours to have divine mercy and pity. But the time for help and assistance to him is coming." But Righteousness says the opposite in this manner, "I pray you that the words which you have spoken are accomplished, so that Adam dies with all his issue. For he has bitten of the apple in breaking the commandment." Mercy answers, "Alas, sir, for what cause have you made me? Righteousness knows well that I am lost if you have not mercy upon me." To the contrary Righteousness says, "If you bide not by your previous sentence, your righteousness shall perish and never dwell any longer with you." This question was spoken by the Father to the Son. And Righteousness and Mercy said the same thing before the Son as they did before the Father. One may not see by way of any manner that Mercy and Righteousness hold together in the deliverance of man. The Son wrote this sentence, namely: "Righteousness says, 'I lose should Adam not die.' And Mercy says, 'I lose should man not obtain mercy.' If he dies a good death, then each one of us shall have what he demands, namely that Adam dies and that he obtains mercy." All marvelled greatly in his wise sayings, and consented that Adam should die and that He should have mercy. But they inquired and questioned how that death might be made good, for it is horrible only to hear of it being named. The king answered, "The death of sinners is evil, but the death of those who are holy is precious, and is the gate and entry into everlasting life. Let us find one then who will die by true charity and without any guilt or having cause to die. And that death would not be grievous to him by reason of sin, but made in him an opening or gateway through which one can easily pass." And surely this advice pleased them all. But they said, "Where might such a man be found?" Righteousness roamed all over the land and never found anyone without sin, not as much as a day old child. And likewise, Mercy sought around everywhere and found none with sufficient charity to do this. And therefore the victory was given to the one who deserved it, for he deserved it since he had so great charity that he gave his soul to please his most undeserving servants. They then returned again on the appointed day, walking sorrowfully and wearily since they had not found what they desired. But Peace comforted them, saying "Do you not know that there is but one only that does well?" Being unable to restrain himself the king understood them and said, "I repent that I made man, for I keep him with great pain. And it is necessary that I suffer pain for man, whom I have made." And then he called the Angel Gabriel and said to him, "Go and say unto the Daughter of Zion: 'See here your sweet king who comes to you.'" And unrestrained the Angel hastened and said, *Adorna thalamum tuum, Sion*, "Oh Daughter of Zion, glorious virgin, prepare your chamber that you may receive the king of kings in it."

Oh, you creature, you therefore say how great how great was the danger, and how great was the sin, and how very difficult it was to find a remedy? For this reason they consented to the foregoing virtues, after which Scriptures were accomplished, and Mercy and Righteousness met together.

Pope Leo says about this: "But because the devil had not shown himself so violent in his attack on the first man as to bring him over to his side without the consent of his free will, man's voluntary sin and hostile desires were to be destroyed so that the standard of righteousness should not stand in the way of the gift of grace. Then, in the entire human race there was rationally but one remedy which could give assistance to the fallen, and which ought to be innocent and free from the original transgression of Adam's sons, and win over the rest by example and merits. And it is for this reason that the natural generation may not proceed from David's Lord that he is made David's Son. And in the same manner the line of descent is born without vice, of the fruit of the promised line." About which Saint Anselm says, "Our nature at the beginning was made in God's image, so that it might ever more have abundance in time to come with God himself, and afterwards be a partner of His glory without the blemish of sin or change. But it had easily lost all His great goodness when our forefathers fell into this miserable world; and yet more poorly shall they fall into everlasting pains when this life comes to an end. The time is over and I pass away. The greatness of damnation of the sons of men has been ever enforced and strengthened, that the sovereign wisdom of God may not find any other manner in all of humanity's history by which He was also disposed to come to win back the world which was in such decay and condition, up to the time when the Virgin had come. But unrestrained as she came to the world by the line of human nature, she was resplendent and shone so much in all goodness, virtue and steadfastness that the wisdom of God engendered her to be truly worthy that he would come by her and become man. And He would not only do this because of the sins of our father, but for those of the whole world; and He would snatch them from the hands of the devil, his enemy. And so he would renew man, who had lost his way to heavenly glory by his sins. Having then had great concern about these things, man might have greater admiration for the praise and dignity she has deserved before all other creatures through such great goodness." Saint Anselm also says about this: "A man ought not to believe that this Virgin was by chance and suddenly found, but she was pre-elected and predestined by God before the beginning of the world, which really means ever without end." John of Damascus, the Damascene, says: "This mother of God was predestined by divine counsel, and provided

by God everlasting and before all time. And she was chosen beforehand, imaged and figured by the Patriarchs and
Prophets by the inspiration of the Holy Spirit in various
images, figures and holy works."

Now let us lift up our mind's intellect and desires in acts
and deeds of grace, and let us offer affections to God for
the great pity He had on us, saying with Saint Anselm: "Oh
Jesus Christ, king of kings, we pray to you, who art the light
of people, the prince of princes of the earth, the Lord of
heavenly hosts and the virtue and strength of almighty God.
We pray to you, being the precious price of our redemption,
to delete and appease what by the inestimable sweetness
of your odour or taste has made the Father who dwells on
high to behold what is lowly, and returned it to the sons
of anger, to pacify and bring peace with your compassion.
Oh Jesus Christ, we offer ourselves in all abundance in the
mirror of your sweetness. To you, Jesus Christ, we make sacrifice with affection for the greatness of all your sweetness,
which you have shown to us evil abodes and children of
perdition. Oh Lord, though we are still your enemies and
ancient death still exercises its lordship on us creatures,
which we have owing to the culpability of our forefathers,
remember your sweet mercy, looking from your abode on
high at this miserable vale so full of tears. Oh Lord, you
have seen the affliction of your people, and has smitten
them with the intensity of your charity, and are willing to
provide for our peace and redemption." It is Saint Anselm
who speaks of these things.

And afterwards, in the twenty-seventh year of emperor
August, the Blessed Virgin was born of the root of Jesse.
She was saintly owing to her poverty, tender by meekness,
righteous by intent and charitable. She has brought forth
to us the passing fair flower, Our Saviour Jesus Christ, and
upon her rested the grace of the Holy Spirit with his seven
gifts. This Blessed Virgin was prefigured by the gate which
God showed to Ezekiel, which never ought to open, but it
is only the Lord who can will to pass through it, and in
being ever standing it is closed and shut. For in the same
manner as a flower neither blemishes nor defiles a herb
garden, but makes it fair and sweeter, in the same manner

the Son of God does not blemish the Virgin, but makes her even more fair and sweet with great gifts of graces.

She was born of her father Joachim from Nazareth, and of her mother Anne, hailing from the castle town of Sepphoris, sited some two miles from Nazareth. They were two just people before the eyes of God. The Virgin was descended from the line of Judah and David; for as Chrysostom says, it was worthy and appropriate for the divine mystery that Mary, who should be the mother of the Son of God, accord‚ ing to what was written should be born of royal descent, and the Son of God, who is the eternal king and priest, has taken human nature from her.

The Virgin's parents, having no child after twenty years, heartily prayed God to send them one; and they vowed that should they have a child they would offer it to God. And when Issachar, the Old Testament priest, notices Joachim there offering oblations to God, he despised him along with those around him calling him barren or one who could not beget any children. When Joachim heard this, thinking that this was shameful for this to happen, he went alone into the fields to tend his herds. And there the angel of God appeared to him comforting him and saying that his prayers were heard by God. Then Joachim gave a third of his goods to poor people, and the other third to the temple and its ministers, while sustaining himself and his household with what remained. And the angel said to him: "Your wife Anne shall conceive a child, whom you shall name Mary. And she shall be consecrated to God as you have vowed. And she shall be filled with the Holy Spirit in her mother's womb. And she will lead her life in the temple of God." And the angel also announced this message and gave it to Anne. And as the angel bid them, they both went to Jerusalem to give praise and thanks to Our Lord God, after which they went back to their house. When all this was accomplished, Anne conceived and was with child, a daughter, who she called Mary.

She was prefigured in the king's daughter, called Astiagis, who, as it is written in Scholastica's stories, he had seen in a vision where a fair vine grew and sprang from his daughter's womb, which was so delicious to see, all replete with flowers and branches and bearing very fair fruit which gave shadow over all his realm. He was then told that his daughter would give birth to a great king, who was after to beget king Cyrus, the deliverer of the children of Israel from their captivity in Babylon. The same was said to Joachim, that he should have a daughter who should bear the king of kings, Jesus Christ, who was to deliver us from the captivity and servitude of the devil; he was the true vine which is the delight and comfort of the whole world.

The Virgin was by singular privilege purged and preserved in her mother's womb from any culpable original sin. Saint Bernard says about this: "Amongst the fair prerogatives of the Virgin Mary, this is a great one, for without doubt she was a saint before her birth. I think that a greater multitude of blessings descended in her when she was in her mother's womb than in any other saintly persons in their mother's womb; which not only made holy or kept her nativity holy, but in the same manner preserved and kept her life clean from sins. For it was seemly that due to her singular privilege of living a clean and sinless life, she was bound to bear and bring forth God, the destroyer of sin and eternal death. And so it was reasonable that she had and obtained the gift of holy life and righteousness before all others." As Saint Augustine says, before conceiving the Son of God the Blessed Virgin was sanctified and made holy in only that she might commit venial sins, but after the conception of the Son of God she might commit neither venial nor mortal sin. And this thing was proved by the fountain or well that was at the Jordan, which was enclosed on every side; for the Holy Spirit made her holy while she was in her mother's womb. And he blessed her in such manner with the sign of the Trinity in that nothing has ever since entered her that might foul or infect her.

And some time later when the Blessed Virgin was three years old, she was brought into the temple where she was presented by her parents; there she dwelt with other virgins in the inner part of the temple, that she should be taught good conduct and serve Our Saviour and Redeemer Jesus Christ, dwelling in that place until she was fourteen years old. And this Virgin's oblation was shown by the Son's presentation table, about which Scholastica recounts that certain preachers cast a net into the holy sea and by chance drew out a table all made of gold. This was materially presented to the Son's temple where they prayed, built on the shore of the sea of Zebulun. Similarly the Virgin was offered into the temple of the everlasting Son. And it fits that she might be compared to the golden table, for the heavenly food is given to us on it; for she has born us the Son of God, Our Saviour Jesus Christ, who has made us partners with his flesh and blood. She was also compared to the temple built by Solomon to God. This temple was built with polished stones, and very preciously adorned inside with gold and precious stones. And the Virgin Mary was very white too endowed with the whiteness of the pure chastity within her, and the precious stones inside stood for the very pure charity within her. She was also prefigured by Jephthah's daughter, who was offered in thanksgiving for the victory over her temporal enemies. Mary was also offered before the victor, or winner, that we may obtain victory over our spiritual enemy. And where she was first chosen close to the Ark of the Covenant which contained the Law tablets. For Mary had two tablets on which the ten commandments were written and which she kept diligently. There was also in the Ark the Book in which the Law was written, in which Mary found great delight to know and to read the Holy Scripture. And Aaron's rod, which had blossomed, was in the Ark, just as Mary bore in her womb the blessed blossom or fruit of life. In the Ark there was also the manna which God had sent to Moses to keep in witness, just as Mary has borne unto us the heavenly manna itself. The Ark was made of acacia wood that it might never get rotten, the same as Mary does not return to ashes or dust. The Ark had in its four corners four golden rings; and Mary held within her the four cardinal virtues, and these are at the root and head of all other virtues. The Ark was gilded on the inside and outside, as Mary shines and casts her light both within and outside of herself by her fairness of virtues. How Mary served God and led her life was prefigured at the garden which the king of Persia planted for his wife on a high building from where she could see her land which was far from theirs. And this showed the contemplative life which Mary led, who in the temple she contemplated and imaged eternal peace.

By divine grace she started reasoning, and when her parents had left her to abide in the temple, she thought in her heart how she would now have God the Father and the Son to teach her the Law. Many times she thought devoutly of what she might do to please God, so that she might please Him so well that He would bestow His grace on her. She very earnestly yearned for God's grace to keep His commandments, and that it pleased him to make her to love all those things He loved, and hate all those He hated. And she also asked for all the virtues by which she might find grace in God's sight. And so she profited in an ever better way in God's service. At all times she was beside herself in contemplation, prayers, reading or doing virtuous works, as she prayed unceasingly for man's salvation. And she read gladly in the holy books about the coming of Our Saviour Christ. She read all that she found about the Incarnation of the Son of God twice over, sweetly kissing and hugging the book. She was the first among the faithful, the utmost shown of God's divine wisdom, the meekest of all, and the most joyful in God's service, the most gracious in loving God and the purest, the most clean and the most perfect in all virtues. She was constant and not inconsistent, passing her time ever for a better purpose. She was never enraged nor angry, for her words were so full of grace that a man might know God from what she said. She always kept herself busy among her company, for the purpose that none should ever be offended in anything she told them. And she never raised her voice in laughing or cheer. And she never showed pride nor offence amongst her companions by which they might offend God who she blessed at all times. And so that she might not surrender herself to pride or be troubled with it, she answered and said *Deo gratias*, thank God, to whoever greeted her. And so it was she who first said and answered *Deo gratias* when a holy person greeted another. She was also the first who made the vow of virginity to God, unless God ordered her to do something else, and that vow had never been made since the beginning of the world. She kept herself going so wisely, meekly and devoutly, that her life was an example of good living to all others. This is what Saint Ambrose says about her: "The life of Mary is written before our mind's eye as a fair mirror, lighting up the beauty of chastity and the form or mould of all virtues. For she is a virgin in body and thought, humble of heart, agreeable of speech, wise of conduct, fast in speaking, always studying the Holy Scripture, setting her hope in prayer for the poor and not in vainglory or in riches. She paid heed to her works, was modest of speech and eager in all her being to please God and not the world, ever glad to worship her elders, not envying anyone in her company, fleeing temptations and rewards, inclined towards reason's judgments, and praising and commending virtues. Who can say that this maid was ever found to have any guilt in deed or in thought? Or that she despised the meek or mocked the simple? She held no resentment in her sight and was not bold in her speech, all her deeds being modest and her body representing her thoughts. The glorious Virgin Mary was such that her life alone was an example and a rule to all those who wanted to lead a good life. And therefore, if she led such a holy life as she would please to show us by her works, she did it for the purpose that we may desire to have merit with her and follow her by example."

This is our guide, prefigured and provided by the star that Balaam had prophesied to be born of the line of Jacob. Similarly, Mary makes the star to light up and give shine to those who swim in the waves of this world's sea, leading them to a good haven. And without her we may not pass the danger of this troubled sea, nor come to the haven of the heavenly region.

And Saint Anselm says about her: "Since when this Virgin was born and passed her childhood years, who can ever think or fathom how she ordered herself and how she persevered devoutly in following God's ways? Certainly, there is no doubt that her very chaste body and soul were ever preserved by angels, continuously keeping her from all sins, as she was the hall in which the maker of the whole world should take his dwelling, and of which he ought to take our human nature, and herself in union with him by marvellous divine actions. And there should be no marvel in this, for if anyone may find among earthly beings this kind of behaviour, how much more should no one compare heavenly things with earthly things. For we see that when a great lord or a rich man wants to lodge in any place, his messengers seek an honest place and keep it and make it ready, so that it may be proper and pleasant to their lord who will abide in it. And if men make such furnishings to receive an earthly lord and persons of worldly might, what may we think of what was furnished in the heart of the most Holy Virgin for the coming of the heavenly king, who was not only in passing to lodge in her, but was to be made of her substance in this act and take the form of man?

She was also provided for mankind when at her nativity she was born and issued forth from the root and line of Jesse, father of David, from whose staff the most sweet Jesus Christ descended upon her and did proceed from her, she upon whom rest the seven gifts of the Holy Spirit.

Then let a devout soul diligently consider these virtues and good works of the Virgin Mary. And with your power enforce yourself to follow them.

CHAPTER 3
OF OUR BLESSED LADY'S WEDDING

IMILARLY, when the Virgin Mary increased in age and from day to day in virtues and since her parents had left her, Our Lord made her his own and sent her his angels to visit her every day. And he gave her solace that would keep her from going astray and caused her goodness to abound. She kept on living so in the temple until she was fourteen years old. It was then that the overseer demanded and let it be known that all maidens who were in the temple and had reached that age, should return home to their houses, from there to be united in marriage. They were all ready to obey this command, except the Virgin Mary, who answered that she might not do this since her parents had given her, as she said, to the service of God, and so had she also promised in her vow of virginity. The overseer was then very angry, for he might not go against the Holy Scripture which says, "You who have made any vow to God, give him that which you have promised him." And also he would not set upon something or bring up any new customs among the Jewish people, such as the vow of virginity.

By counsel of the elders he commanded everyone to pray, so that it might please God to show his will. And unrestrained, there was a voice heard by them all, which according to the prophecy of Isaiah said *Egredietur virga de radice Jesse,* "A rod or branch shall spring from the root of Jess," so that now they had to seek a man to whom Mary should be married. Then, in terms of the prophecy, he commanded that all those of the house of David who were not married and were able to marry, to take and hold in their hands a rod to the temple waters. Unrestrainedly, without waiting at all, Joseph's rod flourished, with a dove coming down from heaven sitting on its end; by which men knew that this was the man to whom this Blessed Virgin should be married. And although, according to Saint Augustine, Mary and Joseph had before being married commonly agreed to keep their virginity, they gave mutual consent to the marriage by revelation of the Holy Spirit. Neither had known of the other's vow, but when they had told of their vow to each other, they again vowed their virginity in being together.

Hugh of Saint Victor says about this, that although the Virgin had vowed virginity and her friends wanted her to marry, she dreaded being disobedient to her friends and would in no way abandon her vow of virginity, which was assigned to her by the Holy Spirit, whom she considered as the holy one of God, in having in him such trust that his divine mercy should keep her so that she might still be obedient to her friends in taking the state of marriage, while never being constrained to break the vow of virginity. She mentioned Abraham as an example. Acting rationally, Abraham had obeyed God's command and God gave him remission in his son Isaac after he had offered him up for his love on the mountain. Even so, however, this command was seen to go against the promise. Even more, in terms of seeing all things as being possible for God, Abraham believed that by being obedient in making his offering, God might accomplish his promise. Likewise it so happened that his obedience helped to deserve God's merit, and here the promise followed the effect. This might also be the Blessed Virgin Mary's purpose.

Saint Anselm says about this that Mary certainly loved greatly these two things: virginity and fertility. Virginity, for she knew well that virginity was in everything most pleasant to God. Fertility or motherhood, for she dreaded the curse of carnal law that men marked off those who were sterile or did not bear children. So there were two things in the Virgin's soul that fought strongly against each other. These were her wish to keep her virginity to God, while yet dreading the Law's curse or anathema. Her constant wish to keep her virginity won over the dread of deserving the curse of the Law. Then, this tender and delicate Virgin of royal lineage and descent, and the fairest of the most fair, with all her intellect, love and study, intended none else but to consecrate herself and make her body and soul holy to God for ever with the vow of virginity. For she knew well that the holier the vow of virginity was seen in her, so much more did He, who is the utmost chaste king and is chastity himself, would draw near to her. And then, embracing that which she knew as being most pleasant to the Lord of the Law, she believed that she would plainly go against the curse given by the Law. Generally believing that she had within herself that which was so good and of such great wisdom, she was certain that according to her conscience she might not think of anything else better or more true which might make her abstain from all sins. And she was not deceived in this. Who is he that having had hope in God was left astray or forsaken? No one. In the Virgin there was holy intent, chaste purpose, steadfast faith and such constant hope, and charity never failed in her. Here may we see how the Father of mercy had sent upon her his blessed oil, so that she did not depart from her intention, nor would such great virginity be fouled and steadfast faith diminished, nor that her steadfastness and hope should ever change, or that the great bounty of charity that was in her should ever change or fail. And his help was given to her to deliver her from what she feared, and he kept her so that what he loved in her should not be cast away. And so that no one would think about her that she had deserved the curse of the Law, he gave her fertility, and with her virginity the fruit of motherhood.

And this helps us to know about the line of Mary. It is mentioned many times in the Gospel that Saint Anne had three husbands in succession. The first was Joachim; the second, Cleophas, brother of Joseph; and the third, Salome. And she had a daughter from each of them, whom they always called Mary. And each of them had a husband. The first had Joseph; the second, Alpheus; and the third, Zebedee. From the first was born Our Saviour Jesus Christ; from the second, Saint James the Lesser and Joseph the Just, who is called Barsabbas, with Saint Simeon and Saint Jude; and from the third, Saint James the Greater and Saint John the Evangelist. And although Saint James son of Zebedee is the last, yet he is ever called the Greater, because he was the first to be called by Our Lord; and owing to this distinction Saint James son of Alpheus is called the Lesser. For which reason Saint James the Lesser and his three brethren are above all others called the brethren of Our Lord, for they were not only cousins of two sisters, but so also sons of the two brothers Joseph and Cleophas. Nevertheless, among all others Saint James the Lesser is called the brother of Our Lord by a figure of speech called antonomasia, for he resembled him very much in face and physical stature.

And it should be known that Our Lord wished his mother to be a married woman and that he would be born of her in a state of marriage for many reasons. Some causes affected the child, others the mother, while there were also other causes.

There are five reasons on the child's part. The first being, according to Saint Jerome, to declare her nativity, so that the line of the Virgin Mary was shown by Joseph's descent, whose cousin she was, and that the genealogy of Our Lord was according to the Scripture written by man and not by a woman. The second, according to Saint Ambrose, is to put away all suspicion, since it was not to be seen that men broke the Law, when she was with child although not being married. The third, also according to Saint Ambrose, in order to put away all doubts, so that Herod and the Jews were not to be justly seen as Our Lord's prosecutors as if he was begotten in adultery, and that he was not presented by misbelievers as one who was begotten out of wedlock. The fourth, according to Origen, for the child's sustenance on being taken to Egypt, that it might be nourished by the holy man Joseph. And for this cause Joseph is called Our Lord's carer. The fifth, according to Origen, Ambrose and Jerome, that the nativity of Our Lord was to be kept concealed or secret, so that the mystery and the upbringing of Our Lord was kept concealed from the devil who was to think that he was not born of a virgin but of a wedded woman.

Another five reasons concern the mother's part. The first, according to Saint Ambrose, so that she would not be defamed when people saw her with child without being married. And for this cause, Our Lord provided that men should not doubt about his nativity, nor that his mother is defamed. The second, according to Bede and Jerome, so as to put away the guilt and not to be openly shamed and stoned to death as an adulteress by the Jews according to their Law. The third, according to Saint Jerome and Origen, to give her solace so that in going to Egypt and returning from there she should be sustained by the service of the good man Joseph. The fourth, according to the *Interpretation*, to inspire the faith, so that men should even put greater confidence and belief in the words of the Virgin Mary. For if she had been with child and was not married, it would have been thought she had spoken aberrantly, and men would not have believed her in saying she should be called a virgin. The fifth, for she ought to be included in another family status, such that Our Lord's mother should have something to do with each state of virginity, marriage and widowhood.

Additionally, five reasons are given for other causes. The first, according to Saint Ambrose, in order to cast away all false justifications of sin, to the end that she should not cover shameless virgins leading an evil life with an excuse by which they should think that the Mother of God were defamed. The second, according to Origen, to confirm marriage, contrary to certain heretics who say that marriage was not good; so that the two states of virginity and wedlock should be proved, when men see that Jesus was born of a maiden and a wife. The third is to put away all chidings and shame, so that in the person of the Virgin Mary all the rebuke which Eve, the first woman received is removed as she was put away from the status of women, as well as virgins, wives and widows. The fourth is to give example, whereby it is shown that after being married, and before being thoroughly acquainted with each other, one may freely choose a better status and make more solemn vows as to enter into religion, without the husband's consent; this was the case as shown in the Virgin Mary. The fifth, according to Chrysostom, to show the mystery that the Holy Church is the spouse of Our Lord Jesus Christ, who is ever a virgin without spot or blemish, of which virgin we are children in the faith of Our Lord. For according to Pope Leo, Christendom is born from the body of the Church from the same spirit as Our Lord Jesus Christ is born from the body of the Virgin, namely from the Holy Spirit. And on this account, according to Chrysostom, the Virgin Mary was wedded to a hewer of wood, that is to say to a carpenter, since Jesus Christ, spouse of the Church, should labour for the salvation of all by the wood of the cross. And according to Saint Augustine, Our Lord Jesus Christ, born of his mother who was married to a hewer, killed and murdered all the pride and growth of fleshly states.

This Virgin was prefigured by the virgin Sarah, daughter of Raguel, married to young Tobias, who kept her soul from all carnal lustfulness. Even much more and stronger was the Virgin Mary, the wife of Joseph, who remained virgin for ever without spot of defilement. Similarly this Virgin is compared to the very strong tower that was called Baras, which, as it is written in the story of Scholastica, may only be defended by two men against all their enemies. So too the Virgin Mary has been very strong and invincible, of whom the sovereign God, who is eternal wisdom, was her principal safeguard. Her life was also compared to the tower of David, where a thousand shields and bucklers hung, their light surpassing brightness; she too was light in all her virtues, whereby her life was defended against all her enemies in overcoming all sins and temptations. This she did not do on her own, but it was by the grace of God which was in her that she put away all temptations of whatever kind from her heart.

Now let us consider how many women and maidens came before this Virgin, and yet she has deserved to be the mother of the Son of God before them all. For certain, this is a great grace and hard to know that only one among so many thousands is exalted to this dignity. She was exalted before all women, for she exceeded them in living a holy life. Saint Anselm says about this: "God has searched the hearts and minds, and before all that existed in the world, He only chose this Virgin. He has consecrated her, so that he would make His dwelling in the flesh in her, whom He had before nourished full of virtues and spiritual things. I believe she surpassed all women in holiness, as men may see if they consider it. For while others have deserved having some part of grace from God, this Virgin was hailed by the angel as being full of all grace."

CHAPTER 4
OF SAINT JOHN THE BAPTIST'S CONCEPTION

N the time of the reign of Herod, king of the Jews, there was a priest called Zechariah descending from the line of Abijah, who had a wife called Elizabeth descending from the line of Aaron. Both of them were just people before God. Unlike what these hypocrites do, in doing good works for the eyes of the world and toiling in all the commandments while pretending to observe the moral commands, these two were just before God and observed the commandments justly. Their conduct with their close neighbours was peaceful. Yet they were childless, because she was barren and past her child bearing age, and similarly old age was his cause like that of her barrenness. Because of this it appeared that Saint John's conception was miraculous since it was not only by nature, but by nature joined to the grace of God.

It should be known that it was a custom each month to have instituted or set in place a one and only special priest who, when he should die, another one by order would be his successor. Then David, who was willing to help in the divine service in the temple of God, set there twentyfour of his household, descended from the line of Aaron, of whom only one was preeminent and was called the prince of priests. He also ordained that each one of them was to take his turn of service each week, from Saturday to Saturday. Their week's work being to study in all chastity, they should not then return to their own house but dwell in little cottages erected close to the temple, where they would abide. And for each one of them he ordained his week by lot; and the lot fell and came to Abijah, from whom Zechariah, father of Saint John the Baptist, was descended. It was him who in his order might do the priestly service, as the lot fell, and that was the eighth week. Then, going out of the house where he had worn the priest's clothing, he went into the temple to offer incense to God. That was the fourth day of the seventh month, that is to say September. Meanwhile the people prayed outside the temple for no way were they allowed to enter into God's temple. This indicates that Zechariah was not the chief and sovereign priest, but a simple one.

Morally, this is interpreted as Zechariah having his mind set on Our Lord, meaning that the good prelate should bear close to his heart and remember God for his salvation and that of those committed to him. A good prelate should enter God's temple exercising diligently the service of God, offering incense by devout prayers while the people pray as taught by him and his learning. For one ought to have in mind three elements existing in God, which are His might, in regard to His works of creation; His wisdom, in regard to His works of creating anew; and His goodness, in regard to His works of reward. The first is said as to the Father; the second as to the Son; and the third, to the Holy Spirit.

The angel Gabriel appeared to Zechariah standing at the altar's right side, where he offered incense. On beholding him, he feared greatly, seeing the high and mighty nature of an angel, which he had never seen before. There is a great difference between a good angel and an evil one since the evil angel is always dreadful and horrible to whoever sees him. And according to Bede, there is nothing that shall sooner overcome this angel than steadfast and fearless faith. The good angel, on the other hand, instantly comforts and consoles a person. So because of this the angel immediately said to Zechariah: "Do not be afraid;" as if to say, "I am come to comfort you and that you may have joy." He afterwards said, "Your prayer has been heard." Zechariah had not prayed God in order to have a child, for he did not believe that; but he prayed for the sins of the people and for the coming of the Messiah. And for the people to be saved by the coming of Our Lord Jesus, the angel showed him that he should have a son, who should prepare the people's hearts by preaching, penance and true faith. And he gave him the child's name, John. Bede says about this: "John means the place where grace abides, or grace of God, this name being first declared to his friends, by which they might see that this son, who these old people had, was given and came by the grace of God. He was also declared John for his self-understanding, namely that he should be great before God, for the Holy Spirit showed him to be alive even in his mother's womb. The children of Israel too were given to understand that John was the one who should convert them to their Lord God."

The angel also showed his father Zechariah that he ought to be happy deep down inside while being outwardly cheer-ful. Properly speaking elation is a joy which is so great deep inside the heart that it cannot be understood unless it is outwardly shown. The angel also promised that many would be glad when he was born, for it would not only be a joyful event for his parents, but also for many others. To this day we see this happening, when not only Christians keep and feast the day of John's nativity, but also the Sara-cens and others too. Bede says: "As it was dutiful to do and not without cause the father found great joy in having a child full of such graces in his old age. And it was not only John who was joyful, but he also gave joy to all those who, entering the heavenly realm, had not yet even been born or had the Gospel preached to them." Saint Ambrose says: "Men ought to have great joy and delight in the generation and nativity of the righteous, for John did not only bring glory or gladness to his parents, but also because this should be the cause of salvation for many. And we must be admonished because of this in order to have joy in the saints' nativity."

Morally, in each one of us we may find Zechariah and his wife Elizabeth who has borne him a son who was to be called John. And man ought to be joyful and to exult in this, and many ought to be joyful in his nativity. Through Elizabeth, wife of Zechariah, a man may perceive flesh joined to the spirit. Similarly as a man governs and chastises his wife, so ought the spirit to govern and chastise the flesh, that it might not become mistress and fall into the sin of fornication; like with the child John who was being incit-ing by the spirit to exercise good works, as in giving alms and clothing to the poor, in visiting the poor and the sick, in burying the dead and doing other works of mercy; and so is the wife, like the vine abounding in all good, in her husband's house. The child should be named John, just as saying the grace of God, for none ought to attribute the good which he does other than to the grace of God. And to him this same child shall bring joy and exultation in finding his joy in God through his good works and the gift of the Spirit shall be everlasting joy. Many then shall have great joy in the nativity of Saint John, for each should then find joy in one another.

So that we ought to take heed patiently that in enjoying ourselves outwardly in any solemnity, we also enjoy ourselves spiritually in our souls, and that our bodily joy is linked to spiritual joy, so that what remains of our thoughts may feast Our Lord. Doubtlessly, those who are evil may not have this joy as long as they persevere in it; so let us cleanse our souls from all sins that we may be worthy to obtain the joy and solace of such solemnity.

The angel has also shown greatness and magnificence that the child should be similar to God in virtue, holiness and worthiness. This greatness is found in four elements, according to four dimensions, as Saint Paul says, namely in being of very good conduct, in profound meekness, in being generous in charity, and finally, in the endurance of perseverance. Saint John had all these four elements as, according to Our Saviour's testimony, none is born of woman greater than John. Yet in these practices, the angel variously exalts the child's greatness and magnificence. He recalls many privileges the child should be having in saying that he should live in abstinence all his life; that he ought not to drink anything that might derange him, such as wine, beer or ale, for he should not fill and serve the dedicated or holy vessel of heavenly grace in exchange for the ways of the world. So that it appears that he ought to be clean of all vices which might subvert the state and desire of the soul. The angel also said he ought to be filled with the Holy Spirit both as to being purified from original sins and as to his virtuous works, wherein it is shown that in being born into this world he ought to bear fruit and shine in all virtues. He also says that he was to convert many of the children of Israel to the Lord Jesus Christ, and he did this in preaching and in giving testimony about him to others.

And yet the angel said that he should precede Our Lord and go before him in virtue and in the Spirit or likeness of Elijah. First, as to the similarity of the office; for just as Elijah shall precede or come before at the second coming of Our Lord, so has Saint John preceded him at the first coming. Secondly, as to the similarity of their lives; for they were both alike in their food and clothing. Thirdly, as to the similarity of doctrine; for both have constantly overcome the vices of renowned persons. It is for this reason that he ought to precede and go before, to convert the hearts of what the fathers believed to the sons by rendering the same understanding of the Scripture to them. And also he ought to convert the hearts of sceptics to make them just by observance and obedient to the faith. And he ought to prepare perfect people for Our Lord, to the grace of the New Testament as the Holy Gospel says. For the Old Law does not lead the soul along the perfect way. And this why it is called the law of fear, for they only withdrew from evil because of the pain suffered by those who are imperfect or evil. But the law of the Gospel, or the New Law, is called the law of love, since it departs from doing evil and accepts love for what is good. That belongs to those who are perfect and good.

Similarly then, as such a great child is born of barren parents, it often also happens that some who are in an advanced age and are barren, do good works by the gift and grace of God, making great fruit in the Church. This is the case with Saint Augustine and Saint Denis, who were in quite an advanced age when they were called to the faith of Our Lord.

Yet Zechariah, considering his wife's barrenness and his own age, did not believe what the angel had told him. And for this reason, he was as if dumb or one who did not speak, up to the nativity of the child; this means that at the coming of Jesus Christ the Law and the Prophets were to cease foretelling their prophecies. Whereupon Chrysostom says: "This is why Zechariah, a priest of the Jews, was dumb in understanding, since the sacrifices which he had offered for the sins of the people should now end. For the Only Priest had come who should offer himself to God in sacrifice for the sins of the whole world." It was also because he was in doubt and so deemed to be capricious; for his prayer was neither pleasant nor acceptable to God. He was also dumb after the revelation made to him because it is a sign that after a revelation or vision is made to man, one ought not to say anything as if one was unable speak, for in no manner should a person be lifted in elation.

When his days of office were over, Zechariah returned home, to the house where he was not allowed to go during the term of his office, nor drink any wine or anything that might derange him. And so this priest of the Law was to keep such continence of abstinence and reverence in performing his office, that this same cleansing and purifying ought to be done by all the priests of the world who consecrate so great a sacrament. As an example of this, some religious have an honest custom that the hebdomadary or governor, namely the one intervening between monks and God, does not depart for a whole week from the cloister and performs action outside the walls of the monastery, but only sets his mind on divine matters. Also in various rites, the hebdomadary does not speak for a whole week with his brethren; and in some canonries the hebdomadary has a dormitory room where he sleeps and lies.

After this, Elizabeth conceived, that is to say on the eighth day before the first day of October, on the sixth weekday, a Friday. And since she was quite advanced in age, she kept herself still for five months by holy modesty, up to the time when the Virgin Mary conceived, as Saint John her child had prophesied. And then she was glad in her soul of the coming of Our Lord; and although she was glad to have conceived and that the reprobation of barrenness was cast away from her, yet she was always badly ashamed due to her age, in having been so involved at her age as with such things as pertained to youth. For those who were aged and had no hope of having any more children, neither convened nor went along together. Bede says: "Elizabeth shows that her heart and mind ought to be in angels' keeping, since she kept nothing in her of which she ought to be ashamed so that her renown by that was not diminished, in bearing shame in herself about what she had herself desired to have." Be now ashamed of all that which is contrary to your soul and abstain from it, not only before man, but even more so before God and his angels. For as Boethius bears record, it is of great necessity that we live righteously, that we do all our works before the eyes of the judge who sees and takes heed of all things. And Saint Augustine says: "God is present in all I do, as He is the sovereign beholder of all thoughts, intentions and works. When I ponder deeply I am very confused. In all goodness and in all fear, I am confounded. I see Him present in all places, seeing all my secret thoughts. Certainly, there are many things in me which are evil and make me feel ashamed before him." And yet Anselm says: "When you sin by yourself alone, where do you suppose God to be if not there beside you?" And another doctor says: "When you do anything of which you would be ashamed if people see you, how can you not be more ashamed to do so before God, who sees all things, be it sin or breaking his commandments?' Certainly, one of the traits of man is for him to be modest in not doing evil or causing evil to be done. So that those who are shameless are unrepentant; for they deliberately avoid honesty and are like beasts of burden, and are brutes and forest dwellers among rational beings. 🙟🙝

CHAPTER 5
OF THE CONCEPTION OF THE SON OF GOD AND OF THE ANGEL'S WELCOME OR GREETING

N the sixth month after the conception of the precursor or forerunner of Our Lord, the fullness of the holiest and most fortunate time had arrived. It was the beginning of the sixth age, when the sovereign everlasting Trinity had ordained and provided to help the human race with the Incarnation of the Word, of the Son of God. God almighty, calling the Angel Gabriel, one of the first princes of his realm, and sending him into the city of Galilee called Nazareth to the Virgin Mary, wife of Joseph, and to her blood relation, for they were both of the house of David, and of the royal line, and above all the other most noble and religious houses, as Saint Bernard says. It has pleased God to reconcile man with him in the manner and order which he knew that he had fallen. For he fell when the devil sent the evil spirit to enter into a dialogue, or speak with the woman, and Eve consented. It was also this way, although in an opposite manner, namely that God sent the holy angel to enter into a dialogue with the Virgin who consented. The following words are full of great mysteries. And because of this, as Bede says, men ought to take good and solemn heed of them, and to go as far as putting them in the very depth of our hearts, for it is seen that all our redemption lies in them. We ought to willingly remember the beginning of our redemption.

It is then to be noted that the number six is not lacking of great mystery. Our Lord Jesus Christ has been conceived in the sixth age, for by him all things ought to be perfect. Six is a perfect number. He was also conceived in the sixth millennium, namely during the six thousand years from the beginning of the world, signifying that he is the purpose and end of all created things. He was also conceived in the sixth month, since the world was made in that month, as it ought to be put in good order by him similarly as it had

been first made by him. It was also the sixth day of the
week, Friday, for man was created on that day, which ought
to be remade by him. And similarly in the same age, in the
same month, and in the same day of the week, he has suffered death for us after thirty-three years had passed. And
perhaps, so that all things might be brought about together,
men might say that he was conceived in the sixth hour; for
in this hour he suffered death and in this hour had man
sinned. And similarly, by some analogy to the hour when
the first woman was overcome by the devil, Mary was shown
the mystery of our redemption by the angel.

Missus est igitur angelus Gabriel, "then the angel Gabriel,"
who is interpreted as being the strength of God, "was sent"
to show that the virtue and wisdom of God came together
to take our human nature, appearing meek to fight against
the power of the devil. And it is proper that this angel
ought to be in the order of archangels, for he was to show
great things. When men say that God sends the angel, in
saying God men may understand all the Blessed Trinity. At
all times this special mission is attributed to the Father.
The Father then sent him, since it was He who had to
show the providence of the spouse, and of the mother, and
of the Son. Also, that the Son of God was sent, for it was
him who ought to come into the Virgin. The Holy Spirit
was also sent, for he ought to make this mother holy and
surround her all around.

The angel was sent into the city of Galilee, which means
transmigration, for there one ought to leave the Law of
the Jews and return to the faith of Our Lord. The name of
the city was Nazareth, which is as much to say a flower.
It is very appropriate that the true flower which is Our
Lord Jesus Christ, was conceived in the flower which is
the Virgin Mary, along with flowers, that is in the time of
flowers. Similarly we shall say, the flower of flowers among
the flowers. Our Lord Jesus is called flower by the plenitude
or fullness and beauty of his holy conduct, for the fruit of
his passion, for the odour and pleasantness of his good
works, and for the profit and utility of the ways of life of
all true Christians. This flower flourished in the conception,
appears in his nativity, and was withered in the passion,

but resumes its figure in his resurrection. If you will gather this flower, follow the beauty of his conduct, preach the sweetness of his works, and in this manner you shall have the fruit of his passion. Our Lord had no will in his weddings to choose great cities, as these worldly kings do, at which nuptial feast he joined humanity to himself. But he wanted to choose Nazareth, a little city, there to show an example of meekness and to show us to always choose small and meek places. He has also chosen to suffer in Jerusalem, which is a great city, to show us that we ought not to be ashamed to suffer rebukes and injuries for his love in the presence of a great mass.

So Gabriel is sent to the Virgin of thought, body and vow. Our Lord would be conceived and born of a virgin. First, according to Saint Bernard, because it was agreeable that if God should be conceived and be born, this should not be but of a virgin. Similarly, if the virgin ought to conceive and be delivered, it should be no other but God. The second reason, according to the Damascene, was that in the same manner as God in heaven had a Father without a mother, so had He on earth a mother without a father. The third, according to Saint Augustine, was in showing that His mystical members according to the Holy Spirit had to be born of the mystical Church, which is a virgin. It is for this reason that he, being the head or overlord, wanted to be born of a virgin. The fourth, since just as the First Adam had been made of virgin earth, so should the Second Adam be made man by the Virgin Mary. The fifth, since just as man's downfall had been brought about by the virgin Eve, so was his restoration to be made by the Virgin Mary.

The angel was then sent to the Virgin wedded to a man. Wherefore God had will to be conceived and born at the time when his mother was wedded, as has been said before at the feast of Mary's espousal. And should be noted that four men of great renown are found in the Scripture bearing the name Joseph. The first was Joseph the son of Jacob, known for his prudence, for he discreetly explained the Pharaoh's dream. The second Joseph was the spouse of the Virgin Mary, known for his self-denial, for he kept the Virgin Mary in good renown. The third was Joseph of Arimathea, known

for his strength, for he went boldly to Pilate to demand
Our Lord's body which hung on the cross. The fourth was
Joseph the Just, known for his justice, and this is why he
was called just. The Gospel calls Joseph spouse of the Virgin, a man. And according to Saint Bernard, not only as a
husband, but because he was a man of great virtues and
since he was just, and similarly known to be legitimate.
And because of that, Joseph is said to be growing, which
means that he constantly profited in virtues. Mary's spouse
was then bound to have such a name, in whom men may
find the mysteries and secrets of all virtues. The Gospel has
added "of the house of David" so as to show that Our Lord
is descended from the line of David, as had been foretold
by the prophets. For although Joseph was not Our Saviour's
Father, the Virgin Mary, of whom he has taken our human
nature, was nevertheless of the same line and kin like her
spouse Joseph, from the line of David.

Also not without cause is the name Mary justified, for
her honourable name could be interpreted in three manners
according to three languages. In Hebrew it is interpreted
as *Stella maris*, star of the sea giving light. In Latin it is
ethymologie Mare amarum, bitter of bitterness. In the Syriac
tongue she is called *Domina*, a lady. This glorious Virgin
was star of the sea in the nativity of the Son of God, for
then she sent her light to illuminate the whole world. She
was bitter of bitterness in the passion of her son, for then
the sword, that is the passion of her son, went through
her soul which was full of anguish. But she was a Lady in
her assumption, when she was lifted up above all orders
of angels. She is also called the star of the sea in leading
sinners, and she leads them through the rough seas of this
world to the port or haven of penance and salvation, so that
afterwards they may come to her Son. And in this context,
the star appeared to the three kings in the nativity of Our
Lord and brought them to the place where the child was
born. And because of this, all the eyes of the sinners ought
to take heed, similarly as did "the eyes of" those seamen
in beholding their star. Saint Bernard says: "If you are not
overthrown by the tempest, then take heed you turn not
your eyes from this star. Now then, if you perceive that in

the world you are more amongst the floods and perils of the sea than secure on land, do not turn your eyes away, but behold the light of this star and call upon Mary. If you are cast out by the tempest and all covered and drowned in the waves of this sea, behold this star and call upon Mary. If you find yourself in the winds of temptation, and when you are driven against the rocks of tribulation, behold this star and call upon Mary. If anger, avarice or sensual pleasure bruise or break your ship or the vessel of your soul, behold this star and call upon Mary. If you are cast out by vainglory, or if you are troubled by the multitude of your sins, or if you are infected in your conscience, or if you are in fear of God's horrible judgment, or if you think that beginning now is too late to suffer for the love of God, or if you are all cast in darkness or heaviness or sorrow, think upon Mary. In perils, in anguish, in situations of fear, call upon Mary. See that she departs not from your mouth, or that she may not be out of your heart. And so that you should obtain the assistance of praying to her, do not ignore the example of her ways of life. And when you shall follow her, see that you do not depart from your way. When you shall pray to her, mind that you do not fall in despair. When you shall think about her, see that your mind keeps steadfast and does not err. When Mary shall hold you, you shall not fall, nor do you have anything to fear. Being under her protection, you shall never go astray; but she will bring you back again. And by her sweetness, she will make you arrive at what you desire. And similarly, in doing these things you shall surely see that by good right the name of the Virgin Mary means star of the sea."

She is also called *Illuminatrix* or she who lights, for she lights the world by example of her most holy life and by grace shining within her. And it is because of this that the Church sings about her as the one whose fair life lights up all churches. Saint Bernard says: "Put away from this world the Son, where should the light of grace appear? Put away darkness from me, blessed Mary star of the sea, that no obscurity may abide in me which might put me in the shadow of everlasting pain and darkness." This is the same star of the same great sea of darkness, where much evil abides that it cannot be numbered. The sky has many stars, but the sea has none but one, which is more clear than all of them, and even better. This Mary shines by merits when she enlightens by examples, since the true son of righteousness, by whom all things are enlightened, is only born of her. She was shown to Balaam by the star a long time before that she should be born of the line of Jacob. For Mary, the single female leader over all floods, and helper in every need, is the sovereign star without whom no man may pass this perilous sea.

She is also called bitter of bitterness in the conversion of sinners, whom she desired to convert from their sins, as if changing in them the water of carnal delights into the wine of compunction. This is also an adapt and proper name, for in all her life the sea of this present world was bitter and tasteless for her due to the desire she had to see her son in his heavenly realm. This is the person from whom came the abundance of all grace, the same as all waters come from the sea. Even according to Latin she is a river of the sea, inasmuch that there is a confluence of all graces in her as all rivers and streams return and flow to the sea.

She is also called Lady because of her help in all temptations and in delivering us from all perils and anguish, for she may both do it and will do it as the heavenly queen and mother of mercy. The name Lady is appropriate to her inasmuch as she is a lady, not only of man on earth, but also of angels in heaven and devils in hell. And because of this, in all the temptations and incitement of our spiritual enemy, men ought to call upon Mary. For according to Saint Bernard, the visible worry of the enemy is not so much caused by the great multitude of enemies they see coming towards them, as it is for the great powers of the air, the devils, who fear the invocation of Mary's name, her help and examples. For just as the dust flies before the wind, and as wax melts besides the fire, so do the enemies flee and depart when a man devoutly calls upon the name of Mary. And moreover it is said that the devil flees from the place where the name of Mary is called, and pardon is thereby given to the sinners, medicine to the sick, strength to the feeble, consolation to anything having affliction, help to pilgrims.

Or even so, men may say that she signifies by her name the three states of salvation. For in being bitter of bitterness, she stands for the active state; in being illuminatrix, the female illuminator, she stands for the contemplative state; and in being a lady, she stands for the state of prelates.

So then the angel was sent from God to the Virgin Mary to show her and say that the Son of God had coveted her beauty and had exalted her to be his mother, showing her and saying that she should receive this child in all joy, for God had ordained that it was by her than by that of any man that salvation should come. Saint Bernard says: "The Virgin Mary, in whom neither humility nor virginity ever failed, is very fortunate. For the purpose that she might conceive the saint of saints while still bearing a child and be holy of body, she observed the gift of virginity. And also for the purpose of being holy in thought, she had the gift of humility. Undoubtedly, she was by all this the royal Virgin, the most precious of precious stones, of virtuous lighting, of double beauty of body and soul, so that by her appear-ance and singular beauty and by the respect she evoked in the heavenly citizens in such manner that she made them covet and incline themselves before her, God sent to her a heavenly angel to greet her. *Et ingressus angelus ad eam*, "And the angel went unto her." Saint Bernard says: "I believe that where the angel entered before her was at the secret place of the chaste chamber or closet while she secretly prayed to the Father with the door closed and shut behind her. And men ought not suspect that the angel found the Virgin's door open, since this was shut to refuse man's company and to deliberately avoid vain speech, so as not to trouble the rest and the silence of her prayer, nor to let go of her good purpose of keeping chastity. Certainly, this very wise Virgin had at that hour the door of her dwelling place firmly shut to men, but not to angels." Mary then was not in any place where she could waste time, nor did she dwell in many places amongst people, but she was in her little chamber. And there she was not by herself alone, but surrounded by such a great company of her fairest virtues. Chrysostom says: "The angel did not find Mary walking around, but mind-fully entreating her contemplations. And since she did not

seek grace before the world, she found it there with God."
Ambrose says: "When the angel entered, Mary was found
in her secret chamber and without company, so that nobody
should interrupt or hinder her prayer. Neither did she desire
the company of women, as she had and was accompanied
by many good thoughts. Wherefore she thought she was
not alone when she was alone. How might she be alone,
having so many fair books with her and so many archangels
and prophets? Certainly, the Angel Gabriel found her there
where he was accustomed to visit her." Saint Jerome says:
"You shall have a little chamber where you shall be alone.
Yet you shall not be alone there, for the multitude of angels
shall dwell there with you. As many companions you shall
have there with you as there are saints in heaven. And, as
we read in the Gospel, the apostles and prophets and Jesus
himself shall speak with you. I ask you, whether you could
have better company than these that you may speak with
them all? Certainly not." Saint Bernard says: "I am never
less alone, than when I am all alone."

Men ought to believe that at that hour the Virgin was
there all uplifted in uttering devout prayers or contemplating inwardly, perhaps especially on her meditations about
human salvation, and how man ought to be saved by means
of a virgin. Some say about this that at that hour she was
reading what was said by Isaiah, that "A virgin shall conceive." This was a reasonable thing, that at the same time
as the Eternal Word would corporally be in one substance
with her, so at such hour would she spiritually be one with
him on high.

Then the angel entered before the Virgin and appeared to
her in the figure of a man, greeting her and saying *Ave gracia
plena dominus tecum*, "I great you, full of grace, Our Lord is
with you, you are blessed above all women." And saying
so the angel showed her that he who was invisible in her
would take a visible body in her. Although this was something admissible, it was hard to perceive. He appeared to
her in human likeness and had the form of a fair and most
shining body. According to Saint Augustine, he appeared
to the Virgin with a reddish face and in white clothing.
Then, most appropriately, the Incarnation of the Word is

shown to the Virgin so that first of all she should conceive by faith in her heart, and carnally in her womb. And the angel prompted or put together the name of Eve with this calling *Ave*, and said to the Virgin *Ave*, in showing that she was delivered from all curses. He also said well that she was full of grace, since to others grace is given by measure, but she had only deserved that grace which before her none ever had, that is to say being fulfilled with him who gives all grace. If this Virgin was already full of grace before her son's conception, who is it that might doubt the abundance of grace she had after such conception? Saint Jerome says: "And it is well said full of grace. For to others, grace is lent by portion, but in Mary all the fullness of grace is shed." Truly she is really full of grace, by which the dew of the Holy Spirit is distilled in all creatures, having given glory to them in heaven and shed peace upon earth.

The angel also said to her, *Dominus tecum*, "Our Lord be with you." That is namely, he who is in your thought and soul, be also in your womb. And he who has filled your soul, also fills your womb; and is now with you not only by essence, might and presence, as he is in everything, not even by grace, as he is in holy men, but also by assuming flesh and your most pure blood. And you should know that of the whole greeting of the angel, the most agreeable is the clause *Dominus tecum*, for in it she marvellously rejoiced. And for this men ought to say it in every devotion. And although he was now with the Virgin, yet he sent to her new messengers, for he would be with her in more singular ways. It is also to her that it is only said that she is blessed before all other women. For all defiled women were subject to the curse of God, saying that women should be delivered of child in pain. And all virgins were cursed in the Law, for they who bore no descent for Israel were cursed. But the Virgin Mary deliberately avoided both of these curses, namely God's curse by remaining a virgin ever after her nativity, and the curse of the Law when she had a child. And it is because of this that when she first of all offered her virginity to God, she cast away the curse of the Law. Thus she may appropriately be called blessed, for by her blessing the world is delivered from all imprecations and cursing.

It should be noted by this greeting, which God the Father has said and shown to the Virgin by the angel, that no man might ever attain to such understanding and high-ness. Nor could anyone salute Mary with a sweeter or more gracious greeting in her sight, for in each word very sweet mysteries are enclosed. Certainly, God the Father had that confirmed by his might, as she who bears this name *Ave* was free from all imprecations. The Son similarly shines upon her by his might, since she was the fair star by which heaven and earth should be lit up. For this is signified by the name Mary which means the star of the sea. The Holy Spirit, in penetrating her sweetness, makes her so gracious that all those seeking grace through her shall find it. This is meant by the two words *Dominus tecum*, about the union and ineffable operation by which all the Blessed Trinity is perfectly in her when the divine nature in one person has been united in the natural substance of her flesh, in such manner that God is made man and man is made God. Of the joy and sweetness she had at that hour, no one ever had full experience of this. By this clause *Benedicta tu in mulieribus*, all creatures marvel in her of the knowledge, and witness to her being blessed and exalted above all creatures, both in heaven and on earth. And also by the words *Benedictus fructus ventris tui*, "The fruit of your womb is blessed and exalted as the most excellent fruit of the Virgin, who has given life, sanctified and blessed all creatures without end."

This Blessed Virgin, hearing the angel's greeting, was astonished or troubled in her mind, and answered nothing. And her tribulation was never one of incredulity, as had been that of Zechariah or of others who were culpable, neither was the vision of the angel, for she had seen angels many times before; but she was mostly troubled, accord-ing to Chrysostom, since the angel was again appearing to her. For although she was accustomed to seeing angels, the angel appeared this time in a new physical form and with very clearly, and that is why she was somewhat moved and troubled. And it is because of this that the Church sings, *Expavescit Virgo de lumine*, "The Virgin was afraid of the light." Secondly, owing to the modesty of her virginity, since as Saint Ambrose says, it befits pure virgins to fear men approaching them and to doubt what they said to them. Thirdly, for the new manner and form of greeting the angel showed by what was said. For the angels were not used to greet her in that manner, nor had she ever heard such words before. So she, being wise and modest, answered nothing but thought in herself and examined these words deeply in her mind. Saint Ambrose says: "The Virgin marvelled in the new manner of greeting, which had never before been said to anyone, for it was kept only for Mary." Fourthly, she feared the high praise which the angel tendered her in what was said, as this meek Lady seeing herself so much honoured and praised had good cause to be disturbed in her mind. For it is a condition of very meek persons that the more they see men exalt and honour them by praise and commendations, the more fearful and modest they become. She was then disturbed by modesty and by virtuous and honest shame, and not moved into anger or being displeased. Whereupon Saint Bernard says: "The cause why Mary was disturbed was due to her virginal modesty. And in not being displeased in anything this was given to her by the gift of strength and since she thought within herself and said that nothing came her way by the gift of prudence and discretion."

Now the angel, beholding the Virgin and knowing completely that she had various thoughts in her heart, and also knowing why she felt annoyed, sweetly conferred with her again as though he was familiarly acquainted to her. And he called her gently by her name and encouraged her in no way to be afraid, *Ne timeas Maria* "Mary, do not doubt these things I am telling you. And be neither dismayed nor ashamed of the tidings I bring you, for all truth is in them." As if he would say, according to Chrysostom: "He ought not fear anything he who only yearns to find grace with God."

"Your haste," the angel said, "has found grace with God by the merits of your humility, your goodness, your chastity and the poverty of your conscience." About the first merit Chrysostom says: "How could anyone receive God's grace if it were not by humility? For God does not give his grace other than those who are meek." About the other two merits Saint Gregory says: "The Virgin has found grace with God, for she has prepared a dwelling place suitable for God in preparing her own soul with the beauty of chastity. And she did not only study in this virtue, but she also kept her conscience fully clean." Then, Holy Virgin, you have found grace, namely the peace between God and man, the destruction of death and restoration of life, in such manner that through you God has both enlightened and called back the world to everlasting life. She, then, who was there full of grace, has found grace, but it is so that she might spend it among others. Saint Augustine says: "Oh Mary, you have found the grace from God which you have desired and which you have dispensed throughout the whole world. And it is because of this that the angel said 'you have found,' and not 'you had' or 'would have had grace.' For what a man has and justly earns, he may as a result retain it as his own. But if he finds something which has been lost, he is bound to return it."

So Mary has found the grace which Eve had lost; and she found it not only for herself but for us all. For if we had not been sinners, God would have not taken our "mortal" human nature. And therefore, all we who have lost the grace of God because of our sins must surely return to her who has found it, and let us beseech her by repentance and devout prayers that it would please her to restore it to us again. For she is so liberal and merciful and rather willing and ever helpful that she may not deny it to anyone asking for it. She is so much disposed towards all sinners that whoever petitions her with good heart, is granted his request. Saint Bernard says: "Mary is ready at all times, and she opens the bosom of mercy to all creatures, so that the whole world might have of what she has in abundance. She redeems prisoners, gives health to the sick and consolation to those who are comfortless. She gives remission to sinners, grace to the righteous, joy the angels, and glory to all of the Trinity. ... Yet additionally, this Virgin is the ladder of sinners. In her I put my greatest trust as she brings effect to my hope and yearning. ... And I promise you that if she is called by us or is pitifully desired, she will have compassion and will never fail us in our needs, neither in will nor in deed, for she is the heavenly queen and mother of mercy. ... And for this reason no good Christian can worthily prosper unless once a day he presents her with some fervent prayer, and in so doing he need not doubt that she is there every day to help him, as well as in everything in which he needs help. Now my friends, let us prepare ourselves to serve her well and devoutly as we are bound to do. And moreover, I pray you, let us truly behold her in the profound honour ordained by God, and in the great honours this Virgin has and the abundance of full goodness in her, so that we might know that if there is any hope of salvation or grace in us, all comes as a gift from Mary. And also that all good Christians ought in their troubles to have their hearts and thoughts always set on the sweetest and most worthy Virgin Mary, for she is ever more kind and loving in helping us when we call her to our aid, and then for as much as we desire help. And so, my very sweet friends, do remember in your hearts, in all your minds and in all your thoughts, this most sweet and worthy Lady, mother of Our Lord Jesus Christ. Also Our Lord has ordained to give us nothing, unless it were with Mary's consent." Now since the Lord and master has given this power to her, let us be eager to present her with our devout prayers. I now say to you, blessed Lady, that you have found grace, for you are the woman who ought to receive the maker of grace, and you shall conceive in your womb without sin a child, of whom you shall be delivered without pain, and remain a virgin both at his birth and at his conception. And the angel said well that she should conceive him in her womb, for she had conceived him in her heart by her belief and devotion. And so ought we also to conceive him by devotion and be great with him by doing holy works.

"And the name of this child shall be Jesus." The angel did not say, "You shall name him so," for this name was given to him by the everlasting God the Father, and shown by the angel to Mary and Joseph, and by them to others. Also this name was bestowed upon him according to propriety and figure, for the human race ought to recover salvation by Jesus, and his name is interpreted as meaning salvation. And the angel then said about this that Jesus was to save and deliver his people from their sins. Indeed, these were the people whom he had joined him in faith and followed him in good works. And by this the angel showed God who himself alone could pardon sins and redeem men. And as Chrysostom says, those of Jesus Christ are not only those of the Jewish nation, but all those who come to the knowledge of him by true faith.

"Then this son whom you shall bear, shall be a great man," for he is and ever shall be great God. And the greatness which the Son of God has by his everlasting divine nature, he himself, as the Son of the Virgin, ought to take by grace in the time of his greatness when he is grown to manhood. And he shall not then be great like Saint John, of whom it is said that he should be great with God as a man, but this child shall be great as God and Son of God, as it here follows. "And he shall be called the natural son of the sovereign God, who alone is most high above all creatures. And the Lord God shall give him the seat of David his father," namely the realm. According to Bede, and about what the angel first said that Jesus Christ is son of the most high and after named David his father, that was a clear sign that in Christ is one person of two natures, that is the divine according to which he is the Son of God, and according to human nature that he is the Son of David. Then God shall give him the seat of David, not in this world, but in heaven; and not figuratively, but in all truth, what is said to belong to David; for the seat in which he sits corporally stood for the eternal seat which is in heaven. Bede says: "Our Lord has taken the seat or kingdom of David, for just as David, who was a temporal king, gave governance and an example of justice of his realm to the people and brought him to kindle the faith and love of his maker by the twelve hymns and spiritual songs which he sang, similarly Our Lord called the people of David's realm by works, words, pardons and permissions to his heavenly and immortal realm and has led them to the eternal vision of his Father."

The angel does not speak here of any temporal realm, for Our Saviour and Redeemer Jesus Christ has denied it before Pilate saying "My kingdom is not of this world," even though rightfully by inheritance he was king of the Jews. But he abode according to the heavenly and spiritual realm, for Jesus Christ shall reign in the Holy Church in this world as in heaven. And it is because of this that he after says that he shall reign in the House of Jacob and to be exalted for ever above all else. For certain persons from the house of Abraham and of Isaac were reputed to be wrongdoers, but all of Jacob's children were reputed by holy doctors among those who were exalted. For although some of them sinned, they always did penance. Therefore Jacob is interpreted to be "supplanted" by Our Lord. And he reigns as one who keeps their vices and sins low, but the devil reigns in those who make sins seem large. And Jesus Christ shall not only reign in the house of David, who hails from the tribe of Judah, but with him in the house of Jacob, that is to say in all the people of Israel, and in all the Church, and in all those who follow the faith and justice of David and Jacob. For they are the spiritual everlasting seats of David and of the house of Jacob where Jesus Christ shall sit and reign without end, now by grace and afterwards by glory. Blessed be all those in whom Jesus shall reign here, for they shall afterwards reign with him in his glory. "And his realm shall never end", for Our Lord Jesus Christ shall reign for ever, not only for being God, but also with what makes him human; and not only over men, but also over angels. Saint Bernard says about this: "Oh, how so glorious is the realm in which all kings are assembled together to laud and praise him who is above all kings, king of kings and lord of lords. Doubtless to say, by most deeply contemplating him the righteous shall shine, as the Son does in the Father's realm. Oh, if Jesus remembers me, a sinner, and it might please him to count me among his people when he comes into his realm! Or that it would please him to visit me on the day when he gives his realm to God, his Father, and to those who he has exalted, who shall there see him and find joy in him! Oh Lord Jesus, I pray you that while awaiting and abiding here, you would put away all rebukes from your realm, rather from my soul, so that only you may reign therein. For you are my king and my God, who sent salvation to Jacob."

And when the angel had finished recounting these great things, the Virgin was confused, for according to Saint Ambrose, she ought to believe in what the angel had said to her and not fear heavenly things. And willing to be assured about this, she first inquired as to the manner of conception, saying *Quomodo fiet istud*, "Angel of God, how is it that you promise me that I shall bear a son, if I have never known any man intimately and have vowed in my mind to keep my virginity before God?" As although she would say, "I believe well what you say, but I ask how I shall do it." Ambrose says: "She doubted not that she might do it, but she asked *how* she might do it. For she had read *Ecce virgo concipiet et aperiet filium*, "A virgin shall conceive and bear a son." And it is because of this that she believed he should come, but she had neither read nor found how it should happen. For this was never shown to any prophet, nor to anyone else, but only told to the angel who was to announce and show it to the Virgin." And the angel answered her, "I tell you that this shall not be done the human way, but in a divine manner. Not by man, but by the works of the Holy Spirit, who shall come from above into you and as divine fire shall kindle your thoughts and make your flesh holy, which, owing to your very great poverty, ought to be one with the Son of God. And you shall conceive in a singular way, saving your virginity." The Holy Spirit first of all enters Mary in the first sanctification, purging her of her original sins; but in the conception of the Son of God he comes in even greater abundance, confirming to the Virgin a much greater gift of grace and descending upon her as does the virtue of the Son upon the rose and lily, giving her virtue to conceive.

And although this marvellous conception is done by the action of all the Holy Trinity, for the works of the Trinity are outwardly indivisible, yet it is even more especially attributed to the Holy Spirit for many reasons. The first, according to Saint Augustine, in order to show that the grace of God is given without merit. For by what men say that Mary had conceived by the Holy Spirit, this show that it is by his grace only and not by the merit of any creature. For no merit has preceded so great a grace than when the grace is attributed or given to the Holy Spirit. As the Interpretation says, the Holy Spirit is he to whom is given all the grace which is inspired by God. The second cause, according to Saint Ambrose, is owing to the virtue of the work. For she conceived by the action and virtue of the Holy Spirit who is given the virtue of piety and meekness. The third, according to the Master of Sentence, is in order to show his overabundant charity, as given to the Holy Spirit, to show that the Incarnation of the Son of God is done by an inestimable charity God had towards man in giving up his only child for him unto death. *Et virtus altissimi obumbrabit tibi,* "And the most high virtue," namely the Word or the Son of God the Father, who according to the Apostle is called the Father's wisdom and virtue; and "shall shade or shadow him in you," that is to say that he will take a body from you who will be like a shadow, in whom he would be enclosed, as the clove spice is hidden and mingled in the midst of meat. Divine virtue was to conceal him within the shadow of the Blessed Virgin Mary's body. Or otherwise, he shall there shadow the presence of the divine majesty so that you may endure these things, by means of the body he shall take in you, which are impossible for any mortal woman. This, according to divine wisdom, is inaccessible like the sun which, when it does not shine, it is because it is covered by some kind of cloud between it and us, like the sky or anything else. Saint Bernard says: "This is why we say that God is spiritual, and we are creatures, for He is drawn to us under the shadow of Mary's body, since through his human nature we see the eternal Word in mortal body, as the sun in the sky and the light in the covert, or close place, and a tapering lantern light."

This is what men sing in the Preface of Our Lady, namely that the Virgin has conceived the Only Son by the shadowing of the Holy Spirit. Do not deny what we say that the shadowing of the light has been made by means of Our Lord's body. Since for both the Son and the Holy Spirit by the virtues of the Father, and the body of Jesus Christ agreed or set together one virtue to the other, namely as regards the Son as to the two to whom he is united or is one, and the Holy Spirit as to the Son whom he forms. By this it appears that these relationships may as well pertain to one as to the other.

Now consider here how the angel showed the Virgin all the Trinity. First, he called him the Holy Spirit in his own name; and after, the Son under this virtuous name; and so forth the Father was called the most high. And this was shown in the works of the Incarnation, in giving to the

Father the authority, the Son the taking of the body, and the Holy Spirit the works, in such manner that what one did, the other does as well. So that it is only the Son who has taken our human nature, and not the Father, nor the Holy Spirit, so that the world might be restored by the same Wisdom by which God had created it. And likewise, he was Son of God in divinity and Son of Man in his human nature so that the name of the Son might not pass to anyone who was not the Son of God by eternal birth. Just as having three maidens who are clad all in one clothing, about whom men might say that they all did one work, and what one did, the other did too, and still only one is clothed.

Ideo et quod nascetur ex te, "And for this, he himself who is holy shall be born of you and be called the Son of God," him who has always been the Son without end, but he was neither so called nor shown by any name but when God wanted. Saint Bernard says: "Who will say this that you shall conceive of the Holy Spirit, and not of man? Certainly, glorious Virgin, you shall conceive sovereign virtue, the Son of God. He who shall be born of your precious body shall be holy and called the Son of God. That is, not only he who comes from the Father's bosom into your precious womb there to protect him shall be called the Son of God, but for what he has taken of your substance and has been with you, he shall be called and reputed to be your son, engendered of the Father before the world. And so, he that is of Him, shall be yours, and he who shall be born of you, shall be His, for he shall be one only son and not two. And although he has taken other things from you than from Him, yet for all that he shall have neither there, but he shall be only one son to both." And take heed how the angel told the Virgin the Son of God would be *Sanctum*, "holy," without joining any other word; for if he had said "the holy flesh", "the holy man" or such other similar word, it would have seemed like not enough was said, nor that his holiness was expressed well enough. He has then been indeterminately called *Sanctum*, "holy," for undoubtedly what the Virgin had conceived was exceptionally holy.

And so that the Virgin shall might not in any way doubt that she was with child, and also for the angel that the Law was confirmed by example, the disparaging sterility and barrenness of the old woman Elizabeth was mentioned, for she was shown that all things were possible for God, saying "He who has given to the barren to conceive, which was something above nature, so he might also give to the Virgin. And for the reason that it may be easier for you to believe my words," the angel said to the Virgin, "I shall show you that your cousin Elizabeth, although she was reputed to be old and barren, in order for her not to despair that she could not have a child, six months have now passed since she has conceived a son by God's power." And since saying this does not perfectly mean the same thing to everyone, as it is much greater for a virgin to conceive than a barren woman, the angel showed the special cause of reason for God's power saying that nothing is impossible for God. So that consequently, God could also accomplish what had been promised by the angel's words. For God's word is understood as being done in deed, as it is written that God spoke the word and it was done or created. Without any contradic- tion everything is possible for God, like the Virgin being with child. Yet those things having contradiction in them, like when two persons contradict each other on anything, with their mind set on proving the truth, or what is done or not to be done, or other similar things, are in no way impossible to God, not for the possibility that were in God, but for the thing being impossible. As though the angel had said that neither the virgin nor the barren woman might not conceive by the virtue and works of nature, but that they might by divine power.

According to Saint Bernard, the angel only spoke to the Virgin verbally and not by any signs or symbols. For just as it is easier to speak and show what one would say, then also might God sooner accomplish what He desires by saying it verbally or in any similar kind of speech. Also according to the aforesaid Saint Bernard, the conception of Saint John is made known to the Virgin that she should increase her joy in seeing one miracle complementing another. Elizabeth too, his mother, kept this close to her heart for six months. This was reasonable, as it was expected of the Virgin to be the first to know that she might as well witness to the works of the Son of God as the might of the Father, and to later teach them to Gospel preachers. Elizabeth's conception was also shown to Mary owing to the holiness of Saint John, whom Our Lord Jesus had made holy while yet in his mother's womb. Also for the purpose that Mary would go serve her cousin who was then old, and to accomplish the virtue of humility. Mary and Elizabeth were second cousins, being the daughters of two sisters, that is to say of Anne and of Sobe, and both were of the same family of Judah.

Notice well and remember how all the Blessed Trinity is present in this closet, each one waiting for the answer of their outstanding daughter. Let us lovingly and sweetly take heed of the Virgin's very kind and sweet countenance and hearing her sweet words. Oh, how fortunate is that house where such company is found and where devotion is kept! For although the Trinity is in all places, the Son is ever here more eminently because of singular works. Notice also with great heed how the angel in all reverence and with sweet countenance encouraged diligently his Lady, and how wisely he put his words, that in this marvellous work the Lord's will might be performed and accomplished. And also take heed how the sweet Virgin did not hold back in great fear which she did bear meekly, and how her face was greatly embarrassed with shamefulness, when she was suddenly found by the angel and was not prepared about what to say and answer. Most certainly, she did not exalt herself to any extent by what which she had heard, although she heard great things being said to her, indeed so great that they had never been said to any other creature before her, and so with great wisdom she remitted them all to divine grace.

The angel, unrestricted after having accomplished the ordained task and announced the message, awaited the Virgin's answer. Saint Bernard says: "Oh Virgin, who has heard that you shall conceive, and not by human works but by the Holy Spirit, the angel tarries for your answer, now being time to return to the Lord. And we, sweet Lady, await the words of compassion, for we are under the sentence of a miserable damnation. Oh sweet Lady, see that you are being offered the price of our salvation. If you will now consent, we shall be delivered without any restrain. Oh most compassionate and meek Virgin , this is what Adam beseeches you together with all his poor posterity, having been exiled and cast out of paradise, and also David, your father, with the other good patriarchs, who desire and pray to you to consent to this message, for they dwell in the region of the mortal shadow. And similarly the whole world, glorious Virgin, falls flat down to your feet in expectation of this answer. Oh Lady, answer the words upon which heaven and hell and the whole world depends. Answer one word, and receive the eternal word. Show yourself, and receive the divine. Cast out what is transitory, and embrace what is without end." As Saint Augustine says: "Oh glorious Virgin Mary, the whole world, which is in captivity, prays to you to consent to these things. Oh Lady, the world sets before you their faith in pledge. Oh Virgin, do not wait any longer, but answer easily and hastily one word to the messenger and receive a son."

Then this most wise Virgin, hearing the angel's the words, consented. And as it is said, she bowed her knees in deepest devotion, and lifting her hands and casting her eyes towards heaven, so that in the lowliest way she uttered these words most eagerly from her heart that they might be in full and fervent affection, saying *Ecce ancilla Domini*, "See here the handmaid of God." Oh see here, she, who is exalted to be the mother of God, calls herself the handmaid or servant of God, in keeping ever before her eyes her fragility and the mercy shown to her by God. As though she should say, "I am nothing from my nature, other than this coming from Him and which He has given me. And because of this all is in his might, so let it be with me as you say." Oh most mighty and most virtuous word of the glorious Virgin, *Fiat* "Let it be," by which the sovereign God the Father created all things at the beginning, for he said *Fiat* and all things were made. We too, who were lost, the glorious Virgin has restored to life when answering *Fiat* to the angel. Saint Augustine states and says on these words: "Oh most fortu-nate obedience! Oh great and marvellous grace which was in this Virgin, who, when she meekly showed her belief to what the angel had told her, deserved the Son of God to take human nature in her." Anselm says: "Oh faith most acceptable to God! Oh humility most agreeable! Oh great obedience offered to God, and being more pleasant to Him than any other sacrifice! Oh sovereign Virgin and mother of God! Oh mother, most meek handmaid of God! What might be any higher? Oh mother, humble chambermaid of God! Who may perceive in you even more humility?" Behold her devotion. She calls herself chambermaid, she who is exalted to become mother. She was not so exalted suddenly with the promise made to her by the angel, nor did she again give the angel the prerogative of such grace, as though she would not have done what she was commanded to do. For it would not have been appropriate that she, who ought to bear the most sweet and meek child, that meekness was to be found in her before all others. And as Saint Bernard says, the virtue of humility is ever ready to receive the divine grace, for God removes grace from the proud and bestows it upon the meek. So then the Virgin's humility answered the angel saying that the seat or place was prepared, *Ecce ancilla Domini*, "Here is the helper or handmaid of God." Oh, what so high humility is this that does not start when such a great honour is done to her, nor that she will exalt herself of what is in her? Certainly, it is no great virtue to be meek in rejection, but it is great virtue and pain to find a meek person when having so many honours.

The Blessed Virgin was exalted in honour before all that is in the world by the angel's annunciation to her, and yet she still humbled herself in the meekest and most lowly manner. And for this reason incomparable humility is praised in her before all other virtues. For above all things the humility of the Virgin Mary pleased the Son of God so well that she made him to descend from heaven and take human nature in her, similarly as the iron is drawn or gotten from ore buried in the earth. Saint Augustine says: "Oh blessed meekness by which God has given life to man and to those who were dead, heaven was opened, and their souls delivered from pain. Mary's humility is made heaven's ladder by means of which God has descended on earth." It was most appropriate, as Bede says, that in the same way as death entered into the world by Eve's pride, so was readmission to life opened by Mary's meekness. The words which the Virgin said, *Ecce ancilla Domini*, were so pleasant to the Son of God that in Scripture he often calls himself more the "son of the" handmaid than the Son of the Virgin; whereby it appears that Mary's humility pleased him more than her virginity.

And although this Evangelist's words are full of great mysteries, the words which the Virgin said in giving her consent to the angel, show mainly many fair virtues in her. Since the six terms she used showed six virtues which were in her. She said *Ecce*, "See here," in which she showed the instant obedience which was in her. *Ancilla*, "the handmaid," which shows her perfect meekness. *Domini*, "of the Lord," whereby her unblemished virginity without spot of defilement is shown. *Fiat*, "Let it be," signifying her ardent charity which she had towards God and man. *Michi*, "to me," in which she shows her singular hope and belief. *Secundum verbum tuum*, "according to your words," whereby we may perceive her great faith in what the angel had said. And faultlessly the very faith was very much within the Virgin, for she believed that what had never been heard, nor found, nor seen, nor thought of by any in this world, might and ought to be done in her in the same manner as the angel had told her. About this Saint Bernard speaks of three marvellous things which God did in this Incarnation. The first, that God and man may be conjoined together. Secondly, that the woman in whom this conjoining is made is both mother and maid. Thirdly, that in these things man's heart and humanity have joined in perfect faith. And although this third conjoining is less than the first two, yet it is no less strong. It is very marvellous thing that the human heart had power to join faith to these two things, for how might one believe that God had become man, and that the mother who bore Him was a virgin before and after his birth? Because those "two" things may not be in agreement but by virtue of the Holy Spirit.

When the Virgin said these words, and unrestrainedly in this most holy hour, the Holy Spirit descended in her, and the glorious Virgin conceived the Son of God who entered into her precious womb in which he took our human nature and dwelt fully in the Father's bosom. Our Lord's body was all formed in an instant or one thought, and the reasoning soul created, and both were conjoined to the divinity in the person of the Son of God, because he was both God and man, in saving the property of two natures. The body of the Son of God took its form from the Virgin's purest blood and not the flesh. And in one instant the blood was separate, and the body made and formed, *anime et deifie*. And in this moment God was full and perfect man in body and soul according to all the members of his body. But he was so little that it was only with keen human sight that one might see his members distinctly, since he naturally grew in his mother's womb as others do. However, the distinction of his members or the insertion of the soul was not prolonged from him as with others. Also, he was a perfect man according to human nature, having a human body and a reasoning soul. And he was God and man, by the conjoining of the eternal Word to the soul and to the body in one person. For similarly as the Trinity is of one essence and three persons, also in opposite Our Lord Jesus Christ is one person and three essences ⁓ God, the soul and the body ⁓ that is to say the eternal, the new and the old. God is eternal; the soul, what is new; and the flesh, the old, proceeding of the old Adam. Our Lord is then engendered as to divine nature; he is created as to the soul; and he is made as to the body. And there were three unions in him, that is to say, the Trinity, or God to the soul, and the soul to God; and God to the body, and the body to God; the soul to the body, and the body to the soul. The two unions which come first ever remain in him, but the third was separated in his death. Then the union of divinity to humanity is not for the union of one nature, but it is in one person. And not only human person, but also divine, which is only the eternal Word. For it is impossible that the divine should conjoin with any other, or that it should be mingled in others or others in it. And because of this the divine and humanity are not united in one nature, but in one person. And this unity may not be in the person and as sustaining man, but from God. And because of this, God is made in one of these three persons sustaining human nature. Hugh of Saint Victor says: "When God took human nature, he took the full nature of man, that is the body, the soul. And not the person, but the man in the person, for the body and the soul before they were ever joined by the Word in one person, were not conjoined together in one person, and only by one union of the Word and the flesh and the soul were made one together. But not the body and the Word were not conjoined before there was the soul there, nor the Word and the soul before the body was formed there, nor the body and the soul before the Word, but all in one assembly; the Word, the soul and the body. And because of this, the Word in the person took the nature of man and not the person, so that he who received and what he had received were one person in the Trinity. And because of this, Our Lord Jesus Christ descended into Hades in one only person of the soul, and lay in the sepulchre in terms only of the body, and was overall in person according only to divinity. But you may ask wherefore is it written that Our Saviour Jesus Christ was and lay in the sepulchre, when he was but in one part, and why was he laid there in all parts. It seems that this gives man some occasion to think that three things should have composed or made Our Lord Jesus Christ, being namely the divinity, the soul, and the body. It is of no concern, since there were not many parts in him, as the Trinity being one part and human nature another, but he was fully man and fully God. Since divinity was not in him by parts, so that he may not be divided. But there were two parts in his human nature: the soul and the body. And where one of either two is found, the part of the man is there with it. So it is true that Our Saviour and Redeemer Jesus Christ lay in the sepulchre, and not as fully man, although he was there fully man, for the soul and the body were united in one person of the eternal Word. And it is because of this that where the body was, so were the Word and the Trinity."

Saint Anselm speaks thus of this Incarnation: "Oh Lord and king, who has seen the affliction of your people by your great mercy, and has willed thinking about us with thoughts of peace and redemption. And as you are the eternal Son of God, and of one single substance with God the Father and the Holy Spirit, dwelling in inaccessible light and governing all things only by your word, not scorning to decline bowing your high majesty into this world, which is a place full of misery and captivity, that you might take the taste of our wretchedness and bring us back to eternal happiness. Oh Lord Jesus Christ, it seemed to you by your great love which you have for us, that it was not enough for you to complete our salvation by sending us cherub or seraph or some other angel, but it has pleased you to come to us yourself by your Father's command. Certainly, Lord, we perceive well in this work the great love which you have for us. you are come in this world, not moving from place to place, but by showing your presence under the cover of our human nature, in descending from your royal seat into a maid who saw herself to be meek and discarded as to her reputation whom you named your chambermaid. So that she had made a vow to you of continual virginity, in whose womb by the singular virtue of the Holy Spirit, who is most marvellous in his works, has made her to conceive and be delivered in our human nature, in such manner that the occasion of this birth shall neither violate or defile your divinity nor her entire virginity." As so did Saint Anselm say to his sister: "I will first of all, being in your chamber, oversee the books which speak and prophesy the coming of Our Saviour and Redeemer Jesus Christ. And there behold seeing the angel and hear how the Virgin Mary is hailed. And there, with great joy, hail your most sweet Lady with the Angel saying *Ave Maria*, oftentimes reputing that she had this fullness of grace, of which the whole world has received salvation, by the eternal Word of God, who is made man. And thus continue with the great marvels that the Lord, who has fulfilled heaven and earth, is enclosed within the body of a maid, whom the Father has sanctified, the Son has glorified, and the Holy Spirit is covered in her. Oh sweet Lady, what heaviness might you now suffer or grieve, and by what love are you inflamed, when you felt in your soul and in your body the presence of such majesty, and when you saw that he took the human nature of your body, wherein there ought to dwell the fullness of the whole Trinity. Oh sister, if you might feel what ardent love was sent to this Virgin, and what consolation was put in her, and in what height this Blessed Virgin was exalted, and to what nobleness was human descent exalted, and how the divine majesty descended to us. If you might hear the sweet sung very joyfully by this Virgin, I think you would sing with her because of these great benefits shown to us and never cease giving thanks to God. So that you may have many times in your heart the joy which this Virgin had, do not depart from following her devoutly with the sweet welcome with which the angel hailed her. And in this greeting, sweetly fall on your knees at her feet as near as you may, kissing them and commending yourself to her holy protection and in confer-ring upon her *Ave Maria*. Saint Bernard says about this: "Oh Virgin Mary, I believe that you find great pleasure to hear this little verse all full of sweetness with which the Angel hailed you, the *Ave Maria*, as when men offer you a great amount of good. And because of this, my brethren, we ought to go to the image of this Virgin and kneel down before her offering this sweet present to her saying *Ave Maria*." And moreover, "When we say Ave Maria, heaven smiles, the angels sing, the world has joy, hell's devils tremble in fear."

Morally, six conditions are referred to here which the soul ought to have that it might conceive spiritually Our Lord Jesus Christ. It ought first to dwell in some secret place far from all worldly delights, like dwelling in Galilee, which is a transmigration, by taking no pleasure in any created thing unless it casts light on the Creator's image and perfection, like saying not loving anything which goes against either God or man. Secondly, such a soul ought to dwell in a field flourishing with flowers of works pleasant to God, like this Virgin who dwelt in Nazareth, who stands for the flower of holiness and good conduct. And such a soul ought to flourish by the whiteness of innocence, by the sweetness of divine influence, and by the shine of righteousness. Thirdly, such a soul ought to be a virgin, namely not only in restraining herself from all sensuality, but also from all other delights, in such manner that nothing might enter into her which might blemish or defile her, nor might she by way of her understanding let anything enter to defray her pure curi-osity. Certainly, as Saint Augustine says, a soul having such conditions may well be called a virgin. The fourth, such a soul ought to be married, that is to say that she directs her faith and love to one good thing, namely to one God, so that she does not set her mind on uncertain things as do those who now love one thing and tomorrow another. And she ought to be married to Joseph, which is interpreted as increasing, since she increased in faith and in love. For in a spiritual way, whoever does not advance in this, regresses and is deceived. And not without cause it is written that Joseph was of the House of David, which is interpreted as might and strength; for whoever wants to prevail in spiritual life, must bring himself forcefully to do virtuous works, for he must exercise spiritually this task. The fifth, it is written that the name of this Virgin was Mary, which means that the soul ought to be elated, so that the divine light would be upon her who has always had in her heart the spiritual joy which comes from God. The sixth, it is written that the angel Gabriel entered and hailed her and comforted her, which means that such a soul ought to be comforted by God with the gift of strength, which is the gift of the Holy Spirit, for the angel Gabriel is interpreted as the might of God. And when the contemplative soul is fortified by God, this enhances its hope and desire for God's presence, the fullness of grace and some extraordinary benediction above all other creatures.

And it is to be seen mostly in the third condition that mystically, since Our Lord was conceived and formed by the works of the Holy Spirit in the virginal womb of Mary, this signifies that he is conceived spiritually and formed in her thought by the pure operation of the Holy Spirit. For it is inevitable that the thought which will receive the eternal Word should be fully a virgin, not only from sin, but also from all kinds of created things, from all delights and corruptions; such thought will defer and abstain from all things which might foul it. For when the soul is not drawn away from all worldly things, it is subject and conjoined to all vanities. And then it may not raise to the divine contemplation of divine things, for it is somewhat defiled by being inclined too much to worldly things and living forgetful of its creator. Saint Denis exhorts about such withdrawal and Saint Paul says to Timothy: "Oh you, my friend Timothy, shun stupid and senseless controversies, calling upon the

Lord from a pure heart, he who is all substance and knowledge." Certainly, in withdrawing from such dissensions you
will be made perfect and blessed by divine favour. For Our
Lord says about this, "Blessed are those who have clean
hearts, for they shall see God." And the heart is made clean
when it is purged of all kinds of sin against man's salvation.

The conception of the Son of God was prefigured and
shown by the green hawthorn that was set on fire and yet
did not lose either its foliage or its greenness. The Blessed
Virgin too conceived a son and yet did not lose her virginity. And God dwelt in the green hawthorn bush and in the
Virgin's womb, which kept her luxuriant virginity. And as
God descended to deliver the Jews from the land of Egypt,
so did He descend into Mary to deliver us from damnation
when by taking our human nature from the Virgin, whom
He exalted above all women. And this was figured by the
wool or golden fleece of Gideon, which retained all the
dew of heaven, while all the surrounding ground was dry.
And similarly the Virgin was fulfilled with divine dew, for
no being in the world was found to be worthier than her.

This conception is done by the annunciation of the Angel
Gabriel, who was figured in the servant of Abraham and
in Rebekah, daughter of Bethuel. Abraham sent his servant
to provide for his only son a wife who was a virgin. And
the virgin Rebekah gave drink to the messenger, and he
thereby knew that it was she who should have his lord's
son in marriage. So did the heavenly Father by sending his
angel to seek a mother who was a virgin for his Son and
found a most suitable virgin who gave him drink, for she
consented to what he had told her. Rebekah gave not only
drink to the messenger, but also to his camels. Mary too
has given the fountain or well of life as much to man as
to the angels.

Then the angel Gabriel, having delivered the message
and what was ordained to be said, paid respect to her and
with great reverence took leave of the Lady. And so, having departed and being at once out of her sight, the angel
returned with great joy to the kingdom of heaven and in
recounting to the company what had been accomplished,
they feasted and rejoiced in great jubilation, for the spouse

was now come. And when this happened, the messenger departed, leaving the spouse in the most holy chamber of his spouse, for the marriage was then accomplished. The angel departed from the Virgin in the assumed form or shape taken on earth, yet still many thousands of angels abode with her in due reverence of their Lord, who was in her.

Men ought well here consider how great a solemnity is this day. Such thing was never heard in this world, since this day is the feast of God the Father who made his Son's marriage a wedding between God and the human nature he had taken; and God the Son united himself with this love and took it inseparably in himself. And as this day is the solemnity of the wedding of the Son of God in the Virgin's womb, it is also the solemnity of the Holy Spirit for this marvellous work which is attributed to him or thus given, for it is on this day that he began to show his kindness and sweetness to mankind. And this day is the solemnity of our glorious Lady, who is now known and taken for the daughter of the heavenly Father, and the Son in her as in his mother, and the Holy Spirit in marriage. This day is also the solemnity of all heavenly courts, for their restoration has now started. Yet this day is also the solemnity of all earthly creatures, for now their salvation has started as has the redemption and consolation of the whole world. And this day is much exalted and worshipped, for the Son of God did not take the angels' nature in one person, but only in human nature. And also on this day the Son of God has received a new bidding from his Father to bring about our salvation. This day he went out of the sovereign heaven, and joined himself and took pleasure in taking a course to our salvation, and closeted himself in the Virgin's womb. On this day too he becomes like man and our brother, and started being a pilgrim like us. Also on this day the very true and perfect light of heaven was descended here below to take us out from all darkness. And on this day the very bread of life, which gives life to the world, is moulded in the Virgin's womb and shall be fully baked and dried on the cross, like bread in the oven. As on this day God, the eternal Word, is made man to dwell with us; and he is called Emmanuel, which is as much as to say God is with us, namely meaning God and man. As on this day all Scripture figures, symbols and prophets' desires have been fulfilled, and because of this the coming of Our Lord is called the fulfilment of time. For the patriarchs desired this coming with more fervent desire than any man may recount, and with the most ardent desire expected the journey of this most blessed day. Certainly, the solemnity of this day is the beginning of all other feasts and the beginning of all good-ness. For up to this day God was displeased with man for the sins of our forefathers, and seeing that his Son is made man, He may now cease being displeased with us ever again. So consider how greatly this feast and this work ought to be solemnised, for all that which is done is most delightful, full of all pleasure and most desirable, and it ought to be received with all due veneration, devotion and spiritual joy. Now study by meditating on the aforesaid matters, and take delight and pleasure in them. And in doing so, you shall abound in all spiritual joy, and God shall perhaps show you even greater things.

CHAPTER 6
OF SAINT JOHN THE BAPTIST'S NATIVITY AND CIRCUMCISION

ITH the foregoing having been accomplished, and Mary thinking on the words which the angel had said to her about her cousin, she then wanted to visit her and to be joyful with her in her company and do her service (so that Jesus, who was in her womb, would sanctify Saint John and make him holy, although still being in his mother's womb). So the Virgin rose from the place where she had been, namely her place of rest and contemplation and prayers, since above all else she was used to spending her time in contemplation and prayers. Then, with Joseph's permission, she went from the city of Nazareth to the mountain where the Zechariah's house was built. And the path she took was very stony and hard to go over. Yet she kept going with a fast and hasty pace, showing that a virgin ought not to loiter in any public place, nor have any communication with any man. By this we might also be instructed as to how we too ought to hasten in doing good works, and that without any waiting we ought to do all the good we can. For as Chrysostom says, there is nothing more grievous to our life than to give a false impression we will do good works only to put them off from day to day. And many a time such things make man to fall from good deeds, for when a man would then want to do them, he would not be able. And a wise man says about this that we never ought to put off a good deed, for fear that when one would do it, one would otherwise stay away doing other things; yet men ought always to abstain from doing evil.

Then Mary, having conceived the eternal Word of God, went to visit Elizabeth. And according to Saint Ambrose, she did not misbelieve what the angel had told her, nor had she any doubt as to the messenger sent to her, or doubted Elizabeth's example about which she was told, but she was most glad to accomplish her holy desire and willing to perform an office and service of meekness. She was brisk with joy that she had conceived, and so she hastened to go to her. Notice now how the Lady of heaven and earth did not go there on horseback, but on foot, with some virgins who were with her, by a long and painful way. The distance from Nazareth to Jerusalem was thirty-five miles and from there to the house of Zechariah four miles, proving to be a tiresome journey. But shyness, meekness, poverty and honesty, besides all virtues, went with her as did he who is the Lord of virtues. This Lady had a great and honourable company, and they were not of this world full of pompous vanities. Nor was she grieved or heavy-hearted about the conception of the Son of God, as other women might be of their children, for Our Lord Jesus was neither a burden nor a charge to his mother. Oh, how fortunate was anyone who met Mary in this way and might have been worthy to have been greeted by her! When the Virgin came to the mountain, she entered Zechariah's house, and on entering she greeted Elizabeth, who was really joyful of the gift she had received in conceiving her son, Saint John the Baptist. And it is because of these two things that Mary greeted Elizabeth, first because she was very meek, and secondly, since she was above her cousin in dignity. The first reason is according to the manner of regions and lands where it is the least or most unworthy who first greet the eldest and most worthy, thus showing a sign of reverence. The second is according to the custom of the places where those who are greatest greet the least, thus showing that all kindness comes from above.

Morally, we are here taught six things by Mary's example. The first is to steer us away from all idleness, negligence and all worldly desires in which we have long dwelt by our negligence. The second, that we may climb up the mountain of perfect life and approach heaven by good works. The third, that we ought to hasten to do good deeds. The fourth, that we may enter into the city of Judea, which is interpreted as confessing the Church, to render thanks to the holy name of God and serve him with all our might. The fifth, that we enter into the house of Zechariah not pursuing our vain thoughts, but rather that we ought to keep in our minds God's commandments, since Zechariah is interpreted as having the mind of God. The sixth, that we greet Elizabeth by keeping in disregard evil love and only set the affection of our desire in God, who alone may satisfy us with all goodness, since Elizabeth means the abundance or fullness of God.

And yet we are thus shown that we ought to describe the goods which God gives us to our next of kin, the same way Mary did with Elizabeth and her son. For being unrestrained when the Virgin greeted her, Saint John was filled with the Holy Spirit, as the angel had promised. And he, perceiving the presence of his Lord, moved and stirred himself for great joy in his mother's womb, as though he would rise, leap and go forward to meet his Lord. And then Our Lord made his precursor John the first to prophesy. And he, being willing to begin the office of precursor or forerunner, what he could not say by mouth he showed by sign and by moving himself with very great joy. For as he was still in his mother's womb, he foretold the coming of the Son of God as though he would have spoken with a loud voice, "See here the Lamb of God; it is him who puts away the sins of the world." Chrysostom says: "The reason why Our Lord caused Elizabeth to be first greeted by Mary is so that the words uttered out of the Virgin's mouth and womb, where the Lord dwelled, went into Elizabeth's ears and so descended to John, for the purpose of being anointed in prophecy. For as soon as the words were heard by his mother, the child was full of unrestrained joy and began to prophesy. Oh child, a true prophet who may be properly called more than a prophet, tell us from where you receive this rejoicing by which you show this great joy? You are not yet born, and you already prophesy and know about Our Lord's coming, which you might not express by speech but only by rejoicing, and do what you can do. Oh, how you could merely go before him if you had been out of the prison in which you were! Oh you, yet being held in your mother's womb, who knew him and made a great effort to go before him!"

The mother was then filled with the Holy Spirit by the merits of her son, for Jesus Christ, being full of grace within him, shed grace by the Virgin's greeting into John of such abundant holiness that it rebounded, or resounded, on his mother. And because of that, being full of joy and kindled with the Holy Spirit, she embraced and hugged most ten-derly the sweet Virgin, so that she not only greeted her, but also cried for joy with her with great devotion such that her cry might be heard from heaven. And it is, namely, that she cried for joy not with a loud voice, but by showing the great desire which was in her heart, the same way as Moses did when God said to him: "Oh Moses, why are you crying out to me?" But Moses never cried by any shouting, but by his heart's desire. Saint Augustine says: "The crying which man ought to make to God ought to come out from the root of the heart and it should be one of fervent love." For the spirit of the child who could not cry, made his mother cry with a high voice as a sign of great affection, because she knew the great gift of God and that she carried in her womb him who was the voice of the eternal Word.

Then Elizabeth said to the Virgin: "Blessed are you above all women, and among those who are blessed the most excel-lent and full of divine favour, for no one has ever been as worthy to have grace before you as you have been, nor shall anyone be found after you to be so. You are then blessed and very much so, and yet you shall be filled with much greater blessings. And may the fruit of your womb also be blessed, for it is from him that all divine favour comes. And inasmuch as he is man, he is blessed by the divine favour of grace, for he is full of all the gifts of the Holy Spirit. And inasmuch as he is God, he is blessed with the divine favour of glory, since before the beginning of the world, and he shall be without end. And for this you are blessed, because he has provided you in divine favour and all sweetness." Mary is blessed in like manner as the angel had said to her before, for she has restored the ruin, or loss, and triumph of the Church. But here she is blessed by Elizabeth, because she has restored the Church's glorification, which had been as much as fully dead. Bede says: "This Virgin is blessed by all in the angel's and Elizabeth singular voice. And here you may see with what glory she is honoured by all, both angels and earthly creatures." And we should here note the five fruits to be gathered from the Blessed Virgin. The first is the fruit of her womb, and this is the begetting by which

we are shown the fruit of life. The second is the fruit of her
soul and of her thought, which is the compassion which she
shows to those in affliction and those who are sinners. The
third is the fruit of her mouth, which is prayer. The fourth
is the fruit of all good works, and that is called protection.
The fifth is her name, which means devotion, or that which
both good and evil ought to have in calling her blessed
name, for men ought to call on her in all perils and needs.

And Elizabeth says *Et unde michi hoc*, "On what merits do
I deserve this, and from where does this come to me, being
old and barren and cursed as to how men repute me? How
is it that the mother of my Lord, a Virgin, comes to me so
meekly, when it is me who ought to serve her? This is not
by my merits, for neither perfection nor nobleness do make
me worthy of this great honour or of this great fortune, but
only by the grace of God. Oh Virgin, I rather ought to go
to you, but your son's and your own meekness have constrained you to come to me." And let it be known that Our
Lord's mother first comes to sinners by compassion, since
her name is interpreted to mean bitterness, so giving them
the bitterness of contrition. She also comes to those who
are in affliction, in so much as she is a lady who defends
and delivers them. And she also comes to those who are
in grief, affording them comfort and consolation, and also
as she is the star of the sea. Saint Augustine says: "*Sancta
Maria, succurre miseris*, Oh Mary, Holy Virgin, help the poor
sinners, and this is what she does first. *Iuva pusillanimes*,
Give help to those who are feeble and dishonest, and this
is what she secondly does. Comfort those who are sorrowful
and grieving, and this she does thirdly.

"You are blessed, indeed, and blessed is the fruit of your
womb. Certainly, oh Virgin, I marvel seeing this visitation
which you undertake by your meekness because of the great
magnificence of virtue which appears in you. For I often find
joy in your coming and greeting, as does the child who is
still in my womb; and what he cannot express in speaking,
he shows by gladness and joy." Thus did Elizabeth come to
know of the Incarnation of the Word and of the miracle,
and she was well aware that Mary was the mother of God,
that she was filled with grace and that she had conceived

by the Holy Spirit; and that the great happiness shown by her child meant that his mother was coming from him of whom he was the forerunner. And because of this she, who was before ashamed to have conceived and kept herself closed because she was with child and knew not as yet God's secrets, now thanking God and blessing Him found joy in herself that she was the mother of such a prophet. And what she had known by secret inspiration, she now showed openly to all those who would hear her, in saying *Et benedicta que credidisti*, Oh Virgin, you are blessed since you have believed what the angel said, and by consenting with your faith you have conceived. Certainly, at the time things were announced to you by the angel, God showed them to you, and enlightened your soul through the Holy Spirit, and without being taught or any other means your instructions shall be perfect in you." Hearing this, a man may see clearly that Elizabeth knew from the Holy Spirit the words which the angel had spoken to Mary: "Blessed are you who has believed, and blessed too are those who shall hear of these marvels and believe them." Oh man, consider the great virtue of this greeting to the Virgin Mary, endowing joy and comfort, and making the Holy Spirit reveal divine secrets and the spirit of prophecy. And for this we ought every day to salute her, that we may be saluted back by her.

Then the Virgin, hearing Elizabeth's answer prophesying to her that she would be the mother of God, by calling her blessed and greatly praising her faith, could no longer keep matters private nor withhold the gifts she had received from God. For what she had before kept secret by her meekness and virginal goodness, namely the marvellous conception of the Son of God, she now showed it at the most relevant time and of utmost need. And in doing this she found joy within her, so that being so overjoyed she chanted a song, saying *Magnificat anima mea Dominum*. The Jews had a custom of composing a song which they chanted to God whenever they made something worthy of praise or when God did for them any marvellous thing. And certainly, the Virgin before and even more than all others, was justified in magnifying our Lord. So she, while holding on to her meekness, did not immediately tell everyone about the great mystery shown to her, but kept it secret so that it might be shown by others, like Elizabeth. And inasmuch as she knew that Elizabeth knew of these things through the Holy Spirit, she understood God willed it to be shown. And so she showed it in magnifying God saying *Magnificat*, that is to say that she lauds and praises Him in all his works, that is in him whom she coveted in her to grow and increase; as if to say, "Oh Elizabeth, you magnify me for the goodness which you have seen in me, but it is my soul in what you said to me which magnifies, shows and praises God, her Creator."

Et *exultavit spiritus meus*, And my spirit finds joy in God, my saviour, that is the blessed Son of God, through whom the world's salvation is restored." And although he is Saviour of all, he was ever eminently so of his mother owing to the dignities and prerogatives she had been given. This Virgin understood all of the soul's might in these two words, *Anima et spiritus*, "the soul and the spirit". For the soul comprises the inferior powers, hence the body. And the spirit bears the substance of the soul, and according to the superior power, she was sent in rapture by this power and lifted high above by her sweetness and contemplation. Then Mary rendered devoutly thanks and praises to God with her soul and spirit, that is with all her might, for the benefits He was pleased to do her. As though, according to Saint Ambrose, she would say: "God has so exalted me by the gifts He wanted to shed upon me, that I cannot recount them all. But I offer to render Him thanks inwardly with all the affection of my soul, and all my life I will serve Him for all that He has given me, for my soul, my intelligence and understanding, and in contemplating his great magnificence and keeping his commandments. For I ought to praise and magnify Our Lord, so that God's goodness ought to be praised and magnified, similarly as the master is commended by his servants and workmen in their work." God then is praised and magnified when our soul, made after his image, conforms itself with Jesus Christ, who is the Father's image, by justice and virtuous works; through which it is made great in living according to God's commandments, and when it shines by good works and studies to show good examples to every creature. The Apostle says about this: "Magnify and bear God in your bodies." So take heed that God is to be magnified and praised for his benefits in three methods. First, when a man gives back to God what he has from Him, namely His benefits. Secondly, when a man renders thanks to God for all His goodness. Thirdly, when a man performs and gets involved in the work which God has shown him to be done and the good which He was pleased to give us, as He did to the Holy Virgin, who found delight in her actions of grace, as can be seen in this song.

Let it also be known that it is not found in any Scripture that the Blessed Virgin Mary spoke other than very little nor that she uttered but only a few words. And she spoke seven times in all, as a sign that she was full of the seven gifts of the Holy Spirit. She spoke twice with the angel, the first time being, *Quomodo fiet istud*, "Angel, how is it that what you are saying can be done?" The second time was *Ecce ancilla Domini*, "Angel, Behold the handmaid of the Lord." And twice she spoke with Elizabeth; first when she greeted her; then when she said *Magnificat anima mea Dominum*, "My soul and my body give praise to God." And she spoke twice with her son. First when she said to him *Filii, quid fecisti nobis sic*, "Son, why have you done this to us?" The second time was at the wedding of Cana, when she said to him *Vinum non habent*, "They have no wine." And at another time too during the same wedding when she spoke to the servants, telling them, *Quodcumque dixerit vobis, facite*, "Do whatever my son bids you to do." And it is to be noted that she spoke these seven sentences during four events. Each time she spoke them she showed that something had to be done, for they were followed by four miracles. These were the angel's annunciation, in which she conceived the Son of God; her visit to Elizabeth, where the child John rejoiced greatly in his mother's womb; at the nuptial feast, where water was changed into wine; and at the temple, since it was there that the Son of God made himself subject to her. Also in these seven citations she spoke words with four persons, namely with the angel, with Elizabeth, with her son and with the servants. In these we are shown the passing on of fair teachings, mostly to the young maidens and mainly to those in religion, for very little they ought to speak unless it was with the angel, that is with their spiritual father, whom the prophet calls God's angel; in confession to confess herself, or else with some honest and holy old mother of religion, and this should be in short and a few words of consolation; or with the Son of God, in devout reading and praying; or with His servants, when asking for her needs.

Consider now, devout soul, how these two mothers were very joyful and how both praised God of having conceived, and so passing the season in gracious works and delighting in virtue. Indeed, how fortunate are these houses where such mothers like Mary and Elizabeth rest and dwell, great with such children! Oh devout ladies of religion, if you could climb upon the mountain with your Lady and mistress Mary, and you could consider them sweetly hugging each other and lovingly greeting each other, I believe that you would sing this holy chant of the *Magnificat* in full sweetness with the Virgin Mary, and with the little child Saint John you would prophesy in gladness and great happiness, and pray to the Virgin's marvellous conception. Whereupon Saint Anselm writing to his sister says: "Oh my sister, go now and climb with your most sweet Lady up the mountain of the barren Elizabeth and the Virgin Mary. And consider the hugging and the greeting which the servant does to the master, the herald to the sovereign, the voice to the Word shut fast within the Virgin's womb, and yet knowing and prophesying with great joy. Blessed be the wombs from whom all the salvation of the world ought to spring." Now follow these examples of humility and see if any greater example of humility might be shown than when Mary came to Elizabeth, Jesus Christ to Saint John, the lady to the chambermaid, the lord to the servant. And certainly, the Virgin glorified herself specially in her chant of all these virtues of humility, being full of all virtues in saying *Quia respexit humilitatem*. And by virtue of Mary's example you may not feel anything in you but meekness and such goodness as she gives you, heed to her again and consider you do not have anything by your merits.

Then Mary stayed with Elizabeth for three months to comfort and serve her meekly in all that she might need, as though she had forgotten she was the mother of God and queen of the whole world, since she would always accom-plish the perfectness of humility. And though getting on with her contemplations she never left her active life, nor did she lessen her contemplations by her active life. And so men read in what she did what is written in the Gospel about Martha's active life, and Mary Magdalene's contempla-tive life. For she led an active life in the service she gave to Elizabeth, and a contemplative life by keeping in her mind and contemplating all of her son's doings. Mary dwelt with Elizabeth until she saw the nativity of her Lord's forerun-ner, for which reason she had gone there, and to serve him together with his mother. And so she only tarried there no longer than she wanted to be seen to be in the way or at that place by people, and that she might ever increase in virtue. And certainly, this lord, Saint John, and his mother, were filled with the Holy Spirit by the coming of Mary and her son, and had even more graces in waiting with such an extraordinary mother and so worthy a child.

When it was time for Elizabeth to be delivered, she gave birth to a son. This was on the eighth day of July, on the sixth weekday, a Friday, that in all meekness the Blessed Virgin Mary served him at his birth and his mother, having leave to serve in a another's house rather than in her own house. *Et audierunt vicini et cognati eius*; when her neighbours and cousins and those of her lineage then heard how Our Lord had shown mercy to Elizabeth by delivering her from the lowliness of being barren and giving her such a son, who had also been marvellously shown by the angel and conceived above nature, then they all rejoiced greatly with her for this great gift which God had given her, the same as the angel had told Zechariah that many people should have great joy in his birth. This joy meant the holiness which ought to be in little John. So that every man ought to have joy when things go well for his neighbour, unlike our spiritual enemy who wills all that is evil and hates all that is good. And let it be known that the lesson read on this day was for the passing of Saint John the Evangelist. Yet for the great service given by both of them, Baptist and Evangelist, the Church may not keep that feast on this day, so that it has as of now been carried to the day when it is kept, for this day was the dedication of his Church. And the solemnity of Saint John the Baptist shall abide and be on this day as of old times, for the angel had shown that on this day there should be gladness and solace for the birth of Our Lord's precursor. And for this, dear brethren, let us worship these two great friends of God, so bright amongst the company of angels, that we may see them before the throne of grace, and pray that through them we may find mercy and grace in all times of need.

Now someone might ask, why do we keep and make solemn the nativity of Saint John the Baptist more than that of any other saint? According to Saint Augustine there were no other saints before being born who believed in Jesus Christ, but only after being born was true faith given to them that they might believe what was found in Holy Scripture while being in this world. Now the nativity of Saint John was a prophecy which he himself had made about the coming of the Son of God into this world, when he greeted him while he still was in his mother's womb. And so is his nativity celebrated and kept, since it was given by God's grace. He was also born at the beginning of the time of grace, and he had to preach the grace of the New Testament by which he was filled after he was born. Many light up and make great fires and torch lights on the day of the nativity of Saint John, really meaning that this is the nativity of him about whom Our Lord said, *Ecce erat lucerna ardens et lucens*, "John the Baptist was a burning light and an illumination."

On the eighth day after the precursor's birth, his kinsfolk came together to circumcise the child according to what was ordained in the Law. As custom required in this circumcision men put or gave the name of the child, as nowadays done in christening, so that it is written in the Gospel of Saint Luke: *Et vocabit eum*, "They named him." And they would have given him his father's name, Zechariah, for the custom was to give the fathers' name to the firstborn, and even more to those who had no hope of having any more children, as to their latter children. And let the reason be known why men give the name during circumcision, for no one is worthy to have his name written in the Book of Life unless he first sheds himself of all carnal desires as required by circumcision. On hearing this the mother answered, *Nequaquam*, "In no way will he be named Zechariah, but John, for so it has been shown to him by God." And his father, not having heard of the name John before for he was deemed dumb, was questioning in his inner self and mulling over the meaning of the child's name; so that we may surmise that Zechariah was not only dumb but also deaf. Then Zechariah demanded, by making a sign or giving an indication and not by word of mouth, a *pugillarem*, or a little small tablet which may be held, on which he wrote, *Iohannes est nomen eius*, "The name of the child is John." He did not say, "His name should be," but "is John"; as though he would say "His name is now given and set by God as well as by the angel." And it is to be noted that this name John was given to him for three reasons. First, for the fullness of grace which was in him. Secondly, for the new time of grace which he began. Thirdly, for the excellent grace which he first preached, namely the remission of sins and the comfort of grace. Then all those present were greatly marvelled of the intimacy and agreement existing between his parents about the name of the child, for then the father's mouth was opened and his tongue set free, faith opening up that which misbelief had closed. These events show how the grace of the New Testament has been now opened and made manifest.

Then Zechariah spoke and thanked God for all the good He had done him. Then, a great marvel and fear fell upon all his neighbours about the events which happened regarding the nativity of Saint John. These were the birth of a child from a woman who was barren and past childbearing age, how the child was named, and the restoring of Zechariah's speech. And they might have feared God's punishment in seeing a man leading such a good life being so punished for doubting and failing to believe what the angel had told him, considering that it was not permitted to offend God. And all these things, being great miracles, were made public and shown all over the hilly area where they dwelt and in every place. And all those hearing about this kept it in their hearts and mind, thinking between

themselves what things should come to this child, saying *Quis putas puer iste erit?* as though saying "This child
shall be a person of great reputation." This was no marvel
although they spoke thus about this child, for the might
of God wrought in him these marvels which were done to
him, so that men might reasonably perceive the greatness
of this child before God.

And his father Zechariah was filled with the Holy Spirit.
Prophesying, he composed and made a fair chant of divine
praise, saying all along *Benedictus Dominus Deus Israel.* It says
that the Lord's goodness and divine generosity are great
with us if we are ready to receive them, when we see that
the speech, which only had been taken away from him for
having mistrusted and doubted, was restored to him when
he believed with the spirit of prophecy; and that where
sin did first abound, virtue was renewed with prophecy.
By this we may perceive that Our Lord often gives to man
more than he takes from him, for those whom he healed
bodily, he had first healed spiritually in their souls. Ambrose
says: "See how good and light God is to pardon sins, for
he restores not only what is taken away, but gives other
gifts together with them, as we see in him who was dumb
and now foretells prophecies. It is by God's great grace that
Zechariah now confesses Him to any unbeliever. So that, no
man ought to have any mistrust in God's goodness, or ought
he to despair of God's mercy due to any sin committed by
him. For God may change your sentence if you convert from
evil to good, from sin to virtue."

When these things were done the Virgin took her leave
of Elizabeth and Zechariah, and blessed the child Saint John.
And she returned to Nazareth after the nativity of Saint
John, such as doctors more commonly hold. By returning to
her house after her cousin had given birth, we are shown
that it is not an honest thing to abide in a stranger's house
without doing something kind. It would be fair here to think
of the anxiety and trouble in which Zechariah and Elizabeth
had found themselves, and how she wept tenderly when the
Virgin departed, for the joy of the world and the star of
the sea was returning to her house. It should also not be
doubted that Saint John was sorry, being so happy about

her coming home. Meditate and recollect yourself about the poverty to which Mary returned, for she went to her house where neither bread nor wine were found, nor anything else of necessity. She had been in Zechariah's house for about three months where there was much abundance but now, returning to her poverty, she needed to seek there her living with the labour of her hands. Do then have compassion on her and inflame yourself with loving poverty.

The child Saint John grew as to both increasing grace and virtues, for as he grew physically so did he in virtue. And he perfected his way of life in the desert, which is a place fit for prayer and contemplation. There he dwelt from when he was eight years old up to the time it pleased God to show him to the people of Israel. This was when he came to the waters of Jordan to preach the baptism of penance, which he began doing in the fifteenth year of the Emperor Tiberius Caesar. It was then that he came out of the desert to preach to the people. Do consider by the aforesaid the grandeur of Saint John, together with many other privileges relating to him.

CHAPTER 7

OF OUR LORD'S GENEALOGY, OR LINE OF DESCENT

AVING written about the birth of Our Lord's precursor, I must consequently write about the genealogy of Our Saviour. It precedes his nativity, and Saint Matthew says about this, *Liber generationis*, that is to say the Book of the temporal generation of Jesus Christ, son of David and of Abraham etc. The Book which Saint Matthew wrote is called the Book of the Generation of Jesus Christ, which he wrote in Hebrew. He begins his Gospel with the generation of Our Saviour, for Jews have a custom that in the beginning of their book they name the person or persons about whom they would speak. So then Saint Matthew, beginning from Abraham and descending by line or lineally until David, the first king in the line of Judah, writes the full generation descending from David until Joseph. He wanted to show how Our Lord Jesus Christ is descended according to his human nature from the seed of Abraham, who was the first in importance among patriarchs, and of the line of David, who was similarly the first among the kings, and of the line of Judah, which was the principal line among the twelve lines, He also wanted to show that the dignity of priesthood pertained as of right to Our Lord Jesus Christ, as it did to Abraham, and the realm to be king as it did to David, for in the Old Testament it was only to Abraham and David that an express promise was made about Our Lord, who was to descend from them bodily, and about whom it was prophesied by Jacob that he should by birthright come from Judah's line.

The Evangelist has first put David, then Abraham, although Abraham came before David in time. This was done for two reasons: first because royal dignity is worthier than temporal antiquity and priority; secondly, because David, being a great sinner, is put before the just man to show us that Our Lord has come into this world by his own mercy. And also since this promise was made

to David more often and in a steadfast and evident manner; and so that the order of the genealogy is kept the
beginning consists of one clause followed by the other.
And so, after the beginning, he wrote: *Abraham genuit Isaac*,
descending until Joseph. And he says about the extraordinary number in the book of the generation, that although
many generations had been recounted in order, yet this
was all done to seek one generation, that of Our Saviour
Jesus Christ, while all others were repeated. And he is
called *Jesus* owing to his Trinitarian nature, and *Christus*
as relating to his human nature. And the name Jesus is a
proper name, and Christus is an added name and one of
grace. It should also be considered that Saint Matthew put
the generation of Jesus Christ in descending order when
he was speaking of his human nature through which he
came down to us, showing that he has taken our infirmity.
And so he begins from Abraham, in showing the manner
how God comes into the world, descending according to
his human nature from the line of the ancient fathers, and
then proceeds to Joseph, Mary's husband, of which Virgin
he would only be born materially, just as he is born in
essence from the Father.

Saint Luke writes this generation in an opposite manner, by construction, so as to show how the children of
grace should rise to their Father's realm, and how man's
nature is in union with God through Jesus Christ. And to
do this, he starts with Our Lord's baptism, for whom the
children of grace are made and engendered, and he so
proceeds till Adam, since the spiritual generation comprehends all those as will become the children of God. And
so, as Saint Hilary says, Saint Luke writes his genealogy
according to the priestly order, while Saint Matthew writes
according to royal dignity, so as to prove Our Lord's glory
and dignity, that he is king and eternal priest in one line
and the other. For Joseph descended from Salome, and the
Virgin Mary from Nathan, his brother. And therefore both
Evangelists are in agreement that David is the father. Saint
Augustine says: "In the Law only the priest and the king
were anointed, by whom was understood Jesus Christ, in
order to show that he, being king and priest, governs us

and prays for us in making us his members, because he is in us and we are with him."

This genealogy is written by three of fourteen generations, some of whom were before and some in the time of the Law, and the last, namely the genealogy of Our Lord Jesus Christ, is in the time of grace which began at his conception. And this means that some were saved during these three times by faith in Jesus Christ. For according to Chrysostom, when the three by fourteen generations were accomplished, the state of the Jewish people was changed. For from Abraham to David they were under the Jews, from David to the transmigration they were under the kings, and from the transmigration to Jesus Christ they were under overseers; showing men that just as the three by fourteen generations were accomplished, the state of the Jews was changed, so was the state of the world changed after the coming of Jesus Christ; also showing that he is judge, king and overseer; and that obedience of the commandments was accomplished in him just as much as the truth of the Gospel, which is founded in faith in the Holy Trinity, by which we were given power to be made Sons of God; and that by observing all the foregoing he, as the son of justice, may come in us by spiritual enlightenment. It should also be understood that three multiplied by fourteen make forty-two generations, by which we come to Jesus Christ, who is promised to us for our reward, in the same manner as the children of Israel came by forty-two sojourns to the land which was promised to them. These three by fourteen also mean three times, that is to say the time before the Law, that under the Law, and the time of grace. The first fourteen generations are from Abraham till David; the second from David to the transmigration to Babylon of the children of Israel; and the third from the transmigration to Babylon to Jesus Christ. The first contains the patriarchs; the second, the kings; the third, the overseers and leaders. First in order are those who were born before that went to Egypt, about whom it is said *Iudas autem genuit Phares.* Second in order come those who were born in Egypt, about whom it is said *Phares autem genuit Esrom.* And in the third order are those who were born after those who came out of Egypt, about whom it is said *Naason autem genuit Salmon.*

The first fourteen generations stand for the engendering of Jesus Christ by the grace which Our Lord affords to the penitent soul. The second, for what he makes in the soul growing in perfection; and the third, for what he makes in the perfect soul.

The spiritual generation made by Our Lord in the penitent soul is shown according to the three degrees of penance: the first is at the beginning; the second in growing in perfection; and the third in accomplishing and ending or consuming it. To start showing true penance, three elements are required; they are the preliminary elements, the ordained elements and the conserving elements. There are two introductory elements as well, namely faith in God's goodness, as seen in Abraham, and the hope of pardon, as seen in Isaac. The ordained elements are three, that is to say contrition, where doing battle is to detest the sin which was loved before, as seen in Jacob; confession, as seen in Judas; and restitution, as seen in his brethren. The elements conserving penance are three, that is to say the fear of displeasing God, as seen in Pharez, which is interpreted as division; love of the everlasting glory, as seen in Zarah, just as saying *oriens*, springing; horror and fear of perpetual pain, as seen in Hezron, just as saying *sagitta*, an arrow. Following these comes the spiritual generation made by Our Lord in that soul which has started doing penance, which contains four generations according to the three elements expedient to this end. The first is the choice between good and evil, as seen in Aram, which is interpreted as *electus*, chosen. The second is to have perfect will to follow what is good, as seen in Aminadab, just as saying *spontaneus*, of his good will. The third is prudence to discern good from evil, as seen in Nahshon, just as saying cunning, like a serpent. The fourth is the joy one has in pleasing himself, as seen in Solomon, just as saying sensible. Afterwards comes the third generation which Our Lord makes in the fulfilment of penance, which for it to take effect four generations are required, according to the four elements required for it to be done. The first is strength against temptations and the evil of the guilt or deed, as seen in Boaz, just as saying strength. The second is the readiness to take heed of the warnings which God sends, by means of his grace, to his creature, as seen in Obed, just as much as saying keeping. The third is that of being constant against persecutions of all pains, as seen in Jesse, as much as saying the coast of Libya, whose shore is ceaselessly smitten by the waves of the sea. The fourth is strength of final perseverance in penance, as seen in David, just as saying strong and manually dexterous.

There after begin the second of the fourteen generations, meaning the spiritual generation Our Lord makes in the soul's growth in perfection according to four degrees. The first is in the will of doing good things; the second in declining from evil; the third in keeping the commandments; and the fourth in observing the counsels. Three elements belong to the first degree, namely the rejoicing of heart, which a person ought to have in himself, as seen in Solomon, just as saying peaceable. One also ought to be generous in charity, as towards his neighbour, as seen in Rehoboam, just as saying the generosity of the people. And also to have one's will subjected to God, as seen in Abijah, which means the Lord is my father, or just as saying the subjection of love and of fear. Also three things pertain to the second degree, which is to decline from evil, that is to say that a man ought to deliberately avoid slander, as seen in Asa, just as saying plenty. One ought also to deliberately avoid foolish judgment, as seen in Josaphat, just as saying judging; and to keep oneself from abhorring or despising one's neighbour, as seen in Joram, just as saying excellent. By the first is shown how a man should deliberately avoid evil in effect; by the second, in thought; and by the third, in affection. As to the third degree, relating to the perfection of the commandments, there pertain four generations, for a man ought to keep God's commandments both in time of adversity and of prosperity. As to the time of adversity there pertain two things, that is to say strength to undertake hard things, as seen in Uzziah, just as saying the strength of Our Lord; and patience in sustaining contrariness, as seen in Ioathan, just as saying perfect, for patience can do perfect work. It should also be stated that two things pertain to prosperity, that is to say that one ought to keep oneself back from having too great delight in variable and transitory goods, that is to say in the good things of this world, and departing from his maker, as seen in Ahaz, just as saying being continent; having comfort in goods which are unalterable and invariable, as seen in Hezekiah, just as saying comfort of Our Lord. To the fourth degree, as seen in Rehoboam accomplishing the counsels, four things are necessary. First, to forget the earthly things of this world, as foretold in Manasseh, just as saying forgetting. The second is the succession of Gods grace, which is a spiritual nourishing of the soul, as foretold by Amon, just as saying nourished; so that he says elsewhere: "Come to me and I shall feed you." The third is the devotion that one has to serve God and to keep what He ordains to be kept, as seen in Josiah, just as saying God's incense or good taste. The fourth is the preparation that the creature makes in this present world in order to receive some reward from God after this present life, as seen in Jeconiah, just as saying preparation.

Lastly there begins the third of the fourteen generations, just as saying the generation of Jesus Christ made by grace in the perfect soul according to the four degrees, the first of which is to consider as to the perfection of religious men; the second, of prelates; the third, of committed men; and the fourth commonly refers to all those who persevere. Then after the transmigration of Babylon, that is to say after that a man passes from the state of imperfection to the state of perfection, which is the state of religious men, there pertain three things, that is to say prompt obedience, as seen in Jeconiah, just as saying preparation; voluntary poverty, which is such as a man who seeks nothing else in this world but God, as seen in Salathiel, just as saying my petition, that is to say God; as to all good example and discipline, as seen in Zerubbabel, just as saying the master correcting the confusion of sin. Also as to the prelate's perfection there pertain four things, that is to say paternal care of his subjects, as seen in Abihud, just as saying this is my Father; doctrine which stirs those who are slow and negligent, as seen in Eliakim, just as saying lifting up again; knowledge in order to teach the unlearned, as seen in Azor, just as saying seeing light; holiness of life in order to give others good example, as seen in Sadoc, just as saying justice. There also pertain four things as to the perfection of committed men, that is to say the perfection of charity towards their neighbours, as seen in Achim, that is to say my brother; perfect love to God, as seen in Eliud, just as saying my God; perfect hope and trust in God in adversity, as seen in Eleazar, just as saying my God helper; perfect humility in prosperity, which is when a man reputes all that comes or happens as coming from God, as seen in Nathan, just as saying gift. Also to the common perfection of those who persevere there pertain three things: to supplant vices and sins, as seen in Jacob, that is the sign of a supplanter; continual labour in order to get virtues, as seen in Joseph, just as saying accruing; and firm and constant faith without doubting, as seen in the fact that Joseph is called the husband of Mary, just as saying star of the sea, being a fixed star which never moves. These three things are all necessary for perseverance.

Oh man, consider here Our Lord's relatives, and how he is not scorned in being born in his human nature of such persons of low reputation and sinners, showing that you ought not seek glory in the nobleness of your relatives and descent, nor in your virtues or the good works which you do, so that you will not altogether diminish or lessen the reward which God should give you. Chrysostom says: "The dignity of Our Saviour is shown here, not for having in his genealogy great and mighty relatives according to human nature, but for being of little reputation and considered of little use; for the glory is great and very marvellous when great persons humble themselves by their own will to be lower than they are. If anyone says that it is a marvellous thing that the Son of God would not only receive death for us, but also that he would be crucified and buried, one may also say that in his generation it is not only worthy to be marvelled in having taken our human nature and becoming man, but in having been pleased to have such relatives as one who had no shame of our vileness and filth; thus giving us example that we should never be ashamed of our relatives' reputation, whether that derives from nobility or work, since we must seek to become noble only by the nobility of virtues. Truly no man is either to be praised or even blamed for his relatives' virtues or vices, since he is neither more fair nor more foul because of them. And to speak clearly, we do not know of what reputation a man is worthy who is born of relatives who are vicious and sinners or of small or low descent according to the body, and who sees how to make himself noble by acquiring virtues. So then, no one ought to grow proud or elevate oneself by virtue of those relatives of his descending from nobility, since taking into account Our Lord's relatives according to the body we ought to push down and remove all pride from our thoughts, and one only ought to be glorified in virtues. We see that the Pharisee, who glorified himself as to his merits, was made worse than the publican, who called himself a sinner. Then you, whoever you might be, do not cast away in vain nor spoil the fruit of your labours. Do not let your pain wither away for nothing, nor cast away the fruit of your merits, for certainly your God knows better than you the merits of your virtues. So let us not be proud, but let us say about ourselves that we are useless servants, so that we may be counted among those who are profitable. Certainly, if you say that you are worthy of praise, you are worthy of rebuke, notwithstanding that before you were worthy of being praised. And if you say and repute yourself useless, you are then made profitable before God, though you were before worthy of chiding. And so, if we want to profit, it is necessary to forget all past virtues and all the good which we have done. For if we glorify ourselves and convince ourselves, like those who want to sell some merchandise, we would be arming and provoking our enemy against us, and he will mock us, and we provoke him to all deceit and guile. But if no one else knows of the good we do but only Him to whom nothing is hidden, then our good deeds, which are precious things, are placed securely. And so do not blow your trumpets far and wide nor should you uncover the good deeds which you have done, for you to lose all as the Pharisee did, who could only vaunt of all the good he had done verbally; and then the devil had it all. Let us then withhold ourselves from boasting or do anything from which our own praise may come, for such things make us to be hated by men and be abominable before God. And in the greater things we do, which are worthy of praise, so even more should we think less of ourselves and always repute ourselves as useless servants of God. And in so doing we shall be honoured by men, and obtain from God glory and great reward as well as perfect retribution, for undoubtedly, when we do anything worthy of praise for love of Him, we make Him our debtor. And when we feel in our heart, without pretending, that what we do is not worth anything, we draw more of God's benevolence towards us than for all the other works we do. And so, the goodness of humility overcomes the merits of all virtues, for if it fails there, all other works would not deserve any reward. If you will then make your works great before God, do not repute them to be great, nor should you praise yourself, for they shall neither be great nor fruitful. Follow the example of the Centurion, who said to God: 'I am not worthy that you should enter into my house'; and by this humility he deserved that God went with him and praised him above all Jews. And Saint Paul too said: 'I am not worthy to be called apostle'; and because of this he was called the principal one of apostles. Saint John the Baptist too said: 'I am not worthy to untie the straps of his sandals.' He was the friend of the spouse, and with the same hand which he said was unworthy and insuffi-cient to undo the strap of Our Lord's sandal, he afterwards baptised him in the waters of the Jordan. Saint Peter too said to Our Lord: 'Oh Master, depart from me, for I am a sinner'; and for this same confession he deserved to be the foundation of the Church. For there is nothing that makes the creature so agreeable and friendly to God, than when it reputes itself as the least and most humble of all others. So that this virtue of humility neither springs from, nor is it nourished, by anything else but of the soul which has compunction for its sins, and which departs not from arguing about oneself, and which has contrition for one's failures, and is not overcome by vainglory, nor hurt with the wound of envy, nor tormented with the fury of anger, nor when any other passion afflicts one's soul. Listen to what Our Lord says: 'Learn of me who am humble and meek of heart, and you shall find rest in your souls.' To this end, then, that in this world and in the other we might have true rest in our souls, let us plant and graft humility above all else, which is the mother of all goodness, so that by means of it we may securely pass the great sea of this world without mental distress, and come to the most affable port of salvation, being God himself. Amen."

CHAPTER 8
ABOUT WHEN JOSEPH WOULD HAVE LEFT OUR LADY

INCE in the aforesaid genealogy of Jesus Christ Saint Matthew has shown the true human nature of Our Lord, he consequently showed his divinity in the manner of his marvellous conception, saying *Christi autem generacio sic erat*; as though he would say: "It is not to believe that Jesus Christ, inasmuch as human, was engendered by the conjoining of man and woman, as are the aforesaid men named in his genealogy, but he was conceived and engendered in a more marvellous manner." Which after Saint Matthew declares, saying *Cum esset desponsata*.

When Mary returned from Elizabeth's to her own house in Nazareth, Joseph, her spouse, came from Judea to Galilee, and would have brought her there as his wife into his house. Whether they ever came together, that is to say whether bridal solemnity was made in a holy manner, or he had just brought her away and they dwelt together in one house (for after that they were married Joseph returned to his house and the Virgin to hers, seeing that it was not lawful according to Jewish custom that husband and wife should dwell together in one house before the wedding feasts were done); before that they came both together (that is not to say before that they came together in deed of marriage, in the manner some false heretics will affirm, but by manner of a figure called *tropus*, in the same manner as if one should say "Before that such a man repented himself, death prevented him," that is not to say that after his death he had repentance); *Inventa est Maria*, Mary was found by Joseph to be pregnant with child, and Joseph did not openly know that it was of the Holy Spirit. And he was troubled, seeing such a thing and not knowing the secret of such a marvellous mystery. And he would have left her there privately with her friends from whom he had taken her, and he would also bring her into his house so as to dwell with him.

Let us here consider that Mary did not pass through this world without anguish. She saw that Joseph was troubled, and not without cause if she too was troubled. Yet she always held her peace humbly and kept the gift of God close to her heart, cherishing more to be reputed as evil and vile then to reveal God's secret and to regain her repute whereby she might have or show any boasting; yet she prayed Our Lord that it would please Him to send her some remedy for this. See in what anguish and anxiety both the Virgin and Joseph found themselves, and how God suffered his friends to be tempted and troubled so as to increase their merits, and also how Our Lord did not leave them, but provided for both of them. In seeing Joseph pondering upon leaving the Virgin Mary, we have been taught that we ought to take long when considering anything carefully, and to be neither overwhelmed nor hasty in anything which is doubtful and uncertain, so that we may not fall in the sin of mental acuity.

Then Our Lord sent Joseph his angel Gabriel. This was, according to Saint Augustine, and according to Chrysostom this was for three reasons. First, that Joseph, the just man, should not do anything unrighteous deliberately. Secondly, for the honour of Our Lord's mother, that she should not abide alone and that she should not be viewed with foul suspicion. Thirdly, since Joseph had to understand the manner of the conception and that he ought to behave more reverently with regard to the Virgin. The angel appeared to him in his sleep, not openly and in a clear vision as his intellect was oppressed with doubt, in the same manner as when one is in the slumber of infidelity. And the angel said to him: "Oh Joseph, son of David." According to Chrysostom, in calling him son of David the angel was recalling the promise made to David of the coming of the Son of God. *Noli timere*, "Do not have any dread or doubt or fear not to take Mary as your wife and to dwell with her." It should not be understood that the angel warned him to take Mary to consume and bear semblance to marriage, for it seems that Saint Augustine would say that the first betrothal, of which we have spoken before, was made by words *de presenti*, and that then the marriage between them was fulfilled. According to the example of Mary and Joseph, if any true Christian persons in marriage commonly agree and consent to abide in a state of continence and to abstain from each other, they can do it while still being called and considered to be married. This may be seen in Joseph and Mary, who were called and considered to be married, for marriage is not only by the conjoining of bodies, but by a perpetual and inviolate affection of the will. And Joseph is in like manner called the husband of Mary for so much as he kept faith towards her and the loyalty of marriage in being devoutly and courageously dedicated to each other.

The angel then said to Joseph: "Do not suspect at all that this conception is through man's carnal deeds, for the One who is conceived in Mary is work and operation of the blessed Holy Spirit." To be born in her is as much worth as to be conceived, and to be born of her is to be given birth and brought forth into light and to the world. Whereupon it is to be known that there is a double nativity, that is to say in the womb and into the world. We are born in the womb when we are conceived. But we are born from the womb when we are brought forth into the light of this world. Joseph before knew that in the Virgin there was something heavenly and he believed that she was a holy woman, but now the angel opens and declares her virtue and holiness in saying to him, *Quod in ea*, "That which is carried and conceived in her is the work of God," which regards the first nativity. In announcing to him and saying *Pariet filium*, "She shall bring forth a child," namely when the time is due for his outward birth, which is the second nativity, the same as the star sheds its light and the tree the flower. "And you shall call him Jesus, that is to say Saviour." The angel then speaks of the cause: "For he shall save and deliver his people from sin"; which is not a little thing, for it can be none more miserable and wretched than to serve sin which is so vile and detestable. In this matter the Angel shows that Jesus Christ is very much human, inasmuch as he should be born of a woman, and that he was very much God, in that he should pardon sins.

Joseph being so ascertained of Mary's goodness, rose up from his sleep of infidelity and, at the voice of the angel, he took his spouse and served her as his lady. You are by this instructed, oh man, that you are bound to accomplish all that which God commands unconditionally so long as you can do so; and especially as to indefinite vows, these ought to be fulfilled as soon as possible. Chrysostom says: "Joseph is taught and admonished by the angel about the divine and heavenly mystery and secret, gladly obeying such advice and fulfilling in great joy the divine commands, for he took the holy virgin. And inwardly rejoicing, he was glorified in desiring to hear from the angel that he was the spouse of the virgin who was the mother of so great a majesty." By saying that Joseph was thinking of leaving Mary and that, having ascertained himself of the cause, he believed the angel, we take it to mean as a man who having doubts about his faith or in a good work, is yet obedient to his preacher or confessor, and so submits himself to his good advice.

Joseph knew her not until she had given birth her first child, that is to say when the child was born, he came to know of the mother's great dignity. Chrysostom says: "Indeed, Joseph did not know before of Mary's dignity, but came to know of it after she was delivered, for she was fairer and worthier than the whole world in only receiving him, whom the whole world might neither comprehend nor contain, in the little strait chamber of her womb. For Joseph knew her not in the marriage act due to what he had been told by the angel." One ought to take this word *donec* for "never", for here it is negative of all time, and it replaces *numquam*, that is to say "never". Wherefore it should be noted that this word *donec* stands for a determined time which, when it passes, one would do something, as if to say "He ate not *donec*, until, it was noon; when he then ate." Sometimes it is also affirmative of all time, and is taken for "evermore"; as when it is said *Sede a dextris meis, donec ponam*, that is to say "Sit always and for evermore on my right hand," says God the Father to the Son. Sometimes this word *donec* is taken for "never", as in this context: we say that if Joseph knew her not before giving birth, by greater reason than that he knew her not after giving birth, seeing so many signs and miracles in the nativity of the Son of God, and knowing that he was God and man. Indeed, neither before nor after her giving birth Joseph never knew her carnally. Some expound this knowledge referring to the Virgin's face, saying that, by virtue of the presence of Our Lord who was in her womb, her face shined with such brightness that Joseph might never look at her fully in the face till after the birth of the Son of God. It is the same as we read that the children of Israel might not look at the face of Moses since it shone to such an extent owing to his familiarity in speaking with Our Lord.

It is also said that he thought leaving Our Lady not for the vice of incredulity, but because he reputed himself unworthy to be in her company. Saint Jerome says: "This is in witness of Mary's virginity, namely that Joseph knew of her chastity and marvelling about what had happened, he held his peace and kept the mystery which he might not comprehend close to his heart." Chrysostom says: "Oh what inestimable praise of Mary, Joseph esteemed much more her chastity and even more for the grace he saw in her, than he would have had for her had she by carnal and natural work done any harm or sin. He saw the conception, and yet he did not suspect it came from fornication. He believed that it was more possible that a virgin might conceive without a man, than that Mary might do any sin."

And when his anguish passed, the good man Joseph was very much comforted and consoled since, after the angel's counsel, he abode happily with his holy and blessed spouse and ever loved her with a more chaste love than any man can recount. And he was diligent about her in all faithfulness, and the Lady dwelt with him confidently. And both lived together happily in their poverty. The same might happen to us if we have patience in our anguish.

So too, the blessed Jesus kept himself hidden for nine months in his mother's womb, like other children, that he might again take upon himself all that which was in this world's misery and closed in hell to his company of the nine orders of angels. He kept himself there, comely and sustained patiently, waiting for the time due for his birth. Have compassion of him and look at the profound humility to which he comes, and do not raise your head as to anything good you might have. And since it was only for our benefit that he was in his mother's womb for so long and we cannot be of any worth to him, let us at least acknowledge him with all our heart and give thanks to him with all our affection for having been pleased to take us among others and to shelter us so as to be constantly in his service; for all comes from him, and nothing from our merits. This great benefit ought to be very acceptable, adorable and greatly approved by us, for he has not sheltered us to hurt us but only carefully in the most secure and high tower of religion, where the arrows of this cursed world cannot pierce with all their poison nor reach it unless it is through our boldness and malice. Let us then fortify ourselves with all our heart to be sheltered and cast away from our thoughts the bad affections of this world; without doing anything which little profits us to shut ourselves in our own body. Saint Gregory says: "Of what profit is it to attend to your body if you lack taking care of your soul?" What profit do you have if your body dwells in the cloister while your heart is in the world?

Let us also fortify ourselves in everything to give him thanks and praise him with all our heart, for among the virtues it is a very noble and shining thing before God that man, at the beginning of his obedience being in exile, powerless, undeterred and not extolled in praise, shutting himself bodily and spiritually, can just as well bless God and praise Him happily in all His works. Saint Bernard says: "Very happy is the man who puts in order the passions of his body according to the rule of justice, and when all he bears and suffers is for the love of the Son of God, in such manner that all murmuring is cast out of his heart and his mouth only utters thanksgiving with a voice of praise." Certainly, anyone who could take into account that all things turn good for those who love God perfectly, should rejoice greatly in thinking about Him and he shall find in Him what the Man of Wisdom says: "The righteous man shall not be heavy-hearted for anything that happens to him." For all that happens to us, according to Saint Augustine, is through the promise of God, and not through the power of our enemies. And he might also say, as the holy man Job did, "As it has pleased Our Lord God, so has it been done;

the name of Our Lord is blessed." So then you ought not doubt any troubles, for God will not suffer that these visit his friends other than for their profit. For there comes a time when a man turns himself away from worldly love, falls out with praise for temporal delights, and converts himself to God desiring eternal joys. And Saint Augustine says that a person does not convert himself perfectly to God unless he turns himself away from worldly love. And he cannot be more appropriately turned from present worldly love unless God mingles in his cursed pleasures and delights, laborious pains, sorrows and anguish. And if God ceased to mingle the bitterness of this world with bliss, we would soon forget Him. And by virtue of this the Psalmist says: "You have multiplied their sorrows," that is to say, to such as are in the world you have given persecution, "and they have made haste to love You." Sometimes God gives us troubles in order to correct our sins. And therefore Saint Augustine says that in the same way a file knocks off the rust from iron, and the furnace the filth from gold, and the thrashing tool the sheaf from the grain, so anguish does to the righteous man. And so, Joseph's brethren said: "As it should be, we suffer this misfortune of hunger since we have sinned against our brother." Sometimes God also sends anguish to some man so that in finding himself helpless, he might get to know of his imperfection more clearly. And the Psalmist again says: "I have said in my prosperity that perpetually I shall never decline from your love. But so that You should clearly show me my impotence and that without You I may do nothing, You have turned Your face from me and I have become hindered and troubled." Sometimes he gives us troubles in order to hold us on an even keel in having more fear and humility so that we should neither be presumptuous about our merits nor proud. And the Apostle says about this: "Since by many revelations God showed me I should not lift up myself by pride, the thorn of my flesh was given to me; that was the fallen angel Satan, who deals many a great blow." Sometimes, owing to that, one should know what great harm it is to leave God and to be abandoned by God. Jeremiah says about this: "Look and see what great harm it is to have abandoned your God and not to harbour His fear around you." At times it is in order to show us a man's patience, and by the example of holy men to teach everyone the virtue of patience. And Job has this to say: "Let this be to me a comfort which God gives for my affliction. And if it pleases Him, let Him yet give me more sorrow, for I shall never complain against it." Sometimes it is also done so that evil men should fear more and convert themselves sooner to good conduct. The Man of Wisdom says about this: "The foul and evil man, seeing the fool and sinner scourged, shall be even wiser." Sometimes it would be unto God's acclaim and praise, that He sends anguish, as was the sickness of the man born blind and the death of Lazarus; at others so that we should think and come to know again by signs that God loves us. Saint Jerome says about this that it is great mercy for those who have adversities in this world and bear them patiently when God does not take them away. Saint Augustine says: "When God does not correct the sinner in this world, it is a sign that He is very angry with him, for He suffers him to fall from one sin to another." Sometimes too, for the purpose of a person having greater trust and hope in Him. Saint Augustine says: "In being prosperous in this world, you ought to fear greatly. Should it not be better to be tempted and proven than not to be tempted at all and reprimanded by God?' Saint Bernard says that the greatest anger God has against his creature is in not being angry with him. For when a person feels angry by some anguish sent to him by God, he should have great hope of being afterwards pardoned; and also if he is very angered, God remembers him out of mercy. Sometimes God also sends anguish so that a person might know that He is always ready to help when one recurs to Him with all his heart. And so, the Psalmist says: "I cried unto God when I was troubled, and He has graciously heard me." Sometimes it is for the purpose of proving a person's love for God and whether there is true virtue in him. Saint Gregory says: "The person is vexed by anguish and pain if it so perfectly pleases God, for in time of peace no one knows his strength." Certainly, in fighting battles and anguish, the trials of virtue do not show themselves outwardly. Sometimes it so happens that a person is tried even more so that he may get an even greater crown through the merits of his patience, as it can be seen in Job and in the holy martyrs. Saint James says: "Blessed is he who suffers and sustains temptation and anguish, for when he shall be proven, he shall have the crown of life, which God promises to those who love him." And according to Chrysostom, whoever is in anguish ought to show some sign that he has something good in himself, which the enemy struggles to make him lose, for he would not feel safe to come to him were he not to see some honour in him; as we have of the first man, whom the enemy saw in great honour and dignity, and therefore rose against him to tempt him. And he also rose against the holy man Job seeing that he was highly revered by God. And moreover, we are sometimes troubled in this world not that we might be purged, but to start feeling the pain one shall suffer ceaselessly, such as when being reprimanded and as it happened to Antiochus and to Herod. And so that what the prophet says, "Lord, trouble them with twofold affliction," is accomplished, namely in this world and in the other. But Our Lord moves with mercy with his friends, and permits for their profit that they suffer much harm. And so he ought to be praised always and in everything. Saint Augustine says: "The very humility of the friends of God is no way as to grow proud or to murmur in his heart, nor to be unkind or to complain, but to give thanks to God and praise Him in all His judgments, whose works are all rightful, meaning benign and merciful."

Considering the aforesaid, study also to make steady, set and put yourself in order so that you may not be sorry for anything which God sends you, but receive it patiently and happily. And exercise yourself in this manner, in the way of the Holy Spirit, that even for the love of sweet Jesus you may desire to have anguish, which he held in himself and in his members, in showing the right path and giving example to all who would walk by this way. He really desires that the children of his realm suffer something in this present world, for according to what the Apostle says, those who do not come from the Father's discipline and instruction are not worthy to be called sons, but wrongdoers. And according to Saint Augustine, whoever is in this world exempt from anguish and scourging, is exempt from the world of the children of God. And so no man ought to presume or think having any other thing but what the Gospel promises him, namely anguish in this world, which is necessary until the very end, as we read in Scripture which promises us nothing else in this world but tribulations, anguish, and increasing sorrow and temptations. And mainly it is thus that we should prepare ourselves for such things, that we might not fail whenever it pleases God to send them to us.

Now let it be known that the sinners of this world are sometimes only scourged but a little. This is because there is no hope for their correction. Yet for those to whom eternal life is ordained, it is necessary that they have anguish in this world, for their Father scourges them and beats them with anguish as much as they receive or ought to receive in eternal inheritance. Note well that it is said "as much", since He scourged his own son who was without sin. So would He, who scourged His own and natural son who is without sin, leave the son who is none else than adopted and in sin without scourging? No, for sure. His son was without sin, yet for all that he was not left without scourging. He has shown us well an example in his sufferings. And so let us not trouble ourselves when we see any holy person suffer great persecutions, but let us think what things did the most righteous of all righteous men and the holiest of all holy men suffer, who held in disparage all earthly things to show us by example how to despise them, and sustained all the harm of the world so that no man should seek happiness in worldly things, and that in seeking less anguish we should fear that instead we find unhappiness. It is then expedient that we are afflicted, for oftentimes anguish keeps us back from doing evil. And so they should not perturb or make us impatient, but we ought to have appetite for them and desire them, and flee all that goes against adversity, such as pleasure and prosperity, which often induce us to evil. ✤

CHAPTER 9
OF OUR LORD JESUS CHRIST'S NATIVITY

T that time, namely when Mary was pregnant with child, *Exiit edictum a Caesare Augusto,* "an edict was issued by Caesar Augusto," who was the second emperor after Octavian and in whose time he first began the population censuses. Since he was willing to know the number of regions, cities and countries of all the world, he commanded that the whole world should be written and described, so that he might by this know the number of cities in all countries, and in every city the number of heads of households. Now it should be noted that the first emperor of the Romans was Julius Caesar who, according to Isidore, was called Caesar because after his mother had dies, her womb was cut for him to be taken out of it; or maybe he was so called since he fought his enemies valiantly. And so the emperors after him retained this name Caesar. So then when Julius Caesar was dead, Octavian succeeded him, being his nephew, and was called Augustus since he greatly augmented the Roman commonwealth and empire. And so were the other emperors who came after him who were also called *Augusti,* "augmenters." So that Octavian, retaining the surname of his uncle, that is to say Caesar, with his first name Augustus, was called Caesar Augustus. From this also came the name of the month then called Sextilis, and now August since he was born or had victory over his enemies in that month. And when he started holding sway as emperor, he reigned for fifty-seven and a half years; and the twelfth year before the nativity of Jesus Christ, was one in full peace. It is in this peace that Jesus Christ was born, for peace is subject to him and he sought it with all his might, looking upon those who have it. He is the king and prince of peace, and so it was a proper thing that peace should precede the maker, and that it should be the messenger of whom, coming into the world, dwelling therein and departing from it, preached about it and left it behind him. Whereby it is also understood that God only dwells in a peaceful heart,

according to what the Psalmist says: "His place is in peace."

The emperor made the said census so that all realms and regions throughout the world might generally be in peace. This census was first made by Quirinius, governor of Syria, who had been sent by the emperor to govern that country. The country of Judah had no proper governor at the time who was descended from the Jews, but was governed by the commissary and governor of Syria for it then formed part of the province of Syria. It might also be said that the said census was taken in that place since Judea was in the centre of the world, and so it was ordained that it was Quirinius who should begin, to be followed by other governors in nearby regions. Rather, that the first census, counting heads, was made in the governor's city. The second, that of cities, was made in the region, in the country by Caesar's legate. The third, that of regions, was made in the city of Rome before Caesar. Seemingly, this was done every year, as it is written in the Gospel, *Magister vester etc*, "Your master," said the receiving officer of the tribute to Peter, "has not paid the tribute this year." It was called census because the number of heads of every household found in the city was put down in writing. Saint Gregory says: "The world is written in the nativity of Our Lord, for he who should write his chosen children in his eternity came under our human nature." I pray you Lord, that you keep me among your chosen children, that I may be written in your book of eternity.

So they went into their metropolitan city, where every man was to confess himself subject to the Roman empire, giving to the prince of the city one penny, which was worth the current ten half-pence or little pence. And in giving it to the province governor each man was bound to put it under his head, and in his own confession acknowledge himself subject to the Roman emperor, which was written. And so every man made himself subject to the emperor in three ways. Namely in deed, by paying the penny; in word, by confessing himself subject to the emperor; and in writing, as the name of each man was written. We ought also to act likewise, for we ought to pay and confess to our King our penny of faith and of justice; to whom we owe one penny, meaning our soul, marked and formed in His image. Or rather the ten commandments of the law, in which we find God's law and what should be done and what is to be omitted. For just as no man was exempt from paying his penny, so no man was exempt from observing God's commandments.

As the term of nine months was drawing to a close, Joseph departed from Nazareth in Galilee where he dwelt, and went up with Mary, his spouse who was pregnant with child and ready to give birth, to a Judean city called Beth-lehem. This was David's city since he was born there and anointed king, and Mary and Joseph too were of the House of David, and there they had to make profession to the emperor of Rome as all others. See, here, how Our Lord is for those written on earth, in that they are written in heaven where an example of perfect humility is given, which he began at his nativity and continued until his death on the cross. Bede says: "One ought not to pass on without considering the great and benign humility of Our Saviour and Redeemer Jesus Christ. He would not only take our human nature to save us, but also take with it complete and effective consent at the time when the world would be written to pay tribute to the emperor Caesar, so that it was him who was written to show us that he submitted himself to slavery for our deliverance."

Consider even more that although the Blessed Virgin had conceived the Lord of heaven and earth, yet she would still obey the emperor's order so that she might say with her son: "It is our duty to accomplish all justice in giving an example of obedience and pleasing our sovereigns who have power over us." So the Lady now travels and goes a long way; it is thirty-five miles from Nazareth to Jerusalem, and four miles from Jerusalem to Bethlehem, so she went thirty-nine miles. One may see that although the Virgin was pregnant with child and ready to give birth, still the fruit she bore in her womb was not heavy in her body, although she went from province to province. As Saint Augustine says, knowing that she was a virgin and pregnant with child, she rejoiced with flawless joy. For certainly, the resplendent light she bore had no weight.

Joseph's name is interpreted as growing, and we morally take it to mean the spiritual growth each man desires to go through. This man, paying to the sovereign king the tribute of devotion, ought to walk in the path of virtues and to go from Galilee, that is to say worldly pleasures, to Judea, which is the confession or praise of God. And while proceeding he shall also go up from Nazareth to Bethlehem, that is from active life which is action flourishing with virtues, to the vigour of the contemplative life where the repose of holy souls is found. Joseph then went along with Mary, for we always ought to have with us Mary, that is to say bitter sea, by which we understand penance.

And when they arrived in Bethlehem they could not find any lodging since they were poor and many were attending at the same place for the census. Have now compassion of this Lady, and look upon the tender and delicate of the fifteen year old maid, weary from travelling such a long a way and standing ashamedly in the midst of men, seeking and asking where she might find repose, but none would lodge her yet bid her to seek where she might find any. And so she walked into a rock shelter which was a stable on the way to the city, near one of the gates, under a rock, and she stayed there; this stable had no other covering than the said rock. According to Bede, a rock shelter is a place and space found between two streets, bounded on each side by a wall and a gate, so that there might be an exit and outlet from each street. It had a covering over it to keep people coming into it on holy days dry from rain or inclement weather. It now stands for the Church, which has a low status between paradise and the world, receiving all those whom she will recover for itself and turn them away from the world's follies. In this place those coming to do business in the city were accustomed to lodge their beasts there; and that is why it was called a rock shelter, that is to say some place where to turn in, for men took refuge in that place. And so it is well to believed that they were lodged among beasts. Chrysostom says: "You poor man, whoever you are, be comforted here, for Joseph and Mary, mother of Our Lord, had neither servant nor maid here. They came from Galilee all alone and had no beasts to ease. They are Lords and servants, a new and very marvellous thing. They go to the rock shelter because they have no lodging in the city. They are afraid in their poverty, for they dare not start relationships with rich men."

In this place, when the full time for the Virgin's delivery had come, namely at midnight on the holy day of Sunday, surely the day on which God said, *Fiat lux* "Let there be light," and light was made; the very light of the east visited us and the Virgin delivered her first child. Not that she had any afterwards, but he is called the first child since she had none ever before. The Son of God would be born of his mother temporally, according to human nature, because he should get many brethren by spiritual generation. Also, he is better called *primogenitus* in the Gospel than *unigenitus*; first begotten rather than only begotten. For as Bede says, Our Lord Jesus Christ is one only according to divine substance, but he is first born in assuming our human nature. He was born in the night, for he came privately, since he brings back those living in the night of error to the light of truth.

When the child was born, his mother worshipped him as God, and was herself who wrapped him in clothes that were of little value. That is why poor men are called patched, because their clothes are sown with poor pieces of cloth. And there she laid him down, not in a great noble bed or one splendidly decorated, but in an old manger amidst two beasts, for there was no other place where she might put him. See the great poverty of Our Lord. Not only that he had no proper house at his nativity where to be born, but then also no place in the rock shelter where he might be put, if not amongst beasts; and yet he might hardly get any place there. And Scripture was fulfilled in all this, saying that earth's beasts have dens, and the heaven's birds have nests, but the Son of Man, that is to say of the Virgin, has not where to repose his head.

Consider then by what is said that he began to teach us by example the state of perfection, which is found in humility, austerity and poverty; namely the poverty which he had and the places where he took rest. First he took repose in his mother's womb; secondly, on the rack or in the manger; thirdly, on the gibbet of the cross; and fourthly, in a sepulchre which was not his; so that he might truly say along with the Psalmist: *Pauper sum ego*: "I am poor, and in the excruciating labour of my childhood." Here are condemned the honours, pomp and vanities of this world, the enticing delights of the flesh, all excess and abundance in riches.

Saint Anselm says: "Oh for the consent! Oh for the love! Oh for the marvel! You, who are sovereign God of glory, have not scorned being made like a contemptible worm. You, who are Lord of all things, would appear as a servant. You have thought it but little to be our Father, so that by your pity you would be made our brother. And you, king of all things, with no imperfection at the beginning of your nativity, found no horror to taste the austerity of the most abject and dire poverty. For as Scripture says, when you were born in this world "there was neither place nor cradle in the rock shelter" where one might have reposed or received your tender human nature. But in a vile manger and in a foul stable you were swaddled and wrapped in cheap clothes, you, who comprises and encloses all the earth. And yet your mother was constrained to borrow the place of reasonless beasts. Comfort yourself, You who are nourished in poverty, for God is with you in all poverty. He is not laid in enticing or royally laid out places. He is not found with those who find pleasures in this world. Oh you rich man, who are nothing else but earth, why do you glorify yourself in beds, paintings and delights, when the king of kings would honour in his bed the straw, the hay and the bedding of poor men? Why do you detest hard things, when the tender child, in whose hand are all the realms of the world, rather chose to be born in the hard place where beasts were laid to rest, rather than in a place where there were fair and quite large beds of silk and comfort?" Bernard says: "The childhood of Jesus Christ comforts not those who are talkative or contin- ual chatterers; nor do his tears comfort those who mock the poor and simple people; nor do his clothes comfort those who walk in this world in great pomp and honours; nor the stable and manger as those who love the highest positions and those who are called lords. But the joy of this nativity is shown and announced to shepherds who were awake, to whom it was said that the Saviour was born. This nativity was announced to poor men and not to rich men who find their comfort in this world and not in God." Saint Bernard says again: "The Son of God, who might have chosen any such time as he wanted for his nativity, chose the hardest time, especially for him, a little child, and for his poor mother, who hardly had any clothes in which to wrap him, but only a manger where to lay him. And notwithstanding such great need, for all that I heard no mention was made of either skins or linen clothing. For sure Our Saviour, who might not be deceived, chose what was most hard for the body, to teach us that we should choose it as the best and most profitable thing. And if anyone else teaches anything else, we ought to forgo him deliberately as a traitor and seducer. And that notwithstanding, my brethren, this child was promised long before by Isaiah, who says about him that he could choose what is good and abstain from evil. Whereby it appears that the will of the body is evil, and its affliction is good, which the child chose and reproved the other; he who is the eternal Word of God, enclosed himself in a tender body which is weak to all labour. And therefore, men of flesh, flee away from sensual pleasure and voluptuousness, for it is only followed by perpetual death. Do penance, through which one comes to the realm of paradise. What I am saying is being preached to us by this stable, by the limbs of the little child which are announcing it, as well as by his tears which are evangelising and showing it. Oh what great hardness of my heart! To my will, good Lord, in the same manner as you, the eternal Word of God, are made flesh for us, so let my heart be made of flesh, the same way as you have promised by your Prophet's mouth saying: 'I shall take away the heart of stone which is without any sweetness, and I shall give them a sweet loving heart made of flesh.'"

Do you see then, oh creature, the nativity of so high and mighty Lord and prince? Have you seen in the same manner the birth of the queen of heaven? You may also see the great poverty which is found in both. This is the virtue which, in the Gospel, is called the precious stone, which so that it might be had and bought all other things ought to be sold. This is the foundation of all spiritual edifices and the way of salvation, as the foundation of humility is the root of perfection, from which plentiful fruit comes, although now it is secret and hidden. You may also consider the most profound humility of both. They did not despise either the stable, or the manger, or the hay, or other vile things, in giving us an example of perfect humility; without this virtue a creature can never be saved, for no sort of work done in pride may please God. Certainly, humility deserves that God gives other virtues to the person, and that he conforms to them and brings them to a good end. You may moreover think about the corporal affliction they had, and even much more that of the little child Jesus. Amongst other things one affliction was that when his mother laid him in the manger, she had neither cushion, nor even any other respectable thing to lay on this tender child or under his head. But she laid there a big hard stone, though she did this with great bitterness of heart. And perhaps there was a little hay between the child and the stone, which she took before the beasts that were there; and as it is said, the stone is still in the same place in memory of this.

Meditate then with all your mind and power how to embrace and follow poverty, humility and affliction of the body. Saint Bernard says: "He has shown us by three examples the way by which we should follow him. The first is poverty, for in this world he would have no riches; this virtue makes a man light and expedient to run along the way of the commandments. The second is humility, for he did not praise the glory of this world; this humility makes a man little so as to be more hidden against the enemy's temptations. The third is wisdom, for he has sustained for us very great harm; for patience makes a man strong and powerful to bear anguish."

According to Saint Anselm, our Redeemer has put upon our eyes, blinded with the very light, the ointment of his Incarnation, so that we, who may not see God in the secret of His majesty, might see Him through our human nature. And in seeing Him we might know Him; and in knowing Him we might love Him; in loving Him we might grow strong and come to His blessed glory. He is seen in this world according to human nature so that he might call us back into the heavenly realm. He partakes in our mutability, that He might make us participants in His immutability. He deigns to our humility, that He might lift us up to His extreme goodness.

And according to Chrysostom, the natural Son of God would be also son of David for the purpose of making us too sons of God. He would want that his servant should be his Father, so that he should make God our Father. He is born according to the flesh, so that we should be born according to the spirit. And because childbirth comes after conception, it was a proper thing that Jesus Christ, who had been conceived in a flower, that is to say in Nazareth which means a flower, should be born in fruit, that is in Bethlehem which means the house of bread or of the vigour which belongs to fruit; for Jesus Christ is the very bread descended from heaven, who refreshes the souls of chosen men by eternal vigour. He is born in Bethlehem, which is the least of all cities in Judea, to show that he sought no glory or exaltation in any earthly city. Every hour he is conceived in Nazareth and born in Bethlehem, whenever any creature takes the flower of the Holy Scripture and in correcting himself makes himself the Son of God's dwelling, he who is heavenly bread. Also, he would not be born in his relatives' house, but along the way, to show that he was a pilgrim and that his realm was not of this world; as he himself said, *Ego sum via, veritas et vita,* "I am the way by which man comes to paradise."

He was made little to make us great and to take away all pride from us. He was wrapped in little clothes, since he should deliver us from the grave clothes of death and give us back the first stole, which is that of immortality. His feet and hands were strained and bound, so that ours would be free and able to work good deeds, and our feet dressed in the way of peace. He suffered being put in the rock shelter, so that he might prepare for us great mansions in his Father's house. Also, he is put in a tight manger, for he would rebuke delicate things and great edifices and other worldly grandeurs, and so that he should exceedingly fill us with the joys of the heavenly realm, that we should give only to him the place of our heart, the same manner as he wants, saying *Fili prebe cor tuum,* "My son, give me your heart." He is laid down on a little hay betwixt beasts, which miraculously knew him and worshipped him on their knees and in so much as they could, loved and praised him, so as to show that man, who is made beast by sin, acknowledged his maker and afterwards was as innocent. The ox, which meant the Jewish people, and the ass, which meant the heathens, have had Jesus Christ in their midst, and they miraculously knew him and worshipped him. Saint Ambrose says: "Oh creature, do understand the cry of the child and do hear the cry of the ox. The ox knew his possessor, and the ass his Lord's manger." Gregory Nazianzen says: "Honour this manger, by which you have the vigour of living heavenly bread." You who before were like a beast without reason, know your possessor like the ox. And so that you might count yourself among the beasts which chew meat, and gather for God's sacrifice pure and clean, keep often thinking in your mind how the eternal Word God would be made man for you. By Mary may we understand our Holy Mother the Church, and by Joseph, her spouse, the overseer, who as a spouse wears a ring on his finger. And the same way as Mary was delivered by grace, so has the Church brought forth Christian men by the grace of God; going to Bethlehem, their heavenly city, and acknowledging to be servants of the emperor of the whole world. The Church brings forth a child in every person when one puts in effect the good thing conceived, and wraps it in clothes; when he hides his good deeds so that he would have no praise, one puts it in the manger; when a man takes no pride in such a good deed, but rather humbles himself.

When Our Saviour and Redeemer Jesus Christ was born, the angels were all around him and worshipped him without any concern. *Et pastores erant in regione eadem.* And the shepherds were in the same region, tending their beasts a mile from that place, near a tower called the tower of the flock of beasts. *Et ecce angelus Domini.* The Angel of God, Gabriel, who had made the annunciation about the fourth watch of the night, for the night has four watches, came to them and held himself near them in white vestments with a glowing and cheerful face, for the angel Gabriel was cheerful and made others joyful in the fulfilment of this news. *Et claritas Dei.* And God's brightness encircled them on all parts, in the body and outside it, as also in the soul within, in sign that the son of justice was born. The angel came full of light to announce him who in this world enlightens every man.

The angel rather appeared to shepherds than to anyone else. First, because they were poor, and the Son of God come into this world for poor men; as Jesus said: "It is for the misery and wailing of poor men that I am come into this world being made human." Secondly, because they were simple people, for as it is written in the Book of *Proverbs*: "The simple man believes every word." Thirdly, that they might keep awake, for as it is again written in the Book of *Proverbs*: "Those who watch for me early in the morning shall find me." Fourthly, for the mystery, so that the doctrine of the prelates and pastors ought to come to the subjects. *Et timuerunt timore magno.* And these shepherds feared greatly seeing the angels' vision, which they were not used seeing, and also because of the sudden brightness with which they were surrounded. But the angel comforted them, saying *Nolite timere*, "Have no doubts about anything." And they were told why they should not fear what they were seeing: *Ecce evangelizo vobis gaudium magnum quod erit omni populo*, "Behold, I bear tidings of great joy to you which shall be tidings for the whole world", namely to all the Church which was to bring together Jews and heathens, for he who is born today is born both for your benefit and profit, and for that of all men when Jews and heathens are assembled together. And it should be noted that the angel did not say "tonight" but "today" since that night shone with divine brightness as if it were day; even now that night has already preceded day. The Saviour is born, that is to say the lover who restores salvation, being Christ according to human nature, in which he was anointed by God the Father and by all the Trinity through plenty of grace, and Lord according to his divinity, is born in Bethlehem, the city where David was born. This is why Christus means "anointed", for he was king and overseer and, as viewed in the Old Law, was the one who only ought to be anointed. According to Bede, the angel taught Mary in one way, Joseph in another, and the shepherds their way; for Mary was instructed that she should conceive, Joseph of who was conceived, and the shepherds of who was born; so that the angel should sufficiently instruct man and should constantly serve God, his maker. *Et hoc vobis signum*, "And this shall be a sign for you," in the manner of the Jews who asked for signs. *Invenietis*, "You shall find him, as if the little child were hidden and not showing himself or speaking, and yet still being the Word and the Son of God, wrapped in clothes and not in silk." See the poverty of God. So that the shepherds who were poor, simple and humble should not fear seeing this mystery, the sign of poverty and humility in Jesus Christ was given to them in his first coming, but he shall have another sign at his second coming. *Et positum in presepio*, "And he was put in the manger, not in a cradle or in a bed of gold."

By these things we are morally instructed by whom and how Jesus Christ is found, namely only by simple persons and poor men, as his childhood proves to us; and by poor men as is proven by being wrapped in clothes; and by humble men and such as deem themselves unimportant, as is proven to us by being laid in the manger. And these three things are understood in the three vows of religion: that is in chastity as to the first, poverty as to the second, and obedience as to the others. Very appropriately the angel appeared to the tending shepherds when the great and sovereign pastor was born, so as to show that they should be the pastors of the Church, that is to say to be humble and aware of the ways of their subjects and of their souls, that they would not perish being bitten by hell's wolves. And Bede says that, speaking mystically, the night signifies the peril of temptations during which perfect arousers do not cease from keeping watch over those committed to them. And the angel keeps close to them and keeps them, and the brightness of God surrounds them, leading them on the right path. And not only the bishops, priests, deacons or monastery priors ought to be called pastors, but also all those running a household, for they should diligently keep wake over what God has put under them, and not waste themselves unreasonably. And a person may also be called a pastor when he nourishes with spiritual vigour the powers of his soul and keeps the night watches over those who are entrusted to him, in gathering good meditations about God and Holy Scripture, and all that which might cause harm to his good purpose and desire.

And when the shepherds marvelled about what they had seen and heard as the angel's witness should not be seen of little authority, there came at once many witnesses, that is to say a great multitude of angels or armoured men of the sovereign king, who fought for us against the powers of hell, suddenly appearing with the angel who had announced the nativity of Our Lord. And they loved and blessed God for His nativity because they knew that through him who was born their fall and ruin was restored. And they all together chanted a song, *Gloria in excelsis Deo etc*, "Glory be to God in heaven", for the glory of God shines more in heaven than on earth. According to Bede, while one angel was announcing the nativity of the Son of God, a great multitude of angels suddenly began to praise our maker together, accomplishing the reason of their existence and always teaching us that whenever we hear any learning being uttered by our brethren reminding us of the things to which we are bound, we ought at once to give praise to God with our heart, mouth and works. This is the same as was done to show us that through this nativity men should be converted to the peace of one faith, one hope and one charity; and in order to give praise and glory to God, the angel said, "God is not praised by many on earth, yet He is glorified by all in heaven."

And the angel afterwards says *Et in terra pax*, "Peace be on earth to men, and not to all, but to only to those who are of good will." Man is simply called good through good will, more than because of any other power of the soul, for the will moves the other powers to their works, so that their goodness or cursedness rebounds on the other powers. For there is no true peace in evil men; they will be separated from God by their evil and through their evil life; but true peace is only for those who love Our Lord's name and do not say anything against it. To have peace with God, according to Pope Leo, is to accomplish what He commands and not to will doing that which He prohibits. And the true peace of a Christian is not wanting to be freed from God's will so as only to delight himself in his own things. It also appears from the angel's word that this peace, which was also mainly promised by the prophets when Our Lord would come, was to be an inner peace for those who had good will. It is what we actually desire during Mass at the third

Agnus Dei, as Albert the Great says, and not the ephemeral peace of worldly prosperity. For temporal peace, like that at the time of this nativity when the Roman empire was in such great calm, was not but a figure of this inner peace which God mainly asks of us. For Jesus Christ lives only in a peace-loving heart, as the Psalmist says: "His dwelling and His place is made in peace." It is also well said that glory be to God, and peace to men, for God the Father is glorified by Our Lord Jesus Christ, and peace is made between God and man, between angel and man, and between Jews and heathens. It is said that Saint Hilary further said about this: *Laudamus te*. And Pope Anastasius ordained it to be chanted on certain days in the Mass. About the joy of this holy day, on this verse of the *Psalms*, Cassiodorus says: *Haec est dies quam fecit Dominus*, "This is the day which Our Lord made. How can it be that although Our Lord made and created all other days, yet He has particularly made the day which is dedicated and sacred to the nativity of Our Lord Jesus Christ? It is not without cause that every man ought to rejoice, for by him the devil lost all power he had over the creature, and the world received salvation through him."

After the angels had given thanks to their maker for such a great gift as He had shown and given to human creatures, they rose high into heaven and showed their companions the deed and the event, also giving thanks and praise to God the Father. Then they all came according to their hierarchy to see the face of their Lord, and they worshipped him together with his glorious mother with all due reverence and praise. Certainly, no one of them could come to such great pride that, hearing such news, would not visit their Lord so humbly set in the world. Whereupon the Apostle says: "When God the Father sent his only son into the world, He said, *Et adorent eum omnes angeli Dei*, 'Let all the angels of God worship Him.'" And Saint Augustine says: "The Son of God was born in a stable, swaddled by his mother in poor clothes and laid in a beasts' manger, for she had no house made of precious cedar, nor bed of great array whose bedstead was made of ivory, where to bring forth her maker, nor a place where she might place the Redeemer." So that, like a stranger or pilgrim, she brought forth the Lord of the world in a strange house; and as a poor woman wrapped him not in silk, but in poor clothes; and she at once worshipped him as God after giving him birth. Oh happy stable, oh blessed manger where the Son of God is born and in which God of all creatures is laid! The midwives were the cohorts of angels and this Virgin's comfort came from angels, for there were a million angels giving thanks to God and for such special purpose making great mirth in heaven. Our Lord wept in the stable, and yet the great multitude of angels found joy in him, saying "Glory be to the sovereign God of heaven, and peace on earth to men of good will, for the goodness of heaven is born on earth." The very peace had descended from heaven and the angels rejoiced before him, about whom his sweet mother had before been very worried but now rejoiced in great anxiety and persevered in apprehension and exaltation.

When these songs had been chanted and these words told to them, the shepherds conferred and said, "Let us go to Bethlehem and see this *Verbum* and worthy and laudable Word." The word *Verbum* or Word often stands in Holy Scripture for something worthy and honourable; the same as is written in *Isaiah* about king Hezekiah: *Quod non erat Verbum*, "There was nothing in his house that he had not shown to the messengers the king of Babylon had sent him." *Quod Dominus fecit*, "Which God had made," since no other man could make it. *Et ostendit nobis*, "And He has shown it to us by the angel." Or it may be explained otherwise: "Let us go and see the Word who was at the beginning of the world in God the Father and is now made man, he whom all the Holy Trinity has so ordained to be, that he might not be seen by us as a person in the Trinity." And they came hastily and with great joy and desire to see the child. In this they showed their devotion and care to seek him; for no man deserves to see Jesus Christ if he seeks him in idleness and envy. Going there, according to Bede, is not only going with bodily feet, but to profit daily in oneself and from one virtue to another.

Et invenerunt Mariam et Ioseph, "And they found Mary and Joseph and the child at the beasts' manger." Owing to the great peace there was then in the world, the city gates were open for the great multitude of people who came and went through Bethlehem, so that the shepherds too could go in and out as they wanted. They found Jesus Christ with Joseph and Mary in the manger, whereby we understand that whosoever wants to have Jesus Christ ought to be himself clean of heart as seen in Mary, just towards his neighbour as seen in Joseph and humble and reverent towards God as seen in the humble manger. And they, seeing the child according to their physical eyes, knew by inner faith that this was the Son of God and that all that had been said to them was about him; by means of which it appears that a man comes to know about the Trinity by knowing human nature. And in worshipping the child they recounted to the mother and to good Joseph, and afterwards to all others, what the angel had told them, by which the listeners were greatly marvelled of the mysteries of this Incarnation and of what the shepherds had said and testified.

Morally, by these things you may take heed that three things are necessary for those who want to find Jesus Christ, namely by speech, study and meditations of the Scripture; to pass by thinking about creatures; in having him by tasting and savouring grace. Or they who desire to find Jesus must speak by confessing their sins, and move forward by objecting to bodily and temporal things, and of having them by fervent desire; and so also to come to Bethlehem, the house of bread, by smelling divine things. And they found the child Jesus in the crib, which shows us his delicious presence, for he has said that his pleasure is to be amongst men.

Also morally, Bethlehem, signifying the house of bread, is a sign of the kingdom of heaven where bread as spoken of is found in the Gospel: "Blessed is he that eats the bread in God's kingdom." And in order to arrive there we ought to pass through three passages. The first is from vice to virtue. The second, from one virtue to another. The third, from death to life and from this world to God, our Father. Now according to Bede, let us go by the example of these shepherds to Bethlehem, the city of David, which worthily feasted the Incarnation of the Son of God. Let us now pass on to Bethlehem, the sovereign city and the house of the bread of life, by putting out of us all carnal lustfulness, while remembering that the Son of God was made man for our sake and that he has ascended into his heavenly house and there sits on the right hand of his Father. And so let us follow him with all our power in chastising our flesh, so that, the same as the shepherds see him in the crib, so may we see him in his Father's kingdom on high. Certainly, we may not seek such divine favour in idleness or negligence, but by diligently following the way which Our Lord Jesus Christ has shown us. And in the same manner that when they saw him they knew him, let us also make haste to embrace by love all that which is said of Our Lord, so that we may have perfect joy after this present life.

For Mary, who was very wise, kept in her heart all the aforesaid words, namely the angel's annunciation, the great joy shown by Saint John in his mother's womb, the nativity of Our Saviour, the melody made by the angels on this day, the shepherds' faith. And she preserved and bound them all in her heart along with what the prophets said in Scripture. You may see here the very good disciple, who keeps in her mind what she had herd, and does not forget anything, but recalls it many times thinking about it in it great pleasure. This was later to profit the Church greatly, for men wrote all that she taught to the apostles and evangelists, who knew through her many of the doings of Our Lord, and especially what he did before he called them; afterwards they resorted to her as they would to their Lady. And for this reason after the ascension of her Son she was the best person in this world who could teach them in the best and easiest manner and to show them his ways. She was the ark containing the divine secrets of God, and since she had read the Holy Scripture and knew the prophecies, she considered prudently how the prophecies were fulfilled in this newly born child, while even more truly believing and praying to him as to God. For she had read in *Isaiah* "A virgin shall conceive and bear a child," and she knew well that she was a virgin and that she had conceived and was delivered while still remaining a virgin. And she had read *Bos cognovit possessorem suum*, namely that "The ox has known his owner, and the ass his master's crib," and she saw her child between these two beasts. Moreover she had read *Egredietur virga de radice Iesse*, "A rod shall sprout from the line of Jesse," and so did she see him born of David's line. And she had read *Nazareus vocabitur*, "He shall be called Nazarene," and so did she see that she had conceived of the Holy Spirit in Nazareth. She had read also *Et tu Bethlem, terra Iuda*, "And thou Bethlehem, land of Judea, you shall not be the least among the princes of the Jews," and she similarly saw that what the Prophets had foretold of this child was accomplished in deed. And what she had heard spoken before, she now saw with her own eyes taking heed of the agreement between one term and another, and had earnest faith in them. Still she would never tell about any secrets she knew about Our Lord. And she was just as chaste of her mouth as of her body, for she was reverently expecting the agreed and appropriate time when and how God would have it shown. Oh, only to think of the joy this Virgin had when she saw herself become the mother of God! For as Saint Anselm says, to say only of the Virgin Mary that she is the Mother of God exceeds all highness and dignity of what any man might say or think besides God.

After this, the shepherds went back to tender their beasts, glorifying God with great joy in their hearts, verbally prais' ing Him for the great benefit which God had given and shown to the whole world, and which was especially shown to them. For they found that what the angel had told them before was all true. They then commended themselves to devotion, so that after contemplating the Saviour they went back and started doing virtuous works. This ought to be an example for the heads and rulers of the Church how they ought to watch when others sleep, and often visit a contemplative Bethlehem and study the Holy Scripture, so that they too may taste the vigour of the bread of doctrine and learning and return in a more composed manner to their parishioners. It is owing to this that it is written in Ezekiel that the beasts went and came again.

And so, oh soul, you ought to go and see the Word by which all things are made, he who has become man for your sake. And kneeling, pray your maker and his sweet mother, and most reverently Joseph the just man, to sweetly kiss the feet of this little child Jesus laid in the crib. And pray the Lady that it would please her to let you kiss him or to allow you to take him in your arms, and diligently behold his most sweet face which the angels have the utmost desire to see, and do kiss him reverently and delight in him with all your heart. You may do this very boldly since the sweet Lord comes so meekly into this world for you and all sinners, that he shall forgive you and will patiently allow you to do this. Then give him back to his mother, and prepare yourself to help and serve this Lady, who so diligently suckles him, swaddles him and cares for him with such great reverence and fear. Do so that you may not be presumed unworthy and shunned from this company. Anselm says: "Go with the mother of this child to Bethlehem in all reverence and devotion, and be present with her to the place where she lodges, and serve this little child laid in the crib in all that you can do, saying Isaiah in high pitch and in exultation, *Parvulus natus est nobis*, 'A little child is born unto us, and the Son of God is given to us,' while kissing this divine crib where the child is laid. Do this in such manner that love itself, sweet modesty and affection drive away all fear from you when setting your mouth to the feet of the sweetest and most holy child and kissing them sweetly. And then consider how the shepherds came to him by night, in the wonder of worship which the heavenly hosts made at the coming of this king, and sing with heart and mouth with them *Gloria in excelsis Deo etc*, 'Glory be to God in heaven, and peace on earth to men of good will.'" Augustine says: "When men read the Gospel of the nativity of Our Lord Jesus Christ, we hear in it angels' voices, the delivering of the Virgin's child, the news given to the shepherds at this nativity, and how the angels sang *Gloria in excelsis Deo*. This night is much of a great joy and mirth for the Virgin Mary, and not only for her who had given birth to a child without the work or knowledge of any man, but also to all earthly creatures, for when she had given birth to this child, Saviour and Redeemer of the whole world. let us now say with very devout hearts and with high voice *Gloria in excelsis Deo etc*, and let us seriously think of these divine words with our utmost strength, being greatly comforted in faith, hope and charity. For these are God's praises, the angels' chant and the joy of all earthly creatures." And Gregory Nazianzen says: "Worship this child with the shepherds and sing this hymn with the angels. And if you may not find joy in yourself as Saint John did in his mother's womb, at least be joyful as David did before God's ark. Honour this nativity through which you are delivered of the shrouds of earthly nativity." Also, come every day and see Jesus in the spiritual crib, that is at the table of the altar, so that with the holy wheat of his flesh there you may be satisfied with the holiest things.

Now it comes to mind that Our Saviour and Redeemer Jesus Christ has three nativities, namely the divine, the human and the gratuitous. The first is the Father's, who is everlasting and without mother; the second temporal, of a mother without a father; and the third takes place spiritu-ally in the soul, having both father and mother, according to which Jesus says "Whoever does the will of my Father who is in heaven, is my brother, my sister and my mother." Of the Father since ever born, of the mother born only once, and in the soul born many times. These three nativities of Our Lord Jesus Christ represent the Church on the day of this nativity. The first is found in the midnight mass. The second in that celebrated at dawn or the first light of the day, since the human nativity was partly hidden, as con-cerning the genre and assembly of persons on which it has effect. The third is represented in the great or high mass said during the day, for the gratuitous nativity is shown in the soul where God is conceived by affection, born by effect, and nourished by good works.

Do worship now the little city of Bethlehem, which was before called Ephrath, which except for a woman who came to that land was called Bethlehem, the house of bread, for the abundance of food found in it. And in it David was born and anointed king. And Ruth and Boaz there celebrated their marriage, which had been figured on the union of the divine and human nature in Jesus Christ. It was in Bethlehem that a sturdy and triumphant great cathedral church in honour of the Virgin Mary was made and consecrated, as Saint Helen, mother of the Emperor Constantine, had ordered to be made. And in it there is a beautiful marble altar, hewn in a rock, where the Virgin was delivered. There is in this church the sepulchre of the innocents, and of Saint Jerome, and of Paul and Eustace. And there is a cistern, in which according to some the kings' star fell, as well as that of many honest persons who because of this noble nativity were willing to leave great cities and towns and went to dwell there. And the said Church or wayside shelter where the Son of righ-teousness, that is Our Lord, was born is sited on a stony place on a long and narrow ridge facing the east. And four or five feet from there facing the western part was the animals' crib where the sweet child was laid. Bethlehem then is not less than any other city in both excellence and dignity. And Saint Bernard says about it: "Oh Bethlehem, small city, you are greatly exalted by God, and He has truly magnified you, for in you He being great was made little! Oh city of God, great things are spoken about you, for men truly say that the Saviour was born in you to deliver humanity which was in captivity!" This was very much like the Pharaoh's butler who, while in prison, a vine with three branches grew on the ground before him, and it began to flourish and bear fruit, such as grapes of raisins; and he took them and strained out the juice into the Pharaoh's cup and gave it to him to drink; and then, as to how his dream was interpreted, he was delivered. In this manner, when the poor human lineage was in miserable captivity, the vine, that is Our Lord Jesus Christ, grew off the ground, that is from Mary; and had three branches in him, the body, the soul and the Trinity. And the third day after his precious blood was shed for us on the cross and offered to God the Father, he delivered man from his captivity and pardoned him of all his offences. And this wine he left with us here in the holy sacrament of the altar, so that every day it should be offered to God for all people. And this why in the nativity of the Son of God the vines of Angadì flourish, so as to show that the very wine has come. The manner of this nativity was prefigured in Aaron's rod, which flourished and bore fruit, namely almonds. For just as the rod flourished miraculously and contrary to nature and it bore fruit, so did Mary marvellously conceive the Son of God above the order of nature. Without being planted Aaron's rod bore fruit. Also, as Chrysostom says, Mary has borne a child without man's seed, like the nut joined to the tree of the cross; and at times it is called flower and at others fruit. For according to Saint Ambrose, he is like the fruit of a good tree, and he now flourishes and again bears fruit by increasing the virtues he gives us; and in us he is repaired by the resurrection. In both Testaments, he is flower in the Scripture and fruit in the spirit; flower in the Law and fruit in time of grace; flower of the first tabernacle and fruit at the second; flower in the observances of the sacrifices of the Law and fruit of the spiritual understanding of the mysteries which these meant. Similarly as the flower comes first and the fruit after it, so was Jesus Christ meant to come by the ceremonies or mysteries that were in the Old Law. And in the same way as the fruit does not appear while the flower is still flourishing, so has Our Lord's truth not been shown as long as such observances lasted. But when the flower is dry and fallen, men afterwards perceive the fruit; for when the Law fails, the grace and truth brought about by Our Lord Jesus Christ are beheld. Similarly as under the shell of the almond the sweet kernel is cracked, so under the shell of the flesh of Jesus Christ was the most mighty Trinity split open. Just as in the Aaron' rod we find the foliage or greenery of the branches, the taste of the flowers, and the abundance of fruits; so did Mary contain within her the greenery of virginity, the sweetness of piety and the abundance of per-petual vigour and fullness.

By his nativity Jesus Christ did not only show salvation to the Jews but also to the heathens, showing that he was the same one who would save and redeem all men. And for this reason the emperor Octavian was in his time lord of the whole world and was reputed by the Romans as their god. And he once took counsel from a Sibyl prophetess, desiring to know from her whether one should come into the world who was greater than him. On the day when Our Lord was born, she saw near the sun a fair and pleasant circle within which there was a passing fair virgin who held upon her lap a fair and pleasant child. And she showed this sight to the emperor Octavian, saying to him that this little child whom the virgin held in her lap was already born and that he was a much mightier king than he was.

You ought now, by holy meditation and by being joyful in hearing this, to think about the great solemnity of this day, for on this day Our Lord Jesus Christ is born; this is the very day of the birth of the eternal king and Son of God. On this day the little child, the Son of God, is born and given to us. And on this day the Son of righteousness who is above in heaven has clearly manifested himself to us. As on this day the spouse of the Church, who is head of the chosen ones, has come out of his chamber and come openly. And on this day the fairest of all the sons of men has shown his most yearning face to the world. On this day of our redemption, we have been enlightened with the restoration promised to us since long before and with his eternal felicity. And on this day peace is shown and made with men of good will, as sung in the holy hymn of angels. And for love of this solemnity, men sing this chant throughout the whole world and heavens and the sky are made distillers of honey. On this day the kindness and humanity of Our Saviour is shown and perceived. For as Saint Bernard says, His might appeared in the creation of the things of the world, and his wisdom in governing them, and now his sweetness and divine favour has appeared in his humanity. On this day we are spiritually engendered with Our Lord Jesus Christ, for the generation of the Son of God is the beginning and birth of all Christians. And on this day these two miracles are fulfilled, superseding all human understanding saving that only faith understands them, namely that God is born and that she who bore him is a virgin. And on this day many other marvels have appeared in the world, for all things spoken of the Incarnation of the Son of God appeared on this day more clearly than they did before. Then, not without cause, this day ought to be of great solemnity, joy, jubilation and gladness.

CHAPTER 10
OF OUR LORD JESUS CHRIST'S CIRCUMCISION

IGHT days passed from the nativity of Our Lord, including the first and last day prescribing, according to the Law, the time set and ordained for the circumcision of the child. Men then named their children, and the name Jesus had already been shown by the angel to the Virgin before she had even conceived. It was then that our Lord Jesus began practising humility, which is the root which governs all virtues. He was circumcised to show that he did not desire to shy away from shedding his precious blood for us, and that he was the Saviour who had been promised to the Fathers, and was equal to us in everything but ignorance and sin.

Two great things happen on this day. The first is that the name of Jesus is shown and manifested; this name, according to Origen, is sweet and glorious and the worthiest to be honoured and held in reverence and adoration. It was not fitting that the name which is above all names were given first by man, nor by man brought first into this world, but it ought and was worthy to be given by the most excellent nature of an angel. And so however that the name Jesus in Hebrew, just as saying Saviour in Latin, was given before to others as well as to him, yet it was ever still appropriate for him inasmuch as it was given to him as he was in the main a Saviour, and such attribution was not given to others since it generally referred to the saviour and deliverer of man. So however that various men in delivering and doing great feats upon their adversaries are called saviours for what they achieve in battle. But he is first of all called Saviour because of his power to save all, and so he had to keep this name for ever. Secondly, he is called Saviour by his quality and aspect of saving, as given by the angel at the beginning of his conception. Thirdly, it was given to him at his circumcision since he was to save man by his passion. And because of this, according to Chrysostom, the name of Our Lord, which is Jesus, was in the same manner given to him in his mother's womb, so that it was not new but old. And he is called Saviour according to his human nature, since he also derived from divinity.

The dignity of this name is shown in fourteen ways. The first, that he was ordained and consecrated as everlasting. The second, that he was named by the mouth of God. The third, that Patriarchs and Prophets desired him. The fourth, that he was prophesied by the prophets. The fifth, that it is said that the name of Jesus was prefigured in Joshua since old times. The sixth, that he was shown by the angel to Joseph and Mary. The seventh, that he was made public by the Virgin. The eighth, that Joseph gave to him this name on this day. The ninth, that he was declared by the angel. The tenth, that he was magnified by the apostles. The eleventh, that he was witnessed by the martyrs. The twelfth, that he was commended by the confessors. The thirteenth, that he gives the smell and taste of oil spread by holy virgins. The fourteenth, that he is honoured by all Christians.

There is, as Saint Augustine says, a difference between the name Jesus and Christus, for the name Jesus is a proper name, but Christus is a common name and one of mystery. And Christus is a name of grace too, and Jesus is a name of glory. Similarly, just as in this world by the grace of baptism into this name Christus we are called Christians or Christian people, so in heaven being of Jesus we shall be called persons belonging to Jesus and saved people. Now inasmuch as there is a difference between grace and glory, so much is there a difference between Jesus and Christus. This is then the name which is above all names, and there is no name under heaven by which we may be saved but by this one. For according to Saint Bernard, the name Jesus is honey in the mouth, melody in the ear, and joy in the heart of those who keep it in mind, and a dispenser of sweetness to whoever calls it. And according to Peter of Ravenna, this is the name that has made the blind see, the deaf hear, the lame walk and the dumb speak, besides giving life to the dead. He puts to flight all of the devil's might and power from the bodies of those who are possessed by him. And Saint Anselm says: "The name Jesus is sweet and very palatable in comforting the sinners, and is good and wholesome to have trust in it. Now, Jesus, be with me Jesus, abide with me etc." It is a virtuous name according

to the Apostle who says: "Be cleansed, sanctified and justified by the name of Our Lord Jesus Christ." The name Jesus
has power to wash away sin's filth and deformities. It is
virtuous in making holy, in cleansing both culpability and
the guilty, and it has also the virtue and might to justify
and pardon the pain and bondage of sin. As it is found that
there are three things relating to sins, namely its spot or
blemish, the culpability, and the pain that comes along with
the culpability, it appears that all three are pardoned by the
name of Jesus. Then Saint John says that "By the name of
Jesus our sins are forgiven." And in honour of this name all
kneels incline and bow, both in heaven as well in hell and
on earth. And so whoever calls upon this name in full faith
and belief shall be saved. For Jesus himself says: "Whatever
you shall desire of my Father in my name, it shall be given to
you." And to this end we ought to use this name with all our
prayers in making our petitions to God. And because of this,
Church prayers are made and formed in this manner saying
Per Dominum nostrum Jesum. But all those who do not pray
in the name of Jesus and desire anything that goes against
divine will, work against their salvation. By every right and
reason then, he is appropriately called Jesus that we might
not obtain salvation in any other way than only by the name
Jesus. And because of this Jesus says about himself: "I am the
beginning and the end"; for just as by the eternal Word all
things are done, also by this same Word in union with the
body all things are restored and finished.

The second great thing happening on this day, is that
Jesus began to shed his precious blood and duly starting
to suffer for us. He who had never sinned, started as from
this day to suffer pain for our sins. And not only now in
his frail strength and age, but also in his childhood when
he would shed his precious blood for us. The child Jesus
wept on this day for the pain he felt in his body. And then
his sweet mother, seeing him weep so pitifully, could no
way hold back from weeping with him in as most tenderly
a manner as one could think.

Do now you have compassion of them and weep with
the little child Jesus, for on this day he wept bitterly and
vigorously. And the same as in these solemnities we rightly

ought to be joyful for the salvation he sought for us, yet we ought to have even more compassion for him due to the anguish he suffered for us. And we would do well to suffer some sort of pain for our own sins seeing that he has suffered so much for the sins of others. Saint Bernard says about this, "Who is he that ought not to be ashamed of refusing to suffer some small pain in this world for his sins, when he knows that the Son of God has suffered so much not for himself but for us?"

And it should be noted that it was six times that he shed his precious blood in this world for us. The first time was in this circumcision, which was the beginning of our redemption. The second, in prayer, where he showed his desire for our redemption. Third, in his flagellation or scourging. Fourth, when he was crowned with thorns, which was the merit of our redemption, that we may be made whole by the pain of his wounds. Fifth, in his crucifixion, for that was the price of our redemption, for there he did not pay for anything that was due to us but through his compassion for us. Sixth, when his side was pierced and opened, that being the sacrament of our redemption since by it he gave us a mark and sign to be cleansed by the sacrament of baptism, which has as much power as Our Lord's precious blood. By the first we are shown that we spiritually ought to be circumcised so as to put out of us all sins. By the second, that we willingly ought to endure some sort of pain for our salvation. By the third, that we ought to chastise our bodies. By the fourth, that we ought to fill our souls with virtues. By the fifth, that we ought to bind our members to God's commandments and fulfil them. And by the sixth, to have our hearts wounded in Our Lord Jesus Christ's love and charity. You now say how many times Our Lord has shed his precious blood for our redemption? Where are our tears, sighs and doings of grace now, which we render to him for the great outpouring of his blood which he has shed for us? For as Saint Bernard says, that only one drop of his precious blood would have been enough for the redemption of the whole world. Yet he would shed his blood in great abundance, so that the lover's virtue may be shown in remembering the benefits, for in him there is plenty as to our redemption.

Circumcision was brought about and had its beginning with the holy man Abraham, when those of his namesake started increasing. For in the same way as before he was called Abram, just like saying high father, in the same manner after the circumcision, by merit of the faith which he had, he was called Abraham, that is to say father of many people. And also his venerable wife deserved her name to be changed. At first she was called Saraj, just as saying my princess, and only by her house; but after she was called Sarah, that is to say princess of women who leave all to follow God. And it was due to this that according to custom children's names were given to them in their circumcision. Abraham believed before this circumcision that he should have a son, just as God had promised him, and as a sign of what God said, he received the circumcision because he saw that the law which he had before received and kept was justified. This circumcision was first given to Abraham for the merit of his faith, so that just as he was different by faith from other people, so was he by circumcision. It was also given to the end that people who were to be born from his descent were to be known by some sign as being the people of God, and that they were descended from the seed of Abraham who received this sign from God by his faith. And also so that when they were slain in battle with other people, they were to be known by such sign that they were of noble and holy descent, so that they might be buried. But this circumcision was not done in the desert, for there they were alone not mixing with other people. Also this circumcision was given to remedy original sins and to reprieve sins of the flesh. Circumcision was also given to restore the acceptance of faith, for being a profession and witness to the Law of Moses, it has to be kept, the same as baptism in the New Law. For by observing their circumcision persons showed they were disposed to receive the law of grace. Circumcision then was a commandment and sign of the promise of Our Lord Jesus Christ. And they used this sign even at the time when Our Lord, who had been promised to Abraham, was born and this meant that the sign and marking of the promise should not cease. And this circumcision was done with stone knives, for it ought to join the two walls together, namely Jews and heathens.

Our Lord would be circumcised by many causes, although he was not at all subject to the Law. First, it was to show that he was descended from the line of Abraham who was first circumcised. Second, because he was like the Jews' fathers to satisfy them in putting away all kinds of shame and sinful occasions. Third, because he approved the Old Law which God had ordained, showing that it was good and holy. Fourth, because he would show by example the virtue of obedience and meekness in keeping the commandment of the Law to which he was not at all bound. Fifth, since he would himself fulfil the Law which he had given to others and not despise the remedy by which the creature ought to be cleansed of sin, although he had come into this world only in the likeness of sin. Sixth, that he would himself sustain the burdens of the Law and deliver others so that he would not bear the penalty which the Law ordained, since he submitted himself to the Law to buy back those who were under the Law. Seventh, since it was not only that he shed his blood for us in his perfect nature, but in like manner in his young age, and that he would duly begin to suffer for us. Eighth, so as to show in himself the truth of his human nature, to confound the heretics who said that he has not taken true human nature, but a make-believe body. Ninth, so that he would rebuke carnal lustfulness with its great dominance, remarkably in that same member of the body. And this is why the circumcision was done on that member through which original sin entered into the world, since where the way to sin lies there ought men to put the remedy. Tenth, to complete and bring an end to carnal circumcision and begin the spiritual one, as likewise signified in the command that it should be kept. For just as he was born for us and suffered passion and death, he is also circumcised for us and not for himself. Certainly, as the Apostle says, he is the end of the Law to all true Christians.

And on this day the circumcision of the flesh is ended. We so now have baptism, which has much greater power and grace and less pain. Saint Gregory says "That now the water of baptism is as worthy for us, as much as the faith of the old fathers was worthy to them; or for those who were great and rich, was the virtue of sacrifice; or for those who descended from Abraham, was the mystery of the circumcision." But as Bede says, there is a difference, for the circumcision does not open the heavenly gates as baptism does now, although baptism does not do it of itself except for the merits of the passion are joined to it. And if the passion were on the same level as circumcision, circumcision had opened the heavenly gates.

It now comes to mind that the spiritual circumcision, by which the soul is purified from sins, is likened to bodily circumcision. For according to Saint Bernard, it is a double circumcision which ought to be done to us, namely the inner one and the outward one. The outward circumcision is found in three elements: namely in our clothes, which should not be exuberant; in not being disgraceful in our works; and in not being despised and scorned in our speech. In the same manner and equally inner circumcision is found in three elements, namely as to our thought being pure and clean in intention; in being holy in affection; and in all being done rightly. We ought then to be circumcised in our hearts of foul and annoying thoughts, of false and foolish judgments and of evil intentions. We should also be ashamed of having in our hearts things before God of which we should be ashamed to speak or do before people in the world. We also ought to be circumcised in the tongue from foul and infamous speech, lies, foolishness and other vain words. For we shall render account of all evil words we speak in ignorance on judgment day, as much as of the least thoughts which we can think.

We also ought to be circumcised in all members and places of our body by withdrawing them from vices, and to abstain ourselves from all voluptuousness and excesses; and not only from sin, but from all sinful occasions. For according to the Holy Pope Pius I, nothing like fasting, praying or doing other good deeds profits man unless he keeps his mind away from evil thoughts and his tongue from belittling others. Bede says that "No one should think when hearing anyone speak of this circumcision that they ought to suffer but to have only one member circumcised, as doing one good deed only, like keeping oneself away from fornication, or truly keeping wedlock, or being a virgin, while sinning in any other way. It is not so, for we are commanded to circumcise ourselves from all the vain thoughts and uselessness of our hearts, and from all works of defilement. Truly circumcised is whoever stops his ears from hearing anything which might delay or hinder his soul from gaining spiritual profit; who leaves nothing on his tongue, but washes his hands from all evil to be innocent; who keeps his feet away from all evil ways; who above all keeps his body chaste; who renders himself subject to his good angel; and who keeps his heart away from all evil things, so that his soul's life takes root in his good deeds." For as so many times as man turns himself to penance after his sins, so in as many times he is circumcised. For carnal circumcision is nothing else than the mere incision of excesses of the flesh, and in man there is no excess without sin, for all other things in him are made by God and are very good. And if this circumcision is not done, the soul shall be called the daughter of perdition, for which reason it is said in *Genesis* that "The flesh of whoever shall not be circumcised, shall be banished and excluded from his people."

And it is fitting that in the soul eight illuminations should precede this circumcision, as signified by the following eight days. The circumcision is likewise kept on the eighth day, and the time is that of the turning of the sinner to God, of knowing his sins, having contrition, confessing them, being self-satisfied and loathing one's sins, besides keeping oneself well and safe from then onwards. And then comes the eighth day, when justice is made of sins by the grace of God, meaning that they are shed in him, who takes away the excesses of sin from him. Also these eight days may be called the seven gifts of the Holy Spirit, or the seven principal virtues, when final perseverance is called the eighth gift.

And it should be noted that in all these there are three circumcisions. The first is the sacrament itself, namely what was done to his body. The two others are the effect of this sacrament, that is to say the circumcision of sin which is done by those who desire and love God in their souls; the other is that by which we ought to put away all branches of sin which might delay us in our last resurrection in body and soul.

CHAPTER 11
OF OUR LORD'S EPIPHANY AND HAPPENINGS

HE eighth day after the nativity, the child Jesus showed himself to three heathen kings called *magi* or wise men. They were called so not because they were trained in necromancy, but for their great knowledge of astrology. For those whom the Hebrews called scribes, and the Greeks philosophers, and the Romans sages, the Persians called magi. And this is why they are called kings, for at that time it was philosophers and sages or wise men who reigned in Persia. And Seneca says, speaking of happy bygone times: "Heathens were very happy since no man could be king among them unless he was the best." And in that golden time they were called and held the office of commanders and not rulers. And so they governed, without the need of special skill or any other difficulty. As we read about Diogenes, who, on seeing a child drinking at a well with his hand, he broke his own cup from which he was used to drink, saying in great anger, "Oh, what a fool of me! What burden have I borne ignorantly, in carrying this vessel for such a long time." Saint Gregory says: "The holy men are called kings since they can rule well and govern over temptations of the flesh, and they will not be subdued in any way or consent to any inordinate thing." And according to Isidore, kings are called kings because of the righteous works they do. So that whoever does well may be called a king, and those whoever does evil loses that name. See how different it is now between our governors and those of whom we speak! For now they do all opposite things, desiring none else but honour, riches and worldly pleasure.

Et *venerunt ab oriente*, "And these three kings came from the Orient or eastern parts"; namely from those parts east of Jerusalem, to show, as Chrysostom says, that faith's commandment proceeds from the place where the day appears, since faith is the light of souls. And according to Saint Bernard, it is not without cause that these kings came from the orient, which shows the son of righteousness who is newly born unto us and by which the whole world is enlightened. Some say that these kings reigned in the region of Saba, which takes its name from a sea called Saba; others say that they descended from the race of Balaam, who prophesied, as it is written in the book of *Numbers*, that a star should come from Jacob's lineage. And as they felt certain that this prophecy might be accomplished in their time, they inquired with great diligence the time where this star should appear. As it may be seen from these two things, namely that they were from Balaam's line and that they arrived at the place where Our Lord was then in a very short time, they did not come from the forest of Arabia adjoining the land of India where it is always day, as this land lies far from Jerusalem taking a year's voyage to arrive there. But they came from that Arabia which is near to the land of Judea and Persia, and to Medes and Chaldee, where the sea of Saba flows. It is from this sea that the region of Saba takes its name and Saba is also close to Arabia where Balaam was born. And the star was first seen there, by these three kings only and none else. And when it first appeared a little child was recognised, with a shining golden cross on his head. And then they heard a voice saying to them: "Go you into the land of Judea and there you shall find the newly born king."

So they did as they were ordained and followed the star, which was not an ordinary star in various ways. First, as to its substance, for star matter is of a heavenly nature and of the fifth essence; but this star had a corruptible nature. Second, as to its making and beginning, for the others were created and made by God without any creature's help; but this was made by God through the service of angels. Third, as to its endurance, since other stars were created at the beginning of the world and will perpetually endure; but this was made at the birth of Jesus Christ and lost its state of being within a short time. Fourth, since the place of other stars is in the firmament; but this appeared in the air close to earth. Fifth, as to its greatness, since according to Ptolemy every cognizable star in the sky is much greater than all earth; but this current star was no more than two or three cubits great and was very small in size. Sixth, in its movement, since other stars have a circular motion like earth; but this went straight forward from the orient or east to the middle of the firmament. Seventh, since other stars never stopped; but this ceased its movement and moved on in the same manner as the magi. Eighth, since this star first appeared then hid itself, reappearing when the magi entered Jerusalem. Ninth, for the other stars only shone by night, but this one kept on shining day and night; for according to Chrysostom, the sun gave light day at noon, but this star shone brightly more than the sun with its rays superseding the sun's shine. Tenth, in being a sign, for stars marked days and years; but this foretold the nativity of Jesus Christ. Eleventh, as to its own effect, since other stars evolve independently over time; but this was only made to show the nativity. Twelfth, since this star only did service to God; but other stars did service to the whole world. Thirteenth, since when this star appeared it was only seen by the magi and none else; but other stars were seen by all others are under their orbits. Fourteenth, since this star had an angel guiding it; but all others had none.

Then by this new star these magi came to know by divine inspiration about him who was to subdue the pride of the whole world by his meekness; and many a great thing was done on this day by Our Lord Jesus Christ towards his Church. First, the Church is received from him in marriage to heathens as represented by the three magi, since on the day of his nativity he appeared to the Jews as represented by shepherds, who received but a little the word of God. But as on this day he appeared to the heathens who have fulfilled the Holy Church, it is proper to say that this day is the feast of the Christian Church. And because of this, it is called the Epiphany, just as saying apparition or appearance done from above, as by the star. Secondly, as on this day the Church is joined to her head Jesus Christ by baptism, which he was pleased to take on this day when he was thirty. And because of this men sing with great gladness on this day, *Hodie celesti sponso iuncta est ecclesia*, "On this day the Church is joined to her heavenly spouse." For by its baptism, which has taken virtue in the baptism of Jesus Christ, the soul is made his spouse. And because of this the Church is none else but a congregation of baptised souls. There are some who call this feast a Theophany, just as saying apparition of God, because on this day the Father glorified his son saying "See that you hear my well beloved son." Thirdly, as on this day, twelve months after his baptism, he made the first miracle at the marriage feast, when he turned water into wine. And for this cause many call it a Bethphany, or an apparition done in the house. Others say, according to Origen, that on this day he fed four thousand people with five loaves and five fishes. And Maximus the Bishop says in the old books that "This feast is named *Dies Epiphaniarum*, the day of appearances in many ways." But we shall now speak only of the first.

And according to Micah's prophecy, about when Our Saviour and Redeemer Jesus was born in Bethlehem, a region of the Jews, this is different from the other Bethlehem, which is in the land of the tribe of Zebulun. In those days Herod reigned, and this was in the thirtieth year of his reign, making it appear that the time for the coming of the Son of God had come. For the Patriarch Jacob had prophesied that the Messiah should come when the king or leader will rise from the lineage of Israel, and this was accomplished by king Herod the Ascalonite, who came from Idumea, and was the first king from a foreign land who had reigned amongst the Jews. Then these foreign magi, who represented all the Church, came from the Orient to Jerusalem, the royal city, inquiring about the coming of Our Lord and saying "Where is the king of Jews who has just been born?" See here the title of this king, which is announced and shown by the magi, being reproved by the Jews when they said to Pilate, "We would like you not to write that he is king of Jews." Then in order to confirm what he had written, he answered them, "What I have written, is written."

These magi said, "We have seen his star in the orient, which he has created and made by which to show himself. And that is why we have come to worship him." According to some doctors, when the magi entered into the land of Judea the star was no longer seen by them, so that they, having lost what had showed them the way, should be constrained to return to the royal city and ask about the place where the new king was born. Others say that when the magi entered the city to enquire about the child, the star failed to appear any longer. For in demanding worldly help, they rightly deserved to lose God's help, meaning that that those who put their trust in worldly help were not worthy of receiving divine help. By this star men may understand the light of grace, for when the good ask for counsel from those who are evil they lose the true light of grace. But whether this star shone or not before or after they entered into the land of Judea, it was all done by God for various causes. The first cause was that these magi were admonished, as they had been before, by heavenly signs and portents, so being also confirmed by what the Prophet and the city doctors had said. The second was so that the nativity of Our Lord would be made public in the city where the prophecy of his birthplace was shown to have been accomplished. The third was so that the idleness of the Jews would be condemned by the zeal of these magi who were so diligent as to enquire and seek Jesus Christ; since the Jews did not understand anything in this. The fourth, so that the Jews might have no excuse were they not to receive Our Lord and believe that he was not come as he did; since the magi showed the time to the Jews, and the Jews the place to the magi.

The magi were steadfast in their belief in God and confirmed in faith, for although they knew that the custom was that whoever named any other king than the one subject to the Roman emperor would lose his head, yet they still confessed Our Lord Jesus Christ boldly. Chrysostom says, "Did not these magi know only too well that Herod reigned in Jerusalem and that whoever named any other king but him ought to have his head struck off? Certainly they did. But when they considered the newly come king, they did not fear Herod at all; and they had not as yet seen Our Lord, and yet were ready to die for him. Oh blessed magi who before even seeing Our Saviour were ready to receive death for him from one who was a most cruel king! They were the true confessors of his name."

On hearing these things King Herod was troubled in his mind, fearing lest this child should reign over him as he was a stranger. Augustine says: "What shall be said of this king when he shall sit in judgment, seeing that he, being a little child in a crib, frightened these proud kings of the world? Let us then fear this king who is seated on the right hand of his Father, who that evil king feared while he was still suckling at his mother's breast." And it was not only Herod who was so sorely troubled, but all the city. For the greater part of Jerusalem were willing to favour Herod since they approved of him, with the greater part of the people holding him in great favour since he often judged them unjustly that their minds were more set on fear than on love. So it was already common for evil kings and princes to have evil servants and flatterers around them. Now they were also troubled among themselves, for those who were evil might not be happy with those who came and were good.

Then Herod assembled the wisest Jews and asked them if they knew where Jesus should be born. And they answered him that it was in Bethlehem, which is in the land of Judea, just as the prophet Micah had said. According to Saint Augustine, the Jews, in showing others the fountain of life, were themselves dead dry; and although they were much like milestones showing the way men should go, yet they neither moved nor stirred. The latter was a reference to those doctors who teach men to do and live well, while themselves living an evil life.

Then Herod secretly called these kings apart inquiring as to the time when the star first appeared to them. For while knowing from the Jews of Our Lord's birthplace, he wanted to know from the magi the time of his birth; so that were they not to return, he might still put Our Lord to death if he knew the place and the time. Since he was a foreigner, he would not confess anything about this to the Jews, nor would he tell them what he thought on this matter. So he sent these kings to Bethlehem, saying feignedly to them: "Go to Bethlehem and there ask diligently for the child who has been born recently, so that when you come again you may tell me where he is that I may also go and honour him." According to Chrysostom, in promising devotion Herod was sharpening his sword for, under the guise of humility, he was only drawing the spite which he had. The external appearance of evil ones is that, while privately annoying someone else, they would first show some feigned sign of love and meekness. According to Rabanus, Herod feigned a very fair face and manner of speech to honour him who he was already thinking to kill; and he did that so that the magi might be more willing to return and the Jews, whose king he was, would then hide and carry Jesus away so no one should find him. Herod here stands for all those hyp- ocrites who may never find God, for they seek him falsely and with trickery. The same as Herod under the shadow of doing good would have slain Our Lord Jesus Christ, so would hypocrites do inasmuch as it lies within them to slay and murder him. As the Apostle says: "Ceaselessly in themselves the hypocrites crucified the Son of God." And as Saint Gregory says, feigned holiness is a double sin. And according to Chrysostom, those who unworthily use the sac- rament of the altar are like Herod, for they feign to worship him but with as much as is found in them they slay him. As the Apostle says: "Those who eat and drink unworthily God's precious flesh and blood, condemn themselves."

Now when the magi had heard Herod, they departed from him not ever suspecting anything was evil, going towards Bethlehem as they had been instructed in the prophecy. Yet when they exited Jerusalem the star, which had before with- drawn its light from them, appeared to them again, thus in living according to the worldly counsel they had been given they recovered divine counsel. And so the star went before them and showed them the way, till it came over the place where the child was lying. There it stopped, still in the air, over the child's head, as though it would have said "Here is he that is born and whom you seek, of whom I bear record that he is a king." As this could not be said by words, it was shown by standing still over the child Jesus; and so they went down with great joy to the place where Our Lord was. A difficulty arises here, namely whether when these magi were in the Orient, they saw this star in the east and it led them into the land of Judea, or they saw it over the land of Judea as not moving at all. The common opinion of the doctors and Chrysostom is that this star might be made in the Orient, guiding and leading them into the land of Judea. But it seem to the doctor Fulgence that first they saw it immoveable over the land of Judea, giving them a sign to go into that land and on to Jerusalem, which was a royal city and capital of all that land.

The magi, entering into that house or wayside shelter, found the child with Mary his mother, perhaps sitting at that hour and holding him on her lap. And when they saw this they marvelled with joy. Chrysostom says: "Great joy and consolation are felt by these magi since they had found what they had long been seeking and desiring. Besides, they were also messengers of the truth, and had not travelled from so far away countries without cause." Oh, how fortunate Mary is! For Jesus is not without Mary, for she had served in his Incarnation; also Jesus is not found without Mary, for she was his carer; and he was not crucified without Mary, for she was company and partner in his passion. According to Chrysostom, there is no mention of Joseph, since men were not speaking about anything having to do with nourishing the child. According to Hilary and Rabanus, it might have been ordained by divine dispensation that would be absent at that hour, so that these magi would not think he was the child's father and so that they should not have any reason to think that this child to whom they had come to offer gifts was not God.

Then they entered and prostrated low before him with all their heart and body, while meekly bowing their knees before the child Jesus, worshipping the Son of God there in body. They honoured him as a king, and prayed to him as to God, clearly showing that they had come to know of his divinity by divine inspiration. For one should not think that they, seeing the child wrapped in poor clothes and being held on his poor mother's lap without showing any sign of royal dignity, would show him such great reverence had they not seen something supernatural in him. Saint Bernard says: "The magi worshipped and offered gifts to him who was yet feeding on his mother's breasts. Oh you magi, where are the purple robes and royal clothing of this king? He had none but poor clothes in which he was wrapped. If he is a king, where is his crown? You certainly see the very crown with which his mother crowned him, which is the sackcloth of our mortality about which he speaks in his resurrection: *Concidisti saccum meum.*" "Oh you strangers, from where does it come to you to worship Jesus Christ in such manner? We find no such faith in Israel. You are not ashamed nor do you scorn the poor dwelling and stable where this child is lodged, nor of the poor crib where he is laid, nor of the presence of his poor mother whom you see feeding him from her breasts." Oh you kings, what are you doing? Are you worshipping this little child who is being breastfed by his mother in a poor place and wrapped in small clothes? Would you think that this little poor child should be God? Certainly, he is God in his holy temple, and his seat is in heaven, while you seek him in an old stable lying on his mother's lap. What would you be doing when you offer him gold? It seems he should be a king, but it appears not so by his royal hall. Where are his royal towers? Where are the lords who haunt his court and royal palace? Would it seem to you that the stable should be his hall, the crib his tower or tabernacle, and Joseph and Mary the lords and attendants of his court? Oh, how these kings can be made fools. Alas, they worship a poor child who men neither endure nor heed because he was young and those around him were poor. In worshipping they might be seen to be made fools, even though they were wise since they were taught by Holy Scripture. The Apostle says: "Whoever wants to be wise must first be a fool, so that after he may be wise." Men ought not to think, as Saint Bernard says, that these magi were not ashamed, although men were mocking them, in seeing such state of poverty and things unworthy of royalty in the state in which they found this child. Men sent them from the royal city, where they thought the child had been born and where they were seeking him, to the little city of Bethlehem. And when they were there, they entered a stable and found a little child wrapped in clothes; kneeling down before him they worshipped him as God and honoured him as king. They were not annoyed by the stable, nor did they scorn the small clothes in which he lay, nor did they have any shame of the child before them who was so young that his mother had to breastfeed him. Certainly, it was him who had led and taught them, admonished them outwardly by revelation of the star, and taught them the secrets of their inner hearts by divine inspiration. Augustine says: "The newly born child was laid in the crib with a little body, despicable by his poverty. But certainly some great things were hidden in him showing these magi that he was God."

Et intrantes domum invenerunt puerum cum Maria mater eius, "These kings went into the house and found the child with his mother Mary." I say his mother, although she was not crowned with a shining royal headband, nor did she lie in a royally adorned bed; not even scarcely having one gown with which to adorn her body; not still to cover her and keep her from being seen naked. I ask what adornments and clothing might the wife of a poor carpenter have, being so far away from home? Therefore if these three magi had come to seek a worldly king, they might have felt being more heavy-hearted than glad, for instead of what they had come from so far away to seek they found such great poverty. But they were happy because they were seeking the king of heaven. Although in him they could see with their bodily eyes no sign of royalty, yet they were still happy and pleased only with having seen the star. And the Holy Spirit showed them in their hearts that this child was mighty and to be feared. Pope Leo says: "Not without cause these three magi, whom the new star led them to worship the child, did not find the child showing his might and power in commanding the devils and restoring life to the dead; in giving speech to the dumb, sight to the blind, mobility to the lame and crippled; and showed by his power many other great and divine virtues. But they found this child still and in peace under his mother's control, without any sign of royalty, showing them a miracle and an example of perfect humility. For during all his lifetime the child has not ever been but full of meekness, patience and kindness, by which he has subdued the enemy and the whole world. He passed all his days in becoming ever more perfect and in great suffering. When still a child he did not forget the memory, anguish and pain of his passion; nor when he was a grown man did he ever fail being humble. Also in the sweetness of his childhood, he never had pleasure in worldly business, nor in pleasant speech, nor in any deceit or curiosity of disputation, nor in desiring honour or glory, but ever in faithful and voluntary meekness; who, from the instant he was born of his mother up to when he was tormented on the cross, despite of all his might, power and lordship, he chose to preach and teach." And so that you might vanquish the devil and the world following Our Lord's example, find force in all your might to keep the virtue of humility and patience. For when you are adorned with these two virtues, you may even subdue all your visible and invisible enemies more easily.

And when the magi had found the child, they opened their treasures; which morally these mean and teach us that in no manner we ought not to open our treasures at the time when our enemies have passed and we are with God. *Et obtulerunt ei*, "And they offered each of them to the child Jesus gold, incense and myrrh." The age old custom was that no man should go either to God or to king barren or with empty hand, but that he ought to take with him some sort of present. Now the Arabians, who abound in gold and many other sorts of ornaments, were accustomed to offer such presents. And since these magi hailed from the same country, they offered such gifts to Our Lord. And in performing their country's custom in their offering, this was being done by divine inspiration that they might show the mystery and confess the true faith through mystical gifts, by worshiping the Holy Trinity in the person of Our Lord, signifying that he was God and mortal man, and by honouring his divine might, majesty and human mortality.

For the three magi knew these three things to be found in Our Lord Jesus Christ; as it appeared when they said, *Ubi est qui natus est?* or "Where is he who was born?" Here we see the humanity. *Rex Iudeorum*, "King of the Jews," regarding his royal power. *Venimus adorare eum*, "We have come to adore him," regarding his divinity. The gold which they offered stands for his royal power which was in Our Lord, since gold, due to its nobleness and preciousness is a royal gift; in gifting him gold they showed that this child was a King, and such thing should belong to him. Incense also stands for divine majesty as this is the incense which men offer to God in sacrifice; in gifting incense they showed that this child was God. Also because incense was an oblation which ought to be done by priests, and this child was a Priest to whom no priest was ever his equal. The myrrh also stood for human mortality, and by it men were accustomed to anoint the bodies of the dead; since Our Lord was both King and Priest, he would die for the salvation of the whole world. Augustine says: "Men offer to him gold as to a great king, incense as to God, and myrrh to show that he ought to die for all men." According to Saint Gregory, these kings did not offer each for themselves gold, incense and myrrh, but each one of them offered all three. And similarly by these three gifts each one of them confessed and foretold that he was king, God and man. That meaning was suitable too to that mystery, for every good Christian ought to confess these three things as being in Our Lord Jesus Christ, while having holy faith in the undivided Trinity. And moreover, whoever desires to see God ought to keep himself away from all evil thoughts, sayings and works, by memory and understanding, and ought to occupy himself in good and holy works. According to Saint Hilary, we have in these three meanings great knowledge of the sacraments. For inasmuch that this child was man, we know of his death; inasmuch as he is God, we know of his resurrection; and inasmuch as he is king, we know of his judgment. According to Saint Bernard, they offered gold for the child's nourishment and in sustenance of his poor mother; incense, which is of sweet taste, against evil air and the stink of the old stable; and myrrh, which is an ointment, to strengthen the little child's tender members. And he further says: "We offer gold to Our Saviour when for his love we utterly leave and abandon the substance of this world. And to do this it is necessary that those who have left the riches of this world should desire heavenly riches with all their hearts. And it suits them to offer incense, which has a good smell and a good name, and a devout prayer, for incense stands for the saints' prayers. And it would serve well not to hold in contempt and despise the world, but to chastise the flesh and make it subject to the spirit, as seen in the myrrh. And when the prayer has its two wings, that is to say contempt of the world and corporal affliction, there is no doubt that it shall fly to heaven and there be presented and offered, like incense is before God."

Then let us similarly offer to God what is His, which is true faith, which He has given to us, by which we ought to believe that He is God and man. Let us also offer to Him what is ours and what He has given us, namely gold, or our souls, which is the most noble of all creatures as seen in gold; myrrh, namely our bodies made bitter by penance; and incense, namely our holy conduct of soul and body, for just as the incense does not smell well until it is put in the fire, so does our way of life not render any good smell to God until it has passed through the fire of anguish.

And these three gifts do please God very well. These magi offered Our Lord three substances, namely from their body, for they bowed their knees before him; from what is spiritual for they gave him from their goods; and man has nothing else save body and soul and his temporal goods. Morally, the Church has gold in its perfect knowledge, doctrine and right faith; incense is the devout prayer to God, and the holy thoughts acceptable to God by right conduct; myrrh is the bitterness of penance and mortification of the flesh, and further by good works. The doctors offer gold; the martyrs and confessors incense; and the sinners myrrh as for their repentance. All oblations and offerings are contained in these three gifts. The magi then offered oblations to Jesus Christ, signifying the truth of the faith, and the whole perfection and discipline of the Church. We too ought to offer Our Lord the gold of love, for that is why he suffered the pain of his passion for our salvation; and the myrrh of compassion in memory of his despondent death; and the incense of devout love and prayer. We also ought to offer him faith, hope and charity, which all those who worship him ought to have.

The three magi were likened to the three *robustes* or strong men that brought to king David water from the cistern in Bethlehem, unfearful of their enemies' army and power, but passing bravely among them to draw water. Nor did these three magi fear Herod's might and power, but went boldly into the land of Judea and diligently sought the newly born king. And just as these three strong men went into Bethlehem to draw water from a worldly cistern, so did these three kings come to Bethlehem to have of the water of eternal grace which they drew at the well of the heavenly butler. This cistern sited in Bethlehem was a sign that there should be born in Bethlehem the heavenly butler who would give the water of grace and life to all those who were thirsty and desired to drink of it.

The figure of this new king and of this offering was shown before in Solomon's reign. He sat on a bright white ivory throne which was draped and covered with the purest gold, so that all kings on earth desired to see Solomon's face, bringing him the most precious gifts of the world; this was seen when Queen Sheba offered him many great gifts as had never been seen before in Jerusalem. The Blessed Virgin Mary is the throne of Solomon where Our Lord sits and dwells, he who is wisdom itself. This throne is made of shining white ivory and of fine and pure gold. Ivory, by its whiteness and coldness, represents chastity and pure virginity. And when the ivory is old, it turns its colour into a reddish hue, which means that lasting chastity is reputed for martyrdom. Gold, whose value supersedes all other metals, stands for charity, the mother of all virtues. So too is the Virgin compared to gold for her most perfect charity. And it is most fitting that charity is joined to virginity, for before God virginity is nothing without charity. Solomon's throne was at the top of six steps; and Mary is exalted above the six estates or orders of saints, namely patriarchs, prophets, apostles, martyrs, confessors and virgins. And on the sixth step there stood twelve little lions which decorated his throne; for the twelve apostles ministered and did service to Mary as to the Queen of Heaven, and also the Twelve Patriarchs were her friends and forebears. And the throne above was all round; for Mary was all pure without sin. And two hands held up the chair of this throne on two parts; for the Heavenly Father and the blessed Holy Spirit held up the mother of the Son of God by grace and never left or departed from her.

After that these three magi had reverently worshipped Our Lord, they kissed his feet with great devotion receiving his blessing, then departed with great joy. And while in the meantime they prayed God to know what road they should take in returning, they had an answer from an angel in their sleep not to return by Herod's way; for it was not fitting that after knowing the truth they should go back to error. By this we are also instructed that we should always shun the company of evil persons. Seneca says: "Man ought to abstain from error and false teachings, as soon as he has come to know that truth is eternal." For this reason, these magi asked God in their conscience to know His will; much the same as Moses cried heartily to God, but did not speak anything verbally. They prayed God with all affection whether it was His will that they should return to Herod, to deserve then having an answer given to them in their inner self through an angel. So then they departed and arrived at Tarshish, taking a boat to the kingdom of Cilicia, and so forth until they returned to their countries by another way. For according to Saint Jerome, they ought not to mix with unbelieving Jews. And, as it is said, this is why king Herod became as angry as a madman and ordered all the ships of Tarshish to be burnt for, according to David's prophecy: *In spiritu vehementi conteres naves Tharsis*, "Oh Herod, you shall destroy the disciples of Tarshish in your furious manner." Chrysostom says: "Behold the faith of these three magi in saying: 'If this child is great and mighty, why should he flee and return in secret?' Certainly this is a sign of great faith not to desire to know the cause of what is justly and truly ordained, but simply to submit themselves to his will." By this we are admonished to set all our hope and belief in Our Lord, and to come devoutly to him, and to take heed of all he ordains, and to keep ourselves from going back along the way we had previously gone or by which we came to him. Augustine says: "We ought not return into that way by which we had come, nor repeat the wrong-doings of our former conduct. For if the way is changed, then life ought to be changed." And Saint Gregory says: "These kings, by returning to their countries by another way than that by which they had come, did a great thing for us, as we understand that our country is heaven, where, after knowing sweet Jesus, we are forbidden to return by the way from which we had come. For we departed out of our country by pride and disobedience, in our pursuit of visible things and in tasting forbidden meat. But it is necessary for us to enter in that place by being obedient in various matters, by being in contempt of visible things, and by refraining sensual and carnal appetite." Then, when these magi returned to their countries, they honoured and glorified God more than they did before, and talked about and taught many the universal faith.

Surely we may believe that the glorious Virgin was very joyful in seeing her recently born child being worshipped as God and honoured as a king. Oh, with what diligence she cared for him! And with what reverence and holy fear did she wrap and nourish him whom she knew to be God, and her son according to human nature! Oh, how willingly did she breastfeed him! And in what joy, gladness, confidence and motherly love did she hug him and pressed him sweetly between her arms to her breasts! Oh, with what motherly desire and affection did she kiss his sweet mouth! And for how many times did she zealously and wisely swaddle his sweet and tender members in little clothes! For just as she was the meekest, she also was the wisest. And so, she served him most busily in everything, not only in his childhood, but in the same manner as he ever grew in his sleep and when he woke. Saint Augustine, in speaking sweetly to her, says: "Oh mother who has from your breast fed Jesus Christ, your son and Lord, you have breastfed the bread descending from heaven and have given your breast to him who has made you the person whom you are, because in you he was made the person whom he is, him who in his conception brought you the gift of fertility and in his nativity has not taken away from you the gift of virginity." Anselm says: "It is a thing of truth upon which to meditate that when this Virgin saw this little child lying between her two sweet breasts and weep as young children do, she was constrained by great affection to change her sweet countenance, and with utmost diligence and calling her most chaste body was always ready to relieve and help him in his needs." Even Saint Bernard recounts of the holy man Joseph, that when he often held the child Jesus upon his knee, the little child showed him so sweet and cheerful countenance that it often made him laugh. And because of this, every devout soul and especially those who are religious ought at least once daily, from the day of his nativity to that of his purification, visit this child and his mother as found in the crib and rock shelter, and with well disposed contemplation have compassion on their poverty, affliction and humility. And by the example we take of the Son of God dwelling in this stable and shelter home for many days, we ought neither to be grieved to dwell for his love in our places of religion, nor in our secret praying chambers.

Have you then seen how many things happened at the nativity of Our Lord proving him to be truly the Son of God? Chrysostom says: "All new things worthy of great admiration are done at the nativity of the Son of God. First, the angel spoke to Zechariah in the temple and promised him that his wife Elizabeth should have a son. And he did not believe the angel, but was dumb and could not speak. Yet both the barren and the Virgin conceived; and John, still in his mother's womb, rejoiced greatly. When the Virgin delivers, the nativity of Jesus Christ is shown to the shepherds, and the news given that he who was born was the saviour of the world; so that a great gladness is shown in heaven by angels and on earth. The star, which is the new sign from heaven, is shown to the magi so that it might be known that the God of heaven and earth and of the Jews is born."

Although his blessed mother had on this day become rich by extraordinary gifts like the gold which the magi had given to her, may men yet piteously believe that she liked more and found greater joy in wilful poverty, and that in not desiring worldly riches she attended to her son's will. And very shortly she gave that gold to poor people; and for this reason when she was bound to make an offering at the temple, she had not so much money as to buy a lamb in spite of all, but made her oblation offering two turtle doves. Behold the noble poverty in two things. First, as on this day Jesus Christ and his mother received their friends as poor people do. Secondly, the Lady gave all away, for not only was her heart set not to desire temporal goods, but also she would not retain those things which were given to her son. And inasmuch as the desire of poverty grew in her, so did profound meekness show in her son, which he would never leave or abandon. Some repute themselves vile and wretched, yet they would abhor being considered and reputed as such by others. But the child Jesus, Lord of all, had no will to do so, rather wanting others to ever see and know his poverty and rejection; and not only the small, but the great, as the magi and all that were in their company. They came subverting their faith to seek the king of the Jews, whom they believed to be God. In seeing now such things, which were so vile against him, they might have doubted they were deceived and so returned without devotion or belief had it not been for the love that they had for humility, which they would never abandon for anything; but they gave us example that we never ought to put apart the hope of anything good in the world, but that we ought to be willing to learn to be prepared with regard to others who are vile and abject showing them that some sort of good is in us. ✠

CHAPTER 12 〰〰〰〰〰〰〰〰
HOW THE CHILD JESUS WAS PRESENTED
IN THE TEMPLE

S the fortieth day from the nativity of Our Lord drew near, which was according to the Law the time of purification and cleansing from sin, the Virgin left the stable with Joseph and the child to accomplish the Law; although there was nothing to purge within her, for she had conceived without sin. In the circumcision the child was purged of the original guilt, which he had received from his parents, and in the purification his mother was purged of the sin which she had in conceiving with carnal pleasure; but none of these two things was found either in the child Jesus, or in his mother Mary.

Et *tulerunt puerum*, "And they brought the child who had been recently circumcised from Bethlehem to Jerusalem", because according to the Law they would offer him to God in the temple and make a gift (that is to say a pair of turtle doves or two pigeon doves) as ordained for him according to the Law.

By this it comes to mind that they had in the Law double commandments for children. The one was general as for all, which is namely that, when the time of cleansing of the mother should be accomplished, the friends should bear the child to the temple and ought to offer for them in sacrifice, if they were rich a year old lamb, and if poor a pair of turtles or two young pigeons. But the law of purification was that all women who were delivered by man's seed of a male child were unclean or defiled for a period of seven days; and keeping away from the company of any men, they were not worthy to enter the temple or touch anything which was holy. The child was to be circumcised on the eighth day after the nativity and the mother rendered pure and proper to be able to dwell in company of men. Yet she would remain unclean up to the thirty-third day with regard to entering the temple and touching holy things; and during all that time she was not due to go out of her house. But when the thirty-three days added to the seven that went before were accomplished, then on the fortieth day she could enter the temple and bear her child and present him unto Our Lord as an offering of sacrifice for herself and for the child, as already said. And if she had a daughter, her days were to be doubled, just as much from staying away from men's company as entering the temple.

The other commandment was a special one for firstborns, for both humans and beasts. For at the time when God made the firstborns of Egypt to die to deliver and save the children of Israel, he commanded that all those who were firstborns of Israel's children should be offered. And in the same way He ordained earth's first fruit to be offered to Him, and also the first increase of clean and meek beasts, and the first of vile and unclean beasts, which would have to be slain, or sold and their price offered. And this was to show that we ought to offer to the Father of all meekness all things which are in us, the first and greatest, the best and most valuable.

For it did not suffice him to submit himself to God, his Father, to whom he is equal, but He has also submitted himself to the meek Virgin and to the Law. And he did this for many causes. First, with consent to the Law. Second, because in keeping the Law he would determine and bring it to an end. Third, to put away from the Jews an occasion for murmuring. Fourth, to deliver us from sin's servitude and burden. Fifth, to give us an example of meekness and obedience. Also that, notwithstanding the Blessed Virgin was not subject to the Law relating to women, for she had conceived not in their manner but by virtue of the Holy Spirit, so as to show that she submitted herself to the Law for many reasons. First, that she did not despise women, but conformed herself to what they did as her son would conform himself to other men. Saint Bernard says about this, "Oh blessed Virgin, truly you have no cause nor need to be purged, as your Son had no need to be circumcised. But you make yourself like other women and as one of them since your Son would be amongst other children and as one of them." The second cause is that, just as her Son submitted himself to the Law to set us free from the bond of the Law, so did she submit herself for us. The third cause, to abstain from the slander and murmur which must have arisen among the Jews saying that she had not been purged. The fourth, to put an end to the Law of purification, as her Son did. The fifth, to show us an example of perfect meekness, which she could not teach us openly by word of mouth because of the frailty of women.

Then Mary and Joseph brought the child Jesus, Lord of the temple, to his sacred place. Although they feared Herod, possibly knowing of his answer to the three magi, yet they never dared offend the Law; which shows us that we ought not offend God or break His commandments due to any fear or dread. When they entered the temple, they brought with them two turtles or two pigeon doves and offered them for him, as was the custom to offer for poor children. Since they were very poor, we rather ought to believe that they bought small pigeons, for they may be had easier and cheaper and come in the lower scale of the Law. The Evangelist does not speak of the lamb, for that offering was made by rich men, as aforesaid. And similarly Our Lord, although he was rich, yet he willed that the offering of poor people would be made for him, so that he might make us rich in faith in this world through his poverty, and inheritors to the heavenly kingdom. Certainly, in the same manner as he would take our mortality to give us immortality, so would he take our poverty to give and grant us his everlasting riches; and so let us be like Our Lord, and love poverty wilfully, and let us be content with our food, drink and clothing. About why one ought not to offer all kinds of doves in general, such as turtles, but only pigeon doves, Saint Bernard states: "Although the Holy Spirit is shown and signified by a dove, yet because it is a libidinous bird, it was not appropriate that it be offered in sacrifice for Our Lord other that in the age when it was pure and clean from all sorts of uncleanliness. Yet it was not ordained, either in the Law or in the Gospel, at what age one ought to offer a turtle, for she is chaste in every age and only keeps one mate which when she loses she will never take any more; this was to reprimand men who are not content with marrying once, and to show by example how to keep the state and deeds of holy widowhood. When a widow is alone she always weeps and keeps herself upon high mountains and trees and never in green places, teaching us to flee the noxious greenness of this world's pleasures and that we should despise love of earthly things. These two things suit those who will and intend to keep holy chastity."

And the renowned Simeon among the priests of the Law was just in well doing and fearful in keeping himself far from evil and sin, so that he was just with his neighbour and feared God; for justice can hardly be maintained without a chaste and sound fear of God. The fear of God is the keeping of virtues, and inasmuch as a just man keeps himself from offending God, so does he love Him more tenderly. And the virtue of justice follows the works of those who are enlightened with the fear of God, as the *Psalms* bear witness saying: "Blessed is the man who fears Our Lord, for he is willing to keep His commandments." Solomon too says that whoever fears God, does not err or forget anything. So Simeon was very just, and behaved righteously towards his neighbour. For it was not only his own salvation that he desired, but also that of the whole world, and expected the people of Israel to be comforted by a great desire and trust of God, as promised in the coming of Our Lord in human form. Those who were imperfect and of less virtue in that Law only expected temporal consolation and to be delivered from Herod's oppression at the coming of Our Lord. But the holy fathers, being filled with sorrow and heavy-heartedness because of original sin, steadfastly believed that they were comforted by his Incarnation. This was the comfort expected by Simeon, whose name means obedience. And at such a ripe old age he wished to be gone from this world, but owing to the great desire he had of seeing Our Lord, he wanted to live on. And the Holy Spirit, being present by supreme goodness, was in him giving him the fullness of grace, for Simeon had not only justifying grace, as just men commonly have, but also special enlightenment and heavenly comfort. And the Evangelist, intending to say that the Holy Spirit was in Simeon, previously mentioned that he was just and fearful, for God abides in the spirit of those who fear Him and keep justice. To have this he asked through the prophet whom he should rest his spirit upon, if not only upon the humble and peace-loving persons and whoever dreads and fears what He says. And Simeon was answered in his devout prayers, in his soul and invisibly, by secret inspiration of the Holy Spirit which was in him by grace, that he should see the Son of God, whom he had seen before with his spiritual eyes, with his bodily eyes before he died. And it appears clearly from this that, before he saw the Son of God in the nature of man, he prayed God to see Him so, trusting and expecting the consolation of Israel. For then it was commonly held by those who understood Scripture that the coming of the Son of God was just about to happen, according to the signs shown by the Patriarchs and Prophets. And therefore Simeon prayed God even more boldly and came to the temple in spirit, namely by revelation of the Holy Spirit who was in him, so that, just as he had an answer and a promise, he might see the Christ of Our Lord before he died, that is to say He who was anointed by God with plenty of grace.

Oh, what a great desire did this blessed old man have, whom old age then forced him to pass from this world, that God's answer kept him eager to see Our Lord! He desired it and cared for it in his soul and mind repeating to himself: "I know that he shall come. I know that I shall see him. But when shall he come? When shall I see him? Oh Lord Jesus, come straight to unbind me of these bonds and let me go in peace." And he wished with a truly great desire, repeating his words to God. And the Holy Spirit said to him: "Behold, here is him whom you were expecting. You shall see the one whom you desire soon enough. Rise up at once and hasten to go to the temple."

And when he entered ardently and hastily into the temple, he saw him; and he immediately knew it was him by the spirit of prophecy. And going before him he bowed his knees low to the ground, and worshipped him in his mother arms, and stretching out his arms said to his kinsfolk: "Give him to me, he is my God; this belongs to my office. This is why I am sent to this place and kept living for this service." The mother, knowing the Son's will, delivered the child to him in his arms. And he, rejoicing with great joy in his heart,

received him and embraced him in his arms. And the feebleness of old age left him instantly and he felt youthful strength.
As the Greek doctor says, the untold simplicity of the child
enlightened the old man Simeon's soul so perfectly that from
then on all future events were open and manifest to him. He
then stood up and took in his arms him of whom he was
born and who bore all things by his virtuous word. Simeon
carried the human nature of him who was born from the
Trinity. And so the Church sings at this feast, *Senex puerum
portabat*, "The old man carried the child; but the child ruled
the old man." It is here that Our Lord's great power appears
just as his great humility, for he whom heaven and earth may
not comprehend subjected himself to be carried between the
arms of an old man. It is not to be doubted that the holy
man Simeon felt a very great consolation when he held so
sweet a child Jesus while he blessed and praised God giving
him thanks for his great gift; namely for the fulfilment of the
promise and for the event that should be our salvation, and
for having seen our redeemer with his bodily eyes. And then
he made this beautiful canticle saying *Nunc dimittis servum
Domine*, "I pray you Lord, let me, your servant, go in peace.
And that I may pass this transitory life to the place where
my soul may rest, that is to say limbo with the holy fathers";
for he knew that the Saviour who was to deliver them by
his passion was now born. But how could this good man go
and die in peace when all descended into the darkness of
hell and limbo? Let it be known that he desired the peace
and rest of the heart, and not the peace of the abundance of
the Trinity, which was deferred till after the passion. Simeon
was truly perfect, taking the life of this world patiently while
desiring death. Wherefore it should be noted that the Old
Testament fathers were in some things as perfect as those
of the New Testament, according to Bede.

Whoever holds Jesus Christ in his hands and embraces
him and lets himself go in peace, ought to bring himself with
all his labour to have the Holy Spirit for his guide; and to
abide in Jerusalem by his heavenly and spiritual way of life,
staying in the temple, there sighing and desiring only one
thing from God, namely that he may always abide in the
house of God, waiting from day to day for his Lord to come.

And so he shall deserve to take and have the Son of God in his hands and embrace him in his arms by faith, hope and charity. The man who studies must be really happy to see Our Lord with the eyes of his heart, for he shall be let to go in peace seeing that he had in his heart Our Lord's life and way, in meditating him who is the peace we look to have after. Saint Bernard says: "He is let to go in inner and outward peace, for he is just with his neighbour and has the fear of God, expecting the consolation of Israel—that is to say the sight of God, as Israel says for seeing God—and the Holy Spirit abides in him with the gift of grace." And it is to such a man that Jesus is given to hold and hug. And he blesses God with the good Simeon, and desires to pass out of this world that he may have full abundance and see his maker.

We morally learn many things by this deed. First, that Jesus Christ is taken in one's arms, which is done by good works. Secondly, that the old man warily bears Jesus Christ, which means we should cast out sin's grasp from us and bear Jesus. Thirdly, in saying that he who bears all things would be borne, we have an example of meekness. Fourthly, in saying that Simeon praised God, we have an example of thanking God for all the good things He has given us

In this canticle sung by Simeon, Our Lord Jesus is commended and praised in four things, briefly containing the perfectness of the Holy Spirit. He is first named peace, since he took low status between God and man; in this word we understand the mysteries of the Incarnation, for he united one nature to the other in one body, giving peace to all far and near and reconciling God to man. He is secondly called light, for he is the very leader; in this word we understand the mysteries of his preaching, way of life, miracles and marvellous works; for as he himself says, "I am the light of the world." But the mysteries of his death and passion and redemption are understood in this word *salutare*, just as saying Saviour and Redeemer. And the mysteries that belong to the resurrection and ascension are understood in the word *gloria*, which is a reward. And since this canticle thus contains all the fullness and praise and consolation of Jesus and the consolation of the holy old man who is about to die, it is sung at the end of the day, at compline.

Et erat pater. And the good man Joseph—who was called the Father of Jesus because he nourished him—and his mother Mary marvelled, not because they doubted, but because they were filled with joy for what was spoken of the child Jesus, which was worthy of great marvel. Ambrose says: "The Incarnation of the Son of God was not only witnessed by the angels, prophets and patriarchs, but also by just old people of both kinds. The Virgin conceived; the barren bears a child; the divine speaks; Elizabeth prophesies; the kings worship him; the child was filled with joy in the mother's womb; the widow confessed him and the good man expected him."

And the good man Simeon blessed his family, namely he desired them to have God's blessing. And since they were much holier than that holy man himself, yet he was above them as to his office of priesthood and according to the Law it was him who was due to give a blessing. And although Joseph was not Our Lord's father, yet he was not omitted from the blessing. And the holy man Simeon knew by revelation of him whom he was holding that he was only the child of Mary and not of Joseph too, and so it was to her that he spoke and told her what was to come. *Ecce positus est hic in ruinam*, "This child by his coming is ordained by God to bring down, confound and ruin proud people," those whose life seems to them to be steadfast and stable; about whom he says, "If I had not come into the world and had not spoken to reprieve sinners of their evil deeds, they had been without sin." *Et in resurrectionem*, "And he comes to raise many again," that is to say meek men who by their faith rise themselves to God from their sins. And it is appropriately said "in Israel", for many Jews fell by their unfaithfulness to know God, and were blind. *Et in signum*, that is in sign of alliance and reconciliation between God and man. *Cui contradicetur*, by whom it shall be disputed, first by Jews, then by heathens and after by heretics and unbelievers in him. Wherefore, according to Origen, it should be noted that these infidels have found contradiction in all that Christians recount about Our Saviour Jesus; about whom he himself complains in the *Psalms* saying: "Evil witnesses have risen against my doctrine, but lies are found in their deceits."

Evil Christians too shall contradict him, in evil works and methods; so that the Apostle says about them that they know God only by word but never by deeds. So the Son of God comes for the ruin of some, for those who think badly of Jesus' deeds would be availing themselves of sin. To some he comes for their being raised, for he is the cause of their salvation. Yet he may come to a man both as to his raising and to his ruin, for a man may not start building on virtues unless he before sheds his vices. Saint Bernard says, "Virtue cannot grow with vice. And for virtue to strengthen the soul, a man should not let vice grow. Cast out from your soul all excesses, and wholesome things shall grow there." One may expound this clause otherwise: that pride is destroyed in Our Lord's meekness; envy is destroyed by his poverty; lustfulness in his chastity; envy in his kindness; gluttony in his soberness; anger in his patience; idleness in his labour. For according to Chrysostom, when the lustful is made chaste, the greedy liberal, and so about the others, then vices are ruined in a person and virtues increased. Likewise Our Lord in building the kingdom of virtues has destroyed vices, for God the Father sent him into the world as the sign to the arrow, so that anyone can say about him what one wills at one's own pleasure.

And Simeon prophesying about his passion said to his mother, *Et tuam ipsius animam pertransibit gladius*, "O Mary, the sword" or the sorrow of his passion "shall pierce your soul." For as Saint Jerome says, since she suffered in that part through which nothing might pass, she was more than a martyr. *Ut revelentur ex multis cordibus cogitationes*. The passion of the Son of God caused the thoughts of many hearts to be shown, for the Prophets' sayings and hidden mysteries were accomplished and finished there. And this was signified by the temple veil, which in Our Lord's death was torn into two parts, so that all mysteries should be opened and made manifest to all people. Yet it should be known that the thoughts of many were shown in this passion, for some believed in Jesus Christ while others would not believe in him. And also according to Bede, a division between Christians and infidel Jews was made there. Yet Origen expounds this in another manner, namely the revelation which was made in the confession of secret sins, which were before hidden, but which are now rightly pardoned by the merit of his passion for those who humbly confess them and do due penance.

And at that time that Simeon spoke in this manner of the sweet Jesus, the good prophetess Anne came by revelation of the Holy Spirit and worshipped him, confessing him as the very Son of God, while praising and thanking him for the great gifts he had given to people. And, in giving witness of the Son of God, she spoke and taught all those who were expecting the redemption of Israel, saying that the Saviour was born, he whom mankind had desired for a long time to deliver it from the hand of cruel Herod and from other bodily and spiritual tyrants. This adorable woman was well worthy to bear witness of the Son of God, whose noble prophecy and continence is praised, her age is commended and the religion is preached. This Anne, according to Origen, justly desired from God the spirit of prophecy, which she received through great fasts and enduring chastity. And as Saint Anselm says, Jesus Christ was offered at the temple and received by the holy widow, thus giving example that whoever wishes to follow him should willingly serve at the house of God where it may be worthy to receive Him. He would be received and loved by the good old Simeon, showing that he loves seriousness and maturity. Let joy then encompass you with this good old Simeon and with this good Anne. Go you before the Son and the mother. Do so that love may vanquish modesty and your body's affliction may extinguish all worry. Take the child in your arms and say with the spouse, *Tenui eum nec dimittam*, "I have held him and I will not leave him." Go and sing with the holy man, saying *Nunc dimittis Domine*.

Morally, the cleansing of Mary, who is interpreted as being the star of the sea or the bitter sea, signifies the soul found in the light of contemplative life or in the bitterness of active life. Both forms of cleansing are necessary: contemplative life ought to purge itself of all pride, which is to be done by fear; and the active soul ought to purge itself of all negligence, which is done through labour and pain, by exercising them in one's body. For no man shall come to the city of the heavenly Jerusalem till the days of his cleansing are accomplished and would be as clean as on the day of his baptism. Such cleansing can be achieved in this world by penance and trials, otherwise by the pains of purgatory.

After this, the good man Simeon delivered gladly the child to his mother who received him with good will; after they went up to the altar in a fair and adorable procession. And although they were few persons, yet they were of great repute. They represented all degrees, kinds and states: men as well as women, old and young, virgins, widows and married people, that all may bear witness to the nativity of him who took human nature for everyone's salvation. These two old holy men, Joseph and Simeon, preceded joyfully, followed by the sweet mother bearing the king Jesus with great joy while the good Anne accompanied them. When they came to the altar, Mary and Joseph, presented as parents the child Jesus to God his Father. And because of that the Virgin Mary is appropriately figured by the golden candlestick in the temple of God in Jerusalem, under which are seven burning lamps, signifying the seven works of mercy found in Mary. We worship this candlestick and candle at her Purification ceremony by bearing burning candles for on that day she offered a candle to God.

And then Simeon sang, *Lumen ad revelationem gentium*, "Oh, the light has come by which the whole world must be enlightened." Our Lord Jesus, the Son of Mary, may be compared to a candle for three elements constituting it, namely the wick, the fire and the wax. So are these elements found in Our Lord, in the flesh, the Trinity and the soul. This candle was offered to God the Father for all mankind and the night of our darkness is enlightened by it. The offering of this blessed candle was prefigured in the child Samuel, who was given by God to his mother Anne who was barren; so was a son given to the Virgin by the inspiration of the Holy Spirit supernaturally and against nature's course. Anne offered her son who was to defend the Jews against their enemies; Mary offered her son who was to redeem the whole world. Anne's child was refused by the Jews; Mary's son was condemned by the Jews to an utterly vile death. This was the child about whom Simeon was prophesying and preaching to the Virgin Mary that his passion was to be so great that it would pierce her soul.

When they arrived at the altar, the mother knelt down with all due reverence and presented her son upon the altar, giving thanks to God the Father of so great a gift that she, being a maid, had a child who in the Trinity was like the Father. And this was the main cause why Mary offered her son to God and for which the child would be offered, namely in thanksgiving to God. And although children were offered in the temple on the fortieth day in order to be consecrated to God and commended to Him, yet the child Jesus was not taken to the temple for that purpose. For as soon as he was conceived, he was fully consecrated by grace to God, and by the union which was the Trinity he was recommended to God and preserved by Him. We do not read the words spoken by the Virgin in her offering, though they might always be similar to these: "Lord God the Father, I present to You your child, born of You eternally and of me temporally. I present him to You that he may always be present with You. I thank You that by Your grace I have so marvellously conceived and brought forth the child. Oh holy Father, I offer You a new oblation which is Your child and mine, who shall offer himself for the salvation of the world in the tree of the cross." Oh, what offering this is, never was there such other! Saint Bernard says: "O holy Virgin, offer your son, and present to God the blessed fruit of your womb. Offer our reconciliation and that of the whole world. Offer the host which is pleasing to God."

After that the priests of the temple were called; and the Lord of the whole world was bought again as a slave with five pieces of silver, then worth ten pence a piece. For all firstborn children had to be bought at that price, but for Levy's descendants who abode at the temple. Jesus Christ descended from Judah, and so he had to be bought according to his descent. And the mother took the birds from Joseph's hand, and kneeling she offered them on the altar as a poor woman. One was for her son, and the other for her sin, submitting herself to the law of sinners, even though she was very holy. Saint Bernard says about this: "Oh my brethren, this oblation is outright precious and readily done, for the Son has been presented at the temple and bought again, the birds having been offered, and he is at once carried back home. Certainly, the time shall come that this child shall not be offered in the temple, nor carried in Simeon's arms, but he shall be offered outside the city of God the Father between the arms of the cross. The time shall come that he shall not be bought again with others' money, but he shall buy again others with his precious blood. And this oblation is the morning sacrifice, but the other shall be the evening sacrifice."

Speaking mystically, it is meant by oblation of firstborn children *that* only child of God who by His mercy would be firstborn of all creatures in dignity, for he is very holy and offered to God for our sins.

Speaking morally, it is meant by firstborn the beginnings of our good deeds, by which we are with child by the grace of God. Then let us be warned to offer to God our firstborn children, namely that of all the good in us which we shall refer to God and thank Him for it saying *Non nobis Domine,* "Lord, the good which we do comes not from us but by your grace." And if we be with child together with an unclean beast, that is any sin, we must kill it by correcting our ways in a holy manner and by casting away evil and doing good. We are also warned that if in our few good works we find the innocent lamb, that is to say charity, chastity, humility, patience and similar virtues, we should offer them to God saying that without Him who encourages us, gives us will and enables us to achieve what is good, we fail in doing anything. And if we are so poor that we have neither lamb, nor riches to offer Him, we should at least offer Him two turtles or two little doves, these being two kinds of compunction, that is to say fear and love, both for our neighbours' sins and for our own, and also to obtain all virtues and heavenly glory.

Morally, we should consider here three things, namely the mystery of Mary's cleansing; the sacrament of bearing Jesus to the temple; and the meaning of the offering. As to the first we know that Mary, who is called star of the sea or the bitter sea, means the soul, which is either in the light of contemplative life or in the bitterness of active life. For either one life or the other, cleansing is necessary. Contemplative life ought to be clean of pride by fear, and active life ought to be clean of negligence by work. For no man comes into

Jerusalem, or into paradise which is a vision and temple of peace, without first fully accomplishing days of cleansing, either in this world by penance or in purgatory, and unless he is again in a state of innocence as he was after baptism.

As to the second, we ought to know that Jesus Christ was born in five places, that is in Jerusalem, in Egypt, in the desert, on the high mountain and on the pinnacle of the temple. They all signify five places where Jesus Christ is found. Jerusalem means contemplative life or the vision of peace; Egypt is the active life where there are always pain, anguish and trials; the desert stands for religion, where there are fasts and the hardness of life; the mountains signifies the dignity and height of clerical order; and the pinnacle of the temple represents the seat of doctors, judges and lords. And Jesus Christ is found in all these places. But consider who carried him to Jerusalem and Egypt, and you shall find that it was his mother and Joseph, that is to say the star of the sea and growing faith, which is charity. The Holy Spirit brought him to the desert, but it was the devil who brought him on the mountain and the pinnacle of the temple. So that these prelates, masters, lords and judges ought to have fear lest it is the devil who brought them to such honour.

As to the third, it should be noted that it had to be resolved whether the offering was to be turtle or dove. The turtle, being a solitary bird, signifies contemplative life; the dove, which flies in company, means active life. Yet both of them sing as though they were weeping, but in different manners. The turtle's wailing belongs to the contemplatives, and it has two aspects since there were two turtles. The first weeping comes from love, about which the Apostle says: "We weep expecting to be God's adoptive children." The second weeping is that of devotion, about which the apostles say that she prays for us with untold grief and tears. The dove's wailing belongs to active life, and is twofold, for there were two doves. One is for our own sins, according to what Isaiah says: "We weep like doves, in thinking." The other is for the sins of others, as it is written in Jeremiah's *Lamentations*: "All the gates of Jerusalem were destroyed, and so the priests wept." These four types of grief ought then to be offered by those who do not have the lamb of innocence.

Combining all the foregoing, let it be known that this cleansing, carrying to the temple, and oblation are a sign that anyone who is purged of original sin and negligence, is well disposed to rise to the contemplation of God and to be lowly in self-consideration; while rising he weeps out of love and devotion, and on descending he weeps out of contrition and compassion. In these things is found the perfection of a devout soul to God. And since both ways, namely the contemplative and the active, are acceptable to God, it was not determined whether turtles or doves were to be offered for Jesus Christ, but it is set in contrast: turtles or doves. You have seen through this the poverty of Jesus Christ and of his parents, who could only make the offerings of poor people. If you want to know about his meekness, look at his offering, how he was bought from bondage and how he kept the Law. Also behold how he grew, for in his nativity he was naked like a poor man, in his circumcision a poor man and like a sinner, but on this day he was as a poor man, a sinner and a bondman. I say, on this day he made himself poor, for he would choose the offering of poor people. He showed himself as a sinner in that he would be as though bought from bondage by obla-tion with his mother, and as bondman in that he would again be redeemed. And after the circumcision of the Son and the cleansing of the mother, the child was brought to the temple and presented to God.

By means of these three things let all Christians be taught that when on entering the stone temple of God, that is the church, they ought to conform themselves to Jesus Christ and to his blessed mother in all three circumstances, namely of being purged and circumcised of all sins, as to the first; and that they are carried in the arms of the holy mother Church, as to the second; and that they are always governed and living in order for the purpose of having right intent, as to the third.

First of all then, whoever enters a church must not have a sinful conscience and must be circumcised, for Jesus Christ was circumcised and his mother purged, although there was no need that they should enter in such manner into the temple. This reminds us that no one ought to enter in mortal sin unless having first gone to confession, or at least, if there is no priest to confess him, to have general contrition; unless one is not aware of any mortal or venial sin, particularly at that time, since good men are accustomed to seeing blame where there is none, in the example of the Blessed Virgin who had no need to be purified. Therefore the custom is that one shall cast holy water on entering the church, because whoever enters there should be purged by the sprinkling of water at least from venial sins like those having no mortal sin. And in figure of this a basin was set at the temple entrance where Aaron and his children washed their hands and feet when they entered. Secondly, we ought to be carried in the arms of the Holy Church as Jesus Christ was. For the heretics who err in the faith, the schismatics who depart from the way of charity, and all cursed people are cut off and out of the arms and body of the Holy Church and are unable to enter therein. Cyprian said: "None may have God as Father who is not all one with the holy mother Church," about whom it might not be said as it is written in Hosea: "I took them in my arms." Thirdly, we ought to enter into the church with right intent, namely to pray and show devotion, and not because of vain pretence, as these hypocrites do; neither because of conceit and vainglory, like those who dress up in curious clothing when they go to church do to look well before others; nor for sensuality, as do those who go to see women and desire them, and women who go there to be seen and desired; not even for vanity, laughter and comfort, like those blab-bermouths who only tell tales and speak useless words; or because of avarice and money, as clerics do who only go there for their portion of revenue. All these kinds of people who have no right intent are unworthy of entering God's temple. And therefore, not seeing Jesus Christ they cannot embrace him in the spiritual arms of their souls.

Since Our Lord was carried into the temple, all other temples were made holy and were dedicated in his name; the same thing happened when his holy flesh touched a part of the water of the river Jordan and all water was made holy. And so it was ordained that the bodily presence of Our Lord should always be in the sacrament of the eucharist in all churches, and also that the relics of holy bodies should be shown, there where the angels' mystery was made. And so it is well worth keeping the church in great reverence and that one exercises in it with great devotion, for as it is written: "Oh Lord God, holiness suits your temple."

This may also be said of the spiritual temple, namely the soul, where the eternal Word is always received by those who prepare a worthy dwelling for it. About this temple the Apostle says: "The temple of God is holy, and you are this temple."

And since all nobleness appears according to the cause, the nobleness of this temple is shown by four causes. The first is by the nobleness of the effective cause. The second is the preciousness of its material. The third, the beauty of its shape. The fourth is the greatness of its purpose. So great nobleness is shown by the first cause of this temple, which is the reasoning soul created by Our Lord God without men's help; in its making He did not call any creature but only said, *Faciamus hominem ad imaginem*, "Let us make man as in his soul according to our image and appearance." Saint Augustine says that these words were not spoken by God to angels, but that God the Father was speaking to the other persons of the Trinity; wherefore it is shown that this is only the work of the Holy Trinity. As to the second cause, let it be known that the reasoning soul was not made nor created of any matter existing before, but out of nothing. For since it is more noble than the four elements, and than the sun and the heavenly bodies or the heavens, no matter nobler enough could be found out of which it might be made. As to the third, it appears that the shape of the rea-soning soul is truly noble since it is made in God's image. For God has not imprinted there the image of any created thing, but only of Himself, in such manner that the form of the reasoning soul is none else than a reappearance of the Blessed Trinity. Nor can the Blessed Trinity not ennoble the soul more than to make it like itself, because just as sameness or resemblance is cause of love, so should the soul turn all its affection and love to its Creator, considering that it cannot find anything like itself among all created things. The fourth appears in that God did not make the reasoning soul for any other intent than for Him to abide in it and that it should be His temple and dwelling. And since it was made for that cause, He mostly desires to dwell with it, as He himself demands in the *Proverbs* saying *Fili prebe cor tuum michi*, "My son, give me your heart." For as He says in the *Book of Wisdom*: "My delight and pleasure is to dwell with the sons of men." And when God comes into a soul which is so prepared, He may say what is written, *Haec requies mea*, "This is my resting place to dwell in such a soul. I will abide in it and I have chosen it for my dwelling."

Oh devout soul, if you were to consider your nobleness by the aforesaid, then you should never sin. Saint Bernard says: "Oh you reasoning soul, if you knew your nobleness and dignity, you should consider your sin in disgrace; for it is noble pride to repute all worldly things as obsolete and transitory, vain and useless, and in which it ought not to blemish or soil itself." It is where pride dwelt as Seneca said in a poem: "If I knew that my gods would pardon me and men did not know of my sin, yet for the vileness found in sin I would sin no more."

Since this spiritual temple pleases God, it ought to be painted in a motley of hues, that is to say by various virtues: like white, which means chastity; red, showing a man is ready to suffer for the love of God; blue, showing a man's desire to enter heaven; orange-brown, for spiritual joy; green, for the exercise of virtues; gold, which is charity; and black, as a sign of humility. Into this temple so adorned, we ought to bring the child Jesus and offer him there all our works and affections.

Three things make this a solemn feast. First, because Our Lord was carried to the temple in his own person, and for that this feast is called the Presentation. Secondly, since his parents made for him the offering commanded in the Law for those women who were to be cleansed, albeit Mary did not need to do this. The third was the pleasant consolation old Simeon had, and so it is called Candlemas or the feast of light, for on this day the light of candles is carried in procession.

This holy temple of Our Lord is built on Mount Moriah where Abraham would offer his son Isaac. And Jacob also saw a ladder upon it in his sleep reaching straight up from earth to heaven; there too David saw the angel frighten-ing his people, and falling to the ground he prayed and worshipped God, and the angel ceased its doing. In this mountain was silver and golden vessels of the Jebusites, which David had bought to build the temple of God, finding pardon on the same mountain.

It is on this mountain that Solomon built the temple of God, and after offered a sacrifice to Him; and a cloud came which filled the temple and there the glory of Our Lord appeared, and fire descended from heaven and con-sumed all the sacrifices. And Solomon fell on his knees and made his prayer to God, desiring that the prayers of whosoever entered into the temple to ask any gift from God might be received. God appeared to him and said that his prayers were heard and that He had chosen that place and dedicated it and made it holy. Heliodorus had also sent word to king Antiochus to destroy the temple and pull it down, and because of this he was hurt and beaten sustain-ing many wounds. In time past it was called the temple of God, and now it is made holy in honour of the Saviour of the world and of Mary his mother. It has been destroyed by the Babylonians and by the Romans, but it was repaired by good religious people and Christians in the manner of an octagon. In this temple the Virgin Mary and the other maidens served God, and made priests' vestments and tem-ple curtains, besides learning the Law and other Scripture; there they also fasted, watched and prayed. In this place the angel appeared to Zechariah who was praying and doing sacrifice, saying to him that his prayers were heard and that he should have a fair son called John. In this place also, as the Gospel says, Jesus Christ was offered to God by his parents, and taken and received by Simeon, preached about and foretold by Anne the widow and holy woman to all those who expecting man's redemption. In this temple Jesus Christ was found by his mother and Joseph when he was twelve years of age disputing with doctors about the Law. It was upon the pinnacle of this temple that Jesus Christ was taken by the devil when tempting him to cast himself down. It was from this temple that Jesus Christ cast out the stall keepers, buyers and sellers of doves and brawny animals, sheep and other beasts. He preached and taught contemptible Jews in this temple, and here too he delivered the adulteress from her accusers. As his passion drew near he was all day in this temple, at night going to Bethany. At his death the temple veil and curtain were so torn asunder that one might see the *Sancta sanctorum*, the temple's secret area. From the pinnacle of this temple Saint James, the first bishop of Jerusalem, was cast down, bruised and martyred with a clothmaker's teasle. Between this temple and the altar outside the door facing south was Zechariah, son of Barachias, martyred.

This temple is octagonal and enclosed with stone, and there are marvellous marble pillars divided by three within it, and its middle part is closed in a manner similar to a furnace. And there is written on high, at the first degree and order of the pillars within: "Lord, hear the prayer your servant makes to you today, and open your eyes and your ears day and night upon this house." Even outside, at the entrance of the wall, these verses are written in so huge letters that one might read them from all over the city. The writing on the wall facing the city is "The everlasting peace of the everlasting Father is in this house." On the part facing the temple of the knights there is written "The house of God is founded upon sturdy stone." On its part facing the temple cloister there is written "All people must love God and give Him glory in His house." On the part facing the Mount of Olives "Blessed are those who abide in your house." On the part facing the Mount of Jehoshaphat "Blessed and loved be God in his place." On the part facing Mount Zion "The temple of Our Lord is holy. This is the place where He is worshipped, this is a fortress and a building." Also on that facing the other part of the city is written "We shall enter gladly into the temple of God." This temple is built on the lower side of the city on the part against the east wall and on the other part towards the south wall. This church has canons ruled by an abbot of the Order of Saint Augustine.

Near this place there is another very big and honourable temple which Solomon built; there he did justice and judgment and taught the people; differently from the temple of God, it is called the house of the tree of Lebanon or Solomon's temple.

In this temple we ought to make holy spiritually a procession of the four aforesaid persons. In Simeon, whose name is like saying hearing, we mean that one ought to hear gladly the word of God in this temple. In Anne, whose name is like saying grace, since she did not leave day and night from the temple, we mean that one ought to pray constantly in this spiritual temple. In Joseph, whose name is like saying growth and who had busy care and labour with the child Jesus, we mean that we ought not cease from gathering good works in our temple which is our soul. In Mary, whose name is like saying enlightened, who carried Our Lord Jesus, we mean the true perfect union we ought to have with our maker. Simeon bears holy meditation; Anne, the light of devotion; Joseph has that of making good works grow; and Mary, that of sovereign contemplation.

Then after that Mary and Joseph had done their duty according to the Law, they departed from Jerusalem, willing to return to their city of Nazareth. So should you always go with them and help them to bear the child Jesus, serving them in whatever way you can.

CHAPTER 13
ABOUT WHEN JESUS WAS CARRIED INTO EGYPT AND OF THE DEATH OF THE INNOCENTS

 HEN when Mary and Joseph went towards the city of Nazareth, not yet knowing God's counsel nor what He would do with that child of great renown, the angel of God appeared to Joseph in his sleep and said to him that he should arise, take the child and his mother and flee to Egypt as Herod was seeking to catch him and kill him. It should here be noted that perfect meekness ought especially to be ordered and accompanied with three other virtues, namely poverty, in fleeing riches and all other things which might induce pride; patience, in suffering all persecution; and obedience, in obeying others for the love of God. For that purpose the child Jesus was carried to Egypt as a poor pilgrim. He was slain in the little children that were slain for him. And when he had returned from Egypt to his country Nazareth, he was very obedient to his parents, who feared for him when he was away from them, except when he was twelve years old and he abode in the temple; then his good mother sought him with great sorrow and found him with great joy.

When Joseph woke up, he called the mother and told her what the angel had said to him; so she arose hastily and without delay prepared to walk away. When hearing what the angel had said, her body began to tremble, fearing for her child, since she did not want to be found negligent in caring for him. Behold and think on these things well, and how while the child Jesus slept, the mother arose; and how she awoke in such an untimely manner and wept like her son did. If any pity abides in you, have compassion of them.

The sweet woman, who had just delivered the child, departed with her very tender child and old Joseph by night to a strange, idolatrous and faraway country, going towards those areas of Egypt where he might escape all peril more secretly. For since this had been revealed to them by God, yet they ought not do what was in their power to do in man's ways. So Jesus is then seen fleeing by night to show that fleeing, which was a hard thing to do, was even harder by the darkness of the night. He fled to Egypt so that he would first enlighten and heal with the light of grace those whom he had prosecuted at other times. Saint Augustine says: "Take heed of a great and secret mystery. In Moses' time, the evil people of Egypt were deprived from the brightness of the day; and now Our Lord, going to that country, gave light again to those who sat in darkness and in the shadow of death." Chrysostom says: "God, who does not punish twice, remembered which punishments and how many of them he had done to the country of Egypt, and He therefore sent his blessed Son there, showing a sign of reconciliation and perpetual friendship, so that the doctor Jesus might heal the ten wounds Our Lord had given them." Oh what change of God's right hand and might! For the people who were persecutors to God's first people were afterwards kept by His Son. The little child was also sent into Egypt to embrace that region which was before embraced with the fire of wickedness, with the fire of faith, giving to understand that by his coming all heathens ought to be improved. This had also to teach us that from the beginning of our life we ought to prepare ourselves for temptations, as Our Lord Jesus Christ started having them from his childhood; he gave us example that when we have trials or persecutions, we should not fear them but suffer them mainly for His love, knowing that trials are cousins to virtues. Also he would flee to Egypt rather than to any other place or country to show himself as being truly Moses. For Moses had delivered his people of Israel from their subjection to Pharaoh and Egypt, and brought them to the land ordained to him. The Son of God delivered Christians from the power of the devil and the prison of hell, and brought them to the everlasting kingdom of paradise.

One may think of many fair issues in this present work and matter. First, how after prosperity Our Saviour and Redeemer Jesus Christ had adversity in his person. In his nativity he was magnified and honoured by the shepherds as being truly God; and after that he was circumcised like a sinner. The magi came, and meticulously honoured him; and yet he always kept himself in the stable and wept as a poor man's child. He was later presented in the temple where Sim-eon and Anne praised him marvellously, yet the angel soon enough showed that he should flee to Egypt. Besides many other similar events we may seen happening throughout his life which we may use for our instruction. Chrysostom says: "Our Lord, being merciful to all desolate and hurt people, sometimes mingles joy with sorrow for all those he loves. For in this world he suffered none to either have continual joy or sorrow, but in the life of just people in this wretched world both adversity and prosperity are sown together; as we see here. For when the holy Joseph saw the virgin pregnant, he was greatly anguished, but the angel of God appeared, at once casting away from him all suspicion and expunging from him all worry. So that this holy man was filled with joy and gladness at the child's birth. And immediately after this joy a great trouble comes, for all the city of Jerusalem was moved when Herod sought the place where the child was born; but after the three magi felt joy when the splendid and new star appeared. After joy a new peril and doubt returns when Herod seeks the child to slay him, so that he had to flee to a foreign region." So when you have any consolation, look out after for the anguish. And on the contrary, when you have trouble, look for comfort after. And so, whatsoever comfort we have, we ought not to resort to self-advancement, nor should we be downcast in trials. Out of his bounty and grace God grants us comfort to push on with our hope that we might not fail along the way. He also sends us trials to keep us ever meek, so that in knowing our misery and infir-mity we keep ourselves ever in fear of Him.

Secondly, one may consider God's comforts and bene-fits saying that whoever receives them ought not to prefer himself to any other person who does not receive them. And also, whoever does not receive them, ought not to cast himself into any shattering sorrow and to inveigh against anyone to whom God has given them. And to show this, the Angel spoke to Joseph and not to Mary, though being below her in dignity. Also, whoever receives God's solace, even if he does not receive it in the manner he desires, ought not therefore to be unkind or to fall in murmuring, seeing that Joseph, a man so great with God, did not receive the warning openly but in sleep.

Thirdly, consider how God suffers his friends to be vexed with trials and persecutions. What could have been more grievous to the Blessed Virgin and to the good man Joseph than to hear the angel say that someone was seeking to slay the child Jesus? Then be patient when you are visited with trials for you ought not believe that God would give others privileges which He gave to himself and to his mother.

Fourthly, consider our blessed Saviour Jesus Christ's bounty and courtesy . Behold how soon he sustained perfection in such manner that he appeared to flee from where he was born and courteously gave occasion to his persecutor, whom he might have slain in a moment. He had great patience, even more showing his meekness there. For he, to whom angels minister, fled from the place of his persecutor. Although he is God, he flees like man. And he who gives support to all would not pay back evil for evil to his persecutor, nor offend him, but in fleeing he would avoid his ruses. This doctrine would teach us that there are times when the good are cast out by evil from their dignities; in which instance we ought not to seek vengeance, but patiently endure and make way for pretenders, and as taught elsewhere, pray for them. The good people sometimes must give place to the persecution of evil, when their fleeing profits the Holy Church, as Saint Paul did. Morally, this fleeing to Egypt shows how the just should flee the peril and danger of sin and do penance, and to continue doing this up to Herod's death or when the devil's temptations will cease.

So Our Lord fled from before his servant, rather the devil's servant, not because he feared death, but to undertake it in a timely manner. And his sweet mother, a tender and delicate maid, carried him while the good old man Joseph went before them along the very great and long way in the woods which were dark and uninhabited; as said, for a man riding on horseback it was a twelve or fifteen day journey. And perhaps for them it took some two months or more, for it is said they went along the desert where the children of Israel had tarried for forty years. But what did they do about their fare, and how did they carry him, and where did they rest their head during the night? For in such wilderness one could not easily find houses where to lodge. I have compassion on them and behold what comfort that sweet mother, who was a delicate maid, might have had. Their labour and travelling was very hard. Go with them and help to bear Jesus, serving them in all whatever way you can. The labour of penance which we do for our sins ought not to seem long for us, nor suffering any adversity, seeing them making such an effort for us. Anselm says: "Do not in your meditation and thoughts forget him who fled into Egypt, beholding the little child Jesus breastfeeding at the sweet teats of the glorious Virgin and mother. What might you see to be of greater joy and delight? Behold him who is above all creatures, hanging about the neck of his mother, embracing her with his pretty arms, and say to yourself: "I am happy, for I see him whom kings desired to see and saw not." One ought well desire to see him, the fairest of all of men's children. Think well and again with what affection his sweet mother held him in her arms, she who knew what person and Lord he was, and how glad she was; and how she saw him weep upon her knees, comforting him as much as she might; and how sweetly she beheld him, giving him all the honour and service she might give him.

Some say that they met thieves in the desert in whose company was the son of the prince of thieves. Beholding the child Jesus in his mother's lap, the prince's son saw shin- ing out from his truly fair face a brightness of his majesty, thus knowing that he was above and more than man. And calling and embracing him with great love he said to him: "Oh truly blessed above all children, I pray you that, if in future I have anything to do with you, you would remember me and not forget the present time when I am delivering you from the hands of my companions, who would have otherwise slain you." Some say that this was the thief who was crucified at Jesus' right hand and who reproved the thief who was a blasphemer, saying "You have no fear, for we deserve death by right but this man does not deserve it." And in so saying he turned his face towards Our Lord on the cross, and saw in him the shining glory he had seen in the desert when he was a child. And he reminded him of the request he had made to him and said to him: "Master, remember me when you come to your kingdom." "Now," as says Saint Anselm says, "one may well devoutly believe this, putting aside all personal opinion."

On seeing that the magi neither returned to him nor went by the way they took to Bethlehem, Herod thought they were deceived in seeing the star and were ashamed to return to him, and had so departed without further enquiring about the child. Yet later, on hearing what took place in the temple, and what the holy man Simeon had said of the child, and what Anne had prophesied, and that the fame and renown of the child was increasing, he had great fear and became even more troubled than before both since the magi had mocked and despised him and because he feared losing his kingdom. And so he thought how he might make the innocent children die so that in that manner Jesus Christ, who was unknown to him, might be slain amongst them. Being a mischievous man, he never thought that there is no counsel or wisdom which man can take against God.

In the opinion of many it was currently said that Herod was cited to the court of Rome by the emperor's command and was so delayed for a while from persecuting Jesus Christ. The voyage took him about a year and on returning from Rome he ordered all children born after Our Lord's nativity to be slain. He knew from the time passed that Our Lord's age was of about one year and a few days. And so he ordered all children of that age to be slain, that is to say from one to two years old to those who were one day old, trusting that the child whom the stars obeyed and served could not change his countenance and make him look any older than he was. Then was fulfilled what Jeremiah said: *Vox in Rama audita est*, "The voice is heard on high"; which on one side and on the other is spread far and wide, for there was such miserable weeping by children and so many crying mothers. In seeing such cruelty neither man nor woman could keep themselves from crying. Or otherwise "the voice is heard on high" may be expounded as the blood of innocents demand- ing vengeance from heaven against those who killed them, as God said to Cain about his brother Abel: "The voice of the blood of your brother Abel cries to me." Rabanus the doctor says: "Herod had no limits to his cruelty, for he not only wanted the children of Bethlehem to be slain, but also with them all the children of surrounding places." And it is written that Rachel wept for the children of Judah who were in Bethlehem born to her sister Leah, as if they had been her own children; or since may be that Rachel had land in Bethlehem; or also that the family of Judah and Benjamin dwelt nearby, and Herod commanded that not only the children of Bethlehem should be slain, but also them who were in places thereabouts. So that many of Rachel's and Benjamin's children were slain since they dwelt nearby. *Noluit autem consolari.* "Rachel would not be comforted," since her children were slain and they were all she had. Rachel's weeping stands for the Church which bewails good men as a mother does for her children when she sees her children being unjustly persecuted. But when it sees that they go to bliss and glory through this, it will receive no temporal but only eternal comfort. And besides, it bewails the evil men whom it sees going to damnation, though it will take no comfort in this, as it sees them condemned and lost without remedy.

For it should be known there are three kinds of martyrs. Some are those who suffer in deed and will, as Saint Stephen. Some in will and not in deed, as Saint John. Some in deed and not in will, as the Innocents. And therefore their feasts are ordained after the nativity of Our Lord according to the dignity of their martyrdom. The first is Saint Stephen, the second is Saint John, the third are the Holy Innocents. One may also be martyred for various causes, namely for justice, as Abel. For the law of God, as the Maccabees. To sustain truth, as Isaiah and Jeremiah. To reprieve sin, as Saint John the Baptist. To save people, as our Saviour Jesus. In the name of faith in Jesus, as Saint Stephen. To keep Church liberties, as Saint Thomas of Canterbury. For Jesus Christ or instead of Jesus Christ, as the Innocents who, though they could not confess him by mouth, yet they bore witness to him in dying; and God fulfilled that shortfall of their will. Chrysostom says: "In Bethlehem all the Innocents are slain, who since they die for Our Lord ought to be called the first martyrs and witnesses. And they have had the perfect praise of martyrdom." Saint Augustine says: "Oh blessed children, even now born and never tempted, you never battled and yet you are crowned." "Did not your adversary just as much benefit you in loving you as he did in hating you, for as much as his anger burned against you, so much did the grace of God grow within you." Saint Augustine says: "When Herod persecuted Our Lord in these children, he sent him for company a great number of clear and shining stars."

Consider here how Jesus Christ, who was still a really sweet child, began suffering in himself as well as in those around him in having compassion of him. Anselm says: "O Son of God, Jesus Christ, your tender age of infancy was not without the persecution of you enemies. When you were still between your mother's breasts, the angel appeared to Joseph in his sleep saying 'Arise and take the child and mother and flee to Egypt, and be there till I speak again to you.' Oh good Jesus, after that time you began to suffer. And it was not only you who were frustrated in your infancy, but also those around you when Herod was seeking you and slew thousands of children clinging to their mothers' breasts."

King Herod's cruelty, which killed the Innocents, signifies the persecutors of martyrs who thought scorning Christianity; while the slain Innocents stand for the meek and innocent sufferers of persecution. But the religion founded by Jesus Christ shall be neither so abated nor diminished; rather, as Saint Pope Leo says, the Church is increased and augmented even more. According to Bede and Saint Bernard, if any man blames that which belongs to another man's salvation or to the growth of religion or to the Holy Church, he is like those who ordained the children to be slain in Egypt and to Herod who persecuted the nativity of Our Lord, the Son of God.

Our Lord's persecution in his infancy means that while still in this world there shall always be persecutors who shall keep on oppressing the chosen ones of God to the end; as God says in the Gospel: "If they have persecuted me, they shall persecute you." And the Apostle says: "All those who will justly live in God shall suffer persecution." That the children were slain and Our Lord escaped, is a sign that evil people may kill the body and take the goods from faithful persons, but they may not take Jesus Christ from their heart in whose name they suffered death and persecution. For whether we die or we live, if we are good we always have God with us and we belong to Him.

Morally, these children are slain in various and several ways. The king Pharaoh ordained that they were to be cast into the river. Herod caused their heads to be smitten off. Antiochus ordained that they would be hung. And the Medes caused them to be shot by bow and to die with arrows. The casting into the waters means the delight of this life. The cutting off of heads foretells this world's distress through adversity. Those who were hung stand for the world's ambition. Arrows striking afar signify the fear of suffering in time to come. And the devil appears too through Pharaoh, Herod, Antiochus and the Medes, to condemn the world in various ways.

When Mary and Joseph entered Egypt with the child, all the idols of the province collapsed in their temples, as it was prophesied by Isaiah. Some say that also when the children of Israel went out of Egypt, there was no house but where the best died in it; neither now was there any Egyptian temple where the idols did not fall to the ground, as Dagon fell when God's ark was placed next to him. We also read in *Scholastic History* that Jeremiah was brought into Egypt where he prophesied that a maid would in future bear a child who should destroy all the temple gods and idols. The Egyptians had caused an image of a virgin holding a child on her lap to be made and commanded it to be worshipped, but when Our Lord entered into Egypt with his mother, this prophecy was fulfilled. By this fall the idols gave witness to the Virgin having a child. This thing was figured by Moses and the Pharaoh. For, as it is written in the Book of *Ecclesiastes*, Pharaoh, the king of Egypt, had a royal crown with an image of his god Hammon. And the Pharaoh's daughter, who had taken Moses for her son, thought at one time to bring him to her father to see him. While the Pharaoh was playing with the child he put the crown on the child's head. Moses, seeing this, took the crown and cast it to the ground, and it was broken. And as the king would have slain him, the wise men around said

that the child had done it foolishly, so that Moses escaped
the hands of the Pharaoh. So did Our Lord escape Herod's
sword by God's will. Moses was born to deliver the children
of Israel from the Pharaoh's bondage; and God was made
man to deliver us from the power of the enemy from hell.
Moses broke the god of the king of Egypt and his crown;
Jesus Christ brought to nothing all of Egypt's gods and
idols. This fall and destruction of the idols was figured
in the image which Nebuchadnezzar saw in his sleep. It
seemed to him that he saw an image where a stone was
drawn from a mountain without either hammer, sticks or
hands appearing, and it fell down forcefully to the feet of
the image and broke it, crumbling it to powder. This stone
afterwards grew into a great mountain and now stands for
Jesus Christ, who was taken from the mountain, namely
born of the Virgin. He was without hands, that is without
any embracing by man or sensuality, and he broke and fell
to pieces all of Egypt's idols of whatever matter they were
made of. Then he grew into a great mountain, because after
that idolatry was destroyed and the faith of Jesus Christ
increased greatly. And now it has grown so great and so
high that it has filled heaven and earth with its greatness.
According to Chrysostom, the carrying of Jesus Christ from
the land of Judea to Egypt means that the apostles should
pass on to the heathens through the persecution of the
Jews. Joseph stands for the preachers; the child for faith
and knowledge of Jesus Christ; Mary for the Church and
Holy Scripture; and Herod's persecution for the persecution
of the apostles by the Jews.

Then Our Lord took away from Egypt the darkness of
ignorance and made the country to serve God, so that soon
afterwards the deserts of Egypt were filled with holy persons
who burned with God's love. Chrysostom says about this:
"If one considers the deserts of Egypt, they shall seem to
him more worthy and solemn than heaven itself. There are
many holy men who are pleasing to God like angels, and a
company of armoured men to serve them. Certainly, heaven
does not shine so much by many different stars and planets
as much as Egypt shines by the many different dwellings,
chambers and monasteries of monks and religious. The

nights there are occupied in holy meditation, and the days are assigned for holy labour in the manner of the apostles."

When the Blessed Virgin Mary and the holy man Joseph were in Egypt, they went into a city called Heliopolis in the country of Thebaid and dwelt in a little house for seven years. We read that the Blessed Virgin Mary spun and sewed and thereby earned her living and that of her child. One may well think that these poor strangers had not all they wanted and were often in dire straits, yet they still suffered patiently. Now think what if when the child asks for bread and his mother has none, what sorrow and heaviness she would pass through though still comforting him as well as she could, while sometimes keeping from her own food to give it to the child when he asks for it. And if it was necessary for her to get her living by work and manual labour, what shall we say of their clothing and other household needs? I believe their clothes were neither matching, extravagant or peculiar, seeing that such things go against poverty. And although they had little shelter, yet for the love of poverty they set in it the way it was. Also, Our Lady in sowing or doing any other work, did not sin by being curious and in doing dissolute work, for that is a truly dangerous and really evil thing to do, as shall be said further on.

Behold then the sweet lady working and having great pain in governing the house and in frequent prayer watches. Do have compassion on her and think how, although she was the mistress of heaven, she did not have heaven for cheap. The good man Joseph, who was a smith and carpenter, worked for some time at his craft. So that when you have dwelt in your holy meditations amongst these three for a while in this manner, having great compassion on them, ask them to let you humbly depart and, kneeling before them and with deep tears, ask them devoutly for their blessing. First ask the little child, and after his holy mother, and then the good man Joseph. And greet them thinking that they are foreigners and banished and exiled from their country without cause, abiding in pilgrimage and living for seven years by the sweat and labour of their bodies. ❧

CHAPTER 14

OF OUR LORD'S RETURN FROM EGYPT AND OF SAINT JOHN'S PENANCE

 LMOST at the end of the seven years of Our Lord's pilgrimage in Egypt, and Herod having died, God called again his son Jesus Christ. And according to historians, Our Lord was born in the thirtieth year of Herod's reign; and in the thirty-seventh year Herod died. All this was done so that the Scripture should be fulfilled about what God said through the prophet, *Ex Egipto vocavi filium meum*, "I have called my son out of the land of Egypt." This authority, although literally understood as the people of Israel who were the children of God and delivered from the land of Egypt, would however be better understood as the natural Son of God, for the others were only adoptive children.

Then in the first year of the reign of Archelaus, who was Herod's first son, and Our Lord being then eight years old, the angel appeared to Joseph and said: "Take the child and his mother and return to the land of Israel, that is Judea, for those seeking to put him to death, that is to say Herod and those who favoured him, are dead." According to Josephus, Herod ordained the taking of certain little children of the most noble of Israel and commanded that after his death they should be killed, to make the Jews weep and be sorry since he knew and was certain that they would gladly welcome his death. According to Saint Jerome, the scribes and Pharisees favoured Herod so as to obtain Our Lord's death. And Saint Remigius says that by the fact that the Angel appeared to Joseph in his sleep, it is mystically signified that those who never occupy themselves with earthly things and secular business are worthy of having vision of the angel and God's comfort.

Then Joseph arose, ready to serve the child and his mother with zeal and to return at once to Israel, to the ordained land and that of Judea. They went and passed again through the desert by which they had come, renewing the labours and pains they had sustained when coming to Egypt. And what David had prophesied in the person of Our Lord was fulfilled: "I am poor and in labour from the beginning of my childhood and as soon as I was born"; for Our Lord sustained great labours and hard bodily afflictions in an outright constant manner, for it seemed like he hated himself because of his love for us. Certainly, the holy labour about which we now speak had sufficed greatly for our redemption. Go devout soul with him and consider all, and have compassion and pity about all this, for this is something great.

It is said that Saint John the Baptist, though being without sin, started doing penance at the far end of that desert; for it is that he entered the desert at the age of seven. And the children of Israel also passed by this place when they came from Egypt. Whoever should preach penance started as soon as he could leading a hard and intense life in the desert, giving up his youth for this excruciating life, that his heirs might take his example and depart from this world by being more inclined to attend to contemplation, and to come to the deep fountain of wisdom which he was later to show to the people. He gave us an example that it is good to bear God's yoke and charge when young, and to accustom oneself doing good things. By this, one may take example that these imperfections ought not to become our masters. Saint John abode in the desert where it is most clear, the eyes are more wide open, and God is most familiar. In the desert he might, before the time of his baptism and preaching, attend to prayer and be familiar with angels, without later being ashamed or afraid to censure any man, and worthy of the faith to witness to the coming of the Son of God. And none may bear witness of another person unless he cannot bear witness to himself. He then flees the world intending neither to take nor to be spoilt with an evil name, and that his life is not blemished with vain and sweet speech, or with any manner of sin. For according to Chrysostom, as it is impossible that a tree planted on the highway may keep its fruit until it is ripe, so it is impossible that those men who are always in the world and live according to it should, as long as their life is concerned, keep life's innocence and purity. And although some trees are planted in gardens surrounded with walls and enclosed so that goers-by cannot touch them, sometimes they still grow branches outside the walls from which passers-by may take the fruit. The same goes for these religious who concentrate on worldly deeds, as they lose easily the fruit of good works.

The life of this child Saint John is very worthy, excellent and marvellous. The doctor Peter of Ravenna writes so about this and says, "This blessed young child in his young age was by inspiration brought to the desert. For although according to his young age he was feeble to endure such labour, yet God gave him strength to bear all the pain, since he left the world altogether and fled from men for His love. He left his country and despised his family, and only kept his eyes and concern on contemplation of God's bounty and heavenly things. Oh marvellous conduct of a man who entered the world with pain and left it craving so much, forgetting all and seeking only to dwell and to be with God. This child forgets his age and the nobleness of his family only to serve the Trinity, showing the manner to religious, anchorites and monks and being the manner and an example to all religion." Chrysostom says: "As the apostles are the princes of priests, so is John the prince of the religious."

Oh you religious, consider your dignity, for Saint John is the prince of your life, and as to his way of life he was monk and hermit from the instant he was born, then going into the desert where he was nourished and abode as a son of God in the wilderness. He would not abide in the mountain where men dwelt but led his life among the angels. He would learn true knowledge in the desert and in being alone. Truly happy is such conduct to despise men, to seek angels, to leave cities, to seek and find Jesus Christ in the wilderness and in being alone. He did not seek him at the temple or in an open place but in the desert. Truly happy are those who follow the penance and life of Saint John, to whom none can be compared nor is so worthy amongst women's children. The religious and cloistered monks who do not follow Saint John, their prince and patron, but rather desire to be familiar with worldly people, and for whom the wilderness is prison and towns and castles are paradise, are really cursed and unhappy. Saint Jerome agrees, saying:

"Let them go and say what they want, each man according to what he thinks. As to myself, it seems to me the town is like a stronghold or prison, and being solitary and reclusive are like paradise to me." The monk ought to know his name. "*Monos*" in Greek means "alone" and "*achos*" means "sorry". And so as to the monk it is just as saying alone and sorry. Let him sit then as alone and sorry, and heed to what his name teaches him, and not usurp another man's office. But if he will preach and teach others, let him hear the counsel of Hugh of Saint Victor, who says: "Oh monk, the coarseness of your habit, the innocence of your cheer and the holi-ness of your conduct must teach men; and you shall teach them better in fleeing from them than in following them." And according to Saint Gregory, the religious ought to bear reverence to his habit, as shown in his works, words and thoughts. And he ought to study and live perfectly in this world, so that what he shows to men in his habit, is what he pretends to have in his conscience before God with a good way of life. Oh religious, glorify then not yourself of your state in religion or in solitude or that you have been a long time, if you do not do your best to live well. For it does not profit you at all but vexes all greatly so to be called religious and not to live accordingly. Jerome says: "There is no praise in having been to Jerusalem, but there is great praise in living in Jerusalem." And Saint Augustine said to his brethren hermits: "My brethren, we shall have no profit in leaving the world but still live according to the world. What profit can we have in abiding in a secret place, if anger or malice reigns in our soul, or when we do our works more to please the world than to please God? Or when although being out of the world yet we still hold the world enclosed within us owing to various passions, so that we are more in need of the prayers of those whom we ought to help than they are of our prayers? It is undoubted that the soul where lustfulness and self-indulgence reign, and where vain conduct lodges and dwells, cannot be wor-thy to have God's kingdom within it as long as it is in that state. And therefore, my brethren," Saint Augustine says: "consider your calling. For it is a sovereign perfection to leave the world and to come to the desert and hermitage;

but not living according to the state which is taken, is great damnation. What profit is there in the body being in a peace-loving and secret place while the soul is troubled and tossed about with disordered passions and affections? I asked, what profit is there in keeping silence in the monastery if the conscience of its inhabitants is troubled with vices and sins? What if we keep a clean and peaceful life outwardly but have a tempest and trouble within us? Certainly, we have not come into this place so that the world should follow and serve us, and for us to abound in all delights and have whatever we want and pleasure, nor have we come into this place to have rest or to be secure. But we have come here to fight against the vices and passions which reign in us and rule over us, to refrain our tongue or again to pay evil for evil, and so that when men do evil to us, we suffer it patiently for the love of God." But help us Our Lady, since nowadays only a few men of religion are found who profit from study to improve themselves considerably and to increase in virtue. Saint Bernard says: "Much easier and sooner will it be that you find a secular man who turns himself to the service of God, than a man of religion who profits from improving himself. It is seldom found on earth that the religious study to increase from one degree to another as earlier taken in religion. It is otherwise essential that a man either increases or decreases, for in holding fast to one state a man falls." "A man ought not to be called good unless he sees how to become better, since in omitting to be good he feels to be better."

Then Joseph, Mary and the child passed the river Jordan and came to the land of Israel, according to what the Angel had commanded them. Now the angel had neither determined nor set any special place in the land of Israel where they should dwell, so Joseph was in constant fear and doubt. And the angel returned and comforted him; and he too was more sure and more contented by the angel's continual visits. And Joseph, hearing that Archelaus, Herod's eldest son and heir preceding all his brethren, reigned in the land of Judea, which was the land of two descents, namely that of Jews and of Benjamin, feared going to that place as Archelaus was bold and would keep his father's commands. And Joseph was warned in his sleep by the angel that he was to go into Galilee, where Herod's other son Herod Antipas dwelt. For although his brother had deprived him of his heritage, yet the Romans had given him that part of the kingdom of the land of Judea. And so the young Herod dwelt in the city of Nazareth where he might feel safe, since he kept to his father's doings very little after he had disinherited him.

All this was done that Scripture should be fulfilled where it says that this child should be called a Nazarene, that is to say consecrated and holy to God. This name was very appropriate to him, as in that place he had also been con-ceived and nourished. The name, meaning flourished, sig-nified that he is essentially the flower of all holiness and the saint of saints.

It may be seen that when the child Jesus returns from Egypt, Our Lady's sisters and friends called to visit her. And they dwelt in Nazareth where they led a poor life. The good Joseph, just as he had was set doing, occupied himself working his craft. And the Virgin laboured in spinning and sewing as well as she might while caring diligently and busily for the child. Saint Anselm says that there is no kind of device or knowledge one might think of, nor tongue that might speak and recount the sweetness with which the Virgin nourished this little child and with what service she served him in his young age. And in like manner, as shown afterwards to a certain devout person, when she often held her child upon her lap, she bowed down her head tenderly weeping over him out of the great sweetness of devotion which she had for him, such that she wetted and watered her child's head and face with the tears of her eyes strained out of true love; she used saying to him: "Oh you joy and salvation of my soul!" Who can keep himself from weeping in hearing or in thinking of such things in his heart?

It was heard no more of the child Jesus or of his par-ents up to when he was twelve years old. Men say—and it is a truth—that there is still a little fountain or well in Nazareth where the child Jesus drew water to wash the herbs which he had gathered in the fields to eat. Oh, if a man might have found him there alone doing these works of humility, and if a man might have heard his sweet words, what pleasure he might have felt! For in such service he served his sweet mother, and she had none other but him to help her in her needs. The master of meekness very soon began practising this humility, glorifying himself above all others in saying: "Learn from me, for I am meek and sweet and lowly of heart." Anselm says: "Think you not that it is something small if you might see in your meditations the child Jesus in Nazareth with the other children, and if you also see how sweetly and meekly he serves his mother and his nourisher Joseph in all that he may do according to his human nature." ❧

CHAPTER 15

ABOUT WHEN JESUS CHRIST DWELT IN THE TEMPLE AND HOW HE WAS FOUND THERE BY HIS MOTHER

CCORDING to the Gospel of Saint Luke, the child Jesus increased and grew, and was big both in greatness and in vigour. And so that no man should imagine or think that he grew in terms of the soul as he did with the body, the Gospel says that he was "full of wisdom" as to the soul for the grace of God was in him in both, namely just as much in the soul as in the body. For since the fullness of the Trinity dwelt in the child Jesus, he was already full of wisdom and had no need of any increasing or comfort, for he was the eternal Word of God. But inasmuch as he was man he had grace in him, given to him to be great according to his human nature, so that he was perfect and fully made as soon as he was man. Similarly as John writes about him, he was full of grace and of truth, for he had the fullness of all virtues and the gifts of the Holy Spirit except faith and hope instead of which he had conviction of knowledge and secure possession, being especially blessed since the time of his conception. Then when men say that Our Lord was strengthened and grew, or any suchlike thing, men ought to consider this is in terms of the body. Saint Bernard says: "The child Jesus was man for he was born not according to age but to wisdom, and according to the soul but not the body, for he had no less consciousness in his conception than in his nativity, nor was he either little or great with regard to the soul; yet he did not show this power which was much less in the body and around him. So that while he was in his mother's womb or in being born, or while he argued with wise doctors or touched people in the temple, he was full of the Holy Spirit." He always prophesied according to his intellectual knowledge and experience, for his perception of new matters converted them into new matters not previously perceived; as the Apostle says, he has taken obedience from the things through which he passed.

The Apostle does not say that he was the first who desired the virtue of obedience, but he says that he took it by the experience of actually obeying God, his mother and Joseph.

Bernard says: "To have compassion on the misery of others, you must first know your own misery, for in recalling yours you find what is in others. And similarly in having this knowledge, you shall learn how you ought to obey Him. Before the blessed Son of God humbled himself and took the form and shape of God's servant, he did not know by experience—whether this was out of mercy or obedience—for he had not experienced whether this was out of misery or subjection. But when he had humbled himself and took our human nature, in which he might suffer passion and subjection, he then experienced mercy and obedience. By this experience too knowledge was neither increased nor augmented, but he did all this that we should believe even more in him when we see that he resembles us so much and from whom we departed by our misery. Who is he in this world who might have courage to draw near to him if he had still dwelt in his majesty? We are now warned that by true faith we shall go to the throne of his grace, knowing that he has sustained our sorrows and weariness in his body. And because of this we ought not doubt that what he suffered was by way of the compassion he had on us."

Jesus' parents went to Jerusalem every year for the feast and solemnity of Easter, in being devout people of their religion and keepers of the Law. And it must be understood that the Jews did not have by their Law only one common solemnity, like the Sabbath in remembrance of the day when God had ceased creating, and the Neomenia which was the first day of the lunar month in memory of the Creator who had created all things. They have also solemnised Easter in remembrance of their deliverance from Egypt and Pentecost fifty days later when the Law was given to Moses. On the first day of September they feasted with trumpets for they then blew trumpets and horns in remembrance of the day when Isaac was delivered from the sacrifice in which Abraham would have offered him up; then on the tenth day of September was the feast of the Propitiation, or of Expiation, when Moses brought those on whom God's anger was appeased upon them, which anger was because of their prayers and their worshipping of calves; and on the fourteenth day of September they kept the feast of the Tabernacles, dwelling in tents in remembrance of the forty years their fathers had no houses but lived in tents. But above all these feasts there were three principal ones, namely Easter, Whitsuntide and Scenophagia, or of the Tabernacles; each lasting seven days. On these three solemnities all people ought to go and stand before God; and not only those women who were in some sort of need but even more those who went there by devotion. And because of this the Blessed Virgin went there, for she would not leave her child behind her without him being kept or cared for.

So then the child Jesus, being twelve years old, went to the feast with his parents according to the custom of the Law; by which it is shown that men ought to accustom themselves to serve God as from their young age. Now the child Jesus took a longer way to travel to that place, and went to the temple to honour his heavenly Father in the solemnities done to Him, while meekly keeping the Law of which he was himself its Lord. And it was for this that he had come into the world, to give an example of humility and of full perfection in keeping the Law as long as he dwelt in this life. Bede says: "The sweet Jesus kept the Law he had given, to show us that we, poor creatures of this world, ought to keep all that God has commanded us. Then if we desire to see him in his majesty and glory, we must meditate on following him by the way and conduct of his human nature." We servants ought then to come to the solemnities and busily keep God's commandments, taking Our Lord's example of great diligence and a good heart by doing good works. There was a man of religion which had such devotion to the feasts of Our Lord and Our Lady and to all saints that before every feast he prepared himself by fasting, praying and chastising his body to receive such solemnity; then as long as it lasted he occupied his soul in devout meditations, according to the feast he was observing.

Morally, we are here taught that on feastdays and holidays, every Christian ought particularly to attend at the place in which Our Lord has chosen for us to pray, namely in church, and not at sports and plays or at the tavern. For on feasts or holidays men ought to apply themselves, serve and love God and deliberately avoid all vanities and worldly pleasures. Men ought to tend to almsgiving and not to usury or theft. But you must strive to do good works and not to give yourself to dainty affairs, gluttony or ribaldry. And to those who do otherwise God speaks through Isaiah, saying "My soul has hated your solemnities and songs."

Then afterwards, when Our Lord was twelve years old, he showed his wisdom by giving witness as to what was due to his heavenly Father and to his mother according to human nature. Twelve was a sign of the number of those who are saved by the doctrine of the twelve apostles, by the religion and way of life of the twelve Patriarchs and in the election of the twelve tribes. Similarly, in rendering to his parents what he owed them, he went with them as man to Jerusalem there to offer sacrifice to God; he would thus also render what was due to his heavenly Father, by expounding the doctrine and by holy preaching.

When the solemnity and the following eight days, namely the octaves, were accomplished, the child Jesus dwelt in the city of Jerusalem since his parents and friends had left. Not that this was by their negligence or that they had forgotten him, but all was done according to what he ordained and willed, so that in his childhood age he would show and teach all the love he had for spiritual and divine things. His parents, meanwhile, were unaware that he was being left behind, but rather thought he had been in the company of some other father or mother, or amongst his friends, return- ing with them. The reason why he would remain there in this manner without their knowledge was not because he was abandoned by them, or that he was unwilling to obey and go with them, by which they might have thought that he scorned them. But it was done to teach and show by example that children, without waiting for father or mother or any other friends or kinsfolk, should choose the life of perfection as their state of holy religion. And for this reason the custom was, so as to keep better purity or cleanliness and chastity, that men went on one part and women on the other, even in travelling to and from, while the children might have gone and went to and from one party to the other, some time with their fathers and others with their mothers, and at other times too with their other friends.

And the Virgin believed that her child Jesus had been in the company of Joseph, his father as held and esteemed; and Joseph on his part supposed otherwise and thought that he was in the Virgin's company, his true mother indeed. And so they went along for a day's journey until night and came to a place where they should lodge. And Our Lady, his mother, seeing that the child Jesus was not in her husband Joseph's company was in great anguish and misery and, out of her mind as she was, she sought him with Joseph from house to house and in all inns in great sorrow and weeping bitterly.

Go you, devout soul, ever with them and seek the child Jesus, your master, until you find him. Take good heed also of this sweet mother and have compassion on her, since from the hour that she was born until now, she has neither been in such anguish nor trial. What joy or consolation might she have having lost Jesus? And although her friends supported her as much as they could, yet she did not find any comfort. So let us not be disturbed or impatient when God sends us trials, no matter how great they may be, for He did not spare His own mother but courted her with them. In suffering His friends to have trials, he shows them by it a sign of love.

When the Lady could not find the child she returned to her inn and went into her chamber, giving herself to weeping, lamentations and prayers therein. And throughout all night her heart was tormented with sorrowful bitterness about the departing of her son and much beloved child. And when it was morning, she departed with Joseph from the inn and sought him along the ways and streets through which men coming from Jerusalem passed. And she asked for him many times from their friends, kinsfolk and cousins and all those who knew him and were in their company, and all others. And not having found him, the sweet mother without any hope of finding him again was in a most constant anguish. Who might not meditate on the wounds piercing her heart at that hour, and on her sighing and sobbing, and the anguish and heaviness she must have felt in her heart?

Certainly, she now started experiencing the forthcoming sorrow of the passion which Simeon had foretold her, not knowing what to do or say for now she had lost the trea- sure entrusted to her to keep by God. She might well say with great weeping and tears what Reuben said about his brother Joseph as it is written in *Genesis*, "Alas, I cannot find the child; and as for me, in this poverty, where shall I go?"

Oh Christian, consider now that the Virgin had not lost her child Jesus when she was in Egypt, which was a foreign country, nor at any time when she was in trial; but she lost him when she went joyfully to the feast. Whereby we should understand that Jerusalem is ever kept in adversity, but many times men lose it in fortune and prosperity.

And on the third day they returned to Jerusalem. Men may well think that this was not without great labour and pain. And the Virgin might well properly say what is written in the *Song of Songs*: "I have sought him who my soul loves. I have sought him and I have not found him"; namely amongst his friends and cousins. "I shall arise in seeking him from place to place, and go around the city in places and streets, and shall seek him whom my soul desires."

And after the third day that he had been absent from his mother, thereby prefiguring the three days of his death during which some thought that he had been lost and that he would never rise again, that is on the fourth day in the morning they found him in the temple. According to Saint Ambrose he, whom men had believed had been dead, wanted to make them aware that he would rise again after the third day of his passion's victory, to be found in the glory of his immortality. They found him not playing nor in the market place, as men commonly find other children, but in a holy place which had been set for learning and prayer, for the Son dwelt gladly in his Father's house. Whoever loves to dwell and tarry in the Church shows that he is a son of God; and whoever keeps himself and loves to dwell in the tavern shows that he is the devil's son. I ask now, was he was found in the temple running here and there as other children do? No, but like the fountain of wisdom he sat in a seat in the midst of doctors, since he was better off here in opposing and arguing with them while showing a sign of humility. And he examined and heard them; first by teaching them in giving an example to those wise and doctors who were more ready to hear than to teach; for a person who answers before or even having heard shows himself to be a fool. He opposed them, not that he had any need to do this nor that he would learn, but because he would give us the manner and form of learning; and for us to have good will and love for Holy Scripture; and so that we should not be ashamed to ask and learn what we do not or cannot understand, which is something not done by many who are proud for they would ever remain in their ignorance rather than ask. According to Bede, in order to show that he was man, he meekly heard the men. And in order to prove that he was God, when they spoke he answered them so highly that all those who heard him were greatly marvelled, seeing this childhood and wisdom which were in him in his arguing, opposing and answering. They considered this child to be man and not God, seeing that he heard meekly, asked wisely and answered prudently. He, who was still a child, opposed them and answered their questions, keeping the manner of a wise master who teaches, examines and answers his scholars.

His parents were greatly marvelled when they saw him sitting in the midst of doctors since they had never seen him before doing such things. When his mother saw him she was sent into raptures from great sorrow to joy, and she rendered praise and thanksgiving to God. On seeing his mother the child Jesus went to her and she received him sweetly, kissing and beholding his sweet and pleasant face, saying to him, *Fili, quid fecisti nobis sic?* as if saying "Oh my dear child, how may you suffer that your caring and diligent mother sustains such great sorrow?" The Virgin Mary, after seeking him for three days, was in a state gladness and heaviness after finding him yet she embraced him sweetly again. It was she who spoke and not Joseph for we do not read that he ever spoke. Also Joseph presumed not to speak to Jesus, not that he had any doubt about him. But the mother, who had suffered greater sorrow because of the great love she had for him, trusted in taking him back since excelling love could not be supplanted. Gregory says:

"His mother was determined to have compassion on her son while asking heart-rending questions; for as a mother she set all her desire and affection boldly and meekly on him, saying *Fili*, child, why have you done this to us?" And Saint Anselm similarly says: "Oh doubtful soul, if only you had diligently sought with his mother the twelve-year-old child Jesus for three days! Oh, who might keep anyone from weeping seeing how sweetly the mother chastised her child saying to him, 'Oh son, why have you done this thing to us?' It might be said that she did not blame him, but gently chided him about having been for such a long time away from her, saying to him, *Ecce pater tuus et ego*, 'Oh my child, you see your father—who is so called since he is your nourisher—and me with him. We sought you with a heavy heart since you lost us; for your presence is most sweet to us.'"

Here we have to be morally instructed that we ought to have a heavy heart when we lose Jesus by sinning. And we ought to seek him by doing three days of penance, with sorrowful contrition, sincere confession and compensating penance. And if we so seek him, we shall undoubtedly find him. But alas, there are many nowadays who are more angry and loathe losing temporal rather than spiritual goods, such as eternal salvation. Bernard says: "The beast falls and finds relief or help, but the soul perishes and there is no one to help it."

Hearing his mother telling him so the child said to her, more in manner of teaching than of blame, "Why do you seek me? Do you not know that I am expected to be with what belongs to my Father?" just like saying, in the temple of doctrine and in the works through which he is made manifest. As though he would have said: "You ought not to be so marvelled, for I ought to give more heed to the works of Him whose eternal Son I am according to divine nature, than to you mother whose son I am only according to human nature, nor to you Joseph, whose son I am only by upbringing and nourishment." And although he loved his parents and obeyed them, yet he would honour God, his Father, in the main. By which it was being instructed that his parents ought to prefer serving God and showing they are doing so.

Morally, we are taught by this that Our Lord corrected the words of his mother, who had sought him amongst his cousins and friends, that whoever is amongst his friends and pleases his body, may not afterwards come to great perfection but with great pain; and also that many times one lacks perfection owing to the great affection he has for his parents.

And it is to be noted that these words with which he answered his mother were the first we read to have been uttered by him, expressly showing his divinity in them. And they were so high and so great that neither Joseph nor Mary understood them, as it appears from what is written after, for they were not accustomed hearing him utter such words. He would show them that he was due to attend at the temple, as to his Father, and to all spiritual things that matter. For in both there is but one majesty and one glory, one operation, one seat and one house; not only spiritual but material too. Or one may also say that they understood him well, for they firmly believed that he was the Son of God; but that they did not as yet understand so clearly the mysteries and secrets of his divine nature as they did later.

This being done and said, he returned with them at his mother's request to Nazareth, there to console and recompense them for the sorrows they had sustained because of him. Here he shows us his two natures, for as the Son of God he dwelt in the temple, and as the son of man he returned to Nazareth with his parents.

In order to teach us and to confound our pride he remained subject to his parents, as often we do not obey our superiors. I say that he was subject to them insofar as nature is concerned, where he is less than the father for, as Saint Augustine says, in terms of human nature the child Jesus was less than his parents. So see to it that you will be subject and obedient for his love, so that by virtue of the charge and labour of obedience and subjection you may return to him whom you have lost by pride and disobedience. Our Saviour shows us here an example of humility and how to be obedient when he, though being the sovereign emperor to whom the whole world is subject, meekly willed to be subject to man. Do hear, you who have been subjects, and take joy in your meekness and subjection to your king, that he who is the prelate of all has not refused to subject himself to all. Wherefore let priests keep themselves away from pride, for it is often seen that subject persons have much greater merit than some prelates.

Also take heed of the dignity due to the glorious mother and Virgin, like Jesus to whom all creatures are subject, obeys her. Saint Augustine says: "The Virgin had this extraordinary privilege that Jesus was subject to her, to whom not only human nature obeyed but also the nature of angels prayed and revered." Bernard says: "Be marvelled by these two things, namely witnessing to the great kindness of the Son of God and to the great dignity of the Virgin, for they both ought to be greatly marvelled at. This is an incomparable humility that God willed to be subject to a woman, and incomparable dignity that the Virgin had God subject to her." "Oh you man, learn to obey. Oh earth, learn to be subject. Oh dust in the air, learn to fly low. Oh ashes of pride, you ought to be greatly ashamed when God humbles Himself while you exalt yourself. God makes Himself subject to man, but you seek lordship and domination over him. In doing this you put yourself before your Creator; for whenever a man precedes another he forces himself to be before God, and in doing so he does not have the odour of the goodness of God."

It should be noted that the Son is bound to do many things for his parents. First, he ought to love them wholeheartedly. Second, to worship them with works. Third, to help them in need. Fourth, to serve them in what they do. Fifth, to speak to them respectfully. Sixth, to be obedient in honest affairs. Seventh, to implore their pardon when offending them. Eighth, to have compassion in their misfortune.

One might ask what did the child Jesus do during these three days? For an answer take heed diligently how all night he lodged in some poor hostel and ate and drank with poor people. In asking himself, Saint Bernard speaks so about this matter: "Oh Lord, what has sustained you in these three days?" And Bernard answers himself saying: "Oh you Lord Jesus Christ, in conforming yourself in everything to our poverty, you have sought your living in this world from door to door like a poor creature. Alas, who shall let me partake of a morsel of bread which you have begged, that I might be fed with the holy relief you felt in what you ate!" Also take heed of him amongst the doctors, with a face so pleasing and wise, and how in all reverence he argued with them as though he had been untutored, and heard them with meekness that they should not be ashamed of their ignorance hearing his marvellous answers.

Morally, you may perceive in the aforesaid three fairly notable facts. The first is that whoever will unite himself to God ought not to dwell with his carnal parents but to depart from them; for when the child Jesus would attend to his Father he lost his most sweet mother, and she too did not find him with his parents and friends in terms of human nature, for he is not found amongst company. Saint Bernard says: "The sweet Virgin sought the child Jesus amongst her cousins, but she did not find him there. So because of this, flee from your brethren and even from yourself if you want to find your salvation, forget your people and go to your Father's house. And when you do so the king will desire your beauty." And moreover he also says: "Oh good Jesus, if you are not found amongst your parents, how shall I find you among men? How may I find you by merely living in this world when your sweet mother in great heaviness and much pain could scarcely find you?" The sweet Jesus himself may not be found amongst the company of many, as in the multitude of worldly things, for a man can only find him in the inner lodgings of his soul, where the temple of God is sited.

The second teaching is that whoever lives spiritually ought not be either marvelled or embarrassed if there are times when he is all cold and dry in his devotions and desires as to think that he has been abandoned by God, seeing that God has done this to his mother. Yet in seeking Him with all perseverance and diligence, as are good exercises of prayers, meditations and other holy works, he knows that he shall find Him indeed. According to Origen, whoever seeks Jesus ought not to be negligent or slow like those who seek him and do not find him. But whoever wants to find him ought seek him with great labour, diligence and sorrow. Saint Bernard says: "If we do not desire to seek

God in vain, let us seek him righteously; that is to say that we should seek nothing else resembling Him. Therefore let us seek him fervently, for in finding Him we shall desire nothing else. Let us seek Him perseveringly and see that we do not leave Him and return to other things. For this is a very hard thing which heaven and earth determines, that He is not found when someone seeks Him or similarly when one so demands but does not have this experience."

The third instruction or teaching is that none ought to rest or bide by his own intelligence or will, for although Our Lord had said that he must attend to the works of his Father, yet he changed his mind and followed his mother's will and that of the holy man Joseph in going with them and subjecting himself to them.

His mother kept all these things in her heart as great things which had as yet been unheard of him. And she adopted as a law and rule her son's teachings throughout her lifetime, teaching us that in meditating Our Lord's sayings and doings we ought to cast out all evil thoughts from our hearts. Because of this, if any man needs good teaching, he ought to return to her who keeps in her mind the words and works of Our Saviour Jesus.

And the child Jesus grew in age, wisdom and grace towards God and man. Age pertained to the body and wisdom to the soul, and grace to the salvation of both. Men might also say that he triumphed because of his accomplished deeds, similarly as it is said that a wise man prevails in doing things of greater marvel and adopting a wiser doctrine from day to day. For just as he grew in age, he even did more marvellous things. And this is what the Gospel says: *Aput Deum et homines,* "Jesus prevailed toward God and man." Or otherwise according to Saint Ambrose, he prevailed in wisdom, as grace upon grace showed itself in him. Or also according to Saint Gregory, he was of gain to others, namely those who triumph in his doctrine and in his examples, just like we say that a schoolmaster gains when his scholars gain under him. And this gain is owed to God and man, for when God is loved man profits. Or according to Theophilus, this gain is owed to God and man since men ought to please God first and after man.

CHAPTER 16

ABOUT WHEN JESUS WAS FROM HIS TWELFTH YEAR OF AGE UNTIL THE THIR' TIETH YEAR OF AGE

HE Lord then returned from the temple and from the solemn discussion he had in Jerusalem, and went into Nazareth with his parents. He was subject to them and dwelt there with them up to the beginning of his thirtieth year. Now what he did in the meantime is a mar' vellous thing, not found in Scripture. Why should we think that he kept himself idle or doing nothing for so long, or that he did not do anything worthy to be recited or shown? Perhaps Scripture is silent where no speech occurs, since the young child's deeds were not to be made public too soon. But if you take heed patiently and attentively, you may see that in doing nothing he did great things, for in all his doings mystery was never left out. Certainly, just as he spoke and worked in great virtue, so did he virtuously keep his peace and was little in man's way as he might be. It would be well to believe, as the Greek doctor says, that before and after, without openly showing any miracle, he was considered amongst men as if he was one of them up to the time when he arrived at a perfect age. Saint John the Baptist said about this that "He whom you do not know is in your midst."

Saint Luke shortly encapsulates all this time saying that he descended with his parents to Nazareth and was subject to them. Inasmuch as for the duration of this time he did no miracle, as men were not to think that the mystery of the Incarnation was a remarkable thing had he not been seen in his youth to be a child. For this reason he delayed in showing his knowledge and virtue up to the time as others were usually in grown up and relished knowledge and virtue. This sovereign master, who ought to teach the virtues and ways of life, began in his young age to do virtuous works, yet in a marvellous way and unknown to others, and was unheard of for a time, that is he knowingly rendered himself useless and abject to others; and no one expected anything like this from him who ought to think devoutly and consider himself not to have any foolish affection for anything going against it. And with this mitigation I ensure and affirm all that I have said, although the Scripture gives no authority, as I have said in the prologue.

The sweet Jesus then deliberately avoided the company of men and fled their conditions and chatter, for he was chosen to do great prayer and contemplation. He went to the synagogue, that is in church, and there he stood in a low and humble place where he could pray. And after he returned and kept himself with his mother and his carer Joseph, helping them at times. And in being a child he grew in age, wisdom and grace towards God and man. This child grew up until he was between twenty and twenty-five years old. And he did nothing openly which men might see to be worthy of repute and love and men greatly marvelled and derided him for being so young and fair and did not give him no work to do; and they reputed him for being vile and abject, or as one who would not want to learn. The prophet had well said before about himself, "I am a worm and no man, made to be reprimanded by man and rejected by people. All those who see me deride me, both with signs and with words." The sweet Jesus showed himself meekly to all as the most abject of all creatures. Do you not think that these things are of great perfection? Certainly, in all our works there is nothing so great nor more difficult than to be considered lowly with all men. Whoever might come to this degree may be reputed to be at the highest and most difficult stage of perfection. It is indeed not to feign overcoming one's heart and high mind and so condemn his soul and grow inward pride and irritability, which is neither reputed nor praised by men, but rather more to desire not to be praised. And for a man to reach this level, he ought not think about not profiting. For according to the words of Our Lord, we are truly useless and unprofitable servants and we live in fantasies and not in the way of truth so that we might come to this degree of rejection. And we are not deceived about this; for according to the Apostle, when a man thinks that his reputation means something to him, by virtue of being nothing, he would be deceiving himself. Certainly, in all this that we do in order to obtain our salvation there is no better or more useful exercise or medicine for the soul than to censure oneself. And when anyone censures or scorns you, you ought to keep them in your repute as being your helpers and friends, for they do what you should do to be saved; and you ought to show more favour to them than to anyone else. But to whoever you have done any offence and wrong, go and humble yourself before him; but keep him who has done you wrong as your friend. Repute also to your profit the damage and rebukes done to you, and do not cease praying God for those who do this to you.

According to a wise man, a very meek person rejoices himself when he hears himself being despised, and is sad when he is honoured. He weeps in prosperity and enjoys himself in adversity. He fears riches, and finds delight in weeping. Abundance gives him torment, poverty gladness. Despise all passing praise and consider all honour as unworthy, keep all hypocrisy in horror and love all truth. Forget all temporal things and desire what is spiritual. Ignore all that belongs to the world, that you may win heaven. Do not ever be self-presumptuous. Do not give these merits and thankfulness either to yourself or to your detractors before you meekly know that they are gifts of God. So that this might not cause any low pride in you, wish for no one knowing of your virtues, save the good examples you ought to do to your fellow Christian. Now where in this world do you find such a person? If there be, let us duly praise him. Saint Bernard says: "To desire to be praised in your meekness is no sign of humility but rebellion. The very meek will be reputed vicious and not openly called meek, taking pleasure when men censure him."

Then if you will ask why Our Saviour Jesus lived in this manner, I answer you that he did not need doing so but did it to teach us. And because of this, if we do not learn meekness from him and flee the world, we have no excuse. It is very abominable for a poor worm to be proud, where pride is worms' meat, where the Lord of might and majesty is meek. And if it seems to anyone that it was very strange for the Lord to keep himself for such a long time without doing any work worthy to be seen, and that the Gospel narrators have left many of his doings unrecorded, men would better answer whether it is only a little thing to show the exercise of so great a virtue as humility which is the steadfast foundation of all other virtues. As Saint Bernard says, and it is alleged in this book in the chapter on Our Lord's baptism towards the end, the good Lord ought to preach in this manner: "Learn of me, and take heed how meek I am." And this is why he would do that which he did or what he taught; and not out of affection or pretence but with a perfect heart, that no dishonesty might befall him. And this is why he found himself in perfect humility, lowliness and rejection. And he made himself so simple amongst people that until he started preaching divine things and doing great miracles, he was held as being worthless. Then they said mockingly, "Who is this? Is not this the carpenter's son?" besides many other demeaning words which he suffered patiently for he had been used to them for a long time.

Saint Paul the Apostle's words were confirmed in all this when he said that the Son of God is well founded and perfect in taking human nature not in any manner as an indifferent service, but as a useless service by way of a meek and abject life. Consider now all his doings, for in all humility he shone brightly. He has forged and showed how men ought to seek him, that is to say by lowliness and rejection or despising oneself before others, and by the continual meek exercise of doings and works.

Now if you want to seek true humility, being humbled must go before and you ought to exercise yourself in things having to do with meekness and rejection. Bernard says: "Humiliation is the foundation of all spiritual edifices, and humiliation is the way to humility, similarly as patience is to peace and learning to knowing. And if you will desire the virtue of true humility, do not refuse taking the path of humiliation. For unless you go by this path, you may not be meek nor come to this virtue." Yet Saint Bernard says, "Certainly, for men to be aware and knew of my power and feebleness that I may be despised by them should greatly profit me, for it often happens that I am unjustly praised by those who do not know me." "For it is a great danger for a man to hear another speak about him more than he can think of himself. Who shall make me or cause me to be so meek before men, to seeing the faults that really dwell within me, and how falsely and unworthily men have raised and praised me for what is not in me? Certainly, if men do so to me, I shall say within myself so that what the prophet David said may be accomplished: *Exaltatus autem et humilia-tus*, "I am exalted and honoured of men", but certainly not because I am meek. And this prophet himself says to his wife Michal daughter of Saul, *Ludam et vilior fiam*, "I shall play before God and be mocked and made vile and abject before men." God is the *play* of which Michal was angry with all etc, and God took pleasure. Good is the play which is like mockery and folly to men, but gives great delight to angels. I say that the play is good when we are considered to be in public dishonour or persons of no importance and set apart from amongst the proud. It is in the playing of this holy and honest play that Saint Paul the Apostle said: "We are made abject in the sight of the world, of angels and of men." With this play let us play and let us be mocked, so that we may be meek until the day will come that shall depose the proud and exalt the meek to eternal bliss." Yet Saint Bernard says: "Who desires to arrive at high and divine things ought first have the odour of meekness on him; since in thinking about them, great things do not come but rather throw all down. For the high secrets of God may not be obtained but by the virtue of humility; and a humble person is only he who deserves the grace of God. When then you shall see the meek, take it for a good sign and a certain sending of grace that ought to come into your soul. For just as before the heart of man makes him grow in worldly pleasures, in like manner rather than exult himself in great happiness he ought to humble himself. And this is what the Apostle Saint James says, that Our Lord withdrew from the proud and gave his grace to the meek. It is only a little thing to be taken patiently, when God himself humbled himself before us. Of this you may take a marvellous example from the prophet David, who was cursed by his servant, but who felt nothing in his soul by such an offence, for the grace of God took it from him. This prophet was a man who could be well likened to God's actions, rendering good for evil and praying for those who cursed him. And for this he has taken God's justifications, that is for which God was justified. Now let it be seen that true humility justifies us before God, and not humiliation. I say humiliation, for many who are not meek may seem meek. And there are others who humble themselves by force, and some by patience, and others voluntarily by effect of the will. The first are sinners, the second are without guilt, and the third are just. For although innocence is one part of justice, yet its fulfilment leads to humility. Our Lord did not give his grace to those who are meek out of fear, but to those who are meek of heart. Truly meek is the one who converts his humiliation into humility and who may say to God, 'It profits me that you have humbled me.'"

And do appreciate that according to Saint Bernard there are five things which profit and help man to have humiliation and humility. The first is to love vile and abject things and to seek the ways by which man may be mocked. The second is the custom of being subject for long, and to desire to be ever with those whom men fear and honour, because with them he learns to break his proper will. The third is that in practising humility man is ever better before God and more pleasing to Him, so that in his mind he may learn how to have the grace which he ought to have within him, forget what he has and seek what he does not have. The fourth is continual meditation of his proper fragility, putting it before all stirrings of elation, saying many times within himself, "Oh earth and ashes, why should you be proud?" The fifth is to consider high contemplation of God's justice. For just as one who often confesses himself in secret of the words spoken proudly by him, and it so happens that if he returns before such confessor and says the same words to him again, he should be ashamed, similarly, whoever considers well that God knows all and sees all, ought to be ashamed to say or think things before Him which would displease Him. And for this it would be very useful and much easier for man to resist all vices, by having God ever before his eyes and to think that He sees all that which he does, thinks or says.

I pray you then to follow meekness with all your strength, without which you may neither have spiritual profit nor attain any virtues. Saint Bernard says about this: "Humility is more necessary than all other virtues, for without it all other virtues are not virtues. I tell you that whatever virtue God gives to man, whether it be charity or any other, humility is its cause and provider, for it gives grace to the meek and keeps the other virtues in the soul, for the Holy Spirit did not come to us but with humility and peace. It leads all other virtues to perfection." First of all, humility deserves complete perfection and fulfilment of grace, as the prophet says, *Qui emittis fontes in convalibus*, "You are Him, oh Lord, who sends your fountains and valleys"; like saying you give your grace to the meek; *inter medium montium pertransibunt aquae*, "the waters pass between the mountains." Two mountains are two kinds of pride, the first of which proceeds from temporal goods, the other from spiritual ones. And between these two mountains is the vale of humility, not ever declining to any manner of kind or part of pride. And it is through this part, which is humility, that the waters of grace pass. Secondly, humility deserves growth and the help of grace. And for this whoever desires to receive great grace from God ought to feel it meekly within him and he should not enhance himself. There are three measures by which a man may know whether a person is seeking self-respect in the gifts given to him by God. The first is whether he has more reverence for any personal manner of grace or gift which men bestow upon him than to any other. The second, whether he is ready to receive happily and undergo necessity and labour as any other thing. The third is whether when men displease him he believes that men do him no wrong but a right thing. Thirdly, humility is the keeper of grace which God gives to the creature. For just as ashes keep the fire, so does humility keep grace in the soul, which is the spiritual fire. The fire is kept in many methods. First of all, by stoking it with wood; so is the grace of God kept in the soul by stoking it with good works. Secondly, by blowing; so is the grace of God kept by fervent meditation, much like a pair of bellows. Thirdly, by preservation of what goes against it; so is grace kept by prolonging and deferring all sins.

But now let us return to behold the developments and doings and the life of Our Lord Jesus Christ, who is our mirror and the main aim of our purpose. Thus count yourself for nothing in this presence, but do consider this little child with high and blessed humility and with God's gifts in him leading a poor and humble life. The holy man Joseph sought and earned what he might with his craft. And the glorious Virgin sewed and spun to all those who would give her any work by which to get her living. And she dressed the meat and drink for her husband and for her son, and did all other things and business about the house, and she laboured with her hands since she had no servant. Do have compassion on her and also of the sweet Jesus who so faithfully helps her and did work in whatever way he could, just as he said that he came into this world to do service and not to be served. Saint Basil says about this: "The sweet Jesus has been obedient to his parents since he was of age, suffering physical work meekly and reverently from the beginning of his life. His parents were very holy and righteous people and always lived in poverty and suffering, just as it appeared from the crib where they laid the child." Consider how every day these three took their first refreshment of the day seated around a little table. Men might well think how they had no delicate nourishment nor did they lay out great tables for it, but that it was poor and sober. And they spoke together neither vain nor idle words, but words which were full of the Holy Spirit in all wisdom. For it is well to believe that they gave more nourishment to the soul than to the body. Also do take heed how after such recreation each of them applied themselves to prayer in their little chamber, for they had no great house but a little cottage. Do take good heed how the sweet Jesus after his prayer laid himself in his little bed every night. Every devout soul ought every night to behold him in his bed and to have compassion on him who for so long time would suffer such poverty for us. In every kind of poverty which they suffered, the sweet mother was filled with great joy for the presence of her blessed child Jesus. As Saint Anselm says: "For she knew well that he was the Creator and Lord of all things, he whom she saw in her company eat and drink and taught her all that she asked him. Think now what extraordinary love one had for the other."

Consider then the poverty of your Lord. Where are those who seek worldly pleasures and things according to their status, such as superfluous, curious and extravagant clothing? Such people have not learned the lesson of the wise master. I ask you whether we are any wiser than him, seeing that he has taught us to do and see humility, poverty, labour and bodily affliction. Let us follow him then, being the suffering master who neither may nor will deceive any- one, in leading our life according to the Apostle's doctrine; and let us clothe ourselves honestly and not unreasonably, but let us be contented. And then let us meditate and seek other virtues.

Take what Our Lord Jesus said for a learning in your life, censuring yourself and desiring others to censure you, and exercising yourself in vile and abject things. And know that you shall not find anything which may make you more meek and give you more humility than when you earnestly behold in yourself your own guilt, and not that of others. Bernard says: "I would that every soul learned first to know him. Such knowledge does not bloat nor is it any burden, but it edifies and renders a person humble. For the spiritual edifice may not keep standing long unless it is laid on a steadfast foundation of humility. When the soul considers well, there is nothing so fitting nor shall it find any greater humility than in itself. But to find in itself this precious stone of humility, it would suit the soul well not to have in it either fraud or deception." And Saint Augustine says: "It is no little thing for the beginning of beatitude to have knowledge of the soul's poverty and misery." And for this in all our doings, sayings and works, remember and meditate as to compunction, thinking that the good deeds you do are not perfectly good nor are they done with such fervent affection as they should, but are very much soiled and blemished by a great deal of negligence. Do often consider and think very fearfully how all the desire to do good and all your application which you have to seek virtue does not come from you, but that it has been given to you by Jesus Christ out of his only grace, and that if he was willing he might have given it to a villain and sinner and have taken it away from you leaving you in the bond of sin. And how can any man attribute to himself the good that comes from him, he who so many times has had experience of his impossibility in anything good which he does, great or small, and sees and knows that when he may do he will not, and that when he would do he may not unless he is moved by divine grace with a marvellous fervent desire. This grace is not given so lightly by God, since man knows that he may have no goodness by himself without the help of others. And for such an impossibility God suffers a person for a long time, until he learns to be meek and not to let himself in any way grow in pride, but that he attributes all good to God; not only by word of mouth, but by feeling it coming from the depth of his heart.

Consider also that he is not so poor a sinner since, had God given him the grace he gave to you, he has served Him better than you and has acknowledged better His benefits than you have done. Considering this you may judge yourself to be more vile and abject than everyone else; and you ought to have doubts lest Jesus Christ casts you out of his company for your ingratitude. And you ought in some manner to think within yourself on the sins of others, saying in your conscience: "Oh, wretched me, this is homicide, this is fornication" and the same for all others. "And as for me, every day I commit much greater sins, for I have banished myself into being subject to the enemies when I abandoned my Creator and killed my poor soul." You also ought to feel two things within you, namely that you feel you are like a dead body full of worms which all men abhor seeing or beholding; and that were anybody to do you justice by putting out your eyes or cutting off your nose, this should be your just cause for your abandonment, since you have offended God in all your days and are now worthy of all opprobrium and shame. It must also be that it is only you who has trust and confidence in yourself and in all the good deeds which you have done and which you may do in your lifetime, and that only you can rest and incline yourself in the arms of the most sweet Jesus, most poor, meek, despised and suffering death for you. And you ought not to remove yourself from the feeling that you are completely dead and that only the sweet Jesus lives in your heart and in your soul, and that you feel him cordially in your heart, and that you neither desire to hear nor see anything but Jesus hanging on the cross and dead for you.

By the aforesaid this virtue of humility shall be engen-dered in you as the mother and beginning of all other vir-tues. It opens the eyes of understanding to see God, purging human hearts of all the excesses of evil thoughts. For in considering his soul and his own imperfection, a person is vilified, reproved, detested and annulled within himself. So throw out of yourself all temporal occupations and cast them away from your mind and learn to return often to your inner self. And the more you have in you, even more would you draw near to original justice, spiritual brightness and purity, delighting and loving the oil of God's contem-plation and rising up a ladder from where you may con-template the angelic and divine spirit. And let it be known that such soul as desires to come to His purity, must cast out of it all material things; just as whoever wants to see the Son materially must desist from looking at any other material thing. By such contemplation the soul inflames itself to desire heavenly things and is not content with what is temporal. And in doing so charity starts warming up in the soul, consuming all the filth and uncleanliness of the vices found in the soul. And also true love casts these away from the soul in such manner that vanity finds no place in it. So that what man thinks, speaks and works comes and proceeds from the judgment of charity.

For the purpose then that you may persevere, keep your-self constantly in the fear of God and acknowledge that all good comes from Him and ask that it would please Him to give you perseverance. And if you do not want to fall, do not judge anyone else, but always consider your mis-deeds greater than those of others, and excuse all others. And beware against any other person who moves or irks you by any resentment although you see them in anything you observe; but have compassion and pray for them, in thinking that neither they nor you may do anything but as it pleases God to give you His grace. He gives it to us not for our merits, but only out of His goodness and will. If you remember and think about this, you are then safe and purified. I ask you, what is the cause that so many people start doing so much abstinence and other good works of penance, and so few are those who persevere in it, among other things owing to the feebleness of their bodies, or the coldness of their spirit, or such like? Truly, there is no other cause why they do not continue their works and bring them to perfection but their presumption; as in being overconfident and despising others, judging them in their hearts. And because of this God withdraws from them His gift and His grace. And it often happens that they themselves are replete with defects, for it commonly happens that when one judges another to have any guilt, God suffers him in time to come to fall in peril of guilt or in a greater fault than that of the person whom he had judged. And because of this when presumption appears before you, resort to the discipline of self-accusation, so that Our Lord will not be angry with you and you not fall away from the right path. And you should soon follow the very useful doctrine of Saint Anselm which says: "Oh creature, often watch over to what your soul is subject and to which passions, and to all that you do daily; and think well to what end you shall come. And unless you are a fool, I believe you shall do the works by which you may obtain joy and happiness without end, and you shall depart from doing that by which you might bring upon yourself sorrow and heaviness in your soul, or everlasting torment." ❧

CHAPTER 17
OF THE OFFICE AND LIFE OF SAINT JOHN THE BAPTIST

ET us now leave all the other deeds and works of our saviour Jesus Christ's child-hood. The Gospel narrators had desire and wished to write the deeds and words which he did after coming to full age, that is as after becoming a perfect man; and first of his baptism, namely how he was baptised by Saint John the Baptist, and about the preaching and work of this Saint John.

At the time when Jesus dwelt in Nazareth, which was during the fifteen years emperor Tiberius Caesar reigned after emperor Octavian under whom Our Lord was born, Pilate was the emperor's prefect in the land of Judea. For the kingdom of the Jews had at that time ceased there, and the Romans divided the kingdom into four parts and lordships with an aim of abasing and subduing their pride. Of these parts two went to Archelaus, namely the land of Judea and Idumea, while his two brothers Philip and the young Herod took the other two. But since Archelaus was a detestable person, the emperor caused him to be exiled and banished. And the land of Judea then began to be governed by Romans officers, the fifth being Pontius Pilate. And he had his sur-name Pontio, which was the name of an isle where he had dwelt. And he was no ordained prince, but since he was the legal vicar at the time he was called prefect of the land of Judea. And Vitellius presided over the other part of the land of Judea, called Syria. And, according to what Josephus says, Abiline was given to Lysanie, nephew of Herod of Ashkelon. And as the Gospel says these things happened at the time of Annas and Caiaphas, two priests of the Law. These two were joined by affinity and the priests' lordship was governed by them; Annas was sovereign priest in the years Our Lord was baptised, and Caiaphas in the years Our Lord was crucified. And the time spent as sovereign priests between each of the two was of three years, during which there reigned and were three other bishops, namely

Ismael, Eleazer and Simon, although their presence is not mentioned. And by the fact that the preaching of Saint John is so solemnly written, namely by the times of emperors, overseers and princes of the law, excellence is shown in him who came to announce the One who was sovereign emperor, overseer and governor of the whole world.

Now then *factum est verbum Domini*, that is to say, divine inspiration was done in Saint John's soul. Such inspiration is called speech for it speaks inwardly to the soul, as the prophet says, *Audiam quid loquatur*, "I shall hear what Our Lord shall say in my soul". According to Chrysostom speech is taken here as commandment, for Saint John was called to such office not of himself but by God's command. This speech was then made upon Saint John, son of Zechariah, who was in the desert and was then thirty years old, which is a fitting age to start preaching since a man would then be in full strength. In baptising and preaching he showed the coming of the Son of God and the redemption and consolation of the people of Israel.

And so that the baptism of those converted by his preach-ing was not to be laid back by a dearth of water, and so that his preaching might have a much greater effect, he departed from the desert where he had now began preaching about doing penance and came into the region near Jordan, where there was an abundance of waters and many people, and there also to baptise and preach the baptism of penance in remission of sins. By this he gave an example to preachers who ought to seek fruitful places to preach the word of God.

Saint John's baptism prepared people to receive Jesus Christ, so that he baptised nobody else than Jews to whom Jesus Christ was mainly promised. And he also baptised those whom he saw to be penitent, for his baptism was an call or a time for penance. Women were not baptised as it was their husbands' duty to teach them; nor were children, since they did not understand the mystery of baptism, about which knowledge is necessary. But the baptism of Jesus Christ is given to all people indistinctly, to all creatures of all ages, in remission of their sins. When he said that Saint John the Baptist baptised in the remission of sins, we should not understand that his baptism gave, and made man have, the remission of sins as does that of Jesus Christ, which is given to all people, small and great. But what this required for the remission of sins was penance, which went together with baptism, for only by penance could one obtain the remission of sins. Remigius, a Church Doctor, says: "The baptism of Saint John referred to the catechumens, for just as now children are catechised to be worthy of receiving baptism, so did Saint John baptise so that those who were so baptised would after be worthy of receiving Jesus Christ's baptism." Chrysostom says: "It is very appropriate then that later the Gospel set and ordained that Saint John preached a baptism of penance, adding *in remissionem peccatorum*, "in remission of sins", just like having said, 'Saint John encouraged the people to do penance so that those who believed in Jesus Christ might sooner obtain pardon for their sins.' For this baptism was none other than a preparation for the faith of Jesus Christ." And yet Chrysostom says: "The baptism of Saint John was given in penance, and that of Jesus Christ from grace. In that of Saint John there is victory, and in that of Jesus Christ pardon."

And it should be noted according to Saint Gregory Nazianzen that there are five methods of baptism. The first was as a figure with which Moses was baptised; and not only was it with water, but in the sea and in the snow. The second was a preparation, of which we now speak. The third is perfect, which is that of Jesus Christ, of the Father and of the Holy Spirit. The fourth is superabundance, which is in the blood by which martyrs were baptised; and it is more noble than the others because it does not continue after men have received it. The fifth is that done in tears daily for actual sins; and it involves much greater pain than the others.

It should also be noted that Saint John baptised for many reasons. The first is to signify that Jesus Christ's baptism, and in like manner his own baptism, was a sacrament. The second, according to Chrysostom, because under the name and shadow of the baptiser more people ought to come to him for showing them Jesus Christ. The third, according to Saint Gregory, so that men should accustom themselves to Jesus Christ's baptism. The fourth, according to Bede, so that people would prepare themselves for Jesus Christ's baptism.

The fifth, according to Saint John the Evangelist, since the Son of God was shown to the people of Israel by the voice of the Father and of the Holy Spirit.

Adaptly, he baptised at the river Jordan, just as saying descent, or that one should descend from the pride of the old man and come to the new and innocent man, Jesus Christ. Being in the desert and by the river Jordan, Saint John then said to them who were moved by his speech and examples, *Penitenciam agite*, "Do penance for the evil you have done in your life, for the kingdom of heaven is approaching for those who do penance." According to Saint Remigius, the kingdom of heaven is called in four ways. That is to say, Jesus Christ is called the kingdom of heaven in terms of what he says to his apostles: "The kingdom of heaven is within you." The Holy Scripture too is the kingdom of heaven, and it is written about this: "The kingdom of heaven shall be taken from you and it shall be given to those who shall make and bring forth fruit." The Holy Church is also said to be the kingdom of heaven, according to what is written: "The kingdom of heaven is similar to the ten virgins." Then the sovereign heaven is called the kingdom of heaven according to what Our Lord says: "Many people will come from east and west, and shall be received in the kingdom of heaven." And may the kingdom be understood and perceived according to these four ways.

Men ought not to be late in doing penance, like those who have been condemned. Neither should he do it by constraint, as thieves do, or feebly like hypocrites, or even in desperation as those who will be lost. But man ought to do it in truth, which according to Chrysostom cleanses the heart and lights the intelligence, preparing man to receive Jesus Christ worthily in his heart. In like manner as Saint Jerome says: "Saint John preached first of all about the kingdom of heaven, because Our Lord's precursor or forerunner was honoured with this privilege." And Peter of Ravenna says that after Adam's sin and the flood, a great multitude of righteous men arose with whom God spoke face to face and was known by them. And because the Doctor had mentioned the patriarchs, fathers and prophets of the Old Testament, he said that none of them paralleled or recalled the perpetual mansion of the kingdom of heaven, nor is anything mentioned in all their writings, for no prophet has ever prophesied about this. "Should you want to hear great things," this Doctor says: "consider and seek all the elect and chosen ones from the beginning of the world to Saint John the Baptist, and neither in their sermons nor in their works will you find the sweetness of this kingdom of heaven." Come then to Saint John and hear the voice of great happiness and gladness, the words of mercy, the sermon of glory, the largesse of grace; that which God had kept secret, the angels close to their hearts and was neither known by the patriarchs nor ever spoken of by the Prophets. He says *Penitenciam agite*, "Do penance, for it is by it that the kingdom of heaven shall draw near to you." Speaking of penance is sweet and glorious, and mentioning the kingdom heavenly is joyful. And it was proper to consider him the first foundation of the New Testament. From the first father Adam to Saint John the Baptist our joy was turned into weeping because sins abounded and there was no place where to go for penance. But Saint John the Baptist showed the medicine for the wounds, or penance for the sinner, and pardon for evildoing. This is the first voice which he proposed in the desert and it is the purr of the turtle dove which is heard in our land. And because of this we ought to chant a new song to Our Lord and to his actions of grace. For mercy is exalted above judgment, sinners are pardoned, piety reigns, justice appears and the sovereign Saviour seeks occasion to pardon and not punish.

The Gospel writes about the needfulness of Saint John to show that he was replete with testimony of the coming of the Son of God. First by the holiness of his life, for he used to wear hair and a garment made of camel skin; in which we are shown that to restrain our flesh we should use hard and thorny clothes. Jerome says: "Saint John wore skin clothing, not woollen clothes. One is a sign of chastity and the other of provocation to lustfulness." Chrysostom says: "It is not proper to the servants of God to have clothing of pleasure and fair in sight and easy to the flesh, but only to cover the naked body. For Saint John's clothing was neither soft nor easy, but hard, sharp and painful, more sickening to his body than nourishing it, thus showing by his garment the virtue in his soul." Secondly, his appearance is shown in that he had a hard and sharp leather girdle around his waist, where the seat of lustfulness resides, thus showing that he crucified and tormented his flesh against vices and lustfulness as this rightly pertains to those who are on Jesus Christ's side. Chrysostom says: "The Jewish custom was to use woollen girdles, and this is why Saint John would choose harder wearing in using leather girdles." Chrysostom allegorically showed that he signified the Law, which was clothed with camel skins, for he might not wear lambskin as it is written: *Ecce agnus Dei*. And he had a girdle around the clothing on his back, for only the Jews reputed it to be a sin to be worn or shaped on the outside. Another thing, Our Lord Jesus Christ, who was seen in the *Apocalypse* amongst the seven lighters or seven candlesticks, had a girdle all of gold, not around his waist but over his breast. The Law is girded at the clothing on the back of the shoulder. But Jesus Christ—that is the Gospel—not only condemns works done outwardly, but also inward thoughts, as all Christians do. Thirdly, he is shown by the harshness of his food, for he eats locusts, that is to say herbs that were so called and in Latin are called *locusta*, and wild honey, being according to Rabanus the white and tender leaves of a certain tree, which when rubbed between two hands have the smell and taste of bees' honey. Or it may have been some juice and sweet liquor which grew upon bright roses or such other herbs. This name *locusta* has many meanings. It means roots, herbs, fowls. But it should not be believed that Saint John ate any flesh, for he ate nothing that touched fire, or bread, or such fare. The blessed Saint John showed very openly in this that he heeded this life only a little, not even by all that belonging to it, seeing that he used so poor and vile clothing and such sustenance pungent in taste. And although he preached about penance, he showed this as a good master in himself by example as to how penitents should live. For the ground was his bed, and his house was wilderness, and if there were any house it was very little, and his clothing was of skins and hard leather, and his drink was water, and *locusta* his nourishment, his girdle made of skin. And by this he not only showed that he had despised the world, but it also seemed that he wept for the sins of all the human race.

We see the true Gospel preacher in Saint John. First, as regards doctrine, for he ought to preach penance and what causes man to leave sin and wakes him to come to the king-dom of heaven. Secondly, as regards appearance, for it is necessary that whoever preaches has a profile, as it appears figuratively in Jeremiah, to whom God said in sending him to preach, *Accinge lumbos tuos*, that is to say "Gird your loins." Thirdly, with regard to life, for whoever preached penance and heard things, giving evil example to others, is unworthy. But he must show in himself the garment of penance, as in thorny clothing and little fare, for a strait example of life is needed to a great extent by the preacher of the Holy Gospel; as the Apostle says, "I chastise my body and clothe myself in servitude, because I preach to others nothing else than what I do to myself, and so to be reprimanded." Saint Jerome says: "Saint John's clothing, nourishment and drink showed how to chastise one's body and the abstinence those who preach the Holy Gospel should have." Chrysostom says: "It is fitting that Our Lord's precursor was like a prophet and apostle, giving the whole of himself to God in despising all worldly things. And it is because of this that he is called angel by God, because living in this world he despised the world while leading an angel's life." "If he who was so pure and clean and brighter than heaven, much greater than the prophets and all men, and so familiar with God, and likewise so chastised his body by the labours of penance, despised his life by being chaste of all carnal pleasure and the world's riches, what excuse might we have that after so many of God's benefits and such great sins as we have committed, we should not follow doing the least element of chastity and penance as he did, but more pitifully banish ourselves into gluttony and drunkenness? But so we leave him in all ways and make of ourselves a bait and prey for the devil."

Then the people, hearing of Saint John's renown, went over to him at the Jordan with many from Jerusalem, and were baptised in the river confessing their sins and believing in their redemption by the coming of the Son of God. For Saint John could not do it, but only announced and prepared them to receive him. Let us similarly take heed of what is written in the *Acts of the Apostles*, that Saint John baptised the people with the baptism of penance saying "I baptise you in the name of him that shall come after me", that is to say Jesus Christ, so that they believed in him. He then saw many Pharisees and Sadducees come to see his baptisms by faction and to the people's dread, and he said to them, "Oh generation of vipers and full of poison, who has taught you to flee God's anger simply by coming and not doing penance?" As though he would say: "I may show you nothing until you leave your sins and your hypocrisy and do penance, for God knows the dishonesty which you do before the people." This was his sharp censured for them that they should leave their sins and return to penance. According to Saint Gregory, God's anger to come is the day of judgment, which the sinner cannot avoid unless he goes back to doing penance. The priests of the Law are called Pharisees, *a Phares*, just as saying a division; for in clothing, in sustenance and in lying they were distinct from others in a feigned sign of greater humility. Sadducees are called so from the name *Sadoc*, the just ones, and they neither believed in the prophets nor in the last resurrection or the angels. And Saint John seeing amongst the Jews these Pharisees and Sadducees as the greatest and most honoured, rebuked them unrestrainedly for their vices and sins and for the poisonous hypocrisy and error found in them, calling them a generation of vipers.

According to Saint Remigius, the custom of holy writers is to write the names of each according to their deeds and works. And since these mentioned above were all poisonous and serpents, Saint John called them sons of vipers. And because they had need of much greater penance and correction than others, he exhorted them to first leave their poison of hypocrisy that they might be worthy to receive baptism, speaking to them in this manner: "Make worthy and acceptable fruits of penance." Chrysostom says: "It is not enough for penitents to leave their sins, but they must make fruit of penance. For it is written, 'Leave evil and do what is good'; just as it is not enough to heal a wound by pulling out the arrow or what is causing the wound with all flesh around it, but men ought to lay balm on it." Saint John did not only say 'fruit' but 'fruits of penance', showing that men ought to do great penance. And he said not 'all fruits', but he said 'worthy fruits of penance', that is to say according to the amount of guilt or sin. For as Saint Gregory says, the greater the evil that a man has done and by which he has offended God and lost good works, so much more ought he force himself to do acceptable works and fruits of penance. And this is written in the Book of the *Apocalypse*: "As much as man glorifies himself and takes pleasure in sin and vanities, so much torment and bewailing comes to him about it." Peter the Chanter of Paris says: "What should happen to him who has fallen in many sins and is always confessing himself and repenting himself and for some time making amends, but not as to the amount or the gravity of the sin? I tell you that each time he repents, you ought to urge him to be penitent or do penance, not too often according to the amount of his sins lest because of the suffering and gravity of the penance he does not leave all undone and let charity grow cold within him. Certainly, it were better for him to pray that he might do the rest of his penance in purgatory than it should cast him in hell in everlasting punishment. For the sin is not forgiven unless penance is done in this world or in another; for certainly it is either God or man who punishes. And if you know, oh sinner, when the confessor gives you penance according to the amount of your sins, you ought to ask him for more and discharge it as you can. For discretion is as much needed by the penitent as by the confessor, and the pain ought to be measured according to the gravity of the guilt."

The Pharisees glorified themselves because of the noble-ness and holiness of their descent, being descended from Abraham, thus presuming they could be saved without doing penance. And because of this Saint John said to them: "Do not say by words and by thoughts in false esteem that your father, from whom you are descended, is Abraham. And owing to this you presume you are just, believing that you may be saved without penance; for no saint may save a sinner without the fruits of penance". In the same manner many Christians, having some special devotion to a saint, believe that by the merit of such saint they may be saved without either doing any good deed or penance. And this is also what some religious say and glorify themselves in about their holiness and the goodness of their founders and patrons and the fathers of their religion, to whom men may say, "If you are sons of Abraham, do Abraham's deeds and works." Similarly this is the glory of some fools and poor souls who glorify themselves only about the state and noble-ness of their parents and friends. Chrysostom says: "What do great nobleness and descent avail him who does not choose to seek the nobleness of a good life? And who might grieve a low degree or descent if he indulges in living a holy life? For gold comes from the earth and yet it is not earth; and gold is agreeable and loved, but earth is dusted off. It is better to be fair and shining by fair virtues and to be of small descent than to be of noble descent and condemned by God. It were better for a man to see how to make his friends glorify themselves in him rather than glorify himself in them. And it is because of this that Saint John said to the Jews: "Do not glorify yourself in your father saying 'We have Abraham for our father'; but you ought to be ashamed that you are the sons of such a father and that you do not follow him in leading a holy life.' It seems that those who do not follow their fathers in goodness are wrongdoers and worthy to lose the dignity of their descent." Certainly, neither vile nor low descent causes any pain in those who are imbued with fair and great virtues. About which Saint Jerome says: "Jephthah is numbered by Saint Paul amongst the holy men, and yet he was the son of an unchaste woman. Esau was of noble descent for he was born of Isaac and of Rebecca, and yet despite all and being of body and soul obstinate and ungracious he showed that nobleness does not principally come from noble friends but more out of the dignity of good works." Our Lord too did not only will to be born of chaste friends, but similarly of unchaste ones, thus giving us great confidence that whether our friends are good or evil we should only follow the doings and virtues of Jesus Christ; and that we are not separate from his body, which is the Church, of which we are members. And yet Saint Paul preached: "If you are the children of Jesus Christ, then you are certainly the children of Abraham and inheritors of the kingdom of heaven." The Jews were the children of Abraham according to the flesh in their body, but not the children of God in imitating Him. And it is due to this that they lost the faith which Abraham had of Jesus Christ, and also that they lost the title and name of being the children of Abraham. To the contrary, the heathens who had devoutly received the preaching of the apostles on the faith of Jesus Christ are made Abraham's children. And because of this Saint John says that God has the power to raise the children of Abraham from the stones which you see. Men say that in a writing Saint John showed with his finger the twelve stones which Joshua caused to be taken out of the deepest bed of the river Jordan by the twelve leading command-ers of the children of Israel, and caused that they were to be carried on dry land, while causing another twelve to be taken from firm land to be cast into the river Jordan instead of the others. The first stones signified the memory that the Jews, who already had knowledge of God, should be dried, whereas the heathens were to come to the water of baptism and immersed in the light of faith while the Jews drowned in infidelity. The heathens are well likened to stones for they worshipped stone idols, but as to God's things they had hearts as hard as stone. They were made children of Abraham when they were united to him by faith, as it is said. Similarly according to Rabanus, the messenger of truth, wanting to incite the Jews to make acceptable fruits of penance, first called them to humility, without which no man may do acceptable penance.

And since the preacher of the truth ought not only to ardently condemn vices, but also show the pain which sin-ners shall have, Saint John showed the reason why man ought to do penance, saying: "The hatchet or axe is now at the root of the tree"; namely the severity of divine justice is now ready to cut off those sinners who are obstinate in this present life and put them in hell to burn. Or that the axe, which stands for the passing of this life, is put to the root of this tree, for as unrestrained as man is born, he awaits and draws near to his death. And according to Saint Augustine, living is no more than passing from life to death. Night and day are like two carpenters cutting down the tree, and no matter how tall and strong it is and the number of strokes it must take, it is at last constrained to fall. And the place where it shall fall and stay shall be either in heaven or in hell. For as *Ecclesiastes* says, in whatever direction the tree falls, whether towards the north wind or the south wind, which is the wind of the rain, or about the middle of the day, it inevitably remains there. The south, as Saint Bernard says, means good things in Holy Scripture, for it means either height or light things; but from the north comes all evil. Man is very much like the tree; then the tree, which is man, is cut to its death. And in what state God shall find him, in the same state and hour He will judge him, either in joy or in pain; and then there shall be no remedy. Now take good heed in which place we fall, for after we are fallen we shall never rise again. And if you want to know on which side the tree may fall upon, consider that side which has the greatest amount of boughs and branches; for the more boughs there are on that side, even the heavier it is, as it will fall on that side if it is chopped with the boughs growing on it. Our boughs and branches are our desires, which we stretch to noon, and that is the day's peak, if we love heavenly and divine things. But if we extend them to matters of the flesh, we will be putting them in the north wind, which is very cold, drawing the body to it and burdening it even more. And Saint John afterwards says, *Omnis arbor non faciens fructum*, "All men generally, without exception of person, who shall not make in this world good fruit, shall be cut down to death from the company of the good, and put into the everlasting fire of hell without remedy."

By this it appears that it is only omission, or leaving to do good things, condemns the person, as we see in the example of the slow servant. And for this there shall be reproach at the day of judgment, or again telling those who are evil about the good they have lost and not done; for it is not enough that a man leaves doing evil, but also that he is bound to do good. God does not like having unfruitful trees in his vineyard or orchard, just as in the earthly paradise there was no other kind of tree but those bearing fruit. And since those who do not bear good fruit are cast in the fire, what shall then be done to him who does evil? Some trees are sterile and unfruitful, like heathens and unbelievers; and some are green, as false Christians; and amongst these green trees there are some who are unfruitful and who bear no fruit, such as those who live in idleness and sloth. Some do bear fruit but not out of merit, but as hypocrites; and some bear fruit all so full of mortal poison, as do heretics who make fruit by preaching that which is condemned; and all these trees have their place in the fire of hell. There are others who bear good fruit, as those true Christians who obey God's commandments. The roots of the tree are the wills or thoughts, from which there proceed both good and evil works, by which we are raised into heaven or else made worthy to descend into hell. And as Saint Ambrose says, do so that you may have the fruit of grace and that you have the fruit of penance; for undoubtedly God will demand either one or the other fruit of you. And so do those who shall bear good fruit, they shall live for ever; and those who are barren and dry, shall be burnt.

The people hearing of the perils of eternal pains both for their sins as well as for not doing good deeds, asked Saint John *Quid faciemus?* or "What shall we do so that we might not be cast into this eternal fire? We are ready to correct ourselves." And Saint John answered them, *Qui habet duas tunicas*, "Whoever has too much clothing and furnishings, ought to give some to who has none, and in the same manner as to food and drink." And it should be similarly understood as to all other things which man has in abundance, for man ought to help his neighbour or fellow Christian in his need according to his status and power. Go look for him who has nothing, or who is in extreme need such that he may not keep on living without receiving a helping hand. If anyone finds himself in such extreme need, then he who has more of something than he needs ought to be aware that it belongs as much to the poor man as to himself. In keeping it for himself he who ought to help the person in extreme need undergoes much greater hassle and exertion, since he is more bound by the commandments than anyone else. For those in great poverty, superfluous or abundant things belong to them as their own. But if anyone is not so poor and in need, that is if he may lawfully pass this cause without being gifted any goods, man is no further bound than to give him advice. Saint Basil says: "We are instructed about this that all that we have in abundance above our needs and what we require for our living, we ought to give to those who have nothing; and we must do that for the love of God who has given all to us" And Gregory says: "For inasmuch as it is written in the Law 'Love your neighbour as yourself,' whoever is a miser does not love his neighbour, if seeing him in this need he does not help him." For in a little thing a man may be a miser, just as much as he may be for a great thing. "He that gives not his gown for the love of God in time of peace, how will he give his soul in time of persecution? For the purpose then that the virtue of charity is not overcome at the time of persecution and that it is nourished by mercy during the time of peace, man ought to learn first to give of his goods for the love of God, and then himself if need be." Augustine says: "Charity is first born, then nourished and made strong, and finally made perfect." And he then says: "I desire to die and to live with Jesus Christ." Then let not those who are rich to be slow in sustaining and helping the poor, for as Chrysostom says, God has made the rich for the profit and usefulness of the poor, whom He might sustain without any help from the rich, who should afterwards be barren and unfruitful if the poor were not.

Saint John did not command those people who could hardly understand anything which was difficult, like fasting in holy eves or such things, but he only encouraged them to make the works of mercy acceptable fruits of penance. This what God would look for on judgment day, as is written about it, *Date elimosinam*, "Give alms and all your sins shall be forgiven." Bede says: "The filth of the sinner is when after penance he hides the works of mercy, for truly penitent is he who covets forgiveness for himself and for his neighbour when he sees him in need. But on the contrary, whoever turns his ears so that he should not understand the poor man's cry, shall have his prayer void before God. And it is about this that Saint John admonished the people to make worthy and acceptable fruits of penance, so that by their barrenness they are not put in the fire of hell. He therefore gave them advice of salvation, saying 'Whoever has two gowns ought to give one to him who has none, and do the same thing with meat and drink'." According to Saint

Gregory it should be here noted it is a great thing to make acceptable fruits of penance to become valuable works of mercy, being commended above everything else.

Not without cause Saint John mentions the gown, since it covers us inwardly and is needed more than the cloak, and similarly the meat which sustains the body and other things. For to make acceptable fruits of penance it would be proper not only to give fellow Christian material things which are only barely needed, but that we share with him what is most needed in terms of what we have to give. And we can argue about this that in being ordained on this matter that if we have two garments we ought to give one to him who has none, then those who have two benefices are more reasonably ordained to give one benefice to him who has none, for it is not lawful for anyone to serve at two altars. By gowns and meat men understand the soul's virtues and Holy Scripture, which is spiritual food, so that whoever has them ought to give from them and do good to his fellow Christian.

The publicans, who collected tributes and other wares, came to Saint John, thus appearing that after people of low status it was the great and the rich who came to be baptised by him. They asked him *Magister quid faciemus* or "Master what shall we do to have everlasting life?" Saint John answered them: "Do not take in you any other learning more than what you are used to as ordained by the Law and approved by customs." He taught them this doctrine since those who were ordained to assert such arguments were often inclined to do more than what they were ordained to do or what was lawful, so that what was additional stayed with them. At first he did not admonish them about giving plenty of alms, but that they keep away from theft and robbery. For first of all a man ought to refund those who gave alms lawfully and justly, as Bede says.

Noblemen and soldiers also asked Saint John, *Quid faciemus*, "What shall we do to be saved?" And he said to them, "Do not suppress the poor who cannot defend themselves, nor should you do any excess or use force against the wealthy when you suspect their false crimes, nor should you subdue them unreasonably so as to have their money and material goods. But you should be content with the fortunes conferred to you to defend good people." Saint John advised soldiers and noblemen about these things, for they were glad to readily suppress a poor man in taking by force his material goods rather than to defend him. Peter of Blois says about this, "Nowadays the doctrine and good status of soldiers has totally vanished and been brought to nothing. In old days both kings and noblemen bound themselves by their oaths to defend the common cause, not to flee in battle, but to use public things for their own proper living. And yet they even more sharpened their swords upon the altar to confess that they were sons of the Church and defenders of the clergy, who are Jesus Christ's noblemen, and of the people, to revenge themselves of evil doers and to keep peace in the land. But now all has been overturned. For as unrestrained as they are honoured with the name of chivalry, they inflate themselves as slanderers or suppressors against the clergy, and strengthen themselves to lay aside the patrimony of the crucifix, and to despoil and take away by their power the goods of poor subjects, and to suppress unmercifully people of low status, in order to whet their appetites and most extravagant wills." And so these ought to fear greatly that in time to come they will not be liked and they will be denied the kingdom of heaven, which belongs to the poor; according to Saint Augustine, they are condemned by the sentence of Saint John.

The noblemen stand for all the preachers of our Holy Mother the Church, to whom the Apostle Saint Paul spoke of armour saying to them, *Accipe armaturam Dei*, "Take the armour of God and the sword, which is the word of God." As though he would say to them: "Do not despise or confound anyone by your sermonising and doctrine, that it may not be so sharp that it puts off people in despair. And also do not be unworthy in uttering your words, and do not cease preaching." And to the religious too who pretend to be mendicants, as well as all others who preach throughout the world, they are told they ought to be content with the wages and monies assigned and given to them by lords and people.

Oh, how fortunate should common people, merchants and others as noblemen also be, if they keep well Saint John's doctrine! But alas, who is he nowadays who gives one gown to the poor although he has two or many more? Who is the merchant who does his business without fraud or cunning? Who is the high official and officer who does not take more than his due? Who is the lord or the nobleman, whether he be great, rich or mighty, who does not suppress or put to grieve his subjects and poor people although they pay him all their dues to the full? Certainly, only a few are found by men.

And it is to be noted that Saint John preached and uttered his words according to his listeners' temperament, hoping that when they should have accomplished the light things which are left, they might return and accomplish the difficult ones which are the hardest and greatest things. Chrysostom says: "Saint John would induce and lead noblemen, common people, collectors and exactors of people's money by his words to great and high perfection. But, since they were not yet good enough nor adequately prepared to understand, he preached to them a light and small doctrine and commands which were easy to follow, that they should apply them even more willingly and with a greater heart." Saint Ambrose also says: "Saint John Baptist gave to all men and to each status an answer, doctrine and proper rule according to how able and knowledgeable his listeners' were, so that all may understand and not forget from then on what they had been told. He told publicans not to take anything belonging to others more than what was their due and was theirs by right. He commanded the noblemen not to be violent or aggrieve others by taking the goods of the poor. And to all in general, be they publicans, noblemen, merchants, officers or other people, he urged them to be merciful, heart-rending and to have compassion and give alms in charity, which ought to be common to all creatures. And also regarding this, he admonished both noblemen and publicans, rich and poor, to give and part with their goods to those who were in need. So that mercy, which is the perfection and fulfilment of all virtues and is formally found at the forefront all virtues, is proposed, preached and urged to all. And in all men discretion and measure ought to be kept in all things, namely in parting with one's goods by giving them to the poor in terms of the extent of one's possibility to contribute." 🐾

CHAPTER 18
ABOUT WHEN SAINT JOHN WAS SENT BY GOD TO PREACH THE COMING OF JESUS

HE cause mentioned by the Evangelist Saint Luke in the previous chapter referred to what had to befall the Word of God as done to him by Saint John, son of Zechariah who was then in the desert. It is what the Evangelist Saint John declared, saying *Fuit homo missus a Deo*, namely that Saint John was "A man who was sent by God," from the desert where he had been before, to baptise and give testimony about the Son of God. Saint John did not take the office of preaching and baptising with any self-presumption of holiness and by his own authority, but he was sent by God to give testimony of the coming of Jesus Christ in majesty and might, since he is the very light of the Father and by Saint John's testimony all should believe in him. And by being truly obedient and well desiring to preach—for he was full of grace as implied by his name—John preceded the creator of grace.

We should know that in the same Gospel the Evangelist calls the Son of God *Verbum, Verbe*, that is the Word of the Father, *et lucem et lumen*. He called him *lucem*, since *lux* is said to be clearness in its singular poverty with none else. But this name *lumen*, light, is said to be no pure clearness, but is joined to other things; and similarly men say that the air's clearness is not *lux* but light. Saint John was sent to give testimony of Jesus Christ in whom human nature is united with the Word, and the Evangelist says here in the Gospel that he was due to bear witness to the light.

Now the Jews recognised and deemed Saint John to be Jesus Christ. And it is for this reason that the Evangelist put away from them their false opinion saying *Non erat ille lux*, "Saint John was not the very light by essence," for neither himself nor any other saint are either the effective light or that created light, but that he was enlightened by him who made the first light. As Saint John witnessed, this light was the eternal true light, without darkness or shadow, or the involvement of any other light. He was light of himself by essence, lighting by his grace all men coming into a world of darkness. For according to Saint Augustine, no man in this world is enlightened by anything else other than this light. And according to Chrysostom, he lights all men inasmuch as is found in him and which belonged to him. And there are some who are not enlightened, but are in a darkness which does not proceed from the nature of the light, but from the evil that is within them. This evil denies and opposes the true light for, in closing the eyes of their thoughts, they will not receive the rays or resplendence of this light. Because of this not all men can be excused if they choose not to receive the light of grace, this being the wisdom of God the Father by which light the world was made.

In mundo erat. "He was in the world as from the beginning," as the cause is in his effect. By this Son of God all things are made, for he shines in all his creatures, whether by creation or by governance. God is in all places present with His might and power, for the Son's virtue shows and extends Him in everything, as a king in his kingdom. He is also present in all places since everything is naked and bare before His eyes. He is also by essence in everything, giving them not only their existence, but also keeping them whole in their beings.

Mundus per ipsum factus est. "The world is made by Him and by His goodness," so that there might be creatures in it to whom he might give his grace. And the world, that is to say the worldly people and their pleasures, have not known him, since the worldly thoughts they have in their hearts do not let them know divine things. But those who were God's friends knew him before his Incarnation. Otherwise the world has not known him, namely man as dwelling in the world who has not known him owing to his rudeness. For although he was in the world universally in all creatures, yet it does not appear that he was known by all. And in order that he might be seen by all men, he came to this world in His own person taking our human nature, in which he has shown himself in this world. And in a special manner he comes into the land of Judea, the people to whom this promise was made. He was in the world because he was God, but he comes by his human nature. For coming and going occurs according to human nature, while being still pertains to the divine. And so ought men understand *Venit*, namely, that he has visibly appeared or that he was seen by all.

Et sui eum non receperunt. "And his, namely man whom he has made in his image, or the Jews, "would neither receive him by faith nor by charity", for a great part of the world was unwilling to believe in him. It is nowadays the same with several clerics who, like lay people, keep themselves away from him and will not receive him; they cast him away from them by their wayward minds even more than secular people.

Morally, God comes in His proper person, for He comes into the souls of those who completely renounce to their own desires by not living in any manner according to their own will or desires but according to God's will. For those who desire to live by their own will and desires, do not receive Him in their soul. And because of this, those who desire God to come into their souls, ought to be the children of God. The Son of God only comes in his own person, yet some—although few in comparison to all—have received him by faith, being devoted in charity and confessing him to be truly God and man.

Yet you may ask, of what profit is to them who receive him in this manner. I tell you that it profits them greatly. For universally, as to all those who have received him without distinction of status or condition of degree or age, they have received him accepting him as the Son of God only by grace and by the regeneration of baptism. They are indeed all those who have believed in his name, and confessed him to be God and man and the true Saviour of the world. For as Saint John says, all those who believe that Jesus is the very Son of God, are born of God. And it should be noted that the Gospel says *Dedit eis potestatem*, "He has given them power." And he did not say *Fecit eos filios Dei*, "He has made them the sons of God." And he did so for many reasons. The first is, according to Chrysostom, to show that with a lot of inquiry and spiritual work man ought to keep the image of Our Lord's begetting without spot or blemish of sin which is taken away from us by the sacrament of baptism. The second cause signifies that nothing may take away from us this power to save ourselves. The third is meant to show that this grace is not given other than to those who desire it and intend keeping it, for it is God's privilege to give His grace and it is by man's will that he joins faith to it. You have seen the fruit we have by the coming of the Son of God, for by him man is made by grace what he might not be by nature; as the Apostle says: "If we are the Sons of God, we are inheritors of his kingdom." Augustine says: "Oh great benevolence. The only Son of God is born and yet never did he have any will to dwell alone. He did not fear having heretics with him, for his kingdom is nonetheless for the multitude of possessors and inhabitants."

And it is for this reason, that no one may think that this nativity came from the flesh, that the Evangelist says this about how we should obtain this begetting. *Qui non ex sanguinibus*; which means that this nativity is not of the seed of man and woman, nor out of sexual desire or lustfulness, namely from woman. For since the flesh has less strength than the bones, let it be understood that the weakest part is the woman. *Neque ex voluntate viri*, that is to say "not from the lustfulness and delight of man." But these are born from God by the sacrament of baptism and by spiritual generation, by which they receive God's grace and spiritual generation and are built up and made partners of divine nature.

Morally, a man may here learn that nothing human or worldly ought to grow in us, so that we may be only born from God.

Accordingly, the Evangelist showed how the Word, being the Son of God, came into this world. For he would not have come had he not existed before, but now began existing in a new form, humbling himself by assuming our infirmity. And this is what he afterwards says: *Et Verbum caro factum est*, "The Word," who is the Son of God, is united and joined to human nature in comprising and intermingling in one person our humanity with his deity. This name *caro* means here a figure of speech called synecdoche, namely taking one part for all, as though according to Saint Augustine he would say, "The Son of Man has soul and body; the Son of God, which is the eternal Word, has taken man as the soul is to the body. For just as the soul with a body does not make two persons but only one man, so has the Word in taking man has not made two persons, but one, Jesus Christ. What is this that is man? It is the reasoning soul having body. What is this that is Jesus Christ? It is the Word and Son of God the Father having man." Chrysostom says: "Because of Adam's sin all men have incurred and deserved the sentence and pain of death, both of body and of soul, so it was necessary that the Son of God took both of them, so that he should save and redeem them both." The Gospel here will name all, in order to show the extraordinary and great union of the Word to man, which is so great that it is not enough for him only to be man and man to be god, but that each single part of the man is separate, both as to flesh and to soul, for each part is the Word. And although the soul is more noble than the flesh, yet the Evangelist names the flesh even sooner than the soul, to explain this union better to us. For a man might have fallen into greater doubt had the Word taken the flesh or the soul.

To speak morally, the Evangelist appropriately named the most vile part to show the marvellous condescension of God's great kindness and humility. He also confounds the pride of many who, when they recount anything about their descent and kinsfolk, first name those being of utmost dignity saying that they are kin to such a rich and mighty man, but speak nothing of the poor who may perhaps be nearer of kin to them than those whom they call. Such as when men tell by example the fable of a horse mule about which someone asked who was the father; and being ashamed to say that the ass was his father, he answered that the king's horse-groom was his uncle.

Et habitavit in nobis, "And the Word dwelt in us." Not that it had taken help or strength from us, but that it dwelt in us in human nature, which he commonly had amongst us And he is supposed to be the Son of God, and dwells with us perpetually. Or he has dwelt in us, that is in this world, according to what Baruch says: In terris visus est, "He has been seen on earth and considered to be amongst men." Which is morally to say that he came into our souls by grace; for seeing that the Son of God has taken our nature, so has the great God come to us and spiritually dwells in us.

Et *vidimus gloriam eius*, "And we have seen and known
the glorious majesty of him being God." Sight here means
as much as bodily vision as the knowledge of understanding. And both Saint John and the other apostles see him
in these two manners, for they see him bodily; and by the
miracles and virtuous works he did and the doctrine he
taught, they knew he was God mingled and hidden under
the flesh. And he exposed this glory which we have seen,
saying *Quasi unigeniti a patre*, "As the truly only son of his
Father"; not by supposing this but by his very nature. And
take heed that this adverb *quasi* points towards truth. And
according to Chrysostom it is a way of speaking, as if one
had seen the king riding in great glory and triumph, and in
recounting to others he might not tell of all the nobleness
and grandeur which he had seen were he to tell it briefly.
But how much more useful it is to say: "He rode like a
king, and so did they who belonged to him"? In the same
manner here, since the Evangelist might not recount all the
glory of the Son of God whom he had seen, he abridged it
saying *Vidimus gloriam eius*, "We have seen his glory," which
is as the angels glorified him, the shepherds saw him, the
kings were led by the star and came to worship him, the
devils were cast out from bodies, the sick were given back
their health, the dead raised, and briefly all creatures have
testified that God himself, the king of angels, has come and
has the glory which belongs to the Son of God according
to his divinity. And he is the only one engendered by the
Father, and is said to be the firstborn in grace, and our
brother too, inasmuch as he keeps us company.

Now it comes to mind that the knowledge which the
apostles had of the Word, who is God, and those who
believed in him, was according to his both natures. And
it is because of this that the Evangelist said: "After the
divine nature we have seen his glory"; and as to his human
nature he later said: "We have seen him full of grace." For
he received all the gifts of the Holy Spirit without measure.
He was full of grace to purge and cleanse sins. He was full
of truth to accomplish the promises.

And it should be noted that this Gospel is of such great
intellectual depth, and that it contains such profound

mysteries, mainly in this clause *Verbum caro factum est*, that Saint John acknowledged that he was unworthy to declare it. And it should not be doubted that the said words are of such a great authority that it is a good and commendable custom that they are said at the end of each Mass. About their great worthiness and virtue, together with certain other things, I shall now recite by example how, in the land of Guiana in France, there were two *demoniacles mendiens*, or demoniacal beggars, and the one seeing that men gave more to his companion than to himself, told a priest secretly, "If you will do what I shall tell you, that is to read in my fellow's ears the Gospel of Saint John *In principio erat Verbum* while I do not hear it, the enemy shall depart from him." The priest considering the great deceit of this demoniacal and with a high voice began to read *In principio erat Verbum*. And when he came to *Verbum caro factum est*, the devils immediately departed and both men were delivered. Moreover, it is said that the devil once told a holy man that in the Gospel there is one word which the devils greatly feared; and the holy man bid the devil tell him which word was that, but he would not tell him. So the good man told him to pick various words from the Gospel, but the devil said that none of them expressed what he was looking for. As it took a long time the holy man asked him whether it was the sentence *Verbum caro factum est*. And the devil did not answer anything but he flew away with a great and horrible cry. It is also read that the devil appeared to an abbot in the likeness of a fair woman, tempting him to sin; and as they were both alone in a herb garden, the abbot suddenly turned tables and thought of the devil's cleverness and deceit. He blessed him and said, "*Verbum caro factum est, et habitat in nobis*". And the devil immediately fled with a horrible roar and noise. We also read of a monk who heard the Gospel *In principio erat Verbum*; and when men came to *Verbum caro factum est*, he neither bowed his knee nor made any sign of reverence. And the devil unrestrainedly laughed at him saying "If it were read that the eternal Word were made a devil, we should never cease kneeling and revering him." So, let us never cease to bow our knees.

Whereby it appears that man ought to hold this Gospel in great reverence. For him to whom it refers, he has mentioned that we have seen him in such manner full of grace and righteousness, that of his fullness we have received all, as have the twelve apostles and all them who are and shall be. And for this we may well say that he is full. Wherefore it comes to mind that in many ways we may qualify this word "fullness". There is a fullness which relates to quantity and multitude, as generally found in the Church according to various persons, to whom God gives many and various gifts. The other fullness or profusion is one that suffices, as found in Saint Etienne and other saints and with every just man according to their capacity. The third is that of prerogative and abundance. And this pertained to the blessed mother of God, who exceeds all saints in gifts of grace. For just as God has set to the Son the virtues of all the stars, so has God set in Mary the virtues of all the saints. And because of this it does not suffice that she has enough fullness unless she has with it an extraordinary prerogative, and this being in such great abundance that she may rebound and float over sinners; and Jesus Christ is the only author of this grace. The fourth fullness is of consummation or of excellence and richness, which was found in Jesus Christ. And Saint John speaks about this, for not only he had the fullness which other saints might have, but he also had a fullness which might rebound and be sown in others. For the fullness of gifts which all those who were chosen had, proceeded from Jesus Christ as from the head to the other parts and members of the body. And he gave grace by little portions, to each one according to his merits. It is the grace of reconciliation and salvation for the grace of faith, by which we believe in him. It is the grace of eternal life for generated and justifying grace. It is the grace of remuneration for the grace of merit. He gave us grace so that by it we should have the glory of heaven, which is the fulfilment of grace. And in short, all this is joined and is given according to generated grace and is grace for grace, according to these verses: *Quidquid habes meriti*, "All this which you have out of merit," the generated grace of God or which was given to you before you came. For God does not crown us but by his gifts. Augustine says: "The grace, for which we have taken the faith of Jesus Christ, is called a grace which has been given willingly; the sinner first receives this grace when his sins are forgiven." "And by this grace, in which we live in the faith of Jesus Christ, we ought to receive another grace, that is to say eternal life, which keeps together the true faith." And it is for this reason that it is said that as we all have had and taken grace from the abundant grace which is in Jesus Christ, we ought to know that just as in a fountain or well that is full and each vessel may draw out as much as it may contain and hold according to its capacity; if the vessel contains and receives but a little, it is not the fountain's fault, since it is full, but it is the vessel's fault. So it is with us, with regard to Jesus Christ, who is the fountain full of life, that we then receive grace from him according to our hearts' capacity. And in the same manner as a vessel that is low and large takes more than one that is high and narrow, so is the heart which is low by meekness and large by charity, more capable of taking and receiving more grace than a heart which is high by pride and strait and narrow by covetousness. And it is not the giver, who is God, who fails but he who receives. Then let us all do what is within our means to prepare ourselves to receive grace by humility and fervent desire. Isidore says: "There is no other thing which sooner causes man to obtain the grace of God and man than to apply himself to keep humility and charity."

Certainly, as Saint Augustine says, this grace was not found in the Old Testament, since they were led by the Law, and sinners were not delivered. The Law only commanded and showed whether the Jews were defeated and guilty, but did not absolve them. It showed the pain, but did not put it away. It brought the sick to the medicine, but had no remedy for their lack of grace and truth. And because of this the Evangelist has undertaken to show the manner of how to receive this grace, saying *Lex per Moysen data est,* "The Law was given by Moses," who was the messenger of salvation. But the grace given with virtue and with the gifts of the Holy Spirit and the sacraments of the Holy Church, and by which man's salvation is made, and the truth which is fully accomplished by figures and promises made in many ways, is given sufficiently by Our Lord Jesus Christ. Augustine says: "The grace, which was promised in the Law and was not obtained, was the death of Our Lord Jesus Christ, who delivered us from eternal and temporal death as regarding many."

The Evangelist yet shows how this grace and truth have been made, when he says *Deum nemo vidit unquam,* "No creature has ever seen God as He is"; namely by conceptual vision. For as Chrysostom says, neither angel nor archangel, cherubim or seraphim have comprehended the essence and being of God, nor has consequently any mortal man ever seen Him. Yet as Saint Gregory says, in this world man may well see Him by some manner of showing and figures, but not in His nature and being. For whoever would contemplate this ought to dwell in this world in such manner that there should be nothing worldly in his heart to delay him or to withdraw his love from God. Otherwise, according to Saint Augustine, man may not attain this vision.

The Evangelist says: "Who is he that can comprehend this grace in order to see God?' And yet later says *unigenitus filius,* "The only son," who dwells in the bosom of his eternal Father and is comprehended as God, who showed to his friends his essence and nature by teaching them the secrets of the deity, as in the mystery of the Trinity and in various other mysteries, which had neither been shown in the Law nor by the prophets in the manner shown by the Son of God. Similarly, as Chrysostom says, "By this he has opened the way of salvation to all those who believe in him"; and Bede says: "The Son of God being man has declared what was to be believed about the unity of the Trinity, and how man ought to prepare himself to come to the contemplation thereof, and by which works a man may arrive there." 🐾

CHAPTER 19

ABOUT WHEN SAINT JOHN CONFESSED TO THE JEWS THAT HE WAS NOT JESUS CHRIST BUT HIS PRECURSOR OR FOREGOER AND MESSENGER

HE Pharisees hearing what the mobs or multitudes said about judging Saint John to be Jesus Christ promised in the Law, both due to his marvellous nativity and to his holy living and because of his wise doctrine, as well as by the new ways of his baptism, rose against him seeing that he had assumed upon himself the office of baptism against the Law and their ordinance. And doubting inwardly whether he was the Messiah promised to them in the Law, they sent to him the lords of Jerusalem and the priests and prelates of the Law to ask him whom he was and why did he baptise. Yet those who were wise, such as the scribes and others, might well have known that he was not Jesus Christ, for then he should have been descended from Judah, while Saint John was from the line of Levy. So then they asked him: "Who are you, what are you?"

These words give rise to four questions which everyone may ask himself, namely about what he is in nature, in person, in form and in stature. Consider then what you may answer God when He shall enquire of you these things. First, what are you in nature. Then you should answer Him that you are three things. According to the body you are earth, and because of this you ought to make yourself lowly against pride; according to the soul you are a spirit, because you enrich what is on high against avarice; you are according to both of these things a reasonable creature, since you live according to reason, which is against lustfulness. And because of this God asks you: "Oh you proud man, what art you?' You are not natural, for now you are not earth because of your humility, but you are air in making yourself great. You are no spirit in seeking spiritual things, but you are flesh savouring worldly things. You are no man using reason, but you are a beast living like an animal.

The second question is what are you in person, and this question shall be answered when you shall knock at heaven's gates saying "Lord, Lord, let me in." And if anyone asks you what you are, you may perhaps say: "I am a Christian." But listen to what Saint Ambrose says: "Those who call themselves Christians and yet do not do the works they ought to do, are liars." Or perhaps you might say, *Amicus sum*, "I am a friend." Now beware if you who are of those God calls his friends, *Vos amici mei estis etc*, "You are my friends if you do as I command you." So if you are neither one nor the other, you are in error. *Amen dico vobis, nescio vos*, "For certain I say to you that I do not know you."

The third question is what are you in form and likeness, in works and methods, both outwardly and inwardly, for you ought to consider diligently how much you profit or not profit at all.

The fourth question is how are you in spiritual status, for you are little as to humility, and whether you are prepared to enter into eternal life by the narrow gate. Also how great are you as to charity, that you might know the place due to you in heaven.

Saint John then argued and showed them that he had confessed the truth, and that he would abide by it and not deny it for then he would have denied and abandoned Jesus Christ who is all truth. And he confessed saying "I tell you that I am not Jesus Christ." It appears here that he answered in a better way as to what his opponents thought than as to what he said. For although they did not exactly examine him if he were Jesus Christ, yet according to Chrysostom they were thinking about it in their hearts, in the same manner as it appeared from the answer he gave them. He confessed that he was not him they were thinking he was, and he denied being what he appeared to be. In meekly acknowledging his own fragility he had leave to be a member and to count among those acknowledging Jesus Christ, rather than to usurp his name undeservedly and to be separated from him.

Saint John's meekness is here to be greatly commended and lauded, for having such great authority, repute and high virtue among the Jews that they believed he was Jesus Christ. And yet he never boasted about this either by way of pride or by usurping his name and honour, for as Chrysostom says, the manner of good servants is not only to usurp the joy and honour which is due to their Lord, but rather that if men offer it to them they should refuse it. Lucifer did not have Saint John's humility, but would usurp and be above the Trinity. He would then be followed by the tyrants of this world who sit in offices and are kept in high renown and are yet unhappy, but by false means and surmises would inflate themselves above their degree and state. Our fore-fathers too, like heretics and men full of worldly wisdom, did not have the humility of not usurping divine wisdom; yet many presently follow them, like those who know more than they ought to know.

However let us consider the marvellous opinion the Jews had in believing that Saint John was Jesus Christ, but still would not believe that Jesus Christ was the Saviour of the world to whom Saint John himself bore record, gave witness and proved by so many signs. And similarly as the Jews tarried about the coming of Jesus Christ, they also expected and waited for Elijah to precede and go before him. And so, hearing that Saint John was not Jesus Christ, they asked him whether he was Elijah, saying "Are you Elijah?' And he answered them, *Non sum*, "I am not." For he was not Elijah, neither in person nor in body, nor in virtues and spirit, in the same manner as Our Lord testified. Yet in his doings John showed great likeness to Elijah; both had spent time in the desert and lived there in chastity and wore thorny clothing. Elijah was to be the messenger of the coming of the great judge; Saint John was the messenger of the coming of the world's Redeemer and Saviour. And just as Elijah had in him a great and faithful love, so did Saint John die for keeping the truth. And they both reprimanded kings and states, not suffering their evil doings. When Elijah was will-ing to depart from Elisha, he went into an earthly paradise departing from the river Jordan; Saint John converted many people by baptising in the river Jordan. When Saint John told them he was not Elijah, they asked him *Propheta es tu?* "Are you a prophet?" By that they were asking whether he was the one whom Moses had told them that God should raise as a prophet of their line, and whom, hearing him, they assumed it was him. But according to the truth although the same prophet was to be Jesus Christ, the Jews understood otherwise in that before the coming of Jesus Christ there ought to come a great prophet. Saint John said to them that he was not this great prophet, not wanting them to misinterpret or think wrongly about him being Jesus Christ, or Elijah, or this other great prophet. All this goes against those who vaunt about the nobleness of their descent, or of knowing, or other things, or virtues which they have.

And it is because of this that they desired and coveted to know instantly who he was, as they would not return without an answering to those who had sent them. Saint John said to them, *Ego vox clamantis in deserto*, "I am the voice that cried in the desert the straight way of the Lord, as Isaiah has said". This was like saying "I am him about whom Isaiah has shown in the Scripture that a voice should cry in the desert of Judea, so that man might prepare himself for the coming of the Son of God." Saint John had the will and an appropriate manner of what was said by that voice. For just as the voice of man is a sign of what he is thinking, so was Saint John a harbinger and demonstrator of the divine word. And just as the voice precedes the speech, so did Saint John precede and go before Our Lord. We call the voice a sound which comes out of the mouth of whoever speaks; yet it is no speech at all, for speech signifies something other than what the voice does not have. Yet the voice is nearer to speech than sound, for first a man hears the sound and then the voice, and afterwards the speech. In like manner Saint John was nearer to Jesus Christ than the other prophets, for whom prophecy was like the sound made by Saint John; for they showed Jesus Christ from afar, but Saint John showed him as being near when he said, *Ecce agnus Dei*. Saint John is then called rightfully the precursor of Our Lord and the voice is that which proceeded from him, seeing that he had preceded Jesus Christ in his birth, baptising, preaching and dying.

Now Saint Luke says the things Saint John cried in the desert, that is to say, *Parate viam Domini*, "Prepare the way of God," as speaking about accomplishing His commandments; *Rectas facite semitas eius*, "Make straight his pathways," as speaking about acting beyond the call of duty as to his place of dwelling, that it may please Him to come and dwell in us. These are the ways and paths by which man may come easily to Jesus Christ and to heavenly bliss, which man can make more straight by avoiding and deliberately avoiding worldly things, than to be in their midst and esteemed as part of them; for a man can very often go astray rather than look straight before him. There are also others in religion who take paths along which they can neither be seen nor perceived, showing outward holiness but being evil within, and never walk straight in their observances and orders or according to the commandments and Gospel ordinances, by which they can amend their life and mould it in God's image. According to Saint Bernard, those who have deferred and abstained from worldly things and grow inwardly in contemplation and have delight in heavenly things, are called straight. He quotes from the *Song of Songs* about this word, *Recti diligunt te*, "Seek and savour that what is earth makes the soul turn away, but it then strengthens itself again when it desires and thinks of heavenly things." How forthright ought the soul be in itself, for man's stature of the body shows outwardly. Saint Bernard says about this: "It is evil to desire having an erect body and a crooked soul. It is a great simulation for man to have his bodily eyes looking high above while his inner intelligence and affections are cast down on earth."

And Saint John afterwards says: "All valleys shall be filled," that is to say that all those who are meek shall be filled with spiritual goodness. "And all mountains shall be made meek," by which it is understood all those who are proud, who lose the grace and glory of God, which is given to the meek. *Et erunt prava in directa*. "The hearts of the evil," which are not very forthright because of their evil affections, "they shall be addressed by the judge of iniquity." And the hope and thoughts and sorrows which clothe those who are without sweetness of heart shall be converted by the infusion of grace to all kindness and sweetness; for the hearts that have thought evil of Jesus Christ shall be made sweet. *Et videbit omnis caro*. "And all men," that is to say many men "shall see God's blessing," who is Jesus Christ, Son of

God, at his first coming. This may also be understood as
the spiritual sight by which those who are converted to
the faith may see him. Or it may also be understood as the
second coming on judgment day, when he shall be seen by
all in human form, by both good and evil, Jews and heathens,
whose vision was denied to the general nature of ancient
men for then all those who existed were Jews or heathens.

Then the messengers and ambassadors of the Jews, hearing that Saint John was none of these three worthy persons
whom they expected him to be, then asked him: "So why
do you baptise and come up with new observances which
are not customary to our Law and usurp another's office
if you say you are not Jesus Christ," who is only empowered to baptise; for "neither Elijah," when passing this river
Jordan did show this baptism; "nor did any other prophet"
to whom the office of baptism pertains, as was the case
with Elisha who sent Naaman to be baptised. Saint John
was precursor of Jesus Christ and he was Elijah in virtue
but not in person; nor was he the prophet whom the Jews
expected but even more than a prophet. And because of that
he was even more entitled to baptise. Yet in answering them
he always gave witness to Jesus Christ, saying *Ego baptiso
in aqua*, "I baptise in water and in penance and not in the
Holy Spirit, by whom the remission of sins is given. I can
teach you to do penance, but I may not absolve you. I am
seen to baptise in water, in washing and preparing only
the body to show you him who is to come, and who ought
to baptise in the Holy Spirit and has authority to absolve
and wash your souls. So have the old prophets not shown
much by their prophecy and sayings, but by their living and
deeds. And it is for this purpose that I baptise in water and
in penance, for by these are souls purged. I wash the body
to justify the use of baptising and in preparing the way for
him who shall come; he who is stronger and more virtuous
than myself, for he cleanses the soul by virtue of the Holy
Spirit. My baptism is imperfect, because it only washes the
body, while true baptism washes both soul and body. And on
this account you ought not to judge my deed as boldness or
presumption, seeing that I only baptise outwardly in water."
Ambrose says: "Saint John immediately proved that he was

not Jesus Christ owing to the different works done by them. And he said that they should well understand that man is made of two natures, that is of the invisible soul and of the visible body. And the visible, which is visible by mystery, ought to be cleansed outside, and that which is invisible by mystery ought to be sacrificed inside. Visible water is what purges the body, and the invisible Holy Spirit cleanses sin from the soul. Now it is in like manner that Jesus Christ cleansed the soul by the Holy Spirit and by the baptism of grace." "And mine is but only the body in shadow and figure of what is a better baptism. And the form and manner of my baptism is 'I baptise you in the name of the Messiah, who is to come hereafter, and who I am not.'"

Saint John's baptism was yet very profitable to man. For although he did not cleanse sins, he nevertheless showed to all those whom he baptised that they were in bondage to sin and that they should seek and ask for him who might cleanse them of it. And because of this he baptised in penance, that is in the manner that they should do penance by confessing their sins, so that they would be unrestrainedly prepared when Jesus Christ came to receive his baptism; thus seeing that they were now accustomed to Saint John's baptism in three things which were profitable to them, namely to accustom themselves to baptism, to amend their lives, and to show and know Jesus Christ.

And yet he afterwards said, *Medius autem vestrum stetit*, "He whom I have shown you stands in your midst, and he is mediator between God and man; and yet you know him not. And therefore by this baptism I prepare you that you might know him." It should be noted here that it is often read that Our Lord Jesus Christ has always exalted and chosen those in the middle, for it is in that place where those who are meek should always be; in the same manner as he said to his apostles: "I am in your midst, as whoever does service stands in the midst of those who are around him." It is also the common place as whoever is in the middle stands equally before all others; and Saint Peter says that God is not a respecter of persons. It is also the place of union, for both ends are joined in the middle; and Jesus Christ is in the middle for as the Apostle says: "He is our peace who has joined together various things into one." It is also the place of stability, since the centre of the world is firm and stable. It is also a place of nearness or of being close, for whoever is in the middle is next to all those who are around him.

And Saint John said about Our Lord, *Ipse est qui post me venit*, "He is the one who comes after me, whom I have shown to you as his precursor." According to Saint Remigius, Our Lord Jesus has come in five ways according to Saint John. First of all, by his birth. Secondly, by his preaching. Thirdly, by his baptism. Fourthly, by his passion. And fifthly, by his descent into the underworld. *Qui ante me factus est.* This distinction *ante* here means order but not time. As though according to Chrysostom he would say: "If I have come before him to baptise, you should not think that I am greater than him. For although he was born after me, yet he is before and above me in dignity and ought to be magnified by me in nobleness and in dignity." And although Jesus Christ was temporal by way of his birth, he now came into this world when Saint John said these words, yet he said that he was to come as referring to baptism, because he had not as yet shown himself either in preaching, or in doing miracles, or in accomplishing the mysteries of our redemption.

Now Saint John showed that Jesus Christ went before him when he said, *Quia prior me erat*, "He is before me not according to the human nature he took in time, but accord-ing to the Trinity from which he comes and exists before all creatures. He is then everlasting before me, for I am in this world temporally. He is Lord and I am his servant. He is an emperor and I am but a nobleman. And for this he is stronger than me, for he is God most strong and mighty and I am but frail and feeble." Rabanus says: "Saint John is very strong, seeing that he is worthy to have the Holy Spirit in him, yet even of greater might is he who had the power to give it to him. Whoever preaches about the kingdom of heaven is very mighty, but much mightier is he who gives it. Very mighty is he who baptises in confession of sins, yet much mightier is he who forgives all sins."

And Saint John says about his dignity, *Cuius non sum dignus*, "I am not worthy to unbuckle or undo the laces of his shoes", a vile and lowly service. It is as though he would have said, "He is so great and much above me in honour that I am not worthy to do him service, nor am I worthy to be called the least of his servants." Saint John here speaks as men do and as when a man humbles himself and gives praise to another, saying "I am not worthy to touch his shoes." For Jesus Christ never wore shoes, and by this Saint John spoke by likeness. And it is no marvel that Saint John spoke these words about himself. For all creatures, however great they might be, are nothing in comparison to God but dust and ashes; nor is any creature worthy to serve Him, unless He assumes him out of his grace. Or according to another way and the exposition of Saint Gregory, the shoe may stand for humanity, the feet for the Trinity and the fastenings the laces binding the shoe to the feet, the union of soul and body to the Trinity; which neither Saint John nor anyone else is worthy or can show. According to Isaiah, who is he that can recount Christ's generation? Saint Gregory also says about Saint John's humility: "We ought here to think how holy men, in keeping in themselves the virtue of humility although they knew marvellous things, have yet always contemplated on how to bring before the eyes of their thoughts what they did not know for the purpose of knowing their own infirmity or frailty, while their souls were not enhanced by any kind of holiness which was in them. And it is for this reason that the soul, willing to keep in it the virtue of humility, renders itself unworthy of anything it does, so that the wind of vanity and of exhilaration does not carry away all the good it may reap."

Oh my brethren, when you do well always evoke and remember the evil which you have done, so that in coming to know how you have offended, you may never inflate yourself after doing any good deed. Consider your neighbours and like-minded fellows, whom you may perhaps see doing any public fault, and yet you do not know the goods which they do secretly. No good deed is to be allowed or is agreeable to God unless it is not seasoned and mingled with humility. Whoever gathers virtues without humility is like a man who carries or gathers dust in the wind.

After that Saint John said, *Ipse vos baptisabit non solum in aqua etc,* "He shall baptise you not only in water, as I do, but also in the Holy Spirit, by giving you the fire of charity, if you receive him as you ought to do. And as to my baptism, it gives none such grace." Chrysostom says: "The baptism of Saint John was one, and the baptism of Jesus Christ was another. For that of Saint John was in penance; and that of Our Lord in gratification and grace, where the Holy Spirit operates like fire, in burning sins and cleansing the filth of the body and soul of all those who believe in it." Bede says: "We are baptised unto God in the Holy Spirit, not only on that day when we are baptised in water and cleansed of our sins, but also from day to day, when by the grace of the said Holy Spirit we are kindled and stirred to do what pleases God." And it comes to mind that there is one baptism which is done in water, one that is done by fire in penance, and one that is done in blood in martyrdom.

And after Saint John had bore witness to the Jews of the first coming of the Son of God, he gave testimony of the second coming in recommending and praising Jesus Christ for the authority he had to judge. And he said, *Cuius venti-labrum est in manu eius. Ventilabrum* is a tool used to cleanse corn and divide it from straw and chaff. For when corn and chaff are one together, it is cast up high and the wind blows away the chaff while the corn stays in place. In like manner Saint John spoke by similitude, intending by wind divine judgment which divides good from evil. And it is in Christ's hand, that is in his power, for God the Father has given all judgment to the Son. *Et permundabit.* "And perfectly shall he cleanse his Church," where now the chaff is with the corn, for good is mingled with evil. And he shall assemble the wheat, which is now shed in many places. Namely that the good, which in the manner of wheat is white inside by cleansing, red by patience, sound and thick by good works, holy in speech and can be multiplied in the conversion of others, is then laid upon his granary or corn cellar, which is his heavenly kingdom; and the chaff, or those who are reproved by pride, made chaff by envy, frail by anger, dry by avarice, unfruitful by idleness, vile by lustfulness, are burnt in an unquenchable fire. In many other things Saint John exhorted and taught the people, so that it appears that not all his doings and sayings are written.

Morally, Saint John taught a manner of living, preaching and being fruitful. He led a hard life as to his food and drink, as nothing could have been harsher or anyone did more abstinence. As to his clothing none could be coarser, nor did anyone lodge in any harder abode than what he had in the desert. His doctrine was truly that of God as his own, for his promises were true. His works were fruitful, for he baptised many people and taught them God's laws. He set an example first for the religious, then for doctors and lastly for prelates.

The aforesaid things were done in Bethany, on the other side of the river Jordan, where he baptised. This Bethany is a day's journey from Jerusalem, but is not the other Bethany near to Jerusalem only two miles away from it and close to the Mount of Olives. For as Chrysostom says, he did not show the coming of the Son of God in one house, nor in one little place, but he went over the river Jordan in the midst of people and in the presence of all those who were baptised by him. And very appropriately he baptised near the Dead Sea at the mouth of the river Jordan where the land of the heathens started and the land of Judea came to an end. This was to show that baptism comes to all and more commonly it was the heathens, who were non-believers, who should receive baptism, then the Jews who ought to believe in God. ❦❦

CHAPTER 20
OF PENANCE, BY WHICH A MAN APPROACHES THE HEAVENLY KINGDOM

INCE in previously recounted chapters we have referred only to some part of the virtue of the sacrament of penance, through which the heavenly kingdom nears to us and is given to man, and the way to receive Our Lord is thereby laid out and prepared; we presently desire, due to lack of fitting speech and insight, a little longer respite.

Whereupon we first ought to know how to do true penance, which is the cause of God's love to man, and the devil's displeasure. There are two things above all else which are mostly required. Namely that the sinner has displeasure for the sins committed and done by him in past time, and that he ought to have a steadfast purpose never to go back to them again or ever commit them any more. For without these two things, full and true penance cannot be done, nor will God forgive these sins, nor might the priest absolve by his might and authority. As Saint Bernard similarly says about this: "True and acceptable penance is done in having continual repentance of past sins, and in sighing and bewailing them in such manner as to have no will to commit them again. For whoever again commits that of which he is truly contrite, pure and has confessed, is only a mocker deserving to renew his confession for being neither penitent nor truly contrite. Oh sinner, then if you are truly penitent, leave your wicked sins and with this advice keep yourself away from sinning any more. For penance is unfruitful and to no effect if it is defiled with any sin which was once abandoned but taken again." And according to Pope Saint Gregory, to do penance is to sigh and wail the sins done before, willing never to do them again. For whoever bewails his past sins and from then on keeps himself firmly away from them, is truly penitent. And Saint Augustine also says: "Penance is in vain and useless if it is still uncleansed and soiled with the guilt of repeated and newly committed sin." What avails weeping, sighing and crying to God for forgiveness, if the sin is still kept and hidden within him? And yet Saint Augustine says: "Oh you penitents, if you still want to be truly penitent and not mockers, you must change your life and be reconciled with God. Do penance. Bow your knees to the ground, hold your hands together though being mocked by all; you do it to arouse God's patience. If you are truly penitent, you shall repent of your sins; if not, you can have no true repentance. And if the evil which you have committed displeases you, why do it again?'

So that man need do penance. Take heed how Saint Augustine says that there are three things of which man ought to repent. The first is of all his past sins and those which he ever did. For this it is what attracts sinners to goodness and makes man to be good and acceptable now to receive the sacraments of the Holy Church. For all existing creatures act out of their free will in coming to the sacraments of the Holy Church. If he does not repent the old life he led before, he may not begin the new one. Only little children who are baptised are exempt from this penance, for they cannot use their free and arbitrary will. Otherwise all others may not come to Jesus Christ's new life without changing their lives and repenting their old life.

The other manner of penance is for man to meekly and patiently suffer the time of this present and miserable life. For one may not perfectly desire life everlasting, if his pleasure and will are found in temporal life. Who is he that ought not belittle the happiness of this mortal life, even sooner and more easily, to arrive to life without end? Who is he who desires to dwell in the heavenly kingdom, if whoever prepared him for it and to do that pilgrimage, is outside it? Who is he who ought not to weep and show by penance that he will dwell there shorn of his old life? Although many do sins that do not wound the soul unto death, yet small sins gathered together may wound it to death, unless men take every day of the medicine of penance. Certainly, whoever considers well and diligently the perils and dangers of this pilgrimage, shall see the difficulty of coming to Our Lord.

The third manner of penance is what men ought to do for the offences which they do against God's commandments. And in this penance and in each one he ought to consider in himself a great oversight, and he ought to judge himself so that he is not judged by God. For if the man who is a sinner ascends in himself to the place and seat of justice, then it is his reason that would be the judge, and his own thoughts and deeds shall accuse him, the conscience will give witness against him, and fear will convict and do execution. And the accused shall give blood for tears. And then the sentence is pronounced, namely that man renders himself unworthy to partake of the precious body of Our Lord Jesus Christ. For similarly as he ought to be separate from the heavenly kingdom by the last sentence of the sovereign judge, so ought he to render himself unworthy to receive the sacraments of the Holy Church for those sins he has previously done. And in these things he ought to judge himself and convert his will and his life into a better one as soon as he could, so that when he could not do it of his proper will, he will not be judged by God against his will. And if you are in bodily or spiritual despair when you are most burdened with your sins, you should still never be in despair about your salvation, and never add one sin to another. As it is written, *Peccator cum in profundum venerit, contempnit,* "On coming to the depth of his sins the sinner is in contempt of the remedies." But he ought to repent of his great sins and ask God forgiveness, in whichever state he might be. For you see that those who are now little and were great sinners, they yet cry for God's forgiveness, and He grants it to them. Easier was what the prophet had said than the humiliation of their penance. For whichever sin you have done while still living, God will banish you for it if you do not pray Him to heal you from it. Therefore subdue yourself, that the patience of God may bring you to penance and endure you to live so long that you may amend your life.

And as said before, man ought not to do penance only for his great sins, but also for the small ones he commits daily. And although they seem little, yet they too ought to be despised. For as Saint Gregory says, no sin is so little but to grow when men attach little importance to it, or considers it as not being an offence. And even more he says: "The sin which is not overcome by penance does not ever cease until it is accompanied." Saint Ambrose says: "The least sin committed with intentionally is more grievous and much heavier than the whole world." And Saint Augustine says: "Do not lay aside your little and small sins. And if you despise them, consider how much they weigh. For many small things make one big thing. Many drops of water fill a great vessel and make a great river; and many grains make a great heap." And for this man ought not to tarry in getting rid of small sins and faults, nor ought man to despair for greater ones. According to Saint Augustine, no sin is mortal when it is repented, nor is any venial sin if displeasure is shown for it.

Man ought to do penance without delay, and as soon as he can, so that he will not be suddenly surprised and may not desire doing it when God will give him no time for it. Saint Augustine says: "Man ought not to defer from converting himself to God, since in his waiting and delay correction does not come to him. For He who has promised to give forgiveness to the repentant does not defer it from day to day, nor does He act with false pretences with anyone." And yet Saint Augustine says: "If anyone decides in extreme need of sickness, or in his death throes, to do penance, and if he reconciles himself to God, and passes away from this world in such state, I confess that he does not deny penance but we will not dare say that he passes securely out of this world. The Christian man who here lives truly and securely, shall certainly pass from here. Even immediate baptism shall certainly dwell and keep him safe. Whoever does penance and reconciles himself with God while still in health, and leads well what remains of his life, shall pass well and securely out of this world. And whoever does penance in his very last days and then changes his way of life, I am not sure whether he departs so surely. And of what I am sure, I give surety, for I give penance but no surety. I say not that it is given him; but I do not affirm that he is saved. Then if you want to put away this danger and if you want to avoid this uncertainly, do penance while you are still in health. For at the hour of death it is too late; and then you have done penance while you might have sinned. But if you will do penance when you may do no more sin, then sin leaves you, and you do not sin. There are two things in your doings, whether God shall forgive you or not. I cannot say which you shall have of those two. Therefore choose what is certain and leave that which is uncertain." Saint Augustine says: "Woe be to those who do penance at the hour of death and not before. For such people feel better in doing penance out of fear of being condemned, than for the love of God. So, do not delay in doing penance while you still enjoy health, and cast out from you sinful works. For according to Saint Augustine, it is a very foolish thing to live in such a state in which a man fears dying. And it is much harder for him who goes to bed with one mortal sin than for who lies with seven of his mortal enemies.

The world often promises a long life for whoever is young, of good demeanour and strong. But these do not know how short their days are, nor do they think about how few are those who die a natural death, while many are those who die by such sicknesses as fevers, tumours and other diseases which often visit man. And yet they believe that every man dies in his best state and time. Hugh of Saint Victor says: "Know you that there is neither a righteous man nor an evil one, neither child nor anyone else, who dies until they are in the surroundings and at the time of either their goodness or utmost evildoing. And no man passes this, whether he lives for a long or short time." Yet many here are deceived by the hope of a long life. And the cause of this Chrysostom says is that "There is nothing that so much deceives man as to trust in a long life." For as Saint Augustine says, we have certain experience that many are deceased and passed away who kept on deferring from moving on the right path. And although it may be that man might live long, yet he ought not to defer doing penance until he becomes old, seeing that in old age man is more feeble to sustain the hardness of penance. For it is painful to find someone old who aban- don the sins he has committed since his youth. Then it is very good and wholesome counsel and wisdom that man ought to prepare himself while he is still in health by true contrition, full confession and sufficient penance to die well. And that he casts away from him all that might hinder him from coming to eternal life. And that he keeps himself at all times in such a state as though he should die on that very day and leave this life. A man may do penance up to the end of his life, for up to that time he may do sin and obtain forgiveness by God's divine mercy, which is much greater than all the evil which he can do. But it is rare that the penance done at the very end is true, considering that at that hour man has no time or capacity to have sufficient repentance of his sins. And sufficient contrition is requisite so that sins may be forgiven, for the anguish, passion and pain in sensitive parts man commonly has at the moment of death, leave the penitent in such state that using his reason he may not be delivered of his sins.

Take heed then of the penance which you must do, and do it gladly in rendering thanks to God who was pleased in His mercy to give you time to do it. And do not be negligent, for you have the present time during which you may still make amends. If you were evil yesterday, be good today.

Think of how many die today who are not lent even one hour in which to do penance, while a longer respite is lent to you. Therefore run fast to the Church and there kneel down before God sighing and with a contrite heart, up to the time when you have obtained God's forgiveness for your sins. And see how you lose your time in eating, drinking, playing, laughing, idle living, which time God has lent you when to seek His grace and desire heavenly joy. And if the love of God does not soften your heart, yet at least be afraid of death's sudden arrival, of the fearful judgment of God and of hell pains, and beware lest you fall there.

Think how in hell souls are tormented, without any hope of ever having mercy. But alas, only a few nowadays keep this in mind, and these are persons who mostly abuse God's mercy and patience on them. Saint Bernard says: "Nowadays the sons of men despise the salvation of their souls, and fulfil the desires of their bodies in all pleasures. And they do not fear committing sin at all but only seek to be in worldly pleasure; nor do they see how they can obtain any virtue of body or soul, but only to have bodily wellness. These people have gone over to the school of Hippocrates and of the Epicureans. Certainly, this time is given to the souls and not to the bodies. It is the time of salvation and not the time to seek pleasure." "There is nothing so precious as time, which is nowadays not endured. As the days to seek salvation pass, we do not take any heed of them. Everyone knows that a lost minute can never again be recovered." So certainly in this life nothing is as precious as time. For in a short while man may obtain forgiveness for his sins and God's grace and glory, and get and deserve more than the whole world's worth; for there is no short time in which man may do spiritual works, which are of much greater value than the whole world's worth.

Think therefore what the world is and that one day doing penance here is more worth than a whole year in purgatory; in the same manner as God said to Ezekiel, *Diem pro anno dedi tibi.* And yet the pain of purgatory exceeds and overcomes all the pains which man might suffer in this world. For as Saint Augustine says, the fire of purgatory exceeds, overcomes and is even harder than all other pains which man might suffer in this world. And therefore man ought to have a much greater mind and be more diligent in leading a good and holy life which is pleasing to God. Seneca says about this: "A man ought to think how he lives and how he might convert himself to a good life, and not to measure his life according to pleasant and merry living, taking no care of the time."

And it comes to mind that penance has three elements, namely contrition of heart, confession by mouth, and restitution by works. Scripture commands that a man should cut his heart and not his clothes, and also that a man confess himself of his sins to another, and that he makes acceptable fruits of penance. For similarly as all sins are committed by the heart, mouth or deed, they rightfully ought to be purged in the same manner. And in acknowledging his sins with all his heart, by word and by deed, the sinner shows himself to be repenting his sins by deeds. These are the three fares and journeys by which a man goes to the promised land. The book of *Exodus* says about this *Deus Hebreorum etc,* "We call Him the God of Hebrews because we go into the desert for a period of three days and do sacrifice to Our Lord God, so that the pestilence does not slay us." The pestilence is the guilt and sin in this present world, or the sword, which stands for the pain in time to come. The Virgin Mary also sought her son during these three days and on the fourth she found him. This ladder had three little ladders which the patriarch Jacob had seen with their upper end touching heaven. God descended this ladder for three reasons. The first was to sustain. The second, to reach out His hand to whoever was climb it, if he need it. The third was for anyone mounting it and feeling weary and over-travelled, that he may behold Him and desire His help, putting all his trust in Him. Certainly, God is not so cruel as to suffer him to fall.

So the first element of penance is contrition of heart, which is a wilful repentance made wilfully for the sins one intends to confess and do restitution for them, since no one is truly contrite unless he is willing to do this. In contrition he ought to remember all his sins distinctly, accuse himself and have repentance of them in the most bitter way, after which he would confess them. Chrysostom says: "Just as in rays or sun beams men see in the air small motes and filth, which without sun beams could never be seen, so there appear many faults in the soul enlightened by its own deliberation. Yet those who live in idleness and do not care about their salvation cannot perceive this."

Now it comes to mind that for every mortal sin a singular contrition is required, if a man can remember them distinctly, as different ointments should be applied for different sores. Contrition is an extraordinary medicine against every mor-tal sin, and if a man asks for how long he ought to have repentance for his sins, his answer might be that when God absolves man of sin and everlasting pain, He binds him to perpetually loathe it. For it is a matter of rightfulness, that whoever has sinned against the will of God, which is eternal and endless, should loathe and repent eternally or for as long as he lives in this world. And for this it is useful and necessary that when a man confesses himself generally, the priest commits him to some perpetual penance, howsoever light it may be, so that by it he might somehow remember his old past sins and so repent.

Everlasting loathing of sin can be done in two ways. One way is having a lasting and actual remembrance of sins; yet although no one is bound by obligation to do this, whoever does it shows a sign of great perfection. It is the same as reading that Saint Peter wept on for ever after denying Our Lord. And Saint David said: "My sins are every day in my mind." The other loathing is endurance, to which one is bound daily after full remission for one's sins. Saint Augustine says about this: "The penitent ought to consider all the fruits of his penance as small, never thinking of having sufficient repentance. And he should always be sorrowful in his heart and joy within him that he can think so. And yet he ought to be sorry that he never had such repentance and ashamed before God whom he has offended." And yet he says even more: "If he is penitent it would be right for him to be continually repentant for his sins rather than have everlasting torments afflicting his soul." Yet nowadays many greatly bewail their sins, neither because they repent them, nor for the love of God, but owing to the ensuing pain. Some also repent their sins because of the sin's uncleanliness and filth. Fruitful contrition is when a man bewails the sins by which he has offended God; then, for fear of judgment, he repents his evil deed. And the more man is truly penitent, so much sooner would God pardon him, as only He can do, for the forgiveness of his sins. By His grace the penitent would then be released from everlasting pain in this world which was due to him for his sins. Now then, mortal sin deserves eternal pain, but it is commuted into temporal pain. Thus, the delightful and unlawful acts of voluptuousness committed by the soul are purged sufficiently enough while it is in this world, and in the other he would not be rigorously judged any more, for no evil goes unpunished. There are two ways of sighing in penance: the first is when we bewail what we have done wrong, and the second when we bewail what we have omitted to do but which we ought to have done.

The second element of penance is confession by mouth, by which the grief that is in the soul is laid open and shown, hoping for forgiveness. Whereupon it comes to mind that there are two confessions. One is called mental, and it is done only before God, being quite natural. The other is called vocal, made to man, and not quite natural. And this is why before the Incarnation of the Son of God mental confession sufficed, as done only to God for God had not yet assumed human nature. But after God became man, He asked why man did not do confession to Him as to man. And since he might not be present with us in his form and nature in all places, he ordained and left men as his vicars. The first was Saint Peter and the other apostles, and then later the priests, saying to them, "Whatever you bind on earth, shall be bound in heaven." And inasmuch as he has given to ministers the power to bind and to unbind, he showed that confession should be done by them like being judges of the Church. And similarly it appears that Jesus Christ has ordained confession to be done and to be kept secret; and after him the apostles stated and showed to all men that confession ought to be done by man as if he were Jesus Christ's vicar, as our sins should be hidden from the devil. Saint Augustine says: "My well beloved brethren, in all Divine Scripture we are admonished profitably and for our salvation that we ought many times and with great meekness to confess our sins not only to God but also to holy men empowered by Him. For God does not want us to confess our sins to Him, as though we had no other remedy, or that we should think He should not know of them, but He desires us to confess to men who are priests. This goes against the devil's will, who desires to know our sins and would not like us to confess so that on judgment day he might accuse us, desiring that we may rather offend that he may accuse us. It goes contrary to our sweet saviour Jesus Christ, who is so merciful that he wills that in this world we should be confessed, so that we are not confounded in another world because of our sins. And since the devil knows of the virtue of true and holy confession, he enforces a man with all his power to delay his confession. And in the same way as he makes man subject to sin, so does he according to his power cause him to refrain and keep himself away from confession, for he knows well that our sins may not be forgiven in any other way." It is more offensive to deny confession than to do contempt to the Law. It is worse not to please God by restitution of the offences which man has done against God than to offend the goodness of God by sin. And although sin is forgiven by contrition, yet vocal confession done in deed is always required. It reminds us of the need of having the confessor, or of man's purpose and will when he is in need, and that no one should hold in contempt the sacrament or the Church. And similarly it is necessary or requisite that the penitent is confessed after having had contrition, but that is not necessary as a remedy but owing to the bond of the commandment.

Confession is appropriately ordained. First, to show that for whoever first had arbitrary will and would not have offended God if he was unwilful and unless he had given his will and consent, it is not in his power after offending to return to God unless he submits himself by humility and devotion to the judgment of his spiritual father in God's stead and giver of spiritual medicine. To him man ought to resort and show his soul's wounds so that as a sinner, and owing to his much greater humility, he receives from another and not from himself the medicine of restitution; for the sacraments are like plasters. And according to Saint Augustine's advice, the penitent ought only put himself under the power of this judge, by reserving nothing, and he ought to be ready to do all that which he is commanded to do in order to receive the life of his soul, just as he would do to flee bodily death. Also, confession is ordained very reasonably since man would be much more prone to sin in not thinking that he would have to show the shame and filth of his sin to another man as himself.

And it is because of this that confession is the beginning of all good works and very profitable to the soul if one goes often to confession, since it often happens in confession that the heart which had before been contrite and which became meek, is confirmed in holiness. And many times it happens that the sinner presents himself before the priest only out of fear or as a custom of the Church so that then, by the power which is given to the priest, he returns contrite and inflamed with charity. It also happens that some return from confession not so fully contrite, yet notwithstanding the penance they have received nourishes in them more and more humility with charity. They would so often abandon sinning because of their shame in confession, since modesty coupled with humility in confession is a great part of penance, and since modesty does not hinder confession. Chrysostom says: "The confession of sins is a sign of a good soul and gives witness to a good conscience and of him who fears God. But whoever fears God has no shame, for it is whoever does not fear the pains after judgment day that is ashamed to be confessed. And therefore shame is a great pain, on account of which God commands us to confess our sins so as to suffer this shame and take it as part of the pain we have deserved by them." Valerius says: "Whoever in his confession looks for no excuse is worthy to receive forgiveness for his sins. And where such confession is made, there is remission. And because of this, modest confession which is done for the love of Jesus Christ is a means of returning to innocence." Saint Augustine says: "Since it is great shame to confess your sins, whoever is ashamed of having offended Jesus Christ, is worthy to obtain forgiveness. And the bolder a man is in confessing the dirt and filth of his sins hoping for mercy and forgiveness, even more easily shall he obtain grace and remission from God." Yet Saint Augustine says, "Oh fool, why are you ashamed to tell to man what you had no shame to do before God? Put away from you all fear and shame, and run to the priest, and show him your secrets by confessing your sins. Otherwise the contrition of heart does not prevail, unless it is accompanied by the confession of mouth (if it can be done)." "For confession, which the enemy detests, is the salvation of souls, the destroyer of vices and restorer of virtues. And it shuts the mouth and enters into hell, and opens the gates of heaven." And Saint Gregory, in praising confession, says: "There are some who are marvelled with the continual chastity of the good; others of the very perfectness of those who are good; and others of the works of piety which the good exercise in favour of Jesus Christ's members. But I am not marvelled by all these things as long as I do them with humble confession and as a sinner who meekly confesses his sins; and that seems to me to be a much greater thing than all other virtues."

And also it is very profitable and to man's salvation that one confesses many times the sins of which he has to be confessed. For although being confessed twice of one sin is not necessary to save man's soul, yet it is much profitable as long as it happens because a man does not know whether in his first confession he had sufficient contrition and repentance. And the greater the humility and modesty a man has in confession, even more merit does he obtain by it. And also by virtue of confession part of the pain which a man deserved for his sins is diminished every day. And definite grace is given to him, as it is becoming that the priest, by virtue of the authority and power given to him, relieves some part of the pain due to the sin that the man confesses. And a man may confess himself so often that he may attain heaven without any pain of purgatory. And although some will say that only the first absolution has effect by virtue of the given key and authority, and that the other absolutions have no effect inasmuch as there is nothing to absolve, yet according to an even more blessed opinion men ought not cast away what I have said, that is that a man may be confessed several times of one sin. For although such "second" absolution finds no sin, yet it finds the pain binding the sinner for his sins. And if it finds no pain, yet it avails and is in itself a growth of grace, both by the virtue of the key and by the person's contrition. What would be best is to go often to confession, for a hundred or a thousand times, until he is relieved of all his pains by his frequent confessing. And it should be noted that the general confession men do at the beginning of the Mass in the *Confiteor* purges and cleanses forgotten venial and mortal sins.

The confessor ought to be wise and well advised in keeping well the secrets of confession, and to keep and take heed that he tells nothing, nor to confess with permission, since according to the commandment of divine law and the Gospel none may be dispensed about this. And if the confessor has no power to absolve the person of the sin which he has confessed, he ought to send him to one who has the authority to absolve him; or else go himself to enquire better counsel about the penitent's deed of conscience. And in this manner, he ought to make him tell his sins out of confession, and then he may tell them to a confessor above his status, asking for his counsel. And know well, all you confessors, that, even by dying in the seat of confession, you may not, nor ought to show by word or sign any person's secret told to you in confession, nor to give away what you know by any sign or means by which a man may perceive what a person has confessed.

The third part of penance is the restitution of the deed, for he ought to make acceptable payment and according to the quantity of the guilt; like Saint John the Baptist admonishes us to do, when he says: "Make good and acceptable fruits of penance." Saint Gregory says: "Saint John did not only say that men should make fruits of penance, but that they should make worthy and acceptable fruits of penance. For in natural law, whoever has sinned but a little ought not to do such great restitution as he who has fallen in great sins, or, whoever has not sinned as whoever has sinned. It so appears that each time after sinning and according to how his conscience judges him, he ought to seek much greater penance and exchange his sins for good works." "And the more he knows that he has coveted things unlawfully and against his maker's will, so much even more afterwards he ought to abstain himself from lawful things, that he may pay back his Creator. For in the same manner as he has committed things forbidden to him, so, if he will make acceptable restitution, he ought to abstain himself from things which he may lawfully do and which are legitimate for him." Saint Bernard says: "Since we abstain ourselves from forbidden things which we have previously committed these are therefore forgiven us." From this it appears that to make acceptable fruits of penance, man must do the contrary of that in which he has sinned. Chrysostom says: "I call penance not only that we leave our past sins, but also the good fruits with which we ought to fill our souls according to the Saint John's reprimand which says 'Make worthy fruits of penance.' And in what manner we may bear fruit? Certainly, we may act in a contrary manner to what brings us to sin. As for example: Have you unjustly taken anything from another? Start giving him of yours. Have you been a dissolute person for a long time? Abstain yourself from things you can do and apply yourself in the little time you have to live to keeping yourself chaste. Have you done wrong to any man, other than by word or deed? Make amends with him as best as you can. And as to those from whom you have unjustly taken anything from them, make your best to make them full restitution, as at one time by rendering them a service and at others by other benefits. For it does not suffice the hurt or wounded person, if he recovers, to pull the arrow out of the wound, but he must also put balm on the wound. If you are ever haunting taverns, pleasures and sports, make recompense for this lingering about by living by bread and water, so that you may deliberately avoid and escape insupportable hunger. Have you intently seen with your eyes the beauty of women? Now take no more heed of them, nor to anything that may provoke you to sin, but do as Scripture bids you by deliberately avoiding all that is evil and doing all that is good, seeking peace and following it perfectly. I do not mean the peace which only ought to be between man and man, but that peace which joins God and man together. This is little found anywhere, and scarcely can a man find on earth such peace, but it is found in heaven, and we may call for it from there. And moreover, we may have it with us if we cast away from us such impediments as anger and pride, with their residue and everything else keeping man from doing good; and so having sweetness and kindness by conserving himself in the poverty of a clean life."

Now it comes to mind that restitution ought to be done with bitter works or with pain, for it must heal the wounds made by sin in sport and pleasure. And the medicines for sins are every bitterness necessary for restitution. Not that we can cast away or expel anything from us by our own ability, but that the sinner, living in his sin, chooses to cast away and not abide in God's love.

And since restitution is a recompense, the penitent ought in doing his penance withdraw from something which might be done to God's honour, even if this is only a goodness relating to God's honour. Now we have but three goods, which are the soul, the body and exterior goods. By giving alms we may arouse fortune's goods, by fasting, bodily goods, and by prayer we submit our souls and all their power to God's mercy. Also, these three ways of restitution are contrary to the three roots of sin. For fasting goes against the lustfulness of the flesh, almsgiving against the lustfulness of wrath, and prayer against pride. Owing to this, as said before, the severity of the penance ought to be according to the quantity of the guilt; this especially against those who have committed great sins and will not sustain but little penance. And because of this, when the priest does not set sufficient penance, or if he sets such penance and it is not fulfilled, then the penitent is not absolved of the pain due to him for his sins. Saint Bernard says: "I do not flatter you, but I tell you that if a small penance is set for him who has grievously sinned, or since the priest to whom he is confessed is ignorant as to set him a penance, or the sinner himself only pretends to make it, then he shall finish the rest of it in the fire of purgatory. For the Lord of all demands worthy and acceptable works or fruits of penance." Which does not only consist in chastising the body or in being in continual penance, but it is measured according to the contrition of the heart, which thing is most agreeable to God. For God, time and its length are not of so great value as pain and labour, nor is abstinence from food and drink of such great value as the mortification or destruction of vices. And for this cause, canons and laws remit the measure of time to do penance to the will of the confessor, who ought to be wise and discrete in curtailing the penitent's time according to the faith and compunction he sees in him. And also, if he sees him to be negligent in doing penance, he ought to prolong his penance according to his discretion. But a penitent's contrition may be so great that it may put away all the pain which due to him for his sin, for the affection of the heart is more acceptable to God than external works.

Now the sinner is absolved of his guilt and sin by external works. Then by much greater reason, by heartfelt contrition and by his affection for God, he is absolved of all his offences. And it is known that the extent of contrition may be understood in two manners. One relates to charity, causing repentance to whoever offends God. This charity means that man does not only deserve being forgiven for his sins, but also being absolved of all his sins. The other manner of contrition is that which provokes and urges the will, as when a man feels outward pain, or in bodily fasting, weeping and undergoing great abstinence. And this pain and contrition may be so great that it may suffice to put away all guilt and pain.

And if a man may not by himself satisfy or make resti- tution for all his sins, seeing that the pain which he ought to suffer exceeds all his ability, he may still do it with the help of others. For this cause God has ordained by His great mercy that, as to the sinner and for the sin, he ought to make restitution. First, by the merit of the passion of Our Lord Jesus Christ, which has not only redeemed the world but has such virtue that its merits are sufficient for all sinners. Secondly, as it is God's will for the sinner to make restitution, the penitent shall have the merit of the Holy Church. Saint Augustine says about this that the alms and prayers which men do in the Holy Church help and sustain the penitent who confesses and acknowledges his faults. Thirdly, since God wills that the sinner is supported and helped by his own satisfaction. And these three things mentioned above, that is the merit of the passion of Our Lord Jesus Christ, and of the Church, and the proper restitution which man does, makes restitution more weighty than his sins. And it comes to mind, according to Saint Jerome, the same way as the devil sees how to make sinners despair because of the great penance which given to them for their sins, he like- wise sees how to cause tem to have a lighter penance that they may not leave their sins. But as the Man of Wisdom says, in such cause man ought not to incline, nether to the right nor to the left.

Now, that you may be even more inclined to do penance, think that if only one sin of our first father Adam had been so strictly punished during the 900 years and more he was in this miserable life, and he had neither help nor comfort of many tools for man's help and succour like we now have helping us, and that after this life he was for a period of 4,000 years in the darkness of limbo, how ought our sins to be punished, being so great and numerous, keeping in mind that the judge to whom we must render account numbers their multitude, weighs their greatness and measures the length of time during which we have dwelt in them? And for this reason a man ought well see how to purchase back or to do penance for his sins, for which eternal pain is ordained unless many good prayers, fasting and good and acceptable restitution are done.

Do think deeply what you have lost by sin and the danger in which you have stepped. You have lost the friendship of the Blessed Trinity, of the angels, apostles and all the saints, the beauty of your soul, the intercessory petitions of the Church. And you have deserved the punishment of your strong and most cruel enemies. You are in a most perilous state. You have lost the grace of God and incurred the death of your soul. You have offended Him who made you and who has suffered death for you, who has given you so fair gifts and yet, after all this, has promised you everlasting life. Certainly, if you constantly meditate on the above things, I doubt not but that you shall entertain great sorrow within you and repentance for your sins.

But still think deep within you that only a few people have learned well how to do true penance. For although many are those who do penance, yet it is not true penance they do. For according to Saint Ambrose, Saint Augustine and others, there are more people who have kept innocence, than those who have done true penance. And because of this, only a few pass from the fire of purgatory. Saint Bernard says: "Feel and judge in him and each one as he will himself, for certainly I have not yet known one true penitent who has deserved in this life not to pass from the fire of purgatory. I believe that God has great mercy on me if I am right up to judgment day in the fire of purgatory to cleanse all the filth of my sins, and then on that day I may come all clean before the great judge." Now you see what hope may miserable sinners have when such a holy man fears in this manner and has doubts about himself.

Then so that you may do true penance and have perfect remission for your sins by it, you ought to be diligent in being circumcised and purged of your sins by confession. Dwell by Joshua's command in the castle of your thoughts up to the time you are perfectly healed. You may do this by eating the bread of penance and repentance alone and without company, in peace and silence, by abstaining from the events and sights of the world and from the company which gives man occasion to sin. Circumcise then all occasion and suspicion of sin, both persons, places and company with whom and with which you have been accustomed to sin. Circumcise your intelligence by which you have infringed Our Lord God's commandments. And enter into the chamber of your thoughts, and close your door against all sinful temptations, and there pray secretly to the Heavenly Father, for a true penitent in doing penance ought not to riot, or run to feasts, or sports, or such similar things. The blessed Mary Magdalene knelt down at the feet of Our Saviour Jesus Christ, washing them with her tears and weeping and drying them with her hair until she heard that her sins were forgiven.

And so that you may not find discomfort in the labour of penance, think and recall the hard and thorny clothing of Saint John the Baptist, and of the food on which he nevertheless lived; and of the labour and weariness of the waking of Saint Bartholomew; the sack and pain of Saint Jerome; the cold and thorny gown and clothing of Saint Benedict; the sweat and tears of Saint Arsenius; the nakedness and habits of Mary of Egypt; and King David's descent from his throne to do penance in ashes and in his heart. Also think of the penance done by Saint James the Lesser who, although he was a holy man who had received the Holy Spirit in his mother's womb and was of such great merit that he was chosen from among the apostles to be the first bishop of Jerusalem since he was reputed holy and called just by all, was certain of eternal life, yet up to the end of his earthly life he persevered and led a hard and sharp life of penance, in such manner that while still living all his members were dead. He drank no wine and ate no flesh, and did other innumerable penances for the love of God; so much so that by continual kneeling, his knees were as hard as the hoof on a horse's foot.

Be consoled by the foregoing and practise them thoroughly. You may learn how you shall do penance in the following verses: *Sit tibi potus aqua*, Oh you sinner who will do true penance and sustain worthy and acceptable pains for the sins you have committed, see that your drink is water, and your meat hard and unsavoury, and your clothing thorny and painful, with rod smiting your back, short sleep and hard bedding. Bow your knee, beat your breast, pray with a bare head, put your mouth to the ground and your mind in heaven, let your heart and tongue be smitten into one; and let your hand be enlarged in gifts, fast often, humble your soul, listen meekly, cleanse your body with a pitiful heart, proper faith, steadfast hope with heartfelt love, always fervently praying all the holy saints for their continual prayers for you. And even still hear you what Saint Bernard says: "The perfect penitent never loses any time; for he recovers past time by contrition; wins present time with good works; and keeps the time to come by firm purpose by doing well." Have then a good heart, be a true penitent and never abandon or leave your good purpose, for those who sow tears in this world shall reap joy and consolation in heaven. Therefore be joyful in your heart when doing your penance; and know that, according to Chrysostom, those who live in penance may be compared to martyrs. Certainly, a long death is of more pain than a long penance. And also Our Lord has pronounced them to be blessed in promising them consolation, saying *Beati qui lugent, quoniam ipsi consolabuntur*, "Blessed are those who now weep, for they shall after be comforted." Our Lord will recompense with perpetual joy those who weep in penance. Cyprian says in praise of penance: "Oh penance! What is there new that I may say about you? You unbind all that is bound, you open all that is closed, you give comfort in all adversity, you heal all those grieved by sin, you make clear all that is dark, and you comfort those who walk along the way of despair." 🐌

CHAPTER 21 ⟨decorative⟩
OF THE BAPTISM OF OUR LORD JESUS CHRIST

HEN the Lord Jesus Christ had accomplished the age of twenty-nine years, which he had lived in great penance and humbling, and close to his thirtieth year at the time when Saint John the Baptist baptised and preached before being sent to prison, he said to his blessed mother that it was time for him to go to glorify and manifest his Father, and to show himself to the world in which he had been a long time unseen and had not shown himself, and that now he would work for the salvation of souls for which purpose his Father had sent him into the world. We here learn according to Rabanus that man ought not to receive holy orders, or preach the Holy Gospel, or hold any dignity in the Church until he attains perfect age. Yet nowadays such persons who cannot even govern themselves are set to govern others, and those who cannot rule themselves are made rulers of the crucifix, and those who were more in need of being governed are set and preferred before all others. For as Bede says, Jesus was baptised in his thirtieth year and began to work at that age and evidently make signs, preach openly and teach people, in showing that man ought not to take holy orders or the office of preaching until the time comes that he is of perfect age. And if any argue that Daniel and Jeremiah had the spirit of prophecy in their young age, I answer about this that man who ought to work miracles are not taken as examples. And according to Chrysostom, Jesus came to baptism at the age of thirty years, since up to that age he dwelt under the Law by fulfilling it in every detail so that, after breaking it by ordaining a new evangelical order, none might say that he had broken it since he could not accomplish it.

Then, reverently taking leave of his mother and parent Joseph, he departed Nazareth and walked a long way bare-foot to the river Jordan, close to Jericho and where Saint John was, and where also men later made a chapel in honour of Saint John. Take heed of him devoutly and have great compassion upon him, for he did not lead a great company of noblemen and horse-grooms, nor did anyone go before him to seek lodging. There is nothing earthly we may have and find delight in it; yet we only see that whoever has mightily in his royal service thousands and thousands of angels goes there all alone and plods on until he is weary. He had said well that his kingdom was not of this world, having emptied himself and not taken upon himself a king's status but that of a servant, showing he had come to serve and not to be served, and that he would be in this world as a pilgrim and stranger to lead us into his kingdom. He would be a servant, so that he would make us kings. He has shown the way by which we ought to walk and to give great praise; and for this we ought to humble ourselves and be eager in fleeing worldly things. The cause why we love this world's honours is for us to set our kingdom in this world, not thinking of being pilgrims and strangers. And this is the reason why we incur or get into so much evil. Since we choose and accept with all our hearts transitory and vain things, casual matters for certainty and the temporal for the spiritual instead of truthful matters.

Jesus Christ then came to the river Jordan where he found Saint John who was baptising sinners. And great people were come to hear his preaching, for they held him in as great reverence as Jesus Christ. The Lord came to be baptised with his servants, the judge with sinners. It was not inevitable for Jesus Christ to be baptised in water, but for making it holy and to confirm Saint John's baptism of preaching. Anselm says: "Oh innocent lamb, Son of God, when the fullness of time comes when you ought to lay your hand to staunch things, in running for the salvation of man along the way of all our misery. First of all, in order to show yourself equal to us or to your brethren in all matters, you have come as a sinner to your servant who baptised sinners in penance, desiring him to baptise you. What need do you have, oh innocent lamb of God, to be baptised? Or what spot of uncleanliness or blemish of sin is there in you? Certainly, this is for no other cause but that the waters should be made holy through you, and not

you by them; and so that in them you may make us holy."
Chrysostom says: "He who ought to give new baptism for
the salvation and remission of the sins of all men, would
first be baptised himself. Not in order to be himself cleansed
of any sins, or to get by it the grace or fortitude of the
Holy Spirit, but so that he would make holy the waters by
which the sins of good believers are washed away. For in no
way might the water of baptism have power to cleanse sins
unless it was before made holy by touching the precious
body of Our Lord. He would then be baptised, so that we
may be washed of our sins. He would take the washing of
regeneration, so that he would be regenerated or begin a
new law by water and the Holy Spirit. For Jesus Christ's
baptism is the cleansing of our sins and a renewal of the
life of salvation. By baptism we kill sin and life with Jesus
Christ. We are divested of the error of the old man and
recovered the clothing of the new man, or law."

Our Lord worked for our salvation, starting his activities
by teaching. In being baptised by Saint John he started at
the port or gate of the sacraments and the foundation of
virtues, saying to him: "I pray you that you would baptise
me with those who are here." Saint John looked at him,
and came to know by divine revelation that he was God
and man, and being greatly marvelled he meekly said to
him: "Lord, it is me who am a worldly man who ought to
be baptised by you who are of heaven. I baptise sinners
in penance. And you, being without sin, why do you want
to be baptised by me, a sinner? For I am man, but you are
without sin, for you are God." Saint Bernard says: "Oh sweet
Jesus, will you be baptised? And what for? Why do you need
baptism? The healthy man has no need of medicine, and
whoever is clean has no need of cleansing. Why should you
have any sin for which you need baptism? What blemish
might the lamb which never offended have?" Chrysostom
says: "It is necessary, Lord, that you baptise me, that I may
be worthy to enter heaven. But there is no reason for you to
be baptised by me, for all the good that is on earth comes
from you, who are from heaven. And there is nothing that
arises from earth, as it does from me to heaven, who am
but earth." Pope Leo said: "O Lord, what will you do? They

stone me to death as a liar, for I have preached and told them great things about you, and you come as a simple person and as a poor passenger! You are in heaven and in earth as a king's son, but nowhere do you show your royal power! Show now your dignity. Why have you come alone in this great humility? Where is the company of angels? Where is the service of the cherubim, with their six wings? Where is the might and authority to judge? You glorified Moses in the clear sky and in the glimmer of fire, but now do incline your head to me. Oh Lord, do not so to me, for you are head of all creatures. You have shown lowly things, so show now high things. Baptise all those who are here present, and me before all. Why will you be baptised, who has no sort of sin's blemish? And if I would baptise you, the river Jordan would not suffer me, for coming to know its Creator it shall turn back its streams and flow backwards."

Certainly, it is no marvel that Saint John was uneasy, for as Saint Bernard says, the head to which the angels pray and is held in high esteem with heavenly power, is feared by princely powers, and inclines itself for the baptism given by Saint John the Baptist; what marvel is it though man dread and fear to touch the holy head of God? Who may think of this and does not fear? Oh, how high shall this head, now so inclined, be in the day of judgment! Our Lord did not scorn the service done to him by his true servant, since he showed him the secret ordinance of his conferment saying *Sine modo*, "Endure for now that I am baptised by you in water, so that after you may be baptised in the Holy Spirit. For all this I do serves as a mystery." In which, according to Chrysostom, Jesus Christ showed that he afterwards baptised Saint John and said, *Sic enim*, "This thing I do, that is being baptised by you, I who am your master. And there is no need for me to be baptised but that I must accomplish all justice." Justice is not taken here as a special virtue contrary to avarice, but for the accomplishment of all the command-ments, showing that true justice is found in accomplishing God's commandments. As though he would say: "I now submit myself to you, for the great are not scorned in being baptised or governed by those who are less than themselves." Chrysostom says: "Not without cause would Our Lord be

baptised, for it was all for us, so that he would fulfil all
our justice and laws. It is a reasonable thing that whoever
teaches others, should first do something himself. And it is
for this that the master and Lord of mankind has come, to
show by his examples what ought to be done, as disciples
and servants ought to follow their master." Or according to
Rabanus: "It would be suiting that I give such an example
of accomplishing all justice by baptism, without which the
gates of heaven may not be opened, and so that man might
know that no one can be perfect unless he first receives the
sacrament of baptism." *Vel: Omnem justiciam*, that is to say a
superabundance of humility, for humility forms the greatest
part of justice. There is one sufficient humility necessary
for all good people, namely for a man to submit himself
to those who are greater than him, and to those who are
equal to him, for the love of God. And abundant humility,
which is to submit himself to his equal and not to exalt
himself above those who are less than him. And a perfect
and superabundant humility is when a man submits himself
to those who are less than him, and not to grow large over
anyone. And Jesus Christ kept these three degrees of humility
in this world and so accomplished all humility. Saint Bernard
says: "There is one straightforward justice, in such manner
that as soon as you turn your feet you fall into the pit of
sin, namely for a man to consider himself above his equal
and to disobey his sovereign. Thus, the definition of this
justice is to render to each one what is one's own. There is
another greater and more open justice, namely not to make
oneself equal to one's peer, nor to be above anyone less than
him, lording over him with a proud stomach. As well as to
submit oneself to being less in status than one's own, which
is full and perfect justice. Then this is what Saint John the
Baptist said, *Ego debeo a te baptisari*, "It is me who ought to
be baptised by you." And this was the first justice, by which
he submitted himself to his sovereign king. But what Jesus
Christ did was a full and perfect justice in inclining himself
under the hands of his servant. Let anyone who follows
him, or whoever so much exalts himself above all that is of
God (this is the devil of hell), take heed that he humbles
himself so much." "O my friend,' Saint Bernard says: "should

you not be subject to God? I tell you that it is but a little thing to be only subject unless by doing this you are subject to all your fellow Christians for His love, for it suits us in order to fulfil all justice." Saint Bernard has ordained and set the fulfilment of justice in perfecting humility. Go now, you man, to him who is less than you are, if you want to be perfect in justice, and honour the poor. For the justice of humility appears in this, so that everyone is given his rights if man does not usurp the honour due to God, nor attribute to himself what is due to another person, but gives praise to God and to his fellow Christians. And in the same manner as an innocent man does not hurt anyone or judge any soul, nor does he consider himself above anyone, so do hold yourself as least of all and always choose and desire the least and lowest place.

Consider and think well how Our Lord's humility kept on increasing in all things mentioned above. For first he was subject to his parents; and here he is subject to his servant, and he made himself little and low while exalting his servant. Until now he was willing to be considered as an abject person who was little endured; here he would be baptised in the presence of sinners, showing himself amongst men like a sinner. So there is no doubt that in applying himself to teaching doctrine and preaching, he should certainly not be despised as a sinner seeing him being baptised in that manner. Indeed, the master of humility would not delay from humbling himself most profoundly! For in teaching us he would appear that he was subjected, humbled and despised. But we act in an opposite manner, wanting to appear otherwise than what we really are so as to be commended by this world. And if we do anything of value, we will immediately let this to be known. And inasmuch as we can, we hide our full guilt. It is by doing this that Our Lord received baptism and would submit himself to the Law which shines on his great humility. For although he was above the Law, yet he sought no extraordinary prerogative in this world.

When Saint John knew that he must accomplish all justice, the Holy Spirit taught him instantly that he could not do this before. So then he would no longer resist, but consented to what Jesus told him; for humility is true if it is mingled with obedience; and so he devoutly exercised his office, which he had refused to do before. Saint Bernard says: "He obeyed and baptised the lamb of God, and washed him in the water."

Now take heed how the heavenly king puts off his clothes, as all others in that company. And the Creator of heaven and earth has in this manner submitted himself for our sake in time of great cold, and entered into the cold water. He did great things in order to obtain our salvation, showing with what joy his servants ought to run to receive the baptism of their Lord, seeing that the Lord wanted to take the baptism of his servant. And because of this no one ought to refuse the coming of grace and penance, for the master of all would not refuse it. He has now espoused the universal Church, for in baptismal faith all faithful souls are spouses of Jesus Christ, similarly as he says by the prophet's mouth: "I shall be your spouse in faith."

Since Our Lord was baptised in water, and water also issued out of his side in his passion, men consecrate baptism throughout all the Holy Church in water. And men neither ought to, nor could they make it of anything else, since it is done this way in all regions. And so that no one may perish in the absence of baptism, and although the Holy Spirit inwardly cleanses the soul, washing by water is still required. For just as man is composed of two elements, body and soul, so is he regenerated by two essential things into a new life, that is by the Holy Spirit and water.

And in the same manner as he was baptised amongst other people, he came out of the water and prayed for those who were yet to baptise, that they might receive the Holy Spirit. And suddenly as he prayed the heaven opened, that is to say that he was shrouded in such a light as though he had seen the heavenly empire open. Chrysostom says: "The heavens were all open at the baptism of Jesus so that you should learn that when you are baptised the same thing happens, which is invisible to you, because God calls you to his kingdom, urging you not to have in your mind any worldly things." And yet the same doctor says: "The Gospel says that heaven was open at the baptism of Jesus Christ, thus showing that it had been shut before." Now the sovereign garden place is united as one with the park here below, which is the world; and it has only one keeper. Heaven has been opened and humans have been accompanied by angels. Bede says: "Jesus Christ, on being baptised and while still in prayer, heaven opened upon him, for when Jesus with the meekness of his body entered into the waves of the river Jordan, he opened to us by his divine power the gates of heaven. And when his innocent body was shrouded with cold water, he slew and restricted the fiery flow in the opposite direction against to our sins."

Bede shows the reason why Our Lord prayed for himself saying "We ought not to doubt that the prayer which Jesus prayed after his baptism, in which was all that pertained to the Father, was for our instruction, to show us that after receiving the sacrament of baptism we ought not to lead a life of laziness, but one of fasting, prayer and almsgiving. For although all sins are forgiven in baptism, yet the fragile flesh is not yet completely purified of sin. And moreover how the children of Israel greatly rejoiced themselves when they saw their enemies drown, and yet they still had to travel much in the desert. Similarly we rejoice in the sacrament of baptism and in the cleansing of original sins, yet we still dwell in the desert of a worldly way of life, where our enemies often come against us. These we ought to overcome by means of the grace of Our Lord Jesus Christ in the sweat and pain of penance, up to when we may come to our inheritance in heaven."

Now the Holy Spirit visibly descended in the form of a dove, and rested upon him sitting on his head for the purpose, according to Saint Jerome, that it would not be thought that it was Saint John's voice which spoke. I tell you that it descended not by grace, since from the time and instant of his conception he was full of the Holy Spirit; but it descended in a visible sign of three causes and reasons. The first, in order to show others that the fullness of grace was in him. The second, to teach that in baptism the Holy Spirit is given to those who truly receive it, and not in a feigned manner. The third, to show that he was baptising by the Holy Spirit purifying all sins.

The Holy Spirit visibly appeared in the form of a dove to show that he was simple, without any filth or distress, and that he loved to abide with those who were sweet, humble and mainly charitable. Chrysostom says: "The Holy Spirit wanted to show himself in the form of a dove, which above all other fowls signifies charity. Throughout all the likeness of justice which the servant of God has according to truth, even the devil's servants may have this in appearance except for only charity, which the evil spirit might not pursue. And this is why the Holy Spirit has reserved the right to show himself in his form, by which charity is meant, for man may not know any better where the grace of the Holy Spirit lies except where there is charity." And according to Chrysostom, this is according to the Old Testament figure. For just as in Noah's flood the dove brought an olive branch to those who were still in the waters in remembrance of God's piety and that He would have mercy on man, so is he present at Christ's baptism, for the Holy Spirit came at the baptism of Our Lord in the form of a dove in sign that God is very meek with those who are baptised, forgiving them their sins and giving them grace.

But every baptised man ought to be filled with the seven virtues as signified by the dove, for a man who is perfect ought to be as perfect with himself as with his neighbour and God. And all these things are meant by the dove's qualities. As to himself, in two characteristics. The dove weeps when it sings and it has no bent for uncleanliness; similarly man ought to have contrition for his sins, and he ought not to have bitterness in him, such as sin, anger and stubbornness. As to his neighbour, he must have three characteristics. First of all, as the dove hurts no man with its bill, in the same manner you ought not to speak evil of anyone. The dove does not snatch anything with its claws; nor should you take anything from anyone else. The dove nourishes the young pigeons of other fowl as well as its own; you too ought to distribute your goods to poor people who are in need. As to God, he ought to have double characteristics. The dove dwells gladly near the water so that seeing the hawk's shadow in the water flying towards it, it may fall in the water and thus avoid the peril; similarly you ought to dwell upon the river or waters of Holy Scripture, that you might take the oil from there and avoid the wiles and deceits of your spiritual enemy. The dove chose the fairest and best green it may find, and always eats clean things; similarly you ought to choose in the Holy Scripture the fair sentences wherein to find your vigour. And just like the dove dwells in a nest in the midst of stones, so you ought to make your nest in Our Lord's wounds.

Et *vox pater intonuit*. And the Father's voice, giving testimony of his Son, was heard from the sky above, saying *Hic est filius meus dilectus*, "This is my well beloved son amongst all others"; for he is not like all others are but he is natural. Chrysostom says: "He is his not by gifts of grace, nor by creature's choice, but he is his by quality of generation and truth of nature." *In quo michi complacui*. That is to say that in him and by him I have constituted and set what pleased me to do and what he must do, namely to redeem man." The other Gospel says *Tu es filius meus dilectus*, "You are my well beloved son, who has ever pleased me," as if to say that "you have always perfectly obeyed and pleased me." Jesus Christ never displeased God his Father, as we do being anger's first children. Saint Bernard says: "Certainly this is him who in no manner may do anything to displease his Father, nor do any offence in the sight of his majesty." For he sees that he always does what pleases him. According to Bede, this splendour and brightness shall endure as long as men hear the Father's voice, for with that voice He will finish and determine things.

According to the Father we are admonished to hear, believe and obey His son, in saying *Ipsum audite*, "Hear him, to whom we ought to believe, as to God's wisdom, justice and truth." Bernard says: "Hear the word of the Father. Oh Lord Jesus Christ, speak now for you are allowed to speak by your Father, you who are the Father's wisdom and truth. Up to when or for how long will you keep yourself shut? How long will you endure yourself being called son of a carpenter, you who are the most noble heavenly king? Oh most high humility of Our Lord Jesus Christ, you shake the peak of my folly and vanity; that with pain I know or do not know, unless I appear as an untutored fellow, so that others judge me otherwise than I am, ready to speak, easy to learn, late in hearing. When the Son of God kept himself shut, he did it in fear of vainglory. What need has he to doubt, he who is the Father's very glory? Yet with doubt he doubted not for himself, but in order to show us that we ought to fear vainglory. He made us and taught us and uttered no single word, but showed by works what he ought to say later by word, namely *Discite a me, quia mitis sum*, "Learn from me, for I am courteous and meek of heart." Very little do I understand of Christ's childhood, for I can scarcely find anything he did up to his thirtieth year of age. But now he may not keep himself hidden or shut any longer, he who is so manifest of the Father." And because of this take an example from him and be silent. For who does not speak about anything, nothing shall vex him. Therefore I advise you that you apply and force yourself to do this. For as Saint Ambrose says, men find more ease in small talk than profit in lots of babble. You now see that in everything the virtue of humility shines in Jesus Christ, which is so great and necessary. And on this account man ought to busily seek and love him perfectly.

In this baptism all the Trinity appeared in a singular manner. The Father in the voice; the Son in unity of substance, that is the Trinity with human nature; and the Holy Spirit in the dove. We say that the body of the Son of God was united to the Son in unity of substance. And neither the voice nor the dove were united to the substance of the Father or of the Holy Spirit; but the dove was only their sign, for the Holy Spirit was in the dove, and the Holy Spirit was no dove nor united to it, for never was creature united to God saving by human nature. Nor also the Holy Spirit was in the dove by grace, but by sign of vision, for it after returned in the same substance it had before. And it is in the same manner that the other figures in which God appeared should be understood. And by such vision of the Trinity as was done at Our Lord's baptism, it was meant that the baptism ought to be conferred in the name of the Father and of the Son and of the Holy Spirit. Yet in the early days of the Church it was given in the name of Jesus Christ only, so that men should hold it in much greater reverence and cast out the error which says that baptism is given in virtue of a mystery and not from God. Similarly, as Saint Paul says, *Ego sum Pauli*. And these causes having ceased, the Church goes back to its first form.

Here we find three effects which baptism endows in terms of the passion of Jesus Christ. The first is to open heaven, for if a baptised person dies, he should and might go straight to heaven. The second effect is the Holy Spirit's mission and his grace which are given when receiving baptism. The third are the Father's words, which regenerated those who were baptised when still children, since the children of anger are made children of grace by baptism. Consider all these things diligently and let your spirit grow in this sweet Trinity in all meekness. And persevere in it that you may obtain the gifts of the Holy Spirit and be worthy of hearing some of the words of God the Father. Anselm says: "The Son of God, bowing himself at the river Jordan under the hands of Saint John, heard the voice of the Father and received the Holy Spirit in the dove, thus showing us that we ought to dwell in meekness of thought, as understood by the river Jordan which is very much of a descent. And there we ought to be honoured with the words of the sovereign Father, who spoke in simple speech, and to be exalted of the presence of the Holy Spirit, who rests upon the meek. And this ought to be done under the hand of Saint John, as if saying he is the one in whom there is grace, since we do not attribute what we receive from God to our merits but to His grace."

Baptism was prefigured or foreshadowed by the brass washbasin standing before the temple in Jerusalem, where priests entering the temple of God were to wash their hands. In the same manner those who ought to enter into the heavenly temple ought inevitably to be washed with the sacrament of baptism. Twelve oxen carry on their back this cistern, as a sign that the twelve apostles ought to carry the sacrament of baptism throughout the whole world. This cistern was all round and set with precious stones, ornate with glasses, so that whoever entered the temple might see on them if there was any filth or defilement. Likewise does baptism require that a man sees through his conscience, has repentance for his sins and contrition of heart. This baptism is also shown in Naaman the leper, who at the command of Elisha had to be washed seven times in the Jordan waters so that his flesh might become like the flesh of a young child. Baptism cleanses the seven capital sins and renders man in a state of innocence. It was also likened to the only passage through the river Jordan which the children of Israel had to pass before entering the Promised Land; so also all those coming into the true Promised Land must first receive the sacrament of baptism. The Ark of the Covenant, which stopped in the middle of the river Jordan, signified Our Lord Jesus Christ who was to be baptised there. And the twelve stones which the people of Israel carried away for perpetual memory signified the twelve apostles who have given witness to the baptism over the whole world.

It comes to mind that Our Lord instituted the sacraments of the Holy Church in various ways. Some were there before his coming, like marriage and penance, and he then confirmed them and concluded them in the New Law by attending the bridal feast and preaching penance. The other five were given to us by Our Lord Jesus Christ himself. These included baptism, which he instituted, confirmed and made perfect both in receiving it and in passing it on to his disciples for them to baptise throughout the whole world, as well by speech, when he said, "He that will not be cleansed by water and by the Holy Spirit will not enter heaven." He also confirmed it and made it perfect, when water and blood issued out of his side, and verbally when after his resurrection he sent his apostles to baptise. He also instituted the sacraments of confirmation when he lay his hands upon the little children; extreme unction when he sent his disciples to give health to the sick and to anoint them with oil; the priesthood by giving power to bind and unbind and to consecrate; and the eucharist when he gave it to his disciples on Maundy Thursday close to his passion.

The sacraments were instituted for many reasons. First, for humiliation; for it takes great humility to covet salvation of visible things which are less than man if kept in their right order and are lost by pride. The second reason is for us to learn; to this end, men were taught and furthered by visible things that they might understand and know invisible things. The third reason is for proper conduct; for seeing that man was affectionately subjugated to corporal things by his sin, it was most appropriate that God would give him spiritual medicine. The fourth reason is as a means of exercise; so that man may let go idleness and evil things, and exercise himself in good works, in hearing Mass, in receiving the eucharist, and doing other good things. The fifth is to receive the proper medicine; for as spiritual refreshment is good for man, it is also fitting that medicine should have some kind of temporal nature such as that it can be seen. The sixth reason and consistency is what is sick in man; for although sickness is found in man in body and soul, the spirit being in the body may not receive spiritual refresh-ment unless it came to it through the body so that it was proper to give spiritual medicines to what is corporal. The seventh reason is for merit to grow; for it is very worthy to increase merit when man believes in God by means of visible things which man's reason may not have perceived.

The sacrament is in things, deeds and words. The sacra-mental elements are water, oil and visible kindred essentials. What is done in baptism is casting water upon the child's head. Each sacrament has its own words which are req-uisite sayings. This word sacrament is none other than a visible sign of invisible grace; as when we see one baptised, the exterior washing of the body, which we see, is none else than a sign of the washing or inward cleansing of the soul in remission of sins, which is not seen. By baptism we are taken out of Egypt, like going through the Red Sea, through which the children of Israel passed and stands for the precious blood of Our Lord Jesus Christ. And since the sacrament of baptism has its excellent power in the death and effusion of Our Lord's blood, in the same way as all other sacraments have, it has the same effect for those who came before the Law and those who have been in the Law. By baptism then God forgives sin, and helps men to resist it and sin no more, and in the end makes them to come to the place where no sin is committed.

The reason why there are seven sacraments and no more, is so that the sacraments are ordained against three manners of wrongs or guilt and four manners of pains. Baptism is ordained against original sin; penance, against mortal sin; the last holy ointment, against venal sin;

confirmation, against lack of strength and feebleness; the order of priesthood, against ignorance; the sacrament of the eucharist, against malice; marriage, against lustfulness, since marriage tempers and excuses such lustfulness. And it is a character or sign in the soul which may never be wiped out, and it cuts off and divides those who do not have it from those who have it; and it is perpetual—but this is not the case in a sacrament which may still be retained as in the sacrament of penance, marriage, the last unction and the eucharist, but it is in baptism, confirmation and priesthood, which are never repeated—like the character or blemish of sin which are imprinted in man, each one receiving the sacrament is distinct and separate from those who do not receive it. A distinction is made by baptism between those who believe and those who do not believe; by confirmation, between the strong and the feeble; by priesthood, between priests, clerics and lay people. And though these three sacraments may not change or be abandoned again because they impress character, yet it applies commonly to all sacraments that none should be removed just because of only one person, a single matter or for only one reason since men should have no doubts, nor should they scorn the sacraments. So that man might not believe that the sacraments which were first given or dispensed were worthless and ineffective. 🐟🐠

CHAPTER 22

OF THE FASTS AND TEMPTATIONS OF OUR LORD JESUS CHRIST

 FTER being baptised the Lord of the whole world, Jesus Christ, departed from the river Jordan fully replete with the Holy Spirit, of whom all of us may be partners. Then with- out any waiting he was immediately led into the desert or wilderness high on a tall mountain or hill called the Quarantania, rising between Jericho and Jerusa- lem and only two miles away from Jericho and twelve from Jerusalem. In past times it was called *Domyn*, that is blood, for thieves dwelt there causing mischief. And it is there that one who was on the way from Jerusalem to Jericho wounded and hurt and sent to be healed in *Domyn*, otherwise called an old farmhouse midway between Jerusalem and Jericho.

He went to the desert for various reasons. First, because he was tempted by the devil, against whom he came out to fight. He also wanted to show that whoever would perfectly overcome the enemy's craft and deceit ought to flee, even with body at times, but always with the soul; and not only from the multitude of enemies, but also the company of evil people, taking example from him who sat royally and was Lord of all peoples. He said, *Ecce elongavi fugiens*, "I have fled and gone to dwell in the desert and in solitude." The second reason was that here he offered his spirit to God his Father in prayer for us, and that by fasting he would leave his innocent body for us, showing us that we ought to offer ourselves to God in fasting and prayer. The third cause was that he would consecrate the life of perfect followers and hermits teaching us, according to Chrysostom, that those who are baptised ought to leave the pleasures and fantasies of this world and evil company, and give themselves to keeping God's commandments. For since the soul is not surmounted nor overcome by the body, it is required to resist the enemy's temptations besides serving God its Creator. Saint Augustine says: "Would you have your body serve your soul, rather than that you make your soul serve God? You ought to be governed by God, that you may govern your body." The fourth reason, in order to give us example as to how to use and do penance. The fifth, to give us an example of how to do penance, for penance ought to be pure and without mingling or meddling with hypocrisy; rather that man ought not to return to that sin for which he has done penance. It is because of this that Our Lord began doing penance immediately after his baptism, which penance ought to be hard and not pleasure-seeking. For, as Saint Augustine says, it is of no avail to fast every day for a long time, if afterwards the soul is brought low by much sweet and delicate food and drinks. And so did Our Saviour and Redeemer show, in the desert place where he was, that man ought to fight hard against the devil in matters of temptation, since our forefather Adam was overcome by delicious things in a paradise of voluptuousness. So be it also that penance should be secret and the penitent ever desires that he would address all his doings according to God's will. I do not belittle that good doctrine so that by foolish presumption and confidence I do not lose body and soul, as it happens to many. It is because of this that Our Lord was led into the desert by the Holy Spirit, for Jesus Christ's human nature was the organ of the divinity, and it is because of this that he continued along his way of doing. And all those filled with the Holy Spirit are sent to fight spiritually and he gives them strength.

When Our Lord was in the desert he fasted without fare for forty days and forty nights. Men added the nights to days to prevent others from saying "If he fasted all day, he must have eaten by night." I say he fasted to give us example that we ought to overcome temptation by fasting. For according to Basil, soberness is necessary for those who want to subdue temptations. And also to show that baptised innocent persons often fall in peril of worldly pleasure; for whoever joins himself by baptism to Jesus Christ ought to chastise himself and crucify his body from all lustfulness and consider himself and be dead here on earth. Chrysostom says: "So that you might learn the goodness that comes from fasting, what a great defence and shield it is against the devil, and that after baptism a man ought not apply himself to former delights and pleasures, but ought to abstain heedfully, Our

Lord fasted although he had no need to do so. For just as when a man wants to heal a sick person he orders him to do what might restore his health, in the same manner is it that after his baptism Our Lord fasted against the vices of extreme gluttony and other condemnable vices. And it was because of this vice of Adam that he was thrown out of earthly paradise; and because of that abominable sin the waters drowned the whole world in Noah's time. By extreme gluttony, or by wretchedness and unclean living, the sodomites were consumed by lightning from above; and so have the Jews incurred much of that vice by drunkenness and pleasures."

For these causes Our Lord Jesus Christ would fast to show us the way of salvation. Saint Ambrose says: "Our Saviour Jesus Christ made this fast for our salvation, so that we should not say that he taught us only by words what is profitable to us, but also showed us in deed. What a Christian are you? Your Lord is hungry, and your larder is full of meat? He has sustained hunger for your salvation, and you think it is painful to fast for your sins?" "Do you know that there is nothing so blinding nor so perilous as the sweetness of this world which, in beginning to make the spirit sweet, puts away the life of grace and makes the soul lose its intellect. And by his fasting and the desert place where he was, Our Lord has appropriately instructed us against the world's voluptuousness. And he wanted to suffer the enemy's temptations to show us that for his love we ought to apply ourselves and endeavour to overcome all voluptuousness and temptations that may visit us."

It comes to mind that Our Lord has received in himself many medicines that he might heal us. He will make us whole by his abstinence in fasting for us for forty days and forty nights. By a medicinal, when on Maundy Thursday he gave his blessed body to his disciples; by sweat, when he effused like drops of blood running to the ground; by plastering, when his glorious face was all scratched, rent and spat upon; by drink, when he tasted vinegar mingled with gall; by privilege, when he was wounded with a spear and nails. Consider here then and behold Our Lord Jesus Christ, for he gives an example of many virtues. He goes alone in the wilderness, he fasts, prays and keeps wake, he lies and sleeps upon naked ground, contenting himself in a lowly and meek way in the company of wild beasts. Anselm says: "Our Lord Jesus Christ, from your baptism you went straight to the desert with a forceful spirit, to the end that man might take from you an example of solitary life; in which solitude you have sustained forty days of harsh fasting, hunger and temptation" "Oh creature, these things are done for you. Love him in his doings he who has done so much for you."

In this place here four things be touched, namely solitude, fasting, prayer and bodily affliction; they marvellously help one another, and we may come to cleanse our heart by them, which we would do well to desire. As said in the dialogue of the Fathers of the Church, all the exercise of monks ought to be for us to be clean of heart, for by that man deserves to see God, as Our Lord says: "Blessed are all those who are clean of heart, for they shall see God." And according to Saint Bernard, whoever is most clear and pure is next to God; and when he is utterly clear and pure, he then comes to God. To have purity is very worthy of fervent and continual prayer, which man might not have with drunkenness and bodily pleasures. And to achieve this it is necessary to fast up to reaching bodily affliction; and for this to be done, solitude is utterly needed. For with pain, loud noise and many words man may not appropriately lift up his heart to God in fervent prayer. And a man hears and sees many people wanting to delay him, and many things he might do without offence, for often the death of our soul enters through our exterior feelings, and it is good to remember that by this bodily affliction and abstinence are often released. Desire solitude then, if you want to be united with God with a clean heart. Also flee loud words, and yourself too. For the goodness coming from peace would be still for some time unless it is to speak good words. Desire no new acquaintance, for new reflections come from them; and flee as from venom all that which may hinder the peace of your soul. Know well that it is not without cause that the holy fathers desired to go to solitary places; and asked those who dwelt in monasteries whether they were blind, deaf or dumb, for by these things they might be united to God. Chrysostom says: "When the Holy Spirit descended upon Our Lord, he went immediately into the desert. Oh, how many monks dwell in that place with their friends, on whom the Holy Spirit descended and tarried, so that they immediately left their friends and were led by the Holy Spirit into the desert? Certainly the Holy Spirit loves not to dwell where there are many people, nor where there is discord, dissent and noise. But appropriately his seat is in solitude. For this cause Our Lord was by day with his disciples and departed from them by night when he would pray to his Father with great vigour. Then if we will pray secretly and not openly, let us keep ourselves shut, get ourselves into a cell and live there in solitude." Augustine says: "My brethren, as soon as we may, let us see how we can bring about an end to all idle distractions, fleeing with all our might the seductions of this world and taking ourselves to some service where we may occupy ourselves in prayer and reading for the salvation of our souls."

Take also the example of Jesus Christ to be meekly familiar amongst wild beasts, as your Lord God did who lived peacefully amongst wild beasts, lions and other cruel beasts; yet the angels preserved him. Expect to willingly forbear those whom you consider unreasonable; for it is very celestial to dwell and be considered amongst people who are like beasts, and to dwell in a hermitage, that is in holy thought and contemplation, reading and prayer, without any meddling with one's life or blemishing it. Bede says: "Our Lord dwelt amongst beasts as man, but the angels administered to him and served him as they would to God. And as for us, in touching the desert of a holy way of life, let us suffer patiently the evil conditions of people who render themselves as beasts by sin; let us deserve being administered over by angels, by whom we may be brought to heaven after our death." Jerome says: "Beasts are at peace with us when the flesh does not go against the Spirit, and angels are sent to bring us joy and comfort." Therefore visit often your Lord in this solitude and have compassion upon him; for ever and in every place, and especially in this place, his life has been very painful and afflictive to his body. For this the devout soul should visit him daily and see his manifestation until forty days have passed, during which he dwelt in this desert, and give over yourself meekly to him.

This number of forty days is sacred in many ways. For God kept the children of Israel in the desert for forty days; for forty weeks he was in his mother's, the Virgin Mary's, womb; for forty months he preached in the world; for forty hours he was dead; for forty days after his resurrection he was in the world with his disciples; and for forty days he fasted, as we have already said. Also, according to Saint Ambrose, for forty days Noah's flood was rising and falling, by which sinners were drowned; and then came the fair clear cloud, meaning that by fasting for forty days sins were forgiven, and God showed his glorious face. Now it comes to mind that forty is set by four times ten; four stands for the New Testament, as contained in the four Evangelists; ten stands for the Old Testament, containing the ten commandments of the Law. From which it appears that fasting for forty days keeps all that which both testaments command. Yet the Church does not begin fasting immediately after the Epiphany, but about forty days after, this meaning that its fasting ought to begin at once after that of Jesus Christ. And it is also appropriate that Our Lord's resurrection should be at the end of Lent. Bede says: "The Lent of fasting was rooted in the Old Testament in the fasting of Moses and Elijah, and in the Gospel in Our Lord's fasting for so many days to show that the Gospel is in no way averse to either Law or prophecies. The Law was found in the person of Moses, and the prophecies in the person of Elijah; between them Our Lord Jesus Christ showed himself glorious upon the mountain, and the saying of the Apostle was verified accordingly that Our Lord Jesus Christ bears testimony to the Law and to the Prophets." And Albin says: "In the same way as Moses made the Law holy by fasting, and Elijah by prophecy, in the same manner Our Lord Jesus Christ has dedicated and made the Gospel preaching holy by fasting for forty days." Augustine says: "Moses and Elijah and Our Lord himself have fasted to show us, in both Moses and Elijah and in the Gospel, that we ought not in any way to conform ourselves in this present world, but that we ought to crucify the old man (which we have from Adam), and not accomplish the pleasures of our bodies and delights. It is most proper that we, who ought to celebrate the passion of Our Saviour and Redeemer Jesus Christ, make a cross in ourselves to rebuke sexual lust, and the Christian ought to keep this cross throughout his whole life. This is not the time in the present life to pull out the nails; the *Psalms* say about this, *Confinge timore tuo*, "Nail my flesh with the nails of your fear." Thus it is necessary for the Christian to nail himself with the fear of Our Lord God." And moreover by this number forty we pay God man's promises and debts. And in doing so in Lent we ought to apply ourselves more to prayer, abstinence and weeping for our negligence in past times. And similarly as we have fallen from the joy of paradise by the food which was forbidden to our first father, inasmuch as is possible we ought to restore again ourselves with abstinence.

Our Lord neither deferred nor prolonged his fasting over forty-one days and forty nights as this would not have been credible because of his human nature, and also to shut away the virtue of divinity from the devil. For Moses and Elijah did fast for as long a time, although they were hungry at times, but Our Lord did not fast beyond forty days. And yet he was not inevitably hungry but it was only because he wanted to suffer hunger to show the infirmity of human nature in himself, and also to give occasion to the devil to tempt him and to show how man ought to overcome the devil. According to Chrysostom, in that he was not hungry for forty days did not follow his human nature, and even to be later hungry did not pertain to God. And because of that, since the devil doubted about the veracity of Jesus Christ, he came to tempt him.

The devil first tempted Jesus Christ by gluttony, saying *Si filius Dei es dic ut lapides isti panes fiant*, "If you are the natural Son of God," and consequently equal to him in power, "bid these stones to be made bread." According to Saint Hilary, the devil did not only want to now whether he was God, but he would entice and deceive him as man with false delights, since owing to his hunger he might make him sin by gluttony. Yet he might not deceive his master since in being tempted Jesus Christ defended himself as not to be overcome by the devil, nor even yet allowed him to be aware of his being in the Trinity. And yet he did not deny that he was the Son of God, nor did he affirm that he was such. However he only warned him by authority of the Holy Scripture saying *Non in solo pane vivit homo*, "Man does not live by material bread alone, but also by all words uttered by God." This was as if he would say he ought not to change these stones into bread "for although I have hunger, yet God sustains or quenches hunger only with His words." This is true not only with regard to spiritual nourishment but also bodily sustenance, as it appears with Moses who fasted for forty days being only sustained by the word of God. Augustine says: "My truly beloved brother, we very certainly know that the same way as the body which is not nourished for a long time with material food is weak and feeble, so does the soul which is not nourished constantly with the word of God." According to Chrysostom, we here remember the Old Testament which ordains us that in whatever thing we suffer, be it fasting or any other thing, that we never ought to leave God.

Jesus Christ had power to change or turn the stones into bread, but he would not do it for five reasons. First, for his divinity to be kept hidden and shut away from the devil. Second, to show us that temptation is much sooner and lightly overcome by humility and wisdom than by power and trust in oneself. Third, that we might learn to flee all pride. Fourth, to despise the tempter's will; for it was not necessary for Our Lord to do a miracle at the devil's will and command, so much so that the devil is overcome when he sees that he is despised. The fifth, to show us that we ought not do anything when the devil entices us.

Morally, the devil many times warns us that the stone, or the hardness of penance, is under some manner in the likeness of discretion converted into bread, that is into carnal delights and pleasures, when he said, "You are now the son of God and you need no more do such abstinence and penance." And so did Ahaz turning Naboth's vine into a herb garden; and Mount Lebanon in being changed into Carmel, meaning moulds or soft earth; such things being often done in honour of high feasts and company. And so too the Jews asked Pilate that Jesus Christ should not remain on the cross on a feastday.

In Our Lord's example, man ought to first of all resist the vice and sin of gluttony, for it is here where man must begin if he wants to subdue the other vices and sins; for we see that whoever is overcome with the sin of gluttony is made very feeble to overcome other sins. Bede says: "A man labours in vain to subdue sins if he does not first learn how to subdue the sin of gluttony." And it is because of this that the enemy first tempted God with this sin; for it is the first temptation that man has from his childhood, after which comes another for no man may live without being tempted. Saint Bernard says: "I want you, my brethren, to be certain that no creature may live bodily in this world without temptation. For if he is delivered of one, he is sure to have another. And when he prays God to be delivered of one, certainly and soon enough another comes." And Our Lord often lets a man tarry in one temptation, so that he may afterwards come out with a greater and more heartfelt desire and repentance due to his very long wait. Or sometimes He delivers him immediately from some temptation, so that he might do good to others men. We are not certain whether these temptations were all done in one day, or on many days and successively, for Scripture does not say anything about them.

And the devil, seeing that he might not in any way overcome Our Lord, according to Chrysostom thought within himself and said, "This man is reputed as a saint. And if saints are not overcome by gluttony, they are very often overcome by vainglory." And so he took him up and carried him into the holy city of Jerusalem, which is called holy since it was cleansed from all idolatry, and the temples and holy things were there, now being called holy for our redemption. Consider here Our Lord's kindness and patience. He suffered himself to bear that cruel beast which desired his blood and that of all his friends, not for lack of ability according to Chrysostom, but by his meek patience. And there is nothing to marvel about, according to Saint Gregory, if Jesus was patient enough to bear the devil, seeing that he suffered to be crucified by the devil's members and servants. And because of this, if we see that Our Lord has been dealt with in such manner, let us not marvel at being tempted. And for so much as he overcame all, we are even more in need of his help, that we may similarly overcome temptation; and also not to be confident in any of our virtues, but to put all our hope, trust and faith in God. According to the *Interpretation*, true to say that the devil appeared in the form of a man; and according to others, that he bore him between his arms; and still others, that he led him by the hand. And the sweet Jesus followed him as a prize-winner going to be tempted in his good will. Yet he did all this in such manner that none saw him. And he set himself on the pinnacle of the temple. Now it should be known that the temple had three mansions: the first was that nearest to earth; the second was thirty cubits high above that; and the third, it was forty cubits high up to the conning tower or rose above; and each mansion had its gallery. And the devil set Jesus Christ upon the highest of all, or upon the lowest gallery, where the scribes and priests sat when preaching the Law to the people. Similarly, the *Interpretation* says that the devil tempted Jesus Christ with vainglory from the place where before he had deceived many.

Then he tempted him for a second time, saying *Si filius Dei es*. The devil thought that if he descended while still keeping himself in mid-air, being the Son of God and the world marvelling to see these things, he would be given an opportunity of vainglory as all the city praises and magnifies him. Truly, it is really a devil's voice and advice to make him descend and not to ascend, and forces man to fall from a height of virtues, but not to ascend to them. But God relieves those who fall by sin.

And the devil said, *Mitte te deorsum*, "Go down to the ground." He showed his powerlessness, for he might annoy no one unless he was at a lower level than himself. Chrysostom says: "He did not say 'I shall put you down,' so that he would not think he was using any force; but he said *Mitte te deorsum*, to show that each one of us falls into sin by his free will, and then falls from sin to death. He may give us occasion to sin, but it is up to us to overcome him and his sweet talking by observing the law."

And since in the first temptation Jesus Christ used the authority of the Holy Scripture, the devil took also the same Scripture authority; not that by doing so he would increase any virtues for himself, but because he would devise errors. And he said, *Scriptum est quoniam angelis suis mandavit de te*, "It is written about you that God has commanded his angels to keep you whole and no stone will hurt you, or cause your hand or your foot any harm." This authority serves a purpose since, according to Saint Jerome, whoever bears all things and is borne by nothing ought not to understand Our Lord Jesus Christ, but he ought to understand and meddle with all those who are of his ilk and like-mindedness. According to the *Interpretation*, such authority ought to be exposed in this manner: "Oh you righteous man, whoever you are, God has commanded his angels, who are created spirits, to carry you in their hands, that is to say that they help you and keep you so, that you might not hurt your feet, that is the affection of your thought, with stone, that is in any sin." Whereby man may know that angels are appointed to protect the life of those who are good and holy in this world. And they have two hands, that is a double power, namely the power of evil, which is the left hand, and the power which promotes good, and that is the right hand.

But the devil interpreted the Holy Scripture falsely and altered its sense, and similarly alleged it imperfectly; for what had been said of Jesus Christ, what comes after must at least show its validity, namely that *Super aspidem et basilicum ambulabis*. The devil is the basilisk and horned viper, the lion and the dragon, those to whom Jesus Christ was subdued in these temptations. And it was because of this that he spoke with great pride of the Scripture as referring to him, and subtly omitted what was between them. Here it was him who was won and overcome by authority of Scripture, for Our Lord tempered his answer since he was hindered by the intention he would have wanted to reach. He said, *Scriptum est non temptabis dominum Deum tuum*, "It is written and told to everyone not to tempt the Lord your God, insofar as in any other way you might avoid it." "I am man, and because of that I may descend by other means without any hasty boasting." God is tempted in many ways, namely by those who want unduly to prove His power, will or wisdom, or in seeing what man can do on his own. We are instructed and taught by this that when man may do something according to human nature or reason, such as giving advice, helping or doing any other good deed, he ought not, so as to avoid the peril of offending God, to omit it, but to do it, while asking God for knowledge on how to perform it. According to Saint Augustine, if man does not deliberately avoid this peril while he may deliberately do so, he would be tempting God and showing lack of trust in Him. For although God has power over all, yet he said to his disciples: "If men prosecute you in any city or place, flee to another." And he himself fled and hid himself. And because of this the proof of furious jealousy is forbidden as being unlawful in the Law. And lacking human reason and prudence, if a man does not know what to do then he must ask meekly for help and ability from Our Lord; not by tempting Him, but by putting full trust in Him, and putting all of himself in the hands of His providence.

Now in descending from the pinnacle Jesus Christ had good ladders by which he might descend from that gallery and come down. And because of this he said to the devil, *Non temptabis*, "You should not tempt your Lord." Chrysostom says: "Our Lord was neither moved nor displeased with this, for he answered the devil with patience and suffering and in no other way, so that we might not act in whatever way we want to show, or entertain vainglory within us." *Et iterum.* "Take heed how Our Lord is not moved at all or angry, but showed and disputed meekly about Scripture with the devil." So endeavour with all your might to conform yourself to your God.

The devil knew well the arms by which he had to subdue the Son of God, namely humility and kindness. So when you shall see any of your enemies or adversaries, take care to overcome them as Our Lord overcame and vanquished the devil. Watch carefully and take heed of Jesus Christ's example in all your temptations, and adorn yourself with the authority of Holy Scripture; so that, if you are tempted with the appetite of honour answer, *Scriptum est quid superbis terra et cinis*, "It is written: "Oh earth and ashes, why do you find your growth in pride?" Life is very short for those who are in this world. If you are tempted with the appetite of riches, answer the way Job did, *Nudus egressus sum de utero matris mee*, "I am come into the world naked, and naked from here shall I go." And if you are tempted by the devil with carnal pleasures and delights, answer, *Caro et sanguis regnum Dei non possidebunt*, "It is written that flesh and blood," that is to say carnal works, "shall not possess the kingdom of heaven." And so may your answer be to other temptations on other vices.

Morally, the devil builds up many in high places that he may draw them to greater sins even more easily; just as the jackdaw carries the nut high up and then lets it fall so that it will crack and break, so does the wrestler heave up his opponent from the ground to give him a great fall. Many are exalted and led to the height of preferment only to be after cast to earth although they would have been secure before in their meek and simple state and having led a good life. Israel's strongmen fell on the mountains of Gilboa. Augustine says: "The higher the place to which a man is elevated, inasmuch more he is in peril." And according to Chrysostom, promotion has caused many prelates to fall. And because of this Our Lord suffered himself to be carried to that place, and did not consent to the devil, to show that prelates ought to resist the devil.

According to Saint Bernard, since Our Lord showed no sign of him forming part of the Trinity, the devil esteemed him and thought that he had been purely human. And he so tempted him the third time as if he were human, and took him from there and carried him and set him upon a high hill or mountain and showed him all the kingdoms of the world. It was as if, according to Chrysostom, a man had been on a high place and shown from far off, being told, "In this part lies Africa and in this other Palestine and other places like them." *Vel: Ostendit.* That is to say, in a moment he exposed and showed him the pomp, glory and magnitude of all the kingdoms and of all that was to be desired in the world, such as delights, riches and honours, so that he might turn and lust for such things and thus overcome him. This word *momentum*, that is the fourth part of an element, or the fourth part of an hour, means the short and transitory nature of the world's things and goods. Ambrose says: "It is well and appropriately said that in an instant earthly and worldly things are shown. In a timely moment they are all vanquished, and the honour of this world is often gone before it even comes." Thus in tempting him with avarice, he promised him easily what he cannot give him, saying *Hec omnia tibi dabo*, "I shall give you all these things, if you will fall before me praying to me." Truly and justly this was a crestfallen scheme for the devil to submit Jesus Christ in such a manner to him. Chrysostom says: "It is nothing that makes man so much subject to the devil than to make him lust so inordinately to the riches of this world, and to be subdued by desiring and coveting it falsely." Ambrose says: "Ambition shown in clothing is like whoever serves himself first then gives to others. And similarly, when he will be the greatest, he shall be made the least. All power comes from God, but ambition and the lust for power come from the devil. And power is not evil in itself but only to him who uses it evilly. So we are taught by this to despise ambition, because whoever has it submits himself to the devil's power." So when you desire to be made great, beware that the devil will show you the world's kingdoms. And if you want to have what you desire, it is necessary that you fall and pray to the devil. For whoever prays or worships him, before falls, and never is the devil worshipped without falling.

By the order of these temptations it appears that the devil started with the highest, and proceeded with even greater ones, and finally with the most grievous one. He began with the sin of gluttony, and after avarice, and then idolatry. And they are well united one to the other, for avarice is none other than serving idols.

But there this liar and murderer was overthrown, it being said that whoever has nothing, promises all things. And Our Lord Jesus Christ, as a most victorious figure, threatening to put him out by authority, said, *Vade Sathana*, "Go away, Satan, into the fire of hell, which is everlasting." We are taught by this how we ought to suffer patiently our affronts and wrongs, and in no way ought we to sustain those done by man to God. Chrysostom says: "When Jesus Christ had suffered these bruises of temptation which the devil did him in saying to him *Si filius Dei es etc*, he was yet not moved by this, nor did he blame the devil for this. But now when the devil usurped the honour due to God, saying *Hec omnia tibi dabo*, "I shall give you all these things if you will humble yourself before me and pray to me," he was then reprimanded most sharply and cast away from him, saying *Vade Sathana*, for by his example we should learn how we ought to suffer our wrongs patiently, and in no way to suffer or hear the grievances made to God. It is commendable to be patient in human wrongdoings, but it is evil to conceal the insults done to God."

After that Our Lord said, *Dominum Deum tuum adorabis*, it is written for all men that "You should pray and worship your Lord and your God, and only do service to Him." According to Saint Augustine, by this man concludes that this is not the service man does to temporal lords; for according to Bede, this should not be understood as the subjection of a person due to someone in a position of excellence.

And although the Gospel sets only three temptations about Our Lord yet, as Saint Bernard says, whoever cannot find the fourth temptation falls in idleness or overlooks Scripture, which says that man's life on earth is not but temptation. And the Apostle says that Our Lord would be tempted with all things.

And Our Lord would be tempted for many causes and reasons. The first, according to Saint Gregory, so that his temptation might deliver us from ours. The second, according to Saint Augustine, so as to give us example to fight against the devil; and by this we are taught that he is not only a mediator in giving us help but also by example. The third, according to Saint Leon, since in vanquishing the devil he would cast away his might and boldness from him. The fourth, according to the Apostle, because he would have compassion on those who were tempted, and would give us hope and stability out of his mercy; for anyone who is tempted usually has piety and compassion of anyone else who is tempted. The fifth, according to Chrysostom, in order to give us courage to endure, and not to be troubled or moved by any temptations which come to us, seeing that Our Lord has been subjected to temptation. There is much anguish which does not come to every man, but mainly to righteous ones. Those whom God loves, He often chastises, so that afterwards, when they shall be proven, they should receive the crown of glory. Ambrose says: "The Holy Scripture teaches you that you ought not only fight against the flesh, but against all that which may take you away from holy and spiritual works. The crown is set as a priority and is ready, but whoever wants to win it must enter battle; for none may be crowned without having first won and overcome, and none may overcome unless he fights. About this crown, the greater the labour the greater its fruit. And because of this we never ought to fear temptation, but we rather ought to glorify ourselves saying that in being tempted we are most mighty. For remove a martyr from entering battle, and take away from him his crown; remove his torments, and you take away the beatitude. We ought not to fear worldly temptations by means of which eternal life is bought, but we ought rather more pray that we may submit ourselves to them, that we may suffer them according to the condition of our human life." The sixth, according to Saint Hilary, is to make us obedient and so that none may be so holy, to presume that he is secure against anguish. And since after baptism and fasting he would be tempted, to show us by this that whoever enters the desert of penance is more strongly tempted by the enemy than any other. It is as Scripture says, *Fili accedens ad servitutem Dei*, "Oh son, in entering God's service prepare your soul for temptation"; that is to say make ready to resist all temptations which may come to you. For after perceiving grace following the labour of penance and desiring to lead a holy life, the tempter will become even stronger and more eager against us to turn and revert us from the good purpose we have begun. Certainly, he tempts more the good than the evil; for as Saint Gregory says, he is not content to tempt those who are his by right. And because of this a man ought to doubt when he is tempted, and even more so when he is not. For according to Isidore, you are grievously challenged by the devil when you are not aware that you are being tempted. The matter of temptation is reserved to true Christians owing to their great usefulness, so that, in whatever holiness abides in man, he should not take any pride in it although he feels his enemy luring him towards it. The seventh is for the purpose of giving consolation to those who were tempted. Jesus Christ was tempted at once after he was baptised, and when he was called son by the Father, and when the Holy Spirit tarried upon him in the form of a dove, and when the heaven was opened over him, and when he had fasted forty days and forty nights. He showed us by this that if anyone is tempted, by this any less cleansed from sin, inasmuch as he is not less worthy from having his descent from God or to be His child, nor being any less filled with the Holy Spirit, or any less worthy to gain heaven, or any less acceptable to God in his penance. And because of this, if you fast and are tempted, do not therefore say: "I have lost the fruit of my fasting," for if it has not been of profit to you since you were not tempted, yet it shall profit you in not being overcome by temptation. The eighth is to the end that when he overcame temptations, he would give us power to overcome them too, as he suffered death to destroy our death. Our Lord readily won and overcame temptations soon enough and at the beginning, for as soon as the devil presented them to him, he immediately resisted them and cast them away from him. And so ought man do in being unable to control himself when he feels being tempted. For as Saint Jerome says, the old serpent, namely the devil, lies in ambush in such manner that if he is not observed by the head, all the body will at once give him away. The hellish serpent has a head, which is evil suggestion; has a body, which is consent; and a tail, which is the deed or actual work done. And where he sets the head of suggestion, he immediately sets the body of consent; and where there is consent, then at once there is the tail of operation and work. And so because of this if his head, or the beginning of everything, is broken or cut off, he may not annoy anyone any more, neither with his body nor with his tail. For when his head of suggestion is cut off, all his strength is lost.

It comes to mind that the devil mostly tempts in six ways: the good, by excitement; the evil, by despair; the idle, by lustfulness; the merchant, by confusion; the judges or lawyers, by cruelty; the merciful, by adulation and flattering. And although he tempts in many ways, yet he mostly deceives in four. The first, in suggesting what is good for an evil purpose; that is when he finds occasion in an instable person who enters in religion, that he may after become an apostate. The second, in saying evil in the guise of good, as to forswear man to keep and not return the goods of others. The third, in opposing good as being something known, as when he opposes any good man from going into religion fearing he might be sorry for it, in suggesting to him that in taking a blind leap and entering religion, he should be confounded; or when he withdraws a man from prayer or almsgiving, as he will recover or receive no vainglory from these actions. The fourth, in withdrawing from evil things since he may suffer worse things after that, such as on with-drawing from inordinate eating and drinking so as to lead himself into indiscrete abstinence, which is a worse thing.

Then all men ought well to take good heed that they are not taken with spies and liars who serve the devil, and that they are not ensnared in his wills, which wills or dupes he spreads all around in various ways. Pope Leo says: "The enemy, our adversary, who changes himself into an angel's likeness, never stops, but in all places spreads his nets of deceit and beguilement. He knows men well, so he will inflame them with the fire of cupidity, he will make them fall in gluttony, he will move them in lustfulness, he will shed upon them the venom of anger and wrath, he will vex by inordinate fear and worry. He searches every man's conditions, and whenever he sees anyone most virtuously occupied with his inner self, he sets his affections upon him and begins to annoy him most."

And when all the temptation which Lucifer had come to entice was consumed and subdued, and not knowing what he ought to do on hearing the name of God, he left Jesus Christ, whom he had yet never made to fall, and departed from him until some other time. According to Chrysostom, the devil did not depart out of obedience, but the Trinity of Jesus Christ and the Holy Spirit which was in him cast away the devil from there, and this was profitable for our consolation; for the devil does not tempt man as much as he wants, but as much as God suffers him to do so. And if God suffers him at all to tempt us, this is done for our profit and the salvation of our soul. And when he sees that the time has come, He makes him cease owing to our infirmity and debility, for He never suffers us to be tempted any more than we can endure. Saint Augustine says: "If the devil were to annoy man as much as he desires, no righteous man would be left on earth."

In the three aforesaid temptations, yet in which the Christian battles, all temptation is consumed. For in these three, namely gluttony, pride and covetousness, all kinds of sin and vice are contained from which man ought to keep himself well away from their very beginning. For as Saint John says, all that is in this world is lustfulness of the flesh, or lustfulness of the eyes, or a proud life; and against these three arrows thrown by our enemy we must put up three shields to block them, that is fasting against lustfulness, prayer against pride, and almsgiving against avarice. And so, the evil enemy departed from Our Lord for a time, only to return at his passion, not treacherously and secretly but challenging him openly through his ministers who wanted him to be filled with the fear of death. At other times he also ceases tempting us, seeing that he may come by no profit in tempting us, and departs from us up to another time when he will return and assail us with even greater strength than before.

By this we are taught that we should have resistance in us, for although we may subdue any temptation, yet we still ought to be ready to fight against the devil. At the time of Our Lord's passion, the devil was vanquished and bound in hell; and at the time of the Antichrist, he shall be unbound, the same as Saint John says in the *Apocalypse*. Saint Augustine says that it was Lucifer who did this temptation, being the first angel who wanted to be equal to God and who overcame the first man. And the *Interpretation* says: "Do you now see the devil'[s ancient pride?" In the same way as in the beginning he would make himself a fellow and peer to God, so now would he usurp his lordship.

Now it is to be noted that the order of temptations of Our Lord Jesus Christ, which Saint Matthew sets in his Gospel, corresponds to the order of temptations of our first father Adam. Which was first of all, *In quocumque die comederitis*, "On that day when you shall eat", which is the sin of gluttony. Secondly, *Eritis sicut dei*, "You shall be like god", which is vainglory. Thirdly, *Scientes bonum et malum*, "They know good and evil"; namely that avarice which is not only in money and riches but also in extreme goodness and knowledge, when exalted above measure. According to Saint Augustine, we do not know for certain which was the second or the third, for as to the Gospel narrators Saint Matthew and Saint Luke who speak truthfully, one says one thing and the other says another. On this diversity Saint Remigius explains the reasons saying: "For this cause one of the Evangelists sets one thing before the other, for vainglory and avarice grow out one of the other." Then Jesus Christ overcame the devil as to the temptation of gluttony. And this was prefigured in the idol Bel and the dragon to which prayers were made in Babylon as to God. Bel, or Baal ate and drank much, the same as men made the king to believe, and Daniel destroyed him and ordered the priests of this idol to be slain. In Babylon too, a dragon was hidden in a cavern or cave which the people of Babylon held to be God. And the priest of the Law ordained certain drinks and offered them to him with meat; and the prophet Daniel made a loaf of peas, fat and skins, and cast it into the dragon's throat. And as soon as the dragon swallowed it, his belly burst, and so were both idol and dragon destroyed by Daniel. Daniel prefigures and signifies Jesus Christ, who first overcame the vice of gluttony. Secondly, Jesus Christ also overcame the devil in the temptation of pride. This had been a long time before prefigured in David and in the death of Goliath, who was a very proud man and boasted of his strength, and who David threw him to the ground and killed him with his own weapon. David killed Goliath with the torrent stones; and Jesus Christ overwhelmed the devil with three testimonies of the Law. Goliath kept the figure of the proud Lucifer; and David, the pastor or keeper who brought down this pride, is Jesus Christ who meekly conquered the temptation of pride. Thirdly, Jesus Christ overcame the devil in the temptation of avarice or covetousness as prefigured in the lion and the bear slain by David. The lion and the bear stand for avarice, which they committed in ravishing and eating David's sheep. David delivered his sheep from being devoured by the lion and the bear, and he slew them. Similarly Jesus Christ, being tempted with avarice, cast away Satan from him. And as after this victory the children of Israel crowned David king, in like manner after Our Lord's victory angels came and served him.

We find here the order of the beginning of the world as ordained by divine goodness, namely that all those who resist perseveringly their temptations shall after their anguish receive consolation from God. Of which it is written in Tobit: "Sir, you are the one who after the tempest brings tranquillity, and gives gladness and comfort after weeping and lamentation." And Saint Paul says: "Blessed be God the Father of all mercy and God of all consolation, who comforts us in all our anguish." Abraham, Jacob, Joseph, David, Daniel and innumerable others according to this order have been comforted by God when they found themselves in anguish. So were the apostles comforted with the power of the Holy Spirit after the anguish they had suffered in the passion of Our Saviour and Redeemer Jesus Christ.

And it is known that there are three kinds of solace with which the chosen friends of God are comforted after their anguish, these being the diminishing of their temptations, the revelation of divine secrets, and the multiplication of all goodness. The first is a decrease in anguish and confusion, coming when all methods of temptations which have tra-vailed and tormented the devout person are restricted and ceased by the presence of God. Job desired this consolation when he said, *Quis mihi tribuat ut sim iuxta menses pristinos*, "Who is he who shall give me strength to be after months have passed", that is to say "after the days in which God kept me and when his light did shine upon my head." This consolation is much agreeable to those who have been in affliction for a long time. For just as after torrential rain a fair and clear weather is pleasant, and after a severe malady health is most welcome, and after great wars and divisions the sweetness of peace is most delightful, so in long anguish is the tranquillity of consolation most eagerly expected and then possessed with greater joy. On this the prophet Nahum says, *Afflixi te et non affligam te ultra*, "I have afflicted you and shall afflict you no longer; and now I shall break the rod of your back." The second consolation is in divine and secret inspirations, which are in abundance of grace and of spiritual joy; and the more we know about them, much less are we worthy to speak about them. Yet we must put in speech what the holy men who lived much before us said, though they kept all in secret by experience so that those who have tasted by experience understand what we are saying. This consolation then is in the inflaming of charity, in the illustration of wisdom, in the marvellous and ineffable tasting of the sweetness of God, in the revelation of His secrets, in showing His infinite friendship and amity, in the confirmation of perpetual inseparability, in the marvellous and as one continuous visitation of the inner soul, and in the invocation of graces. In many methods God promises His solace by His prophet Isaiah, in saying *Ego ipse consolabor vos*, "I shall comfort you myself." And it is because of this that the comforter is infinite, and the solace he gives of himself is endless. The third consolation is in the delight in good and virtuous works. And how well that the exercise of virtues at the beginning seems to be believed, although by habit they come by long exercises, and then give sweet vigour to the soul and man possesses them with full delight. This third consolation closes the state of man in this life and brings him to plain perfection. Not that he will resist all, but that he falls into silence, *Salutare Dei*, this silence being none other than extinction and rest from all troubles and assaults.

And now oh you disciple of Jesus Christ, desire solitude because of this with your master and be a fellow to wild beasts. Take heed that you are partner of God's secret things, which are shown in secret, silence and devout prayer to those who love long and strict fasting. All your assaults return to Him, for as the Apostle says, we have no bishop who may not have compassion of our infirmities; in setting all your hopes in Him, because you are worthy of the company of angels.

Victory won and the tempter overcome and having gone his way for shame, the angels then, being the Lord's subjects who were for a little while absent from him so that his divinity might be even more hidden from the devil, came to administer to him. And Saint Anselm says about this: "The Son of God after forty days and his fast having come to an end, having subdued the devil and all his company, was glorified by the service of angels; in teaching us that at all times in this present life we ought to despise the delight of worldly things and set the world under our feet with all

its delights. And that way we may feel being kept by angels."
Bernard says: "After that he had overcome the temptations
and the enemy had fled and gone, the angels came and
administered to him." And then if you will have the company of angels and be kept by their service, flee worldly
joys and solace and resist the temptations of the devil and
refuse all worldly desires. Chrysostom says: "As long as he
was doing battle, he would not suffer the angels to appear,
that the devil might not flee before he was subdued and
overcome. Then when he had been vanquished and the Son
of God had commanded him to flee, the angels appeared
and showed themselves. Whereby you ought to learn that,
after you shall have obtained victory over the devil, the
angels shall immediately take joy of you and honour you
in all places. The same way as they act with the leper who,
after great poverty of hunger and much anguish, they receive
him and bear him into the place of rest."

A man may take this word *administrabant* in three ways.
First of all, as to adoration, as and a man shall say, *ministra-*
bant, "The angels prayed to Jesus Christ meekly as to God."
Secondly, as to the praise and joy that they had, *ministrabant*
is as one should say: "They took joy as to how Jesus Christ
had fought and overcome the devil." Thirdly, as to how they
helped him as to his body, it seems that Saint Chrysostom
felt the same way in saying: "The angels of far beheld Jesus
Christ doing battle, so that men should not say that he was
vanquished by their help. But when he had victory, they
came and administered and served him."

And Scripture makes no mention of what service they
did him. Certainly, it is something worth believing that they
ministered somehow providing him with something to eat
as servants and ministers, for the Gospel says he had hunger.
And this was not something inevitable to show Jesus Christ's
incapacity, but to do him reverence and honour his power. It
is not said that they helped him, but that they administered
to him; we read nothing as to the kind of food they brought
him. If we consider his power, he might create and make
such food as he would like to have, and he might have all
that he wished for as he willed. And although he could use
this power for those who followed him, yet the Gospel does

not say anything about him using it for himself or for his disciples. It is known that when his disciples rubbed the ears of corn in their hands, they ate the flour in his presence as they were very hungry. So too when he was weary and he sat down on the side of the well and spoke to the Samaritan woman, it is seen that he did not create any food or bodily sustenance, but sent his disciples into the city to buy food. Neither ought man to believe that he provided for himself by such miracle whenever he was in need of doing so, for he only did his miracles in the presence of many for their edification, and here he had none else than angels with him.

And because of this we may pathetically and devoutly think that two of the angels departed by Our Lord's will and were instantly before his mother. And they saluted and greeted her reverently, recounting to her the state her son was in; and they took with them a little nourishment which she had prepared for herself and Joseph along with other needs. And having returned to him, they lay for a table the plain ground, and making solemn benedictions and calling graces over the food, they served their Lord. Heed now all this that is done here. He inevitably sat down on the ground and ate very soberly, surrounded by angels that served him and made great joy and gladness and sang hymns from the chants of Sion. And it is quite fitting to say, that this feast is mingled with the passion; and we ought to weep much for they beheld him reverently and considered him to be their Lord God and Creator of the whole world; he is the one who sustains and gives food to all those who lead a meek life and require bodily nourishment; and there he ate like any other common person, and they had great compassion on him. And I know that if with a well disposed heart you behold him in this state, if there is any love in you, you will weep very compassionately. After Our Lord Jesus had ate his food and said prayers of grace, he started descending from the mountain in great willingness to return to his mother. Take good heed now how he went barefoot alone, he who is Lord of the whole world. And have compassion on him, and behold him for ever in your own mind, by serving him diligently and in everything.

CHAPTER 23

ABOUT WHEN JESUS CHRIST WAS PRAISED BY SAINT JOHN, WHO SAID, *BEHOLD THE LAMB OF GOD*

 DAY after returning from the desert, Jesus Christ came to the river Jordan. And seeing him coming, Saint John pointed towards him with his finger, calling out and saying *Ecce agnus Dei*, "See here the lamb of God. This is he who puts away and forgives the sinners and poor souls of this world of their sins." This testimony or witness of Our Saviour was given by Saint John in two ways. First, as concerning his true humility, in which he has been sacrificed for us and a made most pleasing host to God. The second as concerning his divinity, by saying *Qui tollit peccata mundi*, as it is only God who forgives sins. He was now come, but he was not yet known, and this is why Saint John pointed to him, as though he would have said, "This is him whom the Patriarchs described, the Prophets pronounced, and the Law prefigured." Now the innocent one, in whom there is no sin, is amongst sinners, the righteous one among the unjust and evil, and the abject one amongst the cruel.

And although men immolate or offer up other beasts according to the Law, like the ox, the goat, the calf and many other animals, yet a lamb is more called for than any other beast for two reasons. First, since the paschal lamb, amongst other Old Testament figures, signified Jesus Christ; for such a lamb was without blemish of sin, and by its immolation the children of Israel were delivered from Egyptian slavery. In the same manner we are delivered from the devil's servitude by the passion of Jesus Christ, who was without sin, but innocent and simple. For the same as the lamb which was brought to be immolated said nothing, so would Jesus Christ suffer for us undefended. The second reason is that although in various times the Jews had and did other sacrifices in the temple, yet they also had a daily custom when a lamb was offered in the morning and another in the evening; and this never changed, but was kept as a principal sacrifice. All did it by times and terms, signifying the perpetuity of beatitude, for Our Lord Jesus Christ is called our perpetual beatitude. Theophilus says: "Saint John did not say that Jesus should put away the sins of the world, but he said that he puts them away, as he did every day. For he has not only put them away when he suffered death for us, but from then to the present time he has put them away." He is not crucified every day, but has only offered an oblation to God his Father which purges our sins every day. He puts away the sins in pleasing God the Father for us by the treasure of his most sorrowful passion and by washing them in his most precious blood, and he helps us not to sin any more while conducting and leading us into a life where we may never sin. Not only did he wash us in shedding his blood for us, or in being baptised, but he also washes us every day in his blood with the daily remembrance of the passion as recounted in the sacrament of the eucharist. There, the bread and wine are transubstantiated into his precious body, flesh and blood, by the inestimable sanctification of the Holy Spirit; and owing to this he puts away our sins and helps us pass this pilgrimage, that we might say in the first two acclamations of the *Agnus Dei* of the Mass, *Miserere nobis*, and in the third, *Dona nobis pacem*, to be found in that beatitude.

According to Chrysostom, Jesus Christ came to Saint John after his baptism for two reasons. The first, for none to think that he came to him for the same reason as others had come to him, namely to confess his sins or to be cleansed by penance. For Saint John, in saying *Ecce agnus Dei*, fully destroyed this suspicion, because it was impossible that Jesus Christ might put away the sins of others unless he himself had been wholly purified from sin. The second, because those who had heard the first testimony which Saint John had given of Jesus Christ, would believe him more firmly in hearing him the second time. And about this Saint John afterward said *Hic est de quo dixi, 'Post me venit vir'*, "This is he whom I have spoken to you before he came to baptism. 'After me the man who comes in dignity will come before me'; for in his eternity he is before me." *Et ego nesciebam eum*, "And I know him not," as regarding the distinct person, "till he comes to me. But so that he may be made manifest to the people of Israel, I am come to baptise in this water, preaching penance. And for this I have left the desert and solitude in order to descend to a plain place, where I have begun to baptise, that I may show him to all people coming from all parts to me." The full office which Saint John did in baptising and preaching, was ordained to show and manifest Jesus Christ to the people. To this end he was commanded by God that he should baptise in the name of he who was to come, and that he should prepare the people to be ready to receive him.

In addition he after gave testimony, saying *Quia vidi Spiritum descentem*, "For on this one about whom I give witness, I have seen the Holy Spirit descending from heaven in the form of a dove which sat and remained upon him." Saint John saw these things when he baptised him. The Holy Spirit abode in Jesus Christ from his conception and not only when he was baptised; but to others he came various times and departed again from them because of their sins. Chrysostom says: "The Holy Spirit descended and abode in Jesus Christ. And on others he descended, but did not tarry with them. For in no way we ought to think that the Holy Spirit abides in us when we are vexed and angry, or when we defame someone else, or when we have any worldly trouble which brings us to death, and when we think too much about bodily pleasures. But when we think of any good thing, it is a sign that the Holy Spirit is with us; and when we think evil, it is sign that he has departed from us" So do we see by experience that when the spirit and the soul abide enclosed within the body, the body may neither drown nor die, though being in water; but if the water enters within, it causes the Spirit to depart and the body to drown. The same with those who are in the waters of this world, if they have the Holy Spirit enclosed within them by their love for God and for their neighbour; for although they are strongly tossed about with waves and temptation, yet they are never drowned; but if the waters of sexual desire of the world enter into us, they drown and kill us. And because of this, it suits whoever desires the Holy Spirit to abide in him to have his spirit shut off from all worldly things, since water never enters a watertight vessel.

And Saint John says, *Ego nesciebam eum*. According to Chrysostom, Saint John did not know Jesus Christ by face before he came to baptism at the river Jordan, for he had dwelt in the desert out of his father's house for a long time. But he knew that he was born of the Virgin, and that he ought to baptise him in the Holy Spirit. But when Jesus Christ came to baptism, Saint John knew by divine revelation that this was him of whose coming he had preached before. Saint Augustine witnesses he had no knowledge of the excellent power which Jesus Christ had reserved for him with regard to his baptism, which he himself had to perform and not pass on to anyone else. And since Saint John was not aware that Jesus had retained for him this excellence of giving baptism, owing to this he afterwards said, *Hic est qui baptizat*, "He is the one who only can baptise," as relating to that excellence.

Whereupon it is to be noted that the power to baptise exists in many ways. The first is about the authority, which God had not shown, nor might He show, any more than the power of creation. The second is under the authority, which, according to the Master of *Sentence*, God might give and has not given; so however that the other Doctors say that He may not give it, since the power of creation is enclosed within it, namely to create grace. The third is about invocation, which might be given, for since it is God who gives baptism, it might have been given in the name of Peter and Paul, which God did not will, that we might not set our belief and trust in man. And also because not as many baptisms had been exceeded as baptisers. The fourth is about excellence, as a man may say and think that the baptism of one should be more effective than of the other, which had not yet been given to anyone. The fifth is about institution, it being only Jesus Christ who instituted this sacrament. The sixth is about restoration, which Saint John had, for whom baptism was like being restored, signifying him who was to come. The seventh is about operation and eternal mystery, as given to Church ministers.

Then Saint John did not know him so highly and subtly until he saw the Holy Spirit descend upon him. And it was because of this he said *Sed qui misit me*, "He who has sent me," namely God and all the Trinity, whose works are undivided, to "baptise in water," and not in the Holy Spirit; "he told me," through his subject creature, an angel or inspiration. *Super quem videris*: "Him upon whom, among those whom you baptise, you shall see the Holy Spirit descend, and abide in a visible sign," that is the dove, "and who only baptised with the authority and power of the Holy Spirit," namely in remission of sins, as done by the Holy Spirit since such remission is only attributed to him. And such power is not given to others, but they have only been committed to do this sacrament without demanding any effort. Jesus Christ baptised without any difficulty; and it is because of this that baptism is given in need by a layman or by a cleric or, if need be, by a woman. Yet this ought not to be done but when need arises. According to Bede, if an heretic or a schismatic or other great sinner baptises any person in confession of the Holy Trinity, there would be no need for that person to be baptised again by the Church or by a good Christian, so that the invocation or confession of this great name is not seen to be annulled or diminished. The power of God is given to none, but the service and administration may be granted to both good and evil. And so that one should keep in dismay administration by evil persons, one ought to take heed of God's power, so that the truth and verity of the sacraments is not diminished by the unworthiness of the ministers.

And Saint John says *Ego vidi*, "And I have seen the Holy Spirit in the manner and form as I have said before, descending upon Jesus Christ, and have brought witness that he is the only Son of God, natural and not feigned." By saying this Saint John shows what he has understood by this vision, that is to say that Jesus Christ is the only true natural Son of God, and by consequence or similarly has the same power as the Father. Saint John thus witnesses that he whom before he called man is the Son of God, and it so follows that he testified that he had both divine and human nature and that he was God and man.

Jesus Christ had already been witnessed in some ways before. First, by the prophets, who called him to be Christ. Secondly by Saint John when he said, *Ecce agnus Dei*. Thirdly, by his Father, when he said *Hic est filius meus dilectus.* Fourthly, by the works he did, as he himself said, *Si non facio opera quae nemo alius fecit,* "If I do no works greater than those of my forebears, you would not believe in me."

You may here think and imagine how Our Lord Jesus Christ was received by Saint John with great joy, and how he tarried with him for some time and ate food which grew near the hermitage, as he did. Stretch out your hand like a poor man of God, in asking for alms, food and drink. With the period of recreation and vigour having come been fulfilled, and thanks and graces rendered, Jesus Christ took leave of Saint John and departed from him. Now you, devout creature, go with him too. But first recommend yourself to Saint John, kissing his feet, for he is the one who bears witness of your Lord, and he is great in the same manner as Jesus Christ gives witness about him. ☙❧

CHAPTER 24

HOW SAINT JOHN YET PRAISED JESUS CHRIST AND OF THE FIRST CALLING OF THE APOSTLES

UR Lord Jesus was yet in those parts owing to his closeness to Saint John, and was also there present to testify about him and make people aware of him. One day Saint John was by the river Jordan, ready to exercise his office of baptising and to teach and tell people how Our Lord had come, giving testimony and speaking of what had happened. Before, he had testified and told people that he was the Son of God; now he testifies and shows him to the disciples who were with him, like Saint Andrew and one and the other, some believing that this was Saint John the Evangelist. And as Saint Stephen was the first martyr, so was Saint Andrew the first Christian and disciple of Jesus Christ. And Saint John, seeing Jesus walking by the river Jordan, said: "See here the lamb of God." By what Saint John did, we see in his commended constancy that he did not give testimony about Jesus Christ only for one day but on several days, so that in preaching the Holy Gospel one ought to be constant in preaching the word of God and diligent in considering how Jesus Christ passed his life. And these two disciples, hearing their master praising and commending Jesus Christ in this manner and believing what he said to them, followed Jesus Christ desiring rather to hear him rather than Saint John encouraging them that they had found him about whom their master had always so much spoken. Have you marvelled about the simple, meek and sudden vocation of his disciples who followed without raising any objection or making any inquiry? And the sweet Lord, who gave confidence to all those who desired him with a perfect heart and mind, and gave hope of mercy, and gives himself back to all those who convert their lives to him, says *Quid queritis?* What are you seeking?' Chrysostom says: "We are here taught that when we start having the will to do well, Jesus Christ gives us many occasions of salvation." Theophilus says: "Take heed

how Our Lord turns his face towards those who follow him and beholds them; for if you do not follow him by good works, you may never come to the sight of his face, or hope to reach his mansion." He did not say to them *Quem queritis?* that is "Who is he whom you seek?" for they were enlight' ened about his person by Saint John, their master. But he said to them: "Whom do you seek?" for he knew well that they were asking for something for their salvation. And they answered him: "Rabbi," that is to say master, "Where do you abide?" or where do you dwell? They did not ask "Where is your house?" for Jesus Christ never had a dwelling place or anything belonging to him in this world except the title which he was given by Pilate on the cross.

Morally speaking, they were asking: "Where do you dwell?" as though they knew it was them who were the ones with whom God ought to dwell, to prepare them to join him. Spiritually speaking, this question brings delight to those who remember the light in which God dwells, as David says: "Sir, I have loved the beauty of your mansion." As diligent disciples they were asking where he dwelt, so that they might come to him to be taught even more often. Bede says: "They would not enjoy their stay with the master of truth only for a short time, but they asked him where he dwelt that they may be taught by him even more easily." And by this reasoning, each time we recall remorsefully the time of his Incarnation which is now past, we ought to pray him diligently that it might please him to show us his eternal dwelling place. He answered liberally to his two disciples, *Venite et videte*, "Come and see"; as though he would say, according to Alcuin, that "Man may not show nor tell of my dwelling place by talking, but rather by work."

And he led them to the lodging where he dwelt; and they dwelt with him for the day, that is abiding with him from the day when he had spoken to them, and the fol' lowing night, hearing from him words about everlasting life. The Evangelist said well that they should abide this day, for there might be no darkness or night where Jesus Christ was, being the light of virtue and the son of justice. Oh, how blessed were such nights and such days, during which these disciples saw and heard him and which so many kings and Prophets desired to see! But who can tell us what it was that they heard Our Lord telling them? Now let us construct in our hearts a dwelling place where he may dwell, and let us adorn a house in ourselves where he may come to us, speak and teach us.

Hora autem erat quasi decima, "It was about ten o'clock," when the disciples spoke to Jesus Christ, this being the time of evensong. Here the great diligence of Our Lord ought to be praised since even though it was late he did not give up teaching his disciples. The disciples too ought to be commended for the great desire they had to hear him, for although it was late, and perhaps they were still fasting, yet they tarried and urged him on. Moreover in the hour of evensong, when everyone ought to return to their houses, they left all and abode with him until the next day, owing to the great desire they had to hear the word of God. According to Chrysostom, we are instructed and taught by this that we ought to set all our time to hear or put into effect the word of God, for all our time is ordained to this end. On this Theophilus says that the Evangelist did not set the time without cause, but to show that doctors and masters ought not to delay teaching people when it was late. Taking the example of these disciples let us not lose any time but be disposed to receive Jesus Christ and to dwell with him, not knowing when he shall come, whether at midnight or at noon, in the morning or in the evening, to judge or condemn the stink of the sins committed by us. Let us seek him in the night of sin. Let us follow him with true penance, that he might behold us mercifully. Let us pray him with perfect heart that it pleases him to show us where he dwells. Let us dwell with him in his house, where blessed are those who dwell in it.

These two disciples followed Jesus Christ for none else, nor were they drawing close to him but to be instructed and told of his doctrine, which pleased them so much that immediately one went and converted the other. First it was Saint Andrew who departed to seek his brother Peter that like him he might hear Jesus Christ's doctrine. So, the Gospel says, did Saint Andrew find his brother Simon; for, according to Albin, man ought not to procure nor tarry from day to day as to faith who shall go first. Saint Andrew was younger than Saint Peter, and yet it was him who first found Jesus Christ. Then he at once told his brother, that he might partake too of the goodness he had received, and for him to be his brother in faith just as he was his brother in the flesh. So it was Saint Andrew who first announced to his brother the treasure he had found. And even had he not found him, then he would have shown and brought the first one he found to Our Saviour, for charity is never envious of another's welfare. This goes contrary to those who withdraw and keep their own friends from entering into religion or into the way of virtue and holy living. Saint Andrew had not found Jesus Christ till he had before diligently sought him, the same as the Gospel shows and says *Invenimus Messiam,* "We have found the Messiah," promised in the Law and by prophecy, and who had been expected for a long time before. And very well and appropriately he says "We have found," for it had been sufficiently shown and prophesied about Jesus Christ that he was the righteous redeemer. It is like what Bede says: "It would be a true discovery of Jesus Christ to love him fervently with your heart and long for your brother's salvation." *Messias* in Hebrew is like saying *Chryste* in Greek, and ointment in Latin, for Jesus Christ was singularly anointed with the invisible oil of the Holy Spirit even more abundantly than any creature ever was. Cyril speaks about Jesus Christ being anointed with the Holy Spirit as man in the form or manner of a servant, while he as God anointed by the Holy Spirit those who believe in him.

Et *aduxit eum ad Jesum,* "And Andrew brought Peter, his brother, to Jesus Christ." He was not confident enough that he might teach sufficiently. This is to the instruction of the Church to use witnesses at the sacrament of baptism and confirmation; these witnesses are presented by those receiv-ing these sacraments, and they are called godfathers and godmothers. Jesus Christ received him gladly, for he knew well how to go about him, and so he beheld him with his inner eyes of mercy. Seeing his devotion, he said to him, *Tu es Simon Bar Iona;* like saying, "You are the Son of obedi-ence and grace, or of the dove, that is the Holy Spirit, and for this your name fits well your character." Simon means obedience; *Bar*, son; *Iona*, dove or grace; *Bar Iona*, son of the dove or of grace, all this showing that obedience is very necessary for those who return to God, and that man comes to Jesus Christ by faith, and that we are confirmed by the blessed Holy Spirit in God's love. *Tu vocaberis Cephas*, "You shall be called Cephas, which is just as saying Petrus in Latin." And this name Peter means in Greek and it means in Latin a head or chief, and it is very fit of him who ought to be constituted by Jesus Christ as the master and head of others and his vicar on earth. Saint Peter was named Simon before his calling and way of life, but after this name Peter was given by Jesus Christ. Simon was his proper name, and Peter was his byname. Bar Jona is a Hebrew name, yet the other Gospel says that he is called the son of Johanna, for according to some this was a holy name of the Father yet made different by omitting a syllable, as in some countries Nicholas is called Nichol or Colin. Notice here Saint Peter's humility and obedience; for he who was the elder brother did not scorn following Saint Andrew who was younger than himself, but he immediately obeyed him and followed him.

And on another day, after Saint Peter's and Saint Andrew's calling, Jesus Christ willing to return from the land of Judea, where Saint John was baptising, to Galilee where his mother was, he found Philip, who came from the city of Bethsaida on the shore of Galilee. He called Peter and Andrew to him and said *Sequere me*, "Follow me." Some say that he followed Jesus Christ who wanted to conform him to his humility and passion, so that he might be in his company in his resurrection and ascension. Saint Philip immediately followed him unquestionably and as a true obedient man. According to this it looks like Saint Philip was the first called by Jesus Christ of all the other apostles. Now these four apostles, namely Andrew, and the other who is not named, and Peter and Philip, were disciples of Saint John the Baptist, and that seeing Saint John's testimony of Jesus Christ they joined him.

Then as Jesus Christ told him to do, Saint Philip, went to seek his brother Nathanael, and found him on a fig tree, and said to him *Quem scripsit Moises in lege etc*, "We have found Jesus of Nazareth, presumptive son of Joseph and

long awaited, about whom Moses has written in the Law
and the Prophets have pronounced him in their prophecies."
Then Nathanael, marvelling that a prophet had come from
the land of Galilee and not from the land of Judea, saying
that Jesus Christ ought to be born in Bethlehem according
to Micah's prophecy, showing his doubt and negation said,
according to Chrysostom, *A Nazareth potest aliquid boni esse?*
"May there come any good from Nazareth?", as though he
would say "No." Or, according to Saint Augustine, that doctor
and man who was wise in the Law who read in the other
prophecies that Jesus Christ should be called the Nazarene,
and might have noted the signs of his coming, on hearing
the word Nazareth had immediately felt great hope and
spoke to affirm what he had heard. And inasmuch as Saint
Philip was not yet well learnt, he brought him to Jesus Christ
to hear him more plainly in saying to him *Veni vide*: "Come
with me, and you shall see him and learn by experience
of the goodness and virtue found in him." *Et aduxit eum
ad Jesum* since according to Chrysostom he brought him
to Jesus Christ believing that if he savoured anything of
his doctrine, he would after say nothing else against him.

And Jesus Christ, seeing Nathanael coming to him, went
towards him with an eye of acceptance and with spirit more
than with body, saying to those around him, *Ecce vere Israelita
in quo dolus non est*, "See here indeed a real Jew who comes
from Israel in whom there is no deceit." He had come to
Jesus Christ simple and lowly to know the truth and having
a true intention. In saying this Jesus Christ did not say that
he was not a sinner, but rather he praised his confession.
Deceiving are those who show and say they are just and
righteous, and are yet sinners. This word *Israelita* is just like
saying seeing God. And Nathanael began now seeing him
first by faith, beginning to believe in him; secondly, he also
saw him by understanding the Scripture which he knew,
for he was doctor in the Law; thirdly, he saw him by the
confession he made when answering Jesus Christ.

When Nathanael then saw that Jesus Christ knew well
what he was thinking, he asked him how was it that he
knew all, saying *Unde*, namely "By what virtue do you know
me? For you tell me it is by virtue of human nature." And

Jesus Christ answered him, telling him many secrets, *Cum esses sub ficu*: "When you were under the fig tree, I saw you, that is to say I have perceived and known the purpose of." Regarding what he was really doing, perhaps this man was resting under the fig tree thinking about the coming of the Saviour. And Saint Philip found him there and told him how the Saviour had indeed come to the world. And by this sign and by others before, he confessed Jesus Christ to be truly the Son of God saying to him, *Rabbi, tu es filius Dei*, "Master, you are the Son of God, king of Israel"; which is like saying "You are Christ awaited since past times by the people of Israel to deliver them from their enemies' captivity." Chrysostom says that although Nathanael had not yet confessed Jesus Christ to be the natural Son of God, yet he did it by grace, and as a man of wisdom, and knowing by revelation God's secrets; for Nathanael had not yet embraced faith in the Trinity. And Our Lord exalted him to even higher things, that is to the knowledge of his divinity in teaching and telling him that the angels showed him honour and reverence as their sovereign, thereby showing him to be the natural Son of God, for no creature is above the nature of angels but the divine. And Jesus Christ told him: "Since I have told you that I have seen you under the fig tree, you believe that I am Jesus Christ, him who has been promised in the Law. Regarding the excellence of grace, you shall see much greater things in me." This is the virtue of my divine substance. *Amen, amen dico vobis*, that is to say "Truly and certainly I tell you", two amens showing a much greater certainty and sureness, "you shall see the heaven in all power and the angels of God ascending and descending on the Son of Man serving his Trinity," which is hidden under his humanity. This was truly accomplished in his nativity, and when the angels served him in the desert and in his passion, when he was strengthened by the angel, and in his resurrection and ascension, when they showed him to the women and to the apostles. Chrysostom says: "Notice how Jesus Christ little by little strengthens Nathanael from an earthly consideration of heavenly things, and taught and instructed him so far as to make himself known to be God and man, for it is not possible that him to whom the angels administer may be pure man." Certainly, by these sayings Jesus Christ showed himself to be the Lord of angels.

It is because Nathanael was a great expert of the Law that Jesus Christ would not choose him as one of his apostles, not even Nicodemus, so that it would not be presumed that that they had been exalted for their knowledge. But he would choose the first foundations of the Church from simple people, from innocent persons not being any men of the cloth, since man's first conversion and the doctrine of faith were not to be thought to come through man's wisdom, as well as to confound the world and all its wisdom. Yet Saint Philip and Nathanael were at the beginning cold to the faith, to the end that it would not appear that the faith of Jesus Christ had only been received and begun by simple people, and so that they would not be held in contempt and rejected because of this; and also for it not to appear that simple persons should have been deceived by ignorance; but since the faith had been confirmed and made public, great members like Saint Paul would be called to it. Saint Andrew and Saint Philip were taught by Jesus Christ and they busied themselves for their brethren's salvation, like those who by their power lead others to follow Jesus Christ. This goes against those who not only give opposite advice not to follow him, but return with all their power and take away others from him.

When these things were accomplished, Jesus Christ and Saint Philip returned to Galilee. At Nazareth he was received with very great joy by his mother. All that year he dwelt in Galilee, but no Gospel specifies what things he did during that year, for we read nothing about him from his baptism up to the marriage feast, other than of his fasting and of the devil's temptations, of Saint John's testimony about him and of the calling of the apostles.

Consider how Jesus Christ after his baptism and victory over the temptations, returned to Nazareth, which means a flower, signifying that in man's cleansing from his sins and in the temptations he overcomes, and in whatever good things he has done, he ever yet ought to repute himself as being in the flower, that is at the beginning, and he ought not to cease or stop labouring as long as he lives. ✿❧❧

CHAPTER 25
HOW JESUS CHANGED WATER INTO WINE

N the following years, namely when Jesus Christ was thirty-one years old, he started doing marvellous signs and wonders, by which the world was enlightened. And since heretics assume confounding the sacrament of marriage, which he has instituted and established, so would he honour it with his bodily presence and approve of it by marvellous signs. And so on that day, after twelve months that he was baptised, he entered into the bridal and wedding house. Bede says: "It is because of this that continence in marriage is good for those who keep it, and surely better is continence in widowhood, but continence in virginity is best of all. The Son of God would approve all states and all degrees, as those who deserve their merits and every one, he being born of a Virgin, and he who kept himself continent after being born of the blessed widow Anne, and in his youth was invited to wed." Then on an unspecified day among others, the third after he was baptised and after Saint John had testified about him, but there are many such days in between which are numbered successively from one to three because of the great things that were done on them, *Nuptie facte sunt*, the wedding was held in Cana in the province of Galilee.

And although men doubt who was the bridegroom in this marriage, we think it might have been Saint John the Evangelist, such as Saint Jerome seemingly affirms in the comments to the prologue of Saint John's Gospel, who being willing to marry, Jesus Christ called him to the nuptial feast, and from then on, owing to the worldliness or the chastity of continual virginity, he was more familiar with him than with others. We also do not find Jesus Christ at any other nuptial feast, so that men may think that the spouse might have been some kin of his and special friend. The mother of Jesus Christ was also there, as at the wedding of her nephew. And it was very unlikely that she had come there unless it was some close next of kin of hers. Similarly she had gone to Elizabeth, her cousin; and we have no more as to where she went any further. She was there not as a stranger, but as the first begotten and oldest of all the family, and as the worthiest of her sisters. And it is also written that Jesus went to this nuptial feast with his disciples since they were not yet firm or steadfast in their master's belief, but only followed him due to some familiarity they had with him, desiring to be taught about his doctrine. Joseph, spouse of the Virgin, is not mentioned here, some saying that he was then deceased, for in all that follows in the Gospel no mention is ever made of him. And it should similarly be believed that at the passion of Jesus Christ he was deceased and dead since the Virgin, his wife, was commended to Saint John the Evangelist.

Now behold the Lord eating meekly along with the others. Together with his company he sat in a low and humble place, not in the highest, nor in the midst of the best and greatest. He did this according to what he had preached, namely that when you are invited to a wedding, sit in the lowest and most humble place. Notice too how this glorious Virgin was ever ready to serve and busied herself to see that nothing was lacking or that anything was at fault. Towards the end of the feast, she perceived while watching out that wine was lacking and that it had finished. She went to her son and said to him, *Vinum non habent*, "They have no wine." She did not tell him: "Give them wine," for she knew well that it was enough for her to show her needs to him, whom she loved, without the need of saying anything more. And she, being filled with the Holy Spirit, foresaw the miracle that her son would do. Saint Jerome says, "She then warned him about what she thought he should have done, and he did it." It is very fitting that the wine of temporal gladness and pleasure should fail at the place where Jesus Christ was attending at a feast, for holy people take no pleasure in that wine which makes them drunk and forgetful of God, kindling all lustfulness in them. And it should not be doubted that Jesus Christ would have never been among them had they been tavern haunters who delighted in wine.

Jesus answered his mother, *Quid mihi et tibi mulier?* or "Oh woman, what does that concern you or me? What do we, you and me, have to do with this shortfall? Why are you goading me?" No wonder marvelling at Jesus Christ's harsh response to his mother, to whom he showed such great reverence. According to Saint Augustine, this response teaches us that we ought not to make known matters relating to God to either father or mother. Whereupon Saint Bernard says: "Oh Lord, is it not that what belongs to her also belongs to you? That what belongs to sons, also belongs to mothers? So why do you ask her about her business if you who are the blessed fruit of her virginal womb? Is she not the same one who has borne you without blemish of sin and brought you into this world? Is she not the one in whose womb you have dwelt for nine months, and have been nourished with the milk of her virginal breasts? Or with whom at twelve years of age you came to Jerusalem, and was subject to her? And now you answer her about your own or her business? Certainly, Lord, it does, and in all ways. But I openly see that you are not answering her unworthily, or that you would confound the tender modesty of your glorious mother and that you do this when she needs you. So why, my brother, would he answer her in this manner? Certainly, for our instruction, and to show us that in being converted to God's service and after our conversion, the great concern of our earthly parents ought not to hinder our spiritual conduct. For as long as we are in this world, we are sweet in serving our parents; but after renouncing to ourselves, by much greater reason ought we to be delivered from their care and business. It is like to what we read in the life of the holy fathers that a certain person visits his brother who dwells in the desert. The brother answered telling him that he should go to one of their other brethren who was then deceased. And marvelling within himself on hearing such words, he told his brother, that he was sending him to a dead man. By this we see that Our Lord readily teaches us that, in hearing Jesus Christ answer his mother in this manner, we ought not to think of our friends more than our state requires. And he did the same thing in another place, when men showed him that his mother and brothers were waiting outside to speak to him. He then chided them, asking who was his mother and who were his brethren. Where are they now those who think much of their earthly friends who are dead, perhaps even more than when they lived with them in this world?"

According to Saint Augustine, Jesus Christ called the Virgin *mulier*, woman, not that she had lost her virginity, but according to the external appearance of the Jews, who call all wedded females "woman". According to Origen, he might well and readily call the glorious Virgin woman for the propriety of her heart, which was softened with pity and compassion for those serving at the nuptial feast when they lacked wine, which was something of which they should have been utterly shamed. According to Chrysostom, with pity in her heart she would show this lack right at the time when it was necessary to do so, and fitting to do a miracle, that there might not appear to be any confusion.

And it was owing to this that this miracle was the first of Jesus Christ's miracles. In order to confirm the apostles, it had to be readily shown and to be pleasing to all those who were present. And this was the more pleasing since wine was lacking compared to what they had before. And for that reason Jesus Christ, who was much wiser than his mother, withdrew for a time, saying *Nondum venit hora mea*, "My hour is not yet come", rather like saying, "Those sitting at this dinner do not yet know about the lack of wine. Let them know about it first, for when they shall know of the need, they will repute the benefit that I do them even more." According to Saint Augustine, it was a proper thing for Jesus Christ to do a miracle there according to his divine nature, which did not pertain to his mother. And because of this, in answering her *Quid mihi etc*, he would show that as to this matter he was not subject to obeying her, as though he would say, "The time to do a miracle is not come to you and to me, but to me only."

Now the Virgin, understanding well her son's words that he would not leave matters as they were, nor entertaining any mistrust in his answer, returned to the servants. She sent them with great hope and trust to her son, saying to them *Quodcumque dixerit vobis, facite*, "Do all that he shall bid you to do." Certainly, she knew well that he had such great mercy and pity that he would have compassion on those who had suffered for him, and do whatever they asked him, although he would speak roughly and he would deny them. The Virgin gives a fair learning here, that in every⁄ thing we ought to obey Jesus Christ and ought not to show any mistrust in him, although it may often seem to us in our prayers that he hardly answers us. Yet in the Virgin's example we ought to wait faithfully for his mercy.

In that house there were six great earthen pots, or big vessels containing water for the rite of Jewish purification. The Jews have a custom of washing their hands after touch⁄ ing any forbidden thing according to the Law, and also to often wash the vessels out of which they ate. According to Isidore, each one of these great pots contained some twenty or thirty sexters, which is a measure reckoned to contain two pounds. And since the water that was in these pots was as to some of it to wash vessels and hands, Jesus Christ said to them *Implete idrias aqua,* "Fill the pots with water." Unhesitatingly, the servants did so, drawing water from the well and filling them to the brim; and the water was immediately converted into very good wine. We do not find written that Jesus Christ said or spoke any words here, nor in a greater miracle on Maundy Thursday at supper in the transubstantiation of the bread into his blessed body and the wine into his precious blood. But he did it by the hidden virtue of his divinity, although he has done some miracles accompanied by words, others by his merciful touching and still others when he wept. And he afterward said to them, *Haurite nunc,* "Now fill out the wine in vessels and take it to the feast steward," who sat at the top table in the hall. Three degrees of table were ordained according to high and low degrees, as is the custom in the dining halls of religious people. This word *triclinium* in Latin is just as saying a couch or reading position, for in old times men were wont to eat and drink while sitting, covered and laid on a bed, so that while eating the members of the body might be at rest. And it might be that this steward of the feast was an old priest of theirs, who was at this nuptial for spiritual welfare and to show how, according to the Law and according to the old order, they ought to proceed there and what to do afterwards.

Two things ought to be noted here. First, Our Lord's discretion, wanting the chief person in that company to be first to assay and taste the wine which had been miraculously provided, for it was what he decided which was most esteemed and so that the miracle would be accepted according to what he recommended. And in doing this he did not accept people's praise, for as Saint Augustine says, in honouring people according to their status, we need not fear to accept people. Secondly, according to his humility, for he sat down very far from the feast's steward in telling the servants "Take it to him", being well beneath and lower than him. *Ut autem gustavit architriclinus.* When the feast's steward saw the water made wine, that is to say changed into wine, and he did not know where it came from, he called the bridegroom to him to censure him, telling him "All men reasonably and wisely making any feast or dinner, at first set good wine before the nuptial feast starts, or food goes around. For then their perception works faster and they reason out things better, so that men then best discern the wine's goodness. And when they are drunk, they may be given small wine, to abate their drunkenness and hinder their intelligent discretion. But you have done the contrary, keeping the good wine up to this time, so that men could not savour well its taste."

It is not to be doubted that the wine changed by Our Lord's power was better than that which grew on the vine. Chrysostom says: "Our Lord changes the water into wine, and not into simple and small wine, but into very good wine. Since Our Lord's miracles are of much greater honour and effect than what nature can do. It is generally seen in Our Lord's miracles that they always end up in better things than those made by nature, as it was seen when he made the lame and the crooked straight and he healed the sick."

The servants showed this miracle to all, for they knew well how it was done. And the Gospel says more, *Hoc fecit Jesus inicium signorum,* "These things Jesus did at the start of his miracles," in the town of Cana in the province of Galilee. And by this he was a sign and showed his glory, that is to say that he would show his glorious Trinity hidden in his human nature, and that he was Lord of virtues and king of glory, who had power to make all things out of nothing and to change the elements at his pleasure and will, and that it is him who gives the vines seasonable weather, and as time passes changes them into wine. And because of this one should not believe—for it is false—the Book called *De infancia Christi*, which foolishly speaks of signs and wonders in his childhood.

The disciples, seeing this miracle, believed in him more perfectly and firmly than before. Scripture does not deter-mine who his disciples were, although it may be said that some of them who were there were recent believers in him. Augustine says: "The Scripture calls not only the disciples of Jesus Christ those twelve it often mentions, but all those who believe in him and desire to be taught by him and by the doctrine of everlasting life and of the heavenly kingdom."

It should be noted here that there are four manners of nuptials, according to the four senses of Scripture. First of all, the nuptials of carnal copulation, according to the literal sense. Secondly, in the allegorical sense, the nuptials of the divine Incarnation of the Son of God. Thirdly, according to the tropological sense, the nuptials of the soul's spiritual union to God. Fourthly, according to the ascendental sense, the nuptials of abundance, namely the soul knowing God in everlasting beatitude. This Gospel relates to the first nup-tials, according to the literal sense, and the mother of God ought to be at this nuptial together with the disciples. By these there ought to be understood three kinds of goodness which are found in marriage. The first is about faith and chastity, which they ought to have towards each other, as seen in the chaste mother of Jesus Christ. The second is the sacrament, just as saying the union of the divinity in human nature in Jesus Christ, or of the Church with Jesus Christ. The third goodness is the line and family that ought to be procreated and nourished by faith in Jesus Christ, as seen in the disciples. The second nuptial, according to the alle-gorical sense, is about the divine Incarnation of the Son of God: the spouse or bridegroom is the Son of God, and the bride is human nature. In that condition there was only the mother of Jesus Christ and Jesus, and his disciples, who were those chosen before the world's creation. The line of these bridal kinsfolk are all those who believe in the Catholic faith and confirm themselves in the faith of the new law. The third nuptial, according to the tropological sense, is the union of the soul to God, as in the cave of Galilee. Cana means zeal or love, and stands for the fervent love which the soul ought to have for its Creator. Galilee is interpreted as transmigration, by which it is shown that worthy to come to these nuptials are those who, by fervent devotion and by God's tender love, leave evil works and delight themselves in doing good. They transmigrate from vices to virtues, from sin to grace, from worldly to heavenly love; and in order to be united and joined with God they abandon their own proper love and will for their Creator's love. The fourth nuptials, according to the ascendental sense, is when the devout soul enters her spouse's chamber and into the secret of the heavenly light, which is the place where our joy is to be accomplished perfectly. In the same manner as Saint John exhorts us in the Book of the *Apocalypse*, saying: "Let us be urged and give glory and praise to God, for the nuptial of the lamb has arrived, and his bride is ready." To these nuptials none enters save the wise virgins; and whoever is called to these nuptials is very fortunate. Similarly as we see that the nuptials are made by the joining of man and woman, so are made the nuptials of God and man by the joining of two natures and by the company of the created and uncreated spirit. And this is when man is on high with God in grace and glory.

According to Saint Augustine, we now see the mysteries and secrets which are contained and hidden in this miracle which Jesus Christ did at these nuptials. For it was proper that what was written about him should be accomplished. The ministers and servants of these nuptials are the doc-tors and masters of Scripture, as to what Alchim says, like Nicodemus, Gamaliel and Paul. Scripture was none else but only water, but Jesus Christ made wine of the water when he exposed and opened his disciples' intellect that they might understand him. For just as the wine has a different taste and of better savour than water, so was it after he had opened their minds or instructed them, they tasted the water which they neither understood nor knew before.

Jesus Christ has kept this good wine, which is the promulgation of the Holy Gospel, up to the sixth age. The six
earthen pots are the five bodily intelligences, with our
understanding. The pots were made of stone, as our understanding and intelligence were hard and obstinate by sin
before the coming of Our Lord's grace, which we fulfil with
water when, because of our failures, we perfectly wash all
our intelligence by compunction and weeping. They hold
two measures, when we weep for what we have committed
by delight and consent. Men can hold three, not only in
bewailing the delight and consent to our sins, but also their
works done in deed.

Jesus Christ changes the water into wine when he turns
good out of evil and casts away sin from man and gives him
his grace; when the water of this world's consolation, which
is tasteless, is turned into the wine of eternal joyful bliss, in
being in God's company and taste. And he did these things
as the Virgin Mary, who always has great compassion for
sinners, prayed him. Water is also turned into wine when
after sorrow it is turned into a consolation of inward devotion. But, as the Scripture says, *Omnis homo primum bonum
vinum ponit*, "Every man takes out the good wine first"; for
the people of this world desire and seek most delightful
things, as signified by good wine, and because of that they
shall after this world receive bitterness. In like manner,
when the devil deceives any man, he first enthuses him
with some kind of thing under the guise of good. And when
because of lack of pleasure man is irked and worn out, the
evil one then lays before him all his wrongdoings according
to various sinful depravities, since he causes man to fall
in despair. Jesus Christ does not first take out the good
wine, for when he tries anyone he first puts out before him
hard and bitter things, which will after bring him spiritual
delights and joys. A good doctor does not give a sick man
powerful and strong wine alone in his sickness until he
recovers perfect health. And when he sees him beginning
to recover his health, he gives him wine mixed with water.
So does Our Lord act with man in this life; for although
he would have departed from the sickness of sinning, yet
since his resistance is feeble and he might fall again, he

gives him wine mixed with the water of anguish. But when later he resumes perfect health, he will give him the pure wine of eternal consolation.

Saint Bernard speaks about these large water pots, say-ings: "Six pots are given and set for those who after their baptism fall again into sin. The first is the cleansing which a man does by contrition and compunction, about which is written that 'In that hour when the sinner beseeches and wails, all his sins shall be forgiven him.' The second is in confession, where all sins are washed away. The third is in almsgiving, about which it is written, *Date elimosinam*, 'Give alms and all shall be forgiven you.' The fourth is in forgiving the wrongs that man may say or do to another, similarly as we pray to God in saying *Dimitte nobis debita nostra*, 'Lord, forgive us our debts, the same as we forgive our debtors.' The fifth is in bodily affliction, and about that we pray at the hour of prime that by abstinence we may sing glory and praise to God. The sixth is in obedience of the command-ments, the same as the disciples heard it being said, and we may at least with good will hear them, *Vos mundi estis*, 'You are pure and clean by the words I have told you.' They had nothing to do with those about whom it is written: *Sermo meus non capit in vobis*, 'My words do not enter into your hearts,' but belonged to those who after hearing him simply obeyed him. See here the six water pots set for our purification, which are empty and full of air if they are just kept for vainglory. And they are full of water when men keep them because they fear and dread God, for the fear of God is the fountain and well of life. I say that the fear and dread of God is water. And although it is but a little tasty, yet it is very refreshing, inasmuch as it cools the soul which is heated up with the evil and irritation of desires. This is the water that may quench the ardent arrows of the devil of hell; but by divine virtue this water is changed into wine when that perfect charity puts away all dread.

It is written that these were stone pots, not only because of their hardness but also for their stability; and each one of them contained two or three measures. The two are the fear to lose the heavenly joy and deserve the pains of hell. And it is since both joy and pain belong to a future time, by which the soul is flattered in saying 'Oh soul, since you lived for a certain time in pleasure and voluptuousness, you shall now do penance, and you shall not lose the joys, and also you shall neither incur nor have any pain,' it would be reasonable to join a third measure, known to devout and spiritual man. It is a measure of the present time, that is one of spiritual nourishment, of the bread of angels, of our daily bread, which the good and those who fear God fear to lose. It is him who promised us that in this world we shall have one hundred for one. In the same manner as men give labourers their daily food and drink when they employ them, and every day they receive their daily wages, so does Our Lord God with us, his workers, rendering us eternal life when we reach our end. And now he has promised to give us a hundredfold while still enduring in his labour. How much then ought he to fear, he who having spoken of this nourishment loses it. See here the third measure, which by lawful right he has set to be disjoined since not all are promised a hundredfold." And yet Saint Bernard says about this: "Let us seek the measures which these earthen pots hold or contain. Certainly, the Saviour has given and set us three kinds of water, and whoever takes them shall profit well. The first is that he wept over the leper and the pit of Jerusalem. The second is that he sweat at the time of his passion. Water proceeds not only from his eyes but from all his body, and it was red and bloody. The third was the water which issued out of his side together with blood. You have the first, if you water the bed of your conscience. You have the second, if in the sweat and pain of your body you eat your bread, and chastise your body with the labour of penance; this water has the hue of blood, both for the labour and the fire of charity which stops a person's sexual desire. But in prevailing to obtain the grace of devotion, then you should be satiated with the water of grace and salvation, which is much sweeter than honey. And it shall make a well of life in you, which will fulfil and help you to have eternal life. And keep in mind that this is the third water that issued out of the side of him who lay on the tree of the cross, in a painless issue for it suits anyone trying to draw this water himself, is dead to this world. The first then cleanses the conscience of past sins; the second quenches sexual desire, since the soul is the body's mistress; and the third, if a man might attain to wash, fulfils or satiates he who is thirsty."

Now when this noble dinner was consumed and finished, Our Lord called Saint John apart and said to him: "Leave this woman and come after me." And this was the first calling of Saint John, by which he came to know and be familiar with Jesus Christ. And his spouse, called Anachita, or according to some others Mary Magdalene, followed Our Lord with other holy women. And it is because of this that it is still held in the Holy Church that before marriage is consummated by copulation, men may lawfully enter into religion since spiritual marriage is much worthier than carnal marriage. ☙❧

CHAPTER 26

OF THE FIRST EJECTION AND DRIVING OUT OF THOSE SELLING AND KEEPING MARKET IN THE TEMPLE, DONE BY JESUS CHRIST

FTER the foregoing miracle done in the month of January, Jesus Christ tarried in Gal-ilee close to the month of April, when the Jewish feast of Easter was due. Then he went from Galilee to Capharnaum, the chief town of Galilee, together with his mother and brethren, that is to say his cousins by way of relationship, and kinsfolk of the Virgin Mary and Joseph, who was reputed and accepted as his father, and his disciples, who were taught by him. He wanted to go to the town of Capharnaum to the end that he would show his glory there, for this was the largest city in all that province. And they did not tarry for a long time in that town since the townsfolk were defiled and would not pay them homage or devoutly receive his doctrine. His time was also drawing near for him to go to Jerusalem for the Jewish feast which was well nigh. Then he went to Jerusalem with his disciples, which was the metropolitan city; and it was ordained by the Law that this feast was assigned for everyone.

Et invenit in templo, "And he found people and changers in the temple who sat there and kept a market. The name temple does not stand here for the house where incense is offered and there are golden candlesticks as on the altar of sacrifices, but it also includes a synagogue where doctors preached and taught. The greedy priests sold animals in the first section of the temple to be offered as a sacrifice on the altar, so that none would fail doing his offering; and also for those who came there and had but little money with which to buy their offering. And for this reason they admitted money changers and usurers, who gave money to the people against pledges; moreover they received principal sums, presents and gifts, but not honestly earned money which was of little value, since they were not openly rebuked for having gone against the Law which defended and forbade priests of usury.

And Our Lord made a whip of cord and drove out of the temple all those who sold such beasts and sheep, and the usurers. He overthrew their tables and cast their money under feet and turned all upside down. And he told the dove-sellers, *Aufferte ista hinc*: "Take away these things from this place; and do not render by your unlawful works the house of my Father a house for doing business or for the provision of needs and wares."

We read that Jesus Christ went twice to Jerusalem for the Easter feast. The first was in the early years of his preaching, as the Gospel says about this. The second was at the time of his passion. Here now, at the beginning of his preaching, he drove out of the temple all those keeping market, and spoke to them courteously. But the second time, before his passion, he drove them out more harshly and cruelly, and rebuked them even more angrily. And it is well to believe that he made a whip of cords. For according to Saint Augustine, the cause for which he punishes us is for our sins; and prolonging and continuing sin is none else but a cord; for just as the cord is made and braided and joined thread by thread, so does sin continue heaping sin upon sin on us. It is for this that an old proverb says that an evil person is bound strongly with the grave shrouds and cords of his sins.

To speak mystically, according to Alchim, God enters spiritually and daily into His Church, and takes heed as to how each person conducts himself in it. Let us beware then that we do not give ourselves to storytelling, laughing, mocking, scorning, hatred or other similar vices, that He may not come and take us unprepared, scourge us and drive us out. According to Saint Augustine, those who sell in the Church are those who seek to make a profit for themselves, and not Jesus Christ's honour. And it should be noted that the sheep which give their wool for our clothing signify the works of pity and cleansing but after doing this they are sold for this world's praise under the hue of hypocrisy which is carried under sheep's clothing, since hypocrites have the mind of a wolf under a sheep's skin. Yet oxen, which draw in the plough, signify the preachers of the holy doctrine of heaven, who labour in the land of Our Lord and sow it with words of salvation. They are sold when they preached not for the love of God but to make some temporal profit. Oxen, which are beasts of great labour and suffer much pain, may also signify those who sustain great labours and pains for their masters and superiors that they may influence and advance in the Holy Church. And they sell the doves which have received the grace of the Holy Spirit, as signified by the dove, and they sell them and distribute them not as they had been given to them, although they do not receive any money for them. And they did all this to receive the glory of the world and not to obtain God's merit. They lent church money, neither by simulation nor covertly, but surely did service to the Church for the goods of this world and for transitory things, looking for their profit and not Jesus Christ's honour. Those who exercise the grace or degree which they have in the Holy Church, not for any simple intention but for worldly retribution, also make the house of God a house of merchandise.

When Jesus Christ put all those mentioned before out of the temple, he banished them from the temple and the glory of God. So they who do not want to be banished from the Holy Church or out of God's holy temple, must endeavour to put away from their works the aforesaid things and cast away from themselves all simony and covetousness, for otherwise Jesus Christ comes to judge him. For those who are counted as good, but their good doings are only feigned and done by hypocrisy, ought to be put out of the company of holy people. Also those who sin openly ought to be put out, as their sins in this world are like the scourge of a whip and at the end they shall be condemned unless they amend their. Our Lord always gave remedy by way of work and deeds in teaching those who have the governance of Holy Church and ought to correct their subjects by word and deed.

If then Our Lord Jesus Christ prohibited and defended merchandise within or in front of the temple, which was only in figure and a lawful and honest thing at that time seeing that this consisted in what men offered in the temple, by much greater reason does he presently forbid men in his Church from doing any sports or games, laughing, noise, or speaking idle words, or any similar things. Then because of this, all of Our Lord Jesus Christ's doings ought to be taken as a law or commandment. It is not lawful to sell in the Church, or to change money, or similar business, even though this may be offered to God, nor to exercise any kind of office unless it is an office pertaining to the Church.

Recordati sunt vero discipuli eius: "The disciples seeing these things, recalled what is written in the *Psalms*: "*Zelus domus tue comedit me*, and it is Jesus Christ who speaks to his Father saying, "The great love that I have had for your house makes me warm-hearted." So that this is a witness to the word *zelus* meaning an intention of love, namely when a person loves God so much that he may not suffer anything that goes against his love. Any Christian is bound to this love and it puts out of them all worldly fear. Augustine says: "Every Christian man ought to force himself to have zeal and love for the house of God, which is the Holy Church. He is endeared and warmed by this love when he sees that things are going amiss in the Church, and it forces him to correct them and keep desiring to see them being corrected." And if you may not correct it, as Saint Augustine says, take it patiently by weeping and sobbing. "By way of example, if you see your brother run to a feast or to a tavern, forbid him and warn him while being sorry for what he is up to; and in doing so you have love for the house of God. If you see others run away from you, get them under your ken inasmuch as you can do so, and if you may not win them in this manner treat them fairly. And do not leave them until you have overcome them by one way or another. For if you are cold in that regard and negligent, what will you think of yourself and say: 'What ado do I have to meddle with others' sins? It is enough for me to keep my soul securely to God.' I pray you, tell me whether you thought of what the servant said when he hid the sum of money given to him by his master to award and yet he would not depart from it at all, so that when his master questioned him he was rebuked for having kept it without winning any happiness with it. Hear you now, my brethren, and see that you cease not, but ever more keep in your ken how to win a soul for God, for He has won you first."

Consider of what merit is the zeal of love for God's house, sparing no friend or anyone who goes against God's will.

Whoever has this zeal or love fears doing anything which might displease God. This is the zeal of the fervent love by which Phineas obtained the perpetual dignity of priesthood, and by which Mathathias defended the Law, and the burning love by which Elijah burnt all the prophets of Baal.

Et *dixerunt ei Iudei.* The Jews asked him by what sign would he show the power with which he was doing these things, as it seemed that he had authority over them. Although the deed was good in itself, yet it did not pertain to common people or to any such men, but only to him who was empowered to correct the excesses of priests, for they were above the people in dignity. But true to say some prophets were sent by God in special manner to correct them. Seeing then that Jesus Christ was not of Aaron' children, nor yet the sovereign priest of the Law, and also that according to how the people esteemed him he was not a king, nor did it appear in any way by what authority he proceeded in this manner although he was not a great prophet sent by God, and since they loathed laying hand upon him, they demanded him to give some sign to show them how he was sent. This would still not help in making them believe in him or honour him, but that they would say what he might not give or do. Upon which he answered them, *Solvite templum hoc,* "Pull down this temple, and in three days I shall build it up again." And according to what the Gospel says, he was saying these things about the temple of his body, for where God abides may be called a temple; and divinity dwells in the body of Jesus Christ, and so he might well be called temple, not only according to his soul but also in terms of his body. And he did not tell them these things to command them, or to counsel them, or to exhort them to this, but to show them what they should do afterwards. As though he would say to them, "You shall dissolve and destroy this temple which is my body." Since in his passion his soul had departed from his body, and his blood from his flesh, and the joints of his members were inwardly broken by the nails and spear, this body which by virtue of the Trinity was hidden in him, was resurrected and revived as though he had slept. So here he was giving them a sign of the resurrection which was to come, for his Trinitarian virtue was marvellously shown in his resurrection; and this was not something for a simple creature to urge him on to his death.

It is because of this that he gave them in figure this sign and marking when he called his body a temple, so that all those who were carnal would rebuke him for what he said in alleging the natural temple within himself. He also said, *Quadraginta et sex annis*, "In forty-six years this material temple has been edified and made by Zerubbabel and Nehemiah, who edified it again after the captivity of Babylon, and you say that in three days you will make it up again." They were not speaking here of Solomon's temple which took seven years to build and was destroyed by Nabuchodonosor. So they mocked him saying this was impossible; and yet they mocked him even more when he told them openly of the resurrection of his body, which is something more difficult and much harder to know than what they understood. Yet since they only wanted to deceive him, they demanded a sign from him, but he would openly give them none, for they were unworthy of it. Yet at the same time many Jews began to believe in his name as they were seeing the signs which he did. What were these signs? The Gospels do not tell. Saint Jerome says: "To many it seemed that it was a great sign made by Jesus Christ when he healed the leper, or when he gave sight to the born blind, or when the Father's voice was heard at the river Jordan, or when his glory was shown in the transfiguration. But as for me, among all the things he did in this world, the most marvellous seems to be when as a man, notwithstanding being esteemed as contemptible and wretched by the people and crucified by heathen scribes and Pharisees seeing that because of him they had lost their flair, he was able to put out of the temple so great a multitude of people and beasts just with a staff, overthrowing tables, benches and stools, and all such things as a great crowd might not have done. Certainly, there came out of his eyes a light as ardent as fire, and the peak of divinity shone in his face." Also in his passion when his voice, which was the instrument of the divinity, cast to the ground a great multitude of men-of-arms.

Jesus autem none credebat se illis. This is to say that he did not show them the great and high mysteries of our faith, knowing them well inside out. Bede said that we are warned in this regard that although we are never sure of our conscience, yet we ever ought to be concerned and to be ever fearful, for what we know of the divine majesty sometimes does not pertain to us by right to know. He knew those who were unstable and left the faith in time of temptation; he knew that their fear did not proceed from steadfast faith, but only out of suspicion since they did not believe by the signs and miracles which he did that he was God, but only that he was a man sent by God. And the Gospel too does not say that they believed in him, but it says that they only believed in his name, that is to say in what men testified about him.

And so it is written that Nicodemus, who was a leader amongst them and one of the Pharisees, and who was in the darkness of this error, came to Our Lord by night. He came by night to the Light that he might be enlightened, out of love for the people of whom he was one of the governors, and so that he would not be banished from the synagogue. He also came by night because he was ashamed yet to learn inasmuch as he was master in the Law and of the people. He then came secretly to Jesus Christ so as to be taught and ever desirous, according to Bede, that in speaking to him he might get to know of his secrets and of the mysteries of his faith, which he might have perceived by some other presentations and shows of miracles. And like a man of wisdom, he kept well in mind the miracles which he had seen Jesus Christ perform, and because of this he deserved to be rather even more taught the mysteries of the faith of the Holy Church. He is also commended and praised for his great diligence in coming by night to seek and be willing to learn the truth unhindered and silently as preached by the Son of God.

Jesus Christ then taught him about his divinity, as well as of his nativity, passion, resurrection and ascension, and of his two comings, and of many other things which were necessary for his salvation. And he specially taught him of the second and spiritual generation of man by baptism, which is a needed sacrament; for it suits whoever wants to be saved to receive this sacrament worthily and in deed, if possible, or in sight or in desire, if he is in the throes of death. For whereas baptism of water is scorned, baptism of fire or of blood does not profit anyone at all. And no one may come to heaven unless he is made a member of Jesus Christ by spiritual regeneration. Nor could any man come by his proper virtue but he who is descended, not simply by moving in leaving heaven for earth, but in taking anew our new human nature. For all they that come to heaven come there by virtue of him who by his own proper virtue comes there. If any man objects that many of the Old Testament have been saved without baptism, a man may answer that at that time baptism was not ordained. Yet they had and won the spiritual life by grace in the faith of Jesus Christ's coming, and also they had the virtue and effect of baptism, which is the reason for it being ordained. They also had baptism in figure and in other corresponding things, like circumcision, by which original sins were cleansed.

Men read this Gospel on the day of the Blessed Trinity because of baptism. There, the Trinity is expressed when men say, *In nomine patris etc*. And also every man is mentioned clearly in this Gospel, for the person of the Son of God is he who speaks; the person of the Father is mentioned in it when Nicodemus says, *Scimus quia a Deo venisti*; and likewise the person of the Holy Spirit when Jesus Christ says, *Nisi quis renatus fuerit ex aqua et spiritu*. So that the three persons of the Trinity are expressed by this which is appropriate to them. The person of the Father with his might and power is expressed there where it is said *Nemo potest hec signa facere*, "None may make the signs and miracles which you make unless God were with you" for doing signs and miracles only belongs to divine power or to the power of God. The person of the Son is expressed with his wisdom when it is said *Scimus quia a Deo venisti*: "Master, we know and believe that you are come from God." It is the master's prerogative to have wisdom to teach his disciple. And the person of the Holy Spirit is expressed with his goodness when it is said *Spiritus ubi vult spirat*, "The Holy Spirit breathes and knocks where it pleases him." For the Spirit is not given to us by our merits, but only by God's great goodness. And although the Father, the Son and the Holy Spirit have only one power, wisdom and goodness, nevertheless, according to our worldly manner of speaking, this name Father bears empowerment because of His age. And since simple persons do not believe such things as there being a Father in heaven, ability or power are attributed to Him. Similarly, the name of the Son bears, as regarding us, lack of knowledge and ignorance for one's youth; and because man should believe no such things about the Son of God, wisdom is attributed to him. Also the name of the Spirit, as we understand it, bears some manner of fury and pride, according to what Isaiah says: "Let the man who breathes the Spirit be in peace." And since man believes no such things about the Holy Spirit, goodness is attributed to him. If a man keeps in mind devout faith and confession in the Holy Trinity, this would be good for him as, among other things, it takes away all anguish from him. For similarly as John Damascene says, there once was a great and extraordinary pestilence in Constantinople. And it so happened that a child was sent in raptures to heaven in the midst of all people, and he was taught by the angels to say this proper prayer to the Holy Trinity: *Sancte deus, sancte fortis, sancte misericors, salvator miserere nobis*: "Oh Holy God, oh God holy and mighty, oh God most holy and most mighty and most merciful, oh God Our Saviour, have mercy on us." And when this child returned and went before the people and read this prayer to them, all the pestilence immediately ceased and was over.

Nicodemus, who came by night to be even more plainly taught of what belongs to the faith, refers to the disciple who ought to be meek and diligent. In coming to a doctor to be instructed, that doctor ought to receive him courteously as Jesus Christ did when he received sweetly Nicodemus and spoke to him very gladly. This goes against those who are very angry and have no fair manner of speaking other than with rigorous fury. To whom the Man of Wisdom gives a very fair instruction to all, saying *Responcio mollis frangit iram*, "A sweet answer quenches anger, but a stubborn and rude word provokes and kindles ire." It is the same as to what Chrysostom says, that if our servants with whom we are sometimes angry take it meekly and peacefully because they fear us, what excuse must we have that we may not suffer a little thing for the love and fear of God; and whereas we may, we will not. 🐾

CHAPTER 27
HOW HEROD PUT SAINT JOHN IN PRISON

HEN the feast day for which he attended in the city of Jerusalem, sited in one part of the land of Judea, had passed, Jesus Christ came with his disciples and the other Jews who believed in him to the other part of the land of Judea, close by the river Jordan; and there he baptised and forgave sins. According to Saint Augustine, Jesus Christ first of all baptised his disciples in water and in the Holy Spirit, then gave the office and exterior operation of baptising to them so that he would attend to preaching and prayer, It is the same as we read that Saint Paul baptised only a few people, for he was occupied with much greater things. This is an example to prelates about how to commit to their subjects what they may lawfully do, so that they may occupy themselves with much higher things. Although Jesus Christ did not baptise with his hands, yet he baptised spiritually.

Saint John also baptised in Ennon, by the borough of Salim on the river Jordan, for there was much water in that area. And he sent to Jesus Christ those who had come to him to be baptised by the Holy Spirit and the true baptism. And they similarly confirmed what he had said of him; and because of that Saint John's disciples were moved by envy, willing to prefer their master's baptism to that of Jesus Christ, murmuring that their master's authority had been thereby diminished. *Et facta est questio de purificatione*, "And a question was asked by Saint John's disciples about their master's baptism." And after seeing him with the Jews who had been previously baptised by Saint John, they said that theirs was a much greater baptism than that of Jesus Christ. This question was made to Jesus Christ's disciples and to those Jews who had come to his baptism, and was reported to Saint John by his disciples. And they complained to him saying *Rabbi qui erat tecum*, "Master, who was with you over the river Jordan, and there you baptised him as your disciple, about whom you have given testimony and have done him great honour; and now, as though he were separate from you, he baptises and usurps your office, for all are flocking to his baptism leaving you alone?" As though they would ask whether those who go to Jesus Christ should be constrained to come to him. Chrysostom says: "Jesus Christ did not baptise, but messengers were willing to inflame and kindle others in sin by speaking thus to him. For vainglory is the cause of all evil, making Saint John's disciples fall into jealousy, and those who were taken and tempted by it were not only provoked to evil, but also to resist the virtues of those who are good, and to belabour them in vain and fruitlessly." Saint John then, willing to abate his disciples' envy, praised Jesus Christ saying to them: "I am not Jesus Christ, but only his messenger; nor a spouse of the Church, but a friend of the spouse." And moreover he said that it was fitting that Jesus Christ should increase in renown and authority, inasmuch as ever increasingly his virtues came to the knowledge of the people by his miracles; and that he ought to be none else but his humble subject. Now Jesus Christ grew in the people's eyes, for he was known for such as he was, the saviour of the world. And Saint John, whom men thought had been Jesus Christ, was discovered to be his prophet. For what Saint John said about being diminished or lessened, that might also be why he had his head smitten off, and Jesus Christ was lifted upon the cross. And also Saint John's birth is celebrated when the days begin to diminish and wax short, while the nativity of Jesus Christ was when days began to increase and lengthen.

It morally suits that all those profiting in the knowledge of Jesus Christ should be little in their own reputation. For as Jesus Christ increases even more in them by grace, the less they ought to repute themselves to their strength and the power of this world. Some religious are like the disciples of Saint John, much sooner affirming themselves and drawing to some worldly opinion for their own profit by some feigned agenda. And as the Philosopher says, if a man had but two or three friends for whom he would do much, yet he ought not to lie for their sakes, for it is something deserving reward to say the truth and abstain from lying. And Plato says about his master Socrates: "Socrates is my great friend, but truth is my greater friend." By this Saint John also rebuked those doctors who taught they ought not to receive any flattery. Those who gladly hear belittling in which men say all evil ought here too take heed how Saint John immediately rebuked his disciples who detracted Jesus Christ, exalting his master and praising him in his humbling. Those who want to take example from this must refrain from hearing detractors, showing them a sullen face. For as the Man of Wisdom says, the north wind lets the east to rain, and a heavy countenance disables a defamer's tongue.

During the foregoing times of these things, Saint John had preached for a year and three months, and had converted many. In what he said he argued and rebuked Herod for keeping his brother's wife. So Herod sent people to take him, bind him and have him brought to Galilee where he would be put in prison for having spoken against Herodias, whom Herod had taken from his brother and made her his wife. Herod had received circumcision that he might be even more pleasing and like the Jews; and so he was bound to keep the laws of Moses above natural law. And because of this, Saint John, as witness and defender of the truth, said to Herod, *Non licet tibi habere illam*, "It is not lawful for you to have your brother's wife." The virtue and constancy of Saint John is well shown in this that he had the audacity to be in Herod's resentment, rather than by adulation forgetting God's commandments. By this he gives example to preachers who ought not to leave their steadfast preaching when such things happen. Whoever came into this world in Elijah's virtue and spirit rebuked Herod and Herodias, in the same manner as Elijah did with Ahab and Jezebel.

The adulteress Herodias took heed how she might bring Saint John to disrepute. For she was afraid lest Herod would by Saint John's preaching repent for his sins and send her home again to her husband. Because of this she sought how he might be put to death, but she could not find any means since Herod dreaded Saint John with worldly fear and held him in reverence because he was a just man both with men and with God. So he kept Saint

John alive, away from Herodias lest she put him to death, not mocking him too by failing to honour him since the people reputed him to be a prophet. And so he dishon- estly deduced many small sermons within himself, not like the main ones, while he willingly feigned legality. And all these things were not but simulation, for the of keeping the people from rebelling against him. But his love for the woman ever overcame him so much that he caused Saint John to be cast in prison.

And Herod accused him of three things. The first was the circumstances surrounding Herodias, because of which Saint John was the principal propagator. The second since Saint John was preaching about righteousness and bap- tism, and many were those who ran and went over to him; wherefore Herod feared lest there should have assembled a great popular revolt against his holy life which would have singled him as a stranger and an open sinner of that land and kingdom. The third because Saint John preached that a great king should come. It was because of this that the Romans had ordained that no one could be named king unless with the senate's authority, and so Herod feared offending the emperor and so he put and kept Saint John in prison. Now it is as Chrysostom says, that the fear of God makes man to amend. The fear of man, even if it puts away the power and occasion of sin, will always leave an opportunity and occasion to commit it; and evil does not depart from his heart until he actually accomplishes what he thinks. But the fear of God is what corrects evil doers, and makes them leave their sins and flee their occasions. It is this that caused and made Saint John to be bound and cast in prison, for charitably arguing and rebuking the king about his evil life. Herod, who bound Saint John in the prison because he charitably rebuked him of his sins, and all those who do like him, are much like feverish persons who caused their good doctor to be slain.

Consider now how Saint John would please God more than man, and feared more offending God than man. Taking his example, take heed that in all your works you should rather desire to please God than man, and with all your power beware that you do not offend Him. Chrysostom says: "When we shall suffer anything of any evil person, let us think and return to our prince and enforcer of our faith, thinking about what he has suffered and of evil people to show us the way to virtue. Certainly, in thinking well of him, what men do to us would be much lighter for us to bear. If a man is recompensed to suffer pain for his friends, then by much greater reason he should be rewarded if he suffers for the love of God. We ought not only to think about the labours, but also about the good which comes after this life, that is the crown which is prepared for those who in this world suffer patiently the anguish for the love of Jesus Christ." ❧

CHAPTER 28
HOW JESUS BEGAN TO PREACH OF PEN-ANCE OPENLY

HEN Jesus Christ heard that Saint John had been given into the hands of Herod according to the will of God, Jesus Christ departed from the land of Judea and returned to Galilee, where pagans dwelt with Jews, doing this for many reasons. It was God's will that Saint John was taken for, as Saint John Chrysostom says, "no creature, whoever he might be, may do any violence to a holy and righteous man unless God suffers him." The Jews reported to Herod that the Pharisees had heard that Jesus Christ had more disci-ples and baptised more of them than Saint John had done, and so they had more envy against him than they had ever before for Saint John. So they gave advice to Herod that Saint John should be taken while they would also persecute Jesus Christ, seeing that because of these two and the doctrine of Jesus Christ their Law was coming to an end and their dom-inance was diminishing. The first reason why Jesus Christ had departed was to give an example of patience and kind tolerance to those who suffered for the truth. The second reason was so that by his absence, he might abate the anger and envy of the evil and for their furious mind to be set at peace. The third reason was to show us how to flee perse-cutions when a man finds himself in peril. The fourth, since he would preach the Holy Gospel to the pagans as much as to them. The fifth, to show that the time of his passion had not yet come. The sixth, to let people know that the word of God was to pass to pagans through the Jews by teaching his disciples that they were to do the same thing after him.

Soon Jesus Christ entered Galilee with the virtue of the Holy Spirit, doing signs and miracles. For although before he was filled with the Holy Spirit, now he started showing more of his might and virtue by making his doctrine pub-lic and in working his miracles, so much so that he was renowned throughout all the land. And the people of Galilee received him honourably because of the marvels they had seen him doing in Jerusalem on the day of the feast, and Nicodemus also believed in him.

On leaving the city of Nazareth, he went to preach and dwell in the city of Capharnaum, close to the Sea of Galilee. There he began to preach openly and to teach that the time of man's redemption was accomplished and that the full-ness of time had come. And he said to the people: "While you are still in time, do penance and believe in the Holy Gospel," for without faith and penance it is impossible to please God. "The heavenly kingdom draws near to us," and its gates are opened to us by the coming of Jesus Christ, from which man has banished himself by sin but now may recover it by doing penance. Bede says: "To draw near to the gates of heaven is nothing else but to have repentance, which man may delay and hesitate to do." "He who desires to eat the kernel must crack the nut, and the sweetness of the apple makes the bitterness of the root sweet. Man's hope of winning drives the merchant to the sea; and that of having health makes him drink bitter medicines."

It is reasonable to say that after Saint John was cast into prison Jesus Christ began his preaching. For in the same manner as Chrysostom says, he would not preach up to the time when Saint John was put in prison, so that the Jews would not be divided in believing about either one or the other. Also that Saint John never did great signs or miracles, as he would reserve all for Jesus Christ, to whom all people would run owing to the marvel of' his signs and miracles. Augustine says: "Saint John was sent before, as the voice before the word, the dawning of the day before the sun, the messenger before the Lord, the servant before the master, the little light before the great; so that the eyes which were half-closed by the oppression of sin and so blinded by the darkness and night of infidelity that they might not know nor see the son of justice, should be accustomed to see the great and excellent light shown in the Incarnation of Jesus Christ. And little by little the mist of sin shall depart and the humour of infidelity shall dry away, and the world shall enjoy this heavenly light."

This is found in three things, namely in works of piety, in the depth of humility and in the commandments of charity.

These are the three things which Our Lord has principally taught. And for this divine Word, which had been made manifest by the mouth of Saint John and of all the other prophets, he would show the kingdom of heaven starting with penance. For if sins are not forgiven by the sacrament of baptism and by true penance, no creature may enter there. Chrysostom says: "Our Lord began not by preaching justice, but penance. Who is so bold as to say that he would be good but that he cannot? Penance is correction of the will, and if evil does not provoke and urge man to do penance, at least the good coming out of penance shall delight him and make him glad to have received it, for by it the heavenly kingdom, or the heavenly beatitude, is given. As though he would tell us to dispose ourselves by penance, for eternal glory is his hire and payment."

Our Lord has preached penance since the end of the world was approaching, so that man should hasten much sooner to convert. For if at the beginning of the world he had come to call sinners to penance, the world's early epochs might have feared this call. But now, seeing through penance that the heavenly kingdom is approaching, the world is undoubtedly nearing its end, and because of this no man may be excused unless he converts to goodness without delay and immediately.

Now Our Lord, after receiving baptism from Saint John who was then put in prison, preached openly in the Jewish synagogue. For just as Saint John was messenger of Jesus Christ, his preaching also ought to precede that of Jesus Christ. By this the sweet Jesus gives us an example of excel-lent humility, for he would defer his doctrine and let Saint John preach although he was much less than him. It is a great pity nowadays that there are many religious who are not only less and lower than their seniors to whom they are bound, much less equal to them, and still they will not show any reverence to their patience and so go against what Jesus Christ taught.

A condition the preacher ought to have among many is that he must be of perfect age, that is thirty years old, which is the proper and necessary age for preaching. This appeared in Jesus Christ when he began preaching in his thirtieth year. It is also a fitting time for priesthood, as it appears in Joseph who was governor and prelate in Egypt at the age of thirty years. That time is requisite to reign, as shown by David, who reigned at that age. Bishops too ought to be of that age. But alas, they do not reach high standards now and fail to study. Let it be known that from Jesus Christ's baptism to his death three years passed; and much more from the Epiphany to the next following Passover or Easter, from the day on which he was baptised as to that day twelve months later, he turned water into wine. The following Easter, that is in the thirty-first year of the age of Our Lord, Saint John was put in prison; and in the other Easter, which was the thirty-second year, he was beheaded; on the third Easter, which was the thirty-third year of Our Lord, he suffered passion and death. So that he lived a full thirty-two years, and in the thirty-third year as much time as from his nativity to Easter, for which half a year is accounted. In the thirtieth year of Our Lord, the Jewish Easter was on the fifth calends of April and the fifth weekday; and in the thirty-first year of his age, Easter fell on the sixth calends of May and the fourth weekday; and in the thirty-second year, Easter was the nones of April and it fell on a Sunday; and in the thirty-third year, Easter was on the eighth calends of April and the sixth weekday, which we call Friday.

Now we may mark three reasons why Jesus Christ was willing to preach for such a short while in this world. The first reason was to show his virtue and power, seeing that in so little time he has converted and changed the world to follow his doctrine and his law. Secondly, to further urge the apostles' desire, so that seeing that he would be corporally with them for only a short while in this life, they would desire him even more. The third reason was to increase the spiritual profit of the disciples. For just as the human nature of Jesus Christ is the way by which man comes to know his divinity, we ought not to rest in this same human nature and put our principal purpose in it, but to reach to God through it. It is because of this that the apostles accepted heartily Jesus Christ's bodily presence, that they might not rest and put their hope as to their purpose and holiness in it, for he would dwell bodily with them but for a short while. And it was because of this that among other things he said to them before his passion: "If I do not depart bodily from you, the Holy Spirit should not come upon you." It was expedient for them that the servant's body and form which Jesus Christ had assumed were taken away from them, so that they would not set their love too much on his body. Our Lord Jesus, who perfectly overcame the world, wanted his disciples to have all their affections set in the same manner, for so they might lightly overcome and despise the world and all its pomps. He also wanted to teach us that if we will turn our hearts to our inheritance, which is heaven, behold Jesus Christ as the prince of our faith and follow his life and conduct, we may even more lightly overcome and hold in contempt all the adversities and prosperities of this world, and so afterwards come to the interior feeling in our conscience. 🦋🦋🦋

CHAPTER 29

ABOUT WHEN AT JESUS CHRIST'S COM/ MAND A GREAT AMOUNT OF FISHES WAS CAUGHT, AND OF THE APOSTLES' SECOND CALLING

FTER Our Lord Jesus Christ had returned from the land of Judea to Galilee, where he had long preached and done things by which his name and renown were greatly increased and made public, the people gathered and came to him in great company and multitude, ever desir/ ous to hear his words. One day, as he was by the side of a pond or body of water in Genezareth, which is also called the sea of Galilee or of Tiberiade, he was pressed by the people to the seashore. Seeing that he could not keep himself or abide on land, he saw two seacraft close to this pond or moat. One boat belonged to Saint Peter and to his brother Andrew, and the other to Saint James and Saint John, who were all fishermen. They had then gone ashore, having their nets and mending thread with them, and were putting out the filth of their nets so as to later fold them up, for all night they had been out at sea but had caught nothing. So Jesus Christ came into one of these boats, the one belonging to Saint Peter, so that he might teach the people even more as it was fit. He asked Saint Peter to take and put his vessel a little out at sea away from the shore, but only so much as people might still hear him. Here we may see Our Lord Jesus Christ's marvellous humility and sweetness as a person who begged even though he might have commanded. By this he teaches prelates that they ought to admonish their subjects more gladly than to command them, and that they ought to be more desirous to be loved than feared. For as Seneca says, man's mind is noble, and more lightly and easily is he brought and led by fair means than drawn by strictness and fear. But in the same way as the prophet Ezekiel says, fools do the contrary, for they command in all harshness of living and with the full suppression of their power.

To speak mystically, the pond stands for the Law, upon which Jesus Christ was its master and maker. And now, when he comes, the ceremonies start failing. The boats are a figure for the Jewish people and the pagans, of whom God called many to the faith and to the New Law by his great mercy. The fishermen are the preachers and doctors of the Holy Church, who by the nets of their preaching and doctrine draw us to the faith and lead us to the shore and land of life. We ought to descend from the highness of preaching and consider and remember our fragility. Our nets stood for the purging and weeping water of contrition for the failures and sins we committed, for the time when we were soiled and uncleansed with vainglory and temporal values. He washes the nets by not praising vainglory, adulation and temporal gains in his doctrine and preaching. Saint Peter's ship is the primitive Church assembled among the Jews, whose preacher was Saint Peter, on which Jesus Christ embarked by faith and from where he taught the people, for in this presence the Church has authority above all and teaches and instructs all. The other ship is the heathens' Church to which Saint Paul is sent and is doctor in it; many Jews were predestined to be saved but they did not convert to the faith. He taught the people in the ship which was near to the land, for we too ought in the same way to teach heavenly things and divine words to people and worldly persons if they understand and desire them, not being harsh with them but instructing them moderately and fairly. So now Jesus Christ sat in the little ship and taught the people on land as a doctor.

Morally, that pond which is called a sea, stands for the world, which in its pride swells the same as the sea, roars by covetousness and foams by lustfulness. To appease this sea Jesus Christ has provided two ships, one of which is not named but signifies the common way of observing and keeping the commandments which all creatures, without exception, are bound to keep under pain of mortal sin. The other ship is named and belonged to Saint Peter, just as saying being submissive and signifying walking along the way of the counsels, especially in the state of religion whose principal aim is obedience. Jesus Christ embarked on this ship and stayed there, asking a few men to put him out from land. For it is in the heart of a religious man, who keeps the counsels and forces himself to abstain willingly from having affection for worldly things, that Jesus Christ descends by grace and sets himself in it by contemplation and finds it pleasing. Jesus taught with the influence of the gifts of the Holy Spirit and he wants men to put him a little out from land, that is to say out of the heart, but not along with the body, so that due to our imperfection our hearts may not return only to God but may also some time touch the depth, to suit providing the body with full holiness. But nowadays there are many who deliberately do not avoid worldly occupations by entering religion, but draw nearer to the world than ever before.

By these two ships too which Jesus Christ saw, we may understand two ways, which he has approved and entered into both, by which men may come to the heavenly king-dom. The first is innocence; the second, penance. For just as in two manners man attains inheritance, that is by lineal birthright and by succession, and by emption or purchase, so does man come to heaven first by way of innocence, like in succession. And Our Lord, who never sinned, embarked on this ship. Men also come to heaven by purchase, that is to say by labour of penance. And Jesus Christ went for us into this ship, and did not disembark until his death. According to Chrysostom, for the ship we have the Church; and for her governance, the cross; and for the governor, Jesus Christ; for the nets, the Father; for the wind, the Holy Spirit; for the sails, the grace of God; for the seamen, the apostles; for the oars, the prophets; for the anchor, the Old and New Testaments. Let us now put ourselves in the depths of this great sea to seek in Holy Scripture the fair precious stone which is hidden in it.

When Jesus Christ had ended his sermon and finished his speech to the people, willing to confirm his doctrine by miracle, he said to Saint Peter: "Bring your ship higher," that is to say into the place where the water was much deeper, "and cast your nets into the water to catch fish." And Saint Peter said to him: "Headman and master to whom we ought to obey, we have laboured throughout the night and caught nothing, although we have worked with full diligence. But at your will and command I shall let fall my net, believing in the virtue of what you are saying." And they immediately closed in their net a great multitude of fish, as much as it pleased God. And not unreasonably, for they obeyed him to whom all that is in the air, on earth and in the waters are subject and obedient, while all disobedient creatures flee him. Anselm says: "Those who are not ashamed of speaking of their evil works which go against the will of God, ought to have no right in things belonging to God." By their behaviour the apostles gave the religious a form of obedience, so that readily and easily they ought to obey to the simple words of their prelates, not by force of command or threats. Also, that it was only to Saint Peter that Jesus Christ said: "Bring your ship over deeper waters," which means that while allowing lesser priests to preach on minor things, he left high and doubtful things to bishops.

This touches three things which a preacher must have. The first is that he must lead a holy life and be of good conduct, for it is said *Duc in altum*, "Bring or steer the ship," that is your life, "into the highness of virtues." The second is that his doctrine is clear and uncomplicated and doubtful, nor full of personal opinions. For as it is said, *Laxate*, "Uncover and unbind your nets," which means see that what you say is understood. The third is having a right intention, for it is said, *In capturam piscium*, "Take fish," not for vainglory, or temporal use, or worldly adulation, but preach to edify people.

The nets of the apostles broke due to the heavy weight of fish they took. Here a double miracle was seen, for not only they had taken a much greater multitude of fish than they could have taken in the normal course, but kept this multitude of fish closed in a broken and rent net. So that Peter and Andrew signalled to John and James, sons of Zebedee, who were in another ship to come and help them. As Theophilus says, they called them by sign as they were very embarrassed by the great multitude of fish they caught and could not speak. When James and John came, they filled both ships near to sinking them. But the Church could not be drowned, nor could it fail, notwithstanding it flees many times and is cast and tossed about by the winds.

Because of this great deed, Saint Peter and his company highly admired and marvelled at this event, but they were also very embarrassed seeing that it was supernatural. Peter fell upon his knees unrestrained and with great humility to Jesus Christ's feet, by way of acknowledging him as his true Lord, saying "Oh Lord, depart and go from me, for I am but man, and you are God and man; I am a sinner, and you are righteous; I am a servant, and you are Lord; and for this you ought to be distant from me by place as I am separate from you by fragility of nature, by vileness of guilt, and by impotence." By saying this he reputed himself unworthy to be in the presence of such a holy person, by which we are taught that a preacher ought to fear touching the holy things of Our Lord and to accede to receiving the holy eucharist and serve at the altar. And Our Lord said to Saint Peter, in comforting him and revealing to him that catching fish meant catching people by his preaching: "Oh Peter, do not doubt. Up till now you have caught fish with nets, but from now on you shall catch people by holy doctrine, in drawing them to the way of salvation." The word of God is compared to the fisherman's fishing hook, for just as the hook does not catch any fish unless the fish first bites the hook, in the same manner the word of God does neither takes nor draws man to the eternal way unless man, in his heart and understanding, first receives the said word. This is why you should humble yourself, that you may have the office to catch men, for humility is a virtue which can be accomplished. And it is something worthy that men precede one over the other, for they cannot be proud out of their own will. It is also because of this that Saint Peter and his company, who had laboured all night and caught nothing, cast the net at the word of Jesus Christ and took a great multitude of fish, but still said he was a sinner. In this manner we understand that the preacher of the Gospels in which he believes in his intelligence and has confidence in his own virtue, does not profit anything, but only profits well when he has confidence in God. And when Saint Peter, having caught this great multitude of fish, humbled himself at the feet of Jesus Christ, it may be understood that if the preacher has caught so many people and saved so many souls by his preaching, he ought to humble himself and attribute this to God and none else to himself than sin. And then he is comforted by Our Lord, who says to him *Nolite timere*, "Do not fear." Our Lord promised Peter much greater profit, telling him: "In time to come you shall not catch fish, but people." After this calling, the said disciples, namely Peter, Andrew, James and John, returned to their boats and houses; for they did not follow Jesus Christ perfectly in all manners since they had not yet been raised to the dignity of apostles, but they left all for a time in due reverence of Jesus Christ.

Soon, however, Our Lord Jesus Christ was walking by the sea of Galilee when he again saw Saint Peter and Saint Andrew casting their nets into the sea to catch fish, then he said to them: "Come follow me, and I shall make you fishers of men," and not of prebendaries, or dimes, but of souls. And you should know that this pond of Genezareth is set between Jerusalem and Damascus, where the space from both cities is of a three days journey. This pond was twelve miles long and five miles wide, and was called a sea according to Jewish custom which calls all fresh waters which gather in one place a sea. And also it might be called the lake or pond of salt waters, because of the salt wells which ran into the said pond where they become sweet. And according to Chrysostom, Our Lord called the apostles when they were doing their job to show that before all other occupations man ought to follow Jesus Christ; so that whoever is occupied in the Church and purchases benefices and dignities, ought to fear greatly that he follows him not perfectly in tarrying in other occupations.

As soon as the apostles heard Jesus Christ calling them, they left their nets and boats and followed him without ever again returning to their houses. And Jesus Christ going a little farther, saw two other brothers, Saint James and Saint John, who were with Zebedee their father, mending and preparing their nets, thus showing their great poverty. Whereupon Saint John Chrysostom says: "Take heed how the Evangelist diligently shows the poverty of these two apostles when he says that Jesus Christ found them repairing their net." They were so poor that they could not afford to buy new nets but mended and patched their old poor broken nets. And yet this is something of greater compassion since their old father was there with them to help as he can his two sons; and they took him along with them to the boat not because he had any work to do but to please them by being there. These things teach us quite a bit, telling us to suffer willingly all poverty and life with our fair labour, and by way of charity for a man to keep with him his poor father and work to sustain him."

All these things shown us the way how to follow Jesus Christ. Chrysostom says: "There are three things which men who will follow Jesus Christ ought to leave, that is to say carnal works, as represented by the nets in which men catch fish, and the world's wealth is signified by the boat. Then the disciples left their boat, because they would be governors of the boat which is the Holy Church. They left their nets, since they would bring no more fish to a worldly city, but might well take man into the heavenly city. And they left one father on land, that they would now be spiritual fathers of all."

Now think of how obedient these four disciples were when, by just hearing one command from God, immediately left everything and would no longer tarry but went along with the will of the possessor of all. By which action, according to Chrysostom, they showed themselves to be the very sons of Abraham who on hearing God calling him left everything. The disciples too, hearing Jesus Christ call, left their occupations to earn a living to obtain eternal life. They left their worldly father so that they might have God as their heavenly Father. And for this they surely deserved being exalted by God. And yet Chrysostom says: "Consider this thing well. Fishing is a very covetous occupation yet they, being in middle of their main fishing when they heard Jesus Christ's voice commanding them, did not tarry about anything or say 'Let us first return to our houses, or let us speak with our friends,' but they left all without delay. Jesus Christ desires such obedience from us, for he does not want us to defer for a single instant when we feel his will calling us. And it is here shown to us by another disciple who came to him, who afterwards prayed him that he would let him go to bury his father, but Our Lord would in no way put up with him to show us that God ought to be obeyed and served before all other needs." And in admonishing us, Saint Gregory says: "We have heard that two disciples have followed the redeemer of the world after only one call, and that they were so quick at his sole command that they left all they possessed. Indeed, what shall we say at the great judgment if we have set nothing apart or cared about following God who has called us so strongly, yet we despise Him and do not amend our ways either by the commandments or by anguish!" And although these disciples had only a little good and wealth, they still left many great things for the love of God, for in this world they intended not to have nor retain any worldly things that might delay them from listening to God. And according to Saint Gregory, by this alone we ought to think even more that their affection was greater than their treasure, for whoever renounces for the love of God the desires which he might have in worldly things, leaves much. He who leaves the world and the goods he has leaves enough. So it appears that those who follow Jesus Christ may desire to leave as much for His love as those who do not follow him; for God considers the heart and not wealth, nor does He take any heed only of what men offer Him and do Him for sacrifice, but with what heart and will it is done. Man fails to assess how much the heavenly kingdom is worth as to external goods, and yet it is no dearer to you than all that you have, and with all that with which you may buy it; for the hand is never empty without offering and gifts before the eyes of God if the heart's urge is fulfilled with good will. For man may not offer to God a far richer thing than his good will. ❧❧

CHAPTER 30

THE BRIEF ACCOUNT AND SUMMARY OF THE APOSTLES' VOCATION OR CALLING, AND OF THE DILIGENCE AND DESIRE WHICH JESUS CHRIST HAD TO PREACH

OU have heard before of these four disciples Peter, Andrew, James and John's three callings. Saint John speaks of the first when they were only called to the faith, and thereby came to know and be familiar with Jesus Christ. Saint Luke speaks of the second calling, or that when they followed him though still wanting to return to their houses; it is at this calling that the disciples began to hear his doctrine. Saint Matthew and Saint Mark speak of the third, that being when they persevered, abode with him and followed his perfection. About Saint Matthew's vocation we shall hear later. About the manner how the other disciples were called, there is nothing either written or determined. Chrysostom says, "Why is it that we have nothing given to us nor written about how or in what manner the disciples were called, save Saints Peter, James, Andrew and John, and Matthew? Certainly, since these five disciples were occupied very lowly, for there is nothing worse or more dangerous than the occupation of a money changer, nor more vile than a fisherman's art and trade."

Now then let us consider and take good heed what Our Lord Jesus Christ did when calling his disciples, and how he was familiar with them as he called them sweetly, in giving them fair and amiable words, in drawing them to him by loving words, in showing them where he dwelled, and later in leading them to his mother's house and in other places where he used to dwell at the time. And familiarly he went with them in their houses, in teaching them and showing them great love, as if he were a mother with her child. It is said that Saint Peter says: "Whenever and at night when Jesus Christ slept with them, he rose and covered them in their sleep. He loved them so tenderly, for he knew well that in time to come he should show sweetness and mercy." And although they were men of rude condition and from a humble nation, yet he made and constituted them princes of the world and leaders of all Christendom in the spiritual battle.

Consider also the obedience of those he called, which is to be highly recommended as they were ever so ready; for as soon as they were called, they followed him. He was also replete, or full and perfect, for by just hearing him they left and forsook all. It was because he was righteous that they so followed him.

The first was perfect; the second, more perfect; and the third, the most perfect of all. But for what cause did they leave all things? Chrysostom answers this saying that by this, the apostles teach us that no creature in possessing worldly things may walk perfectly in the way of paradise. For due to the heaviness of worldly things, they ever weigh down the soul to the ground. A man might argue whether since the apostles had left all they had at Jesus Christ's calling, they took back what they had left, for it seems they did not renounce it fully at all. Yet it might be answered that their obedience was to the full and perfect. For although taking back what they had renounced, yet they did not do it for love of greed or for the pity of seeing it lost, but only for their life's needs.

Consider also and understand well of the kind of persons the Holy Church had its beginnings. Gregory says: "Our Lord Jesus Christ has chosen them who were not wise with worldly wisdom. He has refused the strong, and taken the feeble. He has left the rich, and chosen the poor." The latter he ordained to be preachers so as to gather the people to their Creator. Certainly, those who preach ought to come to announce Jesus Christ, that within them they would have nothing by which to glorify themselves, in that he would know more clearly in seeing their innocence that their works did not proceed from them. Chrysostom says: "Oh, very fortunate are these blessed apostles and preachers whom Our Lord has chosen to the apostolic office and preaching of divine truth, before so many doctors of the Law and scribes, before and above worldly wise men. It was very worthy and proper for the preaching of our faith that such apostles be chosen, to show that in preaching the name of Jesus Christ they shall marvel so much more that what they preach shall be meek and would be fitting for the world's infirmity. And such preachers shall not take nor draw the world by great wisdom of words, but only by simple preaching of the faith, by which they have delivered all mankind from error and deception. Jesus Christ was not willing then to chose the most noble and rich men of the world as the Holy Scripture and preaching were not suspicious to anyone, not even to worldly wise men, so that it would not be thought that in persevering they had deceived mankind. But he chose poor preachers who were not like the clergy, but simple and untutored, so as to show God's grace by evidence. These apostles were meek in the eyes of the world, as can be seen in their craft and labour; but they were great by faith and by the willing service they did to God, for if they had but little reputation according to the world, yet they were both noble and rich of God's gifts and graces which He had given them. God, knowing the hearts of all creatures, knew their minds well or that He had chosen them. He chose those who did not desire the wisdom of the world, but who only the wisdom of God; nor those who desired the riches of the world, but only the treasure of heaven." Consider here the noble and wise and the mighty and proud men of this world, and see that it is the simple, and not the gentle, noble or wise men, who are preferred for their humility and the abatement of their pride.

Now in giving example to our princes and leaders let us leave all obsolete and transitory things and follow Jesus Christ, from whom we receive all perfection. And to do so Saint Chrysostom exhorts us well in saying: "The religious ought to desire to follow the apostles' life. Oh religious man, will you be a disciple of Jesus Christ, or a disciples' disciple? So do so as Peter, James and John did. They had one eye delaying and hindering them, which was their parents and their ship. But Jesus told them to follow him, and they put away the eye that was tarrying and keeping them in wait, and they followed Jesus Christ. The religious are imitators of the apostles, but they may be imperfect unless they do like the above named imitators of Jesus Christ. No religious should say that he has a father or kinsfolk or friends, for these are mortal beings. And what do you desire for yourself, oh religious man? Truly, if you have Jesus, you have parents and all your kin with you. Do not ask any more from the dead, but follow those who live. Leave the dead and bury the dead. We read that one asked Jesus Christ licence to go and bury his father, and asked not but said 'Oh Jesus, master, give me just one hour to be with my father.' And Jesus Christ answered: 'Let the dead bury the dead.' And in one hour you may sin, and in one hour die. And because of this take heed when you will bury the dead, that you die not."

Saint Jerome, speaking of these four disciples called from the fishing trade says: "Mystically, by this character, namely by these four fishermen, we are brought to heaven, in the same manner as Elijah. The first Church is edified by these four corners. By these four letters in Hebrew God's name is made known to us, and by their example we are commanded to hear the voice of the Holy Spirit calling us, so that we should forget our people, that is our sins and the house where we abode with our father. Simon stands for obedience; Andrew for manliness; James as a supplanter or vanquisher; John for grace. By these four we are converted and reformed into God's image, for by obedience we may hear; by manliness and strength we shall fight; by supplanting vices we will persevere; and by grace that so we may be kept by God. These virtues are called cardinal virtues, for by wisdom we are obedient; by justice we do virtuous works; by self-denial we subdue the infernal serpent; and by strength we deserve the grace of God."

As the Gospel says, Jesus walked around all the land of Galilee teaching people in their synagogues, preaching the Holy Gospel, and healing all illnesses, just as all corporal passions and all sicknesses which touch the passions of the soul. And in this he showed he was maker of body and soul, confirming Isaiah's words which said: "Truly, he has drawn our sicknesses from us," or those touching the soul, "and he has borne our sorrows," that is those touching the body. Chrysostom says about this: "Jesus, doctor of life and heavenly medicine, came to teach creatures, to heal the diseases of body and soul by heavenly medicine, and to cast out demons from people's bodies, bringing back to perfect health those who bore various sicknesses. He healed the sicknesses of the body by virtue of the words of his divine power and

the wounds of the soul by the medicine of heavenly doctrine. He is then a true and a perfect doctor who gives and
renders perfect health as much to the body as to the soul."

Our Lord also here showed by his example that prelates
and preachers of the Holy Gospel ought to be diligent, not
being negligent or slow, but diligent and fervent, in sowing
the holy word of God, similarly as he did when he travelled
all over the land. And the Evangelist shows us this here in
what he says, *Circuibat Jesus*, "Jesus went around." Chrysostom
says that "As to what people seek for their grievous sickness
they might not come to Jesus, the true medicine, and so
he was busy wishing good for their health and salvation,
and went to visit them himself." Similarly, the prelates and
preachers of the Holy Gospel ought not say what people
want to hear, but their doctrine ought to be common and
profitable to all. And this is shown when the Evangelist says
totam, namely "all". Nor ought they be carnal, or seek their
pleasures and delights, and this shows the Evangelist in saying *Galileam*, "Galilee"; for Galilee was a poor province. They
also ought not to go by the world without doing some good,
for they ought to teach and preach, as can be understood in
the word *docens*, "teaching". Moreover, their doctrine ought
to be openly shown to many without suspicion of heresy, for
the Gospel says *in sinagogis*, in which Jewish synagogue many
doctors assemble. Also, they ought not to preach any tale or
utter useless words provoking people to laugh, but words
which address souls to salvation. The Evangelist declares this
in saying *predicans evangelium regni*, "that Jesus preached the
Gospel of the realm", namely he who teaches about coming
to the heavenly kingdom. And to conclude, the prelates and
preachers of the Holy Gospel ought to render their doctrine
and preaching worthy and laudable by good works and virtues, not only giving help to their subjects as to their spiritual
needs, but also temporal needs. And here yet the Gospel says,
sanans omnem langorem et infirmitatem in populo, "Jesus healed
all the maladies and sicknesses of poor and lowly people."

And it is because of this that Our Lord Jesus Christ
preached similarly in Galilee as in Judea and his renown
spread into the land of Syria. This is a great and wide province containing the region of Palestine where the Jews dwelt.

And he also went into other provinces, as it is said in the story of *Ecclesiastica* of Abagar, king of Edessa close to the Eufrates, who wrote to Jesus Christ a letter about his illness.

And the people came to Jesus Christ with all kinds of illnesses and sicknesses, and with various infirmities, with demons or devils, lunatic and paralytic. And he healed them all both corporally and spiritually, for it had been but a little thing to have healed them only physically, since bodily health without spiritual salvation was worth only a little. Chrysostom says: "Consider Gospel wisdom in these words, for what Jesus Christ had done to the sick does not particularly recount only about miracles, but it included in a few short words the abundance and multitude of miracles done by him."

And many people and a great number of Galileans followed him, as did many others from other regions and lands, all being of various thought, heart and body. For some followed him to be taught by him as his disciples; others to be healed of their diseases; some for bodily nourishment; and others out of curiosity to see the miracles he did, wanting to know by direct experience whether he truly was whoever men said he was. Some also followed him by envy, like the Jews, who sought and spied on how they might take him to task in word or in deed and accuse him. Yet the sweet Jesus always did good to them, in teaching them, healing them and giving them nourishment, sustaining them both spiritually and bodily. And it was through these: *Morbus, signa, cibus,* that is in sickness, miracles, signs, or nourishment, or in blasphemy or mocking, and doctrine. These are the five things why people followed Jesus Christ. And these five kinds of people in the world followed Jesus Christ, coming from five places and various countries. From Galilee the curious came, according to what is said, "Men of Galilee, how do you take heed of heaven?" The sick and the diseased came from the Decapolis, being of those who observed the commandments. From Jerusalem came the spies and the envious, about whom it is said, "Oh Jerusalem, which slays the prophets." From the land of Judea came those who had been converted, confessing their sins and rendering thanks to God, so that they might be saved in keeping the Gospel commandments. From the river Jordan came the disciples, who after became apostles, to be baptised and taught, that they too might themselves baptise and instruct others. These five places signify the five conditions of the persons who followed Jesus Christ. Galilee, which is interpreted as transmigration, means the state of penitents. The Decapolis is a legal entity and stands for active persons. Jerusalem is a vision of peace and figures the contemplative. The land of Judea means confession, that of the prelates. And the river Jordan means the innocent and those who were newly baptised.

Chrysostom says: "Let us follow him now, we who have various illnesses in our souls, which he will mainly heal. Let us go to him and ask forgiveness for the sins, which we may have unless we are negligent and fail to ask him for it. Oh, what if we only were a little ardent or made some bodily effort, we ought to do our best lest our sins increase and we do not seek help. And our souls are surely sick, and yet we ever defer and delay to heal them! And so we are not healed of our bodily sickness, for we really do not want to be healed. And do not think that you know for sure when you sin and so have no repentance nor be sorry for your sins. You ought to sigh and weep for them even more strongly so that you do not feel the sorrow and distress of your sin. And not because that sins encumber your conscience when you have committed them, but since your soul, which has sinned, is insensitive. First then, it is good not to commit any sin; and secondly, when a man has sinned, let him weep and be sorry for his offence and faults. Consider diligently your own faults and sins, that you may know why you are asking for God's forgiveness. And it is because of this that you render Him great thanks, and for his great benefits; for God is more displeased with man, and man is more resentful when after sinning he does not repent his sin and does yet again the same sin he had committed before. And for this we ought to pray God, in such manner that we may know all our will, intent and desire to be in full goodness that we might be shortly delivered from the evils which surround us on every side, and finally learn of the state by which we may come hereafter to our free liberty of Spirit."

CHAPTER 31

OF THE CALLING OF SAINT MATTHEW AND OF HIS BANQUET

NE day among others, the good Jesus Christ was tarrying near the Sea of Galilee when he saw with his physical eyes and in his soul of compassion a man called Matthew, son of Alpheus. Levy, as he was formerly called, sat at his money changing bench for he had the charge and office of receiving the tribute and the money paid as tribute by men for the passage principally of things which came and were brought by sea. Seeing him, Jesus Christ said, "Come follow me." He would call Saint Matthew in that manner and at the time he was so occupied to show that no creature ought to despair of God's grace, however great a sinner he might be, nor of whatever sinful occupation he might have. Unhesitatingly, Saint Matthew rose up and followed him leaving all, both his own and others' monies which he had gathered by extortion. And he followed Jesus Christ, completely cutting the cord and not undoing or unbinding it, according to the counsel of Saint Jerome that whoever he called outwardly was immediately inflamed in himself with his love. So that he should follow him, Jesus Christ provoked him to come with him. As Jerome says: "The beauty and the majesty of the divine Trinity, which shone so bright in the face of Jesus Christ, might without delay draw to him those whom he beheld or who beheld him. For if amongst precious stones the diamond is of such virtue that it draws iron to it, then by much greater reason the Lord of all that has always been and who has created all, may draw to him those whom he wants to have." And Chrysostom says: "In the same way as you has seen the virtue of the calling, do likewise learn from the obedience of him who is called. For he would not resist, nor tarry, but only obeyed without delay, not even asking Jesus Christ to let him go home to his house to tell his kinsfolk and friends that he was leaving."

Saint Matthew then followed Jesus Christ with great joy and thanked him, receiving him with his disciples at his house. And with great devotion and showing inner pleasure for his coming, he prepared a great banquet for that gathering, so to render and recompense Jesus by worldly fare for the spiritual things which had lately come to him and upon which he had greatly set his heart. And it was very proper that this banquet should be great due to Our Lord's attendance, with a great dinner as it would be for the nourishment and feeding of angels in heaven. And yet it was a greater dinner, for as Saint Ambrose says, whoever receives Jesus in the house of his soul may have a very great nourishment and abundance of delights. And Jesus Christ said: "There is great joy amongst the angels of heaven when a sinner converts and makes penance." And there is no doubt that heaven found great joy in the conversion of such a sinner as Saint Matthew. Chrysostom says: "As soon as Jesus Christ told Saint Matthew to follow him, he did not wait or bide his time any longer, but he rose instantly and followed him without delay; so that following Abraham's example he received Jesus Christ as his guest and made him a great banquet."

Mystically speaking, just as Saint Matthew made a great and honourable banquet according to his manner and condition in his house, similarly ought each one who is converted to Our Lord to make a spiritual banquet in his conscience and heart, having for his nourishment good and holy thoughts, meditations and affections. And this is what the Book of the *Apocalypse* similarly says: "I came at the gate and knocked. If anyone opens, I shall come in and I shall eat with him; and he with me."

Now in the same manner as Jesus Christ and his disciples sat at table, there also came a great multitude of publicans. They were also called that they might openly receive tributes and taxes for the public coffers, or who were employed in other public affairs such as money changers or others who occupy themselves in the reckoning and distribution of money. According to Saint Gregory, these were tasks which may only with great pain be exercised without sin. These people are called publicans *a Publio* after the king of the Romans who first ordained such levies of passage to be paid; and they came to Saint Matthew for the banquet he had ordered to be given for Jesus Christ; and they sat down with him and his disciples, as many of them had repented their sins and followed Our Lord Jesus Christ in the hope of obtaining forgiveness by his sweet mercy. And Saint Jerome says about this: "Since publicans or known sinners had seen one public or open sinner converted to God, and had found where to go for penance, they felt self-confident in similarly finding themselves sitting with Jesus Christ." It is the same like also saying that Saint Matthew had assembled those with whom he had kept company in sin to have keep him company now in penance. And according to the *Interpretation*, it was reasonable that he who was chosen to be Apostle and preacher of the Holy Gospel should draw to him at the beginning of his new way of life a great company of sinners for their salvation.

Jesus Christ had a remedy of salvation for all, not only in disputing, healing or reprieving the evil, but in eating and drinking and showing us that in all times and in all works we may do well if we will it. He did not flee the company of publicans owing to the useful outcome which he saw that should follow; but he did it as a good doctor who unless he touches the wound it cannot be healed. For as Saint Jerome says, he went to the feasts and banquettes of sinners so that he might have occasion to teach them and give spiritual nourishment to those laying out such banquettes. When you read that Jesus Christ had been many times to banquets, you will not read or find anything else other than the miracles and marvellous things which he did there and the doctrine which he taught in those dinners. Thus was his humility in going about with sinners shown, as well as the power of doctrine in the conversion of sinners, so that we may also eat with sinners in the same manner.

The Pharisees considering the Law and their fathers' traditions, fled and declined the medicine's goodness and mercy. They murmured and thought it unworthy of Jesus Christ to be at such a banquet and eating with the publicans. And they said to his disciples by way of reproach: "Why does your master eat with sinners and publicans?" This was as though they would say, "It is forbidden in the Law to do such things. It seems that your master will destroy the Law.

You are all fools to follow such a master." It is the same thing nowadays with detractors; they hold in scorn Jesus Christ's members and servants and their good deeds. In such manner, these Pharisees erred for their pride made them suppose they were righteous, while rebuking those who had become penitents as sinners. They were like the Pharisee who justified himself and condemned the other at the far end of the temple. Yet it is a quality for the truly righteous man to have compassion, and for an unrighteous man to have resentment; for although the righteous hold the sinners in resentment, it is another thing which makes him abandon pride which is done by God's love and discipline. In this they are like Pharisees who praise their own traditions and belittle God's will and commandments; they would like man to obey the least of their commandments while living and forgetting God's commandments. God's mercy is shown immediately against such Pharisees and murmurers, provoking sinners to penance. For all that which Jesus Christ did in this world, like eating, drinking, going about or such similar things, serves to save sinners if we now understand that all the works he did on earth were done to convert us

In answering the Pharisees instead of his disciples, he who was master showed himself as a doctor. He first of all demonstrated reason by saying *Non est opus etc*, "The medicine is not necessary for those who are whole, but for the sick." And not without cause that Jesus Christ rendered himself so familiar with sinners who were sick with a spiritual illness. As though he would have said to the Pharisees, according to the *Interpretation*: "Be you holy as to how you repute yourselves, and for that I will leave you and visit those who leave a place for grace and repute themselves as sinners." According to Chrysostom, he shows by saying this that those who repute themselves to be holy and righteous, deserve neither having nor obtaining any spiritual reward since they are unthankful for Jesus Christ's spiritual medicine. Yet those who are aware of their infirmity, like their own sins, and have steadfast faith shall be healed of it with heavenly medicine. For according to Saint Augustine, no creature is so steadfast or secure but he who feels being infirm.

After that, he answered them and showed their ignorance quoting the authority of the prophet *Hosea* who says, *Euntes autem a temeritate vestra discite etc*, "Go ye and leave and depart from your fear, and learn and diligently consider what God speaks through his prophet: 'I will have mercy and forgive the sins, and not have the sacrifice of beasts.' And if you heed Scripture, you shall find me doing what he said, for it pleases me more only to have mercy without the sacrifice of those who have humble hearts, than sacrifice without mercy of those who are elated and proud." And because of this, the Book of *Proverbs* says: "To do mercy and righteousness pleases God more than any sacrifice." And God loves a sinner even more if in remembering his sins he meekly submits himself to His grace and goodness, than He does with just and proud men who despise and hold in contempt others who presume His justice. According to Chrysostom, the Pharisees and scribes of the Law supposed that all sins were forgiven by the sacrifice of the Law, and so they held in contempt all other virtues, setting their trust and hope in the sacrifice they performed. But Jesus Christ put mercy before sacrifice, showing clearly that sins may not be forgiven by the sacrifice mentioned in the Law, but that they might well be forgiven of God by the works of mercy and pity which man does for the love of God. According to the *Interpretation*, God does not greatly despise sacrifices, but only those which are made without mercy, as those which the Pharisees made to appear to be just before the people; these, however, they did not exercise in works of mercy in which true justice was shown. And Rabanus says: "then Jesus Christ admonished them that they should seek the eternal reward by doing works of mercy, not by believing to please God only by sacrificial offerings without succouring and helping poor people by it in their needs who are in their immediate surroundings."

And with regard to this he proposed to them the meaning of mercy by giving them an example, saying *Non veni vocare iustos*: "I am not come from heaven to call the just to penance, but to urge them to become even much better. I am come to call sinners to penance, that they may correct and amend themselves. Otherwise I am not come to call the just, that is to say those who repute themselves just

in their own conceit and lay aside God's justice and righteousness; for were they to perfectly commit themselves to
God, then they would no longer repute themselves for their
righteousness, but for being sinners, and so of having need
of God's medicine." Or even otherwise he would say, "I am
not come to call the just, for no creature is just. Certainly,
all have sinned, and need the grace of God. I am come to
call the sinners who are aware of their faults and are aware
of having need of heavenly medicine, and who submit themselves by penance to the grace of God." As if, according to
Gregory of Nyssa, he would say, "I know the sinners but do
not despise them, for I have come for them that they might
not remain sinners, but to convert them and make them
good." The Apostle says about this: "By this, Jesus showed
great hope to sinners that he came into the world for their
love." Augustine says: "Jesus Christ comes for none else but
to save sinners. Put away then all sickness and wounds, and
no medicine would be necessary other than the great medicine coming from heaven; for mankind is found to be sick
throughout the whole world." And it is only one without sin
who comes and has delivered many of sin. Certainly, it is
not our merits which have made him descend from heaven,
but our sins. According to Saint Ambrose, those who usurp
justice are not called to grace. Were it to be that grace is
given by means of penance, whoever abhors penance would
be refusing grace.

It is here shown, as much by Jesus Christ's words as
by deeds, that the sinners who will return to the way of
penance ought to be received willingly, for Our Lord shows
himself to be kind and loving in receiving the publican
Saint Matthew. And according to Saint Jerome, the other
Evangelists would not call him by the name of publican for
the shame of others and of him, but for his greater honesty
called him Levi. And it is because of this that Saint Matthew,
according to Solomon's saying that the righteous starts by
accusing himself, called himself as Matthew and a publican
since he wanted to show all those who read his Gospel that
no man ought to despair of his salvation. By this we may
learn that as much as we can, we ought to hide others' sins
so as not to be brought to ken or suspicion either by sign or

by speech, but that we ought to accuse and confess the filth of our sins following Saint Matthew's example. The secular man's calling to religion may be understood by the way he was called. The murmuring Pharisees are the evil people who scorn and withdraw from the sweet state of religion, and it is said to them, "Go ye, and learn that I will have mercy and not sacrifice." It is a great work of mercy to call sinners to penance.

Now then the Pharisees and Saint John the Baptist's disciples came to Jesus Christ and asked him for what cause they fasted so often and so much, but his disciples did not. For the Pharisees still held Saint John's custom of much fasting. It should be here noted here that just like before the Pharisees had come to Jesus Christ's disciples to slander and bring Jesus to rebuke for being familiar with sinners, now they similarly went to him to rebuke his disciples for not keeping fasting times. Likewise this is indeed the custom of those who are evil to speak wrong just as much of one as of the other and to sow discord and dissent amongst those who are good. Yet this time they were deceived for first, they vaunted about their fasting which ought to be done secretly. Secondly, they reproved Jesus Christ since his disciples did not fast, by laying the fault of the disciples on their master. And this applies to hypocrites who stand before the world for their good deeds in contempt of others, saying as the Pharisee did, "I should not be counted among others."

Now Our Lord intervened and excused his disciples by three comparisons, which he put in saying *Nunquid possunt filii etc*, "If the diners are the children of the bride and bridegroom, or of the spouse of the Church, and these are the disciples engendered by their faith in me and in the Church, they may still fast and weep as long as the spouse is with them." According to Saint Jerome, there are three methods of fasting. One is a fast of expectation or waiting, that man should be better; and it is because of this that men fasted in the Old Testament; but the disciples did not need to fast in this manner for the spouse Jesus Christ was still present with them. Another fast is that of frustration and travail, which is ordained to refrain the flesh from carnal delights; this fast disposes man to contemplation, so that fasting is fulfilled with spiritual delights. And the disciples had no need for this fast as they had no affec-tion for carnal pleasures, having with them Jesus Christ; his presence and doctrine even more refrained them from a lustful and inordinate unlawfulness, than did the great abstinence of fasting to others. Because of this they ought not to fast as long as the spouse is physically present with his bridegroom, but they rather ought to enjoy themselves even more by the presence of the spouse, which makes man more perfect in all good than any other bodily abstinence. There is yet another fast, which proceeds from an abun-dance or fullness, and it is one of perfect contemplation. This is the fast which Moses did on Mount Sinai, for the more the soul is exalted in high contemplation, so much more it is contented with little corporal nourishment. But such fasting was not fitting for the disciples, since they were as yet rude and imperfect and had to be renewed first by the charity and grace of the Holy Spirit, which was done on the day of Pentecost, after which they ought to start a new way of living.

Jesus Christ said to them, *Venient dies etc*, "The days shall come, namely those of the passion and ascension when the bodily presence of the spouse shall be withdrawn and taken away from them and then they shall do a fast of weeping and meekness." For such days, according to Saint Augustine, shall be full of sorrow and heaviness, until the joy is rendered again to them by the descent of the Holy Spirit. And the Apostle says about this fast: "The disciples of Jesus Christ were at the time of their master's passion hungry and thirsty, and fasted much." It is to be noted, according to Bede, that the weeping of which Jesus Christ speaks here because of the absence of the spouse, should not be only understood as to what the apostles did after the passion and ascension, but also of what was done before his Incarnation; for before the Virgin was delivered, it was a time when the holy Fathers desired the coming of the Son of God into the world. Afterwards too, after his ascent into heaven, is a time when saints desire his manifestation, which shall be when he shall come to judge both the living and the dead. And this weeping is desired by the Holy Church, which sees none but the little time which Our Saviour and Redeemer Jesus tarried on earth with the apostles.

Although Jesus Christ speaks of his physical presence, yet even morally the days when he is taken from us are the days of guilt and sin, when by sin we cast out from the house of our conscience our soul's true spouse, Jesus Christ, and in his stead put the flattering devil of hell. Then we fast by virtue of spiritual reflection where our souls find true consolation, when we will have the days to weep and be sorry. Because of this, we ought to keep close to the sweet spouse and take heed that we do not lose him by sin. For when we have lost him by mortal sin, then we truly ought to weep and fast by way of penance and sorrow. Some time the sweet Jesus, who is the true spouse, withdraws himself from the soul so that he may be called in much greater desire and after returning by grace, he would be more bound by desire and devout affection. For as long as he is with us, we live gladly, and may neither weep nor fast. Saint Ambrose says: "Those from whose life Jesus Christ is absent ought to fast, for they are in great need of good works. No creature may take away from you Jesus Christ but your own self. Take heed that your vainglorious boasting and your arrogance do not take him away from you."

Spiritually, the soul is the spouse with whom her spouse, Jesus Christ, desires to be, having all the conditions which are desirable and requisite for a spouse or bridegroom. For, first of all, he is very rich; otherwise he could not give anything nor make his spouse or bride rich. And he says in the *Proverbs* of Solomon: "With me are riches and glory." Secondly, he is very wise, otherwise he should be tired and undo all. But it is he to whom all the treasures of knowledge and wisdom are acknowledged, as Saint Paul says. Thirdly, he is very fair, otherwise he would displease his bride. And the *Psalms* speak of him that "His figure is fair, for child born of man was never so fair." Fourthly, he is very noble, otherwise he would not be praised. The Man of Wisdom says about him: "The nobility of this spouse glorifies all others." Fifth, he is very mighty, otherwise he should be oppressed by others. And *Ecclesiasticus* says: "There is a most high and mighty Creator." Sixth, he is the best of all, otherwise he should not be believed. And for this reason, it is said in the *Song of Songs*, "My friend or most beloved one is chosen out of a thousand." And the Apostle says, *Locutus est nobis etc*, "He has spoken to us through His Son"; see here the example of nobleness. "And there he constituted an heir of all", see here the abundance of riches. "By which he has made all things", see here his marvellous wisdom. "He is the one who shines over heaven", see here his beauty. "Bearing all things of pleasure", see here his infinite power. "Who gives remission to sinners', see here his sovereign goodness. Verily, the children of such a spouse have no cause to weep as long as such spouse is with them.

And you must understand that he sometimes calls Jesus Christ the Lord, otherwise Father, and at others spouse. Saint Gregory says about this: "When Jesus is to be feared, he calls him Lord. When he is to be honoured, he calls him Father. And when he is to be beloved, he calls him spouse." Consider now well the order of these names. Certainly, hon-our comes from worry, and love comes from honour. Saint Bernard says: "If I am Lord, where is my worry? If I am father, where is my honour? But when he wants to show himself as a spouse, I think that he will change his voice and say, 'If I am a spouse, where is my love?' Then God wants to be dreaded as a Lord, honoured as a father, and beloved as a spouse. But which of the three is most excellent? It is love, for without love neither worry, nor honour, or glory or grace will prevail. Unless it is made and exhibited by love and honour, worry is bound. What does not proceed from love is unworthy of being called honour, but flattery. And although the Apostle says that God gave him honour and glory, yet he shall not accept either of them unless they are mingled with the honey of love. And because of this, love keeps its excellence and is most noble. It pleases only by its very being. It is man's merit. It is his wages. It is his fruit, for his fruit is his profit." And yet Saint Bernard says: "The devout soul is the spouse of God, for it is betrothed with gifts of grace. It is joined and coupled to him by chaste love, and by the fertility of a virtuous life."

Then Jesus Christ gave the second comparison saying that no man of wisdom who labours discreetly will patch new clothes with old clothes; for new cloth is much stronger and thicker, and so breaks the old and tarnishes the beauty of the cloth. After that, Jesus Christ gave them the third comparison saying that no wise man puts new wine into old bottles; for when wine is new, the force of the wine bursts the old bottles, and the wine spills. And no man likes drinking old wine but, unrestrainedly, they will desire to drink new wine although being accustomed to old wine. Very similarly, it is not expedient to burden blunt people, who have just been converted, with grievous abstinences as it would often be hard for them to leave their custom.

Throughout all the aforesaid comparisons, the good master would conclude that his disciples, who were still innocent and novices, ought not to be constrained to the abstinence and fasting about which the Pharisees spoke. But later, when they became tougher and more renewed in the spiritual life by the grace of the Holy Spirit, they shall fast. And he would also conclude that those who were newly converted, should not be too hardly implored to do penance, lest they despair and leave the good life which they have begun. And also such things as are of high perfection ought not to be put to them until the time when they are divested and snatched out of their old worldly life, for such works would be for those who are not yet perfect, hard and severe to keep, seeing that they have not been accustomed to them. And because of this, whoever will induce and lead anyone to a perfection of virtues, ought first to instruct about small things and later, as these may be easily accomplished, how to achieve them fully. Accordingly, anyone ordering anything or giving penance to a sinner ought to take heed of Jesus Christ's example and better to urge light penance. This might with good will be more accomplished than a great and unbearable penance, which may not be accomplished, thus making one guilty before God. It is the same manner as when it is said that "Too much rigorous is perilous," for ever mercy and pity should in judgment overcome rigour.

CHAPTER 32
OF THE ELECTION OR CHOOSING OF THE TWELVE APOSTLES

FTER Our Lord, seeing the number of people following him, had called many disciples to him, he left them and departed from the row they made and went up all alone on a mountain called Tabor to pray. This mountain is within the circuit of Galilee, and at its foot is at the place where Abraham turned from doing battle which he had done against the kings which led away his brother Lot, and there found Melchisedech. Through that place flow the waters of the river Kishon. On this mountain there has been an abbey of black monks under the metropolitan bishop of Nazianzen; and the said mountain is some four miles away from that city. Or perhaps he went upon another mountain to pray to God, his Father. Anselm says: "Jesus Christ, in preaching the kingdom of heaven, dwells with the people by day, edifying them by miracles and discourses, while he passed the night in prayer and supplication on the mountain. This he did to show all that in accordance with the beat of time man ought to apply himself to doing good to his fellow Christian, with whom he lives, by words and good example, so that with his might and power he may show him the way to eternal life. He will also go up by desire the mountain of virtues and seek the sweetness of contemplation by addressing his intention to sovereign things, that he may not forget the works of mercy."

Then Jesus Christ was all night in prayer, not of this world but of God, to obtain true and very spiritual goodness, and not for himself but for us, This brings to mind that prayer is a supplication to God when man desires to obtain from Him true spiritual goodness. For some are worldly supplications when prayer is said to have earthly things; and some are to the devil, when prayer is said for bodily wills to be fulfilled. Ambrose says: "Jesus Christ was awake and praying by night to give the manner and form of prayer which you ought to follow. What shall you do to obtain salvation when you see that the Son of God keeps awake to grant it to you? Take heed that you must then take the example of Jesus Christ when you wish to do anything for which you desire to have merit, Before sending his apostles to announce and show the kingdom of heaven he first prayed alone, desiring to show that who wanted to be exalted by God must keep himself clean of vainglory and worldly praise and seek a secret place and desire to be alone." Bernard says: "The blessed Son of God commands us in the Holy Gospel and says: "When you pray to God, go into your chamber secretly and shut fast the door behind you, and then pray to God your father." And he who has said and commanded this even did it before you. For in praying to God the Father by night, he would depart not only from people but also from his apostles, giving himself to prayer. Finally he gave up himself to his death and passion. When he would pray God his Father he would leave apart his three apostles though he was more familiar with them in spite of all than with the others." Chrysostom says: "Rise at night when you desire to pray to God secretly, for in the night the soul is more pure in itself because of the darkness and silence surrounding it at such time of rest; so that it may in this manner be sufficiently brought to compunction. When a man prays to God by night, vainglory shall not bother him. And to say the truth, the fire does not depart as long as the iron rod is still red, as night prayer endures what removes sins; for what the sun smites with its heat by day, night sweetens and moistens it again. And also tears shed in prayer by night surpass all other dews and moistures and are good against all lustfulness and pride. If then man is not washed in this dew, he would then immediately go dry. Also man ought to pray to God by night as by day, to show that night not only belongs to the body, but likewise also to the soul." To whoever then desires to speak with God and to obtain divine consolation, must first find a place in solitude or where he would be alone and can leave all worldly comfort. Bede says of this and gives us an example in the Holy Gospel saying: "Each one knows the story how Saint John was brought to the island of Patmos by Domitian due to his preaching, and there God's secrets were shown to him." And similarly men find that many others have in a short time won more alone than they have during their life in company. And Saint Bernard says: "Come and let us mount and go up the mountain of Our Lord to the house of God of Jacob, and there we shall be taught His ways. Oh you, all my intentions, thoughts, wills, affections and all my heart, come to the mountain of God, and let us mount to the place where as God sees so is He there seen. And you, my heart's earnest care, anguish and other pains, tarry here beneath with this ass which is my body, so that I and this child, who is understanding, may go up on high, and after having prayed we shall return to you. Unless it would be too soon that we return to you since in this world a man may not dwell for long in the mountain of contemplation."

Now when it was day, Jesus Christ called his disciples to him and chose twelve of them to remain with him. He called them apostles, or those who are "sent to preach" to announce the heavenly kingdom. Earlier he had called them to be disciples, but now he called them to be apostles. He did his after he had prayed God his Father by day and by night, showing us that when prelates are promoted to a higher position there ought to be prayer before and that they ought to be chosen by devout supplications and not by installations or worldly promises. The *Interpretation* says, "Our Lord going upon the mountain called to him those whom he would have and he chose them. And it was not by their merits that they were chosen to that dignity, but only by goodness and divine grace." It was because of this that he later said to them: "You have not chosen me, but I have chosen you." This shows that in the election of prelates there should be excluded any manner of deception which may be done by worldly means such as money, promotion through descent and worldly honour; for divine grace only appears when in election each and everyone can be chosen. But alas, nowadays many elections are defiled in various ways, and this brings great offence to God. The institution and making of apostles on the mountain also means that bishops, who are the apostles' successors, are persons of the most sovereign degree in the Church. And it is because of this they are called bishops, just as saying being above all others in attending and caring for others, for they ought to be busy and attend to Jesus Christ's sheep which they ought to lead on with all their power and to direct in spiritual life. But woefully, many of them do less good works than people do, and neither have any profit themselves or bring it to others, so that they enjoy the name without the work.

Now just as divine grace was greatly magnified and lauded in the apostles' calling, for they were such simple people, the number twelve had a great meaning too. For twelve, being the number of apostles which Our Lord chose, was figured in many ways. These twelve apostles are first and foremost the twelve Patriarchs, for having engendered all Christians to the spiritual way. Secondly, they are the twelve living fountains or wells of heaven, for by their doctrine they have endowed the Holy Church and the whole world. Thirdly, they are the twelve precious stones or vestments of the high priest of the Law, for by their example they adorn, furnish and make shine the Holy Church. Fourthly, they are the twelve loaves which were set upon the table of the prop-osition in the temple of God, in nourishing holy souls with the words of eternal life. Fifth, they are the twelve princes of the line of Israel, since they declared the commandments of salvation and entirely governed the Holy Church. Sixth, they are the twelve spies or explorers of the Promised Land, for having sought by contemplation the life to come and afterwards showed it to the devout. Seventh, they are the twelve stones which were brought by Joshua's command from the river Jordan, since they have kept in contempt the flux and course of this world. Eighth, they are the twelve stones of Jesus Christ's altar, for the sacrifice was born from them. Ninth, they are the twelve calves sacrificed to God, in sustaining martyrdom for Jesus Christ. Tenth, they are the twelve oxen under the brass cistern, for having preached and ministered the grace of baptism. Eleventh, they are the twelve little lions which were on the throne of Solomon, for having vanquished the world, tyrannies and other obstinate rulers, threatening them with the horrible pains of hell. Twelfth, they are the twelve prophets, for having advised the Holy Church of coming times. Thirteenth, they are the twelve hours of the day, which order the time to be awake according to God's laws. Fourteenth, they are the twelve city gates, opening with the power of their key the kingdom of heaven. Fifteenth, they are the twelve city foundations, sustaining by their merits and prayers all the Holy Church. Sixteenth, they are the twelve stars in the crown of the spouse, enlightening the Holy Church by their doctrine and miracles. Seventeenth, they amount to twice six, which is a perfect number, meaning that those holding the apostolic office ought to be perfect in two manners, namely in life and knowledge, or in works and words.

These apostles, according to Bede, are chosen by Jesus Christ for three times, for by them the faith of the Holy Trinity ought to be preached to the four parts of the world. And because of this it is written about the holy city of Jerusalem that he descended from heaven and had three gates in each of the eastern and western parts, and south- ern and northern parts. Whereby in figure it was given to understand that the law of Jesus Christ ought to be preached throughout the whole world both by the apostles and by their successors. And according to Saint Jerome, Jesus Christ set the number of twelve apostles for them to sit on twelve thrones and judge the twelve tribes of Israel.

The names of the apostles which Jesus Christ chose are as follows: Simon or Peter and Andrew, his brother; James, the son of Zebedee and John, his brother. And Jesus named the latter two Boanerges, that is to say the sons of thunder; for they often heard the terrible voice and the thunder of God the Father resounding over his Son in the sky. Then there came Philip and Bartholomew; Thomas; and Matthew the Publican; James, the son of Alpheus, who is called James the Just for the holiness of his life, and also the Lesser for he was called after his brother, besides being called brother to Our Lord because he was so much like him; and Simon the Publican, his brother, called Canaanite since he hailed from Cana, a town in Galilee, meaning love and because of this he was called the Zealot, that is emulator; Thaddeus, seemingly his brother who is called Judas Jacobi, that is to say brother of James the Lesser. And Judas Iscariot, or hailing from Kerioth, a village in the land of Judea where he was born. He was chosen amongst the apostles of Jesus Christ to accomplish David's prophecy that Jesus Christ was to be given to the Jews by one of his disciples, and also to excuse the good when any evil or falsehood is found in their company. Saint Augustine says: "I am loathe to say that he was better at home than in the company of the apostles." And according to the same Saint Augustine, he was chosen by Jesus Christ since Jesus Christ was well adapted to Judas' evil, and to accomplish the ordaining of his passion, and to give example to his Church of the patience needed to suffer evil. According to Saint Ambrose, he was chosen in order to show that truth is a great thing, which no evil man may defraud or break. He would be abandoned by his apostles and be sold and delivered by one of his apostles to give example that if a man is abandoned or sold or betrayed by his company, he ought to take it patiently and meekly. According to Theophilus, he chose Judas to show that he does not cast away his grace from anyone because of the evil that is to come, but that anyone who is in grace and in virtue is still accepted. Jesus Christ named the apostles by their proper names in order to exclude those false and deceiving apostles who were to come, so as to resist their doctrine, By naming them, men might know those who were not the ones which Jesus Christ chose, and so keep away from them. And also so that it would be shown that the apostles' names and of those who receive their doctrine were written in the Book of Life. It should also be noted that in naming them, he assembled them, as a sign of broth-erly love and in approbation of the company bearing each other's deeds. And in helping one another, they ought to be stronger in the confession of the faith against all the assaults which might come to them.

Now, as Saint Augustine says, Jesus Christ chose as his disciples, whom he called apostles, since they were of little repute and among the people of the world they were con-sidered not to have any knowledge and honour. He wanted to show that all the great and virtuous works which they were about to do and what they did was by him and in him. Ambrose says: "Consider the divine ordinance and heavenly counsel. For God has no will to choose any noble, rich or wise people according to worldly wisdom, to send them about the world to show the heavenly kingdom; but He would choose fishermen and publicans to show that he had not deceived the world by worldly wisdom, nor bought it back by riches or drawn any man to his grace by authority of power and nobleness, and also in order to show that the authority of truth is above all other vain and worldly altercations."

And although he might have taught them in the place where he was, yet he went upon the mountain to pray and preach and to teach his apostles in a more familiar manner, showing that those who teach all others God's righteousness ought to ascend upon the mountain and height of virtues. And he ought not to leave his intent and purpose wishing for low and frivolous things, but he should ever strengthen himself with sovereign things. Chrysostom says: "Whoever is a teacher ought to keep himself in full virtue, for no man may keep himself in the valley and speak about the moun- tain. Take heed that you keep yourself from the place where you have spoken or how you would speak. If your mind is on earth, how can you speak about heavenly things? If you speak of heaven, take heed you keep yourself away from the world. And if you show yourself not being righteous, why do you desire to hear your righteous master? Why do you call him master, if you are not his disciple?" And Richard of Saint Victor says: "The fact that Jesus Christ went upon the hill to teach his disciples shows us that whoever ministers the word of God to others ought not keep himself in the valley of evil works, nor in the field of idleness and negligence, but rise on the mountain of spiritual conduct by exercise of the virtues, for as Isaiah says: Climb upon the mountain you who evangelise the kingdom of heaven." To teach he would also go to the top of the hill as from there he would give the great and high commandments. And just as he would give the lesser commandments to the people of Israel on Mount Sinai, so would he give the great commandments to his disciples on the mountain to show himself to be one only and the same God who had given the Law and who now gave the law of the Gospel. 🔖🔖

CHAPTER 33

OF THE SERMON THAT JESUS CHRIST MADE TO HIS APOSTLES ON THE MOUNTAIN

FTER these things, Our Lord Jesus Christ gave a very sweet and delightful sermon to his apostles. As Saint Augustine says, if any man will pitifully and soberly consider this sermon, he shall find in it all that belongs to perfection and the good ways according to which a Christian ought to live, since it contains all the commandments by which Christian life may come to perfection. This sermon is recounted in variant shades by Saint Matthew and Saint Luke; and because of this, some say that Jesus Christ first made a sermon to his disciples alone on the highest place of the hill as recounted by Saint Matthew. Then later, on the hill or mountainside and at a lower level, he made a very similar one as recounted by Saint Luke which was common for both disciples and those who were present by way of preaching to them and standing before them. Others say that Our Lord first sat down with his disciples at the peak of the mountain, and when he had chosen the twelve, he came down with them much lower on the mountain side, and there gave a passing fair sermon both to his disciples and to the people together. This sermon though recounted by the two Evangelists in different manners yet holds only one truth, although the first is most commonly observed and conforms more with the truth. Because Jesus delivered his sermon in this manner it is the custom in the Holy Church that when the preacher gives a sermon to the people, he stands before them, as in offering himself to doing battle and to fight by doing good works; but when the preacher speaks to clerics and religious, he sits, to show them that they should have rest and contemplation.

Our Lord Jesus at the beginning of this sermon ordained eight beatitudes or blessings, or eight virtues, explaining each one of them accordingly and showing that whoever wants to be recompensed must first study to receive that merit. Saint Augustine says: "No one who is willing may lack fortune. But just as no one runs away from here, so no one ought to refuse the labour and pain. Who is he who would not run with joy if someone told him that he shall be very fortunate and blessed? He should gladly hear this word. Even when he is told that if he does such work he shall be rewarded, and that he ought to exercise himself in virtue, he should not run away from the labour if he wants to have the reward, but he ought to much more force himself happily to labour and distress."

You should know that a beatitude comes in two ways. One is found in hope, namely in this life; the other is real, in truth, namely as it is in heaven. Those who in this world are great and excellent in virtues are in this life blessed in hope, and after they shall be blessed by glory in paradise.

Then Jesus Christ taught the beatitudes to his apostles. And he said, *Beati pauperes spiritu*, "Blessed are they who are poor in spirit," that is those who practise wilful poverty and choice and have not left and abandoned worldly things by force or deceit, "for theirs is the heavenly kingdom." Whereupon it comes to mind that in this place you abide by wilful poverty to abstain yourself here from the love of the world, that is to say from those things which the world desires. Similarly it is also a plain renunciation of all delightful things that may be found in riches, delights or honours. For keeping in contempt such riches grows out of contempt for oneself. Whoever for the love of God truly and meekly keeps himself in contempt in such manner that, although he is a good man yet he reputes himself worst of all the most unworthy, so even more easily he will despise the temporal things which come his way. This beatitude, which means poverty, may just as well be understood as wilful poverty or humility.

According to these two meanings this beatitude holds the first place since first, wilful poverty is the first perfection of those who will follow the blessed Jesus Christ and it is the foundation of all spiritual edifices. For he who is laden with temporal things may not easily follow Jesus Christ who is the mirror of poverty; and whoever submits his affection to transitory things is not free but bound. Certainly, I willingly make myself a servant of what

I love affectionately and because of this there is nothing to love but God, and if I love other things this should be for His love. Saint Ambrose says: "Both Gospels have set this beatitude as the first or in terms of order it comes first as the mother engendering all other virtues. Whoever for the love of God keeps in contempt worldly things deserves spiritual things. He who may not nor will deliver himself of this world's covetousness could not desire to merit the kingdom of heaven." Secondly, humility may be set first as it goes against all vices, mostly pride which is head and lord among other vices. Saint Augustine says about it: "It should be so that by wilful poverty we understand the meek and those who fear God. No beatitudes ought to begin at any other virtue than poverty or humility since by them man comes to sovereign wisdom." Now the beginning of wisdom is the fear of God, and opposite to it the beginning of all evil is pride. Chrysostom says: "Just as among vices pride is the main one which leads the soul to hell, also among virtues humility is the one which makes the soul deserving of being exalted into heaven."

Then here follows the second beatitude, which is *Beati mites*: "Blessed and fortunate are they who are meek and do not think highly of themselves, for they shall possess the kingdom of heaven." Meekness comes after poverty, for the poor often has enemies and suffers and is troubled by many wrongs; and for this he need be patient and meek. Patience and meekness go together, and there is no differ- ence but only in name. He is called meek him who does not offend any man, and patient and enduring him who suffers and endures the evil done to him by men. And a man is called *mansuetus* if he is well accustomed to knowing the meaning of suffering strokes and buffeting, and who does not render evil for evil. Patient is he who is not troubled by anything, but constantly perseveres in goodness of spirit. Accordingly, the patient is held in affection, and the meek is loved. So the patient are called men of gentleness and mildness, or meek and kind, having a lowly disposition, meek and simple, and patient in all injuries which men may do him, without feeling any bitterness in the stomach about anything men do them; and when men mock these people, they take it meekly and wish them no evil, but they ought to overcome the evil with their goodness. And indeed, such people are very fortunate, for they shall possess or be in double possession, that is to say of their proper bodies for having suffered patiently, and then after of the heavenly kingdom, which they represented on earth. I say that they shall possess the land of their proper bodies, for the meek and patient have lordship over themselves; something which angry people do not have, as they will never submit their sensuality to reason. They shall also possess the land of paradise, for God has possessed them in this mortal world, and because they shall possess the land where man lives for ever. According to what the Gospel says, because the patient have studied in this world to have lordship over themselves, it is rightly so that after this world they should enjoy and possess the heritage of the kingdom of heaven. Augustine says: "You shall possess the land when you shall be joined by love to him who made heaven and earth, since to be patient is none else than not to resist, or be obstinate against God; that is to say, whatever comes to you, be pleased with God and thank Him for all. And if you suffer any evil you should not displease God but think of it as coming from your own doing. For you are pleasing to God in your own disfavour, and unpleasant to God in pleasing yourself." Now, in the same manner as Bede says, if the heavenly kingdom is promised to the poor in spirit, and the land of life to the meek and patient, what remains for the proud other than hell?

Here follows the third beatitude, *Beati qui lugent*, "Blessed and fortunate are those who weep, for they shall be greatly comforted." And it is appropriate that this beatitude is set in order as the third. For after holding the world in contempt through poverty in spirit and then the rest of the soul which man obtains by patience, in looking at himself and his state he shall not find anything in him or in others other than things deserving weeping and sighing, and he starts weeping about them. Now he ought not to weep for any temporal losses, but for spiritual misdoings. As indeed, those who weep in this world are very fortunate for Our Lord shall gather the tears of their eyes by the consolation he will afterward give them. And as Saint Bernard says, those tears are very fortunate which deserve to be gathered by the hand of the Lord of pity. And Bishop Maximus of Turin says that tears do not obtain God's forgiveness, but have great merit and acceptance. Although they do not show their cause yet they still win mercy. Certainly, speech does not often recount all the cause, but tears state and show all desire. Let those who weep be comforted both here and in time to come. In this present world they shall be com-forted by the Holy Spirit, who shall give them many joys; and in the next even more, when they shall have heavenly joy. And according to Chrysostom, Our Lord recompenses such weeping with consolation and perpetual joy; for man ought to weep during all this present life, considering he does so much harm, so that, if he would only consider it and reckon one thing and another, it would be of great pain to keep him from weeping. For were a stranger to come out of a foreign country and see the confusion of our way of life and the faults we do against God's commandments, he would undoubtedly judge us as enemies going against God's commandments, and also that we should determine and meditate on how to resent them. So that man ought first to weep for his own sins and miseries. Secondly, for the sins and miseries of others. Thirdly, for the pains and labours which are in this miserable life. Fourthly, for the peril and doubt about eternal life. Fifth, for the delay or love of everlasting joy. Regarding these five aforesaid manners of weeping, those who weep sincerely shall be comforted also in five manners. With regard to the first weeping, they shall find consolation in the remission of their sins. As to the second, they shall be comforted with God's saving power and evil being condemned. As to the third, they shall be comforted of being delivered from this miserable life, and the fourth, they shall find joy in being delivered from eter-nal pains. With regard to the fifth, they shall be comforted by the consolation of perpetual joy. And then they may say according to the Psalm: "My soul has enjoyed your solace after the multitude of sorrows which were in my heart." Saint Gregory agrees with this sentence saying: "There are four qualities by which the soul is by right marvellously affected in compunction. Namely, when a man remembers the evils which he has done, in thinking where he has been; where the sentence of God's great judgment shall judge him, in dreading and thinking what shall become of him; or in considering the evils existing in this present life; or when he thinks of the everlasting and eternal goodness which he may not obtain as long as he is in this world."

After this the fourth beatitude follows, *Beati qui esuriunt et sciciunt iusticiam*, "Blessed are those who have hunger and thirst, which is a great desire to accomplish justice." And according to Bede and Saint Jerome, those who never esteem themselves to be righteous enough, but from day to day kindle themselves to profit in righteousness, doing from better to better and having full desire to act in the manner of him who has hunger, which desire would not only be that justice is accomplished in them but also in all others. And it is not only those doing the works of justice who are fortunate, but also those desiring them to be done. For although they do not perform what they desire, yet they are fortunate for doing what lies in them. Saint Augustine says: "He who perfectly knows and loves justice is himself just if he, and his exterior parties, never did any other exterior work." This resembles justice which is a general virtue of all other virtues, and by which man abandons all that is evil and does all that is good; and after this, man is gen-erally called just by the exercise of virtues. For according to Chrysostom, whoever desires to be converted and keep himself after God's justice has hunger for justice.

It is very fitting that this beatitude follows the first three, since whoever has felt contempt for worldly things, and applies himself to take control of his conditions in meekness and weep for his faults, may well have hunger to accomplish justice as he was not able to do before. For, according to Saint Ambrose, when a sick body is really ill, it does not take any heed of hunger. And because of this, the first three deliver man from this present evil world, in like manner as it appears. For poverty casts out of itself all riches and does not feel what pleasure men have in it. Weeping erases the evil man has committed. And the divine favour which here follows strengthens man for heaven. The first of which being hunger and thirst for justice, distributing to each what is his: to God, to his neighbour and to himself. To God man owes three things, namely honour to his Creator, love to his redeemer, and fear before his judge. To his neighbour too he owes three things, namely obedience to his sovereign, concord and peace with his peers, and mercy and support for whoever is of a lower degree than himself. And three things as to himself, namely being clean of heart, chaste of mouth, and holy of body.

Those who have hunger and thirst for justice are very fortunate indeed. For they shall be satisfied, not only in the life of fortune, of which the *Psalms* say "I shall be satisfied when your glory shall be manifest," but also in this present life. For in like manner as the covetous man has hunger and thirsts after his neighbour's goods, he too that desires anything ought to be content with what he has of his own.

Now comes the fifth beatitude, which is *Beati misericordes*, "Blessed are they who are merciful, for they shall obtain mercy from God." It is very fitting that mercy is set according to justice or righteousness. For the one ought not to be without the other, and the one ought to be tried and mingled with the other. For mercy without justice descends to dissolution, justice without mercy descends to cruelty. Both one and the other proceed out of fairness. Now mercy is none other than having compassion on one's neighbour as on oneself. And it is because of this that those who are very pitiful and fight against the misery of others as their own, are called merciful. Mercy is when a person forgives the wrongs done to him and does not keep any hate or rancour in his heart, and helps his neighbour as much as he can, both bodily and spiritually.

Now it is to be noted that there are three manners how to show mercy. The first is that which man has on his own evil, the same as the Book of *Ecclesiastes* says, "Have pity and mercy on your soul to be pleasing to God." The second is to do well to your neighbour and have compassion on his faults. The third mercy is tender love, which should be shown towards God in having compassion of the death and passion of his blessed redeemer. By the first we obtain from God the remission of our sins. By the second, a lessening or release from our pains and a great increase in intercessors, for whoever diminishes another person's pain deserves that God diminishes his pain. By the third we deserve everlasting joy for, as the Apostle says, if we have the compassion like that our maker suffered for us in this world, we shall reign with him in his glory. And Saint Ambrose says that whoever has true compassion on Jesus Christ, ought to suffer in his body, as much as he can, the anguish which Jesus Christ suffered; the same as Saint Paul did. And for this we ought, with great care, to incite ourselves to mercy seeing that in all we need God's mercy. This virtue is so excellent that it is attributed above all others as belonging to God. And because of this it is said *Deus cui proprium*, "O God, it belongs to you to have pity and mercy and good will."

On judgment day, rebuke the condemned since they had no mercy, and reward the just and those who have had mercy with salvation. Marvellously the works of mercy shall help at the day of judgment those who have performed them. For, as Saint James says, judgment without mercy shall be done to him who has not done mercy in this world. And Saint Augustine recounts that the Son of God says that those who help the miserable and poor are very fortunate, for in such manner they shall be rewarded and delivered from misery. Do then mercy, and it shall be done to you. Certainly, what you shall give him who asks for your forgiveness, the same shall God do to you when you shall ask mercy of Him. And Saint Hilary says: "With what great affection does God delight himself in the mercy of man, giving His mercy only to those who are blessed and merciful." And Chrysostom says: "The God of mercy says that the merciful are very fortunate in showing that each one of us may not obtain mercy of Him unless one has been merciful in this world." Chrysostom yet says that "It seems that it should be equal retribution to render mercy for mercy. But there is a great difference, for there is no equality between human mercy and the divine." So do tyrants and cruel people enforce them, though they perish with their cruelty and tyrannies. And blessed are the merciful, for they shall obtain God's mercy in a time to come, where they shall be exalted from all misery, from guilt and pain in this world, and where their sins shall be forgiven and grace given. And also temporal goods shall be made to raise them up from all miseries, in this that they are expedient for their salvation.

The sixth beatitude follows, which is *Beati mundo corde, quoniam etc*, "Blessed are those who are clean of heart." Not only outwardly, as do these false hypocrites who clean only that which shall appear on the outside; or as do the worldly rich who are concerned about how to keep their bodies clean. But those who have a clean heart and conscience are very fortunate, and then they shall take again no sin upon them, for in this world they will flee from all evil as much as possible for them, and do all the good as they may for a good purpose and with true intent. These are very fortu-nate, for they shall see God in His everlasting vision which cleanses so marvellously that it unites the soul to God. And the heart from which no evil thoughts come, is made the temple of God; and if the heart is clean from evil thoughts, all the body shall be clean from all wickedness. That is the place where the sins come from and where they are rooted; and if they are cut away from there, they will no longer grow.

This beatitude is well and appropriately set in the sixth order. For man, who is created in God's image by love and knowledge is capable of such worldliness when he lost the sixth day. And cleanliness of heart is as of right set after mercy. For according to Saint Ambrose, whoever has done mercy to another, loses his merit if it is not done with a clean heart. For if in any good work he seeks boasting or vainglory, he shall have no merit. Augustine says: "Here is the purpose of our love." For all the good we do is to have the vision of God; which is something we should desire more than anything else; and it is promised to those who are clean of heart. Prepare then all that with which you ought to see Him, for He will not let you see Him if you are not clean of heart and conscience. And in the same manner since to see the Son the oil of the body must be pure and clean, then it is even more reasonably deserving that to see God the oil of the heart, which is understanding, must be clean. Ambrose says: "Cleanse your heart and cast away from you all pollution and unclean thoughts. Let your mind be on simple things and pure intent, that nothing may turn your affection into unclean thoughts. It is to such men that the Lord God shows Himself when death comes." And the more that cleanliness will shine in you, you shall have an even more and better sight of God.

Here follows the seventh beatitude, which is *Beati pacifici:* "Blessed are the peace lovers" that is to say the lovers of peace who diligently apply themselves to make peace, both within themselves and with their neighbours, "for they shall be called the children of God." Peace follows the cleansing of the heart well and suitably. For as Saint Ambrose says, when you shall cleanse your soul from all filth of sin, then peace shall take root in you; and so afterwards you may pacify others. He then says, "Blessed are the peace lovers." He says not "those who have or set their mind to peace," for that is something concerning the second beatitude, which is sweetness or meekness. But the peace lovers are those who first of all have peace within themselves by casting out of their souls all that which they may perceive, as in thoughts, words and works which might hinder them from coming to this peace, and by having nothing living in them which might trouble their soul's kingdom. And if anything goes against their wishes, they will yet live in peace and let nothing deter them, judging nothing so good as having tranquillity of heart. And when they see their neighbour in any discord, they urge them to return to a state of peace ever willing, just as much as for themselves as for their neighbour, to reform themselves and keep peace. These are the offices of the Son of God, who in himself peacefully reforms and calls others to peace. And it is because of this that it is said of such persons that they shall be called the Sons of God.

Peace lovers are also so called here those who by affec- tion unite their soul only to God and seek nothing save only Him, only finding rest in Him to pacify them. And for such resemblance they deserve to be called sons of God, whose characteristic is to have the joy of a spiritual good in themselves and to abide in it. We then ought to be peace lovers, that we may have within us the very Lord of peace, of whom it is written that his place is made in peace. According to Saint Augustine, the mild ones or peace makers are those who ordain all the movements of their soul and submit them to reason; they would have abandoned all carnal lustfulness and come to God's kingdom, to which all things are ordained in such manner that reason, which is essential to man, has lordship above all other powers belonging to us and to beasts. Such reason submits itself to the sovereign truth of God, for it may neither command nor have sovereignty above others unless it obeys the Lord. And in this is the peace which is given on earth to men of good will, this peace being the life accomplished by the perfect and wise man.

Now after comes the eighth beatitude, *Beati qui persecucio-nem*, "Very fortunate are those who not only do good, but also suffer and patiently endure persecution, not for their sins, but for what is right," which is to say according to Chrysostom, for piety, virtue and to defend the goodness of others. Justice is often understood as all the virtue found in the soul. "For such is the heavenly kingdom." According to Chrysostom, after Jesus Christ set the beatitude of patience, so that no one should think that his goodness ought ever to seek peace, he accordingly set the beatitude of suffering persecution, which makes man perfect to endure well, in like manner as all the aforesaid consumes and comes to good work. For just as good works pertain to virtue, so also are pain or the will to suffer to be expected.

Now one may say or ask: "Should I dispose myself to death to defend the liberty and prerogatives of the Church?' The answer is "Yes," for spiritual things and for the love of justice. Although for temporal things it is great peril to a man to risk his life, yet often we put ourselves in danger to do this, for we are more inclined towards it by false desires than by justice. And Saint Ambrose speaks about this question: "If the emperor demanded of me what belongs to me, such as my possessions, money or other things, he namely expects that I should not refuse or deny him any-thing, although all that I have belongs to the poor. But divine things do not belong to imperial power. If he desires my livery, he may take it or leave it. If he asks for my body, I shall present it myself and say, 'If you will take me for your bondman or if you will take me to put me to death, I am pleased, it is my will.' I will not defend myself engaging a multitude of men of arms, nor yet take the privileges of the Church to safeguard my life. But for the things and for what belongs to Holy Church, I am ready to endure and suffer death."

This is the eighth beatitude, and it accomplishes the aforesaid matters and is the epitome of all crowns. For when man is perfect in the mentioned beatitudes, he ought also to be found worthy to suffer the adversities that might come to him in this world for the love of God. Chrysostom says that Our Lord began to declare the first beatitude, he proceeded to make way to the second, and from the second to the third, and so compiling like a fair chain of gold. For whoever shall be meek, shall be patient; and whoever shall be patient, shall weep for his sins; and whoever sheds tears for his sins, has hunger and an urge to accomplish justice and righteousness, and is merciful because of this. And if he is merciful, he must consequently be clean of heart and conscience; and whoever is so, must without doubt be patient. And whoever is perfect in all these eight, is undoubtedly prepared to sustain all adversities, or that anything coming to him cannot overcome him if he is constant in enduring and suffering all. Whoever has in him these virtues is then very fortunate, and he is even more fortunate if he keeps them in all the adversities which may come to him. Then the seven aforesaid beatitudes make man perfect, and the eighth clarifies and shows what is perfect, since patience is a work of fulfilment and perfection. He ought to be inclined to all the aforesaid, since these were approved beatitudes. For the scorpion, which is ever non-combative and does not heave up his head unless he is touched and pricked, then he immediately rises and casts out of his throat and strikes whoever provokes him; so does the unrestrained man who lacks virtue, when pricked by words or a wrong deed like a serpent hurls himself at the throat of some for anger and of others for wrath, or when pierced by injurious words or impatience strengthens himself against those who vexed him; whereupon a man may see that his vessel is empty of all virtues. And to the contrary, if a man smites holy people, they take it patiently for the love of God. They love their enemies, and consider their persecution worthy. Bernard says: "Just as the stars show light by night and do not appear at all by day, so does virtue, which does not appear in prosperity, but shines in adversity." And because of this, it so seems that the eighth should not be a beatitude, nor should it be distinct, for it is an illumination and confirmation of all those aforesaid. For there is only one love which answers man, as in the first, namely the kingdom of heaven, since those who are despised and suffer great persecutions and those who are mocked and despised in this world, are in wilful poverty of spirit. And because of this the two beati-tudes fit in merit together, for wilful poverty is a manner of martyrdom, because in everything man ought to overcome his own will regarding the delights of the world. Each one then hearing these things must consider whether he is con-tained in any of these beatitudes; and if he finds himself there, he ought to be sure that if he continues, he shall be very blessed. For the truth, which does not tell lies, says so.

After generally pronouncing them, Jesus Christ further prevails by conversing with his apostles about what he said, showing them three manners of performance, that is to say of the heart, the mouth and works. He says to them that "you shall be blessed when people have cursed you," as regards the first; "when they shall have persecuted you, you shall be divided and separated from each other, in putting and casting you from their synagogues as unworthy to be there," as regards the third; "and they shall have said all evil and opprobrious words which they may say against you, in hurting your good renown by their evil words, and in having cast your names," that is the name of Christendom, "as evil people and as they that herded together in error," as regards the second. It is not like saying that man ought to seek to suffer such things, but it should be understood that for fear of them he ought not to leave the truth of life, justice or doctrine. These three enemies deny God's Church, and Jesus Christ gives three remedies against them, namely of patience, that is to say that for his love men ought to forgive all offences done to them; and that a man has compassion on his neighbour's sin; and that man prays that he may turn himself away from his evil, that God may forgive him his sins. And it is because of this that not all persecution makes man blessed, but only that which is gladly received for the love of justice which is Jesus Christ himself. Jesus Christ suffered them to say: "You and we shall lie in saying such opprobrious words against you and against the Christian name", for if such evil sayings were true, this would not be a beatitude. Augustine says: "If you suffer any adversity because you have sinned, you suffer it for yourself and not for the love of God. But if you suffer for having kept God's commandments, you certainly suffer for God." And your work shall be perpetual; which is what they now feel in their hearts that they might say: "We glorify ourselves in anguish." This is no great fruit to suffer persecution or adversity in this world without taking it patiently for the love of Jesus Christ.

And because of this he finally sets the reward for such patience, giving us comfort in willingly suffering for him. For according to Saint Jerome, all labour is lighter when a man knows his reward shall be great. And he says, *Gaudete*: "Be joyful in your hearts and exalt yourselves and I shall give you exterior gladness in showing you outward joy, so as to be of an example to your neighbour." For the reward which you shall have in heaven is not only great, but so plentiful and abundant that man may not comprehend it. And it is so copious that it is countless. It is so precious, that it is immeasurable. And it lasts for so long that it is endless. The more that man has patience for the love of God and has suffered the above injuries and anguish to obtain virtues, his wages and reward are even much greater. For God rewards not man justly with as much and no more, but according to how much he has laboured or to his multitude of works. It is the manner and root from which such works proceed, the same as it appeared to Jesus Christ when he sat in the temple and saw the little piece of silver which the widow gave by way of great alms. But alas, we find joy for what we should be weeping, for there is more peril in prosperity than in adversity, in worldly praise than in despising, so that in such manner we are deceived. Let us now find joy with the apostles in all anguish, that we may be greatly rewarded by God. Saint Jerome says: "I know not who of us shall be he who may here accomplish and desire that his renown is held in derision and scorn by opprobrium, and not any less to find his joy in God. This would not be him if he desires to accomplish vainglory and worldly praise." Chrysostom says: "As much as it is man himself who finds joy and takes pleasure in the world, so much is he displeased in being despised and mocked by the world. But whoever only desires the joy of heaven need not fear the rebukes done to him by man in this world." Seneca says: "You are never well in perfect holiness till the world mocks you. Then if you want to be blessed, think first about being despised by the world. If you want to show that you are a good and virtuous man, suffer to be despised and reputed for a fool. For if anyone condemns you or wrongs you, if you have virtue within you, you shall not feel it."

And not only Our Lord Jesus Christ urged the apostles to penance by the recompense or reward which he promised them, but also according to the Prophets' example, by giving them the solace of those who have suffered great persecu' tions to keep on sustaining the truth. And he said: "If the prophets which have been before you," such as Jeremiah, Isaiah and the others, "have suffered so much persecution and torments to do and say the truth, why do you not take an example from them if their beatitude pleases you?" Jesus Christ was here referring to the way of going about with an elephant when, in fighting it, men show him blood or some red colour so as to make him fight even more strongly. It is also proposed to us, according to Our Lord Jesus Christ and the martyrs' example, to comfort us against all adversities and anguish which may come against us. For likewise as the Apostle says, all those who live a holy life following Jesus Christ must suffer persecutions in this world. If you suffer persecution be very courageous for that is a good sign. And if you do not suffer patiently, you will not live a holy life in Jesus Christ. Ambrose says: "When we will not endure the persecution sent to us by God, it is a sign of reprobation and of condemnation; for we will not live like Jesus Christ, and it seems that our intention would not be to follow our master, and that we flee the way in which he walked." But one may say: "No man may come now to the beatitude and to eternal glory by suffering of persecution, for the Church has peace with all parties." To this end a man may answer that in the Holy Church secretly and daily Cain persecutes Abel; Ishmael, Isaac; and Esau, Jacob; that is to say the evil persecute the righteous or the just. And if the just does not suffer from strangers, yet he suffers from false brethren. And if he does not suffer externally, yet he suffers within himself, and those will be none others but his spiritual enemies. And because of this persecutions are not sufficient to win them or to overcome them, so that we would need patience to obtain the promises. Very unfortunate are those who in their anguish lose patience and its crown; for in the short time of having patience a man may get a great reward, which is life everlasting.

Of these eight beatitudes as recounted by Saint Matthew, Saint Luke recounts only four. But according to Saint Ambrose, these eight contain the four, and these four contain the eight. For meekness and peace are contained in patience, purity or cleanliness of heart and conscience, and wilful poverty and mercy for the purpose and to desire to accomplish justice.

And it is because of this that Our Lord, by what has been written above, urges people to faith, and to obtain virtues by the rewards which he has promised them. He consequently upset and frightened them by denouncing, showing and threatening divine punishment with the coming torments they should suffer for the sins and crimes they committed and for which they did no penance or restitution. And he said: "The curse of eternal pain be upon you who are rich; not to all, but to those who have their pleasure in this world." As if he would say, "You who have your pleasures and solace in this world shall not therefore have mine, neither in this world nor in another." He calls here the rich those who pass their life and time in sports and worldly pleasures. For riches are not so much of a sin and guilt as is love and the abuse man takes in it; as it has been similarly said before that the kingdom of heaven belongs to the poor. And he does the contrary and takes away the said kingdom from those who seek the solace and pleasures of this world which go against the kingdom of heaven. Ambrose says: "Those who shall have their sports and consolation in this present life, deserve losing the reward of eternal life." And it is after said: "Cursed be you who live in fullness and gluttony in this world and who attend lavish banquets and give in to drunkenness, for you shall have hunger in another world"; not for lack of food at the most, but of all goods in general. The gluttons shall be tormented with dire fasting and hunger, to the end that a contrary pain answers their sins. The same can be seen from the rich glutton who denied giving alms to the poor. From which it appears that, as in medicinal practice something contrary is the best medicine for man's health, the same applies to spiritual sickness when sin is absolved by contrary penance. Bede says: "If those who in this world have had desire and hunger to accomplish justice are very fortunate, to the contrary it may be esteemed that those who have taken all their desires and pleasures without wanting or desiring to do any kind of good are unfortunate and worthy of confusion."

After Jesus Christ said, *Ve vobis qui nunc ridetis*, "Woe be to you who in this world laugh with boisterous laughter full of vanities. For after that you shall weep and sigh, externally and in your inner self", namely for their lack of good deeds and the presence of their evil which they shall bear in the everlasting fire of hell. Similarly as those who weep for their sins and do penance shall be strengthened in the end, so shall those who laugh be comforted in a contrary manner. And Solomon says about this: "The laughing done in this world shall be fulfilled and mixed with sorrow, and everlasting cries of grief will follow worldly joy and pleasure." Basil says: "Although Our Lord spoke again of those who presently laugh, it is a clear thing that never in this world do we have any time to laugh if we take heed of how many people die every day in their sins; for which reason men may even sooner weep than laugh." And Chrysostom says, "Tell me what occasion you have to laugh and be glad, which might be presented before the mighty judge to render account of what you have done in this world?"

And it is here where it follows in the Gospel: "Be you cursed when the people by adulation, flattering or praise shall bless you." And in praising and commending you they make you blind, so that you shall not know yourself and fail to consider what the Apostle says: "If I please persons, I am not Jesus Christ's servant." Such praise and blessings were likewise done by false prophets and the old fathers of scribes and Pharisees, who praised and blessed in proph-esying by their own proper intelligence, not by God's com-mandment, but falsely, to be honoured and praised by the people. And the *Psalms* say this, that the sinner is praised in the desires of his soul; and who does well is blessed. But cursed are those who laud and praise others in that manner, for a flatterer's tongue is more grievous to man than the sword of persecution. Whoever flatters the evil doer sets him a cushion under his head that he may sleep even more sweetly on the feathers of flattery. If then those who are cursed and despised by malice and the world's evil will are fortunate, then by even greater reason those cursed by God are those who are lauded and praised and flattered by the people. It is of great displeasure and a punishment of God when the sinner is neither punished nor corrected but praised as much of his evil as of his good deeds. So that in such adulation he is nourished and in that manner also condemned. Saint Luke wrote these sentences since the truth of the four beatitudes written here before should appear more clearly in damning the curses which go against the beatitudes.

CHAPTER 34
HOW THE PRELATES OUGHT TO GIVE GOOD EXAMPLE, BOTH AS TO WORKS AND WORDS, TO THEIR PARISHES AND OTHERS

UR Lord Jesus Christ had by the aforesaid things greatly exhorted and admonished his apostles and disciples to suffer and for his love endure all anguish, adversities and torments which man might do them and which might arouse and happen to them. He therefore set four likenesses and comparisons in this regard, comparing them to salt, light, the city and brightness, for them to understand by these that in anguish they ought to be much stronger. As though he would say to them: "You ought not to be annoyed or be weary with anguish, because if you fail you might give occasion for the ruin of many, seeing that you are where you should be as the salt of the world, the light of the world, the city set on a mountain, and the brightness put upon the candlestick." The first two likenesses are affirmatives, since the purpose is shown by them as to the reason why the apostles and Church prelates have been instituted and set; namely to influence and give flavour to affection and desire, as salt does to the pottage, and lights do to understanding. The latter two show why they are not ordained, namely for not having kept their life or doctrine secret, nor have they personally fled.

So the apostles and prelates are called the salt of the earth owing to their life's perfection and honest conduct, by which they have made and seasoned others in teaching the souls of those who still have the taste and smell of worldly things. Salt makes earth dry and barren, but it also savours and seasons food and preserves flesh and keeps it from stinking; it is made by water and fire, and it is offered in all sacrifices. Similarly the example of holiness makes worldly affection dry and barren, and in sweetening holy desire it renders a taste of sweetness to the flesh and keeps it from stinking by restraining it from every desire of luxury and the sin of lustfulness. And it is mingled with the water of devotion and delight in being boiled in the furnace of penance. It is offered at all times to redress and moderate all our works. And principally salt means dissen, sion in Scripture, which goes with spirituality as they ought to address and render savoury the works of their subjects for them to be good and pleasant to God. And even more, by way of the salt metaphor, Jesus Christ admonished his apostles and other prelates to study and apply themselves to virtues. He said that if a priest or a doctor by which others ought to be ordered, is an idiot or deficient by fear of adversity or persecution, or for greediness, or the wealth of prosperity, or by exhilaration in pride and vainglory, or in many other ways, and shows no good example to his parishioners either by word or by deed with which all the people of this world, being so frail, ought to be salted, how will they be seasoned and led well by the life and doctrine of their superiors and of those who have care of them? Or else, if the salt, namely the prelate or doctor, offends and sins, who is he who should correct him? No man for certain. For the same as a sorcerer who is bitten by a serpent would find no one to help him, but would be told as a doctor to help and heal himself, so should discretion, which seasons our works and our faults, fail then all our doings will not be pleasing at all to God. And as a figure of this, in all Old Law sacrifices salt was offered. Salt then, when melted and mixed with water, is not worth anything for it bears no fruit and rather hinders the earth which bears fruit; nor will it do anything else which is good and so men must cast it away. Now the prelate who is ineffectual or unproductive, in being meek, ought to be cast out as one who is somewhat of a nuisance and does not profit others. And he ought to be deposed of the dignity of the orders of the Church so that the prelates' office does not appear to be vile and vicious before the people. And men ought to keep him apart from any Church office or he shall be excluded from the glory of those who are blessed and fortunate. And he shall be scorned by the world by derision, on judgment day by the angels by separation, and by the devils in hell by affliction.

The apostles and prelates are also called the light of the world because of their doctrine, by which light they ought to enlighten those who are untutored that they might believe and act. For similarly as the sun and the stars throw light on bodily eyes, so do doctors enlighten spiritual eyes. The man who wants to preach and teach well ought first to live well; and so, since Jesus Christ first said that they were the salt of the earth in living wisely, he now said they were the light of the world in enlightening those who are in darkness.

The priest then ought to be salt in the world by good living and light by giving good instructions and teaching. He ought to be salt by example, and light by doctrine. This is the right order, for good living comes first then good teaching. God is the enlightening light, but is not Himself enlightened. Light enlightens the apostles, and those who are like them or who belong to the Holy Church, and then they shine out light. Simple righteous folk give out no light, but are enlightened. The first light is like sunlight, the second like moonlight and the third like starlight.

And after salt and streaks or beams of light, there follow the protection of the city and the light given by the torch and the lamp. For the apostles and prelates ought not to keep silent and not to speak clearly of the divine words staying under the barrel and vessel of worldly fear, or under the bed and rest of worldly prosperity; but they ought to be the city set upon the mountain, serving as a place of refuge for those who are done wrong by others. And then they ought to be the light set upon the candlestick, so that the people of the world, seeing their good works, should conduct themselves in doing the same; and so that God is glorified thereby and not themselves praised. They ought then to shine light before others by their works and sayings, so that all those who see them will glorify God the Father who is in heaven. A man shall profit more in good works or doings than in good words; and examples sooner bring another to do good than just speech, for clarity is achieved more by works than by words. Whoever does nothing else but speak preaches by mouth, and then for only one hour a week; but whoever does what he ought to do by work and not only by speech, really preaches according to the truth and at all times. To teach others by mouth and not by deed, is nothing else but vanity. For according to Saint Bernard, it is but a show when the tongue says that man should do well, and the sayer's might and power are void or idle while the doctrine is pleasant and life is dark. Now it should be noted that this does not go against what shall be said after. "Take heed you do no justice before the people," for man ought to do well not due to any worldly honour but for the honour of God. Wherefore man must seek the glory and edification of his neighbour so that, in seeing such good deeds, man may glorify himself mainly before God, and not before whoever does this, and men may then follow in all good works. Men ought to seek divine glory and flee from their own.

Jesus Christ then began to instruct the apostles about what they should teach. He said, *Nolite putare*, "Do not think that you might not fall in error, that I am come into this world to destroy the Law or the prophets, in forbidding that they should not be kept spiritually." For according to Saint Augustine, all Old Testament writings prefigure and are a precedent for the New Testament. "I am not come to destroy the Law, but rather to accomplish it." Our Lord's sentence can be understood in two ways. According to Saint Augustine, to accomplish the Law is to do something which man ought not to do; and this is only what he said. Our Lord, who has added this which was less in the Law, has not destroyed what he found there, but has rather confirmed it by making it more perfect. Also that, what the Law and the prophets have promised about him is for the most part accomplished in him. "And before heaven and earth with the other elements," not as regarding matter but as regarding form, "they are finished, passed and changed, all shall be accomplished in such manner that one *iota*," that is the paint or dye that turns when the dice is cast, "shall not remain that by effect it is not accomplished," either in him as head, or in his saints, who are his bodies and members.

He afterwards showed them how the doctors ought to accomplish by deed what they say by words, taking his example, by dividing doctors into two. For there are some who teach well but lead an evil life, as did the scribes and Pharisees, it being said about them, "Whosoever shall neglect or leave undone one of the least commandments of the Law," and they are called little because they give beginning to man, "shall be called the least in the kingdom of heaven," that is in the triumph of the Church. For according to Saint Gregory, it is proper that men should not be moved by the preaching of anyone leading a scattered life. Indeed, who is it that now-adays appears to be great yet according to this sentence is very little? Augustine says: "It is clear that whoever is least in the heavenly kingdom, namely in the Church militant, shall not enter into the kingdom of heaven in time to come if he destroys by work what he teaches by words, for he may not belong to the company of those who do by works what they teach by words." Chrysostom says: "To teach others and not to do what he ought to do is no winning but a great damage, for it is most damning to work and only speak nice words while leading an evil life." There are other doctors who live well and teach others well, and so should prelates be in the Holy Church, about whom it is said, "Whoever shall teach and do what he speaks of in deed, should be called great in heaven. For those who accomplish the Law shall be justified by God." Now all commandments are reputed to be deeds when all that is not accomplished, is forgiven. And for this we ought many times to say, *Dimitte nobis debita nostra*.

After that, he confirmed what he had said, for he had not destroyed the Law, but accomplished it excessively. And he said that the true Christians who were his do works which are above and more worthy than the Law, and that their justice superseded that of the scribes and Pharisees, who say plenty but do no manner of good. For in saving souls good doctrine is not enough, but it is also requisite to have a good life, without which they may never come to the kingdom of heaven. And because of this he says, *Nisi abundaverit iusticia vestra etc.* Justice in this place is taken not for any cardinal virtue, but in so much as it goes against or quenches sin. For as Saint Jerome says, all the likeness of virtues is contained under the word of justice. And according to that meaning Saint Augustine says that there are two elements of justice, namely to deliberately avoid doing evil and to do good. And similarly justice quenches sin; and just as there are various gifts of grace, in the same manner there are various states and conditions of persons. Because of this men might say to those who are in a state of perfection as regards others,

"If your justice is no greater than that of those who are less than you, you shall not enter into the kingdom heavenly of heaven." And you must take heed that here Our Lord showed the commandments, and incited man to keep them, and that he stated their true and very good meaning. And he erased the Jews' errors in saying that outward works were only defended or forbidden by negative commands and not with the moving of the heart, and that the will in applying them or intending to do evil was no sin unless it was committed in deed. About the commandment *Non occides* they said that manslaughter in deed was forbidden, but not the purpose. And he says, *Audistis quia dictum est antiquis*, "You have heard this that has been said to the old and ancients," that is according to how the ancients interpreted it. You shall slay no man in deed, for so did the ancient Jews interpret it, and spoke nothing of the heart. And Our Lord excluded that error, in forbidding them to be angry without cause. They said that to slay a man justly or righteously with hand or deed pertains to justice and the perfection of the Law. But to slay him unjustly, it is something worthy of judgment and death, for the Law in any manner want it to be so. And to kill him of the heart or of the will is no less a sin.

And Jesus Christ stated more perfectly and forbade anyone from being angry in his heart with his brother without cause; or to show him any sin of inner commotion by voice in saying *Racha*, which is the word or term of an angry man without expression of scorning or blaspheming; or to do any other offence by speech to anyone but by expressing *Fatue*, or fool, which is a much greater offence than *Racha*. So that first, the soul's moving of anger is forbidden; secondly, so is the outward sin of resentment; and thirdly, that of despising expressed in words. As to each of these three kinds of guilt and utterances Our Saviour Jesus Christ taught three different punishments according to each guilt. The first guilt is ire or hatred of the inner heart and the desire to be angry with his brother by vicious ire; and so a man determines a suitable time when to show his hatred outwardly by deed; and the punishment for such ire or anger is to be accused before God although a man may not be accused before man of such secret anger. The second anger is that of a person who shall resentfully and abusively say the general or contemptible *Racha*; and his punishment for being guilty is that he shall be sentenced by the judge, and assigned a punishment, for his guilt is now known by all. The third, which is done by whoever moves on to insulting or especially despising and speaks of despising the person, but not of correcting the vice, with words like fool, beast, and similar words of envy; and his punishment is hellfire and punishment without end. For according to the *Interpretation*, it is no little fury to call him who God has instructed and taught by his salt of wisdom a fool. Moses then has set knife and axe to the tree's bough in forbidding homicide. And in the Gospel Jesus Christ, like a good labourer, puts the knife and axe to the root to wrench the root of sin out of our hearts.

And most suitably Jesus Christ has begun to speak of ire, which, according to the *Interpretation*, is the gate of all vices. If it is closed, we may have our rest; but if it is open, our souls shall be abandoned to all evil. Jerome says: "Anger is all evil moving others and annoying them." Sometimes it gains strength in the soul, and that is a venial sin; but at others it gains strength by careful intention, and that is a mortal sin. You must also know that not all anger is sin, for anger is none else than a desire to do vengeance; now, that a man revenges himself righteously is no sin; and ire is unlawful and unrighteous in four ways. That is to say, when one craves for or wishes evil to anyone who does not deserve it; or when man craves over the form and manner due; or if he desires some evil end or intent which is only to be revenged.

Then Our Lord devoted his doctrine to keeping us ever together in his love, peace and charity, in casting away from us the root of offence and that by which charity might be wounded. But alas, very few look in that direction. Jesus Christ says: "Do not be angry with your brother without cause." Whereupon Chrysostom says that for some it is a much easier thing not to be angry than to suffer any wrong done by him who is angry without cause. Chrysostom still says: "And if for fear of man you suffer and endure what is much greater and stronger, such as the anger and wrongs which men do to you, why do you not endure that which is less? That is not to be angry with others for the love of

God." And if here anger is now forbidden, according to Saint Augustine, much more ought ire to be dug up by the root that resentment might not commit man to hatred.

As to what has been said of ire, Jesus Christ concludes and says that whoever by faith and heart will offer an oblation on God's altar, be it host or alms or fasting, doctrine or prayer, or any other spiritual or corporal thing, he must first be reconciled with his brother if he has offended him by words or in any other manner. For God does not receive the gifts which men offer him unless they are made in charity; and no man can have charity unless he first casts out the root of discord and gratifies his neighbour. Whereupon it should be known that if man has a proper outlook on his offence, he ought to revoke it and call for grace by beseeching the other to pardon him; and if a man does not have it, it would be enough for him to have it in heart, in reverence and submitting to it by humble affection and purpose to gratify himself in time and place. It is this external appearance which the Church of Rome keeps, in absolving the sinner who confesses himself and promises to do penance in time and place. According to Chrysostom, if you have offended in thought, you ought to do penance by thought; if it is by words, it is likewise to be done; and so by works and such other similar things. For in the same manner as sin is committed, so he ought to be cleansed and to do penance. By way of example: if one has offended by belittling another man, he ought to do penance by restoring his good name. Consider these things well, for we are enlightened by them as to God's great mercy, who takes more heed and loves peace and love and man's usefulness, than the honour and sacrifice and gifts given to Him by man. Chrysostom says: "Oh marvellous, great love which God has for us. He leaves and despises His honour when He wills man to have charity with his neighbour or that he should offer or do Him sacrifice. His business is more to assemble or gather us together with the bond of charity, than that we revere Him with any oblation. By such bond, as by charity, all things are assembled, and man is made by them." God's severity also appears here, in refusing the offerings and gifts of those who live in hatred and discord. Gregory says: "We see how God will not receive the sacrifice of those who are at variance and discord; whereby we may see what evil strife is and how it hinders what may be a cause for the forgiveness of sins." Saint Cyprian says: "If whoever is in discord and is not in peace with his brethren, but would suffer himself to be slain only for the love of Our Lord yet does not put away the crime and sin of strife, he will be condemned; consider how great this sin is, seeing that the martyr who is baptised in blood, may not annul or wash it away." But alas, nowadays many are equal to Cain and Judas, going and receiving the eucharist in discord and malice, hatred and sin. About whom Chrysostom says: "If it is so that God has such great business with our reconciliation that he suffers his service to be broken so that man could be reconciled and rejoined to his brother, how much more should we then cast away from our hearts all roots of anger and rancour? And yet to the contrary, many keep for a long time the state of their hearts and their hatreds, and make them longer every day; and yet they know well that the longer they keep them, the longer punishment they will have for them."

And for so much as Jesus Christ spoke of the concord, peace and fraternity which man ought to have with his brother, he afterwards generally said that we, standing in the way, ought to consent immediately to our adversary, that is when we are in the way and passing through this present life, which is the right time and place to do penance and to have merit. And if we can do it today we should not postpone it till tomorrow, for the long wait causes the greatest hurt as no man knows for how long he shall live. There is nothing that may so much subvert man as dishonesty, and lack of courage, or to delay doing good deeds, for lack of courage often makes us fall from all the good we can do into all evil. Let us agree then with our adversary, who has offended us, that he might not be our cause for being brought before God as judge at the time of the last judgment. Let us do this then lest the judge hands us to the servants and the hangman, who is the devil of hell, to revenge himself on us. He will then put us into hell's prison, where we must render account to the last penny and half-penny, and where we shall weep for our sins, both great and small, for there is no sin which goes unpunished.

And for this cause, Jesus Christ said *donec*, "unto this", which is a determined time. According to Saint Augustine *donec* does not here mean an end of punishment, but the continuation of misery, which the sinner shall have both for his venial and mortal sins, which are united and attached to mortal sins. Our Lord Jesus Christ does not intend us here to go to our adversary, the devil of hell, to whom we ought never to consent; but he speaks of our neighbour to whom we have offended and by that has made himself our adversary; and we must ask him forgiveness for this. Also to speak mystically, when we sin we make God our adversary, and then He is against us. Similarly, the divine words are adversaries to all evil for they defend man from doing evil. The faculty of doing moral judgement and conscience are also the adversaries of sinners, since they rebuke them in doing evil. And to this we ought to obey, by abstaining from sin and submitting ourselves humbly to good guidance.

After this, Jesus Christ spoke of another reason, confirming what he had said before, namely that he was not come to destroy the Law, but to accomplish it. He did so by making known and easy to understand another commandment of the Law, *Non concupisces*, "You shall not covet or carnally desire your neighbour's wife." By which commandment the Jews understood only the actual deed and outward sign, as unclean touching, kissing and such doings, to be forbidden, but inner lustfulness was no sin. Which logic is unreasonable, for outward works and signs have no reason to be sinful unless they are done willingly. To this end Our Lord cast away from them such error, saying *Omnis qui viderit mulierem*: "All men who shall behold any woman for the purpose and end to desire doing his will with her, seeing that he neither thinks otherwise or doubts in his purpose, but still affirms and always plainly consents to wilfully accomplishing his carnal wish." And Chrysostom says about this: "If I only desire in my heart, and deliver or consent without anything else the evil of the flesh, then I count myself among adulterers." And I would have given opportunity to my lustfulness and am condemned by the Law and by Jesus Christ, author of all cleanliness. The Law condemns adulterers by deed, and the Gospel condemns lustfulness which is the root of all sins. And in figure of this, Saint John the Baptist, who at that time signified the Old Law, was girded about the loins or beneath the waist, and Jesus Christ around his breast.

Now you must take heed that there is one lustfulness coming from a sudden impulse, without careful consideration of what is good or evil and without consenting, and it is called the first stir to passion, and it is a venial sin. Another is that which is done with deliberation and willing consent and delight in work, and without outward operation, and which is a mortal sin. And Our Lord here speaks of this.

And because seeing and touching actually provoke lustfulness, Jesus Christ consequently taught man to put away all those occasions which might make him fall to such consent. And he said, *Si oculus tuus dexter,* "If your right eye or your right hand induce or draw you to evil, scratch it out or cut it off, in refraining from unlawful works. For it is more expedient that one of your members perishes in leaving an unlawful work undone although it being delightful, than having your body and soul cast in hellfire for it." Gregory says: "It is neither licit nor lawful to behold or covet that thing which is not lawful. And so that the soul might be kept clean in thought, man ought to retain and turn from them his eyes, his kissing and his hands." For according to Chrysostom, whoever gives himself to behold the fair faces of women, kindles the fire of lustfulness in himself. And Saint Bernard also says that he who holds a woman by the hand by way of defilement, then enters the devil's bondage. What shall they say now those who without fear presume to dwell with virgins, and behold them every day for lustfulness? Hearing this, and also for those who often go to common places and so sustain and defile themselves by the occasions which they learn and see there, is Saint Gregory's effective counsel who says: "When the flesh covets, so man ought to remember how it shall be when the soul passes out of it. Nothing refrains man more from his desires and carnal lustfulness than to think what he shall be in the hereafter, and how he is beloved only while his life lasts."

Do also consider, every creature, how the noble stature of man is made vile and loathsome by foul lustfulness. For according to many doctors and religious men of holy life, to behold gladly the favour of the faces of women or of other young people, or to speak with them or touch them inordinately, are signs that the man is inwardly corrupt with debility, annulled and excluded, and that the devil had power over him.

We find here, according to Saint Augustine, that it is not commanded that a man cut or harm any member of his body according to what is written, but that man casts away sinful occasions from him; which occasions may sometimes sound of good works. By way of example: if it so happened that one went into a monastery or a nunnery of women to preach or to give counsel or any such things, and by sight feels being inclined to sin, then he ought to leave such works and keep himself chaste, so that all his other good deeds do not come to ruin. And Alaine de Lille says about this: "If you want to deliberately avoid mortal sin of the flesh, flee the time and the place, for the places which are inappropriate for you are great nourishers of this sin." And such remedy is good against all other sins. Seneca says: "Whoever wants to cast away from him the desire of all that relates to concupiscence, let him put out his eyes and stop his ears. I find myself more greedy, more ambitious, more lustful, more cruel and out of reason when I am in the company of men, than when I am alone and restrain my mind from these things."

And Our Lord says: "Yet if your right eye tempts you, what shall your left eye do?' Jerome says: "Man ought to take heed that this is necessary for us not to fall into vice, for if the soul falls into sin, then soon enough the body must also too, as it is more inclined to sin than the soul." And Chrysostom says: "Jesus Christ neither desires nor means man ought to put out his eyes, nor cut off his hand from his body, but it is the heart, which is a member and feeling of evil lustfulness and carnal desires, that man ought to cut off and held back, for all evil proceeds from it. And this we ought to do for the heavenly kingdom, so that the vice will not dominate us and bring us to hellfire."

After that Jesus Christ had shown how we ought not to desire nor desire any other man's wife, he consequently taught that no man should leave his own wife. And he explained about the declaration of licence or sufferance given to Moses as set in the Law, that is to say for man to leave his wife in giving her the libel and writing of repudiation and licence. And the Jews altogether believed that such things were lawful for them, but it is false. For they were only tolerated for the hardness of heart of those who held their wives in hatred and scorn, so that in such fury they would not murder them. And similarly, he allowed the Law to bear up with what is less evil to omit what is more. And now Jesus Christ commands that leave should not be given other than for fornication, for then she would not be truthful inasmuch as she would not have been faithful in marriage, and since it would be lawful to leave or be denied from dwelling lying together, in spite of the bond of marriage remaining all the days of their life. And because of this, if a man marries another woman, he commits adultery; and so does the woman if she does the same. Yet whoever will put his wife away from him because of her fornication ought first to be clear himself of such vice. For according to Saint Jerome, all that men are commanded, later rebounds on women. And also the man being in adultery ought not to put away his wife because of her adultery.

And after that Jesus Christ had preached and taught how man ought to do no wrong to his neighbour, thereby forbidding wrath and lustfulness, he consequently taught man how to abstain from doing wrong to God by forbidding all others and perjurers. And he declared the commandment not to swear, about which the Jews erred believing the other *men conger* meant that it was only forbidden, and that an oath done in deceit and needlessly though being unlawful ought to be kept. And more than all this, Our Lord ordained that man should not swear about anything of the sort, that is for no cause, unless it was necessary. Now the strength and justice of the Pharisees lay in not being abjured, and Our Lord confirmed this in also forbidding swearing as otherwise man might not enter heaven. And the same as saying that anyone who does not speak does not tell any lies, anyone who does not swear is never abjured. But just as much speech and too many words may not be without sin, similarly much and frequent swearing may not be without unwarranted swearing and perjury. And just as God commanded in the Law to offer sacrifice to Him in the best manner (not that such sacrifice pleased him, but he did it to urge the Jews that they should not resort to idolatry in doing sacrifice to other feigned things, and so become idolaters), so did He give them leave, imperfect as they were, to swear by God. Not that He granted them this with His pleasure but, as Saint Jerome says, so that they should take to no evil custom of swearing by those creatures on whom they would later set their minds and pray to them.

Now the Gospel does not accept any sort of swearing for a Christian's word ought to be so true and just that it ought to be taken for his oath. Chrysostom says: "In no way is it licit for us to swear. Why should we need to swear, seeing that we are forbidden from lying and that our words ought to be so true that they should be taken for our oath? And because of that, Our Lord not only forbade forswearing, but also any swearing, for we should know that although not swearing we would have said the truth and that in our simple words we were just and true, and by that men might believe us. The cause of swearing is to warrant that every word the swearer says is the truth. Now Our Lord wants that there would be no difference between swearing and simple words; for just as in swearing there ought to be no deceit, so in a simple promise there ought to be no lying or deceit, seeing that both the liar and the blasphemer shall be both condemned into eternal punishment in God's just judgment. Then whoever speaks, swears. For it is written: "The witness of truth shall not lie." And that is why the Holy Scripture so often says that a man should not swear, for all that the servant of God says ought to be true and reputed just as much as having been sworn." Seneca says: "There is no difference between affirming and swearing, for when a man speaks in truth he would be treating and speaking of faith and of all good works." Saint Augustine says: "He swears who takes God to witness in what he says. It is a simple thing to think that he does not swear who says: 'I take God to record' or 'God knows that I do not lie.'"

You should yet know that in an inevitable case swearing is not forbidden. And about this he says, *Non iurabis omnino*: "You shall not swear vainly." Here the negation is just as saying "It is sometimes licit to swear." Our Lord then did not forbid all kinds of swearing, otherwise all swearing would be unlawful. But he said that man should not swear without cause, in forbidding all false and deceivable oaths done without cause and for no reason. Saint Augustine says: "Our Lord does not say that man should not swear about anything, as if all swearing was unlawful. But he forbade anyone swearing against the truth, and not light oaths, and without cause and need, so that by the custom of swearing man should not fall into perjury."

Now three things are necessary for swearing to be licit. First, take heed of what you are swearing on, that is to say the truth, as otherwise it would be taken as lying. Secondly, take heed of the motive and the cause why you swear, that is justice and necessity, as otherwise swearing would be evil. Thirdly, take heed of the swearer, for he ought to have discre-tion, as otherwise the oath would not suffice. And Jeremiah says about this: "God has said to me, 'You shall swear truth in judgment and in justice.'" And it is not only unlawful to swear in vain by God's name, but also by creatures, inasmuch as divine virtues are realised in them. And for this Jesus Christ said: "Do not swear by heaven, for it is the throne of God," that is where his glory mainly shines. And also "Swear not by the earth, for that is his footstool," that is earth is the least and lowest of all created things, in the same manner as the footstool is under all the body. "Also swear not by Jerusalem, which is the city of the sovereign king," that is God's who is king of kings and it is assigned as a city in his service. "Also do not swear by your head," for it is divine work and not made by man, which is like saying that "you cannot make one of your horses black or white, nor contrary to its natural colour." By saying these things, Jesus Christ showed that in the same manner as it is unlawful to swear by God, nor is it any more lawful to swear by his creations. For just as all creatures are the work of God, so it is that whoever swears by them swears by God. Also it is forbidden us to swear by them in a manner that we do not hold them in honour and reverence, and that then we might come to know that we were perjurers and liars, when we are forsworn by crea-tures, and that it is no small thing to swear by them. Yet it so happens that a man swears by God's cross, or by Mass or other holy relics, these having been created, much more than by other unreasonable creatures, only because God is more honoured in them and we revere them even more.

After the Saviour had forbidden swearing, he consequently taught how man ought to speak, saying "Your words ought to be none other than yes and no." Namely that man should teach the truth and deny what is false without oaths. And he said twice, yes yes and no no, so that the inner heart may conform itself to the spoken word or to what it speaks. Then what we say must be yes yes and no no, when we affirm or deny what we speak in double measure, that is both verbally and from the heart. And just as we feel in the conscience, so it should be in the tongue; in like manner as we affirm by words what has to be proven by facts. And as a man who swears more than these two words, yes yes and no no, proceeds from evil, imperfection and suspicion, so it is with a man who believes nothing without swearing. A man does no evil in swearing in truth if he is constrained to swear, even though swearing comes from evil and imperfection. For when he sees that anyone is hard to believe anything which is necessary and of profit, he may then affirm what he says on oath. Whereupon it is to conclude that swearing is always evil for whoever swears unless he keeps all the above said conditions, or for whoever causes swearing in not believing what is true and all that is clearly seen. To suffer anyone to swear needlessly is evil and carries the guilt of sin; and not to believe each other by way of truth without swearing, is evil and proceeds from man's frailty.

Let us then always say the truth without swearing, and let us speak with our mouth and not with other members, for it is an evil and inappropriate thing to do. As it is said in *Proverbs*, "The apostate man, who is the man with no dignity, uses and speaks with his finger and is simple and unwise"; and more unwise is he if he spoke with his hand which holds all his fingers. He is even more than a fool if he speaks with his arm and shoulder; and if he speaks with all his members, he is reputed to be out from his mind. The speaker then must retain all his members, and especially the tongue, so that he might not slander his neighbour and not be reputed a fool and a madman.

CHAPTER 35
ABOUT WHEN SAINT PETER FOR HIMSELF AND FOR THE OTHER APOSTLES ACKNOWLEDGED JESUS CHRIST TO BE TRULY THE SON OF GOD

NTIL now no mention has been made of the passion of Jesus Christ, but in the following chapters it is declared well at length together with the things which were done by him after his passion, and so forth about other matters.
After the above said events Jesus Christ, the very beacon of the light of doctrine, came to all places, seeking those who were lost and saving those who were penitents; and he came into the parts of the city called Caesarea Philippi, now called Banias. It is here worth recalling that Philip the Tetrach, who was Herod's brother, had renewed and built this city, calling it Caesarea Philippi in remembrance of his name and to the honour of Tiberius Caesar, who had given him the fourth part of the kingdom. The city stands by the mountain of Lebanon and two fountains or wells spring at its foot. One is called Ior and the other Dan, and their streams and branches unite and set together making Jordan. In taking their own course they make the river Jordan which flows into the sea near the city of Chorazaim. The city is also called Caesarea Philippi as different from Caesarea Palaestinae where the centurion Cornelius dwelled, and as varying from Caesarea, the metropolis of Cappadocia in the region of Turkey. Heathens dwelt in this city of Caesarea Philippi and its suburbs, so that men might know that Jesus preached on the borders of the heathens, upon whom he would found his faith and the Church. Also, this city is in the parts of Phoenicia, which is the region of the heathens, and at the end of the land of Judea in the southwest coast. It was into this city that men brought the onetenth of tribute due to the emperor by each person. As we read, the world had been ordained to pay such tithes and tribute to the emperor Caesar Augustus. It was fitting that in this city the king of kings was confessed and attested to by his apostles,

and that he there received the tribute of their true faith, such tribute being paid by each head of the soul.

And Jesus, praying to God his Father and walking alone, returned to his disciples and scrutinised them, not to learn anything new from them which he did not know or had forgotten, but to teach them the truth so that by their answers he would try to clear the errors people were saying about him. He also wanted to fortify his disciples and even more to confirm their faith, and later to approve them and to make a promise to them by which he would show the difference between the apostles and the people. Jesus Christ then wanted the people's errors to come out because in chiding them and putting them out, he would show the real truth; like the doctor who first rebukes the false doctrine and then sows the good one. So he examined his disciples and asked them whether the people and the world said that he was the Son of Man, that is to say of the Virgin. According to Chrysostom, he would be called the Son of Man, for he wanted that man should believe in the dispensation and coming of his Incarnation, and thereby come to the faith. To be the only son of a virgin pertains to Jesus Christ. Adam, the first man, was son of the earth; and all others are the sons of men, that is of man and woman. But Jesus Christ was son but of the one, for he had no kin but only one on earth and another in heaven. And as Saint Jerome says, Jesus did not say, "What do the people say about who I am," that it might not seem that he would only know by chance what they were saying about him; which is against all those who will ever deem themselves as being of no account with regard to their lineage and personal existence. And thus just as Jesus Christ asked his disciples about the Messiah's renown, in the same manner ought spiritual men and doctors inquire their servants about their renown. For good renown edifies greatly, and an evil renown is the cause of great ruin. Origen says: "Jesus Christ examined his disciples about what other men said of him to teach us that we often ought to enquire what opinion others have of us; so that if they feel or speak any evil of us we may proceed to amend it, and if they speak well we should fortify ourselves to increase it. Even in so acting, the bishops' servants and prelates are instructed when they detect any evil, opinions or evil words spoken about their masters them." When Our Lord asked his apostles to know about the people's faith, we understand that those leading a spiritual life ought to render account and deem the faith of all those who are in their charge.

Now since there were various opinions among the people about the Messiah, his disciples told him that some said the son of man was Saint John Baptist, who felt Jesus Christ's presence in his mother's womb and baptised and led an excellent life; and Herod held this opinion too, namely that, according to Theophilus, Saint John the Baptist had risen back to life and was doing many miracles. Others said he was Elijah, owing to the burning desire he had for the truth and for his power in making fire descend from heaven. Yet others said that he was Jeremiah, who was sanctified in his mother's womb and had been very patient in his anguish and merciful in weeping for the people's sins. Some said that the Messiah was one of the other prophets risen from death to life, as was Elisha for the excellence of his wisdom for he had a double spirit of prophecy. In like manner many are those who nowadays seek their salvation in other ways, since every man places his bliss in what he loves, and worships it as his god. According to Saint Augustine, man worships what he loves most.

Then, hearing these things, Jesus Christ still wanted to hear from his disciples their own confession and opinions, and said to them: "You, who are not common people but my disciples to whom I have given knowledge of the kingdom of heaven, and have made you beacons of this world, and given you to know all that I have heard from my Father, whom do *you* now say that I am?" And Saint Peter, knowing the truth about Jesus Christ's divine and human nature, and believing that he was true God and true man in one substance, answered him: "You are Christ, that is to say true man anointed with the oil of grace above all living beings"; and in saying so he confessed his humanity. "Also you are the Son of God naturally, not by the love of a Father as he had for others, for you are of the one nature of which the Father is"; and in saying so he confessed his divinity and showed he was the living Father, that is to say inconceivable

and eternal, since the Jews were accustomed to call the living God in contrast to false gods made of dead bodies and
other insensible and inanimate things to which heathens
pray. And although all the other apostles well believed what
Saint Peter said to Jesus Christ, yet because he was the eldest
and prince of the whole remnant, he answered with the
mouth of the whole college and company. And this was a
good reason that he, who ought to be and put forth above
all others, should answer before all and for all. It appears
by this that it is mainly incumbent on Saint Peter's successor,
namely the Pope, to validate all doubts relating to the faith
and all that pertaining to it.

And Jesus Christ answered Saint Peter for his making and
rendering of a true confession, and said to him: "Blessed
are you, Simon Barjona," that is Simon son of John, "for
knowing the true faith leading man to blessedness. For flesh
and blood," that is to say mortal man or man's teaching:
"have not shown you this truth, which is faith's secret, but
my Father in heaven has shown it to you." Chrysostom says:
"These words Jesus Christ spoke to Saint Peter pertain to
all Christians, for they may be told to everyone: 'You are
blessed for it is not flesh and blood which have shown you
your very articles of the faith.'"

"You say the truth that I am the Son of the living God.
And for this I, who am steadfast truth, say for you and for
your company that you are a stone, truly so called by me, for
having acknowledged me that I am the very strong stone in
faith and stable in teaching. And upon this stone, of which
you now know and I have laid the foundation, that is upon
you, I shall build my Church." Now Saint Peter before was
called Simon, but this name Peter was given to him by Jesus
Christ to mean the Holy Church. For just as Jesus Christ
is the very stone himself, in the same manner Saint Peter
stands for Christians. Saint Paul agrees with this sentence
when he says: "No man may lay any other foundation in
this Church than that which is laid, that is Jesus Christ."
As though he had said: "There is no other foundation in
the Church but the stone which has been laid and admitted Saint Peter for a foundation." That is Jesus Christ, to
whom Saint Peter had said: "You are the very Son of God,"

for upon the same stone is the all holy Church built. "And the gates of hell," which are the suggestions of our spiritual enemies, the delights of vices, the false doctrines of heretics, the torments and flatteries of persecutors, all evil sayings, works and examples that show the way of all perdition and lead man into the deepest place of hell, "shall have no power over the Holy Church founded in this manner," for they may never separate it from Jesus Christ's faith and charity. Whereby it appears that the Holy Church is founded upon those people who truly know and confess the faith and truth.

Then Our Lord afterwards promised Saint Peter to give him the keys of the kingdom of heaven, although he did not give them to him at the time; precisely because if he had given them to him at that hour, there should never have been found in Saint Peter the place of a perverse confession, about which we shall speak later, nor the error of negation, about which it is spoken in the passion. And the same as Saint Peter answered Our Lord Jesus Christ in all the other apostles' name, Our Lord promised the apostles the keys of the kingdom of heaven in like manner as he did to him, saying: "To you, as above all the others, who have confessed me, I shall give the keys"; that is to say the power of the kingdom of heaven, for in using them well and worthily proceeds the opening or closing of heaven. Bede says: "The keys of the kingdom of heaven were not then given to Saint Peter, but they were promised to him. For they were not as yet forged on the anvil of the cross, nor tempered with the precious blood of Jesus Christ; who might in this manner say to Saint Peter: 'I am the master of the same keys by which, when they shall all be perfectly made and forged in the ardent language or furnace of my passion, I shall first open the gates of heaven for a thief and murderer. And then as for you, I shall after suffer you to enter by my example; as well as publicans and foolish women, for upon them you shall exercise your judgment when they shall truly confess their faults and do penance for them. And in this you shall be ordained to have jurisdiction and power to be able to exercise two requisite things, namely authority to know the guilt or the offence and sin, and the power to absolve and judge man. These two things I shall give you called as the keys.'"

From which it appears that by the keys of the kingdom of heaven Jesus Christ would have meant the power and discretion which those using them ought to have within them. Which is namely the discretion to discern who is worthy and unworthy, and the power to bind and unbind them. In what is here said, the key is none other than a spiritual power which is supernatural, granted and given by God and not required by nature. And in there being two keys, the *Interpretation* says these are the knowledge to discern between one sin and another, and the power to bind or to absolve. For just as in the Son lies the one and only power to soften and to harden, and all proceeds from only one state, yet there are two effects and works; in the same manner that state has but one key, which as said has two effects. For it is a power to judge or give judgment over souls and not over bodies, and this power is divided in two, that is to say the power to discern in the examination of the cause, and the power to define and determine by an absolute or severely rebuking sentence. The first power is called a science, not the same as that which a man obtains by being disposed to have knowledge, but an authority and power to discern and judge between good and evil. The other power is called that which after true judgment receives or excludes any man from the kingdom of heaven. For those who are unworthy ought to be excluded, and the worthy to be received. Saint Bernard says about this: "Saint Peter received the keys in knowledge and in power, which were given to him from above. And these keys are not but a power to open and close, and one discretion to receive the worthy or to exclude the unworthy from the kingdom of heaven."

And yet Jesus Christ says to Saint Peter, "And all that you shall bind on earth," which is namely as a man still living in the world, "shall be bound in heaven," that is to say that the heavenly court shall receive them. "And all that you shall unbind on earth, shall be unbound in heaven." The *Interpretation* says that "All living people whom you shall judge to be unworthy of having remission for their offences, shall be judged unworthy before God. And all those whom you unbind in their lives by judging them to be worthy of remission, shall have God's forgiveness for their sins."

This power was not only given to Saint Peter, but together with him to all the other apostles. And after the apostles, it was given to bishops and the spiritual leaders of all the Holy Church; in such manner that the power of authority is always and lies only in God, who opens by the infusion of grace. Also the power of excellence is in Our Lord Jesus Christ, opening by the merit of his passion. And the power of mystery and service is given to Church prelates, which open it as servants by the mystery of the sacraments. But the reason why Saint Peter especially received from Jesus Christ the keys of the kingdom of heaven and the lordship of judicial power, is to make all Christians understand that whosoever separates himself from those who are chosen and from the company of this faith, by any manner whatsoever, and remains in this error and separation, may not be absolved of his sin, nor may he enter into the kingdom of heaven. And as the *Interpretation* says, Our Lord yet gave that power especially to Saint Peter so that he should ever incite us to good unity and peace. And it is because of this that he would make and accept him as Prince of the Apostles, in order to show that there mainly ought to be in Holy Church one vicar or deputy of God, namely the Pope, from whom members ought to seek help when there is any dissension amongst them. For if there were in the Church various keys, then the true unity of its members would often be broken. Here then we see that Saint Peter is chosen chief prelate of all the Holy Church; but the same power promised to him was later also given to the others in deed when the Apostles were ordained and made bishops after the resurrection, when Our Lord Jesus Christ told them, "Take the Holy Spirit in you." But when he said to Saint Peter, "Keep well my sheep," he ordained and made him pastor and head of all Christians, Prince of the Apostles, and vicar in all the Holy Church. And in hearing these things Church bishops and prelates ought to be joyful for the gift which God has given them, and take no pride in having the power to bind or unbind like Saint Peter; that what they bind, shall be bound, and what they do not bind, shall not be bound. Then they ought to follow him in the discretion and good justice which will follow him in power and authority to bind or unbind.

The foregoing was only said to Saint Peter, so that all other prelates after him should take his example of a good life and works, in binding and unbinding and in not depart-ing from the union of peace and concord, by not presuming to do anything contrary to right and justice, while consider-ing the Apostle's words when he says: "We are not ordained by God to do anything contrary to truth, but we ought to do all according to the Gospel and truth." And, as Origen says, whoever has the power to bind or unbind others, as regards the judgment of the soul, ought to lead their lives in such manner without any disquiet whether he was said to be worthy in heaven to bind or unbind. For all who righteously and discreetly without error, after others who have received the keys, he shall bind or unbind in this world, shall be bound or unbound in heaven. But if the prelate in his judgment did anything unjustly, notwithstanding that the party is judged by the Church militant, yet he shall not be judged by the Church triumphant; although man ought ever to fear and doubt the sentence of his curate, righteously or wrongfully indeed, so that the failure which has not as yet been committed in deed will not be done and committed by exhilaration. Gregory says: "The heads of the Holy Church ought to bind and unbind man's soul with great self-denial and careful consideration. Yet if the pastor obliges and binds his spiritual children, be it righteously or not, his sentence is yet ever to be dreaded, because who-ever is unrighteously bound deserves not to be righteously bound by any new offence. So that the curate who binds or unbinds indiscreetly ought to be feared. And also the spiritual child ought well fear that he is not unrighteously bound or unbound, and well ought to guard himself that, neither by pride nor by any other vice, he will rebuke his Creator's sentence; either by pride since he has not sinned or offended, or by disobedience and pride for having fallen in sin and guilt."

After Saint Peter's confession the disciples' recognition of Our Lord truly being the Son of God, he commanded them to keep themselves well and firmly from telling any living man that he was the one whom the Law promised. And he did this because of his great meekness, and not to cause by this his early death and passion, and not to bring discomfort to those who were frail and of little faith; for if it had been said that he was immortal but everlasting, and then men had seen the opposite, this might have been a matter and means of despair. And this prohibition was to last until after the resurrection, when death would have being vanquished and overcome and men might preach openly the glory of Jesus Christ's majesty. Chrysostom says: "If men had truly known that Jesus Christ was the true Son of God as he was, no man would have been so great or sturdy as to lay his hands upon him, and so he would not have been crucified or risen again from death to life; and so the kingdom of hell would have still been on earth and the devil's dominion would have still been over the whole world." Ambrose says: "Jesus Christ commanded his disciples to keep his secret for many causes. Namely to deceive the devil whom called himself prince of the whole world, and to repudiate his deceits, to show his very meekness; and also for the purpose that, if then they did not know him to be truly the Son of God, they would have preached about his crucifixion more freely before our redemption, for the very joy and gladness of a good Christian is in finding joy in the cross and passion of Jesus Christ. Certainly, all other worldly things may indeed little prevail as regarding man's salvation, except the intention and remembrance of Our Lord Jesus Christ's cross which you should ever keep in your mind as it is of ever great profit to you to rebuke all evil thoughts and temptations, for by it the world is crucified in the heart of man and man in the world. If then the world is crucified in my heart, it is certain that it is death to me and that I should neither love nor desire it. I know well that the world shall pass and vanish away, and so I should abstain from it as a stinking vegetable, and something worse than anything else, and flee from it and abandon it."

The way and manner of speaking and calling to the faith of the Holy Church both heathens and Jews, is shown by Saint Ambrose in saying: "When any misbelievers are called to the faith, we ought to order our words in such manner as in God's commandments. We should first of all teach that there is only one true God, Creator of heaven and earth, from whom we derive our living, our being and our salvation, and whose creatures we are. We not only ought to love Him for the gifts of life and of light, but ever think about Him as the Creator of all things. And then we ought after to destroy the false opinion that they have of idols by showing that neither silver nor any other metal with which they are made has any strength or power, nor anything else of divinity. And when they are thus shown and instructed that He is the only one God, then they may be shown easily that we owe our salvation and redemption to Jesus Christ, and so forth, in teaching them of the miracles and deeds he did in this world where he lived bodily, and that he has risen from death to life by his own virtue and power, and that in him was the power of the Trinity, and that he was above poor creatures. And so, little by little, faith should increase in them, and they should have no doubts that he was not God. For unless you prove and show that he might not have done such great things without virtue and almighty power, how and in what manner can you show that this almighty virtue was in him? It is by such example that Saint Paul instructed the Athenians. And when the apostles spoke to the Jews, they showed them that Jesus Christ was the one promised in the Law and by all prophets, who first of all they did not name him in their authorities as the Son of God, but that he was a man proven to be good and righteous, a man risen from death to life, and that this was the same man of whom the prophet says: 'You are my son, I have as this day engendered or begotten you.' And as to the thing which is hard to be believed, man ought to join thereto the authority of Holy Scripture. Also say and show how the coming of Our Lord has often been prom-ised by the prophets. Show also by the Holy Scripture how the resurrection of the bodies has been promised, and has been shown in the resurrection of Jesus Christ, and that it shall be accomplished in all at the end of the world by God's might. And when you will deal with the sacraments of the Holy Church, if any misbeliever will receive them, ye ought to show and tell him that there is one God which has made all things, and one Jesus Christ by which all things are made; although men ought not to say that there are divided or two Lords. For similarly as the Father is perfect and fully made, so also is the Son fully made; but you ought to say that the Father and Son are of only one substance and inseparable with regard to the divinity."

And so that the apostles are better kept in their master's commandment, that is not to preach before the resurrection that he was both God and man, and that they should not abhor and fear the peril of death if they loved the glory and bliss of heaven, he then showed them his passion. He showed them that it was a proper thing according to divine ordinance, that the Son of Man was to suffer a bitter death and passion in Jerusalem, which lies in the middle of the world and of habitable earth. And that he was to be given there a fair present of myrrh, made of great bitterness, and all kinds of torment. Also in Jerusalem he was then to suffer great pains and afflictions, as to be captured, beaten, spat upon, accused, despoiled of his clothes, scourged, and rebuked by the ancients or old people, who should have led an honourable life, and by the scribes, who seemed to have had the prerogative of knowledge, and by priestly princes, who held the excellence of authority and power; for he was judged to death by them and given to the secular judge, who stood there for the Romans. And yet, he said, the Son of Man should be put upon a cross, on which he would suffer the most bitter death and passion; but on the third day he should arise again. These things he said to them to the end that they should not be too much angered and moved by his death, and also so that by their hope in his resurrection they should be comforted. And you should know that when Jesus Christ spoke of his passion or about anything of human fragility, he ever yet called himself the Son of Man and not the Son of God, in order to show that he suffered according to human nature and not according to his almightiness. Jerome says that it is "As though he said to them: 'Preach about me to the people so and the same as I am, when I shall have suffered what I have told you by other words.' For it was only a little profitable to preach manifestly and openly about his majesty to the people, when shortly after he should be seen by all people crucified and scourged and tormented in many ways."

And when Saint Peter had heard these words, he took Our Lord apart, because it was not seemly that he rebuked his master before the others, showing us by way of example that the subject ought not to rebuke his sovereign or burst out in any open or common place, or before others. And in beholding him, he said to him: "Lord, it is not worthy of you to suffer what you are saying, namely that you, son of the sovereign God, should die so villainously. This is a very hard thing, that the Lord of such great might and majesty shall be so ignorantly entreated and die so shamefully." And when Jesus Christ had heard Saint Peter speak in this manner, he turned his face towards him, since Our Lord was walking before him, that he might behold him even faster, and began to rebuke him. And he said to him: "Oh Satan," that is to say adversary: "go behind me and conform to my will, and not go against me"; as though he had said to him, "Be not my adversary, but conform your will with mine. And do not put stumbling blocks in my passion, but only endeavour to follow the example which I shall give you by this." Origen says: "Very fortunate is the man to whom Jesus Christ responds, indeed if it is done to correct him." And Jesus Christ said to him yet even later, "You discomfort me," that is to say you give me occasion for an offence, "and you offend me by your saying for you do not savour what belongs to God." And as Origen says, God called Saint Peter satan although he had earlier magnified him before all others, and also since, for his own love which he had for Jesus Christ, he would delay his passion which was ordained for the salvation of mankind. Saint Clement says that Saint Peter was so affectionate to the bodily presence of Our Lord that every time after his ascension, when he remembered his most sweet company, his holy way of life and his good master's words, he was resolved himself to tears, in such manner that he had like gutters running down his cheeks owing to the great abundance of tears which fell from his eyes. But for being controlled not by reason for his affection, and that for his own indiscreet love he would delay Jesus Christ's passion, he deserved being rebuked sharply.

Taking then Our Lord Jesus Christ's example, man ought to call as his adversaries all those who would draw him back from doing good and from spiritual profit owing to bodily comfort and ease. And similarly as Jesus Christ here rebuked Saint Peter, whom he had before approved and praised, in the same manner no man ought to be so great or so free a master as not to be corrected for an offence done in this presence, although he would before have done many good deeds. Man ought not then to be ashamed of the cross and opprobrium which the sweet Jesus has suffered on it, but rather find even more joy in it, for it is the sign of our salvation and beginning of all good works. Chrysostom says: "We ought to suffer within us the cross of Jesus Christ as a fair crown, for all goodness comes through it and shall be made perfect by it; and when he shall be baptised the cross is before him. And if he is fed with spiritual nourishment, which is the holy eucharist, or is to consecrate it, or to do any other good work, the sign of victory is present with us. And therefore we ought to be diligent and set it in our houses, bear it on our foreheads and in our thoughts, for it is the sign by means of which we receive our redemption and salvation. Now then when you bless yourself with the sign of the holy cross, you ought to remember all conditions and causes of the cross. For it does not suffice that you only bless yourself with your hand, but you must besides also have great faith and believe in this cross. And then no evil spirit nor the devil of hell may abide around you, seeing the sword and the weapon with which they have all been villainously wounded, and the arms and shield by which Our Lord Jesus Christ has put away all their might and domination."

CHAPTER 36
OF THE EXHORTATION HOW MAN OUGHT TO FOLLOW JESUS CHRIST BY THE EXAM-PLE OF HIS PASSION

FTER that Our Lord Jesus had first told secretly his disciples about the mystery of his passion, he then went openly to the peo-ple. For to follow the passion of Jesus Christ, whether by martyrdom or by penance, per-tains to all those who desire to be saved. And for this he would here speak to all generally, desiring them all to follow him and suffer patiently for his love all the evil that may come to them in this world. And it is because of this that he said, *Si quis vult post me venire*, "If any man," thereby showing the small number of those who would follow him, "come after me by inner love and exterior imitation to the glorious kingdom of heaven." And he reasonably said "if any will," for he left each one in his free choice and will, so that the service would be to him even more pleasing and the reward and recompense would even be much greater for the servant. Chrysostom says: "Just as Our Saviour Jesus is meek and gentle, so does he not desire any servant to go against his will, nor does he want to take any one by constraint, or by force; but he wishes them out of their own good and free will to render him thanks for having pleased him to take them into his service. And due to this, by fairly persuading and promising benefits he would attract all to him, and not by constraint or need." And Chrysostom yet says: "Were anyone to give gold or any other treasure, the whole world would come running to him. So that it is even more reasonable that we ought to force ourselves to run to those things by which man has everlasting rest, such as in serving God."

And yet Jesus Christ says: "Whoever will follow me to lead a perfect Christian life, ought to endeavour to flee from himself, by casting away from him all kinsfolk and friends as well as his understanding and knowledge, in taking the cross by compassion, and in fighting perfectly against the lustfulness of the flesh and worldly desires; for me, he must enlighten against the favour and honour of the world, for he ought to be a guide and leader in doing good works against all of the devil's errors, and he ought to abide in me for the reward of his recompense, as opposed to all temporal profit."

And the perfection of Christian life is set and consists of these three things. As to the first, that is to say in following Jesus Christ, it suits men to leave three things, namely first being external goods, according to what is written that "whoever does not forsake all that he possesses in this world, may not be my disciple." Secondly, his kinsfolk, also as it is written that "If anyone comes to me and does not abandon father and mother, may not be my disciple." Thirdly, his intelligence and his own will, just as it is said namely that he should abandon his old self and know his sins, intellect and affection, this being a much greater thing than all temporal things. The devout doctor Prosper says: "Of what use is it for those who leave their offences and external goods, unless they do not leave their proper will for God's love, which is a much greater thing and of more merit than renouncing and abandoning the goods of this world?"

As regards the second, namely bearing the cross of Jesus Christ, it comes in three manners: by mortification of the body, by compassion on one's neighbour, and by suffering pain and martyrdom which is of two kinds. The first related to the body and is a preparation of the purpose, in being willing to sustain all the pain and peril which may come in this world for the love of Jesus Christ. Saint Hilary says: "Man ought to follow Jesus Christ by taking the cross of his passion; and if he does not do it in deed, yet let him at least bear him company by good will." The second martyrdom is spiritual, as distinct in two manners according to Saint Maximus, namely that of abstinence and that of the cross. One is bodily, namely to resist bravely and with whole mind and will to revoke all the evil ways, delights and such things as may deceive man. The other manner of martyrdom is spiritual, which is more excellent and precious than the first, namely to subdue, refrain and subject to reason the soul's moving, to appease the mental distress and anger which may come to it, to refrain the rashness of vices and to fight against them every day. And this manner of martyrdom and of the spiritual cross is a special gift to religious and perfect men. On this cross Saint Paul says: "The world is crucified to me, and I to the world." And you should know that the Apostle makes both, namely that the world is crucified to him and he to the world. For though it sometimes happens that man does not keep the world in his thought, yet the world retains him in its occupations. And by this lowness of thought, man is dead in the world. And the world retains him as living when it enforces him to occupy it, although this goes contrary to the intent according to which man ought ever to please God. But, as Saint Gregory says, Saint Paul sought not the glory of the world, nor even worldly pleasure. And for this he glorified him who was crucified in the world and the world in him; as though he would have said, according to the *Interpretation*: "The lustfulness of the world has no dominion over me, nor even does the world set any more store by me. And yet I am strongly against it." There are three things, according to Saint John, by which we ought to be crucified and them by us, namely carnal desires, lustful longing for worldly goods, and pride in living. These things are crucified by the three states of religion; and the religious that keep their state well are indeed spiritual martyrs. For, according to Saint Augustine, we bear our cross when by our free will we bear any pain for the honour and love of Jesus Christ.

Then the first manner of martyrdom is in willingly for-saking temporal things. Secondly, in fighting strongly against the delights and lustfulness of the body, for even much stronger than this battle can be, even more glorious is the victory of martyrdom. The third manner is in renouncing and withstanding one's own will and oneself. For, as Saint Gregory says, by obedience one's own will is sacrificed to God, and by constraint the flesh of beasts. And therefore obedience is put before sacrifice. And you should know that Adam lost three things by sin, namely as to what we call freedom, bliss and dignity. And Our Lord teaches here the manner how to recover them by three opposite things, namely by liberty and freedom in denying oneself; by hap-piness when he says that man ought to bear his cross; and by dignity when he says that man should follow him. Man ought also to despise himself in prosperity and in fleeing from evil. Man ought to bear his cross in adversity by doing good. And so would man ever follow the blessed Saviour and Redeemer Jesus Christ in conforming himself to his life and in putting in order all his works according to him.

In the words uttered by our blessed Lord here above there should be excluded six manners of useless and unfruit-ful penance. The first manner is penance done by constraint and force; against which he says, "If anyone wants to come after me." The second is diminished and divided penance, as when any man gives his goods to the poor for the love and honour of God and sets his heart on the world; against which he says that man ought to negate and despise himself. The third manner is sensitivity and living in curiosity, in that living so in this world he will neither feel sorrow nor pain; against which he says that we should take his cross. The fourth is imperfection, and that is when man glorifies and enjoys himself in the pains and passions which his family has suffered for the love of God, yet those who find joy in this manner will suffer nothing; against whom Jesus Christ says that man should bear his cross and not others'. The fifth is to suffer and do penance for some time, and not perseveringly; against whom he says that they ought to bear it constantly. The sixth is by simulation, which is the manner of hypocrites; against whom he says man should follow him and not the world's favour and pleasure.

As regards the third, which is to follow the life of Jesus Christ, we namely ought to know that following his life means nothing else but following the life he led in this world, and to conform ourselves to it with our might and power. Now we must follow him in the three ways he has shown us, namely by poverty, meekness and penance. For when he came into this world by his Incarnation, he showed us a very great example of poverty; and in living in this world, an example of the most perfect meekness; and in his passion, an example of the most bitter pain, sadness and anguish. And so that we ought to follow him perfectly in these three things, that we may be continually reminded of them, he calls us by his prophet saying, as regards the first "Recall my poverty," with regard to the second "and

my profound humility," and as to the third "and the gall
and vinegar of my passion." And you should know that all
that, what true and devout Christians ought to do to follow
Jesus Christ and conform themselves to his appearance, may
be brought and reduced to three, according to the three
benefits we receive from him. And they are the external
goods of this world, our proper bodies and our souls; which
goods or benefits we must all live for his love if we want
to follow him perfectly.

Now then the perfect follower of Jesus Christ must first
of all leave the world and all temporal things for which he
has affection, and therewith prefer and set before him the
service of God above all earthly occupations and worldly
business. He does this by wilful poverty, which Jesus Christ
fully observed while he was in this world, for in all his life
he was very poor. Secondly, he ought to leave and abandon
the affection of his own body, which man does in three
manners. First, by chastising and punishing his flesh by
waking, fasting, praying and other good works by which the
body is made lean and feeble; thus the body does not go
strongly against the spirit and presume not to strengthen it
by pride against the soul which ought to govern it. Secondly,
a man may leave his body by casting off the goods he owns
in this world; for whoever feeds the body of his servant
too delicately shall afterwards find it rebellious, proud and
disobedient to him. And therefore man ought ever to keep
his body low and under subjection, that it may be ceaselessly
subject to the spirit. Thirdly, man may leave the body to
suffer willingly pains and afflictions, like the apostles and
martyrs, having suffered pains willingly for the love of Jesus
Christ. And about all the aforesaid Our Lord Jesus Christ
has given us example through his own self. Thirdly, man
ought to leave his soul, in renouncing and forsaking his
own will and conforming with God's will, in such manner
that he does nothing but that which is pleasing to the
will of God. Jesus Christ did this in the same manner as
he showed when he said that he was not come into this
world to do his own will, but to do the will of Him who
sent him, that is to give witness to God the Father. And
because of this, man ought to be doing the divine will in

such manner by order and measure that in all his works he desires no worldly acclaim, or praises, but rather that his desire ought to be only that the honour of God may be ever increased by him and by all living creatures.

And yet it comes to mind that no man may live Our Lord Jesus Christ's life without also dying the same death as Jesus Christ. And because of this, just like Jesus Christ by his great charity has inclined and humbled himself in taking our human nature, dying by that low status to his divine appearance by which he is equal and of one only substance with the Father, so ought each one of us waiting for this perfect state die in himself by real meekness and by fully despising and reputing himself as being nothing, that he may only live to serve God. Man also ought to think that he has no good virtue in himself and that all comes from God, through His gifts, to which man conforms himself and keeps throughout his life, that he may truly say with Saint Paul, "I live not in myself, for Jesus Christ lives in my soul." And Saint Paul says of such souls which are so perfect and dead in themselves: "You are dead as to the world, and your life is hidden in Jesus Christ." And not without cause he said that "your life is hidden in Jesus Christ" about the life by which the soul shall be perfectly united with God in heaven; and this shall be by continual love and beatific charity, such presence being now hidden owing to the great needs of mortal life. And this love may not be continual or without interruption in this world, but man shall clearly see it in the blessed life in which we shall constantly have abundance of the beatific purpose; for it is only in God that we shall have full delight in all goodness. And Saint Paul says about this: "When Jesus Christ shall appear to be your life, then you shall be with him in his glory."

It is worth knowing that this spiritual death, by which man dies by holding in contempt and despising himself, is accomplished and fully achieved by some degrees. The first is that man ought to repute himself more abject and even less than all others. The second is that he should feel himself to be so in his inner self and say this and conform verbally to it by these words. The third is that he should suffer patiently when others belittle him. The fourth, that he ought to have patience when the honour belonging to his state is not given to him. The fifth is that he must endeavour to love those who so despise him and hold him in contempt. All these degrees shine in Our Lord Jesus Christ, whom you ought to follow and not the devil, as ambitious and proud people do, nor the world, as the greedy and avaricious do, nor our carnal appetite, as the voluptuous and lustful do. And certainly, it would be to no avail for who does not follow Jesus Christ unless he humbles or submits himself to others, or to bear his cross. If you want to follow Jesus Christ, be obedient to God, love your neighbour, and let all that you shall do and suffer be for the love of God, by living through what is evil and doing good. Jesus Christ has taught us about all these things when he was in this world. But Saint Bernard complains within himself saying: "Oh Lord Jesus Christ, how few are those in this world who will go by the way and teaching which you have shown us, yet there is no one who will come to you. Every man will reign gladly, but none will have any of your compassion. They do not value or desire what they might later achieve. They want to have what is good, so that it costs them nothing. They desire to be held as righteous persons, that they may have what is good without pain."

It is because of this that Our Lord has called us to suffer martyrdom that we might know the faith, and so he proposes three things which bring about the confession and knowledge of faith. The first is to have a very great love for him, saying that "Whoever wants to save his soul in this world," that is to keep well his body which had need of bodily sustenance, by fleeing pain or martyrdom for the love of God or by not being afflicted by penance as man ought, "shall lose it in the time to come," for in fleeing bodily death he shall purchase everlasting death. And in holding on to transitory life, he shall lose the spiritual life. "But whoever shall lose his soul," in exposing himself to death in time of need, by rather willing to die than to offend God, or by afflicting himself by penance to be ever willing to appease God's anger, neither for the vanities of the world nor for any other temporal thing, but only for God, "such shall find his soul in everlasting life." Cassiodore says: "Cursed is the flesh which is neither afflicted nor subdued in this world for the love of God. For whoever in this world shall be observed in subjection without being the overlord of the spirit, shall in the end be crowned in heaven." Saint Bernard says: "It is much greater wisdom to lose this world in his soul because afterward he may find it again, than it is to keep it now in order to lose it for ever after this world. What would you say here, you who are diligent to nourish your bodies in this world with so many kinds of meats and who do not abide by the fair composition of virtues? Hippocrates and all his schools taught about the saving of souls in this world, and Jesus Christ and all his disciples taught about losing them. Which of these two masters or teachers will you now pursue and follow? Is it Hippocrates the scholar or Jesus Christ the master? Hippocrates mainly commended the body's pleasure and voluptuousness, Epicurus good and easy living and delicate meats and their nourishment; Jesus Christ taught that these two things should be despised. What may man fear more than what the Gospel says: 'Whoever shall love his soul too much in this world, shall lose it in the other'? Man must lose it in this world, whether by giving it to martyrdom or by subduing it by penance, for mortifying the flesh by abstinence in this world is a great martyrdom in the eyes of God. And although martyrdom by penance is much easier than that by which members are rent and quartered, he is yet even more subdued and in pain owing to its length of time."

Then after, Jesus Christ speaks of the second abstention, which is coveting and desiring temporal goods too much, saying: "Of what good is it to man if he won the whole world, but at the end of his life he would not bear anything from it, nor fare any better for it, but even worse because of his sin?" And what is more, for the more that a man desires to be in this world and enjoy its pleasures, the more he desires to be in hell and to suffer its pains. Saint John says in the Book of the *Apocalypse*: "The more that a man glorifies himself and takes his pleasures and delights, the more they shall cause him to be in torment and pain." If then acquiring worldly goods does not profit the soul but brings it to pain and anguish, for by such things man loses

heavenly bliss and procures eternal pain, man ought not to
have any business in achieving them. It is as though Our
Lord had said: "Nothing concerning the salvation of the
soul may prevail over the acquisition of the goods of this
world." But what is more is that man then loses so much,
namely that what is immortal ought to be exalted above
all corruptible and transitory things. For the soul, which
is created in the image of God, is more precious than all
transitory things of the world. Certainly, covetous man is
very much observed to love money better than himself or
his soul, for by the love of transitory goods he puts himself
in the way of everlasting torments. Men may say that an
avaricious man is worse than the devil of hell, in that he
loves money more than his soul or men's souls, and the devil
loves one soul better than he does to the whole world. And
this appeared when he said to Jesus Christ in tempting him:
"I shall give you all if you will worship me." Origen says:
"When he shall lay these things to us to win the world, let
us take example in the manner of Our Lord and do as he
did." Saint Ambrose says: "Man ought to be feared strongly
if for the love and mind he has for money, or for the delight
of carnal life, he may not attend to his soul's salvation. For
nothing avails temporal goods, if at his last times they make
him lose what is spiritual." Chrysostom puts this example
and says: "If you were in great need and poverty, and you
see that your servants are very joyful and cheerful in the city,
of what benefit or profit would you think it is for you to be
master? In like manner what help can the poor soul seek
from all the amusements and solace which the flesh had in
this world, when because of them it shall be condemned in
the end?" Yet it is more pitiful nowadays with the blind and
foolish people of the world. As Saint Augustine says, if any
man praised silver above gold, he should be called and taken
for a fool by every man; but if anyone praised gold above
God, he should not be blamed, nor his wisdom censured
by any man. Man may also exalt Our Lord's words above
those of who apply them to win others' souls, but fail to act
according to those words as to their own soul. Chrysostom
says: "If you are busy about the salvation of others, and you
do not care about your own, you are just like those who

are in a mine digging for metal, which however often falls upon them and slays them. And because of this, if anyone might have said, 'What if I lose my soul, I can still buy it back by my winnings in this world,' this is false as Our Lord shows, 'Oh, what could there be in the whole world that man may give to buy back his soul, if by mortal sin it is condemned for ever?' " Certainly, if man gave the whole world to redeem his soul, it might still not be delivered. And because of this, there is no comparison between this world's goods and the hurt and damage of the soul. For it is more noble than all the world's goods, and they could not be compared to it. If in this world a man lose any riches, he may somehow recover them. And yet even more, if a man suffers death for the love of God, he may recover immortal life for himself, that for which we wait at judgment day. But if the soul is lost by mortal sin, men may find no other soul that may take its place by which restitution may be made. And as Saint Augustine says, let us now because of this bear willingly in our minds Jesus Christ's death over all transitory things of this world, which whether we want or not we must leave once and for all and abandon that we might not lose what is eternal for what is transitory. If in this world someone said to you that you shall be rich and mighty for one month when you can do whatever you wanted and liked, yet afterwards your eyes shall be pulled out from your head and you shall live in hunger and thirst and all other miseries, would you have such little benefit and then bear so much evil? And certainly, all the time of this life is not one month, one day or one hour as compared to everlasting and endless misery or equivalent pain. Isidore says: "If you have Solomon's wisdom in this world, Absalom's beauty, Samson's strength, Enoch's good life, Croesus' riches and the might of a strong man, to what avail and of help to you might all these be if your body was given to worms and your soul to the devil to be tormented for ever, like the soul of the evil rich man? None of all these should either help or be of profit to you." There are in the Holy Church two times. One is of persecution to which a man, unless he should reject his faith in Jesus Christ, ought to put his soul to all pains and torments until death. The other time is that of peace, to which for the love of God man ought to refrain from all worldly desires and use moderately all the goods that he may have in this world.

Hear then these things, and see that no adversity in this world withdraws your soul from any good purpose, or else that prosperity exalts you to some higher reasoning, or that any falsehood takes away from you or causes you not to keep God's commandments, and that you only set your love on God above all other things. We ought to apply ourselves to do God's will and to please Him, keeping ourselves away from sin and doing all that which may please Him.

Then Jesus Christ put away the third abstention with regard to confession and acknowledging the faith, which is the shame of the world. For, as Saint Gregory says, due to worldly shame we often give up expressing by words the goodness we feel in our hearts, only to do so secretly. And we are much slower in defending the rectitude and goodness of justice before the face of God, feeling even more shame in having to confess it before the world. And as Saint Gregory says, yet there are some who say that they have no shame in acknowledging Jesus Christ's name before all people. Yet in Christian profession it suffices a man not to confess faith by mouth, but at times to suffer to be despised, or to suffer some injuries, or to make restitution when he has offended. Then Jesus Christ lays aside the said third abstention. First of all by speaking of the fruit which comes from openly acknowledging the blessed name of Jesus Christ, and secondly by the pain which man deliberately avoids. For Jesus Christ shall acknowledge and confess in the very end those who in this world shall have acknowledged and confessed him; and he shall not acknowledge at all at his second coming those who in this world have been ashamed to confess him, like unbelievers and those who lack mercy. Then in time of persecution the good and faithful Christian ought not to be ashamed to feel and suffer pain for God's honour and love and if it were indeed necessary to suffer death, nor to lose his worldly goods and substances. And in peacetime, when vices and sins are much greater than at any other time, man ought to refrain from doing them for the love of God. Man should not be ashamed to be despised by his fellow Christians, whether by words or otherwise, for the purpose of truly seeing that he follows the meekness of his master Jesus Christ. And in this manner, he shall be acknowledged in the end.

And so that those who hear such things should not be so much embarrassed, that is that they might submit themselves all together as though it were to bear the cross of Jesus Christ, he after says that which brings comfort and faith: "The Son of Man," that is to say of the Virgin Mary, who calls himself so owing to his great meekness and for the truth of his body and the purity of his soul, "shall come in a glorious form, so that in the glory of his Father, with his angels, he will judge the whole world." In his first coming he comes in all meekness, and in his last coming he shall come in a most glorious and virtuous way. And he shall render to each without preference, or without decreasing from each the good and evil which they shall have done, considering works and not persons. That is to say that he shall give to the soul and body of the righteous the reward and glory, and to evil persons eternal pain, to both body and soul. This world is the place where to obtain merit and to deliver our souls from all evil; and in the other, man shall receive what he has deserved in this world, be it good or evil. Walk so then in this world that the light will be with you, to the end that darkness shall not surround you after on each side. Do suffer death patiently here for the love of God so that you may afterwards find life. First think about dying for the love of God, then consider his triumph and glory. Are you ashamed to bear his cross? Consider and hear how the angels serve and help those who bear it. Consider well the works of Saint Bernard, who says: "Do you want to know what you owe to Jesus Christ? I tell you that you owe him yourself, for he gave the first man his life in order to sustain him for a time."

And it is on this account that the apostles were as yet still rough-hewn, and so that they should not doubt of his coming and be sorely tempted by despair, he yet promised them great solace in this world saying: "I truly say to you that there are some here present among you who shall not pass through death of the body until the time when they see with their own eyes the Son of Man come into his king-dom," that is clearly to say when he shall come and judge the whole world. And as the *Interpretation* says, he showed them in his mortal body the clearness of immortality. And for this we must understand that there are some here pres-ent who shall not pass through death until they see God's kingdom, that is to say the Incarnation and manifestation of the glory of God's kingdom. The sweet Jesus made this sweet promise to them, so that by the glory or gladness of the resurrection that was coming, and the contemplation of the joy of fortunate and good lovers, that they should be even bolder and more willing to suffer the pains and adversities of this present life. And yet at certain times he put off showing them this vision he had promised them, so that they would desire and accept it even more fervently and achieve more by it. ✤

CHAPTER 37
OF OUR LORD'S TRANSFIGURATION

 HEN Jesus Christ would after retreat and perform what he had promised his apostles, the same way as it is now said here. It happened six days after, according to Saint Matthew and Saint Mark, which number is neither the first nor the last, for after the sixth age the holy souls ascend into heaven; or as Saint Luke says eighth days after, counting the first as the day when he promised them and the last when he accomplished his promise. Then, he took with him Saint Peter, James and John, his brother, since these were the three he loved much familiarly, and brought them upon a high mountain called Tabor, four miles from Nazareth. Jesus Christ took with him three disciples, and no more, so that it would be accomplished by the mouths of three true records. It should also be noted that all those who shall keep faith in the Blessed Trinity shall find joy within them in eternal happiness. He took also Peter, James and John, in order to see the glory of God, the high majesty, and to know him by faith, as Peter did; to perturb or suppress vices, as James did; to receive God's grace, as John did. And very appropriately so as to show the glory of his resurrection he led his disciples apart, in giving to understand that if we desire to be partners of this blessed resurrection, it suits us to be divided and separated from the company of evil people and worldly rumours. He also brought them upon a high mountain, and not in a valley, to teach them that we ought to seek the glory of the eternal beatitude on high or here above, and not beneath, and that we shall deserve to see the blessed king of glory, Our Lord Jesus Christ, in his high majesty, and that we may after come to the glory of the last resurrection or day of doom, if by good affection we abandon all worldly things and think spiritually to dwell in heaven.

Jesus Christ also went upon the mountain in order to pray, showing us that to pray to God well and heartily we should ascend upon the mountain of virtues and have our hearts on high and not on worldly things. For this is needed by all those who desire to set their minds upon God alone, that due to voluptuousness they do not abide in worldly things here below, but that they always bring themselves to lift up their hearts on high towards heaven. This mountain was also called Tabor, that is the place from where all light comes and dwells, so that all that man knows and sees, is seen in light. The effect of his prayer is that of transfiguration; and it is not said that he had transfigured himself, but that he was transfigured before them, in order to show that such event was done by God in the human nature of Jesus Christ. Take good heed to these things you will now hear and consider yourself as being present since they are very effective. For the face of the sweet Jesus was radiant and shone as the sun, and even much brighter than the sun, but there is nothing so bright to which man may liken him better than the sun. And his clothes were as white as any snow. According to Saint Augustine, the whiteness of Jesus Christ's clothes proceeded from the brightness of his face, by which it appeared that the real change was in his face and not in his clothes; although because of this he did not lose the very substance of the body, nor its very truth, but only added great brightness to it. And therefore Saint Luke says that the form and figure of his face appeared in another manner, and were not any other; for in this transfiguration he did not take up clarity without doubt, but undoubtedly only likeness. Pope Leo says: "When these things were done the disciples were still clothed and covered with their mortal bodies, and they could not see nor behold this ineffable and inaccessible vision of the divinity, which is kept to be seen by those who shall be pure and clean of heart in eternal life." The brightness of his face represented the pure clarity of Jesus Christ our head; and by the clarity of his clothes we understand, according to Bede, the company of his saints who have despised themselves in this world for the love of God.

Morally, Our Lord did three things in this transfiguration. First of all, he took his three disciples; secondly, he went upon the mountain; thirdly, he prayed God, his Father. All these mean that man may not attain the glory of heaven, unless he is accompanied with fair and good virtues, by the highness of a good life and by devout prayer. So very fortunate is he then who is accompanied by such company, that is with Saint Peter, whose name is just as saying know- ing; for in such a man there are three manners of knowing, of God, of himself and of his neighbour. The knowledge of God is a cause of delight for God and keeps man from falling into despair. By knowing himself man promotes humility and keeps himself far from presumption; and by acknowledging his neighbour man arouses compassion and keeps himself far from cruelty. And the same as man ought to endeavour to know his weaknesses, in the same manner man ought to apply himself to know of the world's vanities, that he may despise them even more. He also ought to be accompanied by Saint James, whose name is just as saying a fighter or man of war, because in such a person there are three kinds of war and of doing battles, which are against the world, against the flesh and against the devil. To the end that he should fight strongly against all the lustfulness of the flesh, the world and the devil's instigations, so that in having a good victory he may throw them under his feet. For no one in heaven shall be crowned unless he fights bravely in this world; as a sign of this, Jacob received his benediction from God after that he had fought faithfully. Then also to keep Saint John in company, whose name is just as saying grace, which ought to be in three manners, that is to say as to good standing, spiritual profit and perfection. Saint Paul says about this: "By the grace of God I am what I am," as regards the first; "His grace which was bestowed upon me was not in vain," as to the second; "but I laboured more abundantly than all the others with the help of God's grace, which has ever been with me," as to the third. And by this lowness a good Christian ought to know the faith, as Saint Peter did; and he ought to subdue the vices, as Saint James did; and he ought to be ever ready to do good works, as Saint John did. For man's full merit lies in pleasing God by believing the truth, banishing all evil and exercising all that is good. And just as Saint John was next and foremost with God by privilege of an excellent love, man ought to love divine goodness in the same manner above all things, and to desire it over all that is transitory. Saint Peter was called Simon, which name is interpreted obedient, meaning obedience; Saint John stands for purity; and Saint James signifies wilful poverty. These three things make man see divine brightness, just as priests see the transfiguration of Jesus Christ. Very fortunate were those who might ascend upon such a mountain, that is to say in the highness of good life, where there are three degrees, namely: to abandon one's own will, to mortify one's flesh, and to be in contempt of worldly prosperity; as mentioned in the former chapter. Even in him who pitifully, faithfully and perseveringly makes his prayer up to the time when the glory of God appears in him, and he is very fortunate. The face of Our Lord signifies the clergy, which ought to be trans-figured like sunshine; for they ought to shine by knowledge, brighten up by charity, and carry others to light by doctrine and good examples. And by clothing let it be understood worldly people, to whom suffices the whiteness of snow by purity of the soul, of the body and of works.

And in this transfiguration Moses appeared to the three apostles in flesh, together with his soul, similarly as the angels appeared together with their body. And with Moses there appeared the prophet Elijah, still living both in body and soul, who was brought from earthly paradise. And Our Lord Jesus Christ was in their midst, as bearing testimony to the Gospel, to the Law and Prophets. Moses was dead and Elijah was alive, this meaning that Jesus Christ is both Lord and master of life and death, of the living and of the dead, and that the righteous dead, for which Moses stands, and the living, signified by Elijah, ought in the end to reign with him. This was also done to show that it was him whom the Law and Prophets have prophesied and promised to come into the world, and of whom they have written. And by this it clearly appeared that the Law and Prophets did not discard anything of the doctrine of Jesus Christ, who is the purpose of the Law and prophecies, and the glory of the faith and of the Law by which they had come. It was also for the purpose that he would show himself to be above the Law, which Law Moses gave to the people of the land of Judea by God's com-mandment, and above the prophets, amongst whom Elijah was one of the most excellent. Then Moses signifies the Law, Elijah the prophets, and Jesus Christ the holy Gospel. One of those who appeared is dead and the other living, in figure that Our Lord ought to die for our salvation and after rise again, thereby showing us that we ought to be dead to the world and only alive in God. Also, Jesus Christ had testimony on every side, namely from heaven that of God the Father, from the air by the sky, from the earthly paradise by Elijah, from the earth by the apostles and from Hades by Moses.

And they told him of the great things he had to accomplish in Jerusalem, namely his passion, where a superabundance of love was to be found, his kindness and his meekness. For in it love was without measure, as it is written that "No man either by delight or so great love has given his soul to death as myself"; and sorrow was my patron, according to Jeremiah, "You all who are suffering, take heed whether there ever was such sorrow as mine"; and humility is above all virtues, the same as he also says, "Have mind and think about my great poverty." These words were uttered to show that the grace of the redemption of the whole world, which had to be accomplished by Jesus Christ, had been prefigured in the Law and by the prophets for a long time. And it is to be noted that they did not speak of this to show Jesus Christ anything which he did not know, but only because they were bound to do so. They also rendered thanks and praise to him for coming into this world by his Incarnation and for the mystery of his passion, which they had predestined a long time before and which they wanted to see him immediately accomplish. And it is not to be doubted but that they were very joyful and glad to see the day of the redemption of the human race approach, although they had great compassion on Jesus Christ as his glorious face was to be spit upon, defiled and scorned, and that by very great envy of the Jews he was to be judged to death and crucified. Moses, who had been leader of the Jews, found joy in Saint Peter seeing him as the prince of Christians; Elijah considered the Virgin and chaste Saint John; and both lauded the privilege of martyrdom and victory in Saint James.

And while these things were happening, Saint Peter and his company were sleeping heavily that the glory which they were about to see might be suppressed; for man's intelligence is suppressed by the great clarity of incomprehensible dignity. And being awakened, they saw Jesus Christ's great

majesty and that of the other two with him, that is to say
Moses and Elijah. Saint Ambrose asks how the apostles knew
who they were, seeing that they had never seen them before.
And the answer he receives is that they knew them by the
great majesty which encompassed them; whereby it is shown
that in the glory to come, each one shall know one another.
According to the *Interpretation*, Elijah is here as the greatest
of prophets, and David the greatest, and Moses the greatest.
Moses was the greatest prophet owing to the familiarity he
had with God, for the extravagance of the astounding sins
he had done, and for the promulgation of the Law. Elijah
was the greater prophet in considering the chastity of his
life, the audacity of reprieve, and the length of his life. David
is the greatest of these two, if we consider the highness of
his prophecy, his royal dignity, and the promise which was
made to him about the Messiah, who descended from him.

And then Saint Peter, who was the most fervent of all, said
to Jesus Christ, "Lord, it would be good if we stay here and
dwell on this mountain and in the sweetness of contemplation." Men set no store by inner feelings when the soul has
an inkling for heavenly sweetness. According to Rabanus, the
more that a man tastes of heavenly sweetness, even more
annoying shall all earthly things become. "If it pleases you,
let us here make tabernacles in which to dwell for ever; that
is one for you, one for Moses, and one for Elijah." He was
not speaking, however, about himself and his company for
he supposed that they should dwell with their master Jesus
in his tabernacle, being his disciples. When Saint Peter saw
the great majesty of his Lord and of his two servants, he
felt such great joy that he forgot all worldly things, willing
to abide in that place for ever. And if Saint Peter was then
so inflamed with heavenly sweetness, how pleasant would
it be when we shall see the mighty and great king in his
royalty and brightness and when we shall be in company
with all the angels and saints? In considering these things,
we should repute nothing in this world as too hard to suffer
for the love of God, neither torments, crucifixion, nor any
kind of pain whatever, or even death itself, that in the end
may bring us to the heavenly mountain on which there is
neither molestation nor evil example of life, but where all

is good. Bede says: "Oh, what happiness of a heavenly life it is to be perpetually in the company of angels and of all the righteous people of the world! If Jesus Christ's humanity transformed in the company but of only two saints, as seen in so short a while, gave the apostles such great delight that Saint Peter prayed Our Lord to still dwell in the place where they were, what joy may man think of having in perpetually abiding in the company of angels and saints?"

Yet in saying these things to Jesus Christ, Saint Peter erred and did not know what he was saying, both because of the manner he was asking for peace, and since in esteeming the shadow of the glory that was to come to be the true glory, he had forgotten that the kingdom of heaven was not promised to those who lived a holy life here on earth but in heaven. He also erred in similarly believing that in the glory that was to come, tabernacles and houses made by the hand of man were necessary, and that he would have a state of immortal life without any tasting of the death of mortal life. And for this his words were unreasonable, for the true and proper beatitude is not constituted or set to behold simply Jesus Christ's human nature, nor that it was expected of him not to suffer to achieve the true heavenly beatitude. And also Peter neither considered the salvation of his fellow Christians, nor that of himself, which ought to proceed by the merits of Our Lord Jesus Christ's passion, which had not as yet been accomplished. Augustine says: "Oh Saint Peter, what are you saying here? That the world shall perish and you will desire a place of certainty? You see so many people being together and having such differences, and you love and desire rest? You see this world's darkness, and you will hide the very light?" The Damascene says: "Oh Peter, this should not have been good for you that Jesus Christ should have still dwelt upon this hill, for if he had abode there, the promise which he made to you would no longer be of any use. For then you would not have had the keys of the kingdom of heaven, nor would evil death have been destroyed." And, as Chrysostom says, after Saint Peter heard that Jesus Christ wanted to return to Jerusalem where he would suffer great pain, and had rebuked him for this when Jesus Christ said to him, *Vade retro Satana,* he then did not dare any more to show openly what he had said. Yet in some manner he would still infer to Jesus Christ that he would not return to Jerusalem with his master, for those who would put him to death dwelt there. Since on this mountain he saw great rest and solitude, he appropriately thought of a fair arrangement for them to keep on dwelling there. And it was because of this that he would infer to Jesus Christ that "It were good that we remained in this place," so willing to ever dwell there. Also because of this he mentioned the tabernacles and houses, saying "If you want, we will make here three tabernacles." And although Saint Peter did not know at the time what he was saying but was all so disconcerted, yet in this he showed the hot ardent thirst he had of the wine of which he had been drunk, in wanting to make three taverns for a single drop of the heavenly wine which he had drunk.

This transfiguration witnesses to the glory of saints in heaven and is first of all written in the majesty of God, for all the Blessed Trinity appeared in it, that is to say the Father in the voice, the Son in the human nature, and the Holy Spirit in the sky. And just as Saint Peter would make there three tabernacles, in the same manner all reasonable creatures have three tabernacles in their souls, where the Blessed Trinity dwells and not Moses or Elijah. The three tabernacles are remembrance, understanding and will. The Son abides and dwells in the tabernacle of understanding, which he fills with his most clear and full knowledge. The Holy Spirit dwells in the tabernacle of will, which he fulfils with his most sweet and enjoyable love. And the Father dwells in the tabernacle of remembrance, which he fulfils with the vigour of very true love and knowledge. By these three the soul is transformed in God in its entirety and is so all worshipped.

Secondly, this transfiguration is written and remembered by the company which was present, being Peter, James and John, Moses and Elijah, for in this place were those who represented the state of the blessed saints and that of the Old and New Testaments. The Saints of the Old Testament are distinct in two orders, that is to say in Patriarchs such like Moses, and in Prophets such as Elijah. The saints of the New Testament are distinguished in three orders, that is in Martyrs, like Saint James; Confessors for being full of wisdom, like Saint Peter, just as saying knowing; and Virgins, as seen in Saint John. It is like saying that Jesus Christ has received the testimony of heavenly beings by his Father; of earthly beings by Peter, James and John; of the earthly paradise by Elijah; and of those who are in hell by Moses. The six persons who were present also stand for such great benefits as God gives to contemplatives themselves. As in order for a soul to come to contemplation, it first suits it to be enlightened, as shown by Saint Peter, just like saying knowing. Secondly, that the flesh is subdued, as shown by Saint James. Thirdly, that God's grace is increased, as shown by Saint John, just as saying in whom grace is found. Fourthly, God gives the contemplative the gift of despising the world, as seen in Moses. Fifthly, it kindles the heart with divine love, as shown by the prophet Elijah. Sixthly, man tastes heavenly sweetness, as seen in Jesus Christ who is sweet, loving and kind to Saint Peter and to all others.

Thirdly, this transfiguration is recounted as relating to the glorification of Jesus Christ's body. For it is said that his body and his face shone as the sun, and his clothes were as white as snow, which means the beatitude and glory with which the bodies of those leading a holy life shall be clothed; in the same manner as it was shown by the angel who appeared in white clothing at the resurrection of Our Lord.

When Saint Peter said to Jesus Christ that it was good to erect three tabernacles in this place, Jesus Christ did not answer him at all. Although Saint Peter spoke with such great love and devotion as were in him, yet for craving so indis-creetly he deserved to have no answer. For whoever erects a tabernacle for Our Lord ought to cleanse and prepare the inner part of his heart, for it would be only there and not elsewhere that the very abode and dwelling place of God of Jacob shall be found. Saint Peter also thought that in wanting to make three tabernacles of earthly matter, such material tab-ernacles were necessary in eternal glory, which is untrue. For there is no kind of adversity, tempest, heat or cold, for God in the temple and house of the Church; and it is because of this that there was no need of cover under the fair and clear sky.

And this is afterwards said, that as Saint Peter thought and spoke of making tabernacles, they were overshadowed by the clear sky, so as to make them understand that the friends of God chosen for eternal life shall not be covered with anything of a material nature, but with the grace and glory of the Holy Spirit. And you ought to understand that, in this manner when Saint Peter had accomplished what Moses and Elijah had said, they departed before, and there immediately came upon them from the heavens above words which were broken in two parts. These heavens were not caused by the dew rising from earth into the air, but proceeded from the great light which was present, just as smoke proceeds from fire.

So as to instruct the apostles' intellect of knowledge about the Trinity of the blessed Son of God, with the testimonies of Moses and Elijah, the Father's voice was heard like thunder in the sky, giving testimony of His only son, saying *Hic est filius meus dilectus*, "This is my well beloved son"; not so by fatherly love, but by nature. That is to say, according to Saint Ambrose: "Neither Elijah nor Moses are my very natural sons, but so is only him whom you see." And as the *Interpretation* says, if Moses and Elijah had stayed on besides Jesus Christ, it would have seemed that the Father's voice was uncertain, for men should not have known about whom of the three had testimony been given. And because of this, they departed before, so that man should understand that only the Father spoke to his Son, Our Lord Jesus Christ, whom He had pleasingly constituted and ordained for the redemption of mankind. For in him is all the Father's delight and repose, inasmuch as he would diligently accomplish all His will and pleasure, although in both of them there is not but only one will. "Hear you him," God called the disciples to do as sovereign and extraordinary master who was much greater than Moses or Elijah. These three disciples were very fortunate, not only deserving to see Jesus Christ's brightness and glory, but also heard the Father's voice in the heavens above. So should we never be estranged nor cast off from all this blessed happiness if we truly believe what they believed, and if we live as they lived, and love God with all our hearts the same as they loved Him.

But so that human fragility may not in this world sustain the great sweetness of the Trinity, as when the apostles heard the Father's voice, they fell face down to the ground; by which they showed their great perfection and holiness, for the evil are accustomed to falling backwards, that is with their back on the ground facing upwards. For many causes righteous men fell many times down on their faces. First, owing to the fear they had, as told here before. Secondly, because of their great meekness, as the three magi did before Our Lord and his sweet mother. Thirdly, for actions of grace, as ancients did in standing before the throne, when they fell on their faces to render thanks to God. And when the apostles heard this voice, they were very afraid; for it was so great as thunder, Ephrem says, that the prophets fled away and the apostles fell to the ground and earth trembled. And it so happened that in being fragile they were strongly deranged, yet their heart-rending master comforted and helped them sweetly by words and deed. For he came to them by his sweet kindness, familiarly and courteously, touching and lifting them up, so that he would fortify their weak members by his touch. And so that they should cast away from their hearts all fear and worry, he sweetly said to them, *Surgite et nolite timere*, "Arise and do not fear anything at all." Most fortunate and blessed are those whom Jesus Christ, the very salvation and life of souls, touches! And when he had touched them, they arose boldly and fearlessly. Now let us pray God it would please Him to touch and waken us from our sleeping idleness and negligence, and open our eyes that we may see Him clearly. He is both meek and courteous in his loving; and in all meekness he comforts those who do not have comfort, and helps them strongly and mightily.

Then having been touched and comforted by Jesus Christ, who pitifully gives his right hand to those who have fallen to lift them up again, the three disciples stood up on their own. And neither Moses nor Elijah saw that they had stood up, but only the sweet Jesus Christ in the human form in which they knew him to be familiar with them.

And while going down from the hill, he commanded and instructed them not to tell anyone about this glory they had seen in the transfiguration till after his resurrection from death to life. He gave this command for many reasons, the first being, according to Saint Jerome, that this event might not seem incredible owing to its greatness. Secondly, according to Saint Thomas, so that the people who had heard such great and glorious things about him, should not fall in despair in seeing him crucified. Thirdly, according to Saint Remigius, so that such event should not delay the fruit of the passion, for if the glory of the majesty had been shown to the people before his passion, many would have fought off the princes of the priests and saved him from such a shameful death. According to Saint Hilary the fourth reason is that the apostles ought then to have been witnesses of Our Lord Jesus Christ's person in the Trinity, since they were filled with the Holy Spirit. Fifth, according to the Damascene, since had they told the other disciples of the event they might have been very sorrowful and sad for not having seen it themselves; and even so, Judas might have been more incited and moved to betray Jesus Christ to the Jews. Sixth, since the resurrection of Jesus Christ for many was hard to believe and they put great doubts in it. And so this vision was reserved only to be shown at the time when it was inevitable to give testimony of the resurrection, when the glory of this transfiguration would have given great testimony; which seemed to be more credible when it was wisely declared after the resurrection. Seventh, in order to give example that in keeping within us what gives us joy and comfort as long as we are in this mortal life is a good thing for, as the Man of Wisdom says, we ought not to either praise or magnify anyone as long as he is still in this world. Also because of this he would show that divine secrets and mysteries should never be made public, but they ought to be shown at the right time and place. And also so that he would give an example to holy people that they should not easily publish any revelation given to them, the same as Saint Paul did when for fourteen years he kept himself from showing what God had radiantly shown him.

Our Lord's transfiguration was at about the time winter was setting in; and so men read about the transfiguration in the Gospel on the Saturday in Lent's ember days. But the feast is celebrated on the sixth day of August, because it was then that the apostles made it public and preached about it and not before, owing to the prohibition which Christ had made them.

CHAPTER 38

OF THE HEALING OF ONE WHO WAS LUNATIC

HE following day Jesus Christ returned from the mountain where he had made his trans⁄figuration and came to his other apostles whom he had left down below; and at once a great multitude of people came to him. This prolific coming denotes that prelates ought to descend to their parishioners with humility, compassion and affability, and that as long as they still keep themselves high above by exaltation or ambition, few come to them and few find in them salvation or healing. We do not read in the Gospel that Our Lord restored health to anyone on the mountain.

And then one of the company came to him requesting him to have pity and compassion on his son who was a lunatic. This sickness was even more grievous in moon changes than at other times. Then saying that he had the foul devil in his body and that the disciples might not deliver him, the child was brought before Jesus Christ. And the devil, feeling that by Jesus Christ's command he had to come out immediately of the body, made the boy fall to the ground and vexed him sorely in all his members, so that owing to extreme pain he frothed at the mouth and grated his teeth. And he was as good as dead, and he cried with great feeling, at times casting himself into the fire and at others in water, in such manner that he could have easily perished had God's providence not kept him alive. And Jesus Christ immediately commanded the devil to come out of his body and not to enter it any more. And he had made the child deaf and dumb owing to the great malice the devil had in him, and it was to make him like him that he made the child deaf and dumb. And seeing that he must immediately come out of him, he tor⁄mented him cause him great ache in passing out of him, in such manner that it seemed like the child had been struck dead. But Jesus Christ took him by the hand and lifted him up, and in lifting him up, he was completely healed and he rendered him again to his father.

Morally, this lunatic body signifies the sinner, whom the devil first takes by delight of sin; secondly, he makes him cry in his desire for sin; thirdly, he makes him dumb in confessing God's love and showing his sins; fourthly, he made him deaf as to the warning given him by God's words; fifthly, the lunatic, by great instability of mind, cried with great pain that he may be separated and leave sin because of its evil custom. And the reason is that when the sinner amends his ways and goes back from sin, he is much strongly vexed by the devil to return to his former evil ways and to take revenge on the body from which he was put out where he dwelt before.

Our Lord did not reprimand the child who was vexed, but he who vexed him. For whoever will heal a sinner ought strongly to despise the vices to which the sinner is inclined; and then after he ought to comfort by love the person who would have withdrawn from evil. Now when the devil, by God's power, departs from the body or soul of any creature, he may never enter it again unless the creature shuts and locks his heart fast with the key of charity and humility. And when he was constrained to come out and be cast away, he tormented strongly the man he had possessed; for when he is put out of the heart which he possesses, he will after put in it many more and greater temptations, in such manner that it shall seem that the patient is stark dead. But he is immediately made whole when he feels the sweet grace of Our Saviour Jesus. For the help of God is much stronger than all of the devil's temptations. Certainly, God will be of great help in all our needs, but after he has helped us he wants us to occupy ourselves in good works.

And when he entered the house, his disciples asked him secretly why they were unable to cast out the devil from this child's body. And he answered them that this was owing to their incredulity. Upon which it is to be noted that the disciples of Our Lord are not called incredulous since they lacked faith, as the Jews did, but for the little desire of fervent faith they had. Their faith was not like the mustard seed for in them there was no desire or the fervent faith required to do such a great miracle as to put out the devil from the body of a person, which is not impossible to do for anyone who has great and fervent faith accompanied with love. And for such faith nothing is impossible; the mustard seed, which is little, like fervent love, is contrary to venom; whereby it appears that Jesus Christ would by this show that he compared faith to a mustard seed, in that man ought to have a little faith by meekness, which is fervent by devotion and bitter in suffering anguish in this world. And that he ought to cast out all error, which is very evil venom, from man's body. For as Saint Ambrose says, the mustard seed is very little by its nature, but when one breaks it between his teeth by chewing, it gives a great smell and shows his strength. In like manner, faith in time of prosperity seems to be little, but in anguish it shows its strength.

And after this, he bound them to meekness, warning them not to glorify themselves for any good deed which they did in this world, but rather more to humble themselves before God, from whom comes all good. And he said to them, "When you have done all that you are commanded to do, then say, not only by mouth but also with your heart so that your humility is not only vocal but real, 'We are useless servants, even though we have done all that we can or ought to do.'" Beware of self-vaunting if you have served well, for you have not done so much as you ought to have done. As if Our Lord had said that by our service we have not deserved that God should give us his grace, but that only by Him have we deliberately avoided the pains. To the contrary proud people, who do not do all the good they are commanded to do but only a few good deeds, not only fail to vaunt themselves of the good they do, but also despise others who according to them are more frail than themselves. Certainly, we are servants, but not to be self-serving. For it was with a great ransom that we were bought back, as with the precious blood of the sweet Jesus. And for this we are well bound to serve him, leaving nothing undone of what we ought to do, or leaving what we ought not to do. The servants ought not to be called useless in receiving the fruit of eternal life by duly accomplishing God's commands. But they are called useless because God has no need of our service; or since all the good which we do in this world is nothing in comparison to the glory and reward God will give us; or also in order to show that all creatures ought to hold themselves as imperfect, whatsoever perfection they might have in this world. Bede says: "The only perfection of the people's faith is, if in doing all the good which they are commanded to do and yet still consider themselves unworthy and useless, but then as long as they are in this world they do many evils of which they ought to bewail and repent, they should do good whereby they might deserve the grace of God. And as Jesus Christ says: 'Without me and my help you may do no good deed worthy of eternal life.' And for this you ought not to think on the length of time or on the merits of the labours, but by good love and service you ought ever to believe in what is best." And it is a good thing to say: "We have done what we ought to do"; for according to Bede, God has strongly bound us to Him, not having come into this world to be served, but to serve, so that we should not put great trust in our good deeds and fear his judgment, saying with the prophet: "What good may we render to God for all the good He has done to us?" For he has shown his great and infinite mercy in us. And for that, we never ought to rest our hope in our merits or good deeds, but only put all our trust and confidence in God's mercy, whom we ought to serve meekly, so that in the end He will take us into His blessed heavenly kingdom. Do here consider well that whoever only does what he is bound to do is reputed as a useless servant. And because of this, so however perfect may a man be in this world, he ought to be meek about himself, and heartily say to God, "Oh Lord Jesus Christ, my God, I know well that before you I am nothing, for I serve evil and I may not do well without your help, which should be profitable to my salvation." Saint Francis often said to his brethren, "Let us begin to serve God yet after many great labours. For until now we have profited a little." And we ought to firmly humble ourselves for having accomplished in deed all that which is commanded to us by God, then we ought more reasonably to humble ourselves in leaving many things which we are commanded to do. And if whoever accomplishes all things which God commands him is called useless, what might men say of whoever leaves such things and fails to accomplish them? Ambrose says: "You will not walk forward in vain if you have served well and accomplished what God commands you, for the sun obeys Him, the moon attends to Him, and all angels do Him service. Hear you what Saint Paul, who was chosen by God, says: 'I am not worthy to be called apostle, for I have persecuted the Church of God.' And in another place he showed that in his conscience he was not caught by sin; and yet for so much he said before God, 'I am not justified nor made good now.' Let us not then demand for our good deeds the lauds and praises of this world. But let us ever have fear, and let us receive the sentence of God, the very true judge, and reserve all to His judgment, which shall be in terms of the truth and according to it."

It is a good thing for man ever to keep himself in fear and presume nothing of himself. For whatever good he might do in this world, howsoever great it may be, yet he is not sure whether it is worthy to have love or hatred before God. Bernard says: "In good truth, I have learnt and known that in this world there is nothing having greater effect to obtain the grace of God, or to keep it when it is obtained, or to recover it when man has lost it, than for a man to keep Him ever in fear and dread and presume nothing of himself. For it is written that very fortunate is him who keeps himself ever in God's fear and dread. Then if you feel the grace of God within you, keep yourself in fear, that it might not seem to you that you should be good now to God. Also, if you perceive by any sign that grace should be withdrawn from you, keep yourself staunchly in the fear of God, for it is because of this that God lets you be in your own keeping and in your virtue, which is very little. And if yet again you call for His grace, still keep yourself in fear, so that owing to your fault He does not withdraw it from you once again, and that would be worse for you than it was before." And Saint Paul, who lived in this fear, exhorts us not to receive the grace of God in vain. It is received in vain by whoever does not exercise himself in good works according to the grace which God gives him. And for this, if we do not want the grace of God to be in us without us bearing spiritual fruit, it is inevitable that we nourish it with good works and exercise them virtuously, keeping ourselves far from all vices and sins as much as possible.

In all our works we also ought to consider that all that we do for the love of God, is well pleasing to Him and not only in terms of works. In considering the works we should be doing with regard to God, Saint Basil says that we ought to be like an artificer who makes a hatchet or some other tool for another person, recalling daily how it should be made, its greatness, quality or mode how and for what purpose it will be used, and moulds his tool according to the will of him who orders the work so as to please him. So too in our works, we ought to see that everything is done soon according to the will of God who has commanded and set us on some work. And we ought to accomplish what the Apostle Saint Paul says, that whatever we do by way of good deeds in this world ought to be done for God's glory and honour, whether we eat or drink or in doing anything else.

Yet after Our Lord showed how according to the aforesaid cause pride and presumptuousness are subdued, saying that these kind of devils found in the body and soul of man may not be put out, or such devils be made to lose their power over man, but by prayer. Such gives salvation to the spirit, as fasting does in giving spiritual healing to the body, as both prayer and fasting are the effect of a well fervent faith founded upon charity. Whereby it seems that such sickness came to this child by too much eating and drinking.

There might also be other causes why the disciples could not make the devils come out of this child's body. For these causes are not all of one power and might, and so one is much harder to put out of a man's body than another. Now, to put out this devil out of a body it was necessary that whoever was to expel it must have his body subject to the Spirit which he achieves by fasting, and that his Spirit was exalted toward God which he obtains by supplication. These two things were not yet found in the apostles, since at that time there they behoved it not that they should fast owing to the presence of the true spouse Jesus who was with them. Even so, neither were they yet perfect with God in everything, being crude and imperfect until the time after the passion and the time when they received the grace of the Holy Spirit in great abundance.

Or one might also say that the devil is not cast out of man just by the power of Church ministers, unless it is done by prayer and fasting; not that the minister usurps and appropriates divine power, which was Lucifer's pride wanting to set a high seat for himself. And as Chrysostom says, Jesus Christ says that these kind of devils, not only of lunatics but of all others, may not be put out of people except by prayer and fasting, since the devil always dwells in the hearts of sinners up to the time that they would have converted to God by true penance. Jerome says: "Our Lord Jesus Christ, in teaching the apostles how the devil should be put out of man, teaches us how we should live in the life of grace," namely that by fasting and prayer all temptations are overcome, as are all the doings of the devil of hell and of the world's evil people. And yet if it so happens that God's displeasure were kindled against us because of our sins and offences, yet we might be certain that by fasting and prayer we may appease it. And so it is a most extraordinary remedy for us; for also, we ought to understand that by fasting man may abstain from all evil, and by prayer he ought to do all that is good. As Saint Augustine says, man's great and perfect fast is not only to abstain from food and drink, but likewise from all evils and from all the evil voluptuousness of this world. Saint Bernard says: "If only the mouth has sinned, it ought to fast alone, and that would suffice. But if the other members have sinned, why do they not fast with it? And because of this, the eye ought to fast from too curious observations, and from all defilement, that it might be humbled to goodness by penance. The ear ought to fast from all rumours, and from hearing about evil doings, and from all other things not related to man's salvation. The tongue ought to fast from all belittling talk, and from lies, and from all other vain words. And yet to show how serious silence is, man ought sometimes to abstain from uttering words, except those which are necessary. And above all, the soul ought to fast from all vices and from its own will; for without this fast, other fasts will be rebuked by God and be of no value. For it is so written that God said to the Jews: "Although your proper will is found in the days of your fasts, they are not pleasing to me." And we ought not to only fast from unlawful things, but also from that which is lawful, if we want God to forgive us of the evils and vices committed by us." Bede says: "In the same manner as man abstains not only from bodily nourishment but also from all kinds of vices and sins, and this is a general fast, just as well prayer is general when we call upon God's divine meekness not only by words, but when in whatever we do we please God with devotion. And by this we accomplish what Saint Paul the Apostle says, namely that we ought to pray constantly to God." For he who ever prays to Him is he who does good works and perseveres in them. ⚓

CHAPTER 39

OF THE TRIBUTE THAT WAS PAID FOR JESUS CHRIST AND SAINT PETER AND HOW THE DISCIPLES DEMANDED OF HIM WHO OF THEM SHOULD BE HELD GREATEST AFTER HIM

WING to the words he had spoken and what he had done in Jerusalem, the Jews sought Jesus Christ to put him to death. And so he would not go to Jerusalem before the feast of Easter. Augustine says: "That Our Lord would not go to Jerusalem was not because he lacked power over anything, but he did it to comfort our fragility. For in future there might have been some men who might timidly hide themselves from tyrants for fear of death. And because of this, he who was master wanted to show that sometimes fleeing is no sin." So then it appears that he tarried with his disciples in Galilee. Yet they did not ask him why they were tarrying all the time because he would have then again told them of his passion, about which they had become used to hearing of it being spoken many times and so that they would not weep in despair when it should come. And he said to them: "Bear well in your minds the words I say to you, namely that the Son of Man must be given of his Father out of very great love. And he must also give himself up obediently and willingly. And he shall be tempted by the devil by evil suggestion; by Judas for his great covetousness; by the Jews for their great and evil avarice; by Pilate for his timidity." (...)

CHAPTER 40

OF THE CENTURION'S SERVANT WHO HAD THE PALSY

FTER the healing of the leper, Jesus Christ went to Capharnaum, the most honoured and main city of that land, but which was now poor and abject. And a centurion, that is to say the prince and governor of a hundred soldiers, who was set there by the Romans to receive the tribute and to keep the land of Galilee that none should rebel against the Romans, came to Jesus Christ full of faith and devotion; but he did not come with his bodily feet, for he was a gentile and reputed himself to be unworthy to come to the presence of Jesus Christ. Origen says: "The centurion came from a foreign country, but he was well-bred and meek of heart, a foreigner by nation, a prince and captain of men of arms by faith, and a fellow to angels."

And then, as he was not a Jew but a heathen, he first sent the most ancient of Jews, as familiar friends and lovers of Jesus Christ, to pray and say to him through them, *Domine*, "Lord," in whose power is both sickness and health, death and life; *puer meus*, "my child," that is my servant and subject, whom tenderly he called his child, more by love or familiarity than by condition; "is sick at home in my house," which is an example to all those who are proud and despise their servants when they are sick and send them to hospital. "He is painfully tormented and is most grievously sick." He asked of him by three words, that is to say that he was taken with "palsy, grievously sick," in order to incline him to compassion. Chrysostom says: "This nobleman only expressed to Jesus Christ his servant's sickness, and did not ask for any remedy nor for a remedy about how he should be made whole, but he left all to the power of his mercy." And now the Jews were sent there by disposition and heavenly providence so that, in seeing a foreigner who hearing of such and so great miracles believed and knew certainly well that his child might be healed, there would be no reason why they should not also believe in Jesus Christ. And this being done, in that the centurion felt very sorrowful and thought well of his servant, we are taught how we should be compassionate and have pity and care for our subjects and servants. He was not like many nowadays who, when they see their subjects sick would not be of great help to them, but would rather be more diligent in keeping their own health and looking after their own wealth than helping or advising their servants in their sickness; and rather more consent to their sensual inclinations than to the needs of other beings who are in need.

Now Jesus Christ, acknowledging this saintly centurion's devotion, answered him through his own messengers and said *Ego veniam*, "I shall come," showing humility, *et curabo eum*, "and I shall heal him," showing pity. And saying this, he went along with them. This doctor acted otherwise and in another manner than those who are only ready to visit the rich and have no store for the poor. Then, when the centurion was close to his house, recalling the great faith which he had and seeing that his messengers had returned, he sent his most beloved and family friends to the majesty and grandeur of this great doctor to pray him that he would not come to his house, saying *Noli vexari*, "Lord, I will not that you take the labour and pain, for I am not worthy that you should enter under my roof," that is in my house, "for in my conscience I am not living the life of a true gentile." In reputing himself unworthy that Jesus Christ should physically come into his house, he still feared greatly to offend him whom he believed to be truly God. According to Saint Augustine the centurion was made worthy by reputing himself unworthy before God and by his great meekness in saying "I do not repute myself so worthy to come to you, but I have sent you my messengers. And therefore, Lord, without the need for your bodily presence, say but only your word, by which all things are created and governed, and I believe that my child shall be made whole." This man had great faith and belief in believing that what Jesus Christ had said by word would also be done in deed. Bede says: "There must be great faith in whom saying is as much worth as doing in deed." And Peter the Chanter says that it is better not to receive the sacrament of holy orders or of the eucharist if whoever receives them has neither good faith nor does he believe in them. I do not say that he abuses them, since such irregularity would exclude all such persons from administering the sacraments. And so we ought to be aware of offending in any manner here. One becomes irregular if he puts himself into such office or service without knowing himself and considering well his state.

Now three great virtues have to be considered in the centurion's act, namely humility, faith and wisdom. He showed humility when Jesus Christ was ready to come to him and into his house, yet he reputed himself to be unworthy. His faith is also shown as well as his wisdom when yet being a heathen, he knew that the Trinity was hidden under the nature of Jesus Christ; he also believed that him who he only saw corporally was in all places, and that he might do anything. And so he said *Nam et ego homo sum sub potestate constitutus*, "I am a man confirmed and set under the emperor's power, and have noblemen and servants under me. And when I say to one of them 'Go there,' he immediately goes, and when I say to the other 'Come here,' he immediately comes to serve me. And to a servant I say 'Do these things,' and he immediately does them without any restraint." By saying this he was then concluding "I, who have but little power and subject to those who are greater than me, and by my only word can do what I want through my servants whom I may command; then by greater reason you, who are God and whom everything obeys, may by a single word of yours save my servant and order the sickness to get out of the body and go away, and to health and salvation to come. And to the sick man of palsy, to do so, and all that he bids him to do, he does. And we may do miracles if you command us; and so there is no need for you to take the trouble of coming here, for you may do it without being here physically present."

Now when Jesus Christ had heard the centurion speak in this manner, showing by his words his great inner faith in acknowledging the excellence of Jesus Christ's divinity under the cover of his human nature, he was marvelled. Namely that in marvelling he showed it in his countenance, teaching us that we ought to be marvelled of God's benefits and give Him praise and thank Him for them. Augustine says: "By this that Our Lord was marvelled shows us that it is ourselves who ought to be marvelled. For as long as we are in this world, there are things which move us. Such emotions as are attributed to God and are said to be coming from Him, are no sign of unease of the soul, but they are only given by way of instruction from the master of faith and truth.

And in praising the centurion's faith, Jesus Christ said to those who follow him, *non inveni tantam fidem in Israel* "I have not found such sign of faith or belief in Israel", that is to say among the Jews who lived in his time. But with the old Fathers, as Abraham, Isaac and Jacob, and many other Patriarchs and Prophets who started our faith, he had found much greater faith and belief. For when men speak of sin or of anyone's merits, they ever ought to do so but with the exception of the Virgin Mary. The apostles too ought not to be included, as it appears he spoke to them in our common manner of speaking. It is like when a principal or chief master enters into a house accompanied by a great number of persons looking for someone, and in finding no one says, "There is nobody in that house"; although he and all his servants and those who entered with him are there. Jerome says: "He says these words about those who were there at the time, and not about the Patriarchs or Prophets. For by this centurion's faith, the faith of the gentiles was commended before the faith of the Jews." Bede says: "The centurion's faith is exalted above that of the Jews who were there present at the time, for they were taught by the Law and under the prophets' guidance to believe in Jesus Christ. And this man, without the Law or anyone's preaching or instruction, still believed in Jesus Christ only by his good will." Chrysostom says: "If we will praise the faith of this man before the faith of the apostles, we may understand that each and everyone is the same man according to the quality found in him. For it is a marvellous thing when a labourer and unlearned man speaks of a great thing and recounts great wisdom, but men fail to marvel when a philosopher or great doctor speaks in the same manner. And so of what then happened there, for it is not a likely thing that a Jew and a heathen both believe alike in God. For at the beginning of their belief the Jews, having seen many miracles and marvels done by Jesus Christ, ought to join him in their faith and believe; but this man had seen neither miracle nor marvel, but having only heard of his great renown, believed in him." And Our Lord, in seeing that the faith of the gentiles and the heathens, as figured in the centurion's faith, grew and increased above the faith of the Jews, was marvelled and commended him in such manner that the Jews were confounded by the centurion's faith. And in this instance, he concluded and predestined the conversion and calling of the gentiles, and on the contrary, the infidelity and reprobation of the Jews, when he said *Amen*, that is to say "Truly and certainly I tell you that in the example of this man, in whom the faith of the heathens is prefigured, many from the east and west," that is according to Saint Augustine, from all parts of the world, "from the north and south, and from all nations of people, as many as keep Christ's laws, shall join in the unity of Holy Church."

Morally, the easterners are those who consider their nature and imperfection or birthright, and those who are obedient to their parents, or who do penance in their youth. And the westerners are those who consider their short life in this world, and that all living creatures must die, and who are converted or do penance while still living. The northern ers are those who in time of prosperity do works of pity, and keep self-denial in time of abundance. The southerners are those who in time of anguish correct and amend their ways, and have patience in all adversity. "And all such men shall be saved and shall find their rest," not in sleeping but spir itually, "with Abraham, Isaac and Jacob," who are especially named since he had mainly covenanted the Promised Land to them, prefiguring the land of God's chosen servants, which is the kingdom of heaven: "and his other friends, in paradise," where light and glory abound together with all goodness.

"And the sons of the kingdom," that is to say the Jews, amongst whom God reigned, who are called the sons of par adise by vocation but not by election, by promise and not by consequence, by reputation and not by deed, "shall be put out of the sight of God into eternal darkness," that is to say into the night of eternal damnation, for inner darkness, that is sin, is in them. According to Saint Gregory, it is inner darkness by lack of sight and blindness of the intellect, and external darkness by the night of eternal damnation. And it is called *tenebres exteriores* since, as Isidore says, in hell God has a fire, which shall be kindled and light up as the pain and misery of wretched sinners condemned to it increases, so that they may see with what they shall have sorrow and heaviness but no comfort. "And there shall be weeping eyes," because of the fire and the smoke, for death caused by sin enters into the soul through their windows, namely by their five senses, and therefore it is not licit to behold anything which is unlawful to desire. "And also there shall be the chattering and grinning of teeth," because of the cold in that place, for here they find joy in their carnal voluptuousness. "Men shall there have weeping," that is to say anguish in the soul, "and chattering teeth," that is to say the grinding of teeth, by the resentment which they shall have for repenting their sins too late in the day. And here are shown the great torments which condemned miserable persons shall have in hell.

And then Our Lord commanded the centurion through the messengers he had sent and said, *Vade*, "Go back safely. And in the same manner as you have perfectly believed, so shall it be done to you in deed; in the salvation and healing of your son." Whereby it should be understood that just as it was by sending messengers to Jesus Christ that he had come, in the same manner he returned into his house through messengers. Rabanus says: "Jesus Christ showed to this centurion that by faith he had implored and obtained health and salvation for his servant, so that the virtue of faith should rather more increase in him in seeing that by imploring in faith he obtained all that he desired." So that although he was physically absent, as soon as he had uttered the word *fiat* by which all things are created, the child was healed; since the centurion's faith was acknowledged immediately after he had confessed that with his word the child might be healed. Chrysostom says: "Jesus Christ being on his way healed the child by a single word, thus showing his mightiness both when in being absent or physically present."

Here a man ought to think how much his proper faith is worth when the others' faith suffices for the healing of this servant. And also consider Our Lord's humility, which was ready to go to the centurion's servant without any great gifts or wages, as he did to the son of the unimportant leader (for whom now the centurion stands here). For although he was begged incessantly, yet he would not go, showing man to deliberately avoid all pomp and worldly honours. According to Saint Gregory, our pride is reprimanded in this if we distinguish between people who pay more honour to riches and honours than to nature, according to which we are created in God's image; in seeing that he who descended from heaven has no scorn in visiting a poor man and a servant here upon earth, while we who are made of this earth will not humble ourselves to the earth. What thing may be more vile and loathsome before God than to worship the people of the world and not fear the eyes of almighty God, the sovereign and dreadful judge? Ambrose says: "Jesus Christ would in no way go to the leader's son, to show that he had no affection for the abundant riches of the child's father. But he went to the centurion's servant, so that it should not seem that he scorned and despised the condition of meek and lowly service; for with God poor and rich, master and servant are all the same."

Morally, the centurion's servant stands for the sinner, since it is by four evils that the sinner deserves to commit sin, which is shown by four conditions, which are here listed in the same order as those of the servant. The first is that the sinner is bound to sin, namely that he is ready to do sin; and this is why it is said that this child was a servant. Saint John says: "All persons who commit sin are bound to sin." And Saint Peter says: "Every man is servant to what overwhelms and overcomes him." Saint Augustine says: "The sinner is servant to as many vices as much as he has in him." For when sin reigns in a man, it makes him ready to do more sin, in such manner that one sin provokes another. Also that sin leads man to another bondage, that is to the devil. For the proud man is Lucifer's servant, the greedy man is Mammon's, and the lustful man of Asmodeus.

The second evil which sin arouses is that of making man feeble and weak to do any good deed; as seen in the servant who lay in his bed, as when the centurion asked Jesus Christ, "Lord, my child lies in the house." Now those who lie down can neither do nor actually do anything. Wherefore it comes to mind that the sinner sometimes lies in the fire of resentment and anger, at others in the pit of lustfulness, and at some other times in the briars and thorns of greediness. And in this it is well said that he lies, for he may not do any deed deserving merit in such state.

The third evil is fear and dread. The sinner ever lives in dread, as shown by the palsy which is caused by the dissolution of physical members. If a man says to sinners that they should give alms or that they should make restitution of what they have unjustly taken from others and gotten by evil ways, they will instantly have fear lest worldly goods shall fail them. If man bids them to fast, they then fear hunger; and if they are bidden to go to confession, they are ashamed of doing this. And if men bids them to make restitution and to do penance for their sins, they fear putting their bodies in the way of any pain or abstinence. And due to all this, man may see and know in these things how this sick man with palsy trembled and feared within himself like an aspen leaf.

The fourth evil is affliction of the spirit, as seen in what is said of this child that he was grievously tormented. Certainly, every sinner is evilly tormented in himself because of the worm of his conscience, which ever pricks and steers the soul. Augustine says: "You have commanded, oh Lord, and it is so that all conscience perturbed and vexed by sin suffers its own pain." And the Man of Wisdom says that an evil and hindered conscience, is ever fearful and thinks evil. The sinner is also tormented about other things, like when he has his mind fully set on how he may get goods and honours, riches and pleasure in this world. He is tormented in prosperity by too much business and excesses, and in adversity by impatience. He finds himself in great torment when he knows of the great disgrace the vices in which he lies bring with them, and the great pains of hell where he shall lie in time to come unless he makes amends. And although the sinful creature often resists grace and heavenly inspiration, yet Our Lord many times comes by his goodness before such sinners by the merits of the saints who pray for them.

Then if you have your soul stricken by palsy, if you feel such evils in you, pray to the saints and send them before God that they may pray Him for you, like the centurion's

messengers prayed for him. And cry to God most devoutly
saying like this man, "Oh Lord, my child," that is my soul,
"lies in the house of my body and is tormented. And I am not
worthy owing to the fragility of nature, to the foul stinking
sin, to the multitude of my miseries, that you should enter
under my roof which is so low, so foul and so loathsome.
But only speak one word, and at your command I shall be
made whole." And since what this centurion said to Jesus
Christ was uttered with such great effect and devotion, he
made it worthy to be a recommendation and prayer. When
a man will receive the holy sacrament of the eucharist, he
may say it, because by its very virtue he may be worthy of
receiving the body of Jesus Christ. Origen says: "When holy
people or prelates, who are the holy servants of God and
of the Holy Church, enter into your house, then Our Lord
enters into your house with them. And so do ever think of
them as if you have received Jesus Christ. And when you
receive his precious body in the sacrament of the eucharist,
he then enters under your roof and into your chamber. And
because of this, in humbling yourself, say devoutly, *Domine,
non sum dignus etc.* For if he enters unworthily in that place,
he enters to the damnation of those who so receive him."

This centurion also stands for the intellect or reason
of those who are servants of their sensual appetite, who
ought to obey reason. But because of defiled nature they are
sick. And therefore when a man, understands his disease
by himself and through others, he ought to pray and make
others to pray to God that He would heal his servant by
His grace. And also since he said about himself that as a
centurion he was set under the domain of others but still
had noblemen and people under him, whom he commanded
and they accomplished his will, so with the virtuous and
perfect soul, Cassian said, as figured by the centurion and
constituted under the power of God, has domain over all
his powers, and it may cast from him all evil thoughts and
keep good ones, and say to the evil to go, and to the good
ones that they may come. And he shall also say this to his
bound man, that is to his body, which ought to serve the
soul, "You shall be chaste", and he shall immediately obey
the spirit, and rule over it as a servant. ✒

CHAPTER 41

HOW OUR LORD HEALED AND REDEEMED ONE WHO WAS VEXED WITH THE DEVIL, AND ALSO HOW HE GAVE HEALTH TO THE MOTHER OF SAINT PETER'S WIFE

ESUS Christ once entered the city of Caphar-naum, which is a name just as saying the field or town of consolation, of beauty and of pleasure. This means the soul of a devout religious person who ought to be adorned with three kinds of ornaments, namely charity, devotion and contemplation. For it is so and into such soul that the sweet Jesus descends, making it a town of beauty and con-solation. Peter of Ravenna says: "As far as I may perceive and my intelligence can or may understand, unless there is religion in this world there is no heaven either in schools and in the study places of divine Scripture, for whatever comes from these two places would be all full of fear and disquiet, of bitterness, business and sorrow." Yet what he here says of schools should be understood as study places of Holy Scripture, not schools of vanities and curious knowl-edge. Hugo says: "There is nothing in this world or in this life which is so sweet or which may sooner depart the soul from the love of the world, or which urges and enforces it so much against temptations, or which so much helps it towards all goodness and to undertake all labour for the love of God, as for a man to exercise himself in the study and to know the Holy Scripture."

And to this end, upon entering into the city Jesus Christ went into the synagogue, as he taught people in the syn-agogue. As Jews were ordained to hear the Holy Scripture being declared on holy days, this was a proper place where he would teach his doctrine. And knowing that he would be attending in the synagogue many assembled there, in the same manner as now every Christian is bound to attend church on Sundays and hear Mass from beginning to end. It should here be noted what Mass actually is as relating to natural, divine and evangelical law. For natural law requires all to serve and pray God regularly and frequently; and the written Law commands that on the Sabbath day men should attend to prayer; and so too have the teachings and holy decrees of the Holy Church ordained and commanded that such supplication should be made at the time of the Mass, where God and man find themselves together. And because of this, as the *Interpretation* says, it is a mortal sin not to hear a whole Mass on Sunday, unless due to grave necessity, as this is one of the commandments; and as for other days one can act according to one's conscience.

And as Our Lord was so teaching people, they were all marvelled to hear his doctrine. For although it seemed to them that he had not formally learned either the prophecies or the Law, yet he could still declare and teach them clearly to them. And they also marvelled greatly when he confirmed them by divine works, as it is written that he taught them as one having power over them, for he taught them by showing signs and miraculous virtues. And he did not hide the truth owing to any kind of fear, as the scribes did in teaching only by words for fear of saying the truth which they did not keep themselves and so were ashamed to preach it to others. Bede says: "The word of a doctor and preacher is very powerful and strong when he does in deed what he says by mouth. And whoever goes in deed against what he speaks by mouth should not be praised. And because Our Lord did in deed what he said by mouth he was held by the people in honour and great reputation. He was not like the scribes who had learned the commandments in the Law, and all that they showed, and preached them to the people. But Jesus Christ taught the Law as if ordaining it, accomplishing and increasing it according to his goodness and liberal choosing or will." Then it is because of this that he confirmed his doctrine by miraculous works, so that now all other doctors and preachers who may not do miracles ought to confirm their doctrine by virtuous works, and not be like the scribes who said many things by mouth but after did nothing by deed; their doctrine was none else but words to be pleasing with people. And it is because of this that Our Lord's power was effectively shown in doing in deed what he spoke by mouth.

As it is written there was a man in their synagogue who might have been brought there to be healed. He had in him a foul and evil spirit, that is the devil, which possessed him. The man started shouting and saying loudly, "Oh, Jesus of Nazareth! Why should you hinder us and cast us out? Why have you come now, to destroy us and torment us and to cast away our power of tempting people?" The devil was saying that it would be to his loss if he were cast out of the man whom he possessed. Without mercy devils torment people, and they seem to suffer evil when they stop vexing them. "I know well," said the devil, "that you are strong and of great might," that is to say that "You are the holiness of God, sent from God above into this world for the salvation of people." The devils knew well of the spoken and written prophesies about Jesus Christ which set the time, place and manner of his coming, as well as by other events, that he was the Christ promised in the Law. But they did not know that he was God, not even after the desert temptations. For if they had known it, according to the Apostle, they should never have asked for his death or sent him to it. We see how perverse and of great rebuke are those who blaspheme God when anything goes wrong, as it would be the devils that preach to them, make them a good name and praise them above all others. Bede says: "This confession which the devil makes here is not out of his own will, for it was of no profit to him, but it was inevitably and forcefully done. It is like when a fugitive servant sees his master after a long time and returns to him; the master takes him back but only to have him beaten even more. The devils too, seeing their Lord and master upon earth believed that he was suddenly come to the world to judge them and cast them into the deepest place in hell; and it is because of this that they cried and paid him honour. For the presence of Our Saviour causes great torment to the devils." The devil is called a foul spirit owing to what he does, for he makes foul and abominable whoever he possesses; the same as it is said of the deaf and dumb spirit, for he also makes whoever he possesses deaf and dumb. Or, according to Chrysostom, he is called the wicked spirit due to his wicked-ness, and because of this he is far from God, and also because he mucks around with all works which are wicked and evil.

Now although the devil gave witness and acknowledged Jesus Christ and said the truth, yet Christ commanded him to keep his peace, since he should not mix up false matters with true ones, and because it should not seem that Christ was coveting anything about the devil after the Pharisees said that it was by the works of Beelzebub that he cast out devils from persons. It was also done too so that the fruit of his passion would not be deferred, and to teach us to abstain from the praises of the evil and from wicked people. Seneca says: "We also ought to be sorrowful and sorely displeased to hear ourselves praised or commended by evil people, as though we were loved and praised by foul things and by sin."

And when Jesus Christ had commanded this evil spirit to come out from the man whom he possessed, he threw the man to the ground in the midst of all, and grievously tormented and vexed him. And then he came out without doing him any more harm and without mutilating any bodily member. Jerome says: "The evil spirit which tormented the man departed from him. For when salvation and peace approached him, temptation came along with them. It happened before with the Pharaoh who, on being abandoned by the people of Israel he started to strongly persecute them. The devil too, seeing that he is despised, he enforces himself to put all evil to work." Yet in the opposite manner out of such evil comes great good. And this is what often happens spiritually, for sometimes the devil causes someone's sin to become public for him to be defamed; but when the sinner sees himself being slandered or openly put to shame in this manner, he leaves his sin, and the devil is then constrained to depart from him. And the Book of *Psalms* says the same thing: *Imple facies eorum ignominia*, "Oh Lord God, make the devils replenish sinners' faces with shame, in provoking them to do sin openly. And fill their faces with shame. And they shall desire your name, for the shame and rebuke which the sinner feels for his sins is great occasion for him to leave his sin." Seneca says: "Man ought ever to abide in this shame, for the more that he is modest, even more shall he be inclined to good hope and correction."

Man also ought to understand by this that the devil vexed this man when coming out of him, so that no man is delivered from the devil's power unless he is separated by compunction and contrition of salvation. Which is especially to be understood of carnal vice, which is not healed here without bodily affliction, that is great pain, for he is tormented of his own right in and by what he has sinned. And if he has sinned by pleasure of his body, then he ought to be purged by repentance. And when the devil tormented this man, he seemed to be dead, so much so that many said that he was dead. Gregory says: "Whoever is delivered from the power of the devil remains dead, for he has by the grace of God overcome all worldly desires and his carnal ways of life. He then seems to the world as being dead, for he leaves and abandons him who possessed him most grievously by foul and detestable desires. And then many believe that he is dead, since whoever despises living spiritually, when he feels tormented and as dead, then begins turning towards penance." Then if it so happens that whoever is delivered of the evil spirit is dead, it follows that whoever lives according the world is not delivered from the evil spirit; which is terrible to think of about those who live according to this world. And when Jesus Christ saw him in this state of affairs, he took his hand and raised him up on his feet; for he gives his hand and helps those who are cast down and vexed.

To speak in terms of our faith, whoever had the evil spirit in the synagogue has is in him a sign of the Jews, swathed and enfolded in the devil's ruses. And while seeming to be bodily cleansed, he is inwardly all stinking, having lost the Holy Spirit after the devil entered the place from where Jesus Christ was cast out. Theophilus says: "We ought to know that there are many nowadays who have the devil in them, like those who accomplish their wicked desires, or those who are madly angry, who have the devil who is empowers the sin of wrath and so also other sins. But Our Lord Jesus Christ comes to the synagogue at the time when man's soul ought be recollected and gathered in spirit far from its occupations, and says to the devil dwelling within a person before his coming, "Go away without uttering a single word"; and the devil shall depart immediately at his command."

Now after that Our Lord had preached and his instruction was confirmed when he ousted the devil, he left the

synagogue and went to Saint Peter's house for bodily nourishment after his work. Cyril says: "Notice well how Jesus
Christ dwells in the house of a poor man, him who has
chosen wilful poverty in this world for our sake; so that after
his example we should learn to be familiar and dwell with
the poor, and neither hold them in contempt nor despise
them." Chrysostom says: "Think of him in fishermen's houses,
and yet Jesus Christ had no scorn to enter under the roof
of such poor people's abodes, so teaching us that we should
with all our affection despise all pride." It is neither read nor
found that Our Lord ever entered into respectable houses
and was clothed according to the pomp of this world, save
in the houses of publicans and of their leaders and in sinners' houses, showing us that we ought to hold in contempt
worldly pride in all our doings. And if you will call him into
your house, furnish it with charitable deeds and prayer, with
supplications and vigils. For no man ought to be ashamed to
dwell or be in a poor house if it is adorned and furnished
with such ornaments and decorations. No matter how rich
he may be, no man ought to consider having a respectable
or pleasant and great house unless it is adorned with the
aforesaid things, because in this world we now receive Jesus
Christ, and in time to come we may be received by him in
his eternal glory.

Here some say that although Saint Peter hailed from
Bethsaida, yet because of his wife he still had a house in
the town of Capharnaum. But it seems as Saint Mark says
the contrary, where he says that Jesus Christ came into the
house of Simon and Andrew. Wherefore it comes to mind
that here the house is not so called as belonging to Saint
Peter, but that when he came to sell his fish, he kept his
market in it, and that owing to the familiarity he had with
the townsfolk, his wife went along with him. This house is
also called the house of Saint Andrew for the inseparable
association which they had in their business together.

And as soon as Jesus Christ entered the house, the disciples prayed and implored him for Saint Peter's mother-in-law,
who was laid with a bout of fever. And Our Lord laid his
hand on her and taking the woman by the hand he commanded the fever to leave her, And she was immediately

healed and no longer felt miserable with fever, such that she rose without delay from the bed where she lay, and served Jesus Christ and his disciples. She might not do this but by divine power, for it is not normal for nature to work immediately but this was the nature of the heavenly doc‑ tor who works in the twinkling of an eye. Bede says: "It is something natural for those having fever that when they start healing, they are confused and feeble, still feeling the shivering and harassment of their former sickness. But the very true health given to her by Jesus Christ's command is given so completely and fully that she after had no remorse or complaint about it. And not only health was rendered to her, but such strength and might with it that she was able to minister and serve those who helped and served her before." Cyril says: "We receive Jesus Christ when he shall visit us in adversity and we bear him in our minds, by patience he shall quench all the height and flame of our vices, and he shall make us whole and sound in such manner that we may minister to others as he pleases."

Morally, we may understand from the above that before being healed of sin none of man's services is pleasing to God. But as soon as the penitent is healed of the fever of sin, he ought to occupy and give himself to serving God totally. As the Apostle says: "Now study and apply yourselves to show your bodily members to serve justice in all holiness, similarly as in past times you have applied them to serve all filth and iniquity." Now then, if your soul is taken with the fever of vice and sin, call to your help the holy saints, so that the grace of God may by their intercession give you health. In all the disciples prayed Our Lord for this woman, we are given an example how to pray God for sick people and others' needs.

Also morally, Saint Peter's mother‑in‑law, who was fever‑ ish and in pain, stands for carnal sexual desire. For when one labours by height of carnal sexual desire, he is like one in a strong, fervent and hot fever. This may be in three manners, as Saint John says, that all this world reckons others by lustfulness of the flesh, or by sight of the eye, or by pride of the body. Because of this we have three kinds of fever, some of which proceed from the corruption of the spirit, the other comes from the corruption of the humours or state of mind, and the third proceeds from the corruption of bodily members. And in all is an inordinate height passing the order of nature, where pride makes the first, lustfulness the second, and avarice the third. Jesus comes to such fevers and washes them by grace, commands them to cease by grace, and touches them with his hand most full of grace. And so the fever is changed into contrition, man is lifted up by confession and he now ministers and serves by restitution.

It is also morally said that Jesus Christ cast his eyes on her, for if that man is not under Jesus Christ by fear and meekness, he shall never be healed in body and soul. Bede says: "If morally we say that the man who was delivered of the devil by Jesus Christ was just as saying he was purified from evil thoughts, then consequently the woman who was tormented with fever and was healed by Jesus Christ's command, stands for the flesh which desists the heat of lustfulness by the command of continence. For all rancour, wrath, resentment, yelling and blasphemy are the fury of the foul and wicked spirit. But filth and fornication, evil lustfulness and avarice, which are the bondage of idols, proceed by fevers from inordinate physical moods."

This woman may also stand for sensuality which, according to Saint Augustine, is like the woman herself; and Jesus Christ is the image of the Father, after whom the creature is made in the image of God. Now then sensuality, which has been tormented by fever caused by the height of lustfulness, is morally healed when it is by reason provoked to the forthright order of virtue. And for this it is said that after her healing, she ministered and served Jesus Christ and his disciples as much as she could recompense them. For when sensuality is reformed by moral virtue, it ministers to reason and serves it well. Then man begins to do good works and to know his sins, which he did not know before, when still living in it. Chrysostom says: "If you will know well the foul stink of sin, think according to its foul and false desire, how you has passed your time in it and what you have lost in committing and doing it, and then you shall see and know its foul filth and disgrace."

Also take heed that by the aforesaid four manners of sickness, man may spiritually understand four kinds of sins. By the leper, one may understand the original guilt. By the palsy, the actual guilt which denies man from doing what he ought to do. By the fever, the actual guilt which does in deed what is forbidden. By the devil's annoyance and tribulation, the guilt of error.

Afterwards, in confirmation of the new law, many miracles were generally made, for it is said that when people heard of this miracle, and in the evening after the sun had set, all city people who had any kind of sickness and were vexed with various diseases, and mostly those who were vexed with the devil, were brought to Jesus Christ and presented to him that he should give them health and salvation. As it was then that he might attend to such matters, one may ask why it was at such a late hour that they brought these sick people to him. Theophilus answers this question saying: "It was because that was the Sabbath day, and the Jews thought it was not lawful for them to heal the sick on the feastday. And so on the Sabbath day, about the time after evening when the sun had set, they presented all such sick people, since it was then that they might bring them to Jesus Christ."

And when they had brought them to him, he laid his hand on each one of them and healed them, for he was not afraid nor did any sickness annoy him; which relates mostly to the proud doctors who despise nature and scorn visiting the poor unlike what they do with the rich. By his word Jesus Christ expelled the evil spirits from the body of those whom they possessed, to show that when the word of God is heard devoutly it causes the devil to come out from the heart of sinners. And although he might heal them all by his word, nevertheless there were times when he laid his hand on them. For just like the workman produces his work with his tools, in the same manner Jesus Christ's heavenly virtue and his might does some things by human operation to show that he was one and united with divinity. Upon which it comes to mind that the miracles done by Jesus Christ were ordained for two things. First of all, to confirm and demonstrate his divinity. Secondly, to confirm his doctrine and teaching, by means of which people may be induced to faith and believe in him. And it was because of this that sick people were healed by the touch of his hand, the leper was cleansed, the blind had their sight, and the dead were raised to life by his voice, and fiends were put out of the bodies in which they abode.

The fact too that it was after evening that the sick and those vexed by the devil were presented to him, means that it will be at the end of the world that Jesus Christ will come and cast out the devils and heal the sick people of this world. And the setting sun also means that in his passion, where the same sun was obscured and darkened, there was a medicine to all spiritual infirmities. Bede says: "Mystically, the death and passion of him who says 'As long as I am in the world, I am the light of the world,' means that when the sun had set many people who were vexed by the devil and others who had other diseases were healed and made more whole than they had been ever before. For being in this world in his human nature he taught many, but only converted a few Jews, compared to those who would have changed course and come to the faith after his passion and ascension." Also morally, the setting or obscuring of the sun may be seen as the fall of this world's prosperity. For after man passes from prosperity to adversity, many are those who in prosperity, when its sun lighted them, were very sick but are now healed.

Be well aware here how many miracles are involved in a few words which, if uttered, they would probably seem incredible. Chrysostom says: "Understand well here the great amount of cures and healings done by Jesus Christ. The Gospels pass briefly, for they do not show us each one on its own, but only as one saying they comprise some. For in this one single recount no particular sick people are mentioned, from those affected by various illnesses and sicknesses, whom they brought to him from all parts and were healed in a short time and rendered fully whole."

Now in healing, the devils came out of the bodies of many whom they had possessed before, saying with great fear that Jesus Christ was the Son of God. And then he reprimanded them, forbade them and would not suffer them to speak nor tell such things about him. Bede says: "The devil confessed that Jesus Christ was the Son of God; and he knew well that it was he who was promised in the Law. For when the devil saw him in the desert, weary and feeble by the long fast he was doing, he came to know that he was very much of a man. But when he saw that he could not overcome him by his temptations, he started doubting whether he was the Son of God. But now, by his signs and miracles which he did with his heavenly power, he understood and inferred that he was the Son of God. But he might not as yet perceive him, for his damnation and determining was in the death of Jesus Christ. For as the Apostle says, this mystery was hidden from all those inhabiting the world; and none who were so great or mighty in this world knew anything about it. For if they had known him well to be King and Lord of glory, they would have never crucified him." And it is because of this that Jesus Christ did not put up with the devils saying such things about him, for the purpose, according to the *Interpretation*, that the people should not hear the devils preach or say their truth to the world, and in time to come counterfeit his words, and so forth by low means make people obey them in error, lies and deceit. For they are such a wicked and deceiving company that they ever meddle in falsehood with truth. This has already been spoken of before in this chapter.

Now when night had passed, early in the morning the next day Jesus Christ departed from the city of Capharnaum and went into the desert. He wanted to flee the people's praise and adulation, and also to pray to his Father even more secretly. This is of an example to preachers and to those who will do holy and heavenly works, to flee vainglory and conceit, showing them that after the labour of preaching men ought to return to the spiritual care of contemplation and secret prayers, in rendering thanks to God for the profit they gained in preaching, being ever ready to dispose themselves to receiving new grace in future time, and to the end that they may gather from God what shall be later denied to others. Also by going into the desert, according to Theophilus, this shows us that all the good we do, ought to be remitted to God, seeing that all comes and descends from Him.

Now we see that Jesus Christ prayed in the desert; not that it was inevitable for him to make supplication or prayer for himself, but to show us the manner and form how we should busy ourselves in good works, and also to teach us to avoid deliberately the world's noise and hassle, and to seek a secret and a solitary place where we could even better offer up our souls to God, and desire to speak with Him in our prayers in all silence. And those people sought him owing to their faith in him, and they came to him by hope and kept him with them by charity, that he should not depart from them and be taught by him even more. Chrysostom says: "The sweet Jesus gladly received the people who came to him. And yet he would feign leaving them and being alone, so that other people too would hear his doctrine." And so he said to them: "It suits that I announce and show the kingdom of heaven to other cities, similarly as I have done to you, and show the way by which man comes to heaven, and show how it can be done, namely by penance." Theophilus says: "Since Our Lord had shown the kingdom of heaven to the city of Capharnaum, he went on to those who were in much greater need of his teaching. For it is not fitting ever to preach and sow his doctrine in one place, but it ought to be shown in all places, just as the sun spreads her rays and strikes over all." Chrysostom says: "Do not think that it is only at the place where Jesus was that he might have attracted all those people to him, but he would not do that for all, for he would give us example that in going out we should seek those who are in the way of being lost; as the shepherd would do and herd in the humble sheep when it is lost, and likewise as the doctor attends to the sick. For in winning one soul which is in the way of perdition, a man may obtain a great part of the remission of his sins and trespasses."

CHAPTER 42

OF THE RAISING FROM DEATH TO LIFE OF THE WIDOW'S SON

NCE, Jesus Christ, went into a city called Naim, which is two miles from Mount Tabor, where Mount Endor rises above Naim, and at the foot of which mount the waters of Kishon pass and run. He went there with his disciples and was followed by a great multitude of people because of the new miracles which he wrought, the sweet-ness of his teaching, the devotion they had towards him and his holiness, And before the gate of this city Jesus Christ found a great company of people who were bringing to the grave the only son of a widow who had dwelt in the city to be buried. In olden times the custom was that tombs and burial places were sited out of town owing to the stink of corpses. And he had assembled there a great multitude of people, so that the miracle would be even more evidently known and better seen by many witnesses. And since these people were involved in doing works of piety, by keeping company to the corpse and in comforting the sorrowful mother, they deserved to see the miracle; for God, who is the comforter of those who weep, marvellously beholds the tears of those who bewail the miseries of others' sins. And when Our Lord saw the sorrowful mother crying her heart out for the death of her only son, he was moved by pity and had great compassion on her, seeing that she was a lonely and an old widow past the time of having any more children in this world. She also had not much of a long life during which she might be comforted or have joy, nor did she know from who could help or support her being old. And Cyril says about this: "Pity and compassion is of such virtue that it provokes others to weep and wail." According to Bede, Our Lord seeing this woman weep was moved to pity and mercy so as to give us an example of how to have pity and compassion on others' misery.

Our Lord comforted her meekly saying *Noli flere*, "Do not weep." Chrysostom says: "He who comforts all those who are comfortless as this woman, commanded this woman to cease weeping, showing us that in this world we ought not to weep too much or to be too sorry for dead bodies, seeing that we shall see them again at the universal resurrection or day of doom. But the heathens and idolaters have cause to weep and to wail those who die in their errors, for they do not see nor take into account this resurrection. But Christians believed it and acknowledged it, and so have no cause to weep."

And then Christ went to the corpse bearers, and took the bier and held it still with his hand, for the effect of saving health ought to come by the touch of his precious hand. And then in the miracle which he wrought it appeared that his body was united to the deity or Trinity, and that in doing miracles his body was but as an instrument of divinity. *Loculus* is the chest or bier where the dead body lies or is laid in the earth. Often, in this mortal life, great mansions or curious dwellings or pleasant places are not enough for us where to dwell, whereas after our death a little coarse coffin will be enough to contain us. And on this account a philosopher says on the death of the great Alexander: "Yesterday this man was not content with the whole world, and the world might not be enough for him. And now today a little coffin contains him and fulfils his mind." And when Our Lord had touched the bier and the coffin, the bearers set them down while they rested. And God spoke, *Adolescens, tibi dico surge,* "Young man, I say unto you, arise." Christ spoke as though he had been God alone, without his part of human nature. So he raised him to life. And then the dead man began to rise up. And he set himself on a bed which had been brought there for him and upon which he had lain before. And he began to speak and show openly that he was truly risen and not just pretending to have risen from death to life. And perhaps the words he said were of praise and thanks to Jesus Christ for that great benefit he had done him. And then Our Lord gave him to his mother, by whose merit he was raised to life so that after her great heaviness she should receive comfort and gladness. Then those who saw this miracle were very much afraid and sorely embarrassed. And this fear was not evil, for it proceeded from an honour and reverence of God's power and goodness. And there they magnified and praised God, and said that He was great. For even as much greater and more grievous the fall is, even more the piety and the grace of God is towards him that arises, and so is the hope of salvation of all penitents the more certain. And they said to him, *Propheta magnus*, "The great prophet. Here is the greatest prophet promised in the Law and Prophets. He has appeared to us, for God has visited his people, by sending them the Saviour and Redeemer of the world, similarly as the doctor visits the sick to make them whole."

To speak mystically, this dead body stands for the man who is dead by mortal sin. His mother is the Holy Church, which is the multitude of believers in Christ and true Christians, of whom those who believe in the true faith of the Holy Church are all her sons. Now the sinner is called the one only son of his mother, that is to say of the Holy Church, which bewails every Christian sinner when he falls in sin, as the mother weeps for her one only child when he passes from this world. The Church is sometimes called a widow, since she has been bought back by the death of her spouse; for as long as he was in this world as a pilgrim, she was taken with her spouse's embraces and hugs. And it is written in the Book of *Psalms* about this widow, *Viduam eius benedicens benedicam*: "I shall give benediction to his widow."

Now the dead body is borne outside when internal consent is put in external operation.

The four bearers of this corpse stand for the four affections of the heart, namely joy, heaviness, hope and dread. And these four bear the dead corpse *par abus*. Saint Bernard says about them: "They loved that which was unlawful to love, and they feared what ought not to have been feared. They took a vain sorrow, and enjoyed themselves more vainly." These four bearers are also the love of sin, which is feared because of the penance which has to be done for its amendment; yet presuming too much upon God's mercy. Therefore these four porters or bearers may be the four things causing the soul to persevere in sin, that is to say the confidence and trust which man has of living a long life, which often deceives man; the consideration of others' offences, by which man often defers and keeps himself from doing penance; the foolish hope that man has of doing penance when he is old, and then trusts to have forgiveness, makes man to presume too much on God's mercy, and this causes him to continue in his sins. Men may also see these four bearers to be the carnal desires, as slanderers, backbiters and all such, as in vain praise, the words of holy preachers, flatterers and those who by word or deed support sinners and vicious people in their sins.

The gates through which this corpse is passed from the town are the bodily senses, through which sin appears more plainly. For whoever sees, hears or speaks anything which is unlawful, is drawn and slain by the gates of each one of his five senses. Bede says: "I think that the gate through which this dead corpse was borne out of the town was some bodily sense of his. For whoever sows strife between brother and brother or speaks proudly and viciously, is borne out stark dead by the gate of his mouth. And whoever looks at a woman to covet her, shows that he is dead by the gate of his eyes. Also whoever gladly gives an ear to fables, belittling and all secular things, is by these made to be borne as a dead corpse in his soul. And whoever does not control his five senses, lays bare his soul to be judged to death."

The covering and the bier or coffin is the sinner's conscience where he rests as a man does in his bed.

Yet such death by mortal sin is revived by the prayers of the Holy Church; and how he is revived, we have here a figure. For similarly as there are three signs of spiritual death, there are also three signs of spiritual awakenings or raisings. The signs and markings of spiritual death follow the example of bodily death. The first sign showing man to be bodily dead, is the lack of good works, which is also a sign of spiritual death. It is written in *Exodus* about this, *Efiant immobiles quasi lapis*, "Sinners are as immobile as a stone." The second sign is a lack of feeling, for when a man smites another and he does not feel anything, that is a sign of death. Also when by warnings and spiritual scourging man could not correct him, that is a sign of spiritual death. And of such spiritual deaths says the Man of Wisdom in his *Proverbs*: "They have beaten me and I have not felt it."

The third sign is rigour. When a man has such a hard heart that he cannot incline to any works of compassion nor can he be obedient to God or to his fellow Christian, this is a sign of spiritual death. And in figure of this, it is said in the *Book of Kings* that the hand of Jeroboam which stretched out to the altar was dry. Pride takes from man his good works, and lustfulness his feelings; and avarice stiffens him.

And to the contrary there are three signs of spiritual raisˊ ings, as relating to when this young man sat up and began to speak again and was given to his mother. By saying that he laid himself down and rose up again, we understand contrition; for in contrition man arises from sin. This is why he says, "began to speak", by which we understand confession, where man speaks in accusing himself. And by what he said when he gave him to his mother, we understand restitution; for when man is absolved and he makes restitution, he is then returned to his mother, the Holy Church and the comˊ munion of Christian saints by spiritual incorporation. And this restitution is done by three things, namely by prayer, fasting and almsgiving. The manner of this resuscitation is related to what Jesus Christ did in touching the bier and the coffin. To speak of this spiritually, Jesus steps forth and draws himself towards the corpse when he gives time and grace before coming to it or showing any good desire of his proper salvation. To touch the bier is when the sinner softens his conscience and his wayward stomach to conscience; in leading himself by his grace to selfˊawareness. It is then that the man who is dead due to sin is raised again.

And this is to witness that the Holy Spirit wills that sin should be signified by death in order to show the gravity of sin, for it is to be abstained from and feared as much as death. And when it is committed, man ought to have great repentance and heaviness, as if it were for the death of a friend. So should anyone who sees his friend in mortal sin weep and be sorry for him as though he were dead. And it is because of this that this death signifies the sinner, just as his resuscitation signifies the conversion of the sinner to a good life. And similarly as man ought to be very mindful of anyone who is dead by sin, so also ought he to find great joy in the sinner's conversion to a good life.

So you who are in sin, pray meekly and humbly to Our Lord that by his grace he will raise you from death to life, and render you back to your mother the Holy Church; to the end that you may cleanse and wash away the sin, which was so great, by the tears which your mother the Holy Church weeps with you in praise and honour of his name. And as Saint Ambrose says, if your sin is so great that you may not wash it away with your own tears, our mother the Holy Church shall weep for you; as it weeps for all sinners as her own children. She has compassion when she sees her children wounded with sin unto death. Augustine says: "The mother of this young man who was brought back to life by Our Lord Jesus Christ, rejoiced greatly. Similarly our mother the Holy Church every day finds great joy about us when we are raised from sin in the spirit. For as he who was raised was bodily dead, so are all sinners spiritually dead."

Morally, Jesus Christ brought back to life three kinds of dead people. Namely the maid in the closed house, just as saying like him who is dead by consenting to evil delight and wilfully wants and has a mind to continue in this state; he is dead in his soul without any sign of life. The second death was like this young man's which this Gospel relates, now being borne out at the city gate towards his grave; which signifies the death by external operation of sin by word, by will or by work. The third dead body was Lazarus who was in his grave; signifying death, which is now accustomed to sin, and is so strong that it exceeds all others by its evil example.

All these three dead persons are raised and healed thoroughly when they return to God by true penance. And the fewer sins each man has, it shall be even easier for him to be raised and brought back to life. And this was shown in the raising of the maid, being raised before a few people and easily, for he said no more to her than *Puella, surge*, "Maid, arise and stand up." But the raising of this young man of Naim was done before many and with greater difficulty, for he touched the coffin in which the body lay saying *Adolescens, tibi dico surge*, "Child, I command you to arise." He raised Lazarus in a more difficult or wonderful manner, for his resuscitation and raising was done with tears, weeping and anxiety, but with a sign of piety crying with a loud voice, *Lazare, veni foras*, "Lazarus, come forth." And as in helping and delivering others, he said: "Unbind him and let him go." And yet the raising of Lazarus was not so difficult or hard for Our Lord, as was the raising of the maid, or of the widow's son. For as Saint Augustine says, no man can awake someone lying in sleep on a bed more easily than Jesus Christ raised a dead body from his grave. But he pretended as though it was something hard to do, so as to show that Our Lord's deeds were examples of other things. For when any man is suppressed or grieved by evil, and has lain in pain and great labour for long, he may be raised. And to raise him Our Lord is constrained to weep. And because of this, we must not necessarily abstain ourselves from all sin, for so it is that we are more accustomed to sin than anything else; for being accustomed to sin is the hardest thing to heal. And this is what Saint Ambrose says: "All sin is reputed as nothing and as being no sin unless it is done by custom, or willingly, or for the purpose of sin." And also to the contrary, all virtues done by good custom are more graciously made and are more acceptable. Then three kinds of the death of guilt are signified by the aforesaid three dead bodies raised by Our Lord, namely the sin of the heart, the sin of work, and the sin of custom. Now it is shown in their resuscitation that Our Lord has power over three kinds of death, namely over natural death, the death of culpability or guilt, and everlasting death. And also, to the contrary, he has power over three lives, namely over the life of nature, of grace, and of glory. And he would not go to the fourth death which was shown to him by his disciples; namely that of whoever is dead by obstinacy or despair, or in the evil custom of excusing himself of his sins. About whom it is said, *Dimitte mortuos sepellire mortuos suos*, "Let the dead bury their dead."

As to those then who are hearing these things, if they have not fallen in sin, let them be aware of presumption and deceit, and be well advised not to fall in them. Also for those who have fallen, let them beware of despair and let them be busy and diligent to relieve and raise themselves to grace. Augustine says: "My very beloved brethren, we have heard these things so that those who live should amend their lives and live a better life, and so that those who are dead may bring themselves to live in the life of grace. For although sin is yet in their heart without outwardly appearing, regardless of this man ought to repent for it and correct such thoughts. And so is the dead man raised to life within his inner conscience. Man ought not to despair, for if he is not raised inwardly, yet he may be raised outwardly if he repents his sin sufficiently and is aware of not sinking to the bottom of the grave, in making sin an evil custom and continuing to live in it for a long time. Yet he ought not to despair, for although he is dead and buried deep, yet since Jesus Christ is almighty to raise him again, he should revert with all his heart to penance." Chrysostom says: "We who are in grace, let us not presume ourselves, but let us ourselves endeavour to take heed that we neither fall nor stumble. Even if we have fallen, we should not despair but say to ourselves: 'Shall he who has fallen not rise again? Yes, by the grace of God.' Many who are now in the kingdom of heaven have been great sinners in this world. And yet after their conversion, they have been so virtuous that they have cast devils out of people, along with many other great miracles which they have done, as all the Holy Scripture says and expresses. And for this, their lives ought to be an example for us. For as the doctors write in their books, great and difficult diseases are there to have even much greater learning, for by great and serious illnesses they might have even know more perfectly less grievous diseases. In like manner God often gives man great mercy as He did with great sinners, so that those who have only a few sins and have offended little should find comfort in it. There is no doubt that if great sinners and those wounded by sin have found salvation to their wounds in the mercy of God, those who have not so much offended Him shall find the same. And so let us arm ourselves with good works. And if it so happens that we are infected by anything, let us wash ourselves, that we may be worthy to obtain the celestial joy of heaven, where after this life we may live in the vision and abundance of our Creator."

It is a very dangerous thing when the sinner lies in the filth and stink of his sins and is dead in his soul, and does not endeavour to rise out of his sin and cleanse himself by penance. For if a man spoke with an angels' tongue and with all the tongues in the world, and his doctrine and preaching converted as many people as there have been since the beginning of the world or as many as there are stars in the sky, but he were in mortal sin and took no heed or caused himself to be cleansed or purged thereof by penance, he becomes like a bell or a brass clapper, or as a thing which in serving and being of use to others consumes itself. And yet even more, if you had all the knowledge of the world in such ways that, by the same and by such good and discrete counsel, all of the world's kings and princes were governed peacefully by your policy and wisdom, but you do not correct your flesh by penance when you feel you are in mortal sin, it will be of no avail for your salvation. And yet if you had such great faith that by it you could bring to Christianity all Jews, heretics and heathens, but you are in mortal sin, this would be of no use to you. Yet even more, if you make a thousand houses of religion and build with your own hands a thousand hospitals or alms houses, and you feed in them and refresh with your own goods all the poor people of the world, as long as you abide in mortal sin, you would not count among the number of those who are saved. And moreover, if you gave your own body to be put on a gridiron, as Saint Lawrence did, or suffered your skin to be flayed, as Saint Bartholomew, or were crucified, as was Jesus Christ, and you abide in any mortal sin, you may never be saved. Yet even more, if after being deceased a thousand million Masses are said for you, and all the saints who are in heaven with all the angels were kneeling before God until doomsday, beseeching him for your soul and weeping with bloody tears, they might not incline divine mercy to have pity or mercy on you if you were deceased in mortal sin. And this is because when man commits mortal sins, he separates himself from the life of grace and submits himself to all impotence and feebleness to rise from sin on his own, so long as it is in him. For no man may rise on his own after having sinned unless he is given grace anew infused by God, who is the sole donor and giver of such things and gifts of grace. And because of this, as long as man is in this world, he may obtain God's grace; but those who are deceased and die without grace, may never recover it. And again, if they do not have it, they may not come to heaven, but suffer perpetual pain. For he shall have but one of these two places after this world, of which one is for them who live well and have done good works in this world, and the other for those who have led a vicious life. Now a good confession would be much better to the sinner who lies sleeping in mortal sin like swine, than all the aforesaid goods and benefits done before by him or by others if he is in mortal sin.

CHAPTER 43
OF THE FALSE SCRIBE

ESUS Christ, finding himself in the midst of a crowd which followed him in all places, ordered his disciples to board a ship to pass over the seas and waters. And he boarded the little boat with them, thus teaching preachers of the blessed Gospel that, above all things, they should abstain and flee the flattery and praise of the world, and not to do anything for the purpose and reason of being seen amongst people. In doing this he also showed one ought to abstain from the world's attentiveness or the business of temporal things. By the crowd of people we understand the world's great responsibilities and business, which ever trouble the soul on both sides, for they delay, hinder and keep back man from doing good deeds; on the right side, since man would not desire eternal things, and on the left, since man should not fear hell torments. Or they may delay man in considering the failures and sins done in past times and keep him from thinking about the life to come; on the right hand, because man fails to consider the dangers and perils found in prosperity; and on the left hand, because man does not also consider the dangers found in adversity. For just as a smith will let a horse bleed, binding or stopping his ears and then striking where he pleases, so does the devil who wants to deceive man first come to his ears with great desires of worldly things, so that he might inflict a better wound on him by sin, then draw from him the blood or the strength of virtues. And because of this, man ought to flee and abstain from such doings and overpowering of evil company. Even though, these may be the things which allowed Zacchaeus to come to Jesus Christ.

And when Jesus Christ was walking along the way, there came to him a scribe, that is a master of the Law, and said to him, *Magister, sequar te,* "Master, I will follow you to all places." Chrysostom says: "This doctor and lawyer did not come to Jesus Christ by faith and in order to believe in him, but by feigned dishonesty." In seeing his heart because of what he said, Jesus did not answer him according to what he uttered by mouth, but according to his thoughts in his heart, and he said to him, *Vulpes foveas habent*, "Foxes have their holes and grounds, and the fouls of the sky their nests," where they to which they resort at night and lodge in them. "But the Son of Man," that is to say of the Virgin Mary, "has no place of his own in this world where he might lay and rest his head."

We see here that according to the poorest and lowliest wise men he named and showed his descent, contrary to those who glorify themselves with their family by starting to recount of the noblest and worthiest of their ancestry. As although Jesus Christ had said to this master of the Law: "The brutes and wild beasts have their places from where they come and go as their lodging. But I am so poor that I have no lodging of my own in this world. And because of this you come to me for nothing and in vain as for any temporal gain or pleasure." This master of the Law came to Jesus Christ to be praised and lauded, and for worldly benefits and profit which he hoped to have had through Jesus Christ's lowness in doing miracles and marvellous things. Similarly to when Simon the Magician, who was an enchanter, would have bought from Saint Peter the grace of the Holy Spirit in order to make money out of it. But on hearing that Jesus Christ was so poor, the master said no more to him. For as Chrysostom says, he neither answered him nor did he say "I shall follow you, howsoever poor you might be", for all that Our Lord might have granted him.

This was inasmuch as the greedy man might behold greed for worldly things, and how he is put away from Christ and not tolerated to follow Jesus Christ. Chrysostom says: "Take heed how Jesus Christ shows by work the poverty which he had taught before. He had neither table nor candlestick in this world, neither a big nor a small house in which he might lodge." His little house was Mary's virginal womb; his cradle was the ox crib and the tree of the cross; his burial too had a strange nature. By foxes men might understood deceit or cunning, and by the sky foul advancement, boasting or elation, which are all hidden in man's heart. As to what Jesus Christ told this master, it was like saying, "You will follow me for the deceit and delight which are in your heart, and due to the greed for vainglory. And because of this I will not receive you into my company; for the Son of Man is simple and not deceiving, meek and lowly against pride and exaltation, and he has not in the world so much as a place on which he may lay his head."

Nowadays, in the Holy Church, the ambitious and those who commit simony follow this Pharisee; they desire to be promoted to high benefices and high dignities, in seeking what is profitable to them in terms of the world, and not what is to God's praise and honour that they might serve Him, that they may serve themselves. And for this they may be well and appropriately likened to the deceit and cunningness of the fox and a foul's flight. This also applies to those who are rich and have great possessions and yet enter religion or into monasteries. For they do not enter by devotion, but so that being poor they may be made rich and there to receive honour, whereas in the world they were held in contempt. And owing to this, they are told, "The foxes have their holes and burrows, and the fouls of the air their nests." That is to say, "It is the devils which are full of deceit and pride who dwell in you, and not Jesus Christ." A man may yet say that the malicious nurture deceit, to which they resort that they might not be caught and found in their wickedness. And the proud seek worldly things for the purpose that they may ever move forward and have prosperity, and that no adversity touches them. But in such order of things, the Son of Man has no place upon which to rest his head. For whoever lives in this world according to the judgment of reason is not delighted by anything nor does he covet such things.

Jesus Christ said to another man, knowing well that his father was dead, *Sequere me*, "Follow me." And he answered him and said, "Lord, I beseech you first let me go and bury my father." Rabanus says: "He did not refuse to be a disciple of Jesus Christ, but he would first accomplish the burial ceremony and funeral rites for his father, that he might follow Jesus Christ even more freely and at leisure"; similarly as Elisha did when Elijah called him answering, "I pray you that first I may kiss my parents, and after that I will follow you." When Jesus Christ had heard this man speak, he told him by way of correction, "Follow me despite all the burying of your father, and let the dead," those who are dead of fault and guilt, "bury their dead," namely those who suffered physical death. When Jesus Christ said, "Let the dead bury their own dead," he implied that this disciple was not dead, but that there was some misbeliever dead in his soul by infidelity and vicious living. For such should be truly called dead inasmuch as they have no faith, which is the life of the soul. For as the Man of Wisdom says, the righteous man lives by faith. It is thus shown that those who follow Jesus Christ ought to live the carnal affection of their kinsfolk in the same manner. And here is an argument against those who excuse themselves to enter in religion for the charge and business which they have with their parents and with the world. And it also goes against those who put off their entering in religion from day to day. For if Jesus Christ would not suffer this disciple to tarry so long from following him because he wanted to bury his father, then in all likelihood he does not want a man to defer from one day to another to follow him.

Notice how he refused and dismissed the first, who was false and proud, and those who came to him with deceit. Yet as to the second, who sought him with a low and meek heart, he provoked him to follow him, and did not give him as much respite as to go and bury his father, but would that without delay he should follow him, not even going into his parents' house. And he said to him: "Go and do not show to the world any fables, or curious or pleasant words, but speak of the kingdom of heaven. Give life and raise those who are dead by mortal sin." We ought well leave and abandon that which is less to follow that which is more. It is of great merit to do service to parents, but it is a much greater merit to preach, indeed though a man may have but only one soul, than it is to bury the dead. Ambrose says: "It is highly commended to a man to bury the dead. So why then did God forbid this disciple from going to bury and lay his own father in his grave? Certainly, this was meant to show that divine and heavenly things should be preferred and put before worldly things. It is a good deed to bury the dead, but God's servants are allowed more than that. For whoever has his mind occupied on many things, may not know so perfectly the cause, condition and disposition of everything. And for this, man ought to apply himself to have first the most special and extraordinary things. How may the dead than bury their dead, unless it means that there are two deaths, namely a physical one, and another of guilt? However there is only one in which we die when we leave sin and live in God. So that this disciple was not forbidden from burying his father, but the piety of Christian religion was more necessary and expedient, and it was put to him before. Burial was left to those of Jewish descent, but it is commanded to all of God's chosen friends to announce God's kingdom." Chrysostom says: "It had not been proper that whoever had put himself in the disposition and true faith of the Son of God, and had taken him for his heavenly Father, should have mind for his carnal father, who was then dead. And because of this, Our Lord showed him that faith and knowledge of him were set before all such works of piety. And this is the cause why we are commanded to leave our parents who are still alive, namely for the purpose of following Jesus Christ. He forbade him from going to bury his Father, not that he despised the honour which he ought to pay to his father, in order to show that there is nothing that is more necessary than to occupy ourselves for our salvation in good works and heavenly things. For it is a much greater and more noble thing to announce the kingdom of heaven and to retract others from sin's death than to bury a dead body that cannot be of any further profit to the world, considering that there were others who were more skilful in go about such burials. It is because of this then that it has been said before that we are only taught that, inasmuch as we can, we should be aware of allowing the time granted to us by God to do good deeds in it. Indeed, there might have been ten thousand people who provoked us to the contrary, yet we should ever prefer and put before those things which are most necessary to us, as in doing all those spiritual things which are best for our salvation."

Morally, the dead bury the dead when sinners nourish and keep their sins close and secret from one another,

covering their vicious life with faint praise. According to
Saint Gregory, a man may get to know himself through the
dead, extollers and flatterers who nourish sinners in their
evil. And they bury them by casting on their heads the earth
of faint praise, so that they may be blinded even more; and
they bind their feet with bonds, that they might not walk
in the way of virtues.

Yet another came to Jesus Christ, saying to him, "Lord,
I will follow you. But first of all allow me to go and tell
about this to my kinsfolk and those in my father's house."
He would tell them he was leaving and bid them farewell,
and also that his company should not seek him in not knowing where he went. Many are those who nowadays put off
from day to day their entering religion or taking up any
new manner of good living, saying, "I must first despise my
goods and my friends, then I will later enter into religion
or amend my life." Saint Jerome advised against this anyone
who tarried too long and delayed too much in putting his
good purpose into effect, saying: "Rather cut the cable which
holds the ship tied to the ground than tarry to unbind
it." Chrysostom says: "Do not say if you are converted and
have changed your life to a good life that you must first
describe and put in order your temporal goods, for that
is the beginning of all idleness, inasmuch that the devil
marvellously forces himself to delay man from putting his
good purpose into effect." And if by any enticing to tarry
the devil may keep him still and then overcome him, so
would his good purpose and desire ever grow colder. And
for this, according to the counsel of the Man of Wisdom,
a man ought not to put off from day to day accomplishing
what he desires doing.

Jesus Christ, hearing this disciple's words, answered him,
Nemo mittens manum suam ad aratrum, No man sets his
hand to allow the withdrawal of penance, by which the
heart is troubled and overthrown, and does this so that
virtues are not sown there. And in order to follow Jesus
Christ, he might repent with intent, so that he would after
behold and look back with deed or purpose, and remember the former state which he first left. "For the kingdom
of heaven should not pertain or belong to such persons;

and he would not be worthy to preach about. Such is the religious who leaves the outward world but clings to it in his inner heart and thought, murmuring in his heart about what he has done or said before in this world, and taking more pleasure in it than in the service of God. Saint Paul, who was one of those who ought to dwell in heaven and ought to preach to others how man may come and dwell there, said to his disciples: "Forget as much as you possibly can the things which you have left in the world." In this authority of Our Lord it is shown that man ought not to wait or delay for any love or pleasure of his friends, but that he accomplishes his good purpose or will when God gives it to him. For it often happens that when man shows his friends his will and purpose, they would never rest until they have taken it away from him and made him change his good purpose. Saint Maximus the Bishop says about this: "All people who hold the plough, and in holding it look behind to see whether the furrow is being made fair and straight, and that it is neither torn not crooked or done uselessly, or that he does not mar or break with his plough the way of his oxen, so it is with him who walks in the right furrow and way of spir-itual life, scraping and cutting from his heart all worldly things, so that after he has started walking in the way of perfection, he does not go back on his determination to useless and vain things. For this shall wound both body and soul, and it shall cover his way in such manner that it shall be so perilous to him that unless God gave him grace, he would fall into many errors and troubles." Saint Augustine also says that he sets hand on the plough who-ever has affection to follow Jesus Christ, but who looks behind when he desires to delay the time he would have been at home and asked counsel of his friends. And Saint Bernard says: "If the disciple who resolves to follow Jesus Christ is rebuked and blamed for wanting to return home to speak to his friends, what then shall be done to them who, without either profit or edification, visit the houses of the friends they would then have abandoned and left before entering into religion?' This is also against all such religious people who will eat and drink too often amongst

secular people or in the houses of their friends. On this
Chrysostom says: "Whoever desires to follow Jesus Christ
and sets his hand to the plough, that is to say who will
make his foundation upon the faith and belief of Jesus
Christ in forsaking the world, ought not to look behind;
that is that he should never again return to the state which
he has left and abandoned in the world, since in doing
this, which is a business of vanities, and also by too much
great cupidity he is made unworthy of the kingdom of
heaven." And Saint Paul admonishes us about this saying
that after we shall be converted to a good life, we should
keep ourselves from returning by lack of affection to what
we have abandoned and left. On this Saint Bernard says:
"Man ought to be aware above all things that neither only
with heart, nor with heart and body together, should he
be an apostate. For we read about the children of Israel
that they returned with heart into Egypt, but they might
not return with body, for the Red Sea was between them
and kept them away from that place; for after they had
passed halfway through it, the sea closed at their heels.
And this is what I doubt, my brethren, that there are some
amongst us who would perhaps be ashamed to be apostate
bodily, but who would not be ashamed to be apostates
spiritually and with heart before God, namely when under
the habit of religion they have their minds on the world
and on secular things, in absorbing all the comfort which
they may find." And since it is for this that they renounce
the world for the love of God, let them then keep themselves well and beware that they look not behind them.
For as Saint Gregory says, there is nothing to angels more
entirely beloved, nor anything to God more pleasing, nor
to man more fruitful, than to persevere up to the end of
his life in the state of religion when he has taken it, in
keeping and accomplishing the rule of obedience. Isidore
says: "In the discussion of divine judgment there shall
be most eagerly rebuked and examined those who have
held in contempt and idleness to accomplish what they
have promised God in their profession." And because of
this we ought to be wise and well advised that the world
does not deceive us or withdraw us from it, nor that we

should look behind; so that we shall not be of the same nature as those like Lot's wife, who looked behind, and was immediately turned into a pillar of salt. On this it is to be noted that a statue has the figure of a man, but that it neither feels nor moves. In the same manner are those people who have left the world to enter into religion, and later they give themselves and their hearts to secular thoughts and distractions. For then they neither have any stirring nor feeling of doing good works. And in the same manner is the earth and land where salt is sown made barren and unfruitful by it.

ABOUT THE TRANSLATOR

DESCRIBING HIMSELF AS A CARTHUSIAN AT heart and a Jesuit in spirit and action, Victor Cauchi was born in 1950 on the island where St Paul was shipwrecked some two thousand years ago. Malta has always been seen as a bastion of the Catholic faith and a cultural crossroad between Byzantine and Latin Christianity after a short brush with Islam.

After receiving a Jesuit education for eight years, the translator was for a time a postulant with the Carthusians at the Order's novitiate at the Farneta Charterhouse in Lucca, Italy. Trained as a lawyer he has worked as a solicitor in private practice since 1974, joining government service at Malta's Attorney General's Office in 1983 where he served until retirement in 2011. His verve for translation was mainly induced in 1985 with the translation of local legislation from English to Maltese and vice-versa.

As the need for a well organised team of permanent translators grew in view of Malta's accession to the European Union, he was entrusted with supervising the translation into Maltese of the voluminous EU *acquis communautaire* and the Union's case-law. He attended various conferences at the time in EU countries on the subject.

His flair for translations into English from Italian and Spanish, as well as Latin and Middle English, started about his reaching pension age and he has to date translated further works of a spiritual nature, like the *Discourses of Isaiah of Schetis*, into Maltese. He has also had a brush with writing a novel and playwriting. Steeped in Catholic church movements, he has been married for over forty years to Marie Therese and they have one daughter, Rebekah.